THE MATHEMATICS OF CODING THEORY

Information, Compression, Error Correction, and Finite Fields

The Mathematics of Coding Theory

Information, Compression, Error Correction, and Finite Fields

Paul Garrett

Department of Mathematics
University of Minnesota, Minneapolis

PEARSON
Prentice
Hall

Upper Saddle River, NJ 07458

Library of Congress Cataloging-in-Publication Data

Garrett, Paul.
  The Mathematics of Coding Theory: Information, Compression, Error Correction,
  and Finite Fields / Paul Garrett.
    p. cm.
  Includes bibliographical references and index.
  ISBN: 0-13-101967-8
CIP data available

Acquisition Editor: *George Lobell*
Executive Editor-in-Chief: *Sally Yagan*
Production Editor: *Jeanne Audino*
Vice-President/Director of Production and Manufacturing: *David W. Riccardi*
Executive Managing Editor: *Kathleen Schiaparelli*
Senior Managing Editor: *Linda Mihatov Behrens*
Assistant Managing Editor: *Bayani Mendoza de Leon*
Assistant Manufacturing Manager/Buyer: *Michael Bell*
Manufacturing Manager: *Trudy Pisciotti*
Marketing Manager: *Halee Dinsey*
Marketing Assistant: *Rachel Beckman*
Art Director: *Jayne Conte*
Cover Designer: *Bruce Kenselaar*
Editorial Assistant: *Jennifer Brady*
Cover Photo: *Global Communications. Herrmann/Starke/CORBIS.*

©2004 Pearson Education, Inc.
Pearson Prentice Hall
Pearson Education, Inc.
Upper Saddle River, New Jersey 07458

Printed in the United States of America

10 9 8 7 6 5 4 3 2 1

ISBN 0-13-101967-8

Pearson Education LTD., *London*
Pearson Education Australia PTY, Limited, *Sydney*
Pearson Education Singapore, Pte. Ltd
Pearson Education North Asia Ltd, *Hong Kong*
Pearson Education Canada, Ltd., *Toronto*
Pearson Educación de Mexico, S.A. de C.V.
Pearson Education -- Japan, *Tokyo*
Pearson Education Malaysia, Pte. Ltd

Contents

Contents

Preface

This book is intended to be accessible to undergraduate students with two years of typical mathematics experience, most likely meaning calculus with a little linear algebra and differential equations. Thus, specifically, there is *no* assumption of a background in abstract algebra or number theory, nor of probability, nor of linear algebra. All these things are introduced and developed to a degree sufficient to address the issues at hand.

We will address the fundamental problem of **transmitting information effectively and accurately**. The specific mode of transmission does not really play a role in our discussion. On the other hand, we should mention that the importance of the issues of efficiency and accuracy has increased largely due to the advent of the internet and, even more so, due to the rapid development of wireless communications. For this reason it makes sense to think of networked computers or wireless devices as archetypical fundamental practical examples.

The underlying concepts of **information** and **information content** of data make sense independently of computers, and are relevant in looking at the operation of **natural languages** such as English, and of other modes of operation by which people acquire and process data.

The issue of **efficiency** is the obvious one: transmitting information costs time, money, and bandwidth. It is important to use as little as possible of each of these resources. **Data compression** is one way to pursue this efficiency. Some well known examples of compression schemes are commonly used for graphics: GIFs, JPEGs, and more recently PNGs. These clever file format schemes are enormously more efficient in terms of filesize than straightforward bitmap descriptions of graphics files. There are also general-purpose compression schemes, such as **gzip**, **bzip2**, **ZIP**, etc.

The issue of **accuracy** is addressed by **detection** and **correction** of errors that occur during transmission or storage of data. The single most important practical example is the TCP/IP protocol, widely used on the internet: one basic aspect of this is that if any of the *packets* composing a message is discovered to be mangled or lost, the packet is simply **retransmitted**. The detection of *lost* packets is based on numbering the collection making up a given message. The detection of *mangled* packets is by use of 16-bit **checksums** in the *headers* of IP and TCP packets. We will not worry about the technical details of TCP/IP here, but only note that **email** and many other types of internet traffic depend upon this protocol, which makes essential use of rudimentary error-detection devices.

And it is a fact of life that dust settles on CD-ROMs, static permeates network lines, etc. That is, there is **noise** in all communication systems. Human natural languages have evolved to include sufficient **redundancy** so that usually much less than 100% of a message need be received to be properly understood. Such redundancy must be *designed* into CD-ROM and other data storage protocols to achieve similar robustness.

There are other uses for detection of *changes in data*: if the data in question is the operating system of your computer, a change not initiated by you is probably a sign of something bad, either failure in hardware or software, or intrusion by hostile agents (whether software or wetware). Therefore, an important component of **systems security** is implementation of a suitable procedure to detect alterations in critical files.

In pre-internet times, various schemes were used to reduce the bulk of communication without losing the content: this influenced the design of the telegraphic alphabet, traffic lights, shorthand, etc. With the advent of the telephone and radio, these matters became even more significant. Communication with exploratory spacecraft having very limited resources available in deep space is a dramatic example of how the need for efficient and accurate transmission of information has increased in our recent history.

In this course we will begin with the model of communication and information made explicit by Claude Shannon in the 1940's, after some preliminary forays by Hartley and others in the preceding decades.

Many things are omitted due to lack of space and time. In spite of their tremendous importance, we do not mention **convolutional** codes at all. This is partly because there is less known about them mathematically. Concatenated codes are mentioned only briefly. Finally, we also omit any discussion of the so-called turbo codes. Turbo codes have been recently developed experimentally. Their remarkably good behavior, seemingly approaching the Shannon bound, has led to the conjecture that they are explicit solutions to the fifty-year old existence results of Shannon. However, at this time there is insufficient understanding of the reasons for their good behavior, and for this reason we will not attempt to study them here. We *do* give a very brief introduction to **geometric Goppa codes**, attached to *algebraic curves*, which are a natural generalization of Reed-Solomon codes (which we discuss), and which exceed the Gilbert-Varshamov lower bound for performance.

The exercises at the ends of the chapters are mostly routine, with a few more difficult exercises indicated by single or double asterisks. Short answers are given at the end of the book for a good fraction of the exercises, indicated by '*(ans.)*' following the exercise.

I offer my sincere thanks to the reviewers of the notes that became this volume. They found many unfortunate errors, and offered many good ideas about improvements to the text. While I did not choose to take absolutely all the advice given, I greatly appreciate the thought and energy these people put into their reviews: John Bowman, University of Alberta; Sergio Lopez, Ohio University; Navin Kashyap, University of California, San Diego; James Osterburg, University of Cincinnati; LeRoy Bearnson, Brigham Young University; David Grant, University of Colorado at Boulder; Jose Voloch, University of Texas.

Paul Garrett
garrett@math.umn.edu
http://www.math.umn.edu/˜garrett/

1

Probability

1.1 Sets and functions

Here we review some relatively elementary but very important terminology and concepts about *sets*, in a slightly abstract setting.

Naively, a **set** is supposed to be a collection of 'things' (?) described by 'listing' them or prescribing them by a 'rule'. Please note that this is *not* a precise description, but will be adequate for most of our purposes. We can also say that a **set** is an *unordered list* of *different* things.

There are standard symbols for some often-used sets:

$$
\begin{aligned}
\phi &= \{\} = \text{empty set} = \text{set with no elements} \\
\mathbf{Z} &= \text{the integers} \\
\mathbf{Q} &= \text{the rational numbers} \\
\mathbf{R} &= \text{the real numbers} \\
\mathbf{C} &= \text{the complex numbers}
\end{aligned}
$$

A set described by a *list* is something like

$$S = \{1, 2, 3, 4, 5, 6, 7, 8\}$$

1

which is the set of integers greater than 0 and less than 9. This set can also be described by a *rule* like

$$S = \{1, 2, 3, 4, 5, 6, 7, 8\} = \{x : x \text{ is an integer and } 1 \leq x \leq 8\}$$

This follows the general format and notation

$$\{x : \ x \text{ has some property}\}$$

If x is in a set S, then write $x \in S$ or $S \ni x$, and say that x is an *element* of S. Thus, a set is the collection of all its elements (although this remark only explains the *language*). It is worth noting that the *ordering* of a listing has no effect on a set, and if in the listing of elements of a set an element is *repeated*, this has no effect. For example,

$$\{1, 2, 3\} = \{1, 1, 2, 3\} = \{3, 2, 1\} = \{1, 3, 2, 1\}$$

A **subset** T of a set S is a set all of whose elements are elements of S. This is written $T \subset S$ or $S \supset T$. So always $S \subset S$ and $\phi \subset S$. If $T \subset S$ and $T \neq \phi$ and $T \neq S$, then T is a **proper** subset of S. Note that the empty set is a subset of *every* set. For a subset T of a set S, the **complement** of T (inside S) is

$$T^c = S - T = \{s \in S : s \notin T\}$$

Sets can also be elements of other sets. For example, $\{\mathbf{Q}, \mathbf{Z}, \mathbf{R}, \mathbf{C}\}$ is the set with 4 elements, each of which is a familiar set of numbers. Or, one can check that

$$\{\{1, 2\}, \{1, 3\}, \{2, 3\}\}$$

is the set of two-element subsets of $\{1, 2, 3\}$.

The **intersection** of two sets A, B is the collection of all elements which lie in *both* sets, and is denoted $A \cap B$. Two sets are **disjoint** if their intersection is ϕ. If the intersection is *not* empty, then we may say that the two sets **meet**. The **union** of two sets A, B is the collection of all elements which lie in *one or the other* of the two sets, and is denoted $A \cup B$.

Note that, for example, $1 \neq \{1\}$, and $\{\{1\}\} \neq \{1\}$. That is, the *set* $\{a\}$ with sole element a is *not* the same thing as the item a itself.

An **ordered pair** (x, y) is just that, a list of two things in which there is a *first* thing, here x, and a *second* thing, here y. Two ordered pairs (x, y) and (x', y') are **equal** if and only if $x = x'$ and $y = y'$.

The **(cartesian) product** of two sets A, B is the set of **ordered pairs** (a, b) where $a \in A$ and $b \in B$. It is denoted $A \times B$. Thus, while $\{a, b\} = \{b, a\}$ might be thought of as an *unordered* pair, for *ordered* pairs $(a, b) \neq (b, a)$ unless by chance $a = b$.

In case $A = B$, the cartesian power $A \times B$ is often denoted A^2. More generally, for a fixed positive integer n, the nth **cartesian power** A^n of a set is the set of ordered n-tuples $(a_1, a_2, \ldots, a_n)$ of elements a_i of A.

Some very important examples of cartesian powers are those of $\mathbf{R}$ or $\mathbf{Q}$ or $\mathbf{C}$, which arise in other contexts as well: for example, $\mathbf{R}^2$ is the collection of ordered pairs of real numbers, which we use to describe points in the plane. And $\mathbf{R}^3$ is the collection of ordered triples of real numbers, which we use to describe points in three-space.

The **power set** of a set S is the *set of subsets* of S. This is sometimes denoted by $\mathcal{P}S$. Thus,

$$\mathcal{P}\phi = \{\phi\}$$

$$\mathcal{P}\{1,2\} = \{\phi, \{1\}, \{2\}, \{1,2\}\}$$

Intuitively, a **function** f from one set A to another set B is supposed to be a 'rule' which assigns to each element $a \in A$ an element $b = f(a) \in B$. This is written as

$$f : A \to B$$

although the latter notation gives no information about the nature of f in any detail.

More rigorously, but less intuitively, we can define a *function* by really telling its *graph*: the formal definition is that a function $f : A \to B$ is a *subset* of the product $A \times B$ with the property that for every $a \in A$ there is a unique $b \in B$ so that $(a, b) \in f$. Then we would write $f(a) = b$.

This formal definition is worth noting at least because it should make clear that there is absolutely no requirement that a function be described by any recognizable or simple 'formula'.

Map and **mapping** are common synonyms for *function*.

As a silly example of the formal definition of function, let $f : \{1, 3\} \to \{2, 6\}$ be the function 'multiply-by-two', so that $f(1) = 2$ and $f(3) = 6$. Then the 'official' definition would say that really f is the subset of the product set $\{1, 3\} \times \{2, 6\}$ consisting of the ordered pairs $(1, 2), (3, 6)$. That is, formally the function f is the *set*

$$f = \{(1, 2), (3, 6)\}$$

Of course, no one usually operates this way, but it is important to have a precise meaning underlying more intuitive usage.

A function $f : A \to B$ is **surjective** (or **onto**) if for every $b \in B$ there is $a \in A$ so that $f(a) = b$. A function $f : A \to B$ is **injective** (or **one-to-one**) if $f(a) = f(a')$ implies $a = a'$. That is, f is *injective* if for every $b \in B$ there is *at most one* $a \in A$ so that $f(a) = b$. A map is a **bijection** if it is both injective and surjective.

The number of elements in a set is its **cardinality**. Two sets are said to **have the same cardinality** if there is a *bijection* between them. Thus, this is a trick so that we don't have to actually *count* two sets to see whether they have the same number of elements. Rather, we can just pair them up by a *bijection* to achieve this purpose.

Since we *can* count the elements in a *finite* set in a traditional way, it is clear that *a finite set has no bijection to a proper subset of itself.* After all, a proper subset has *fewer elements.*

By contrast, for *infinite* sets it is easily possible that *proper* subsets have bijections to the whole set. For example, the set A of *all* natural numbers and the set E of *even* natural numbers have a bijection between them given by

$$n \to 2n$$

But certainly E is a *proper* subset of A! Even more striking examples can be arranged. In the end, we take as the *definition* that a set is **infinite** if it has a bijection to a proper subset of itself.

Let $f : A \to B$ be a function from a set A to a set B, and let $g : B \to C$ be a function from the set B to a set C. The **composite function** $g \circ f$ is defined to be

$$(g \circ f)(a) = g(f(a))$$

for $a \in A$.

The **identity function** on a non-empty set S is the function $f : S \to S$ so that $f(a) = a$ for all $a \in A$. Often the identity function on a set S is denoted by id_S.

Let $f : A \to B$ be a function from a set A to a set B. An **inverse function** $g : B \to A$ for f (if such g exists at all) is a function so that $(f \circ g)(b) = b$ for all $b \in B$, and also $(g \circ f)(a) = a$ for all $a \in A$. That is, the inverse function (if it exists) has the two properties

$$f \circ g = \mathrm{id}_B \qquad g \circ f = \mathrm{id}_A$$

An inverse function to f, if it exists at all, is usually denoted f^{-1}. (This is *not* at all the same as $1/f$!)

Proposition: A function $f : A \to B$ from a set A to a set B has an inverse if and only if f is a bijection. In that case, the inverse is unique (that is, there is only *one* inverse function).

Proof: Suppose that $f : A \to B$ is a bijection. We define a function $g : B \to A$ as follows. Given $b \in B$, let $a \in A$ be an element so that $f(a) = b$. Then define $g(b) = a$. Do this for each $b \in B$ to define g. Note that we use the *surjectivity* to know that there *exists* an a for each b and we use the *injectivity* to be sure of its *uniqueness*.

To check that $g \circ f = \mathrm{id}_A$, compute: first, for any $a \in A$, $f(a) \in B$. Then $g(f(a))$ is, by definition, an element $a' \in A$ so that $f(a') = f(a)$. Since f is injective, it must be that $a' = a$. To check that $f \circ g = \mathrm{id}_B$, take $b \in B$ and compute: by definition of g, $g(b)$ is an element of A so that $f(g(b)) = b$. But that is (after all) just what we want.

On the other hand, suppose that for $f : A \to B$ there is $g : B \to A$ such that $g \circ f = \mathrm{id}_A$ and $f \circ g = \mathrm{id}_B$, and show that f is bijective. Indeed, if $f(a_1) = f(a_2)$, then apply g to both sides of this equality to obtain

$$a_1 = \mathrm{id}_A(a_1) = g(f(a_1)) = g(f(a_2)) = a_2$$

This proves injectivity of f. For surjectivity, given $b \in B$,

$$f(g(b)) = \mathrm{id}_B(b) = b$$

This completes the proof that if f has an inverse then it is a bijection.   ///

1.2 Counting

Here we go through various standard elementary-but-important examples of **counting** as preparation for finite probability computations. Of course, by 'counting' we mean *structured* counting.

Example: Suppose we have n different things, for example the integers from 1 to n inclusive. The question is *how many different* **orderings** *or* **ordered listings**

$$i_1, i_2, i_3, \ldots, i_{n-1}, i_n$$

of these numbers are there? Rather than just tell the formula, let's quickly derive it. The answer is obtained by noting that there are n choices for the first thing i_1, then $n-1$ remaining choices for the second thing i_2 (since we can't reuse whatever i_1 was), $n-2$ remaining choices for i_3 (since we can't reuse i_1 nor i_2, whatever they were!), and so on down to 2 remaining choices for i_{n-1} and then just one choice for i_n. *Thus, there are*

$$n \cdot (n-1) \cdot (n-2) \cdot \ldots \cdot 2 \cdot 1$$

possible **orderings** *of n distinct things.* This kind of product arises often, and there is a notation and name for it: n-**factorial**, denoted $n!$, is the product

$$n! = n \cdot (n-1) \cdot (n-2) \cdot \ldots \cdot 2 \cdot 1$$

It is an important and useful convention that

$$0! = 1$$

The factorial $n!$ is defined only for non-negative integers.

Example: How many **ordered k-tuples** of elements can be chosen (allowing repetition) from a set of n things? There are n possibilities for the first choice. For each choice of the first there are n choices for the second. For each choice of the first and second there are n for the third, and so on down to n choices for the kth for each choice of the first through $(k-1)^{\text{th}}$. That is, altogether there are

$$\underbrace{n \times n \times \ldots \times n}_{k} = n^k$$

ordered k-tuples that can be chosen from a set with n elements.

Example: How many **ordered k-tuples** of **distinct** elements can be chosen from a set of n things? (In a mathematical context *distinct* means *all different from each other.*) There are n possibilities for the first choice. For each choice of the first there are $n-1$ remaining choices for the second, since the second element must be different from the first. For each choice of the first and second there are $n-2$ remaining choices for the third, since it must be different from the first and second. This continues, to $n-(k-1)$ choices for the kth for each choice of the first through $(k-1)^{\text{th}}$, since the $k-1$ distinct element already chosen can't be reused. That is, altogether there are

$$n \times (n-1) \times (n-2) \times \ldots \times (n-(k-2)) \times (n-(k-1)) = n!/(n-k)!$$

ordered k-tuples of *distinct* elements that can be chosen from a set with n elements.

Example: How many (unordered!) **subsets** of k elements are there in a set of n things? There are n possibilities for the first choice, $n-1$ remaining choices for the second (since the first item is removed), $n-2$ for the third (since the first and second items are no longer available), and so on down to $n-(k-1)$ choices for the kth. This number is $n!/(n-k)!$, but is *not* what we want, since it includes a count of all different *orders* of choices, but subsets are not ordered. That is,

$$\frac{n!}{(n-k)!} = k! \times \text{ the actual number}$$

since we saw in a previous example that there are $k!$ possible orderings of k distinct things. Thus, there are

$$\frac{n!}{k!\,(n-k)!}$$

choices of subsets of k elements in a set with n elements.

The number $n!/k!(n-k)!$ also occurs often enough to warrant a name and notation: it is called a **binomial coefficient**, is written

$$\frac{n!}{k!\,(n-k)!} = \binom{n}{k}$$

and is pronounced 'n choose k' in light of the previous example. The name 'binomial coefficient' is explained below in the context of the *Binomial Theorem*.

Example: How many *disjoint pairs* of 3-element and 5-element subsets are there in a set with 10 elements? We just saw that there are $\binom{10}{3}$ choices for the *first* subset with 3 elements. Then the remaining part of the original set has just $10-3=7$ elements, so there are $\binom{7}{5}$ choices for the *second* subset of 5 elements. Therefore, there are

$$\binom{10}{3}\binom{7}{5} = \frac{10!}{7!\,3!}\frac{7!}{5!2!} = \frac{10!}{3!\,5!\,2!}$$

$$= \frac{10!}{5!\,5!} \cdot \frac{5!}{3!\,2!} = \binom{10}{5}\binom{5}{3}$$

pairs of disjoint subsets of 3 and 5 elements inside a set with 10 elements. Note that we obtain the same numerical outcome regardless of whether we first choose the 3-element subset or the 5-element subset.

Example: How many *disjoint pairs* of subsets, each with k elements, are there in a set with n elements, where $2k \leq n$? We saw that there are $\binom{n}{k}$ choices for the *first* subset with k elements. Then the remaining part of the original set has just $n - k$ elements, so there are $\binom{n-k}{k}$ choices for the *second* subset of k elements. But our counting so far inadvertently takes into account a *first* subset and a *second* one, which is not what the question is. By now we know that there are $2! = 2$ choices of ordering of two things (subsets, for example). Therefore, there are

$$\frac{1}{2}\binom{n}{k}\binom{n-k}{k} = \frac{1}{2}\frac{n!}{(n-k)!k!}\frac{(n-k)!}{k!(n-2k)!}$$

$$= \frac{n!}{2\,k!\,k!(n-2k)!}$$

pairs of disjoint subsets of k elements each inside a set with n elements.

Generalizing the previous: For integers n, ℓ, k with $n \geq k\ell$, we could ask *how many families of ℓ disjoint subsets of k elements each are there inside a set of n elements?* There are

$$\binom{n}{k}$$

choices for the first subset,

$$\binom{n-k}{k}$$

for the second,

$$\binom{n-2k}{k}$$

for the third, up to

$$\binom{n-(\ell-1)k}{k}$$

for the ℓth subset. But since *ordering* of these subsets is inadvertently counted here, we have to divide by $\ell!$ to have the actual number of families. There is some cancellation among the factorials, so that the actual number is

$$\text{number of disjoint subsets of } k \text{ elements} = \frac{n!}{\ell!\,(k!)^\ell\,(n-\ell k)!}$$

The **Binomial Theorem** asserts that

$$(x+y)^n = \sum_{k=0}^{n}\binom{n}{k}x^k\,y^{n-k}$$

This identity shows that the binomial coefficients are integers, and is the basis for other identities as well. This identity is proven by induction, as follows. For $n = 1$ the assertion is immediately verified. Assume it is true for exponent n, and prove the corresponding assertion for exponent $n + 1$. Thus,

$$(x + y)^{n+1} = (x + y) \cdot (x + y)^n = (x + y) \cdot \sum_{k=0}^{n} \binom{n}{k} x^k y^{n-k}$$

$$= \sum_{k=0}^{n} \binom{n}{k} \left(x^{k+1} y^{n-k} + x^k y^{n-k+1} \right)$$

$$= x^0 y^{n+1} + x^{n+1} y^0 + + \sum_{k=1}^{n} \left(\binom{n}{k-1} + \binom{n}{k} \right) x^k y^{n+1-k}$$

Thus, to prove the formula of the Binomial Theorem for exponent $n + 1$ we must prove that for $1 \le k \le n$

$$\binom{n}{k-1} + \binom{n}{k} = \binom{n+1}{k}$$

We do this by expressing the left-hand side in terms of binomial coefficients:

$$\binom{n}{k-1} + \binom{n}{k}$$

$$= \frac{n!}{(k-1)!\,(n-k+1)!} + \frac{n!}{k!\,(n-k)!} = \frac{n!\,k}{k!\,(n-k+1)!} + \frac{n!\,(n-k+1)}{k!\,(n-k+1)!}$$

$$= \frac{(n+1)!}{k!\,(n-k+1)!} = \binom{n+1}{k}$$

as claimed.

1.3 Preliminary ideas of probability

This little section moves from an intuitive version of probability toward a more formal and mathematically useful version presented in the next section.

First, there is the conversion from the colloquial notion of the 'chance' of something occurring to the notion of its 'probability'. While usually the 'chance' of something happening is a percentage, a **probability** is a number between 0 and 1, inclusive. The conversion rule is the following: if in colloquial English the 'chance' of something happening is $x\%$, then its probability is $x/100$. (This introduces no new content.) At one extreme, if an event is 'sure' to happen, then its probability is 1 (its chance is 100%), while at the other extreme if something is sure *not* to happen then its probability is 0 (its chance is 0%).

One basic postulate about probability is that the probabilities of all the different possible outcomes of an event or experiment should add up to 1. An analogous rule is taken as true for 'chance': the sum of the percentages of all possible outcomes should be 100%.

But what *is* 'probability'?

Example: A 'fair coin' is presumed to have equal probabilities ('equal chances') of landing heads-up or tails-up. Since the probability of heads is the same as the probability of tails, and since the two numbers should add up to 1, there is no choice but to assign the probability 1/2 to both. Further, each toss of the coin is presumed to have an outcome *independent* of other tosses before and after. That is, there is no mechanism by which the outcome of one toss affects another. Now we come to a *property* which we would *assume* to be *roughly* true: out of (for example) 10 coin tosses we expect about half to be heads and about half to be tails. We expect that it would very seldom happen that 10 out of 10 tosses would all be *heads*. Experience does bear this out. So far, in this vague language, there is no obvious problem.

But, for example, it would be a mistake to be too aggressive, and say that we should expect *exactly* half heads and half tails. Experimentation will show that out of repeated batches of 10 coin flips, only about 1/4 of the time will there be *exactly* 5 heads and 5 tails. (Only once in about $2^{10} = 1024$ times will one get *all* heads.) In fact, about 2/5 of the time there will be *either* 6 heads and 4 tails, or *vice versa*. That is, a 6-4 or 4-6 distribution of outcomes is more likely than the 'expected' 5-5.

But this is not a paradox, since upon reflection our intuition might assure us not that there will be *exactly* half heads and half tails, but only *approximately* half and half. And we can retell the story in a better way as follows. So what does 'approximately' mean, exactly?

In a **trial** of n coin flips, each flip has two possible outcomes, so there are

$$\underbrace{2 \times \ldots \times 2}_{n} = 2^n$$

possible sequences of n outcomes. The assumptions that the coin is 'fair' and that the separate coin tosses do not 'influence' each other is interpreted as saying that *each one of the 2^n possible sequences of coin-toss outcomes is equally likely*. Therefore, the *probability* of any *single* sequence of n outcomes is $1/2^n$. Further, for any subset S of the set A of all 2^n possible sequences of outcomes, we assume that

probability of a sequence of n tosses giving an outcome in S

$$= \frac{\text{number of elements in } S}{\text{number of elements in } A} = \frac{\text{number of elements in } S}{2^n}$$

Then the probability that *exactly* k heads will occur out of n tosses (with $0 \le k \le n$) is computed as

probability of k heads out of n tosses

$$= \frac{\text{number of sequences of } n \text{ heads/tails with exactly } k \text{ heads}}{\text{total number of sequences of } n \text{ heads/tails}}$$

$$= \frac{\text{number of sequences of } n \text{ heads/tails with exactly } k \text{ heads}}{2^n}$$

To count the number of sequences of n heads-or-tails with exactly k heads, we may think of this problem as that of *counting the number of subsets with k elements from a set with n elements*. That is, the *whole set* is the set of all n flips, and the *subset* is the set of flips that come up *heads*. This number is the binomial coefficient

$$n\text{-choose-}k \;=\; \frac{n!}{k!\,(n-k)!} \;=\; \binom{n}{k}$$

Thus, for example, the probability that exactly 5 heads come up in 10 tosses is

$$\frac{\binom{10}{5}}{2^{10}} = \frac{\left(\frac{10\cdot9\cdot8\cdot7\cdot6}{5\cdot4\cdot3\cdot3\cdot1}\right)}{1024} = \frac{252}{1024} \approx \frac{1}{4}$$

as commented just above. And the probability that 6 heads and 4 tails *or* 4 heads and 6 tails occur is

$$\frac{\text{number of sequences of 10 with exactly 6 or exactly 4 heads}}{2^{10}}$$

$$= \frac{\binom{10}{4} + \binom{10}{6}}{1024} = \frac{2 \cdot \frac{10\cdot9\cdot8\cdot7}{4\cdot3\cdot2}}{1024} = \frac{420}{1024} \approx \frac{2}{5}$$

Perhaps not entirely surprisingly, the probability of getting *exactly* half heads and half tails out of $2n$ flips goes *down* as the number of flips goes up, and in fact goes to 0 as the number of flips goes to infinity. Nevertheless, more consistent with our intuition, the sense that the number of heads is *approximately* one half is correct. Still, in terms of the expression

$$P(\text{exactly } n \text{ heads in } 2n \text{ flips}) = \frac{\binom{2n}{n}}{2^{2n}}$$

the fact is that

$$\lim_{n\to\infty} \frac{\binom{2n}{n}}{2^{2n}} = 0$$

It is not so easy to verify this directly, but consideration of some numerical examples is suggestive if not actually persuasive. Quantification of the notion that the number of heads is *approximately* one half is filled in a little later by the *Law of Large Numbers*.

In purely numerical terms some values of the previous expression are

$$
\begin{aligned}
\binom{2}{1}/2^2 &\approx 0.5 \\
\binom{4}{2}/2^4 &\approx 0.375 \\
\binom{6}{3}/2^6 &\approx 0.3125 \\
\binom{8}{4}/2^8 &\approx 0.2734 \\
\binom{10}{5}/2^{10} &\approx 0.2461 \\
\binom{12}{6}/2^{12} &\approx 0.1813 \\
\binom{14}{7}/2^{14} &\approx 0.1683 \\
\binom{20}{10}/2^{20} &\approx 0.176197052002 \\
\binom{30}{15}/2^{30} &\approx 0.144464448094 \\
\binom{40}{20}/2^{40} &\approx 0.12537068762 \\
\binom{50}{25}/2^{50} &\approx 0.112275172659 \\
\binom{60}{30}/2^{60} &\approx 0.102578173009 \\
\binom{70}{35}/2^{70} &\approx 0.0950254735405 \\
\binom{80}{40}/2^{80} &\approx 0.0889278787739 \\
\binom{90}{45}/2^{90} &\approx 0.0838711229887 \\
\binom{100}{50}/2^{100} &\approx 0.0795892373872 \\
\binom{200}{100}/2^{200} &\approx 0.0563484790093 \\
\binom{300}{150}/2^{300} &\approx 0.046027514419 \\
\binom{400}{200}/2^{400} &\approx 0.0398693019638 \\
\binom{500}{250}/2^{500} &\approx 0.0356646455533 \\
\binom{600}{300}/2^{600} &\approx 0.032559931335 \\
\binom{700}{350}/2^{700} &\approx 0.0301464332521 \\
\binom{800}{400}/2^{800} &\approx 0.0282006650947 \\
\binom{900}{450}/2^{900} &\approx 0.0265887652343 \\
\binom{1000}{500}/2^{1000} &\approx 0.0252250181784
\end{aligned}
$$

Remark: We're not really answering the question 'what is probability?', but instead we're telling how to *compute* it.

One attempt to be more quantitative taken in the past, but which has several flaws, is the **limiting frequency** definition of probability, described as follows in the simplest example. Let $N(n)$ be the number of times that a head came up in n trials. Then as n grows larger and larger we might imagine that the ratio $N(n)/n$ should get 'closer and closer' to the 'probability' of heads ($1/2$ for a fair coin). Or, in the language of limits, it should be that

$$
\text{probability of heads} = \lim_{n \to \infty} \frac{\text{number of heads in } n \text{ flips}}{n}
$$

(And probably this limit really is $1/2$.) But there are problems with this definition. It's not that the assertion itself is false, but rather that this isn't a good *definition* of probability from which to start. For example, either in real life or in theory it's not convenient to do infinitely many flips. Second, if we try to do only finitely many flips and *approximate* the probability, how many do we need to do? Third, how do we know that *every* infinite sequence of trials will give the same limiting value? There are many further objections to this as a fundamental definition, but we should be aware of interpretations in this direction. A more supportable viewpoint would make such limiting frequency assertions a *consequence* of other things, called the *Law of Large Numbers*. We'll prove a special case of this a bit later.

Example: The next traditional example involves picking colored balls out of an urn. Suppose, for example, that there are N balls in the urn, r red ones and $b = N - r$ blue ones, and that they are indistinguishable by texture, weight, size, or in any way. Then in choosing a single ball from the urn we are 'equally likely' to choose any one of the N. As in the simpler case of coin flips, there are N possibilities each of which is equally likely, and the probabilities must add up to 1, so the probability of drawing any particular ball must be $1/N$. Further, it may seem reasonable to postulate that the probability of picking out one ball from among a fixed subset of k would be k times the probability of picking a single ball. Granting this, with r red balls and b blue ones, we would plausibly say that the *probability* is r/N that a red ball will be chosen and b/N that a blue ball will be chosen. (We should keep in mind that some subatomic particles do *not* behave in this seemingly reasonable manner!) So without assigning *meaning* to probability, in some cases we can still reach some conclusions about how to compute it.

We suppose that one draw (with replacement) has no effect on the next one, so that they are **independent**. Let $r(n)$ be the number of red balls drawn in a sequence of n trials. Then, in parallel with the discussion just above, we would *presume* that for any infinite sequence of trials

$$\lim_{n \to \infty} \frac{\text{number of red balls drawn in } n \text{ draws}}{n} = \frac{r}{N}$$

But, as noted above, this should not be the *definition*, but rather should be a deducible *consequence* of whatever definition we make.

Running this in the opposite direction: if there are N balls in an urn, some red and some blue, if $r(n)$ denotes the number of red balls chosen in n trials, and if

$$\lim_{n \to \infty} \frac{r(n)}{n} = f$$

then we would *suspect* that

$$\text{number of red balls in the urn} \approx f \cdot N$$

And we would suspect that the *probability* of drawing a red ball in a *single* trial is f, since the *limiting frequency* of drawing red balls is f.

But how close would this equality be? The numbers above show that it is not very likely that a fair coin will give exactly half heads out of any number of flips, so would we always fail to realize that we had a fair coin? Hmmm.

Again, yes, the limiting frequency intuition for probability is accurate, but isn't adequate as a definition. We give a less intuitive definition in the next section, and later return to limiting frequencies with the Law of Large Numbers.

1.4 More formal view of probability

Now we will remove some of the immediacy of the notion of probability, but will replace it with greater precision.

Suppose that an experiment has possible different outcomes $\omega_1, \ldots, \omega_n$. The collection $\Omega = \{\omega_1, \ldots, \omega_n\}$ of all possible outcomes is the **sample space**. Each possible ω_i is an **event**. We suppose that each possible outcome ω_i has a **probability** $P(\omega_i) = p_i \geq 0$, and

$$p_1 + p_2 + \ldots + p_n = 1$$

The function $P()$ on Ω is (nearly) a **probability measure**. The sample space together with the system of attaching probabilities to each event (the probability measure) is a **probability space**.

Remark: Yes, a (finite) probability space is just a set with non-negative numbers attached to its elements, that add up to 1. There is *no* explanation of where the probabilities come from.

Example: Let $\Omega = \{H, T\}$ and assign probabilities by

$$P(H) = \frac{1}{2}$$

$$P(T) = \frac{1}{2}$$

This is the model of a fair coin.

A more general idea of **event** (sometimes called **compound event**) is any subset A of the sample space, that is, of the set $\Omega = \{x_1, \ldots, x_n\}$ of all possible events. In that context, the events $\{x_i\}$ are sometimes called **atomic events**. The **probability of A** is

$$P(A) = \sum_{x_i \in A} P(x_i)$$

where (to repeat) the sum is over the 'points' x_i that lie in A. The function $P()$ *extended* in this fashion is really what a **probability measure** is. The event A **occurs** if any one of the $x_i \in A$ occurs. Thus, for $A = \{x_{i_1}, \ldots, x_{i_k}\}$,

$$P(A) = P(x_{i_1} \text{ or } x_{i_2} \text{ or } \ldots \text{ or } x_{i_k})$$

As extreme cases,

$$P(\Omega) = 1$$

and

$$P(\phi) = 0$$

Generally, for an event A, the event **not-A** is the set-theoretic *complement* $A^c = \Omega - A$ of A inside Ω. Then

$$P(\text{not } A) = P(A^c) = P(\Omega - A) = 1 - P(A)$$

For two events A and B, the event $A - \textbf{or} - B$ is simply $A \cup B$, and

$$P(A \text{ or } B) = P(A \cup B)$$

For two events A and B, the event $A - \textbf{and} - B$ is $A \cap B$, and

$$P(A \text{ and } B) = P(A \cap B)$$

Two events A and B (subsets of $\{x_1, \ldots, x_n\}$) are **mutually disjoint** or **mutually exclusive** if $A \cap B = \phi$. If two events are disjoint, then we have

$$P(A \text{ or } B) = P(A \cup B) = P(A) + P(B)$$

Example: Let $\Omega = \{r_1, r_2, r_3, b_1, b_2, b_3, b_4, b_5, b_6, b_7\}$ (where we imagine that the r_is are red balls and the b_js are blue balls), with

$$P(r_i) = \frac{1}{10}$$

$$P(b_j) = \frac{1}{10}$$

for all i and j. This is the model of 10 balls in an urn. Then the subsets

$$A = \{r_1, r_2, r_3\} = \text{ drawing a red ball}$$

$$B = \{b_1, b_2, b_3, b_4, b_5, b_6, b_7\} = \text{ drawing a blue ball}$$

are 'compound' events, whose probabilities are computed by

$$P(A) = P(r_1) + P(r_2) + P(r_3) = \frac{1}{10} + \frac{1}{10} + \frac{1}{10} = \frac{3}{10}$$

$$P(B) = P(b_1) + P(b_2) + \ldots + P(b_7) = \frac{7}{10}$$

We can assign these probabilities p_i *by intuition*, by using the limiting frequency idea, or by other means. In fact, they might be measured experimentally, or assigned in some operational manner possibly hard to justify rigorously. Let's repeat the limiting frequency story one more time in this situation. We imagine that the same experiment X is conducted over and over, and that subsequent trials are unaffected by the earlier ones, that is, they are **independent trials**. For n such independent trials let $n(\omega_i)$ be the number of times that the event ω_i occurs. Suppose that for any infinite sequence of trials the limit

$$p_i = \lim_{n \to \infty} \frac{n(\omega_i)}{n}$$

exists and is unique. Then this **limiting frequency** p_i should be the **probability of the event** ω_i.

Example: Consider the experiment of drawing a ball from an urn in which there are 3 red balls, 3 blue balls, and 4 white balls (otherwise indistinguishable). As above, we would postulate that the probability of drawing any particular individual ball is 1/10. (These atomic events are indeed mutually exclusive, because we only draw one ball at a time.) Thus, the 'smallest' events $x_1, x_2, \ldots, x_{10}$ are the possible drawings of each one of the 10 balls. Since they have equal chances of being drawn, the probabilities $p_i = P(x_i)$ are all the same (and add up to 1):

$$p_1 = p_2 = p_3 = \ldots = p_{10}$$

Then the ('compound') event A of 'drawing a red ball' is the subset with three elements consisting of 'draw red ball one', 'draw red ball two', and 'draw red ball three'. Thus,

$$P(A) = \frac{1}{10} + \frac{1}{10} + \frac{1}{10} = \frac{3}{10}$$

Let B be the event 'draw a white ball'. Then, since A and B are disjoint events, the probability of drawing *either* a red ball *or* a white ball is the sum:

$$P(\text{ drawing red or white }) = P(A \cup B) = P(A) + P(B) = \frac{3}{10} + \frac{4}{10} = \frac{7}{10}$$

This is reasonable, and argues in favor of this way of modeling.

As an example of a basic systematic computation:

Proposition: Let Ω be a finite probability space with elements $\omega_1, \ldots, \omega_n$. Let A be a subset of the sample space Ω with probability $P(A) = p$. Let $k \leq N$ be integers with $N > 0$ and $k \geq 0$. Then the probability that A occurs in exactly k of N trials is

$$\binom{N}{k} \cdot p^k \, (1-p)^{N-k}$$

Proof: When $N = 1$, the probability that A occurs is p, and the binomial coefficient $\binom{1}{1}$ is 1. The probability that A does not occur is $1-p$, and $\binom{1}{0} = 1$ also. The main part of the argument is an induction on N. Since the different trials are independent, by assumption, we have

$$P(A \text{ occurs in } k \text{ of } N)$$

$$= P(A \text{ occurs in } k \text{ of the first } N-1) \cdot P(A \text{ does not occur in the } N^{\text{th}})$$

$$+ P(A \text{ occurs in } k-1 \text{ of the first } N-1) \cdot P(A \text{ occurs in the } N^{\text{th}})$$

$$= \binom{N-1}{k} p^k (1-p)^{N-1-k} \times (1-p)$$

$$+ \binom{N-1}{k-1} p^{k-1} (1-p)^{N-1-(k-1)} \times p$$

We want to prove that this is equal to

$$\binom{N}{k} p^k (1-p)^{N-k}$$

We can see already that the powers of p and of $1-p$ will match, so it's just a matter of proving that

$$\binom{N-1}{k} + \binom{N-1}{k-1} = \binom{N}{k}$$

which we already verified in proving the Binomial Theorem earlier. This completes the induction and the proof.   ///

Let Ω be a probability space, and let A be a ('compound') event with $P(A) > 0$. Let B be another ('compound') event. Then the **conditional probability**

$$P(B \text{ given that } A \text{ occurs})$$

is denoted $P(B|A)$ and is computed as

$$P(B|A) = \frac{P(A \cap B)}{P(A)}$$

In effect, the phrase 'given that A occurs' means that we replace the 'universe' Ω of possible outcomes by the smaller 'universe' A of possibilities, and 'renormalize' all the probabilities accordingly.

The formula $P(B|A) = P(A \cap B)/P(A)$ allows us to compute the conditional probability in terms of the other two probabilities. In 'real-life' situations, it may be that we know $P(B|A)$ directly, for some other reasons. If we also know $P(A)$, then this gives us the formula for

$$P(A \text{ and } B) = P(A \cap B)$$

namely

$$P(A \cap B) = P(B|A) \cdot P(A)$$

Example: What is the probability that 7 heads appear in 10 flips of a fair coin given that at least 4 heads appear? This is a direct computation of conditional probability:

$$P(7 \text{ heads} \mid \text{at least 4 heads}) = \frac{P(7 \text{ heads and at least 4 heads})}{P(\text{at least 4 heads})}$$

$$= \frac{P(7 \text{ heads})}{P(\text{at least 4 heads})}$$

$$= \frac{\binom{10}{7} \cdot \frac{1}{2^{10}}}{\left(\binom{10}{4} + \binom{10}{5} + \binom{10}{6} + \binom{10}{7} + \binom{10}{8} + \binom{10}{9} + \binom{10}{10}\right) \cdot \frac{1}{2^{10}}}$$

$$= \frac{\binom{10}{7}}{\binom{10}{4} + \binom{10}{5} + \binom{10}{6} + \binom{10}{7} + \binom{10}{8} + \binom{10}{9} + \binom{10}{10}}$$

since the requirement of 7 heads *and* at least 4 is simply the requirement of 7 heads.

Two subsets A, B of a probability space Ω are **independent** if

$$P(A \cap B) = P(A) \cdot P(B)$$

In simple examples, it usually happens that independence of events is due to some fairly obvious independence of 'causality'. Equivalently,

$$P(B) = P(B|A)$$

and equivalently

$$P(A) = P(A|B)$$

Example: Let $\Omega = \{10, 11, \ldots, 99\}$ be the collection of all integers from 10 to 99, inclusive. Let A be the subset of Ω consisting of integers $x \in \Omega$ whose ones'-place digit is 3, and let B be the subset of integers $x \in \Omega$ whose tens'-place digit is 6. Then it turns out that

$$P(A \cap B) = P(A) \cdot P(B)$$

so, by definition, these two ('compound') events are *independent*. Usually we expect an explanation for an independence result, rather than just numerical verification that the probabilities behave as indicated. In the present case, the point is that there is no 'causal relation' between the one's-place and tens'-place digits in this example.

To model *repeated* events in this style, we need to use the set-theoretic idea of **cartesian product**: again, the cartesian product of n sets $X_1, \ldots, X_n$ is simply the collection of all ordered n tuples $(x_1, \ldots, x_n)$ (the parentheses and commas are mandatory), where $x_i \in X_i$. The notation is

$$X_1 \times \ldots \times X_n = \{(x_1, \ldots, x_n) : x_i \in X_i, 1 \le i \le n\}$$

(No, we are not in any sense generalizing the notion of 'multiplication': it's just a notation.) If all the sets X_i are the same set X, then there is a shorter notation,

$$X^n = \underbrace{X \times \ldots \times X}_{n}$$

suggested by exponential notation for repeated multiplication of *numbers*. Likewise, X^n is the nth **cartesian power** of the set X. Also, the word 'cartesian' is indeed often written in lowercase rather than uppercase, despite the fact that it comes from from René Descartes. The adjective is so widely used that it has been 'promoted' to lowercase. This is a peculiar distinction common in mathematics.

To repeat the experiment modeled by a probability space $\Omega = \{\omega_1, \ldots, \omega_t\}$ some number n times, consider the cartesian power Ω^n of Ω, which (by definition) is the collection of all ordered n-tuples of elements of Ω. We assign probabilities by

$$P((\omega_{i_1}, \omega_{i_2}, \ldots, \omega_{i_n})) = P(\omega_{i_1}) \cdot P(\omega_{i_2}) \cdot \ldots \cdot P(\omega_{i_n})$$

for any n-tuple $(\omega_{i_1}, \omega_{i_2}, \ldots, \omega_{i_n})$. It's not hard to check that with this probability measure Ω^n is a probability space. Further, even for 'compound' events A_1, ..., A_n in Ω, it's straightforward to show that

$$P(A_1 \times \ldots \times A_n) = P(A_1) \cdot \ldots \cdot P(A_n)$$

where $A_1 \times \ldots \times A_n$ is the cartesian product of the A_is and naturally sits inside the cartesian product $\Omega \times \ldots \times \Omega = \Omega^n$.

The idea is to imagine that $(\omega_{i_1}, \omega_{i_2}, \ldots, \omega_{i_n})$ is the event that ω_{i_1} occurs on the first trial, ω_{i_2} on the second, and so on until ω_{i_n} occurs on the nth. Implicit in this model is the idea that later events are *independent* of earlier ones. Otherwise that manner of assigning a probability measure on the cartesian power is not appropriate!

Example: Let $\Omega = \{H, T\}$ with $P(H) = 1/2$ and $P(T) = 1/2$, the fair-coin-flipping model. To model flipping a fair coin 10 times, one approach is to look at Ω^{10}, which is the set of all 10-tuples of values which are either heads or tails. Each such 10-tuple is assigned the same probability, $1/2^{10}$. Now consider the ('compound') event

$$A = \text{ exactly 7 heads in 10 flips}$$

This subset of Ω^{10} consists of all (ordered!) 10-tuples with exactly 7 *heads* values among them, and (by definition) the probability of A is the *number* of such multiplied by $1/2^{10}$, since each such 'atomic' event has probability $1/2^{10}$. Thus, to compute $P(A)$ we need only *count* the number of elements of A. It is the number of ways to choose 7 from among 10 things, which is the binomial coefficient $\binom{10}{7}$. Thus,

$$P(\text{7 heads in 10 flips}) = P(A) = \binom{10}{7} \cdot \frac{1}{2^{10}}$$

Example: Let $\Omega = \{r_1, b_1, b_2\}$ with $P(r_1) = P(b_1) = P(b_2) = 1/3$, modeling a red ball and two blue balls in an urn. To model drawing with replacement 5 times, one approach is to look at Ω^5, which is the set of all 5-tuples of values either r_1, b_1, or b_2. Each such 5-tuple is assigned the same probability, $1/3^5$. Now consider the ('compound') event

$$A = \text{ exactly 3 blues in 5 draws (with replacement)}$$

This subset of Ω^5 consists of all (ordered!) 5-tuples with exactly 3 b_1 or b_2 values among them, and (by definition) the probability of A is the *number* of such multiplied by $1/3^5$, since each such 'atomic' event has probability $1/3^5$. Thus, to compute $P(A)$ we could *count* the number of elements of A. But we can be a bit more clever. Let A_o be the subset $A_o = \{b_1, b_2\}$ of Ω corresponding to drawing a blue ball in a single draw. Then $P(A_o) = 2/3$, and A is the set of all 5-tuples in which exactly 3 elements of A_o appear. As noted above, the probability measure on the product space Ω assures that (for example)

$$P(A_o \times A_o \times A_o \times \{r_1\} \times \{r_1\}) = P(A_o) \cdot P(A_o) \cdot P(A_o) \cdot P(r_1) \cdot P(r_1) = \left(\frac{2}{3}\right)^3 \cdot \left(\frac{1}{3}\right)^2$$

Note that the numerical value does not depend on the exact *location* of the A_os and the r_1s, but only on the *number* of them. Thus, the number of ways to choose the 3 locations of the A_o element from among the 5 places is the binomial coefficient $\binom{5}{3}$. Thus,

$$P(3 \text{ blues in } 5 \text{ draws}) = P(A) = \binom{5}{3} \cdot \left(\frac{2}{3}\right)^3 \cdot \left(\frac{1}{3}\right)^2$$

Remark: All our examples so far are **finite** probability spaces, meaning the obvious thing, that there are only finitely many elements of the set, so only finitely-many 'atomic' events. This restriction is not really terribly confining, and already gives ample opportunity to illustrate many fundamental phenomena, but nevertheless we might want to see how to treat some **infinite** probability spaces.

Example: Suppose we take Ω to be the interval $[0, 1]$ of real numbers and that we want every real number in that interval to be equally probable to be selected. If we try to assign values $P(x)$ to $x \in [0, 1]$ since they are all equal, but infinitely many must add up to 1, we find ourselves in an impossible situation. Instead, we give up on the idea of assigning a probability to *every* subset A of $\Omega = [0, 1]$, *and* give up on the too-naive idea that

$$P(A) = \sum_{x \in A} P(x)$$

and instead only assign probabilities to a restricted class of subsets. For example, we might assign

$$P([a, b]) = b - a$$

for any subinterval $[a, b]$ of $[0, 1]$, and then define

$$P([a_1, b_1] \cup \ldots \cup [a_n, b_n]) = P([a_1, b_1]) + \ldots + P([a_n, b_n])$$

for *disjoint* collections of intervals $[a_i, b_i]$. This is a start, but we need more. In fact, for a collection of mutually disjoint intervals

$$[a_1, b_1], \ [a_2, b_2], \ [a_3, b_3], \ \ldots$$

indexed by positive integers, we can compute the probability of the union by the obvious formula

$$P([a_1, b_1] \cup [a_2, b_2] \cup \ldots) = P([a_1, b_1]) + P([a_2, b_2]) + \ldots$$

(A collection indexed by the positive integers is called **countable**.) We could also compute the probability measure of the **complement**

$$\{\omega \in \Omega : \omega \notin A\}$$

of a set A in the reasonable manner, by

$$P(\text{not } A) = 1 - P(A)$$

Further, we can repeat these two types of operations, taking countable unions of disjoint sets, and taking complements, making ever more complicated sets whose probability measure is definable in this example. (The totality of sets created has a name: it is the collection of **Borel sets** in $[0, 1]$.) To know that these processes really define a probability measure requires proof!

Example: A more important example for our immediate applications is

$$\Omega = \{\text{infinite sequences } (s_1, s_2, s_3, \ldots)\}$$

where all the symbols s_i lie in some fixed set Ω_o. Analogous to the previous example, we restrict our attention initially to **cylinders** (also called **cylindrical sets**), which means sets of the form

$$S(s_1, s_2, \ldots, s_n)$$

$$= \{\text{ sequences } (s_1, s_2, \ldots, s_n, s_{n+1}, \ldots) : \text{ where } s_t \text{ is arbitrary for } t > n \}$$

where the length n of the specified initial segment can vary from cylinder set to cylinder set. As in the previous example, we can then assign probability measures to countable unions $\bigcup_{i=1}^{\infty} A_i$ of disjoint sets A_i by

$$P\left(\bigcup_{i=1}^{\infty} A_i\right) = \sum_{i=1}^{\infty} P(A_i)$$

Assign probabilities to the complement $A^c = \{\omega \in \Omega : \omega \notin A\}$ by

$$P(A^c) = 1 - P(A)$$

We can repeat these processes indefinitely, making ever more complicated subsets to which we can assign a probability measure.

1.5 Random variables, expected values, variance

The idea of **expected value** of an uncertain 'experiment' or 'test' or 'trial' exists in colloquial language already, but must be made more precise for mathematical use. In many cases an intuitive version matches very well with the more formal one, but one must be cautious. Likewise, the **variance** of a random variable indicates roughly how much the actual values differ from the expected value, but we can be more precise.

A **random variable** X is a real-valued function X on a probability space Ω (with implicit probability measure $P()$).

Remark: It is possible to consider complex-valued or vector-valued random variables X, or any kind of values that can be added together and multiplied by real numbers, but for our purposes real-valued ones will suffice.

Remark: Yes, due to tradition at least, instead of the 'f' otherwise often used for functions, an 'X' is used, perhaps to be more consonant with the usual use of x for a (non-random?) 'variable'. Further, there is a tradition that makes the *values* of X be labeled 'x_i' (in conflict with the calculus tradition).

For a possible *value* x of X, we extend the notation by writing

$$P(X = x) = P(\{\omega \in \Omega : X(\omega) = x\})$$

That is, the probability that $X = x$ is defined to be the probability of the subset of Ω on which X has the value x.

The **expected value** of such a random variable on a probability space $\Omega = \{\omega_1, \ldots, \omega_n\}$ is defined to be

$$E(X) = P(\omega_1) \cdot X(\omega_1) + P(\omega_2) \cdot X(\omega_2) + \ldots + P(\omega_n) \cdot X(\omega_n)$$

Of course, we may imagine that after a 'large' number of independent trials with outcomes $\omega_{i_1}, \omega_{i_2}, \ldots, \omega_{i_N}$ the *average* value

$$\frac{1}{N}\left(X(\omega_{i_1}) + X(\omega_{i_2}) + \ldots + X(\omega_{i_N}) \right)$$

will be 'close to' $E(X)$. But in fact we can *prove* such a thing, rather than just imagine that it's true: again, it is a *Law of Large Numbers*.

The simplest models for the intuitive content of this idea have their origins in gambling. For example, suppose Alice and Bob ('A' and 'B') have a fair coin (meaning heads and tails both have probability 0.5) and the wager is that if the coin shows *heads* Alice pays Bob a dollar, and if it shows *tails* Bob pays Alice a dollar. Our intuition tells us that this is fair, and the expected value computation corroborates this, as follows. The sample space is $\Omega = \{\omega_0, \omega_1\}$ (index '0' for heads and '1' for tails), with each point having probability 0.5. Let X be the random variable which measures Alice's gain (or loss):

$$X(\omega_0) = -1 \quad X(\omega_1) = +1$$

Then the expected value of X, Alice's *expected* gain, is

$$E(X) = 0.5 \cdot (-1) + 0.5 \cdot (+1) = 0$$

In general, a **fair wager** is one such that everyone's expected gain is 0. (What's the point of it then? Probably that *perceptions* of probabilities can differ, and that some people like pure gambling.)

It is important to notice that an expected value is more sophisticated than the most naive idea of 'average'. For example, suppose we choose an integer at random in the range 1–10 and square it. With equal probabilities assigned, the expected value of the square is

$$\frac{1}{10}0^2 + \frac{1}{10}1^2 + \ldots + \frac{1}{10}10^2 = \frac{1}{10}385 = 38.5$$

It is *not* true that we can take the average of 0–10 first (namely, 5) and square it (getting 25) to obtain the expected value.

Proposition: Let X and Y be two random variables on a sample space $\Omega = \{\omega_1, \ldots, \omega_n\}$, with probabilities $P(\omega_i) = p_i$. The **sum** random variable $X + Y$ is defined in the natural way as

$$(X + Y)(\omega_i) = X(\omega_i) + Y(\omega_i)$$

Then

$$E(X + Y) = E(X) + E(Y)$$

Proof: This is a direct computation from the definition:

$$E(X + Y) = \sum_i p_i \left(X(\omega_i) + Y(\omega_i) \right)$$

$$= \sum_i p_i \, X(\omega_i) + \sum_i p_i \, Y(\omega_i)) = E(X) + E(Y)$$

$$///$$

Proposition: Let X be a random variable on a sample space $\Omega = \{\omega_1, \ldots, \omega_n\}$, with probabilities $P(\omega_i) = p_i$. Let c be a constant. The random variable cX is defined in the natural way as

$$cX(\omega_i) = c \cdot X(\omega_i)$$

Then

$$E(cX) = c \cdot E(X)$$

Proof: This is a direct computation from the definition:

$$E(cX) = \sum_i p_i \, cX(\omega_i) = c \sum_i p_i \, X(\omega_i) = c \cdot E(X)$$

$$///$$

Let Ω be a sample space. Let X and Y be random variables on Ω. The **product random variable** XY is defined on the sample space Ω in the reasonable way:

$$(XY)(\omega) = X(\omega)\, Y(\omega)$$

These two random variables X and Y are **independent random variables** if for every pair x, y of possible *values* of X, Y, we have

$$P(X = x \text{ and } Y = y) = P(X = x) \cdot P(Y = y)$$

(This definition of independence is really just a paraphrase of the earlier definition of independence of *events*, applied to several implicitly defined events.)

The following assertion is not generally true without the hypothesis of independence. We give an example of this after the proof.

Proposition: For two *independent* random variables X, Y on a sample space Ω, the expected value of the product is the product of the expected values:

$$E(XY) = E(X) \cdot E(Y)$$

Proof: The definition of the expected value of the product is

$$E(XY) = \sum_{w \in \Omega} P(w) XY(w)$$

By the definition of XY, this is

$$\sum_{w \in \Omega} P(w) X(w) Y(w)$$

To prove the proposition gracefully it is wise to use the notation introduced above: let x range over possible *values* of X and let y range over possible values of Y. Then we can rewrite the expected value by grouping according to values of X and Y: it is

$$\sum_{x,y} \sum_{w} P(w) X(w) Y(w)$$

where for fixed (x, y) the inner sum is over w so that

$$X(w) = x \quad \text{and} \quad Y(w) = y$$

Then use the new notation to rewrite this as

$$= \sum_{x,y} P(X = x \text{ and } Y = y) \, x \, y$$

The assumption of independence is exactly that

$$P(X = x \text{ and } Y = y) = P(X = x) \cdot P(Y = y)$$

so the expression becomes

$$\sum_{x,y} P(X = x) P(Y = y) \, x \, y$$

which we can now separate as a product

$$= \sum_{x} P(X = x) \, x \; \cdot \; \sum_{y} P(Y = y) \, y = E(X) \cdot E(Y)$$

///

Remark: If X and Y are not independent the conclusion of the previous proposition may be false. For example, let X and Y both be the number of heads obtained in a single flip of a fair coin. Then $XY = X = Y$, and we compute that

$$E(X) = E(Y) = E(XY) = P(\text{head}) \cdot 1 + P(\text{tail}) \cdot 0 = \frac{1}{2} \cdot 1 + \frac{1}{2} \cdot 0 = \frac{1}{2}$$

Then

$$E(XY) = \frac{1}{2} \neq \frac{1}{4} = \frac{1}{2} \cdot \frac{1}{2} = E(X) \cdot E(Y)$$

An important case of independent random variables arises when several independent trials are conducted (with the same 'experiment'). Let Ω be a sample space. Consider N independent trials. Consider the product

$$\Omega^N = \underbrace{\Omega \times \ldots \times \Omega}_{N}$$

consisting of ordered N-tuples of elements from Ω. Let X_i be a random variable on Ω^N whose value only depends upon the *outcome of the ith trial*. Then for $i \neq j$ the two random variables X_i and X_j are independent.

The **variance** $\sigma^2(X)$ of a random variable X with expected value $\mu = E(X)$ is the expected value of the random variable $(X - \mu)^2$:

$$\sigma^2(X) = E\left((X - \mu)^2\right)$$

The (non-negative) square root σ of the variance σ^2 is the **standard deviation** of X.

Finally, we compute the expected value and variance for the **binomial distribution**. That is, fix a positive integer n, fix a real number p in the range $0 \leq p \leq 1$, and let Ω be the probability space consisting of all ordered n-tuples of 0's and 1's, with

$$P(\text{a particular sequence with } i \text{ 1's and } n - i \text{ 0's}) = p^i (1 - p)^{n-i}$$

Let X be the random variable on Ω defined by

$$X(\text{a sequence of } n \text{ 0's and 1's}) = \text{ number of 1's in the sequence}$$

Then from earlier examples we know that

$$P(X = i) = \begin{cases} \binom{n}{i} p^i (1 - p)^{n-i} & (\text{for } 0 \leq i \leq n) \\ 0 & (\text{otherwise}) \end{cases}$$

Proposition: With the random variable X as just above

$$E(X) = pn$$

$$\sigma^2(X) = p(1 - p)n$$

Remark: The expected value assertion is certainly intuitively plausible, and there are also easier arguments than what we give below, but it seems reasonable to warm up to the variance computation by a similar but easier computation of the expected value.

Proof: This computation will illustrate the use of *generating functions* to evaluate naturally occurring but complicated looking expressions. Let $q = 1 - p$.

First, let's get an expression for the expected value of X: from the definition,

$$E\,X = \sum_{i=0}^{n} i \cdot P(X = i) = \sum_{i=0}^{n} i \cdot \binom{n}{i} p^i\, q^{n-i}$$

An astute person who remembered the binomial theorem might remember that it asserts exactly that the analogous summation *without* the factor i in front of each term is simply the expanded form of $(p + q)^n$:

$$\sum_{i=0}^{n} \binom{n}{i} p^i\, q^{n-i} = (p + q)^n$$

This is encouraging! The other key point is to notice that if we *differentiate* the latter expression with respect to p, without continuing to require $q = 1 - p$, we get

$$\sum_{i=0}^{n} \binom{n}{i} i\, p^{i-1}\, q^{n-i} = n\,(p + q)^{n-1}$$

The left-hand side is nearly the desired expression, but we're missing a power of p throughout. To remedy this, multiply both sides of the equality by p, to obtain

$$\sum_{i=0}^{n} \binom{n}{i} i\, p^i\, q^{n-i} = n\,p(p + q)^{n-1}$$

Once again requiring that $p + q = 1$, this simplifies to give the expected value

$$E\,X = \sum_{i=0}^{n} \binom{n}{i} i\, p^i\, q^{n-i} = n\,p$$

To compute the variance, we first do some formal computations: let μ be $E(X)$. Then

$$\sigma^2(X) = E((X - \mu)^2) = E\left(X^2 - 2\mu X + \mu^2\right) = E(X^2) - 2\mu\,E(X) + \mu^2$$

$$= E(X^2) - 2\mu \cdot \mu + \mu^2 = E(X^2) - \mu^2$$

So to compute the variance of X the thing we need to compute is $E(X^2)$

$$E(X^2) = \sum_{k=0}^{n} P(X = k) \cdot k^2$$

As usual, there are $\binom{n}{k}$ ways to have exactly k 1's, and each way occurs with probability $p^k q^{n-k}$. Thus,

$$E(X^2) = \sum_{k=0}^{n} k^2 \cdot \binom{n}{k} p^k q^{n-k}$$

This is very similar to the expression that occurred above in computing the expected value, but now we have the extra factor i^2 in front of each term instead of i. But of course we might *repeat* the trick we used above and see what happens: since

$$p \frac{\partial}{\partial p} p^i = i p^i$$

then by repeating it we have

$$p \frac{\partial}{\partial p} \cdot p \frac{\partial}{\partial p} p^k = k^2 p^k$$

Thus, in the expression for $E(X^2)$, compute

$$\sum_{i=0}^{n} \binom{n}{i} i^2 p^i q^{n-i} = \sum_{i=0}^{n} \binom{n}{i} p \frac{\partial}{\partial p} \cdot p \frac{\partial}{\partial p} p^i q^{n-i}$$

$$= p \frac{\partial}{\partial p} \cdot p \frac{\partial}{\partial p} \sum_{i=0}^{n} \binom{n}{i} p^i q^{n-i} = p \frac{\partial}{\partial p} \cdot p \frac{\partial}{\partial p} (p+q)^n$$

since after getting the i^2 out from inside the sum we can recognize the binomial expansion. Taking derivatives gives

$$p \frac{\partial}{\partial p} \cdot p \frac{\partial}{\partial p} (p+q)^n = p \frac{\partial}{\partial p} \left(p \cdot n(p+q)^{n-1} \right) = p(1 \cdot n(p+q)^{n-1} + p \cdot n(n-1)(p+q)^{n-2})$$

Using $p + q = 1$ gives

$$E(X^2) = p(n + p \cdot n(n-1))$$

So then

$$\sigma^2 = E(X^2) - \mu^2 = p(n + p \cdot n(n-1)) - (pn)^2 = pn + p^2 n^2 - p^2 n - p^2 n^2$$

$$= p(1-p)n$$

This finishes the computation of the variance of a binomial distribution.   ///

Remark: The critical or skeptical reader might notice that there's something suspicious about differentiating with respect to p in the above arguments, as if p and q were independent variables, when in fact $p+q = 1$. Indeed, if a person had decided that p was a *constant*, then they might feel inhibited about differentiating with respect to it at all. But, in fact, there is no imperative to invoke the relationship $p + q = 1$ until *after* the differentiation, so the computation is legitimate.

1.6 Markov's inequality, Chebysheff's inequality

Among other things, this section is the technical preparation to prove a special case of the Law of Large Numbers, which roughly asserts that in the long run the outcomes of a random event don't stray too far from the *expected value* (mean), in a sense relative to the *variance*. To reduce visual clutter, we may suppress some parentheses, writing EX for $E(X)$ and $\sigma^2 X$ for $\sigma^2(X)$, and so on.

Theorem: *(Markov's Inequality)* Let X be a real-valued random variable, and let f be a non-negative-valued function on **R**. Fix $a > 0$. Then

$$P(f(X) \geq a) \leq \frac{Ef(X)}{a}$$

Proof: Let χ be the function

$$\chi(t) = \begin{cases} 1 & \text{(if } f(t) \geq a) \\ 0 & \text{(if } f(t) < a) \end{cases}$$

Then

$$f(X) \geq a \cdot \chi(X)$$

Note that the expected value of the random variable $\chi(X)$ is simply the probability that $f(X) \geq a$:

$$E\chi(X) = \sum_x P(\chi(X) = x) \cdot x = P(\chi(X) = 0) \cdot 0 + P(\chi(X) = 1) \cdot 1 = P(f(X) \geq a)$$

by the definition of χ. Taking the expected value of both sides of this and using $f(X) \geq a \cdot \chi(X)$ gives

$$E\, f(X) \geq a \cdot E\chi(X) = a \cdot P(f(X) \geq a)$$

by the previous observation.   ///

Corollary: *(Chebysheff's Inequality)* Let X be a real-valued random variable. Fix $\varepsilon > 0$. Then

$$P(|X - E(X)| \geq \varepsilon) \leq \frac{\sigma^2 X}{\varepsilon^2}$$

Proof: This follows directly from the Markov inequality, with $f(X) = (X - E(X))^2$ and $a = \varepsilon^2$.   ///

1.7 Law of Large Numbers

A Law of Large Numbers was first proven for the special case of binomial distributions (coin-tossing with a not-necessarily fair coin) by Borel in 1909. The general case was treated by Kolmogorov in 1933. Although 1909 and 1933 may seem distant now, many mathematicians had been interested in these questions since about 1600 because of applications to gambling, so it is in fact a bit strange that the Law of Large Numbers was put on firm ground so late. We'll just treat the binomial distribution case here.

Fix a real number p in the range $0 \leq p \leq 1$, and put $q = 1 - p$. These will be unchanged throughout this section. Let n be a positive integer, which will be thought of as *increasing*. Let Ω_n be the probability space consisting of all ordered n-tuples of 0's and 1's, with

$$P(\text{a sequence with } i \text{ 1s and } n - i \text{ 0s}) = p^i \, (1 - p)^i$$

Let X_n be the random variable on Ω_n defined by

$$X_n(\text{sequence of } n \text{ 0s and 1s}) = \text{number of 1s in the sequence}$$

Then from earlier examples we know that

$$P(X_n = i) = \binom{n}{i} p^i \, q^{n-i}$$

(for $0 \leq i \leq n$, 0 otherwise). We earlier computed the expected value $EX_n = pn$. We also computed the variance

$$\sigma^2(X_n) = p(1 - p)n$$

The following assertion is a very simple example of what can be said:

Theorem: *(Weak Law of Large Numbers)* Let X_n be the random variable just above. Let $\varepsilon > 0$ be an arbitrarily small positive real number. Then

$$\lim_{n \to \infty} P(|X_n - E(X_n)| \geq \varepsilon \cdot n) = 0$$

Proof: We will obtain this by making a good choice of the parameter in Chebycheff's inequality. We know from computations above that $E(X_n) = p \cdot n$ and $\sigma^2(X_n) = p(1 - p)n$. Chebycheff's inequality asserts in general that

$$P\left(|X - E(X)| > t\sigma(X)\right) < \frac{1}{t^2}$$

where $\sigma(X)$ is the variance of X, which here gives

$$P\left(|X_n - p \cdot n| > t \cdot \sqrt{p(1-p)} \cdot \sqrt{n}\right) < \frac{1}{t^2}$$

Now take

$$t = \frac{\varepsilon}{\sqrt{p(1-p)}} \cdot \sqrt{n}$$

to obtain

$$P(|X_n - p \cdot n| > \varepsilon \cdot n) < \frac{p(1-p)}{n \cdot \varepsilon^2}$$

The right-hand side certainly goes to 0 as n goes to infinity, so we're done.   ///

Exercises

1.01 How many elements are in the set $\{1, 2, 2, 3, 3, 3, 4, 5\}$? How many are in the set $\{1, 2, \{2\}, 3, \{3\}, 4, 5\}$? In $\{1, 2, \{2, 3\}, 3, 4, 5\}$? (*ans.*)

1.02 Let $A = \{1, 2, 3, 4, 5\}$ and $B = \{3, 4, 5, 6, 7\}$. List (without repetition) the elements of the sets $A \cup B$, $A \cap B$, and of $\{x \in A : x \notin B\}$. (*ans.*)

1.03 List all the elements of the *power set* (set of subsets) of $\{1, 2, 3\}$. (*ans.*)

1.04 Let $A = \{1, 2, 3\}$ and $B = \{2, 3\}$. List (without repetition) all the elements of the *cartesian product* set $A \times B$. (*ans.*)

1.05 How many different ways are there to *order* the set $\{1, 2, 3, 4\}$? (*ans.*)

1.06 How many choices of 3 things from the list $1, 2, 3, \ldots, 9, 10$ are there? (*ans.*)

1.07 How many subsets of $\{1, 2, 3, 4, 5, 6, 7\}$ are there with exactly 4 elements? (*ans.*)

1.08 How many different choices are there of an *unordered* pair of *distinct* numbers from the set $\{1, 2, \ldots, 9, 10\}$? How many choices of *ordered* pair are there? (*ans.*)

1.09 How many functions are there from the set $\{1, 2, 3\}$ to the set $\{2, 3, 4, 5\}$? (*ans.*)

1.10 How many injective functions are there from $\{1, 2, 3\}$ to $\{1, 2, 3, 4\}$? (*ans.*)

1.11 How many injective functions are there from $\{1, 2, 3\}$ to $\{1, 2, 3, 4, 5\}$?

1.12 How many surjective functions are there from $\{1, 2, 3, 4\}$ to $\{1, 2, 3\}$? (*ans.*)

1.13 How many surjective functions are there from $\{1, 2, 3, 4, 5\}$ to $\{1, 2, 3, 4\}$?

1.14 How many surjective functions are there from $\{1, 2, 3, 4, 5\}$ to $\{1, 2, 3\}$?

1.15 Prove a formula for the number injective functions from an m-element set to an n-element set.

1.16 (*) Let $S(m, n)$ be the number of surjective functions from an m-element set to an n-element set (with $m \geq n$). Prove the recursive formula

$$S(m, n) = n^m - \sum_{i=1}^{n-1} \binom{n}{i} \cdot S(m, i)$$

1.17 Show that if $f : A \to B$ and $g : B \to C$ are functions with inverses, then $g \circ f$ has an inverse, and this inverse is $f^{-1} \circ g^{-1}$.

1.18 Show that for a surjective function $f : A \to B$ there is a **right inverse** g, meaning a function $g : B \to A$ so that $f \circ g = \text{id}_B$ (but not necessarily $g \circ f = \text{id}_A$.)

1.19 Show that for an injective function $f : A \to B$ there is a **left inverse** g, meaning a function $g : B \to A$ so that $g \circ f = \text{id}_A$ (but not necessarily $f \circ g = \text{id}_B$.)

1.20 Verify that the sum of all binomial coefficients $\binom{n}{k}$ with $0 \le k \le n$ is 2^n. (*ans.*)

1.21 Verify that the sum of expressions $(-1)^k \binom{n}{k}$ with $0 \le k \le n$ is 0.

1.22 How many subsets of all sizes are there of a set S with n elements? (*ans.*)

1.23 How many pairs are there of disjoint subsets A, B each with 3 elements inside the set $\{1, 2, 3, 4, 5, 6, 7, 8\}$? (*ans.*)

1.24 Give a *bijection* from the collection $2\mathbf{Z}$ of *even* integers to the collection $\mathbf{Z}$ of *all* integers. (*ans.*)

1.25 Give a *bijection* from the collection of *all* integers to the collection of *non-negative* integers. (*ans.*)

1.26 (*) Give a *bijection* from the collection of all positive integers to the collection of all rational numbers.

1.27 (**) This illustrates a hazard in a too naive notion of a rule for forming a set. Let S be the set of all sets which are not an element of themselves. That is, let

$$S = \{\text{ sets } x : x \notin x\}$$

Is $S \in S$ or is $S \notin S$? (*Hint:* Assuming either that S is or isn't an element of itself leads to a contradiction. What's going on?)

1.28 What is the probability of exactly 3 heads out of 10 flips of a fair coin? (*ans.*)

1.29 What is the probability that there will be *strictly more* heads than tails out of 10 flips of a fair coin? Out of 20 flips? (*ans.*)

1.30 If there are 3 red balls and 7 blue balls in an urn, what is the probability that in two trials two red balls will be drawn? (*ans.*)

1.31 If there are 3 red balls and 7 blue balls in an urn, what is the probability that in 10 trials at least 4 red balls will be drawn?

1.32 Prove that

$$1 + 2 + 3 + 4 + \ldots + (n - 1) + n = \frac{1}{2}n(n + 1)$$

1.33 A *die* is a small cube with numbers 1-6 on its six sides. A roll of two dice has an *outcome* which is the sum of the upward-facing sides of the two, so is an integer in the range 2-12. A die is *fair* if any one of its six sides is as likely to come up as any other. What is the probability that a roll of two fair dice will give either a '7' or an '8'? What is the probability of a '2'?

1.34 What is the probability that there will be fewer than (or exactly) N heads out of $3N$ flips of a fair coin?

1.35 (*) You know that in a certain house there are two children, but you do not know their genders. You know that each child has a 50-50 chance of being either gender. When you go to the door and knock, a girl answers the door. What is the probability of the other child being a boy? (False hint: out of the 4 possibilities girl-girl, girl-boy, boy-girl, boy-boy, only the first 3 occur since you know there is at least one girl in the house. Of those 3 possibilities, in 2/3 of the cases in addition to a girl there is a boy. So (?) if a girl answers the door then the probability is 2/3 that the other child is a boy.) (*Comment:* In the submicroscopic world of elementary particles, the behavior of the family of particles known as *bosons* is contrary to the correct macroscopic principle illustrated by this exercise, while *fermions* behave in the manner indicated by this exercise.)

1.36 The *Birthday Paradox.* Show that the probability is greater than 1/2 that, out of a given group of 24 people, at least two will have the same birthday.

1.37 (*) The *Monty Hall paradox* You are in a game show in which contestants choose one of three doors, knowing that behind one of the three is a good prize, and behind the others nothing of any consequence. After you've chosen one door, the gameshow host (Monty Hall) *always* shows you that behind one of the *other* doors there is *nothing* and offers you the chance to change your selection. Should you change? (What is the probability that the prize is behind the door you did not initially choose? What is the probability that the prize is behind the *other* closed door?)

1.38 (**) Suppose that two real numbers are chosen 'at random' between 0 and 1. What is the probability that their sum is greater than 1? What is the probability that their product is greater than 1/2?

1.39 If there are 3 red balls in an urn and 7 black balls, what is the *expected* number of red balls to be drawn in 20 trials (replacing whatever ball is drawn in each trial)? (*ans.*)

1.40 What is the expected number of consecutive heads as a result of tossing a fair coin? (*ans.*)

1.41 What is the expected number of coin flips before a head comes up (with a fair coin)?

1.42 What is the expected number of coin flips before two consecutive heads come up?

1.43 What is the expected distance between two 'e's in a random character stream where 'e's occur 11% of the time?

1.44 What is the expected distance between two 'ee's in a random character stream where 'e's occur 11% of the time?

1.45 Let X be the random variable defined as 'the number of heads in 10 flips of a fair coin.' The sample space is all 2^{10} different possible sequences of outcomes of 10 flips. The expected value of X itself is 5. What is the expected value of the random variable $(X - 5)^2$?

1.46 (*) What is the expected number of coin flips before n consecutive heads come up?

1.47 (*) Choose two real numbers 'at random' from the interval $[0, 1]$. What is the expected value of their sum? product?

1.48 Compute the variance of the random variable which tells the result of the roll of one fair die.

1.49 Compute the variance of the random variable which tells the sum of the result of the roll of two fair dice.

1.50 Compute the variance of the random variable which tells the sum of the result of the roll of three fair dice.

1.51 (*) Compute the variance of the random variable which tells the sum of the result of the roll of n fair dice.

1.52 (*) Consider a coin which has probability p of heads. Let X be the random variable which tells how long before 2 heads in a row come up. What is the variance of X?

1.53 Gracefully estimate the probability that in 100 flips of a fair coin the number of heads will be at least 40 and no more than 60. (*ans.*)

1.54 Gracefully estimate the probability that in 1000 flips of a fair coin the number of heads will be at least 400 and no more than 600. (*ans.*)

1.55 Gracefully estimate the probability that in 10,000 flips of a fair coin the number of heads will be at least 4000 and no more than 6000. (*ans.*)

1.56 With a coin that has probability only 1/10 of coming up heads, show that the probability is less than 1/9 that in 100 flips the number of heads will be more than 20. (*ans.*)

1.57 With a coin that has probability only 1/10 of coming up heads, show that the probability is less than 1/900 that in 10,000 flips the number of heads will be less than 2000.

2

Information

The words **uncertainty, information,** and **redundancy** all have some intuitive content. The term **entropy** from thermodynamics may suggest a related notion, namely a degree of *disorder*. We can make this more precise, and in our context we will decide that the three things, uncertainty, information, and entropy, all refer to roughly the same thing, while redundancy refers to *lack* of uncertainty.

Noiseless coding addresses the issue of organizing information well for transmission, by adroitly *removing* redundancy. It does *not* address issues about noise or any other sort of errors. The most visible example of noiseless coding is **compression** of data, although abbreviations, shorthand, and symbols are equally important examples.

The other fundamental problem is *noisy coding*, more often called **error-correcting coding**, meaning to adroitly *add* redundancy to make information robust against noise and other errors.

The first big result in noiseless coding is that the **entropy** of a **memoryless source** gives a lower bound on the **length** of a code which encodes the source. And the **average word length** of such a code is bounded in terms of the entropy. This should be interpreted as a not-too-surprising assertion that the entropy of a source correctly embodies the notion of how much information the source emits.

2.1 Uncertainty, acquisition of information

It turns out that a very reasonable list of requirements for a notion of **entropy** *uniquely characterizes* it. This is a theorem!

First, let's try to clarify a bit what we mean by **uncertainty** and **information**.

For example, the outcome of a *fair* coin flip is *more uncertain* than the outcome of a biased coin which gives heads 3/4 of the time and tails 1/4.

The outcome of the roll of a single fair die (with faces 1–6) is more uncertain than the toss of a coin: there are more things that can happen, each of which has rather small probability.

On the other hand, we can talk in a similar manner about acquisition of **information**. For example, in a message consisting of ordinary English, the completion of the fragment

> Because the weather forecast called for rain, she took her...

to

> Because the weather forecast called for rain, she took her umbrella.

imparts very little further information. While it's true that the sentence might have ended *boots* instead, we have a clear picture of where the sentence is going. By contrast, completion of the fragment

> The weather forecast called for...

to

> The weather forecast called for rain.

imparts a relatively large amount of information, since the first part of the sentence gives no clues to its ending. Even more uncertainty remains in trying to complete a sentence like

> Then he surprised everyone by...

and commensurately more information is acquired when we know the completion.

In a related direction: the reason we are able to skim newspapers and other 'lightweight' text so quickly is that most of the words are not at all vital to the content, so if we ignore many of them the message still comes through: the information content is low, and information is repeated. By contrast, technical writing is harder to read, because it is more concise, thereby not allowing us to skip over things. It is usually not as repetitive as more ordinary text. What 'concise' means here is that it **lacks redundancy** (meaning that it does not repeat itself). Equivalently, there is a high **information rate**.

Looking at the somewhat lower-level structure of language: most isolated typographical errors in ordinary text are not hard to correct. This is because of the **redundancy** of natural languages such as English. For example,

> The sun was shining brghtly.

is easy to correct to

> The sun was shining brightly.

In fact, in this particular example, the modifier 'brightly' is hardly necessary at all: the content would be almost identical if the word were omitted entirely. By contrast, typographical errors are somewhat harder to detect and correct in technical writing than in ordinary prose, because there is less redundancy, especially without a larger context.

Note that correction of typos is a lower-level task than replacing missing words, since it relies more upon recognition of what might or might not be an English word rather than upon understanding the content. Corrections based upon *meaning* would be called **semantics**-based correction, while corrections based upon misspelling or grammatical errors would be **syntax**-based correction. Syntax-based correction is clearly easier to automate than semantics-based correction, since the 'rules' for semantics are much more complicated than the 'rules' for spelling and grammar (which many people find complicated enough already).

Still, not every typo is easy to fix, because sometimes they occur at critical points in a sentence:

I cano go with you.

In this example, the 'cano' could be either 'can' with a random 'o' stuck on its end, or else either 'cannot' with two omissions or maybe '*can't*' with two errors. By contrast, errors in a different part of the message, as in

I can go wih you.

are easier to fix. In the first of these two examples, there would be a lot of **information** imparted by fixing the typo, but in the second case very little. In other words, in the first case there was high **uncertainty**, but in the second not.

Let's look at several examples of the loss of intelligibility of a one-line sentence subjected to a 12% rate of random errors. That is, for purposes of this example, we'll randomly change about 12% of the *letters* to something else. We'll do this several times to see the various effects. Starting with

Experiment and pattern recognition are important in number theory.

we get

Dxpbviment and pattecn recognition arx iqporxant in kumder theofy.
Expurkmest and pattetn rncognition zrp impoxtant in number theocv.
Expecimeno and pattern recognition ake imboltanj in number thporq.
Experimect utk pattern regognitoon ame important in nkmber theoxy.
Experiment and pattern rncognltion xre important in yumbwr qheory.
Expkriment and pattern recognition bre importajt ip number tceory.
Ewperiment and gattern ieungnition are impjrtdlt in numwer theory.
Experiment awk gattern recognition are important jr qumbea tkeosj.
Euperiment anm paltern recognition are importanr in numbew tpvory.
Exmeriment and piztkrn recognition are importgnt in number theory.

Several things should be observed here. First, the impact on clarity and correctability depends greatly on which letters get altered. For example, the word 'number' is sensitive in this regard. Second, although the *average* rate of errors is 12%, sometimes more errors than this occur, and sometimes fewer. And the distribution of errors is not regular. That is, a 12% error rate does not simply mean that every 8th letter is changed, but only expresses an *average*. Among the above 10 samples, in at least 2 the meaning seems quite obscure. Third, using more than one of the mangled sentences makes it very easy to infer the correct original.

With an error rate of 20%, there are frequent serious problems in intelligibility: perhaps *none* of the ten samples retains its meaning if presented in isolation. From the same phrase as above

> Dxpbviment and pattecn recognition arx dmpottant in kumder theofy.
> Expurkmest and pathgrn abcognitiom lre imvortanl vn numser teeory.
> Pxpefiment cnd patrern recogibtiyz ure yvmortnnt iy nmmber thodry.
> Edwhriment anh putzern mecovnition arl mmportanq im number theory.
> Experimewt ang patjern recognition ace iepootant in uumber thkory.
> Experiment and patuerj rgcocnitkon gre ihportans in numbej tyeoul.
> Vxhdpiment and patoejc rvcognioion are important in ndtbvr theory.
> Experiment and pattern rfgojsitreq asp ijportant in wvhber theory.
> Exaegiment and paryern rectgrikion aoj imuovtant en thmbyr theory.
> Expedimctt anc katcern recagnition rre impertant in numbzr theory.

In these 10 examples few of the words are recognizable. That is, looking for an English word whose spelling is *close* to the given, presumably *misspelled*, word does not succeed on a majority of the words in these garbled fragments. This is because so many letters have been changed that there are too many equally plausible possibilities for correction. Even using semantic information, these sentences are mostly too garbled to allow recovery of the message.

Notice, though, that when we have, in effect, 9 **retransmissions** of the original (each garbled in its own way) it is possible to make inferences about the original message. For example, the 10 messages can have a **majority vote** on the correct letter at each spot in the true message. Ironically, the fact that there are so many different error possibilities but only one correct possibility makes it easy for the correct message to win such votes. But a large number of repetitions is an inefficient method for compensating for noise in a communications channel.

Another version of noise might result in **erasures** of some characters. Thus, we might be assured that any letter that 'comes through' is correct, but some are simply omitted.

One point of this discussion is that while English (or any other natural language) has quite a bit of redundancy in it, this redundancy is unevenly distributed. In other words, the *information* in English is not uniformly distributed but is concentrated at some spots and thin at others.

Another way to illustrate the redundancy is to recall an advertisement from the New York subways of years ago:

> F u cn rd ths, u cn gt a gd jb.

An adroit selection of about 40% of the letters was removed, but this is still intelligible.

2.2 Definition of entropy

Some very reasonable and intuitive conditions for **entropy** of a *random variable* turn out to uniquely determine what this notion of entropy must be. The list of axioms characterizing entropy is essentially due to Claude Shannon, from about 1948. We give the definition and an important basic inequality here.

We will only talk about a low-level *syntactical* version of **information** and **entropy**, since this can be formalized. More interesting but subtler questions about *semantic* information are too sophisticated for this context.

The intuitive idea of **uncertainty** in some experiment (such as coin flipping or dice rolling) measures how much **information** we will have acquired *after* the experiment is over. **Entropy** is a synonym for uncertainty in this sense. We will use the word 'entropy' from now on to make clear that we refer to these particular issues.

Let $\Omega = \{\omega_1, \ldots, \omega_n\}$ be a finite sample space, with probabilities $P(\omega_i)$, with

$$P(\omega_1) + P(\omega_2) + \ldots + P(\omega_{n-1}) + P(\omega_n) = 1$$

and

$$P(\omega_i) \geq 0 \quad \text{(for all indices } i\text{)}$$

as usual. The **(self-) information** of the event ω_i is defined to be

$$\text{self-information of event } \omega_i \; = I(\omega_i) = -\log_2 P(\omega_i)$$

Thus, a relatively unlikely event has greater (self-) information than a relatively likely event.

For example, for flipping a fair coin, the sample space is $\{\text{H}, \text{T}\}$. Since the coin is *fair*,

$$P(\text{H}) = P(\text{T}) = \frac{1}{2}$$

The self-information of either head or tail is

$$I(\text{H}) = -\log_2 \frac{1}{2} = 1$$

$$I(\text{T}) = -\log_2 \frac{1}{2} = 1$$

This simplest example motivates the name for the **unit** of information, the **bit**.

The **entropy** of a sample space is the *expected value* of the self-information of (atomic) events in Ω. That is, with the notation as just above,

$$\text{entropy of sample space} \; = H(\Omega) = \sum_{1 \leq i \leq n} P(\omega_i) \, I(\omega_i)$$

$$= \sum_{1 \leq i \leq n} -P(\omega_i) \log_2 P(\omega_i)$$

Remark: If $p_i = 0$, then 'interpret' $p_i \log_2 p_i = 0$. This is reasonable, because recall from calculus that

$$\lim_{x \to 0+} x \log_b x = 0$$

for any base $b > 1$.

Thinking of sample spaces as representing some sort of experiments or tests, the **entropy** should be a measure of the information acquired by performing the experiment, or, equivalently, how much *uncertainty* is eliminated. Since we don't care what the *values* of the random variable are, but only care about the probabilities $p_1, \ldots, p_n$, we may also suppress the reference to the sample space itself and just refer to the probabilities: write

$$H(p_1, \ldots, p_n) = \text{ entropy of sample space } \{x_1, \ldots, x_n\} \text{ with } P(\omega_i) = p_i$$

We also can define the entropy of a random variable X in a similar way. Let X be a random variable on a sample space $\Omega = \{\omega_1, \ldots, \omega_n\}$. The entropy of X can be viewed as a sort of expected value:

$$H(X) = \sum_{\text{values } x \text{ of } X} -P(X = x) \log_2 P(X = x)$$

Now we state the axioms for entropy. The point is not to give an axiomatic system, but rather to discuss the desirable features that we're trying to embody. It is worth being conscious and explicit about these requirements.

- $H(p_1, \ldots, p_n)$ is maximum when $p_1 = \ldots = p_n = \frac{1}{n}$. That is, the most pre-existing uncertainty is when all possibilities are equally likely.
- For any permutation $i \to s(i)$ of the indices,

$$H(p_1, \ldots, p_n) = H\left(p_{s(1)}, \ldots, p_{s(n)}\right)$$

That is, only the probabilities matter, not their ordering or labeling.
- $H(p_1, \ldots, p_n) \geq 0$, and is 0 only if one of the p_is is 1. That is, uncertainty disappears entirely only if there is no randomness present.
- $H(p_1, \ldots, p_n) = H(p_1, \ldots, p_n, 0)$. That is, 'impossible' outcomes do not contribute to uncertainty.
-
$$H(\underbrace{\frac{1}{n}, \ldots, \frac{1}{n}}_{n}) \leq H(\underbrace{\frac{1}{n+1}, \ldots, \frac{1}{n+1}}_{n+1})$$

That is, a larger ensemble of equally likely possibilities is more uncertain than a smaller ensemble.
- H should be a continuous function of the probabilities: 'small' changes in the probabilities should not cause 'large' changes in uncertainty.
- For positive integers m, n,

$$H\left(\frac{1}{mn}, \ldots, \frac{1}{mn}\right) = H\left(\frac{1}{m}, \ldots, \frac{1}{m}\right) + H\left(\frac{1}{n}, \ldots, \frac{1}{n}\right)$$

That is, the uncertainty in performing two independent experiments should be the **sum** of the two uncertainties.

- Let $p = p_1 + \ldots + p_m$ and $q = q_1 + \ldots + q_n$ with all p_i and q_j positive, and $p + q = 1$. Then

$$H(p_1, \ldots, p_m, q_1, \ldots, q_n) = H(p, q) + pH(p_1, \ldots, p_m) + qH(q_1, \ldots, q_n)$$

This is about *conditional probabilities* and a sensible requirement about uncertainty in such a situation. That is, we *group* the outcomes of an experiment into two subsets and then say that the uncertainty is the uncertainty of which batch the outcome falls into, plus the *weighted* sum of the uncertainties about exactly where the outcome falls in the subsets.

Theorem: Any entropy function $H(p_1, \ldots, p_n)$ meeting the above conditions is a positive scalar multiple of

$$H(p_1, \ldots, p_n) = \sum_i -p_i \log_2 p_i$$

(For a proof, see [Roman 1992], page 13.)

Remark: Again, if $p_i = 0$, 'interpret' $p_i \log_2 p_i$ as 0, since

$$\lim_{x \to 0^+} x \log_b x = 0$$

Remark: The logarithm is taken base 2 for historical reasons. Changing the base of the logarithm to any other number $b > 1$ merely uniformly divides the values of the entropy function by $\log_2 b$. Thus, for comparison of the relative uncertainty of different sets of probabilities, it doesn't really matter what base is used for the logarithm. But base 2 is traditional and also does make some answers come out nicely. Some early work by Hartley used logarithms base 10 instead, and in that case the unit of information or entropy is the *Hartley*, which possibly sounds more exotic.

Remark: The units for entropy are also *bits*, since we view entropy as an expected value (thus, a kind of *average*) of information, whose unit is the *bit*. This is compatible with the other use of *bit* (for *binary digit*), as the coin-flipping example illustrates.

Example: The entropy in a single toss of a fair coin is

$$H\,(\text{coin}) = H\left(\frac{1}{2}, \frac{1}{2}\right) = \frac{1}{2}\left(-\log_2 \frac{1}{2}\right) + \frac{1}{2}\left(-\log_2 \frac{1}{2}\right)$$

$$= \frac{1}{2}\left(-(-1)\right) + \frac{1}{2}(-(-1))\right) = 1 \text{ bit}$$

Indeed, one might imagine that such a coin toss is a basic unit of information. Further, if we label the coin '0' and '1' instead of 'heads' and 'tails', then such a coin toss exactly determines the value of a *bit*.

Example: The entropy in a single roll of a standard six-sided die is

$$H\,(\text{die}) = H\left(\frac{1}{6},\frac{1}{6},\frac{1}{6},\frac{1}{6},\frac{1}{6},\frac{1}{6}\right) = -\sum_{i=1}^{6}\frac{1}{6}\log_2\frac{1}{6} = \log_2 6 \approx 2.58496250072 \text{ bits}$$

Example: To compute the entropy of the sum-of-two-dice random variable (two dice rolled together, and their sum taken), notice first that there are $6 \cdot 6 = 36$ possible rolls altogether, and among these just 1 way to get 2, 2 ways to get 3, 3 ways to get 4, 4 ways to get 5, 5 ways to get 6, 6 ways to get 7, and then the counting starts to decline: just 5 ways to get 8, 4 ways to get 9, 3 ways to get 10, 2 ways to get 11, and 1 way to get 12. Thus, the entropy is computed as

$$H\,(\text{sum two dice}) = H\left(\frac{1}{36},\frac{2}{36},\frac{3}{36},\frac{4}{36},\frac{5}{36},\frac{6}{36},\frac{5}{36},\frac{4}{36},\frac{3}{36},\frac{2}{36},\frac{1}{36}\right)$$

$$= -\frac{1}{36}\log_2\frac{1}{36} - \frac{2}{36}\log_2\frac{2}{36} - \cdots - \frac{1}{36}\log_2\frac{1}{36} \approx 3.27440191929 \text{ bits}$$

Example: The entropy in a single letter of English (assuming that the various letters will occur with probability equal to their frequencies in typical English) is approximately

$$H(\text{letter of English}) \approx 4.19$$

(This is based on empirical information, that 'e' occurs about 11% of the time, 't' occurs about '9'% of the time, etc.) By contrast, if all letters were equally likely, then the entropy would be somewhat larger, about

$$H\left(\frac{1}{26},\ldots,\frac{1}{26}\right) = \log_2 (26) \approx 4.7$$

Remark: The proof that the axioms uniquely characterize entropy is hard, and not necessary for us, so we'll skip it. But an interested reader can certainly use basic properties of logarithms (and a bit of algebra and basic probability) to verify that

$$H(p_1,\ldots,p_n) = -\sum_i p_i \log_2 p_i$$

meets the conditions, even if it's not so easy to prove that nothing *else* does.

Joint entropy of a collection X_1, ..., X_N of random variables is defined in the reasonably obvious manner

$$H(X_1,\ldots,X_n)$$

$$= -\sum_{x_1,\ldots,x_n} P(X_1 = x_1,\ldots,X_n = x_n) \log_2 P(X_1 = x_1,\ldots,X_n = x_n)$$

To prove a few basic things about entropy, we need:

Lemma: Fix $p_1, \ldots, p_n$ with each $p_i \geq 0$ and $\sum_i p_i = 1$. Let $q_1, \ldots, q_n$ vary, subject only to the restriction that $q_i \geq 0$ for all indices, and $\sum_i q_i = 1$. Then

$$\min_{q_1, \ldots, q_n} -\sum_i p_i \log_2 q_i$$

occurs only when $q_i = p_i$ for all indices.

Proof: First, from looking at the graph of $\ln x$ we see that the tangent line at $x = 1$ lies above the graph of $\ln x$ and touches it only at $x = 1$. That is,

$$\ln x \leq x - 1$$

with equality only for $x = 1$. And since

$$\log_2 x = \log_2 e \cdot \ln x$$

we have

$$\log_2 x \leq (\log_2 e)(x - 1)$$

with equality only for $x = 1$. Then replace x by q/p to obtain

$$\log_2 (q/p) \leq (\log_2 e)(q/p - 1)$$

Multiply through by p to get

$$p \log_2 (q/p) \leq (\log_2 e)(q - p)$$

and then

$$p \log_2 q \leq p \log_2 p + (\log_2 e)(q - p)$$

with equality occurring only for $q = p$. Replacing p, q by p_i and q_i and adding the resulting inequalities, we have

$$\sum_i p_i \log_2 q_i \leq \sum_i p_i \log_2 p_i + (\log_2 e) \sum_i (q_i - p_i)$$

Since $\sum_i p_i = 1$ and $\sum_i q_i = 1$, this simplifies to

$$\sum_i p_i \log_2 q_i \leq \sum_i p_i \log_2 p_i$$

Multiplying through by -1 reverses the order of inequality and gives the assertion.

$/\!/\!/$

Corollary: $H(p_1, \ldots, p_n) \leq \log_2 n$ with equality occurring only when $p_i = \frac{1}{n}$ for all indices.

Proof: This corollary follows from the previous inequality by letting $q_i = \frac{1}{n}$. $/\!/\!/$

Corollary: For two random variables X, Y,

$$H(X,Y) \leq H(X) + H(Y)$$

with equality if and only if X and Y are independent random variables.

Proof: For brevity, let

$$
\begin{aligned}
p_i &= P(X = x_i) \\
q_j &= P(Y = y_j) \\
r_{ij} &= P(X = x_i, Y = y_j)
\end{aligned}
$$

We will use the fact that for fixed i we have $\sum_j r_{ij} = p_i$ and for fixed j we have $\sum_i r_{ij} = q_j$. Then compute directly:

$$H(X) + H(Y) = -\sum_i p_i \log_2 p_i - \sum_j q_j \log_2 q_j$$

$$= -\sum_i \left(\sum_j r_{ij} \right) \log_2 p_i - \sum_j \left(\sum_i r_{ij} \right) \log_2 q_j$$

Then reassemble the sum as

$$-\sum_{ij} r_{ij}(\log_2 p_i + \log_2 q_j) = -\sum_{ij} r_{ij} \log_2 p_i q_j \geq -\sum_{ij} r_{ij} \log_2 r_{ij} = H(X,Y)$$

by the Fundamental Inequality. And, further,

$$P(X = x_i, Y = y_j) = r_{ij} = p_i q_j = P(X = x_i)\, P(Y = y_j)$$

if and only if X and Y are independent.   ///

For an **event** (that is, *subset*) ω in a probability space Ω, and for a random variable X on that probability space, define a **conditional entropy** by

$$H(X|\omega) = -\sum_i P(X = x_i|\omega) \log_2 P(X = x_i|\omega)$$

And then for another random variable Y on Ω, define a **conditional entropy** by

$$H(X|Y) = \sum_j P(Y = y_j)\, H(X|Y = y_j)$$

where we use the previous notion of conditional entropy with respect to the subset ω where $Y = y_j$. The idea here is that $H(X|Y)$ is the amount of uncertainty or entropy remaining in X after Y is known.

It is pretty easy to check that

$$H(X|X) = 0$$

(so knowing the outcome of X removes all uncertainty about the outcome of X, which seems fair) and that

$$H(X|Y) = H(X) \quad \text{if } X \text{ and } Y \text{ are independent}$$

since the independence should presumably mean that no information about X is imparted by knowing about Y.

proto-Theorem: We have $H(X|Y) = 0$ if and only if X is a function of Y.

The previous proto-theorem, which is not a real theorem because the phrase *is a function of* needs clarification, is really a special case of the following genuine theorem.

Theorem: For two random variables X, Y on a probability space Ω, joint entropy is expressed in terms of conditional entropy by

$$H(X,Y) = H(Y) + H(X|Y)$$

Proof: Exercise in unraveling definitions! Try it!   ///

Exercises

2.01 Compute the entropy of a source with probabilities $\frac{1}{2}, \frac{1}{4}, \frac{1}{8}, \frac{1}{16}, \frac{1}{16}, \frac{1}{16}$.
(*ans.*)

2.02 Determine the entropy of a source with probabilities $\frac{1}{3}, \frac{1}{4}, \frac{1}{6}, \frac{1}{8}, \frac{1}{12}, \frac{1}{24}$.

2.03 Determine the entropy of a source with probabilities $\frac{2}{3}, \frac{2}{9}, \frac{2}{27}, \frac{2}{81}, \frac{2}{243}, \frac{1}{243}$.

2.04 Determine the entropy of the random variable which counts the number of heads in flipping three fair coins.

2.05 Determine the entropy of the random variable which counts the sum of three dice.

3

Noiseless Coding

Noiseless coding addresses the issue of organizing information well for transmission, by adroitly *removing* redundancy. It does *not* address issues about noise or any other sort of errors. The most visible example of noiseless coding is **compression** of data, although abbreviations, shorthand, and symbols are equally important examples.

The other fundamental problem is *noisy coding*, more often called **error-correcting coding**, meaning to adroitly *add* redundancy to make information robust against noise and other errors.

The first big result in noiseless coding is that the **entropy** of a **memoryless source** gives a lower bound on the **length** of a code which encodes the source. And the **average word length** of such a code is bounded in terms of the entropy. This should be interpreted as a not-too-surprising assertion that the entropy of a source correctly embodies the notion of how much information the source emits.

3.1 Noiseless coding

Noiseless coding is about expressing information in a good form for economical transmission. These days the idea of **compression** is familiar to everyone, even if the details are not quite so familiar, and compression algorithms are exactly noiseless encodings. In this little section we set up general formalism about noiseless coding.

Intuitively, a **memoryless source** using a set W of **source words** is anything which emits those words with prescribed probabilities, so that the probability that a given word $w \in W$ is emitted does *not* depend upon what came before it.

More formally, a **memoryless source** is a sequence $X_1, X_2, \ldots$ of independent and identically distributed random variables on a probability space, taking values in a set W of **source words**. A common abbreviation for the phrase *independent and identically distributed* is **i.i.d.**

Example: The simplest sort of source is a gadget which emits a stream of 0's and 1's with equal probabilities. In this case, each of the random variables $X_1, X_2, \ldots$ has **distribution**

$$P(X_i = 0) = \frac{1}{2}$$

$$P(X_i = 1) = \frac{1}{2}$$

Example: A very simple model of English is a memoryless source $X_1, X_2, \ldots$ where the possible values of the random variables X_i are characters a–z, where each character occurs with its average frequency:

$$
\begin{aligned}
P(X = \text{`e'}) &= 0.11 \\
P(X = \text{`t'}) &= 0.09
\end{aligned}
$$

$$\cdots$$

That is, the random variables X_i are identical and identically distributed. Of course, this is a rather silly model of English, but it has the virtue of simplicity.

Remark: The most general type of source, with no assumptions about interdependence, would be called a *stochastic source*. Such sources are probably too general to say much about. A more restricted model is a *Markov source*, meaning that there is a fixed T so that the nth word emitted (that is, the value of the random variable X_n) depends only the T previous values, $X_{n-1}, \ldots, X_{n-T}$. A yet more restricted model is a *stationary Markov source*, which is a Markov source in which the form of the dependence of X_n on $X_{n-1}, \ldots, X_{n-T}$ does not depend upon the 'time' index n. But for our present purposes things are complicated enough already for the simpler i.i.d. model.

An **alphabet** Σ is simply a finite set. The elements of the set Σ are the **characters** of the alphabet. For any alphabet Σ, denote by Σ^* the set of all finite **strings** composed of characters from Σ. That is, Σ^* is the collection of finite ordered lists of elements of Σ.

For example, the alphabet might simply be $\Sigma = \{0, 1\}$, or it might be $\Sigma = \{a, b, \ldots, y, z\}$. Or more characters might be included. It is clear that the precise nature of the characters does not matter, but perhaps at most the *number* of characters in the alphabet.

A **code** or **encoding** f of a (memoryless) source $S = X_1, X_2, \ldots$ (emitting sourcewords in a set W) into codeword strings over an alphabet Σ is simply a map (that is, *function*)

$$f : W \to \Sigma^*$$

We extend the definition of the code f by making it behave reasonably with respect to concatenation of strings: define

$$f(\text{ concatenation } w_1 w_2 \ldots w_n) = \text{ concatenation } f(w_1)f(w_2) \ldots f(w_n)$$

Example: For encoding the English alphabet into dots and dashes for telegraph transmission, the alphabet Σ is {dot, dash}, and the collection W of 'words' can be simply the usual English alphabet. An important design feature of this encoding is that more commonly used letters such as 'e' and 't' have shorter expressions in the Morse alphabet, for example. (Notice that in this case the 'words' are not words in the colloquial sense, but instead are letters in the English alphabet.)

Example: Another example is the encoding of the English alphabet (along with numerals, punctuation, and some control characters) into ASCII code, that is, into numbers in the range 0–255. Here the source words are again single characters rather than 'words' in the ordinary sense of being a string of letters. For the code alphabet Σ we have 4 different choices, all of which are actually used: if the numbers 0–255 are written in **binary**, then we just need alphabet $\Sigma = \{0, 1\}$, and the encoding of each 'word' takes up to 8 characters. If the numbers 0–255 are written in **octal**, then we need alphabet $\Sigma = \{0, 1, 2, \ldots, 7\}$, and the encoding of a single source word takes 3 characters. If the numbers 0–255 are written in **decimal**, then we need alphabet $\Sigma = \{0, 1, \ldots, 8, 9\}$, and the encoding of each source word may take 3 characters. If the numbers 0–255 are written in **hexadecimal**, then we need alphabet $\Sigma = \{0, 1, \ldots, 8, 9, A, B, C, D, E, F\}$ and the encoding of a source character takes only 2 characters.

Example: The Braille alphabet system is an encoding of the 26-letter alphabet (along with numerals and some punctuation, as well as a few short common words) into a 3-by-2 pattern of raised-or-not dots. The 3-by-2 grid gives 6 different choices of whether to raise the dot or not, so there are 2^6 available code words. A practical problem with this code is that it has so little *redundancy*: if through use the dots are worn away or damaged, it is impossible to deduce the character. But since the patterns of dots need to be fairly large to be discernible to fingertips, it seems infeasible to add redundancy. By contrast, *printed* letters have enough redundancy so that even if slightly blurred they are often legible.

Example: Systems of abbreviations used in otherwise ordinary English are examples of coding. For example, we may take as the set of 'words' W the set of genuine words in English, and take Σ to be the usual alphabet with numerals and punctuation. Then we can define various encoding maps $f : W \to \Sigma^*$. For example, we might define

$$f(\text{word}) = \begin{cases} \text{`St.'} & \text{if } \text{word} = \text{`Street'} \\ \text{`Ave.'} & \text{if } \text{word} = \text{`Avenue'} \\ \text{`Blvd.'} & \text{if } \text{word} = \text{`Boulevard'} \\ \text{`Rd.'} & \text{if } \text{word} = \text{`Road'} \\ \text{word} & \textit{otherwise} \end{cases}$$

This code doesn't do much. Larger systems of abbreviations were often used in telegraphy, both for efficiency and for secrecy.

Note that depending upon the context 'St.' may be an abbreviation for either 'Street' or for 'Saint'. And 'IP' may be either 'intellectual property' or 'internet protocol'. Without sufficient information from the context, this abbreviation is not *uniquely decipherable*.

We will only consider **uniquely decipherable** codes, that is, codes in which two different messages will never be encoded the same way. That is, no information is *lost* in the encoding! This condition requires that the function $f : W \to \Sigma^*$ is **injective**, meaning (by definition) that

$$f(w_1) = f(w_2) \quad \text{implies} \quad w_1 = w_2$$

(An injective function is sometimes called *one-to-one*, although the latter phrase is a little ambiguous because of its colloquialness.) This hypothesis of unique decipherability simplifies things a bit, and is often a reasonable hypothesis to take. In fact, it might seem that no one would ever want anything *but* uniquely decipherable codes, but this is not the case. In coding of graphics, for example in use of the JPEG file format, it is tolerable to lose a certain amount of certain kinds of information that are apparently not detectable to the human eye. Further, it turns out that in such scenarios giving up the demand for unique decipherability allows much greater economy.

Given two strings

$$s = s_1 s_2 \ldots s_m$$

$$t = t_1 t_2 \ldots t_n$$

in Σ^*, say that s is a **prefix** of t if s is an initial piece of t, that is, if $m \leq n$ and

$$t_1 = s_1, t_2 = s_2, \ldots, t_m = s_m$$

This terminology is compatible with colloquial usage.

A code $f : W \to \Sigma^*$ is an **instantaneous** or **prefix** code if for all words w, w' in the set W of source words,

$$f(w) \text{ is not a prefix of } f(w') \quad \text{for} \quad w \neq w'$$

If a code is instantaneous, then it can be **decoded** without **lookahead**. That is, the correct decoding of codewords can be determined without waiting to see what comes after. This is a obviously a desirable property. Note that natural languages do *not* have this property, since it happens quite often that a legitimate word occurs as an initial fragment of a longer word. For example, 'red' is a prefix of 'reduction', and the two words have little to do with each other.

Example: The code with words 00, 01, 110, and 001 is *not* a prefix code, because the first codeword 00 is the first part of the fourth codeword 001.

Example: If all codewords are of the same (known) length, then we know when a codeword is completed.

Example: A pattern of symbols such as three 0s in a row may be used to signal the end of a codeword, and thus to guarantee the prefix property, but this device has a cost, namely that extra symbols must be used.

As suggested by the example of abbreviations as an encoding, one of the goals of (noiseless) coding is to be as efficient as possible in communication. Various file compression programs are an example of progress toward this goal. The notion of entropy will allow us to understand some theoretical limitations of such techniques.

3.2 Kraft and McMillan inequalities

Kraft's and McMillan's inequalities give some basic theoretical limits on how tersely information can be communicated. Further, they demonstrate the surprising fact that *in principle* there is no reason to use any but *instantaneous* codes. At the very least this simplifies both theoretical and practical considerations quite a bit, since *lookahead* is tricky to discuss theoretically and tricky to program.

The **length** of a string of characters $s = s_1 s_2 \ldots s_t$ from an alphabet Σ is (as one would suspect) the number of characters in it:

$$\text{length}(s_1 s_2 \ldots s_t) = t$$

Given a set W of source words and an encoding $f : W \to \Sigma^*$ of W into strings composed of characters from an alphabet Σ, the set of **word lengths** of f is the set

$$\{\text{length}(f(w)) : w \in W\}$$

of lengths of encodings of words from W.

Theorem: *(Kraft's inequality.)* Let the set W of source words have m elements, and let the encoding alphabet Σ have n characters. A necessary and sufficient condition that there exist an **instantaneous uniquely decipherable** code $f : W \to \Sigma^*$ with lengths $\ell_1, \ldots, \ell_m$ is that

$$\sum_{i=1}^{m} \frac{1}{n^{\ell_i}} \leq 1$$

Theorem: *(McMillan's inequality.)* Let the set W of source words have m elements, and let the encoding alphabet Σ have n characters. A necessary and sufficient condition that there exist a **uniquely decipherable** code $f : W \to \Sigma^*$ with lengths $\ell_1, \ldots, \ell_m$ is that

$$\sum_{i=1}^{m} \frac{1}{n^{\ell_i}} \leq 1$$

Corollary: If there is a uniquely decipherable code with prescribed word lengths, then there is an *instantaneous* (uniquely decipherable) code with those word lengths.

Remark: The corollary follows from the fact that the conditions for the two theorems are the same. We will prove the two theorems simultaneously, in effect proving the *hard* half of each, by proving first that if the indicated inequality holds then there is an instantaneous code with indicated word lengths, and proving second that the word lengths of *any* uniquely decipherable code satisfy the inequality.

Remark: These inequalities give absolute limits on the size of encoding words necessary to encode a 'vocabulary' W of source words of a certain size. These limitations are independent of any probabilistic considerations.

Remark: Note that the quantities ℓ_i that occur in Kraft's and McMillan's inequalities are *integers*. Thus, there is no *justification* in trying to apply these results with non-integer quantities, and in fact some heuristically plausible conclusions reached in such manner are simply false.

Proof: (of Kraft's inequality) Suppose that the set of encoded word lengths satisfies

$$\sum_{i=1}^{m} \frac{1}{n^{\ell_i}} \leq 1$$

Let ℓ be the maximum word length, and let t_j be the number of (encoded) words of length j. Then the supposed inequality can be rewritten as

$$\sum_{i=1}^{\ell} t_i \frac{1}{n^i} \leq 1$$

Multiply through by n^ℓ and rearrange to obtain

$$t_\ell \leq n^\ell - t_1 n^{\ell-1} - t_2 n^{\ell-2} - \ldots - t_{\ell-1} n$$

Since $t_\ell \geq 0$, we get

$$0 \leq n^\ell - t_1 n^{\ell-1} - t_2 n^{\ell-2} - \ldots - t_{\ell-1} n$$

which again can be rearranged to

$$t_{\ell-1} \leq n^{\ell-1} - t_1 n^{\ell-2} - t_2 n^{\ell-3} - \ldots - t_{\ell-2} n$$

Continuing in the same way, using $t_i \geq 0$, we obtain

$$t_{\ell-2} \leq n^{\ell-2} - t_1 n^{\ell-3} - t_2 n^{\ell-4} - \ldots - t_{\ell-3} n$$

$$\ldots$$

$$t_2 \leq n^2 - t_1 n$$

$$t_1 \leq n$$

The last inequality is obviously necessarily true, but the others are not obvious.

We build up the encoding function $f : W \rightarrow \Sigma^*$ beginning with shortest lengths. First choose t_1 words of length 1, and define f to assign these values to some t_1 of the words from the source word set W. (For the present discussion, we don't care about how astutely this choice is made.) This leaves $n - t_1$ single-character encoded words unused, so we could form $(n - t_1)n$ two-character words in Σ^* whose first characters are different from the one-character encodings. This ensures the instantaneous property. But we only need to form t_2 two-character words, and define f to assign some words of W to these. The inequalities above include one which says that this is possible:

$$t_2 \leq n^2 - t_1 n$$

This leaves

$$(n - t_1)n - t_2$$

two-character strings whose first characters are not the encoding of a word, and which themselves are not the encoding of a word. Then there are

$$((n - t_1)n - t_2)n$$

three-character words whose first character is not the encoding of a source word, and whose two-character prefix is not the encoding of a source word. We arbitrarily choose t_3 among these. From the inequality above

$$t_3 \leq n^3 - t_1 n^2 - t_2 n$$

this is possible. Continuing in the obvious way gives the code f. This proves the sufficiency half of the assertion of the Kraft inequality theorem.

Now we prove half of McMillan's inequality, namely that given a uniquely decipherable code $f : W \to \Sigma^*$ the word lengths satisfy the inequality. Let the set of word lengths be $\ell_1, \ldots, \ell_m$. Let ℓ be the maximum length. For any positive integer t, we can re-express

$$\left(n^{-\ell_1} + n^{-\ell_2} + \ldots + n^{-\ell_m}\right)^t$$

by multiplying out and regrouping by powers of n, as

$$\left(n^{-\ell_1} + \ldots + n^{-\ell_m}\right)^t = \sum_{s=0}^{t\ell} C_s n^{-s}$$

for some coefficients C_s (depending on the number of terms in the sum and also upon t). By the nature of multiplication, C_s is the number of ways a string of length s can be created by concatenating t strings with lengths from among $\ell_1, \ell_2, \ldots, \ell_m$. (This style of argument is very similar to use of **generating functions** in counting problems.)

The assumption of unique decipherability implies that any string obtained by sticking together codewords comes from *just one* sequence of codewords. That is, a given string of s characters occurs as a concatenation of encoded words in at most one way. Since there are n^s choices of strings of length s made from the alphabet Σ, the unique decipherability implies that $C_s \leq n^s$, since each such string can occur in at most a single way as a concatenation of encoded words.

Using $C_s \leq n^s$ in the expression above, we have

$$\left(n^{-\ell_1} + \ldots + n^{-\ell_m}\right)^t = \sum_{s=0}^{t\ell} C_s n^{-s} \leq \sum_{s=0}^{t\ell} n^s n^{-s} = \sum_{s=0}^{t\ell} 1 = t\ell$$

Taking t^{th} root of both sides, we have

$$n^{-\ell_1} + \ldots + n^{-\ell_m} \leq \ell^{1/t} t^{1/t}$$

Letting $t \to +\infty$, the right-hand side goes to 1, and we obtain the necessity half of McMillan's theorem.

Now we combine the two halves to easily complete the proof of both theorems. Since *any* uniquely decipherable code must satisfy the inequality (by the half of McMillan's theorem we proved) certainly an *instantaneous* one must. This proves the second half of Kraft's theorem. And, similarly, to prove that a uniquely decipherable code exists for any set of word lengths satisfying the inequality above, it certainly suffices to prove this with the additional condition of instantaneity. Kraft's theorem proved this, so we obtain the second half of the proof of McMillan's theorem. $/\!/\!/$

3.3 Noiseless coding theorem

This theorem is one of Shannon's basic theoretical results from [Shannon 1948] showing that the entropy of a source gives a fundamental limitation on how efficiently the information from that source can be transmitted. The immediate issue is **minimizing the average encoded word length**. That is, minimizing the *expected value* of the length of encoded words, depending upon the probability distribution of the words emitted by the source.

Let $f : W \to \Sigma^*$ be a code with m source words $w_1, \ldots, w_m$ in W, with encoded words $f(w_1), \ldots, f(w_m)$ of lengths $\ell_1, \ldots, \ell_m$. Let $p_1, \ldots, p_m$ be the probabilities that the respective words $w_1, \ldots, w_m$ are emitted by the source. Then the **average length** of an encoded word is

$$\text{average length } f = \sum_{i=1}^{m} p_i \, \ell_i$$

Note that this is the expected value of the random variable which returns the length of the codewords.

Example: Let the source words be *cat* with probability 1/4, *dog* with probability 1/8, *elephant* with probability 1/8, and *zebra* with probability 1/2. Let the code alphabet be $\Sigma = \{0, 1\}$, and let the encoding f be

$$f(\text{`cat'}) = \text{`011'}$$
$$f(\text{`dog'}) = \text{`01'}$$
$$f(\text{`elephant'}) = \text{`0'}$$
$$f(\text{`zebra'}) = \text{`111'}$$

Then the average length of an encoded word is, by definition,

$$\text{average length} = P(\text{`cat'}) \cdot \text{length}(f(\text{`cat'})) + P(\text{`dog'}) \cdot \text{length}(f(\text{`dog'}))$$

$$+ P(\text{`elephant'}) \cdot \text{length}(f(\text{`elephant'})) + P(\text{`zebra'}) \cdot \text{length}(f(\text{`zebra'}))$$

$$= P(\text{`cat'}) \cdot \text{length}(\text{`011'}) + P(\text{`dog'}) \cdot \text{length}(\text{`11'})$$

$$+ P(\text{`elephant'}) \cdot \text{length}(\text{`0'}) + P(\text{`zebra'}) \cdot \text{length}(\text{`111'})$$

$$= P(\text{`cat'}) \cdot 3 + P(\text{`dog'}) \cdot 2 + P(\text{`elephant'}) \cdot 1 + P(\text{`zebra'}) \cdot 3$$

$$= \frac{1}{4} \cdot 3 + \frac{1}{8} \cdot 2 + \frac{1}{8} \cdot 1 + \frac{1}{2} \cdot 3 = \frac{21}{8} = 2.625$$

That is, the average codeword length with this encoding is 2.625. Note that the lengths of the source words play no role in this computation.

Let $|\Sigma|$ denote the number of elements in a finite set Σ (such as an alphabet of symbols).

Theorem: For a memoryless source X with entropy $H(X)$, a uniquely decipherable code $f : W \to \Sigma^*$ into strings made from an alphabet Σ (with $|\Sigma| > 1$) must have average length satisfying

$$\text{average length } f \geq \frac{H(X)}{\log_2 |\Sigma|}$$

Further, there *exists* a code f with

$$\text{average length } f < 1 + \frac{H(X)}{\log_2 |\Sigma|}$$

Remark: This theorem describes the best achievable performance, measured in terms of average word length, of any encoding of a given 'vocabulary' W of source words. The adjective *noiseless* refers to the fact that we are still ignoring errors.

Proof: Let $f : W \to \Sigma^*$ be a uniquely decipherable code with m source words $w_1, \ldots, w_m$ in W, with encoded words $f(w_1), \ldots, f(w_m)$ of lengths $\ell_1, \ldots, \ell_m$. Let $p_1, \ldots, p_m$ be the probabilities that the respective words $w_1, \ldots, w_m$ are emitted by the source. By the Kraft-McMillan inequality, letting n be the cardinality of the alphabet Σ

$$\sum_i n^{-\ell_i} \leq 1$$

Define

$$q_i = n^{-\ell_i} / \sum_i n^{-\ell_i}$$

Since (by construction) the sum of the q_is is 1, and since they are non-negative, the collection of numbers $q_1, \ldots, q_m$ fits the hypotheses of the Fundamental Inequality above, and we conclude that

$$- \sum_i p_i \log_2 p_i \leq - \sum_i p_i \log_2 q_i$$

By its definition

$$\log_2 q_i = \log_2 n^{-\ell_i} - \log_2 \left(\sum_i n^{-\ell_i} \right) = -\ell_i \log_2 n - \log_2 \left(\sum_i n^{-\ell_i} \right)$$

Therefore, substituting the right hand side for $\log_2 q_i$ gives

$$- \sum_i p_i \log_2 p_i \leq \log_2 n \sum_i p_i \ell_i + \left(\log_2 \sum_i n^{-\ell_i} \right) \left(\sum_i p_i \right)$$

By the Kraft-McMillan inequality, $\sum_i n^{-\ell_i} \leq 1$, so $\log_2 \sum_i n^{-\ell_i} \leq 0$, and thus

$$- \sum_i p_i \log_2 p_i \leq \log_2 n \sum_i p_i \ell_i$$

That is, the entropy of the source is less than or equal to the average length of the encoded words times $\log_2$ of the size of the alphabet. This proves the lower bound for the average word length.

For the other half of the theorem, we will try to cleverly choose the word lengths according to the rule that ℓ_i is the smallest integer such that

$$p_i^{-1} \leq n^{\ell_i}$$

Of course, it is not immediately clear that this is possible, but the fact that the probabilities p_i add up to 1 gives

$$\sum_i n^{-\ell_i} \leq 1$$

so by the Kraft-McMillan theorems there *exists* a uniquely decipherable code with these encoded word lengths.

Taking logarithms base 2, and using the fact that the logarithm function is increasing, the condition

$$p_i^{-1} \leq n^{\ell_i}$$

gives

$$\ell_i \log_2 n \geq - \log_2 p_i$$

Since ℓ_i is by definition minimal among all integers fitting into this inequality, for $n > 1$

$$(\ell_i - 1) \log_2 n < - \log_2 p_i$$

or

$$\ell_i < 1 - \frac{\log_2 p_i}{\log_2 n}$$

Multiplying by p_i and adding up, we get

$$\text{average length } f = \sum_i p_i \ell_i < \sum_i p_i \cdot 1 - \frac{1}{\log_2 n} \sum p_i \log_2 p_i = 1 + \frac{H(X)}{\log_2 n}$$

since $\sum_i p_i = 1$. This finishes the proof of the noiseless coding theorem.   ///

3.4 Huffman encoding

The 1953 Huffman encoding scheme achieves optimality for noiseless coding. Further, the underlying idea is used directly or indirectly in many practical coding schemes.

Given a memoryless source X emitting words in a set W with probabilities

$$P(X = w_i) = p_i$$

an encoding

$$f : W \to \Sigma^*$$

which has the smallest possible length is called **efficient** or **compact** or **optimal**. (Other similar modifiers are also used.) From the noiseless coding theorem above,

$$\frac{H(X)}{\log_2 |\Sigma|} \leq \text{ average length } f \leq 1 + \frac{H(X)}{\log_2 |\Sigma|}$$

In the important special case that $\Sigma = \{0, 1\}$, this is simply

$$H(X) \leq \text{ average length } f \leq 1 + H(X)$$

Codes using the alphabet consisting of just 0 and 1 are **binary codes**.

Now we describe **binary Huffman encoding**. Let $W = \{w_1, \ldots, w_n\}$ be the set of source words. Let the source X emit the words with probabilities

$$P(x = w_i) = p_i$$

and suppose (without loss of generality) that the words are ordered by decreasing probability. That is, suppose that

$$p_1 \geq p_2 \geq p_3 \geq \ldots \geq p_{n-1} \geq p_n$$

We create the encoding $f : W \to \{0, 1\}^*$ **recursively**: let

$$W' = \{w'_1, w'_2, \ldots, w'_{n-1}\}$$

be a slightly smaller set of source words, with

$$w'_1 = w_1, w'_2 = w_2, \ldots, w'_{n-2} = w_{n-2}$$

but at the very end w'_{n-1} is a word *representing the case that one or the other of w_{n-1}, w_n is emitted.* And make a source X' with corresponding probabilities

$$P(X' = w'_1) = p_1, P(X' = w'_2) = p_2, \ldots, P(X' = w'_{n-2}) = p_{n-2}$$

and at the very end

$$P(X' = w'_{n-1}) = p_{n-1} + p_n$$

corresponding to the idea that emission of the original source words w_{n-1} and w_n by X are combined into a single emission of w'_{n-1} by the new source X'. Let

$$f' : W' \to \{0,1\}^*$$

be a binary Huffman encoding for X', which we can assume by induction to exist. Then define the encoding for source X by

$$f(w_i) = f'(w_i) \quad \text{for } i = 1, 2, \ldots, n-2$$

and

$$\begin{aligned} f(w_{n-1}) &= f'(w'_{n-1}) + \text{`0'} \\ f(w_n) &= f'(w'_{n-1}) + \text{`1'} \end{aligned}$$

where the '+' denotes concatenation of strings. That is, $f(w_{n-1})$ is obtained by appending a '0' to the encoding $f'(w'_{n-1})$, while $f(w_n)$ is obtained by appending a '1' to the encoding $f'(w'_{n-1})$.

Remark: Note that the source X' has one fewer word in its 'vocabulary' than did the original source X. Thus, if we continue in this manner, the issue of defining the encoding will eventually become the question of defining an encoding on a set of source words with just two items. It is easy to see that an optimal binary encoding of a two-word vocabulary should encode one of the words as '0' and the other as '1'.

Remark: It can happen that there is more than one choice of pair of least likely words. In that case, it doesn't matter which pair is combined in the Huffman process. Of course, the resulting codes will be different, but the average word lengths will be the same.

Example: Let X be a source emitting 3 words w_1, w_2, w_3 with probabilities $\frac{2}{5}, \frac{3}{10}, \frac{3}{10}$, respectively. Then the source X' should combine w_2 and w_3 as a single emission of a word w'_2 with probability

$$\frac{3}{5} = \frac{3}{10} + \frac{3}{10}$$

Thus, X' emits just two words, $w'_1 = w_1$ with probability $\frac{2}{5}$ and w'_2 with probability $\frac{3}{5}$. We make an encoding of X' by

$$\begin{aligned} f'(w'_1) &= \text{`0'} \\ f'(w'_2) &= \text{`1'} \end{aligned}$$

Then an encoding f of X is defined in terms of the encoding f' of X' by

$$\begin{aligned} f(w_1) &= f'(w_1) &= \text{`0'} \\ f(w_2) &= f'(w'_2) + \text{`0'} &= \text{`10'} \\ f(w_3) &= f'(w'_2) + \text{`1'} &= \text{`11'} \end{aligned}$$

The (average) length of the latter encoding is

$$\frac{2}{5} \cdot 1 + \frac{3}{10} \cdot 2 + \frac{3}{10} \cdot 2 = 1.6$$

The entropy of the source is

$$H(X) = -\frac{2}{5}\log_2\frac{2}{5} - \frac{3}{10}\log_2\frac{3}{10} - \frac{3}{10}\log_2\frac{3}{10} \approx 1.57095$$

We can see that the inequality of the Noiseless Coding Theorem is met:

$$H(X) = 1.57095 \leq \text{length} = 1.6 \leq 2.57095 = H(X) + 1$$

Example: Let X be a source emitting 4 words w_1, w_2, w_3, w_4 with probabilities $\frac{1}{3}, \frac{1}{4}, \frac{1}{4}, \frac{1}{6}$. The least likely word w_4 should be combined with one of the next least likely words, say w_3, into a single case w_3' for a new source X'. The probability $P(X' = w_3')$ should be the sum $\frac{1}{4} + \frac{1}{6} = \frac{5}{12}$. The words $w_1' = w_1$ and $w_2' = w_2$ are emitted by X' with the same probabilities as for X. In this example we need to go one step further, creating a new source X'' by combining the two least likely words emitted by X', w_1' with probability $\frac{1}{3}$ and w_2' with probability $\frac{1}{4}$ into a single case, w_2'' emitted by X'' with probability

$$\frac{1}{3} + \frac{1}{4} = \frac{7}{12}$$

Let $w_1'' = w_3'$, emitted by X'' with probability $\frac{5}{12}$. Since X'' emits just two words, to make its good encoding f'' we actually don't care about the probabilities any more:

$$f''(w_1'') = \text{`0'}$$
$$f''(w_2'') = \text{`1'}$$

Working backward, the encoding f' for X' should be

$$f'(w_1') = f''(w_2'') + \text{`0'} = \text{`10'}$$
$$f'(w_2') = f''(w_2'') + \text{`1'} = \text{`11'}$$
$$f'(w_3') = f''(w_1'') = \text{`0'}$$

and then, one step further back, the encoding f for X is

$$f(w_1) = f'(w_1') = \text{`10'}$$
$$f(w_2) = f'(w_2') = \text{`11'}$$
$$f(w_3) = f'(w_3') + \text{`0'} = \text{`00'}$$
$$f(w_4) = f'(w_3') + \text{`1'} = \text{`01'}$$

With hindsight, it is not so surprising that the 4 different two-bit strings were used, but this may not be so if the probability distribution is different, as in the next example.

The (average) length of the latter encoding is

$$\frac{1}{3} \cdot 2 + \frac{1}{4} \cdot 2 + \frac{1}{4} \cdot 2 + \frac{1}{6} \cdot 2 = 2$$

(Of course this is so, since *all* the encoding words are of length 2.) The entropy of the source is

$$H(X) = -\frac{1}{3}\log_2\frac{1}{3} - \frac{1}{4}\log_2\frac{1}{4} - \frac{1}{4}\log_2\frac{1}{4} - \frac{1}{6}\log_2\frac{1}{6} \approx 1.9591$$

We can see that the inequality of the Noiseless Coding Theorem is met:

$$H(X) = 1.9591 \le \text{ length } = 2.0 \le 2.9591 = H(X) + 1$$

Example: Let X be a source emitting 4 words w_1, w_2, w_3, w_4 with probabilities $\frac{1}{2}, \frac{1}{6}, \frac{1}{6}, \frac{1}{6}$. Two of the least likely words, say w_3 and w_4, should be combined into a single case w_3' for a new source X'. The probability $P(X' = w_3')$ should be the sum $\frac{1}{6} + \frac{1}{6} = \frac{1}{3}$. The words $w_1' = w_1$ and $w_2' = w_2$ are emitted by X' with the same probabilities as for X. We need to go one step further, creating a new source X'' by combining the two least likely words emitted by X', w_2' with probability $\frac{1}{6}$ and w_3' with probability $\frac{1}{3}$ into a single case, w_2'' emitted by X'' with probability

$$\frac{1}{6} + \frac{1}{3} = \frac{1}{2}$$

Let $w_1'' = w_1'$, emitted by X'' with probability $\frac{1}{2}$. Since X'' emits just two words, to make its good encoding f'' we actually don't care about the probabilities any more:

$$
\begin{aligned}
f''(w_1'') &= \text{`0'} \\
f''(w_2'') &= \text{`1'}
\end{aligned}
$$

Working backwards, the encoding f' for X' should be

$$
\begin{aligned}
f'(w_1') &= f''(w_1'') &&= \text{`0'} \\
f'(w_2') &= f''(w_2'') + \text{`0'} &&= \text{`10'} \\
f'(w_3') &= f''(w_2'') + \text{`1'} &&= \text{`11'}
\end{aligned}
$$

and then, one step further back, the encoding f for X is

$$
\begin{aligned}
f(w_1) &= f'(w_1') &&= \text{`0'} \\
f(w_2) &= f'(w_2') &&= \text{`10'} \\
f(w_3) &= f'(w_3') + \text{`0'} &&= \text{`110'} \\
f(w_4) &= f'(w_3') + \text{`1'} &&= \text{`111'}
\end{aligned}
$$

In this example, by contrast to the previous one, the word w_1 occurs with such high probability that it is optimal to allocate a very short encoding to it, consisting of a single bit. Evidently the added cost of having to encode two of the other (least likely) words by 3 bits is worthwhile.

The (average) length of the latter encoding is

$$\frac{1}{2}\cdot 1 + \frac{1}{6}\cdot 2 + \frac{1}{6}\cdot 3 + \frac{1}{6}\cdot 3 = 1.83333$$

The entropy of the source is

$$H(X) = -\frac{1}{2}\log_2\frac{1}{2} - \frac{1}{6}\log_2\frac{1}{6} - \frac{1}{6}\log_2\frac{1}{6} - \frac{1}{6}\log_2\frac{1}{6} \approx 1.79248$$

We can see that the inequality of the Noiseless Coding Theorem is met:

$$H(X) = 1.79248 \leq \text{ length } = 1.83333 \leq 2.79248 = H(X) + 1$$

Proof of optimality/compactness of Huffman encoding: First we make some observations.

- By the Kraft-McMillan inequality, in principle we may as well look for an *instantaneous* optimal code.
- Note that in the simplest case, for a source emitting just two words $W = \{w_1, w_2\}$, the binary encoding

$$f(w_1) = 0 \quad f(w_2) = 1$$

is optimal, regardless of the probabilities with which the two words are emitted. This is clear from the fact that the encodings can't be any shorter than a single character.

- For a **compact** *instantaneous* code $f : W \to \{0,1\}$ if

$$P(X = w_1) > P(X = w_2)$$

for two words w_1, w_2, then necessarily

$$\text{length}(f(w_1)) \leq \text{length}(f(w_2))$$

Indeed, if instead

$$\text{length}(f(w_1)) > \text{length}(f(w_2))$$

then make a new code g by having g be the same as f *except* interchanging the encoding of w_1 and w_2:

$$g(w_1) = f(w_2) \quad g(w_2) = f(w_1)$$

We can check that the new code g has strictly shorter average length than f (and it is certainly still instantaneous): in the expression for average length, the only thing that will change is the subsum for the two words w_1, w_2. Letting $p_1 = P(X = w_1)$, $p_2 = P(X = w_2)$, and $\ell_1 = \text{length}(f(w_1))$, $\ell_2 = \text{length}(f(w_2))$,

$$P(X = w_1) \cdot \text{length}(g(w_1)) + P(X = w_2) \cdot \text{length}(g(w_2)) = p_1 \cdot \ell_2 + p_2 \cdot \ell_1$$

$$= p_2\ell_2 + (p_1 - p_2)\ell_2 + p_1\ell_1 + (p_2 - p_1)\ell_1$$

$$= (p_1\ell_1 + p_2\ell_2) + (p_1 - p_2)(\ell_2 - \ell_1) < p_1\ell_1 + p_2\ell_2$$

since both $p_1 - p_2 > 0$ and $\ell_2 - \ell_1 < 0$, by assumption. This verifies that the code g has strictly smaller average length than f, thereby proving that f was not optimal.

- For **compact** instantaneous code f, among longest encodings there must be two which differ only in their last character. To see this, suppose the assertion were false and obtain a contradiction. That is, suppose that *any two* encodings of maximal length differed in *more* than their last character. Then we could simply drop the last character of each one and still distinguish them. By the instantaneousness, this truncation does not cause any of these encoded words to become the (shorter) encoding of a different source word. This shortening of the longest encodings certainly decreases the average word length (except in the case that the probabilities of these words are 0, which we should exclude as irrelevant!).

Now we prove optimality of the Huffman encoding. By induction, suppose that the Huffman encoding f' for source X' is optimal. Suppose that the encoding Huffman f for X is *not* optimal (and get a contradiction). Let $g : W \to \{0,1\}^*$ be an encoding of X with a smaller average word length than f. We may assume that g is optimal. Then as noted just above two of the longest encodings in g differ only in the last character: there are two source words w_{n-1}, w_n and a prefix s so that

$$\begin{aligned} g(w_{n-1}) &= s + \text{`0'} \\ g(w_n) &= s + \text{`1'} \end{aligned}$$

Now we will use g (assumed shorter than f) to construct an encoding of X' strictly shorter than f', contradicting the inductive hypothesis that f' was optimal.

Let $w_1, w_2, \ldots, w_n$ be all the words emitted by source X, emitted with probabilities $p_1 \geq p_2 \geq \ldots \geq p_n$. As prescribed by the Huffman encoding, the two words w_{n-1}, w_n of least probability are merged to a single word w'_{n-1} for the source X', with probability $p_{n-1} + p_n$, and all other words and probabilities are the same for X' as for X. From the encoding g of X we make an encoding g' of X' by having g' be the same as g except that

$$g'(w'_{n-1}) = s$$

where the string s is the common prefix shared by $g(w_{n-1})$ and $g(w_n)$. (Since g is instantaneous, so is g'.) For brevity let

$$\ell_i = \text{ length } (g(w_i))$$

Note that

$$\ell_{n-1} = \ell_n = \text{length}(s) + 1$$

since $g(w_{n-1})$ and $g(w_n)$ have the common prefix s and differ only in the last bit. That is,

$$\text{length}(s) = \ell_n - 1 = \ell_{n-1} - 1$$

Then, writing simply 'length' for 'average length', we have

$$\text{length } g' = p_1\ell_1 + \ldots + p_{n-2}\ell_{n-2} + (p_{n-1} + p_n)(\ell_n - 1)$$

$$= p_1\ell_1 + \ldots + p_{n-2}\ell_{n-2} + p_{n-1}\ell_{n-1} + p_n\ell_n - p_{n-1} - p_n$$

$$= \text{ length } g - p_{n-1} - p_n$$

using the fact that $\ell_{n-1} = \ell_n$. An essentially identical computation gives

$$\text{length} f' = \text{length} f - p_{n-1} - p_n$$

Thus, if g were really shorter than f, then we'd have

$$\text{length}(f') = \text{length}(f) - p_{n-1} - p_n > \text{length}(g) - p_{n-1} - p_n = \text{length}(g')$$

which shows that g' is shorter than f'. But by induction f' was assumed an optimal encoding of X', so we reach a contradiction.

This proves that the Huffman encoding is optimal.   ///

Exercises

3.01 What is the maximum number of words in an *instantaneous* binary code with maximum word length 5? (*ans.*)

3.02 What is the maximum number of words in an *instantaneous* binary code with maximum word length 6?

3.03 How many source words must there be to *require* that any (binary) encoding of the source have *average* word length at least 4? (*ans.*)

3.04 Determine the Huffman encoding of a source with probabilities $\frac{1}{2}$, $\frac{1}{4}$, $\frac{1}{8}$, $\frac{1}{16}$, $\frac{1}{16}$, $\frac{1}{16}$. Compare the average word length to the entropy of the source. (*ans.*)

3.05 Determine the Huffman encoding of a source with probabilities $\frac{1}{3}$, $\frac{1}{4}$, $\frac{1}{6}$, $\frac{1}{8}$, $\frac{1}{12}$, $\frac{1}{24}$. Compare the average word length to the entropy of the source.

3.06 Determine the Huffman encoding of a source with probabilities $\frac{2}{3}$, $\frac{2}{9}$, $\frac{2}{27}$, $\frac{2}{81}$, $\frac{2}{243}$, $\frac{1}{243}$. Compare the average word length to the entropy of the source.

3.07 In what circumstances will an optimal encoding include a code word of length 1? 2 of length 2? 4 of length 3? (*ans.*)

4

Noisy Coding

This chapter describes a simple version of another of Shannon's basic results from [Shannon 1948].

4.1 Noisy channels

Now we consider the case that there is **noise** that interferes with communication. This presents new problems.

For simplicity, we will only consider **discrete memoryless channels** C, described as follows. There is a finite **input alphabet** $\Sigma_{\text{in}} = \{x_1, \ldots, x_m\}$ and a finite **output alphabet** $\Sigma_{\text{out}} = \{y_1, \ldots, y_n\}$. When input character x_i is sent into the channel, character y_j is received at the other end with probability p_{ij}. We might write this as

$$p_{ij} = P_C(\text{received} = y_j | \text{sent} = x_i)$$

Since these are conditional probabilities, necessarily for each fixed index i for input character x_i,

$$\sum_j p_{ij} = 1$$

That is, the sum of the probabilities of all the possible output characters that might be received (for given input x_i) is 1.

Further, we suppose that the channel operates in a manner so that the transmission and receipt of each character are **independent** of the transmission and receipt of other characters: the probabilities are independent of what has come before or what comes after.

The collection of probabilities

$$M = \{p_{ij} : 1 \le i \le m, 1 \le j \le n\}$$

is the **channel matrix**. The probability p_{ij} is the entry in the ith row and j^{th} column. A matrix with the property that rows and columns are non-negative and sum to 1 is a **stochastic matrix**.

Remark: These stochastic matrices also occur in the study of *Markov processes*, and in that context the p_{ij} are called **transition probabilities**.

Example: The **binary symmetric channel** model is the simplest meaningful example, and for that reason is very important: the input alphabet is $\Sigma_{\text{in}} = \{0,1\}$ and the output alphabet is $\Sigma_{\text{out}} = \{0,1\}$ as well. The probability that the channel transmits '0' as '1' or '1' as '0' (that is, makes a mistake) is p, while the probability that a character is transmitted correctly is $1-p$. Often q is a convenient shorthand for $1-p$. The quantity p is the **(bit) error probability** of the channel.

Example: *Erasure channel:* The case that a channel occasionally loses some characters entirely is included in this model since the number of possible output characters need not be the same as the number of input characters. For example, let the input alphabet Σ_{in} be just $\Sigma_{\text{in}} = \{0,1\}$, and the output alphabet $\Sigma_{\text{out}} = \{0,1,*\}$ where $*$ is considered to be an **erasure** of a character. Let ε be a small positive real number, and let the transition probabilities be given by

in\out	0	1	$*$
0	$1-\varepsilon$	0	ε
1	0	$1-\varepsilon$	ε

That is, the two characters '0' and '1' never transmute into each other, but either one may be *erased* with probability ε. This is the **binary erasure channel**.

The Nth **extension** $C^{(N)}$ of a channel C is a channel whose input alphabet is all N-tuples of characters from the input alphabet of C, whose output alphabet is the collection of N-tuples of characters from the output alphabet of C, and so that the transition probabilities are what would occur if we had N copies of the original channel working independently in parallel:

$$P_{C^{(N)}}(\text{out} = b_1 \ldots b_N | \text{in} = a_1 \ldots a_N)$$
$$= P_C(\text{out} = b_1 | \text{in} = a_1) \ldots P_C(\text{out} = b_N | \text{in} = a_N)$$

The situation we'll consider is that a source X emits words $w_1, \ldots, w_m$ with probabilities $p_i = P(X = x_i)$, which are encoded (perhaps by Huffman encoding) into binary, then sent across a binary symmetric channel C, and decoded on the other side. The encoding to binary is noiseless and is known to the decoder. In a picture, this is

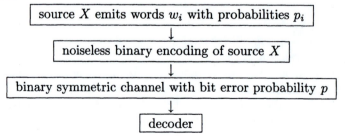

   With our independence assumptions, the probability that a string $a_1 \ldots a_N$ of
N bits in binary will be transmitted correctly is the product of the probabilities
that a_1 is transmitted correctly, that a_2 is transmitted correctly, $\ldots$, and that a_N
is transmitted correctly, which is

$$(1-p)^N$$

The fundamental question is **can we do better than this?**
   (Of course, the answer is 'yes' or we wouldn't *be* here talking about it.)
   And there are two parts to the question of improvement: **detection** of errors,
and **correction** of errors. Obviously detection is generally easier than correction.
Sometimes *detection* is good enough: maybe we can ask for a retransmission. In
other cases *correction* of errors is necessary.

4.2 Example: parity checks

The simplest method to detect single bit errors is that of a **parity check**. And,
in fact, this approach is so simple that it gets used a lot in practice. But it is *not*
an error-*correction* device by itself, so sometimes it's just useless. And even as a
detection device it is too simple to be very effective.
   Given a binary (noiseless) encoding $f : X \to \{0,1\}^*$ of a source X into strings
of 0s and 1s, we can add just a little bit of redundancy and thereby detect certain
simple sorts of errors. That is, replace the encoding f by an encoding $\tilde{f}$ where for
any binary source word w

$$\begin{aligned} \tilde{f}(w) &= f(w) + \text{'0'} \quad \text{if the string } f(w) \text{ has } \textit{even} \text{ number of 1s} \\ \tilde{f}(w) &= f(w) + \text{'1'} \quad \text{if the string } f(w) \text{ has } \textit{odd} \text{ number of 1s} \end{aligned}$$

where (as is common) the '+' denotes concatenation of strings. The **decoding**
involves rejection of any word so that the last bit does not correctly reflect the
odd/even-ness of the rest of the word. (If the code is *instantaneous* then adding
this parity-check bit does not create any conflicts.) Note now that if any single bit
(including the last one) of the new codewords is changed, then this can be **detected**
because the last bit will not correctly reflect the odd/even-ness of the first part of
the word. That is, *all single-bit errors are detected by a parity-check bit.*

Example: Suppose that a source emits 2-bit binary codewords $00, 01, 10, 11$. Let
C be a symmetric binary channel with bit error probability $1/8$. Then the probability that *at least one bit error* occurs (and will necessarily be undetected!) in
transmission of one of these 2-bit words is

$$\frac{1}{8} \cdot \frac{7}{8} + \frac{7}{8} \cdot \frac{1}{8} + \frac{1}{8} \cdot \frac{1}{8} = \frac{15}{64} = 0.234375$$

Add a single parity-check bit to this code by replacing these words with
$000, 011, 101, 110$, respectively. What kind of errors will be detected? If just one bit
of the 3 bits is changed, then the last bit will not correctly reflect the even/odd-ness
of the first 2 bits, so this error will be detected. However, if 2 of the 3 bits are

changed, this will *not* be detected. If all 3 bits change, this will be detected. So the probability of an *undetected* bit error is the probability of exactly 2 bit errors, which is

$$\frac{1}{8}\frac{1}{8}\frac{7}{8} + \frac{1}{8}\frac{1}{8}\frac{7}{8} + \frac{1}{8}\frac{1}{8}\frac{7}{8} = \binom{3}{2}\left(\frac{1}{8}\right)^2\left(\frac{7}{8}\right) = \frac{21}{512} = 0.041016$$

This is a huge improvement over the previous 0.234375 probability of undetected error. Of course, there remains the responsibility of **correcting** an error once it's detected.

Example: Let's look at what happens if there's even more noise on the channel. Suppose that a source emits 2-bit binary codewords $00, 01, 10, 11$. Let C be a symmetric binary channel with bit error probability $1/3$. Then the probability that *at least one bit error* occurs in transmission of one of these 2-bit words is

$$\frac{1}{3}\cdot\frac{2}{3} + \frac{2}{3}\cdot\frac{1}{3} + \frac{1}{3}\cdot\frac{1}{3} = \frac{5}{9} \approx 0.5555$$

So we'd have scant chance of succesful transmission! Add a single parity-check bit to this code by replacing these words with $000, 011, 101, 110$, respectively. Again, if just one bit of the 3 bits is changed, then the last bit will not correctly reflect the even/odd-ness of the first 2 bits, so this error will be detected. However, if 2 of the 3 bits are changed, this will *not* be detected. If all 3 bits change, this will be detected. So the probability of at least one *undetected* bit error is

$$\frac{1}{3}\frac{1}{3}\frac{2}{3} + \frac{1}{3}\frac{2}{3}\frac{1}{3} + \frac{2}{3}\frac{1}{3}\frac{1}{3} = \binom{3}{2}\left(\frac{1}{3}\right)^2\left(\frac{2}{3}\right) = \frac{6}{27} \approx 0.22222$$

Thus, by use of parity-check bits added to the code, in this example we can reduce the probability of undetected bit error within a word to well below $1/2$, though it's still quite high.

Example: Finally, let's look at what happens if the channel is as noisy as possible: suppose that the bit error probability is $1/2$. Suppose that a source emits 2-bit binary codewords $00, 01, 10, 11$. Then the probability that *at least one bit error* occurs in transmission of one of these 2-bit words is

$$\frac{1}{2}\cdot\frac{1}{2} + \frac{1}{2}\cdot\frac{1}{2} + \frac{1}{2}\cdot\frac{1}{2} = \frac{3}{4} = 0.75 > 0.5$$

Add a single parity-check bit to this code by replacing these words with $000, 011, 101, 110$, respectively. Again, if just one bit of the 3 bits is changed, then the last bit will not correctly reflect the even/odd-ness of the first 2 bits, so this error will be detected. However, if 2 of the 3 bits are changed, this will *not* be detected. If all 3 bits change, this will be detected. So the probability of at least one *undetected* bit error is

$$\frac{1}{2}\frac{1}{2}\frac{1}{2} + \frac{1}{2}\frac{1}{2}\frac{1}{2} + \frac{1}{2}\frac{1}{2}\frac{1}{2} = \binom{3}{2}\left(\frac{1}{2}\right)^2\left(\frac{1}{2}\right) = \frac{3}{8} = 0.375 < 0.5$$

Thus, by use of parity-check bits added to the code, even with a maximally noisy channel, we can still reduce the probability of *undetected* bit error within a word to 3/8, significantly below 1/2.

Example: In the case of 3-bit binary words, adding a parity-check bit creates 4-bit words so that an *odd* number of bit errors will be detected. Suppose that a binary symmetric channel has bit error probability 1/8. Then the probability that at least one bit error will occur in transmission of a 3-bit word is

$$\binom{3}{1}\left(\frac{1}{8}\right)\left(\frac{7}{8}\right)^2 + \binom{3}{2}\left(\frac{1}{8}\right)^2\left(\frac{7}{8}\right) + \binom{3}{3}\left(\frac{1}{8}\right)^3 \approx 0.33$$

Of course, any such error is undetected. When a parity-check bit is added, the probability of an *undetected* error is the probability of a positive even number of bit errors, which is

$$\binom{4}{2}\left(\frac{1}{8}\right)^2\left(\frac{7}{8}\right)^2 + \binom{4}{4}\left(\frac{1}{8}\right)^4 \approx 0.072$$

which is less than 1/4 of the undetected errors that would occur without the parity-check bit.

Example: A symmetric binary channel has bit error probability 1/5. A source emits words w_1, w_2, w_3, w_4 with probabilities $1/2, 1/4, 1/8, 1/8$. These words are Huffman-encoded as $0, 10, 110, 111$, respectively. The probability that a word is transmitted with some error is

$$P(X = w_1) \cdot \binom{1}{1}\frac{1}{5} + P(X = w_2) \cdot \left(\binom{2}{1}\frac{1}{5}\frac{4}{5} + \binom{2}{2}\frac{1}{5}\frac{1}{5}\right)$$

$$+ P(X = w_3) \cdot \left(\binom{3}{1}\left(\frac{1}{5}\right)\left(\frac{4}{5}\right)^2 + \binom{3}{2}\left(\frac{1}{5}\right)^2\left(\frac{4}{5}\right) + \binom{3}{3}\left(\frac{1}{5}\right)^3\right)$$

$$+ P(X = w_4) \cdot \left(\binom{3}{1}\left(\frac{1}{5}\right)\left(\frac{4}{5}\right)^2 + \binom{3}{2}\left(\frac{1}{5}\right)^2\left(\frac{4}{5}\right) + \binom{3}{3}\left(\frac{1}{5}\right)^3\right)$$

$$= \frac{1}{2}\cdot\frac{1}{5} + \frac{1}{4}\cdot\frac{9}{25} + \frac{1}{8}\cdot\frac{61}{125} + \frac{1}{8}\cdot\frac{61}{125} \approx 0.312$$

Now add a parity-check bit, giving codewords $00, 101, 1100, 1111$. The probability that there is an *undetected* error in transmission of a word now becomes

$$P(X = w_1) \cdot \binom{2}{2}\left(\frac{1}{5}\right)^2 + P(X = w_2) \cdot \binom{3}{2}\left(\frac{1}{5}\right)^2\left(\frac{4}{5}\right)$$

$$+ P(X = w_3) \cdot \binom{4}{2}\left(\frac{1}{5}\right)^2\left(\frac{4}{5}\right)^2 + P(X = w_3) \cdot \binom{4}{4}\left(\frac{4}{5}\right)^4$$

$$+ P(X = w_4) \cdot \binom{4}{2}\left(\frac{1}{5}\right)^2\left(\frac{4}{5}\right)^2 + P(X = w_4) \cdot \binom{4}{4}\left(\frac{4}{5}\right)^4$$

$$\approx 0.084$$

It is important to realize that mere *detection* of errors is silly or worthless if it is impossible or too expensive to retransmit, such as in the case of satellite or deep space transmissions, or also in the case of video, especially live video. More generally, a high volume of highly structured or synchronized information will make retransmission complicated, impossible, or pointless. Therefore, in the sequel we'll worry mostly about not just detection but *correction* of errors.

4.3 Decoding from a noisy channel

To understand how error-correction mechanisms might be implemented, it is necessary to consider the possible rules for *decoding*.

A first attempt at deciding how to decode messages sent across a noisy channel might be the following reasonable-sounding one. Let $x_1, \ldots, x_m$ be the possible words sent into the channel, and suppose y is received at the other end. We might try to choose to decode y as x_{i_0} where the index i_0 is so that for all indices i

$$P(x_{i_0} \text{ sent}|y \text{ received}) \geq P(x_i \text{ sent}|y \text{ received})$$

That is, in words, given the fact that y was received, the probability that x_{i_0} was sent is the greatest among the probabilities that any of the x_is was sent. This rule is the **ideal observer** or **minimum-error** rule. This rule certainly seems reasonable, but it has a flaw which is fatal for many applications: the receiver must know quite a bit about the probabilities that the various x_i might be sent.

A better rule, which is used very often in practice, is the **maximum-likelihood** ('ML') decoding rule. Using the notation of the last paragraph, this rule decodes a received word y into x_i to maximize

$$P(y \text{ received}|x_i \text{ sent})$$

(This is similar to a *maximum-likelihood estimator* in statistics.) The point is that we do not need to know the probabilities that the various source words x_i may be sent.

Remark: If the probabilities of the code words x_i are all the same, then the maximum-likelihood rule will certainly give the same answer as the minimum-error rule, but not in general.

For a binary symmetric channel, we can describe the maximum-likelihood decoding in convenient quantitative terms, using the **Hamming distance** between strings of 0s and 1s. Let V^n be the collection of **vectors** (ordered n-tuples) of 0s and 1s, of length n. Define the **Hamming distance** $d(x,y)$ between two vectors $x = (x_1, \ldots, x_n)$, $y = (y_1, \ldots, y_n)$ in V^n by

$$d(x,y) = \text{ number of indices } i \text{ so that } x_i \neq y_i$$

The **Hamming weight** of a vector of 0s and 1s is the number of non-zero entries, that is, the number of entries that are 1.

Minimum-distance decoding says to decode a received vector as the codeword x_i closest (in terms of the Hamming distance) to y. (If there is more than one closest, choose arbitrarily.)

Proposition: For a binary symmetric channel with error probability $p \leq \frac{1}{2}$, minimum-distance decoding is equivalent to maximum-likelihood decoding.

Proof: Let y be a received vector in V^n, and let $x \in V^n$ be a possible decoding. The probability that the channel converted x to y is $p^{d(x,y)}q^{n-d(x,y)}$ since exactly $d(x,y)$ specified bits have to be changed. Since $p \leq \frac{1}{2}$, $p \leq q$, so that

$$p^{d(x,y)}q^{n-d(x,y)} \leq p^{d(z,y)}q^{n-d(z,y)}$$

when $d(x,y) \leq d(z,y)$. That is, the probability is greatest exactly when the codeword x is closest to the received word y (When $p = \frac{1}{2}$ it doesn't matter since the situation is symmetrical.) ///

4.4 Channel capacity

To state Shannon's theorem about error-correcting codes for noisy channels, it is necessary to make precise what we mean by the **capacity** of a channel to carry information. We'll only look seriously at the case of memoryless discrete binary channels and memoryless sources.

Let C be a memoryless discrete channel with input alphabet Σ_{in} and output alphabet Σ_{out} and (for $x_i \in \Sigma_{\text{in}}$ and $y_j \in \Sigma_{\text{out}}$) transition probabilities

$$p_{ij} = P(y_j \text{ received } |x_i \text{ sent})$$

Consider a memoryless source X emitting elements of Σ_{in}. Let

$$p_i = P(X \text{ emits } x_i)$$

Then the **output** of the channel C with X connected to its input end can be viewed as another memoryless source Y emitting elements of Σ_{out} with probabilities

$$p_j' = \sum_{i=1}^{m} P(y_j \text{ received } |x_i \text{ sent }) P(X \text{ sent } x_i) = \sum_{i=1}^{m} p_{ij}p_i$$

where m is the number of elements in the input alphabet.

The **information about X given Y** is defined in a reasonable way as the decrease in entropy:

$$I(X|Y) = H(X) - H(X|Y) = H(X) + H(Y) - H(X,Y)$$

Since entropy depends only upon the probability distributions, this measure of information depends only upon the probability distribution of X, and the transition probabilities of the channel (and not on the alphabets, etc.) Define the **capacity** of the channel C as

$$\text{capacity }(C) = \max_{X} I(X|Y)$$

where the maximum is taken over all probability distributions for sources emitting the alphabet accepted as inputs by the channel, and where for each X the source Y is constructed from X and from the channel as just above.

Remark: Note that the expression

$$I(X|Y) = H(X) - H(X|Y) = H(X) + H(Y) - H(X,Y)$$

is actually symmetrical in the two random variables, so

$$I(X|Y) = I(Y|X)$$

In words, more intuitively, but less precisely, the amount of information about X imparted by Y is equal to the amount of information about Y imparted by X.

Remark: Since the definition of capacity depends *continuously* upon the probabilities $p_1, \ldots, p_m$ for the source's emissions and since the collection of all such m-tuples of probabilities is a closed and bounded set in $\mathbf{R}^m$, the maximum really occurs. This is a special case of the fact that the maximum of a continuous function on a closed and bounded set in $\mathbf{R}^m$ is achieved, that is, is bounded above and there is some point where the bounding value actually occurs.

Remark: The *units* for channel capacity are **bits per symbol**.

Theorem: Let C be a binary symmetric channel with bit error probability p. Then the channel capacity of C is

$$1 + p \log_2 p + (1 - p) \log_2(1 - p)$$

bits per symbol.

Proof: Let $q = 1 - p$, and suppose that we consider a source X which emits '0' with probability r and '1' with probability $s = 1 - r$. Let Y be the new source obtained by connecting the channel to the source X. Then

$$P(Y = \text{`0'}) = P(X = \text{`0'}) \cdot P(\text{`0' received} \,|\text{`0' sent})$$

$$+ P(X = \text{`1'}) \cdot P(\text{`0' received} \,|\text{`1' sent})$$

$$= r \cdot q + s \cdot p$$

$$P(Y = \text{`1'}) = P(X = \text{`0'}) \cdot P(\text{`1' received} \,|\text{`0' sent})$$

$$+ P(X = \text{`1'}) \cdot P(\text{`1' received} \,|\text{`1' sent})$$

$$= r \cdot p + s \cdot q$$

The joint entropy $H(X,Y)$ is just the entropy of the joint probability distribution (pr, ps, qr, qs), so

$$I(X|Y) = H(X) + H(Y) - H(X,Y)$$

$$= -r \log_2 r - s \log_2 s - (rq + sp) \log_2(rq + sp) - (rp + sq) \log_2(rp + sq)$$

$$+ (pr) \log_2(pr) + (ps) \log_2(ps) + (qr) \log_2(qr) + (qs) \log_2(qs)$$

Expand each expression $\log_2(xy)$ as

$$\log_2(xy) = \log_2 x + \log_2 y$$

and then use $p + q = 1$ and $r + s = 1$ to simplify the expression for $I(X|Y)$ to

$$p \log_2 p + q \log_2 q - (rq + sp) \log_2(rq + sp) - (rp + sq) \log_2(rp + sq)$$

To maximize this with respect to choice of r, differentiate with respect to r, set the derivative equal to zero, and solve for r (keeping in mind that $s = 1 - r$). This will show that $r = 1/2$ gives the maximum, which is then

$$p \log_2 p + q \log_2 q - \left(\frac{q+p}{2}\right) \log_2 \left(\frac{q+p}{2}\right) - \left(\frac{q+p}{2}\right) \log_2 \left(\frac{q+p}{2}\right)$$

$$= p \log_2 p + q \log_2 q - \left(\frac{1}{2}\right) \log_2 \left(\frac{1}{2}\right) - \left(\frac{1}{2}\right) \log_2 \left(\frac{1}{2}\right) = 1 + p \log_2 p + q \log_2 q$$

This proves the assertion of the theorem. $///$

Remark: When $p = \frac{1}{2}$ the channel capacity is 0. This makes sense, since if we lack any other recourse, then what we get over the channel is worthless. While we can *detect* errors (for example, by adding parity-check bits) we cannot *correct* them.

Proposition: Let C be a memoryless channel with capacity c. Then for any positive integer n the nth *extension* $C^{(n)}$ of C has capacity nc.

Remark: This assertion is reasonable sounding, and the proof contains no surprises, but it is a good exercise in the use of definitions.

Proof: Let $c^{(n)}$ be the capacity of the nth extension. Let $X = (X_1, \ldots, X_n)$ be a source for $C^{(n)}$, in which each X_i is a source for C. Let $Y = (Y_1, \ldots, Y_n)$ be the corresponding outputs from the channel C. By definition

$$c^{(n)} = \max_X I(X|Y) = \max_X H(X) - H(X|Y)$$

Since almost by definition

$$H(X) - H(X|Y) = H(X) + H(Y) - H(X,Y)$$

we have the symmetry

$$I(X|Y) = I(Y|X)$$

so also

$$c^{(n)} = \max_X H(Y) - H(Y|X)$$

Computing,

$$H(Y|X) = \sum_x P(X = x) H(Y|X = x)$$

Since the channel is memoryless, the results of the various Y_j are independent of each other. More precisely,

$$H(Y|X = x) = \sum_i H(Y_i|X = x)$$

Further, since Y_j only depends upon X_j, we have

$$H(Y|X = x) = \sum_i H(Y_i|X = x) = \sum_i H(Y_i|X_i = x_i)$$

where $x = (\ldots, x_i, \ldots)$. Putting this back into the expression for $H(Y|X)$, we obtain

$$H(Y|X) = \sum_{x_1, \ldots, x_n} P(X_1 = x_1, \ldots, X_n = x_n) \sum_i H(Y_i|X_i = x_i)$$

$$= \sum_i \sum_\xi P(X_i = \xi) H(Y_i|X_i = \xi)$$

Regardless of the independence of the X_is,

$$\sum_{x_2, x_3, \ldots, x_n} P(X_1 = x_1, X_2 = x_2, \ldots, X_n = x_n) = P(X_1 = x_1)$$

and so on. Thus,

$$H(Y|X) = \sum_i H(Y_i|X_i)$$

whether or not the X_i are independent, due to the *memorylessness* of the channel.

In the general inequality

$$H(Y_1, \ldots, Y_n) \leq H(Y_1) + \ldots + H(Y_n)$$

we have equality if and only if the Y_i are independent. Therefore,

$$c^{(n)} = \max_X I(X|Y) = \max_X H(Y) - H(Y|X)$$

$$\leq \max_X \left(\sum_i H(Y_i) - \sum_i H(Y_i|X_i) \right)$$

with equality if and only if the Y_is are independent. This proves

$$\text{capacity } c^{(n)} \text{ of } C^{(n)} \ \leq n \cdot (\text{capacity } c \text{ of } C)$$

The equality can be achieved by taking the Y_is to be independent, and taking the X_is to be independent and having the probability distribution that achieved the capacity of the channel C.   ///

4.5 Noisy coding theorem

Here is Shannon's 1948 theorem proving that by suitable choice of **error-correcting** encoding, information can be sent through a noisy channel at a rate arbitrarily close to the *capacity* of the channel.

For a choice of decoding mechanism for a code f, the **word error probability** of f is the 'average' probability of error in decoding, assuming (due to lack of information) that all words $w_1, \ldots, w_N$ in the code f are sent with equal probability. This expression is

$$\text{word error probability of } f = \frac{1}{N} \sum_{i=1}^{N} P(\text{error } |w_i \text{ sent})$$

Apart from the obvious objection that this might allow unacceptably large errors in decoding rare words, it seems that in practice a slightly different measure is used:

The **maximum word error probability** is

$$\text{maximum word error probability} = \max_i P(\text{error}|w_i \text{ sent})$$

Certainly

$$\text{maximum word error probability of } f \geq \text{ average word error probability of } f$$

so if we make the maximum error probability small then certainly the 'plain' error probability will be small. And there is the virtue that we have made no unwarranted assumptions about the probabilities that various codewords were sent. On the other hand, minimizing maximum word error probability requires that we perhaps overly concern ourselves with rare source words.

Now we return to the simple situation that all codes are **binary**, meaning that everything is expressed in 0s and 1s. That means that we think of a binary symmetric channel and its extensions. We use **maximum-likelihood** (equivalently, **minimum-distance**) decoding. From our earlier computation, a symmetric binary channel C with bit error probability p has capacity

$$c = 1 + p \log_2 p + (1 - p) \log_2(1 - p)$$

The **rate** of a binary code with maximum word length n and with t codewords is defined to be

$$\text{rate} = \frac{\log_2 t}{n} = \frac{\log_2(\text{number of codewords})}{\text{maximum word length}}$$

Remark: The maximum possible rate is 1, which can occur only for a binary code with maximum word length n where *all* the 2^n binary codewords of length n are used in the code. This represents the fullest possible transmission of information through a channel.

Remark: In a **noisy** channel, that is, in a channel whose bit error probability is greater than 0, it is not reasonable to try to use a code with rate too close to 1, because such a code will not have enough *redundancy* in it to allow either **detection** or **correction** of errors.

Theorem: *(Noisy Coding Theorem)* Let C be a symmetric binary channel with bit error probability $p < \frac{1}{2}$. Let $q = 1 - p$. Recall that the channel capacity of C is defined to be $1 + p \log_2 p + q \log_2 q$. Let R be a rate satisfying

$$0 < R < 1 + p \log_2 p + q \log_2 q$$

Then there is a sequence $C_1, C_2, \ldots$ of codes of lengths n_i with respective rates R_i approaching R (from below) such that

$$\lim_i \text{ word length } (C_i) = \infty$$

and the maximum word error probabilities of the C_is go to zero:

$$\lim_i \text{ max word error probability } (C_i) = 0$$

A little more specifically: given $\varepsilon > 0$, for sufficiently large n there is a code C of length n with rate $R_0 \leq R$ such that

$$|R_0 - R| \leq \frac{1}{n}$$

and

$$\text{max word error probability } (C) < \varepsilon$$

Remark: Due to the nature of the proof, the theorem gives no explanation of how to *find* or *create* the codes, nor is there a concrete indication of how rapidly the maximum word error probability decreases to 0.

Proof: To set the context, we review some basic probabilistic aspects of the situation. Let p be the bit error probability, and let $q = 1 - p$ for brevity. Then the expected number of bit errors in a binary word of length n is pn. The variance of the random variable that counts the bit errors in a binary word of length n is npq. The probability of *any specific pattern* of t bit errors in a word of length n is $p^t q^{n-t}$, as usual independent of the exact pattern, but rather depending only upon the *number* of bit errors, not their *location*.

Fix $\varepsilon > 0$, and let

$$b = \sqrt{\frac{npq}{\varepsilon/2}}$$

Then, by Chebyshev's inequality,

$$P(\text{number of expected bit errors } > np + b) \leq \frac{\varepsilon}{2}$$

Since $p < \frac{1}{2}$, for fixed ε and sufficiently large n the integer $r = \text{floor}(np + b)$ is surely strictly less than $\frac{n}{2}$. Recall that the **floor function** $\text{floor}(x)$ is the greatest integer less than or equal x.

For fixed word length n, let

$$B_r(x) = \{\text{words } y : d(x, y) \le r\}$$

(where $d(\ ,\ )$ is Hamming distance) denote the ball of radius r centered at the word x. The 'volume' $\text{vol}\, B_r(x)$ of the ball $B_r(x)$ is the number of words in it, which is the sum of the numbers of words with 0 bit errors (just x itself!), with 1 bit error, with 2 bit errors, ..., with t errors:

$$\text{vol}\, B_r(x) = \sum_{0 \le t \le r} \binom{n}{t}$$

Next, we recall the **big-oh notation**: let $f(n)$, $g(n)$, and $h(n)$ be three functions of positive integers n and K a constant with the property that for all sufficiently large positive integers n

$$|f(n) - g(n)| \le K \cdot h(n)$$

If we don't care much about the specific value of K, then we can write instead

$$f(n) - g(n) = O(h(n))$$

or

$$f(n) = g(n) + O(h(n))$$

For example,

$$\frac{1}{n+1} = \frac{1}{n} + O\left(\frac{1}{n^2}\right)$$

This sort of notation is useful when we're trying to *simplify* things and don't care too much about relatively small details.

Now we start the proof in earnest, keeping the notation above. Define a function of two length n words w, w' by

$$f(w, w') = \begin{cases} 1 & (\text{for } d(w, w') \le r) \\ 0 & (\text{for } d(w, w') > r) \end{cases}$$

where $r = \text{floor}(np + b)$. Certainly r depends on n, and is approximately $p \cdot n$. For x in the collection C of codewords, define

$$F_x(w) = 1 - f(w, x) + \sum_{y \in C,\, y \ne x} f(w, y)$$

This quantity $F_x(y)$ indicates roughly how many decoding errors we might make in decoding y as x. In particular, if there is no codeword within distance r of y other than x, then $F_x(y) = 0$. Otherwise, if there are other codewords within distance r of y, then $F_x(y) \geq 1$.

Let $C = \{x_1, \ldots, x_t\}$ be the codewords. We use the following decoding rule: for a received word y if there is a unique codeword x_i within distance r of y, then decode y as x_i, otherwise declare an error (or decode as some fixed default codeword x_1). It is clear from its description that this is a sloppier rule than minimum-distance decoding, so if we can arrange to have *this* decoding rule achieve a good error rate then minimum-distance (equivalently, maximum-likelihood) decoding will do at least as well.

Keep in mind that p is the channel's bit error probability. Let P_i be the probability of an incorrect decoding given that $x_i \in C$ is transmitted. We assume that codewords are transmitted with equal probabilities, each of which would have to be $1/t$ since there are t codewords in C. Thus, the expected probability of error in decoding the code C is

expected decoding error probability of code C

$$= P_C = \frac{1}{t} \cdot \sum_{1 \leq i \leq t} P_i$$

Let

$$P_{\text{best}} = \text{minimum } P_C \text{ for length } n \text{ codes } C \text{ with } t \text{ codewords}$$

Now we compute some things. Let V_n denote the collection of all binary words of length n. For brevity, for codeword $x_i \in C$ and received word $y \in V_n$, write

$$P(y|x_i) = P(y \text{ received } |x_i \text{ sent})$$

For a codeword x_i, the probability of incorrectly decoding the received word given that x_i was sent is

$$P_i \leq \sum_{y \in V_n} P(y|x_i) \, F_{x_i}(y) = \sum_{y \in V_n} P(y|x_i) \, (1 - f(x_i, y)) + \sum_{y \in V_n} \sum_{j \neq i} P(y|x_i) \, f(x_j, y)$$

The expression

$$\sum_{y \in V_n} P(y|x_i) \, (1 - f(x_i, y))$$

is the probability that the received word is *not* inside the ball $B_r(x_i)$ of radius r around x_i. By the choice of b and r above (for given ε and n), we have arranged that Chebysheff's inequality gives

$$\sum_{y \in V_n} P(y|x_i) \, (1 - f(x_i, y)) < \varepsilon/2$$

Thus, summing over $x_i \in C$,

expected decoding error probability of C

$$= P_C \le \frac{\varepsilon}{2} + \frac{1}{t} \sum_{1 \le i \le t} \sum_{y \in V_n} \sum_{j \neq i} P(y|x_i)\, f(x_j, y)$$

Shannon's insight was that whatever the *average* value P_{avg} of P_C is (averaged over all length n codes C with t codewords), there must be at least one code C_0 which has

$$P_{C_0} \le P_{\mathrm{avg}}$$

This is a relatively elementary assertion about numbers: let $a_1, \ldots, a_N$ be real numbers, and let

$$A = \frac{a_1 + \ldots + a_N}{N}$$

be the average. We are claiming that there is at least one a_i (though we can't really predict which one) with $a_i \le A$. To understand why this is so, suppose to the contrary that $a_i > A$ for all a_i. Then (by elementary properties of inequalities)

$$a_1 + \ldots + a_N > A + \ldots + A = N \cdot A$$

and

$$\frac{a_1 + \ldots + a_N}{N} > A$$

contradicting the fact that equality holds (since A is the average).

So we want to compute the *average* of P_C over all codes C of length n with t codewords. In fact, it turns out to be good to enlarge the class of codes to include some *degenerate* codes where some of the t codewords are *the same*. Yes, this means that information is lost at the very outset, and received words nearest such identical codewords can never be reliably decoded. Yes, this will make the average probability of word error greater. Yet making this 'sacrifice' of information makes the computation feasible, and we reach the desired conclusion despite having been profligate! So for the rest of the proof a 'code' with t words allows the possibility that various bunches of the codewords *may* be the same, as silly as this may seem.

Then

$$P_{\mathrm{best}} \le \ \mathrm{average}\ (P_C) \le \ \mathrm{average}\ \left(\frac{\varepsilon}{2} + \frac{1}{t} \sum_{1 \le i \le t} \sum_{y \in V_n} \sum_{j \neq i} P(y|x_i)\, f(x_j, y) \right)$$

$$= \frac{\varepsilon}{2} + \frac{1}{t}\ \mathrm{average}\ \left(\sum_{1 \le i \le t} \sum_{j \neq i} \sum_{y \in V_n} P(y|x_i)\, f(x_j, y) \right)$$

Since the various codewords x_k are chosen independently of each other (because we've given up the requirement that they be distinct from each other!), the averaging processes with respect to $x_1, x_2, \ldots$ can be done independently of each other, allowing smaller and easier computations. In particular, for each j

$$\mathrm{average\ over\ } x_j \mathrm{\ of\ } f(x_j, y) = \frac{\sum_{x_j \in V_n} f(x_j, y)}{2^n} = \frac{\mathrm{vol}\, B_r(y)}{2^n}$$

Thus, doing the inner averaging first, we have

$$\frac{\varepsilon}{2} + \frac{1}{t} \sum_{1 \leq i \leq t} \text{avg over } x_i \sum_{y \in V_n} P(y|x_i) \sum_{j \neq i} \frac{\text{vol } B_r(y)}{2^n}$$

Since the volume of that ball of radius r doesn't depend upon the center, but only upon the radius, we can write

$$\text{vol } B_r = \text{ volume of } any \text{ ball of radius } r$$

Then this constant can be brought outside. Thus, so far,

$$P_{\text{best}} \leq \frac{\varepsilon}{2} + \frac{\text{vol } B_r}{t \cdot 2^n} \sum_{1 \leq i \leq t} \text{avg over } x_i \sum_{y \in V_n} P(y|x_i) \cdot (t-1)$$

since there are $t - 1$ codewords other than x_i. Since $\frac{t-1}{t} \leq 1$, we can simplify this a bit and say

$$P_{\text{best}} \leq \frac{\varepsilon}{2} + \frac{\text{vol } B_r}{2^n} \sum_{1 \leq i \leq t} \text{avg over } x_i \sum_{y \in V_n} P(y|x_i)$$

Next, of course

$$\sum_{y \in V_n} P(y|x_i) = 1$$

for any codeword x_i, since *some* word is received when x_i is sent! This simplifies things further to

$$P_{\text{best}} \leq \frac{\varepsilon}{2} + \frac{\text{vol } B_r}{2^n} \sum_{1 \leq i \leq t} \text{avg over } x_i \ (1) = \frac{\varepsilon}{2} + \frac{\text{vol } B_r}{2^n} \cdot t$$

The factor of t comes from the 'outer' sum over the t codewords x_i in each code.
Next, we use the estimate (from the lemma below) on the volume vol B_r:

$$\text{vol } B_r \leq \frac{n}{2} \cdot \frac{n^n}{r^r \, (n-r)^{n-r}}$$

and rearrange to obtain

$$P_{\text{best}} - \frac{\varepsilon}{2} \leq \frac{t}{2^n} \cdot \frac{n}{2} \cdot \frac{n^n}{r^r \, (n-r)^{n-r}} = \frac{t}{2^n} \cdot \frac{n}{2} \cdot \frac{1}{(r/n)^r \, ((n-r)/n)^{n-r}}$$

If $P_{\text{best}} - \frac{\varepsilon}{2} \leq 0$ we're already done, so we can assume without loss of generality that $P_{\text{best}} - \frac{\varepsilon}{2} > 0$, which allows us to take logarithms base 2 to obtain

$$\log_2 \left(P_{\text{best}} - \frac{\varepsilon}{2} \right) \leq \log_2 t - n + \log_2 n - 1 - r \log_2 \frac{r}{n} - (n-r) \log_2 \frac{(n-r)}{n}$$

Divide through by n:

$$\frac{1}{n}\log_2\left(P_{\text{best}} - \frac{\varepsilon}{2}\right) \leq \frac{1}{n}\log_2 t - 1 + \frac{\log_2 n}{n} - \frac{1}{n} - \frac{r}{n}\log_2\frac{r}{n} - \frac{(n-r)}{n}\log_2\frac{(n-r)}{n}$$

Now r/n is roughly p, and $(n-r)/n$ is roughly q. The other lemma below makes this precise, and gives us

$$\frac{1}{n}\log_2\left(P_{\text{best}} - \frac{\varepsilon}{2}\right) \leq \frac{\log_2 t + \log_2 n - 1}{n} - (1 + p\log_2 p + q\log_2 q) + O\left(n^{-1/2}\right)$$

The summand $(\log_2 n - 1)/n$ is *also* $O(n^{-1/2})$, so we have

$$\frac{1}{n}\log_2\left(P_{\text{best}} - \frac{\varepsilon}{2}\right) \leq \frac{\log_2 t}{n} - (1 + p\log_2 p + q\log_2 q) + O\left(n^{-1/2}\right)$$

For a choice of rate R in the allowed range $0 < R < 1 + p\log_2 p + q\log_2 q$, and for corresponding number of words $t = 2^{\text{floor}(R \cdot n)}$,

$$\frac{\log_2 t}{n} = \frac{\text{floor}(R \cdot n)}{n} = R + O\left(n^{-1}\right) = R + O\left(n^{-1/2}\right)$$

Note that this says that the rate $\text{floor}(R \cdot n)/n$ is within $1/n$ of the limiting rate R. Thus, we have

$$\frac{1}{n}\log_2\left(P_{\text{best}} - \frac{\varepsilon}{2}\right) \leq R - (1 + p\log_2 p + q\log_2 q) + O\left(n^{-1/2}\right)$$

Define

$$\delta = \frac{1}{2} \cdot (1 + p\log_2 p + q\log_2 q - R)$$

From the inequality $0 < R < 1 + p\log_2 p + q\log_2 q$, we have $\delta > 0$. Likewise, by that inequality, for sufficiently large n

$$R - (1 + p\log_2 p + q\log_2 q) + O\left(n^{-1/2}\right) < -\delta$$

For such large n we multiply the equation

$$\frac{\log_2 t}{n} = \frac{\text{floor}(R \cdot n)}{n} = R + O\left(n^{-1}\right) = R + O\left(n^{-1/2}\right)$$

through by n, exponentiate base 2, and move the $\varepsilon/2$ to the other side to obtain

$$P_{\text{best}} \leq \frac{\varepsilon}{2} + 2^{-\delta n}$$

Take n large enough so that $2^{-\delta n} < \varepsilon/2$ (since $\delta > 0$). For such n we have $P_{\text{best}} \leq \varepsilon$, finishing the proof of Shannon's theorem. ///

Here is the simple estimate on volumes used above in the proof of Shannon's theorem:

Lemma: For $0 \le r \le n/2$

$$\operatorname{vol} B_r(x) \le \frac{n}{2} \cdot \frac{n^n}{r^r (n-r)^{n-r}}$$

Proof: First note that since $r \le n/2$

$$\binom{n}{0} \le \binom{n}{1} \le \binom{n}{2} \le \cdots \le \binom{n}{r}$$

from which

$$\operatorname{vol} B_r(x) = \sum_{0 \le t \le r} \binom{n}{t} \le \sum_{0 \le t \le r} \binom{n}{r} = r \cdot \binom{n}{r} \le \frac{n}{2}\binom{n}{r}$$

Then, from the Binomial Theorem,

$$n^n = (r + (n-r))^n = \sum_{0 \le i \le n} \binom{n}{i} r^i (n-r)^{n-i} \ge \binom{n}{r} r^r (n-r)^{n-r}$$

By rearranging, this shows that

$$\binom{n}{r} \le \frac{n^n}{r^r (n-r)^{n-r}}$$

Putting these together, we get

$$\operatorname{vol} B_r(x) \le \frac{n}{2}\binom{n}{r} \le \frac{n}{2} \frac{n^n}{r^r (n-r)^{n-r}}$$

as claimed.   ///

Here is another estimate used in the proof of Shannon's theorem. It is a typical result coming from calculus, using the Mean Value Theorem.

Lemma: Fix $\varepsilon > 0$ and fix p with $0 \le p \le \frac{1}{2}$. Let $b = \sqrt{2npq/\varepsilon}$ and $r = \operatorname{floor}(np + b)$. Using the big-oh notation,

$$\frac{r}{n} \log_2 \frac{r}{n} = p \log_2 p + O(n^{-1/2})$$

That is, for some constant K (which we don't care about),

$$\left| \frac{r}{n} \log_2 \frac{r}{n} - p \log_2 p \right| \le \frac{K}{\sqrt{n}}$$

Proof: First, because of the way r is defined via the floor function,

$$|r - (np + b)| \leq 1$$

from which, dividing through by n, we have

$$\left| \frac{r}{n} - (p + \frac{b}{n}) \right| \leq \frac{1}{n} = O\left(\frac{1}{n}\right)$$

For fixed $\varepsilon > 0$ and for fixed p (and q), by the definition of b we have

$$b = O(\sqrt{n})$$

and then, dividing by n,

$$\frac{b}{n} = O\left(\frac{1}{\sqrt{n}}\right)$$

Since $\sqrt{n} \leq n$ we have

$$O\left(\frac{1}{n}\right) + O\left(\frac{1}{\sqrt{n}}\right) = O\left(\frac{1}{\sqrt{n}}\right)$$

and therefore

$$\left| \frac{r}{n} - p \right| \leq \left| \frac{r}{n} - (p + \frac{b}{n}) \right| + \left| \frac{b}{n} \right| \leq \frac{1}{n} + O\left(\frac{1}{\sqrt{n}}\right) = O\left(\frac{1}{\sqrt{n}}\right)$$

Abstracting the situation slightly, fix $y = p$ in the range $0 < y < 1$, and let $x_n = r/n$ with $x_n - y = O(n^{-1/2})$. We claim that

$$x_n \log_2 x_n - y \log_2 y = O(n^{-1/2})$$

To prove this, we need the Mean Value Theorem from calculus: for any differentiable function f, given $a < b$, for some ξ between a and b we have

$$f(b) - f(a) = f'(\xi) \cdot (b - a)$$

for differentiable f and for some ξ between a and b. Also recall that

$$\frac{d}{dx}(x \ln x) = 1 + \ln x$$

and that

$$\log_2 A = \frac{\ln A}{\ln 2}$$

so

$$\frac{d}{dx}(x \log_2 x) = \frac{1}{\ln 2}(1 + \ln x)$$

Then we have

$$x_n \log_2 x_n - y \log_2 y = \frac{1}{\ln 2} (\ln \xi + 1) \cdot (x_n - y)$$

$$= \left(\frac{1}{\ln 2} + \log_2 \xi \right) \cdot (x_n - y)$$

for some ξ between x_n and y.. For n large enough, $x_n \le 2y$, so $y \le \xi \le 2y$. Thus, by the monotonicity of $\log_2$,

$$\log_2 y \le \log_2 \xi \le \log_2 2y$$

This gives a bound on $\log_2 \xi$ which does not depend on n at all, so, in terms of the parameter n, this says

$$x_n \log_2 x_n - y \log_2 y = O(x_n - y) = O\left(\frac{1}{\sqrt{n}} \right)$$

as desired.   ///

Exercises

4.01 A symmetric binary channel has error probability $1/4$. What is the probability that the binary word '01' is transmitted correctly?   (*ans.*)

4.02 A symmetric binary channel has error probability $1/6$. What is the probability that *at least one error* occurs in transmission of the binary word '0011'?   (*ans.*)

4.03 A message of N binary digits is transmitted through a binary symmetric channel with error probability p. Verify that the *expected number* of errors is Np.   (*ans.*)

4.04 A symmetric binary channel has error probability $1/4$. A source is encoded to the set of codewords $\{000, 001, 010, 011, 100, 101, 110, 111\}$. A single-digit parity check is added, turning the codewords into

$$\{0000, 0011, 0101, 0110, 1001, 1010, 1100, 1111\}$$

What is the probability that one of these new 4-bit codewords is transmitted with an error *that goes undetected?* By contrast, what is the probability that at least one error occurs in transmission of a 4-bit word by this channel?

4.05 A symmetric binary channel has error probability $1/4$. A source emits words w_1, w_2, w_3, w_4, w_5 with probabilities $1/2, 1/4, 1/8, 1/16, 1/16$. These words are Huffman-encoded as $0, 10, 110, 1110, 1111$, respectively. What is the probability that there will be at least one (undetected!) error transmission of a word? Now add a parity-check bit, giving codewords $00, 100, 1100, 11101, 11110$. What is the probability that there is an *undetected* error in transmission of a word?

4.06 Why is there no point in considering a binary symmetric channel with error probability $p > \frac{1}{2}$?

4.07 What is the channel capacity of the binary erasure channel with erasure probability ε?

4.08 What is the *(information) rate* of a code consisting of all binary codewords of length 4 with a parity check bit added (making them of length 5)? (*ans.*)

4.09 A code consisting of all binary source words of length 4 makes codewords by sending every source word twice in a row in order to detect allow the decoder to detect errors. (An 8-bit codeword is rejected if the first 4 bits and the last 4 bits don't agree.) What is its *rate*? (*ans.*)

4.10 A code with binary source words of length 4 makes codewords by sending every source word twice in a row in order to detect allow the decoder to detect errors. (An 8-bit codeword is rejected if the first 4 bits and the last 4 bits don't agree.) In a binary symmetric channel with error probability $1/10$, what is the probability that an error will go undetected? (*ans.*)

4.11 What is the *rate* of a code with binary source words of length 4 in which codewords are made by sending a source word 3 times in a row (thereby making them of length 12)? (The correct decoding is decided by a 2/3 vote, or the word is rejected if no 2 of the 3 4-bit pieces agree.)

4.12 A code with binary source words of length 4 makes codewords by sending a source word 3 times in a row (thereby making them of length 12). (The correct decoding is decided by a 2/3 vote, or the word is rejected if no 2 of the 3 4-bit pieces agree.) In a binary symmetric channel with error probability $1/10$, what is the probability that an error will go undetected? What is the probability that an error will be detected but not be correctable?

5

Cyclic Redundancy Checks

The idea of **parity check bit** can be extended in various ways to detect more errors. (Recall that a single parity check bit only *detects* an *odd* number of bit-errors, and certainly cannot *correct* any errors at all.)

5.1 The finite field with 2 elements

The set $GF(2) = \mathbf{F}_2 = \{0, 1\}$ with suitable operations of addition and multiplication is the simplest example of what is called a **finite field**. Fortunately, we can do many things with $\mathbf{F}_2$ without worrying about the general case right away.

The **finite field** with 2 elements can be taken to be the set $\{0, 1\}$ with the addition and multiplication operations $+$ and $\times$ defined by

$$0 + 0 = 0 \quad 0 + 1 = 1 \quad 1 + 0 = 1 \quad 1 + 1 = 0$$
$$0 \times 0 = 0 \quad 0 \times 1 = 0 \quad 1 \times 0 = 0 \quad 1 \times 1 = 1$$

Various notations are used for this set with these operations: $\mathbf{F}_2$ and $GF(2)$ are the most common. Also $\mathbf{Z}/2$. The notation $\mathbf{Z}_2$ is sometimes used, but this is not so good since in other contexts $\mathbf{Z}_2$ is an entirely different thing, the 2-adic integers. Also, sometimes this finite field is called a **Galois field**, in honor of Evariste Galois, who first systematically studied finite fields such as $\mathbf{F}_2$.

Remark: Since $1 + 1 = 0$, it is reasonable to say that

$$-1 = 1$$

if by '-1' we mean something which when added to 1 gives 0. Similarly,

$$-0 = 0$$

since, after all, $0 + 0 = 0$.

Remark: It is not possible to tell, except from context, whether symbols 1 and 0 refer to elements of $\mathbf{F}_2$ or, instead, refer to the 1 and 0 in the real or complex numbers. At the same time, it is probably misguided to add notational baggage in an attempt to systematically overcome this ambiguity. In fact, context will almost always sufficiently clarify this point.

Remark: If these 0s and 1s are viewed as *bits*, then the possibly suspicious-looking addition in $\mathbf{F}_2$ can instead be understood as being **exclusive or**. This is worth noting, but in fact there are two more general abstractions both of which will subsume this addition operation in a way that is more sensible in the long run, making it seem more like an extension of arithmetic and algebra. The first is the construction of $\mathbf{Z}/p$, **the integers modulo** p. The case here is just the case of $p = 2$. The other abstraction is to **finite fields**, which we will also look at a little later.

5.2 Polynomials over $GF(2)$

We can do basic algebra with polynomials having coefficients in the finite field $\mathbf{F}_2$ in almost exactly the same fashion as with polynomials having real or complex coefficients. The algebra of such polynomials is used extensively in the sequel. The immediate application will be to *cyclic redundancy checks* just below.

A **polynomial** $P(x)$ in the **indeterminate** x with **coefficients** which are *real numbers* is a sum of powers of x with real numbers in front of them, like

$$P(x) = 3 \cdot x^5 - 2.017 \cdot x^2 + 17 \cdot x - 7.123$$

The numbers in front of the powers of x are the **coefficients**. The **degree** of a polynomial is the highest power of x that appears with a non-zero coefficient. We assign the 0-polynomial degree $-\infty$. This choice makes various results hold without making exceptions for the 0-polynomial. For example, *the degree of the product of two polynomials is the sum of their degrees.*

As usual, if the coefficient of some power of x is 0, we don't write that term at all. A polynomial like this certainly gives rise to an associated **polynomial function**, usually denoted by the same symbol, into which we can plug real numbers. With the example just given, to **evaluate** at $x = 1.234$ means to replace x by 1.234 throughout:

$$P(1.234) = 3 \cdot (1.234)^5 - 2.017 \cdot (1.234)^2 + 17 \cdot (1.234) - 7.123 \approx 19.3677$$

Analogously, a **polynomial** in the indeterminate x with **coefficients** in the finite field $\mathbf{F}_2$ will look exactly like a polynomial with 'ordinary' coefficients, except that the only coefficients we'll use will be 0 or 1. It is important to realize that **the exponents of x are still ordinary integers.** For example,

$$P(x) = 1 \cdot x^3 + 0 \cdot x^2 + 0 \cdot x + 1 \cdot x^0 = x^3 + 1$$

is such a polynomial. Notice that since the only possible coefficients are 0 and 1, we don't really have to write coefficients at all: if the coefficient of some power of

x is 0, we don't write it at all, and if the coefficient is 1 we just write the power of x. As usual, such a polynomial gives rise to a **polynomial function** from $\mathbf{F}_2$ to $\mathbf{F}_2$, by **evaluation** inside the finite field $\mathbf{F}_2$:

$$P(0) = 0^3 + 1 = 1$$
$$P(1) = 1^3 + 1 = 0$$

Unlike the case of real numbers, however, different polynomials can give rise to the same function: for example the two polynomials $P(x) = x^2 + x + 1$ and $Q(x) = 1$ have the same values for any input in $\mathbf{F}_2$.

Addition of polynomials with coefficients in $\mathbf{F}_2$ is as usual: add the coefficients of corresponding powers of x, but now inside the finite field $\mathbf{F}_2$. For example,

$$(x^3 + 1) + (x^3 + x^2 + x + 1) = (1+1) \cdot x^3 + (0+1) \cdot x^2 + (0+1)x + (1+1) = x^2 + x$$

Multiplication of polynomials is as usual, satisfying the distributive law. To multiply polynomials is akin to multiplying decimal integers, but keeping track of powers of x instead of tens' place, hundreds' place, etc. And the multiplication of polynomials is somewhat simpler in that there is *no carry*, unlike integer multiplication. First, the integer multiplication case is something like

$$
\begin{array}{r}
2\ 0\ 3 \\
\times\ 1\ 2\ 3 \\
\hline
6\ 0\ 9 \\
4\ 0\ 6 \quad\ \\
2\ 0\ 3 \quad\quad\ \\
\hline
2\ 4\ 9\ 6\ 9 \\
\end{array}
$$

(This example did not have any *carries* in it.) The polynomial multiplication is very similar. For example, with coefficients in the real numbers:

$$
\begin{array}{rrrr}
2x^3 & 3x^2 & +x & -3 \\
 & 2x^2 & -3x & +2 \\
\hline
 & +4x^3 & +6x^2 & +2x & -6 \\
-6x^4 & -9x^3 & -3x^2 & +9x \\
4x^5 & +6x^4 & +2x^3 & -6x^2 \\
\hline
4x^5 & & -3x^3 & -3x^2 & +11x & -6 \\
\end{array}
$$

That is, **each term in the first polynomial multiplies each term in the second polynomial.** Entirely analogously we can multiply polynomials with coefficients in the finite field $\mathbf{F}_2$: again, each term in the first polynomial multiplies each term in the second one, and then we add them all up. Now it's actually easier than for real or complex coefficients, because the arithmetic of the 'numbers' is so easy to do. For example, keeping in mind that $1 + 1 = 0$ in $\mathbf{F}_2$:

$$
\begin{array}{rrrr}
x^3 & & +x & +1 \\
 & x^2 & +x & +1 \\
\hline
 & +x^3 & & +x & +1 \\
+x^4 & & +x^2 & +x \\
x^5 & & +x^3 & +x^2 \\
\hline
x^5 & +x^4 & & & +1 \\
\end{array}
$$

Note that in all cases we preserved the vertical alignment of like powers of x as a precaution against miscopying errors. This is much like keeping the tens' places, hundreds' places, etc., lined up when doing integer arithmetic by hand, except that there is no *carrying*.

Division of one polynomial by another is also analogous to long division (with remainder) of integers, except again there is no 'borrowing' or 'carrying'. First we do an example with coefficients viewed as being ordinary integers or real numbers:

$$
\begin{array}{r}
x^3 +x^2 -x^1 -1 \;\; \text{R}\;\; x^4+0 \;\; +0 \;\; +3x +2 \\
x^5 \;\; +0 \;\; +x^3 +0 \;\; +x^1 +x^0 \overline{)\; x^8 +x^7 +0 \;\; +0 \;\; +x^4 +x^3 +0 \;\; +x^1 +x^0} \\
x^8 +0 \;\; +x^6 +0 \;\; +x^4 +x^3 +0 \;\; +0 \;\; +0 \\
\hline
x^7 -x^6 +0 \;\; +0 \;\; +0 \;\; +0 \;\; +x^1 +x^0 \\
x^7 +0 \;\; +x^5 +0 \;\; +x^3 +x^2 +0 \;\; +0 \\
\hline
-x^6 -x^5 +0 \;\; -x^3 -x^2 +x^1 +x^0 \\
-x^6 +0 \;\; -x^4 +0 \;\; -x^2 -x^1 +0 \\
\hline
-x^5 +x^4 -x^3 +0 \;\; +2x^1 +x^0 \\
-x^5 +0 \;\; -x^3 +0 \;\; -x^1 -x^0 \\
\hline
x^4 +0 \;\; +0 \;\; +3x^1+2
\end{array}
$$

Thus, in effect, at first we ask how many x^5s go into x^8 (exactly x^3), multiply the divisor by x^3 and subtract from the dividend, getting a temporary remainder, in this case $x^7 - x^6 + x + 1$. Next, how many x^5s go into x^7? Certainly x^2. Multiply the divisor by x^2 and subtract from the temporary remainder, giving a newer temporary remainder $-x^6 - x^5 - x^3 - x^2 + x + 1$. Continue until the **degree** of the remainder is strictly less than the degree of the divisor.

Now we use the same dividend and divisor, but viewed as having coefficients in $\mathbf{F}_2$, so that $-1 = 1$, $1 + 1 = 0$, etc:

$$
\begin{array}{r}
x^3 +x^2 +x^1 +1 \;\; \text{R}\;\; x^4+0 \;\; +0 \;\; +x^1 +0 \\
x^5 \;\; +0 \;\; +x^3 +0 \;\; +x^1 +x^0 \overline{)\; x^8 +x^7 +0 \;\; +0 \;\; +x^4 +x^3 +0 \;\; +x^1 +x^0} \\
x^8 +0 \;\; +x^6 +0 \;\; +x^4 +x^3 +0 \;\; +0 \;\; +0 \\
\hline
x^7 +x^6 +0 \;\; +0 \;\; +0 \;\; +0 \;\; +x^1 +x^0 \\
x^7 +0 \;\; +x^5 +0 \;\; +x^3 +x^2 +0 \;\; +0 \\
\hline
x^6 +x^5 +0 \;\; +x^3 +x^2 +x^1 +x^0 \\
x^6 +0 \;\; +x^4 +0 \;\; +x^2 +x^1 +0 \\
\hline
x^5 +x^4 +x^3 +0 \;\; +0 \;\; +x^0 \\
x^5 +0 \;\; +x^3 +0 \;\; +x^1 +x^0 \\
\hline
x^4 +0 \;\; +0 \;\; +x^1 +0
\end{array}
$$

Because in $\mathbf{F}_2$ we have $-1 = +1$, addition and subtraction are conveniently the same thing. Thus, at each line we have the liberty of adding rather than subtracting, which is a little bit easier since it is a symmetric function of its inputs (rather than being unsymmetric as subtraction is in general).

Remark: No, it is not possible to tell what kind of numbers the coefficients of a polynomial are intended to be without knowing the context. This is especially true of the simplest expressions such as 1 or 0, and all the more so when we suppress the coefficients, like in $x^3 + x$.

Remark: In any case, regardless of what kind of *coefficients* we're using, the *exponents* of the indeterminate x are still just ordinary non-negative integers.

5.3 Cyclic redundancy checks (CRCs)

If we don't care about *correcting* errors, but only about *detecting* them, there are very effective standard methods available, called **cyclic redundancy checks**, abbreviated as **CRCs**. These are natural generalizations of **parity check bits**, and in effect are able to keep track of more information.

The CRC's can be chosen to fit the circumstance: if arranged optimally, an n-bit CRC will fail to detect only 1 error out of 2^n. Common values of the bit-size n are 12, 16, and 32.

Given data expressed as a stream of bits such as 11100010100, create a **data polynomial** with coefficients in the finite field $\mathbf{F}_2$ from it by using the 0s and 1s as coefficients:

$$11100010100 \rightarrow x^{10} + x^9 + x^8 + x^4 + x^2$$

A CRC-computing algorithm is specified by its **generating polynomial**, which is also a polynomial with coefficients in the finite field $\mathbf{F}_2$. For example, we might take as generating polynomial

$$x^3 + x + 1$$

Then the CRC of the data is computed by **finding the remainder when the data polynomial is divided by the generating polynomial**: With data polynomial and generating polynomial as above, we'd get

```
                           x⁷  +x⁶  +0   +0   +x³  +0   +0   +1  R  x²+x¹ +x⁰
x³    +0  +x¹ +x⁰ | x¹⁰ +x⁹  +x⁸  +0   +0   +0   +x⁴  +0   +x²  +0   +0
                    x¹⁰ +0   +x⁸  +x⁷  +0   +0   +0   +0   +0   +0   +0
                    ────────────────────────────────────────────────────
                         x⁹  +0   +x⁷  +0   +0   +x⁴  +0   +x²  +0   +0
                         x⁹  +0   +x⁷  +x⁶  +0   +0   +0   +0   +0   +0
                         ───────────────────────────────────────────────
                                      x⁶  +0   +x⁴  +0   +x²  +0   +0
                                      x⁶  +0   +x⁴  +x³  +0   +0   +0
                                      ───────────────────────────────────
                                                x³  +x²  +0   +0
                                                x³  +0   +x¹  +x⁰
                                                ─────────────────────
                                                     x²  +x¹  +x⁰
```

Thus, the remainder is $x^2 + x + 1$, which we translate back to bits as 111. That is

CRC with generating polynomial $x^3 + x + 1$ computed for $11100010100 = 111$

Remark: In real life, the long-division process can be implemented cleverly so that the CRC of quite large chunks of data can be computed quickly.

Remark: In some cases the long-division algorithm is run in the opposite direction bit-wise, meaning that the bit string is interpreted as coefficients in *ascending* rather than *descending* order as we have done. This doesn't change the idea of the thing, but certainly changes the interpretation in terms of polynomials.

• Computation of a **single parity bit** is computation of a CRC with generating polynomial $x + 1$.

Remark: For generating polynomials of degree n there are 2^n different possible values of the CRC of data streams, since the remainder after division can (in principle) be any polynomial of degree $n - 1$ or less with coefficients in the finite field $\mathbf{F}_2$. For each of the coefficients from $n - 1$ down to 0 there are 2 choices, so altogether there are

$$\underbrace{2 \times 2 \times \ldots \times 2}_{} = 2^n$$

possible remainders. Therefore, if we are confident (!?) that these remainders are uniformly distributed among all 2^n possibilities we can claim that the CRC misses only 1 out of 2^n bit errors.

Remark: A common too-simple type of **redundant information** computed to detect errors or changes in data is an **XOR checksum**. Here *XOR* means **exclusive-or**. This is very easy in terms of typical computer operations: **XOR all the *bytes* together**. This produces a single-byte checksum value. This is an appealing kind of redundancy to compute because it is very easy and very fast. Since there are 2^8 different possible checksum values (because of the common 8-bit ASCII bytes), superficially it would seem that these checksums should be good at detecting errors. **However**, due to the fact that some 8-bit bytes are much more common than others, these checksum values are *not* uniformly distributed among the 2^8 possibilities, which means that the effectiveness is sharply reduced. This will be discussed further later.

Remark: Another type of checksum, sometimes called an **arithmetic checksum**, is obtained by viewing each byte (8-bit chunk) of the data as an 8-bit number (in binary), and add them all together, discarding any carries that go above the 2^7s place. That is, only the 'bottom' 8 digits/bits of the sum are kept. (One could also express this as **reduction modulo** 2^8.) Again, there are 2^8 different possible checksum values, so superficially it would seem that these checksums should be good at detecting errors. **However**, again due to the fact that some 8-bit bytes are much more common than others, these checksum values are *not* uniformly distributed among the 2^8 possibilities, which means that the effectiveness is sharply reduced for the same reason as inthe previous example.

The XOR checksum computation can be understood in a more structured fashion in the larger context of CRC's. View each *byte* (ordered 8-tuple of bits) as a **vector** with components in $\mathbf{F}_2$. Then the CRC is computed by adding up all the resulting vectors from the whole chunk of data. For example, for data (grouped into 3 bytes)

$$111000110010101101111001$$

we'd create vectors

$$(1,1,1,0,0,0,1,1) \quad (0,0,1,0,1,0,1,1) \quad (0,1,1,1,1,0,0,1)$$

and add them using the addition operation from $\mathbf{F}_2$:

$$(1,1,1,0,0,0,1,1) + (0,0,1,0,1,0,1,1) + (0,1,1,1,1,0,0,1)$$

$$= (1+0+0, 1+0+1, 1+1+1, 0+0+1, 0+1+1, 0+0+0, 1+1+0, 1+1+1)$$

$$= (1,0,1,1,0,0,0,1)$$

To view this as a CRC, instead of *vectors* we make *polynomials* from 8-bit bunches. Then **computing the XOR checksum is the same as computing a CRC with generating polynomial**

$$x^8 - 1$$

But now we realize that if we are unhappy with the statistical (error-detecting) properties of a CRC with a given generating polynomial then we can try a different generating polynomial. **There are choices.**

Better CRC's in real life are the ones computed with standard choices for generating polynomials:

$$x^{12} + x^{11} + x^3 + x + 1$$

$$x^{16} + x^{12} + x^5 + 1$$

$$x^{32} + x^{26} + x^{23} + x^{22} + x^{16} + x^{12} + x^{11} + x^{10} + x^8 + x^7 + x^5 + x^4 + x^2 + x + 1$$

Why these? Because they catch all two-bit errors in very long strings. Specifically, the above degree 12 CRC catches all two-bit errors up to distance $2^{12} - 1$ apart, the degree 16 CRC catches all two-bit errors up to distance $2^{16} - 1$ apart, and the degree 32 CRC catches all two-bit errors up to distance $2^{32} - 1$ apart, because these polynomials are all *primitive*, in a sense discussed subsequently.

5.4 What errors does a CRC catch?

A little algebra can explain what errors will be detected by a CRC and how different choices of the generating polynomial affect this. Generally, the higher the degree of the generating polynomial the better the CRC will function, but there are other significant issues as well.

For a CRC with generating polynomial $g = g(x)$, and for data (stream of 0s and 1s) turned into a polynomial $d = d(x)$ (both with coefficients in $\mathbf{F}_2$), suppose that $d = d(x)$ is transmitted or played back with some errors, and becomes $\tilde{d} = \tilde{d}(x)$ instead. (We may suppress the reference to the indeterminate x in the polynomials here, to reduce the clutter in the notation.)

The **error vector** or **error polynomial** is obtained by subtracting:

$$e = e(x) = d(x) - \tilde{d}(x) = d - \tilde{d}$$

(Since the coefficients are in $\mathbf{F}_2$ it doesn't really matter whether we subtract or add.) The number of non-zero coefficients in $e(x)$ is its **Hamming weight**. The number of non-zero coefficients in $e(x)$ is the number of bit errors.

Let $r = r(x)$ be the CRC of $d(x)$. It is the remainder when $d(x)$ is divided by $g(x)$, so we can write

$$d(x) = q(x) \cdot g(x) + r(x) = q \cdot g + r$$

where $q(x)$ is the quotient obtained by dividing $d(x)$ by $g(x)$. Let $\tilde{r}(x)$ be the CRC of $\tilde{d}(x)$, and let

$$\tilde{d}(x) = \tilde{q}(x) \cdot g(x) + \tilde{r}(x) = \tilde{q} \cdot g + \tilde{r}$$

where $\tilde{q}(x)$ is the quotient obtained by dividing $\tilde{d}(x)$ by $g(x)$. Then the error is expressible as

$$e(x) = d(x) - \tilde{d}(x) = (q \cdot g + r) - (\tilde{q} \cdot g + \tilde{r})$$

$$= (q - \tilde{q}) \cdot g + r - \tilde{r}$$

This means that **the remainder upon dividing $e(x)$ by $g(x)$ is $r - \tilde{r}$.**

- For the CRC to **fail** to detect an error $e = d - \tilde{d}$, that remainder $r - \tilde{r}$ must be 0, which is to say that $g(x)$ **divides** $e(x)$ (with remainder 0).

Remark: Divisibility properties of polynomials with coefficients in $\mathbf{F}_2$ are entirely reasonable and are abstractly consistent with divisibility properties of polynomials with real or complex coefficients. Later we will look at such issues more carefully, but for the moment we will take some things for granted.

- If there is **just one bit error**, at the ith position, then the error polynomial is

$$e(x) = x^i$$

  This will fail to be detected by the CRC if and only if $g(x)$ divides $e(x) = x^i$. Since x^i is just the product of i copies of the factor x, $g(x)$ cannot divide x^i unless $g(x)$ is x^j for some $j \le i$. So already $g(x) = x + 1$ will detect single bit errors. **Single bit errors are easy to detect.**

- If there are **just two bit errors**, at the mth and n^{th} positions (with $m < n$), then the error polynomial is

$$e(x) = x^m + x^n$$

  This will fail to be detected by the CRC if and only if $g(x)$ divides $e(x) = x^m + x^n$. This error polynomial can be factored as

$$e(x) = x^m + x^n = x^m(1 + x^{n-m})$$

  If $g(x)$ has no *factor* of x, which is easy to arrange by having the **constant term** be non-zero, then for such an error to go undetected it must be that $g(x)$ divides $1 + x^{n-m}$ (with remainder 0). Already this is mysterious if we don't know anything else.

Example: We consider an example to assess detectability of two-bit errors: let's look at the case of the XOR checksum, with $g(x) = x^8 - 1$. Recall the high-school algebra identities

$$\begin{aligned}
x^2 - 1 &= (x-1)(x+1) \\
x^3 - 1 &= (x-1)(x^2 + x + 1) \\
x^4 - 1 &= (x-1)(x^3 + x^2 + x + 1) \\
x^5 - 1 &= (x-1)(x^4 + x^3 + x^2 + x + 1) \\
&\cdots \\
x^N - 1 &= (x-1)(x^{N-1} + x^{N-2} + \ldots + x + 1)
\end{aligned}$$

(The fact that we are working with coefficients in $\mathbf{F}_2$, and that $-1 = +1$, does not harm these identities.) Replacing x by x^8, we find

$$\begin{aligned}
x^{16} - 1 &= (x^8 - 1)(x^8 + 1) \\
x^{24} - 1 &= (x^8 - 1)(x^{16} + x^8 + 1) \\
x^{32} - 1 &= (x^8 - 1)(x^{24} + x^{16} + x^8 + 1) \\
x^{40} - 1 &= (x^8 - 1)(x^{32} + x^{24} + x^{16} + x^8 + 1) \\
&\cdots \\
x^{8N} - 1 &= (x^8 - 1)(x^{8(N-1)} + \ldots + x^8 + 1)
\end{aligned}$$

That is, $x^8 - 1$ divides (with remainder 0) any polynomial $x^{8N} - 1$. For error detection, that means that if two bit errors occur a distance apart which is a multiple of 8, the XOR checksum CRC will **not** detect it.

Example: But that level of performance can already be achieved by a *smaller* CRC: using the CRC with generating polynomial $x^3 + x + 1$, even though it's only of degree 3 rather than degree 8, we only fail to detect two-bit errors when they're a multiple of 7 apart. That is, $x^3 + x + 1$ divides $x^N - 1$ (with remainder 0) only when N is a multiple of 7. You can certainly check by trying to divide that no smaller N works. Again, this property is referred to by saying the polynomial is *primitive*. This will be discussed further subsequently.

Example: Still thinking about 2-bit errors: using the CRC with generating polynomial $x^4 + x + 1$, even though it's only of degree 4, fails to detect two-bit errors only when they're a multiple of 15 apart. That is, $x^4 + x + 1$ divides $x^N - 1$ (with remainder 0) only when N is a multiple of 15. You can certainly check by trying to divide that no smaller N works. This is some sort of **proof that the XOR checksum is inefficient**.

Example: Still thinking about 2-bit errors: using the CRC with generating polynomial $x^5 + x^2 + 1$, even though it's only of degree 5, fails to detect two-bit errors only when they're a multiple of 31 apart. That is, $x^5 + x^2 + 1$ divides $x^N - 1$ (with remainder 0) only when N is a multiple of 32. You can certainly check by trying to divide that no smaller N works, but this is not the intelligent way to verify the property.

Example: Still thinking about 2-bit errors: let's change the generating polynomial from the previous example slightly, from $x^5 + x^2 + 1$ to $x^5 + x + 1$. Mysteriously, the performance deteriorates from the previous example, so that two-bit errors which are a multiple of 21 apart will pass undetected.

Example: Further, changing again to generating polynomial $x^5 + x^4 + x + 1$ mysteriously causes a further degradation of performance: two-bit errors which are a multiple of 8 apart will pass undetected. This is as bad as the XOR checksum CRC with generator $x^8 - 1$, but at least it is achieved with only a 5-bit CRC. A rough explanation for this is that while the degree of the polynomial is higher, so that the CRC's report contains more bits, the choice of how these bits are computed is suboptimal. The polynomial is far from being *primitive* (in a sense discussed precisely later).

Example: By contrast, the CRC with generator

$$x^{16} + x^{15} + x^2 + 1 = (x+1)(x^{15} + x + 1)$$

will fail to detect two-bit errors only if they are a multiple of $32767 = 2^{15} - 1$ apart! (Obviously this fact is not discovered by direct computation!)

Remark: As in the last example, the most effective CRC's are obtained by taking generating polynomials which have a factor like $x^{15} + x + 1$ which is **irreducible**, meaning that it can't be factored further into smaller-degree polynomials with coefficients in $\mathbf{F}_2$. This is the polynomial analogue of being a *prime number*. Further, not only is this polynomial irreducible, it is **primitive**, meaning that the smallest integer N such that the polynomial divides $x^N - 1$ is $N = 2^d - 1$ where d is the degree of the polynomial. Of course this definition by itself is pointless: it is completely unclear whether there are many such things, how to find them, how to verify the property, etc.

Remark: Further, the 16-bit CRC just above also can detect **all** 3-bit errors in data of 32767 bits or less because it is obtained as the product of $x + 1$ with a primitive degree 15 polynomial. That is, the primitive degree 15 polynomial detects two-bit errors within distance of 32767 of each other, while the factor of $x + 1$ detects all errors consisting of an odd number of bit errors.

   Burst errors are bit errors that occur close together. A CRC of degree n with non-zero constant term can always detect a burst error of length $< n$. To see this, let the generating polynomial be $g(x)$, and the error polynomial be $e(x)$. Since it is a burst error of length $< n$, the error can be written as

$$e(x) = x^n \cdot p(x)$$

where $p(x)$ is a polynomial of degree $< n$. For the CRC to fail to detect this, it must be that $g(x)$ divides $e(x)$ (with remainder 0). Since $g(x)$ has non-zero constant term it has no factors of x, so for $g(x)$ to divide $x^n \cdot p(x)$ it must be that $g(x)$ actually divides $p(x)$. But if the degree of $p(x)$ is less than the degree of $g(x)$ this is impossible. Thus, the error will be detected.

Remark: In this little discussion of burst errors, we implicitly used the **unique factorization** of polynomials with coefficients in $\mathbf{F}_2$. This is not too surprising, but deserves proof, and will be proven later.

Remark: It is useful to note that polynomials $f(x)$ with coefficients in $\mathbf{F}_2$ have the possibly unexpected property that

$$f(x^2) = f(x)^2$$

Indeed, let $f(x) = x^n + g(x)$ with $g(x)$ being the lower-degree terms in $f(x)$. Then

$$f(x)^2 = (x^n)^2 + 2x^n g(x) + g(x)^2 = (x^n)^2 + 0 + g(x)^2$$

since $2 = 0$ in $\mathbf{F}_2$. By induction on the number of terms in the polynomial, we can assume that $g(x)^2 = g(x^2)$, so this gives

$$f(x)^2 = (x^n)^2 + g(x^2) = (x^2)^n + g(x^2) = f(x^2)$$

as asserted.

Exercises

5.01 Compute $1 + 1 + 1 + 1 + 1$ in the finite field $\mathbf{F}_2$.

5.02 Compute

$$\underbrace{1 + 1 + 1 + \ldots + 1}_{107}$$

in the finite field $\mathbf{F}_2$.

5.03 Compute $(1 + x + x^2)^4$ as a polynomial with coefficients in $\mathbf{F}_2$.

5.04 Compute the product $(x^4 + x^3 + x^2 + x + 1)(x^4 + x + 1)(x^4 + x^3 + 1)$ in the collection of polynomials with coefficients in $\mathbf{F}_2$.

5.05 Let $g(x) = x^3 + x + 1$ be a generating polynomial for a CRC. Compute the CRC for the byte 11100011. (*ans.*)

5.06 Let $g(x) = x^3 + x + 1$ be a generating polynomial for a CRC. Figure out how to be a little clever in computing the CRC for the bytes

$$1110001101010001100111110$$

so that you don't fill up a whole sheet of paper with an enormous long division.

5.07 Verify that the CRC with generating polynomial $1 + x + x^2 + x^3$ fails to detect two-bit errors that are a multiple of 4 bits apart. (*ans.*)

5.08 Verify that the CRC with generating polynomial $1 + x^2 + x^3 + x^4$ fails to detect two-bit errors that are a multiple of 7 bits apart.

6

The Integers

6.1 The reduction algorithm

This **reduction algorithm**, also called **division with remainder**, is of fundamental importance.

For a non-zero integer m, there is the process of **reduction modulo** m, which can be applied to arbitrary integers N. At least if m and N are *positive*, this is exactly the division-with-remainder process of elementary arithmetic, with the quotient discarded: the **reduction modulo** m **of** N is the remainder when N is divided by m. This procedure is also called the **Division Algorithm**, for that reason. More precisely, the reduction modulo m of N is the unique integer r so that N can be written as

$$N = q \cdot m + r$$

with an integer q and with

$$0 \le r < |m|$$

(Very often the word 'modulo' is abbreviated as 'mod'.) The non-negative integer m is the **modulus**. For example,

$$10 \text{ reduced modulo } 7 = 3$$

$$10 \text{ reduced modulo } 5 = 0$$

$$12 \text{ reduced modulo } 2 = 0$$

$$15 \text{ reduced modulo } 7 = 1$$

$$100 \text{ reduced modulo } 7 = 2$$

$$1000 \text{ reduced modulo } 2 = 0$$

$$1001 \text{ reduced modulo } 2 = 1$$

Remark: In some sources, and sometimes for brevity, this terminology is abused by replacing the phrase 'N reduced mod m' by 'N mod m'. This is not so terrible, but there is also a related but significantly different meaning that 'N mod m' has. Usually the context will make clear what the phrase 'N mod m' means, but watch out. We will use a notation which is fairly compatible with many computer languages: write

$$x \% m = \text{ reduced modulo } m$$

The little theorem which describes existence and uniqueness, enabling us to prove things but not necessarily do numerical computations, is:

Theorem: Given a non-zero integer m and an arbitrary integer x, there are *unique* integers q (for 'quotient') and r (for 'remainder') with $0 \le r < |m|$ such that

$$x = q \cdot m + r$$

Proof: Let's do the proof just for positive x and m. Let S be the set of all non-negative integers expressible in the form $x - sm$ for some integer s. The set S is non-empty since $x = x - 0 \cdot m$ lies in it. Let $r = x - qm$ be the *least* non-negative element of the set S. (This exists by the *well-orderedness* of the non-negative integers.) We claim that $r < m$. (Keep in mind that we're treating only $m > 0$, so $m = |m|$.) If not, that is, if $r \ge m$, then still $r - m \ge 0$, and also

$$r - m = (x - qm) - m = x - (q+1)m$$

is still in the set S. But this would contradict the fact that r is the smallest non-negative element in S. Thus, $r < m$. For uniqueness, suppose that both $x = qm + r$ and $x = q'm + r'$. Then subtract to find

$$r - r' = m \cdot (q' - q)$$

Thus, $r - r'$ is a multiple of m. For such quantities $r - r'$ in the obvious range $-m < r - r' < m$, the only one divisible by m is 0, so $r = r'$. Then it follows easily that $q = q'$ also.   ///

Reductions mod m can be computed by hand by the familiar *long-division* algorithm. For m and N both *positive*, even a simple hand calculator can be used to easily compute reductions. For example: divide N by m, obtaining a decimal. Remove (by subtracting) the integer part of the decimal, and multiply back by m to obtain the reduction mod m of N. Of course round-off error is a hazard.

The process of reduction mod m can also be applied to negative integers. For example,

$$-10 \% 7 = 4 \text{ since } -10 = (-2) \cdot 7 + 4$$

$$-10 \% 5 = 0 \text{ since } -10 = (-2) \cdot 5 + 0$$

$$-15 \% 7 = 6 \text{ since } -15 = (-3) \cdot 7 + 6$$

But neither the hand algorithm nor the calculator algorithm mentioned above give the correct output directly: for one thing, it is not true that the reduction mod m of $-N$ is the negative of the reduction mod m of N. And all our reductions mod m are supposed to be non-negative, besides. For example,

$$10 = 1 \cdot 7 + 3$$

shows that the reduction of 10 mod 7 is 3, but if we simply negate both sides of this equation we get

$$-10 = (-1) \cdot 7 + (-3)$$

That '-3' does not fit our requirements. The trick is to add another multiple of 7 to that '-3', while subtracting it from the $(-1) \cdot 7$, getting

$$-10 = (-1 - 1) \cdot 7 + (-3 + 7)$$

or finally

$$-10 = (-2) \cdot 7 + 4$$

And there is one last 'gotcha': in case the remainder is 0, as in

$$14 = 2 \cdot 7 + 0$$

when we negate to get

$$-14 = (-2) \cdot 7 + 0$$

nothing further needs to be done, since that 0 is already in the right range. (If we *did* add another 7 to it, we'd be in the wrong range.) Thus, in summary, let r be the reduction of N mod m. Then the reduction of $-N$ mod m is $m - r$ if $r \neq 0$, and is 0 if $r = 0$.

The modulus can be negative, as well: however, it happens that always the reduction of N modulo m is just the reduction of N mod $|m|$, so this introduces nothing new.

Note that by our definition the reduction mod m of any integer is always non-negative. This is at variance with several computer languages, where the reduction of a negative integer $-N$ is the negative of the reduction of N. This difference has to be remembered when writing code.

A **multiplicative inverse mod** m of an integer N is another integer t so that $(N \cdot t)\%m = 1$. It is important to realize that this new notion of 'inverse' has no simple relation to more elementary notions of 'inverse'.

For example, since $2 \cdot 3 = 6$ which reduces mod 5 to 1, we can say that 3 is a multiplicative inverse mod 5 to 2. This is *not* to say that '$3 = \frac{1}{2}$' or '$3 = 0.5$' or any such thing. As another example, 143 is a multiplicative inverse to 7 modulo 100, since $7 \times 143 = 1001$, which reduces mod 100 to 1. On the other hand, we can anticipate that, for example, 2 has no multiplicative inverse modulo 10, because any multiple $2 \cdot t$ is an *even* number, but all expressions $q \cdot 10 + 1$ are *odd*.

At this point we might acknowledge that it is not clear which integers might or might not have multiplicative inverses, and that it is even less clear how we might efficiently *find* such inverses. We will leave this as a small mystery for the moment, but resolve it decisively shortly.

6.2 Divisibility

The ordinary integers **Z** with operations of addition, subtraction, multiplication, and division (*when possible,* since not every quotient x/y of integers is an integer itself), are intuitive and familiar. In this section we establish some terminology and basic facts. In particular, at the end we resolve the question of when an integer x has a multiplicative inverse modulo m.

For two integers d, n, the integer d **divides** n (or is a **divisor** of n) if n/d is an integer. This is equivalent to there being another integer k so that $n = kd$. We may also (equivalently) say that n is a **multiple** of d if d divides n. We write

$$a | b$$

if a divides b. As a good sample of how to prove things about divisibility, we have:

Proposition:
- If $a|b$ and $b|c$ then $a|c$.
- If $d|x$ and $d|y$, then for any integers a, b we have $d|(ax + by)$.

Proof: If $a|b$ then there is an integer k so that $ak = b$. If $b|c$ then there is an integer ℓ so that $b\ell = c$. Then, replacing b by ak in the latter equation, we have

$$c = b\ell = (ak) \cdot \ell = a \cdot (k\ell)$$

so $a|c$.

If $d|x$ then there is an integer m so that $dm = x$. If $d|y$ then there is an integer n so that $dn = y$. Then

$$ax + by = a(md) + b(nd) = (am + bn) \cdot d$$

Thus, $ax + by$ is a multiple of d.   ///

A divisor d of n is **proper** if it is neither $\pm n$ nor ± 1. A multiple N of n is **proper** if it is neither $\pm n$ nor 0. *Any* integer d divides 0, since $d \cdot 0 = 0$. On the other hand, the *only* integer 0 divides is itself. A positive integer p is **prime** if it has no proper divisors and if $p > 1$. That is, p has no divisors but itself, its negative, and ± 1, *and* $p > 1$.

Remark: It is very convenient to declare 1 *not* to be a prime, despite its having features in common with primes.

The following is the simplest but far from most efficient test for primality. It does have the virtue that if a number is not prime then this process finds the smallest divisor $d > 1$ of the number.

Proposition: A positive integer n is prime if and only if it is not divisible by any of the integers d with $1 < d \le \sqrt{n}$.

Proof: First, if $d|n$ and $2 \le d \le \sqrt{n}$, then the integer n/d satisfies

$$\sqrt{n} \le \frac{n}{d} \le \frac{n}{2}$$

(where we are looking at inequalities among *real* numbers!). Therefore, neither of the two factors d nor n/d is ± 1 nor $\pm n$. So n is not prime.

On the other hand, suppose that n has a proper factorization $n = d \cdot e$, where e is the larger of the two factors. Then

$$d = \frac{n}{e} \le \frac{n}{d}$$

gives $d^2 \le n$, so $d \le \sqrt{n}$.   ///

Two integers are **relatively prime** or **coprime** or **mutually prime** if for every integer d if $d|m$ and $d|n$ then $d = \pm 1$. Also we may say that m is **prime to** n if they are relatively prime. For a positive integer n, the number of positive integers less than n and relatively prime to n is denoted by $\varphi(n)$. This is called the **Euler phi-function** or **Euler totient function**. (The trial-and-error approach to computing $\varphi(n)$ is suboptimal, but works.)

An integer d is a **common divisor** of a family of integers $n_1, \ldots, n_m$ if d divides each of the integers n_i. An integer N is a **common multiple** of a family of integers $n_1, \ldots, n_m$ if N is a multiple of each of the integers n_i. The following theorem gives an unexpected and strange-looking characterization of the greatest common divisor of two integers.

Theorem: Let m, n be integers, not both zero. Among all *common* divisors of m, n there is a unique one, call it d, so that for *every* other common divisor e of m, n we have $e|d$, and also $d > 0$. This divisor d is the *greatest common divisor* or **gcd** of m, n, denoted $\gcd(m, n)$. The greatest common divisor of two integers m, n (not both zero) is the *least positive integer* of the form $xm + yn$ with $x, y \in \mathbf{Z}$.

Proof: Let $D = x_o m + y_o n$ be the least positive integer expressible in the form $xm + yn$. First, we show that any divisor d of both m and n surely divides D. Write $m = m'd$ and $n = n'd$ with $m', n' \in \mathbf{Z}$. Then by the proposition just above

$$D = x_o m + y_o n = x_o(m'd) + y_o(n'd) = (x_o m' + y_o n') \cdot d$$

which certainly presents D as a multiple of d.

On the other hand, apply the reduction algorithm to write $m = qD + r$ with $0 \le r < D$. Then

$$0 \le r = m - qD = m - q(x_o m + y_o n) = (1 - qx_o) \cdot m + (-y_o) \cdot n$$

That is, this r is also expressible as $x'm + y'n$ for integers x', y'. Since $r < D$, and since D is the smallest positive integer so expressible, it must be that $r = 0$. Therefore, $D|m$. Similarly, $D|n$.   ///

A companion or 'dual' notion concerning *multiples* instead of *divisors* is:

Corollary: Let m, n be integers, not both zero. Among all *common* multiples of m, n there is a unique one, call it N, so that for *every* other common multiple M of m, n we have $N|M$, and also $N > 0$. This multiple N is the *least common multiple* or **lcm** of m, n, denoted $\text{lcm}(m, n)$. In particular,

$$\text{lcm}(m, n) = \frac{mn}{\gcd(m, n)}$$

Proof: This is a corollary of the previous result because we use the existence and form of the *gcd* to prove that of the *lcm*. Indeed, we will grant the existence of the *gcd* and show that the quantity

$$L = \frac{mn}{\gcd(m, n)}$$

is the least common multiple of m and n. First we show that this L is a multiple of both. Indeed, $\gcd(m, n)$ divides n, so $n/\gcd(m, n)$ is an integer, so

$$L = m \cdot \frac{n}{\gcd(m, n)}$$

is an expression of L as an integer multiple of m. Similarly, L is an integer multiple of n. On the other hand, let M be a multiple of both m and n, and prove that it is a multiple of L. Let $g = am + bn$ be an expression of the *gcd* g of m and n in the form mentioned in the proposition. Then

$$1 = a \cdot \frac{m}{g} + b \cdot \frac{n}{g}$$

and m/g and n/g are integers. Let $N = rm$ and $N = sn$ be expressions of N as integer multiples of m and n. Then

$$N = 1 \cdot N = \left(a \cdot \frac{m}{g} + b \cdot \frac{n}{g} \right) \cdot N = a \cdot \frac{m \cdot sn}{g} + b \cdot \frac{n \cdot rm}{g}$$

$$= (as + br) \cdot \left(\frac{m}{g} + \frac{rm}{g} \right) = (as + br) \cdot L$$

as claimed.   ///

Remark: If we *already have* the prime factorizations of two numbers m, n, then we can easily find the greatest common divisor and least common multiple. Specifically, for each prime number p, the power of p dividing the *gcd* is the *minimum* of the powers of p dividing m and dividing n. Since this is true for each prime, we know the prime factorization of the greatest common divisor. For example,

$$\gcd(2^3 \ 3^5 \ 5^2 \ 11, \ 3^2 \ 5^3 \ 7^2 \ 11^2) = 3^2 \ 5^2 \ 11$$

since 2^0 is the smaller of the two powers of 2 occurring, 3^2 is the smaller of the two powers of 3 occurring, 5^2 is the smaller of the two powers of 5 occurring, 7^0 is the smaller of the two powers of 7 occurring, and 11^1 is the smaller of the two powers of 11 occurring. Similarly, the least common multiple is obtained by taking the *larger* of the two powers of each prime occurring in the factorizations of m, n. But this approach to computing greatest common divisors or least common multiples (by way of prime factorizations) is very inefficient.

Corollary: Fix a non-zero integer m. Let x be an integer. Then x has a multiplicative inverse modulo m if and only if $\gcd(x, m) = 1$. In particular, if $\gcd(x, m) = 1$, then invoke the theorem above to write $ax + bm = 1$. Then a is a multiplicative inverse of x mod m (and b is a multiplicative inverse of m mod x).

Proof: First, suppose that $d = \gcd(x, m) > 1$. Suppose that y is a multiplicative inverse of x modulo m. That is, $yx = qm + 1$ for some 'quotient' q. We can rearrange that as $1 = qm - yx$. Write $x = d \cdot x'$ and $m = d \cdot m'$ for some integers x' and m', and then we have

$$1 = qm - yx = q(dm') - y(dx') = d \cdot (qm' - yx')$$

This says that 1 is an integer multiple of d, but $d > 1$, so this is not possible. This proves that $\gcd(x, m) > 1$ prevents there from being a multiplicative inverse to x modulo m.

On the other hand, suppose that $\gcd(x, m) = 1$. Then from above there are integers a, b so that $ax + bm = 1$. That is, $ax = (-b)m + 1$. The latter equation shows that $ax \% m = 1$, so a is a multiplicative inverse to x modulo m.   ///

6.3   Factorization into primes

We now can prove the *unique factorization of integers into primes*. This may already seem 'obvious', since our experience with small integers bears witness to the truth of the assertion. But it is worth paying attention to *how* such a thing can be proven, especially since we will later want to *try* to prove unique factorization for fancier entities, for which our intuition is not adequate. Since it is *not* true in general that 'all kinds' of numbers can be factored uniquely into primes, we must be alert. An example of *failure* of unique factorization is given in the next section.

We also give a formula for Euler's phi-function $\varphi(n)$, defined inititally as

$\varphi(n) =$ number of integers i in the range $1 \le i \le n$ relatively prime to n

We also look at the most naive algorithm to obtain the **factorization** of an integer into primes.

Theorem: *Unique Factorization* Every integer n can be written in an *essentially unique* way as $\pm$ a product of primes:

$$n = \pm\, p_1^{e_1}\, p_2^{e_2} \ldots p_m^{e_m}$$

with positive integer exponents and distinct primes $p_1, \ldots, p_m$.

Remark: The 'essentially unique' means that of course writing the product in a different order does not count as truly 'different'.

Corollary: Let N be a positive integer factored into primes as

$$n = p_1^{e_1}\, p_2^{e_2}\, \ldots\, p_n^{e_n}$$

where $p_1, \ldots p_n$ are distinct primes, and the exponents e_i are all positive integers. Then the Euler *phi*-function of N has the value

$$\varphi(N) = (p_1 - 1)p_1^{e_1 - 1}\, (p_2 - 1)p_2^{e_2 - 1}\, \ldots\, (p_n - 1)p_n^{e_n - 1}$$

The proof of the theorem starts from the following key lemma, which may *feel* obvious, but is not. It makes essential use of the peculiar characterization of greatest common divisors given in the previous section.

Lemma: Let p be a prime number, and suppose that a and b are integers, with $p|(ab)$. Then either $p|a$ or $p|b$, or both.

Proof: *(of Lemma)* If $p|a$ we are done. So suppose that p does not divide a. Then the greatest common divisor $\gcd(p, a)$ cannot be p. But this greatest common divisor is also a divisor of p, and is positive. Since p is *prime*, the only positive divisor of p other than p itself is just 1. Therefore, $\gcd(p, a) = 1$. We saw that there exist integers x, y so that $xp + ya = 1$.

Since $p|(ab)$, we can write $ab = hp$ for some integer h.

$$b = b \cdot 1 = b \cdot (xp + ya) = bxp + yba = (bx + yh) \cdot p$$

This shows that b is a multiple of p.   ///

Corollary: *(of Lemma)* If a prime p divides a product $a_1 a_2 \ldots a_n$ then necessarily p divides at least one of the factors a_i.

Proof: *(of Corollary)* This is by induction on n. The Lemma is the assertion for $n = 2$. Suppose $p|(a_1 \ldots a_n)$. Then write the latter product as

$$a_1 \ldots a_n = (a_1 \ldots a_{n-1}) \cdot a_n$$

By the lemma, either p divides a_n or p divides $a_1 a_2 \ldots a_{n-1}$. If $p|a_n$ we are done. If not, then $p|(a_1 \ldots a_{n-1})$. By induction, this implies that p divides one of the factors $a_1, a_2, \ldots, a_{n-1}$. Altogether, we conclude that in any case p divides one of the factors $a_1, \ldots, a_n$.   ///

Proof: *(of Theorem)* First we prove that for every integer there *exists* a factorization, and then that it is *unique*. It certainly suffices to treat only factorizations of *positive* integers, since factorizations for $-n$ and n are obviously related.

For *existence*, suppose that some integer $n > 1$ did *not* have a factorization into primes. Then n cannot be prime itself, or just '$n = n$' is a factorization into primes. Therefore n has a proper factorization $n = xy$ with $x, y > 0$. Since the factorization is *proper*, both x and y are strictly smaller than n. Thus, x and y both can be factored into primes. Putting together the two factorizations gives the factorization of n. This contradicts the assumption that there exist integers lacking prime factorizations.

Now we prove *uniqueness*. Suppose we have

$$q_1^{e_1} \ldots q_m^{e_m} = N = p_1^{f_1} \ldots p_n^{f_n}$$

where (without loss of generality)

$$q_1 < q_2 < \ldots < q_m$$

are primes, and also

$$p_1 < p_2 < \ldots < p_n$$

are all primes. And the exponents e_i and f_i are positive integers. We must show that $m = n$, $q_i = p_i$ for all i, and $e_i = f_i$ for all i.

Since q_1 divides the left-hand side of the equality, it must divide the right-hand side. Therefore, by the corollary to the lemma just above, q_1 must divide one of the factors on the right-hand side. So q_1 must divide some p_i. Since p_i is prime, it must be that $q_1 = p_i$.

We claim that $i = 1$. Indeed, if $i > 1$ then $p_1 < p_i$. And p_1 divides the left-hand side, so divides one of the q_j, so is equal to some q_j. But then we string these inequalities together:

$$p_1 = q_j \geq q_1 = p_i > p_1$$

which is impossible. Therefore, $q_1 = p_1$.

Without loss of generality, $e_1 \leq f_1$. Thus, by dividing through by e_1 factors $q_1 = p_1$, we see that the corresponding exponents e_1 and f_1 must also be equal.

The rest of the argument about uniqueness is by induction on N. First, 1 has a unique factorization (of sorts), namely the *empty* product. In any case, since 2 is prime *it* has the factorization $2 = 2$. This begins the induction. Suppose that all integers $N' < N$ have unique factorizations into primes (and prove that N likewise has a unique factorization):

From

$$q_1^{e_1} \ldots q_m^{e_m} = N = p_1^{f_1} \ldots p_n^{f_n}$$

by dividing by $q_1^{e_1} = p_1^{f_1}$ we obtain

$$q_2^{e_2} \ldots q_m^{e_m} = \frac{N}{q_1^{e_1}} = p_2^{f_2} \ldots p_n^{f_n}$$

We had assumed that all the exponents e_i were positive, so $N/q_1^{e_1} < N$. Thus, by induction, $N/q_1^{e_1}$ has unique factorization, and we conclude that all the remaining factors must match up. This finishes the proof of the unique factorization theorem.

///

Now we prove the corollary, giving the formula for Euler's *phi*-function:

$$\varphi(N) = (p_1 - 1)p_1^{e_1-1} (p_2 - 1)p_2^{e_2-1} \ldots (p_n - 1)p_n^{e_n-1}$$

where $n = p_1^{e_1} \ldots p_n^{e_n}$ is the factorization into *distinct* prime factors p_i, and all exponents are positive integers. The argument is by *counting*: we'll count the number of numbers x in the range from 0 through $N-1$ which *do* have a common factor with N, and subtract. And, by unique factorization, if x has a common factor with N then it has a common *prime* factor with N. There are exactly N/p_i numbers divisible by p_i between 0 and $N-1$, so we would be tempted to say that the number of numbers in that range with *no* common factor with N would be

$$N - \frac{N}{p_1} - \frac{N}{p_2} - \ldots \frac{N}{p_n}$$

However, this is not correct in general: we have accounted for numbers divisible by two *different* p_is *twice*, so we should add back in all the expressions N/p_ip_j with $i \neq j$. But then we've added back in too many things, and have to *subtract* all the expressions $M/p_ip_jp_k$ with i, j, k distinct. And so on:

$$\varphi(N) = N - \sum_i \frac{N}{p_i} + \sum_{i \neq j} \frac{N}{p_ip_j} - \sum_{i,j,k \text{ distinct}} \frac{N}{p_ip_jp_k} + \ldots$$

$$= N \cdot \left(1 - \frac{1}{p_1}\right)\left(1 - \frac{1}{p_2}\right) \ldots \left(1 - \frac{1}{p_n}\right)$$

$$= p_1^{e_1}\left(1 - \frac{1}{p_1}\right) \cdot p_2^{e_2}\left(1 - \frac{1}{p_2}\right) \ldots p_n^{e_n}\left(1 - \frac{1}{p_n}\right)$$

$$= (p_1 - 1)p_1^{e_1-1}(p_2 - 1)p_2^{e_2-1} \ldots (p_n - 1)p_n^{e_n-1}$$

This is the desired formula.   ///

We'll give another proof later, using Sun-Ze's theorem.

The most obvious (but not most efficient) means to *obtain* the **prime factorization** and simultaneously to **test primality** of a positive integer N is what is called **trial division**, which runs as follows. Attempt division by integers $d = 2, 3, 4, 5, 6, 7, \ldots \leq \sqrt{N}$ until either the smallest divisor $d_1 > 1$ of N is found, or it is determined that N has no proper divisors $\leq \sqrt{N}$. In the latter case, N is prime, by the proposition above on primality testing. In the former case, attempt division by integers $d = d_1, d_1 + 1, d_1 + 2, \ldots \leq \sqrt{N/d_1}$ until either the smallest divisor $d_2 > 1$ of N/d_1 is found, or it is determined that N/d_1 has no proper divisors $\leq \sqrt{N/d_1}$. In the latter case, N/d_1 is prime. In the former case, attempt division by integers $d = d_2, d_2 + 1, d_2 + 2, \ldots \leq \sqrt{N/d_1d_2}$ until either the smallest divisor

$d_3 > 1$ of N/d_1d_2 is found, or it is determined that N/d_1d_2 has no proper divisors $\leq \sqrt{N/d_1d_2}$. In the latter case N/d_1d_2 is prime. In the former case...

This *recursive* procedure ends when some $N/(d_1d_2\ldots d_m)$ is prime. At the same time, if N has no divisor d in the range $1 < d \leq \sqrt{N}$ then N is prime.

6.4 A failure of unique factorization

We will give the simplest meaningful example of the *failure* of unique factorization among numbers just a little more complicated than the ordinary integers $\mathbf{Z}$.

First, note that the fact that 12 can be factored in two different-*looking* manners

$$12 = 4 \cdot 3 = 6 \cdot 2$$

is not at all an indication of problems with unique factorization in the ordinary integers $\mathbf{Z}$, since in the latter two different-looking factorizations of 12 we hadn't actually completed the factorization *into primes*. The complete factorization of 12 is, of course,

$$12 = 2^2 \cdot 3$$

The simplest meaningful example of the failure of unique factorization into primes is in the collection of numbers

$$R = \{a + b\sqrt{-5} : a, b \in \mathbf{Z}\}$$

where we have *adjoined* $\sqrt{-5}$ to $\mathbf{Z}$. The relation

$$6 = 2 \cdot 3 = (1 + \sqrt{-5})(1 - \sqrt{5})$$

gives two different-*looking* factorizations of 6 in R. But to genuinely verify that we've factored 6 in two different ways *into primes* we should verify that 2, 3, $1 + \sqrt{-5}$, and $1 - \sqrt{-5}$ are *primes* in R, in the sense that they cannot be further factored.

To prove this, we use *complex conjugation*, usually denoted by putting a bar over the quantity to be conjugated: for real numbers a and b,

$$\overline{a + b\sqrt{-5}} = a - b\sqrt{-5}$$

For α, β in R, we have the property

$$\overline{\alpha \cdot \beta} = \overline{\alpha} \cdot \overline{\beta}$$

proven by direct computation as follows. Let $\alpha = a + b\sqrt{-5}$ and $\beta = c + d\sqrt{-5}$. Then

$$\overline{\alpha \cdot \beta} = \overline{\left(a + b\sqrt{-5}\right) \cdot \left(c + d\sqrt{-5}\right)} = \overline{(ab - 5cd) + (ad + bc)\sqrt{-5}}$$

$$= (ab - 5cd) - (ad + bc)\sqrt{-5} = \left(a - b\sqrt{-5}\right) \cdot \left(c - d\sqrt{-5}\right) = \overline{\alpha} \cdot \overline{\beta}$$

This computation is a special case of more general ones, as is already visible from the fact that the 5 played no serious role.

Next, introduce a **norm**

$$N(\alpha) = \alpha \cdot \overline{\alpha}$$

The property

$$N(\alpha \cdot \beta) = N(\alpha) \cdot N(\beta)$$

follows from the corresponding property of the conjugation:

$$N(\alpha) \cdot N(\beta) = \alpha\overline{\alpha}\beta\overline{\beta} = (\alpha\beta) \cdot (\overline{\alpha}\,\overline{\beta})$$

$$= (\alpha\beta) \cdot (\overline{\alpha\beta}) = N(\alpha\beta)$$

Note that $0 \le N(\alpha) \in \mathbf{Z}$ for α in R.

The last preparation we need is to check that for $\alpha \in R$ if $N(\alpha) < 4$ then $\alpha = \pm 1$. Indeed, for integers a, b, if

$$4 > N\left(a + b\sqrt{-5}\right) = a^2 + 5b^2$$

then b must be 0 (since otherwise $5b^2 \ge 5 > 1$). And then $a^2 < 4$ which for integer a implies $a = \pm 1$.

Now suppose that $2 = \alpha\beta$ with α, β in R. Then apply N to obtain

$$4 = N(2) = N(\alpha\beta) = N(\alpha) \cdot N(\beta)$$

By unique factorization in the ordinary integers $\mathbf{Z}$, and since these norms are non-negative integers, the integers $N(\alpha)$ and $N(\beta)$ must either be $1, 4$, $2, 2$, or $4, 1$. The middle case is impossible, by our observation on small values of the norm. In the other two cases, one of α or β is ± 1, and the factorization is not *proper*. That is, 2 cannot be factored further in R.

Similarly, 3 cannot be factored further in R.

If $1 + \sqrt{-5} = \alpha\beta$ with α, β in R, then again

$$6 = N\left(1 + \sqrt{-5}\right) = N(\alpha\beta) = N(\alpha) \cdot N(\beta)$$

By unique factorization in the ordinary integers $\mathbf{Z}$, and since these norms are non-negative integers, the integers $N(\alpha)$ and $N(\beta)$ must either be $1, 6$, $2, 3$, $3, 2$, or $6, 1$. By our observation on the possible small values of the norm, the middle two cases are impossible. In the remaining two cases, one of α or β is ± 1, and the factorization is not *proper*. That is, $1 + \sqrt{-5}$ cannot be factored further in R. An essentially identical discussion applies to $1 - \sqrt{-5}$. Thus,

$$6 = 2 \cdot 3 = \left(1 + \sqrt{-5}\right)\left(1 - \sqrt{5}\right)$$

is a factorization of 6 in two different ways *into primes* in R. Therefore, R does not have unique factorization.

6.5 The Euclidean Algorithm

The **Euclidean Algorithm** is a very important, efficient, and non-obvious systematic procedure to find the *greatest common divisor d* of two integers x, m, and *also* to find integers a, b so that

$$ax + bm = d$$

from which we also obtain multiplicative inverses modulo m. (Recall that this odd sort of expression comes up in the proof that greatest common divisors exist). Each step in the Euclidean Algorithm is an instance of the Division/Reduction Algorithm. One important aspect of the Euclidean Algorithm is that it *avoids* factorization of integers into primes.

We'll describe the Euclidean Algorithm by examples. To perform the Euclidean Algorithm for the two integers $513, 614$:

$$
\begin{array}{rcll}
614 - 1 \cdot 513 & = & 101 & \text{(reduction of 614 mod 513)} \\
513 - 5 \cdot 101 & = & 8 & \text{(reduction of 513 mod 101)} \\
101 - 12 \cdot 8 & = & 5 & \text{(reduction of 101 mod 8)} \\
8 - 1 \cdot 5 & = & 3 & \text{(reduction of 8 mod 5)} \\
5 - 1 \cdot 3 & = & 2 & \text{(reduction of 5 mod 3)} \\
3 - 1 \cdot 2 & = & 1 & \text{(reduction of 3 mod 2)}
\end{array}
$$

Notice that the first step is reduction of the larger of the given numbers modulo the smaller of the two. The second step is reduction of the smaller of the two modulo the remainder from the first step. At each step, the 'modulus' of the previous step becomes the 'dividend' for the next step, and the 'remainder' from the previous step becomes the 'modulus' for the next step.

In this example, since we obtained a 1 as the last non-zero remainder, we know that the greatest common divisor of 614 and 513 is just 1, that is, that 614 and 513 are *relatively prime*. By the time we got close to the end, it could have been clear that we were going to get 1 as the gcd, but we carried out the procedure through the final step.

Notice that we did not need to find prime factorizations in order to use the Euclidean Algorithm to find the greatest common divisor. Since it turns out to be a time-consuming task to factor numbers into primes, this fact is worth something.

As another example, let's find the gcd of 1024 and 888:

$$
\begin{array}{rcll}
1024 - 1 \cdot 888 & = & 136 & \text{(reduction of 1024 mod 888)} \\
888 - 6 \cdot 136 & = & 72 & \text{(reduction of 888 mod 136)} \\
136 - 1 \cdot 72 & = & 64 & \text{(reduction of 136 mod 72)} \\
72 - 1 \cdot 64 & = & 8 & \text{(reduction of 72 mod 64)} \\
64 - 8 \cdot 8 & = & 0 & \text{(reduction of 64 mod 8)}
\end{array}
$$

In this case, since we got a remainder 0, we must look at the remainder on the *previous* line: 8. The conclusion is that 8 is the greatest common divisor of 1024 and 888.

At this point it is worthwhile to give a simple estimate of the number of steps the Euclidean Algorithm might take in the *worst case scenario*. In particular, the estimate we give shows that this method for finding *gcd*'s is *much* faster than factoring the numbers into primes and then comparing the factors explicitly. The advantage increases as the sizes of the numbers increase.

Proposition: The number of steps required to use the Euclidean Algorithm to compute the *gcd* of two integers $x > y$ is less than or equal to

$$1 + 2 \cdot \log_2 |y|$$

Proof: We look at several consecutive steps in the execution of the algorithm. This would look something like

$$
\begin{aligned}
x_1 - q_1 y_1 &= r_1 \\
y_1 - q_2 r_1 &= r_2 \\
r_1 - q_3 r_2 &= r_3
\end{aligned}
$$

where $0 \le r_1 < |y_1|$, $0 \le r_2 < r_1$, and $0 \le r_3 < r_2$. We claim that $r_3 < r_1/2$. That is, we claim that in each *two* steps of the algorithm the remainder decreases at least by a factor of $1/2$. (Keep in mind that all the remainders are non-negative integers).

If already $r_2 \le r_1/2$, then since $r_3 < r_2$ we certainly have what we want. On the other hand, if $r_2 > r_1/2$ (but still $r_2 < r_1$), then evidently $q_3 = 1$, and

$$r_3 = r_1 - q_3 r_2 = r_1 - r_2 < r_1 - \frac{1}{2}r_1 = \frac{1}{2}r_1$$

as desired.

Since in the first step the remainder is (strictly) smaller than $|y|$, after $1 + 2n$ steps the remainder is (strictly) smaller than $|y|/2^n$. The algorithm stops when this remainder is 0 or 1. The remainder is an integer, so we can say that the algorithm stops when the remainder is strictly less than 2. Thus, the algorithms stops when

$$2^{-n} \cdot |y| < 2$$

which is equivalent to

$$\log_2 |y| < 1 + n$$

or

$$2 \log_2 |y| - 1 < 1 + 2n = \text{number of steps}$$

The way we have arranged it here, the number of steps is an odd integer, and the latter inequality is satisfied for an odd integer at most $2 \log_2 |y| + 1$. This proves the proposition.   ///

So far we've only seen how to find $gcd(x, y)$. For small numbers we might feel that it's not terribly hard to do this just by factoring x, y into primes and comparing factorizations, as mentioned above. However, the problem of finding integers a, b so that

$$gcd(x, y) = ax + by$$

is much more difficult even for moderately large integers x, y.

The Euclidean Algorithm provides means to find these a, b with just a bit more trouble, requiring that we have kept track of all the numbers occurring in the Euclidean Algorithm, and that we *run it backward*, as follows.

In the case of 614 and 513:

$$
\begin{aligned}
1 &= 3 - 1 \cdot 2 \\
&\quad \text{(from the last line of the 'forward' algorithm)} \\
&= 3 - 1 \cdot (5 - 1 \cdot 3) \\
&\quad \text{(replacing 2 by its expression from the previous line)} \\
&= -1 \cdot 5 + 2 \cdot 3 \\
&\quad \text{(rearranging as sum of 5s and 3s)} \\
&= -1 \cdot 5 + 2 \cdot (8 - 1 \cdot 5) \\
&\quad \text{(replacing 3 by its expression from the previous line)} \\
&= 2 \cdot 8 - 3 \cdot 5 \\
&\quad \text{(rearranging as sum of 8s and 5s)} \\
&= 2 \cdot 8 - 3 \cdot (101 - 12 \cdot 8) \\
&\quad \text{(replacing 5 by its expression from the previous line)} \\
&= -3 \cdot 101 + 38 \cdot 8 \\
&\quad \text{(rearranging as sum of 101s and 8s)} \\
&= -3 \cdot 101 + 38 \cdot (513 - 5 \cdot 101) \\
&\quad \text{(replacing 8 by its expression from the previous line)} \\
&= 38 \cdot 513 - 193 \cdot 101 \\
&\quad \text{(rearranging as sum of 513s and 101s)} \\
&= 38 \cdot 513 - 193 \cdot (614 - 513) \\
&\quad \text{(replacing 101 by its expression from the previous line)} \\
&= 231 \cdot 513 - 193 \cdot 614 \\
&\quad \text{(rearranging as sum of 614s and 513s)}
\end{aligned}
$$

That is, we have achieved our goal: we now know that

$$1 = 231 \cdot 513 - 193 \cdot 614$$

In order to successfully execute this algorithm, it is important to keep track of which numbers are mere *coefficients* and which are the numbers to be *replaced* by more complicated expressions coming from the earlier part of the algorithm. Thus, there is considerable reason to write it out as done just here, with the *coefficients first*, with the numbers to be substituted-for *second*.

Now we apply the Euclidean Algorithm to find **multiplicative inverses** mod m. First, recall what we proved above:

Proposition: Let m be an integer not $0, \pm 1$, and let x be an integer *relatively prime* to m. Then x has a multiplicative inverse modulo m. In particular, in any expression $ax + bm = 1$, the integer a is a multiplicative inverse for x modulo m.

Corollary: Let m be an integer other than $0, \pm 1$. Let x be an integer. Then the Euclidean Algorithm finds the *gcd* of x and m. If this *gcd* is 1, then the expression $ax + bm = 1$ obtained by 'reversing' the Euclidean Algorithm yields the multiplicative inverse a of x modulo m.

Remark: We still didn't prove that the Euclidean Algorithm really works! Let's do that now.

Proof: *(that the Euclidean Algorithm computes greatest common divisors):* The crucial claim is that if

$$x - qy = r$$

with $0 \leq r < |q|$ then $\gcd(x, y) = \gcd(y, r)$. If we can prove this claim, then we know that the gcd of the two numbers at each step of the algorithm is the same as the gcd of the two initial inputs to the algorithm. And, at the end, when the remainder is 0, the last two equations will be of the form

$$x' - q'y' = d$$

$$y' - q''d = 0$$

This shows that d divides y', so $\gcd(y', d) = d$. At the same time, if we grant the crucial claim just above, $\gcd(y', d)$ is the same as the gcd $\gcd(x, y)$ of the original inputs. Thus, the gcd of the two original inputs is indeed the last non-zero remainder.

Now we prove that crucial claim, that if

$$x - qy = r$$

with $0 \leq r < |q|$ then $\gcd(x, y) = \gcd(y, r)$. On one hand, if d divides both x and y, say $x = Ad$ and $y = Bd$, then

$$r = x - qy = Ad - qBd = (A - qB) \cdot d$$

so d divides r. On the other hand, if d divides both y and r, say $y = Bd$ and $r = Cd$, then

$$x = qy + r = qBd + Cd = (qB + C) \cdot d$$

so d divides x. This proves that the two gcd's are the same.   ///

6.6 Equivalence relations

The idea of thinking of *integers modulo m* as necessarily having something to do with *reduction modulo m* is dangerously seductive, but is a trap. A richer vocabulary of concepts is necessary.

The idea of **equivalence relation** (defined below) is an important extension and generalization of the traditional idea of *equality*, and occurs throughout mathematics. The associated idea of **equivalence class** (also defined just below) is equally important.

The goal here is to make precise both the idea and the notation in writing something like '$x \sim y$' to mean that x and y have some specified common feature. We can set up a general framework for this without worrying about the specifics of what the features might be.

Recall the 'formal' definition of a *function* f from a set S to a set T: while we *think of* f as being some sort of rule which to an input $s \in S$ 'computes' or 'associates' an output $f(s) \in T$, this way of talking is inadequate, for many reasons.

Rather, the formal (possibly non-intuitive) definition of function f from a set S to a set T is that it is a subset G of the cartesian product $S \times T$ with the property

- For each $s \in S$ there is exactly one $t \in T$ so that $(s,t) \in G$.

Then connect this to the usual notation by

$$f(s) = t \quad \text{if} \quad (s,t) \in G$$

(Again, this G would be the *graph* of f if S and T were simply the real line, for example).

In this somewhat formal context, first there is the primitive general notion of **relation** R on a set S: a *relation* R on a set S is simply a subset of the cartesian product $S \times S$. Write

$$x \, R \, y$$

if the ordered pair (x,y) lies in the subset R of $S \times S$.

This definition of 'relation' compared to the formal definition of 'function' makes it clear that every function is a relation. But most relations do not meet the condition to be functions. This definition of 'relation' is not very interesting except as set-up for further development.

An **equivalence relation** R on a set S is a special kind of relation, satisfying

- **Reflexivity**: $x \, R \, x$ for all $x \in S$
- **Symmetry**: If $x \, R \, y$ then $y \, R \, x$
- **Transitivity**: If $x \, R \, y$ and $y \, R \, z$ then $x \, R \, z$

The fundamental example of an equivalence relation is ordinary equality of numbers. Or equality of sets. Or any other version of 'equality' to which we are accustomed. It should also be noted that a very popular notation for an equivalence relation is

$$x \sim y$$

(that is, with a tilde rather than an 'R'). Sometimes this is simply read as x *tilde* y, but also sometimes as x **is equivalent to** y with only *implicit* reference to the equivalence relation.

A simple example of an equivalence relation on the set $\mathbf{R}^2$ can be defined by

$$(x,y) \sim (x',y') \quad \text{if and only if} \quad x = x'$$

That is, in terms of analytic geometry, two points are *equivalent* if and only if they lie on the same vertical line. Verification of the three required properties in this case is easy, and should be carried out by the reader.

Let $\sim$ be an equivalence relation on a set S. For $x \in S$, the $\sim$ - **equivalence class** $\bar{x}$ containing x is the subset

$$\bar{x} = \{x' \in S : x' \sim x\}$$

The **set of equivalence classes** of $\sim$ on S is denoted by

$$S/\sim$$

(as if we were taking a quotient of some sort). Every element $z \in S$ is certainly contained in an equivalence class, namely the equivalence class of all $s \in S$ so that $s \sim z$.

Note that in general an equality $\bar{x} = \bar{y}$ of equivalence classes $\bar{x}, \bar{y}$ is no indication whatsoever that $x = y$. While it *is* always true that $x = y$ implies $\bar{x} = \bar{y}$, in general there are many *other* elements in $\bar{x}$ than just x itself.

Proposition: Let $\sim$ be an equivalence relation on a set S. If two equivalence classes $\bar{x}, \bar{y}$ have any common element z, then $\bar{x} = \bar{y}$.

Proof: If $z \in \bar{x} \cap \bar{y}$, then $z \sim x$ and $z \sim y$. Then for any $x' \in \bar{x}$, we have

$$x' \sim x \sim z \sim y$$

so $x' \sim y$ by transitivity of $\sim$. Thus, every element $x' \in \bar{x}$ actually lies in $\bar{y}$. That is, $\bar{x} \subset \bar{y}$. A symmetrical argument, reversing the roles of x and y, shows that $\bar{y} \subset \bar{x}$. Therefore, $\bar{x} = \bar{y}$.   ///

It is important to realize that while we tend to refer to an equivalence class in the notational style $\bar{x}$ for some x in the class, there is no requirement to do so. Thus, it is legitimate to say 'an equivalence class A for the equivalence relation $\sim$ on the set S'.

But of course, given an equivalence class A inside S, it may be convenient to *find* x in the set S so that $\bar{x} = A$. Such an x is a **representative** for the equivalence class. Any element of the subset A is a representative, so in general we certainly should *not* imagine that there is a *unique* representative for an equivalence class.

Proposition: Let $\sim$ be an equivalence relation on a set S. Then the equivalence classes of $\sim$ on S are mutually disjoint sets, and their union is all of S.

Proof: The fact that the union of the equivalence classes is the whole thing is not so amazing: given $x \in S$, x certainly lies inside the equivalence class

$$\{y \in S : y \sim x\}$$

Now let A and B be two equivalence classes. Suppose that $A \cap B \neq \phi$, and show that then $A = B$ (as sets). Since the intersection is non-empty, there is some element $y \in A \cap B$. Then, by the definition of 'equivalence class', for all $a \in A$ we have $a \sim y$, and likewise for all $b \in B$ we have $b \sim y$. By transitivity, $a \sim b$. This is true for all $a \in A$ and $b \in B$, so (since A and B are equivalence classes) we have $A = B$.   ///

A set $\mathcal{S}$ of non-empty subsets of a set S whose union is the whole set S, and which are mutually disjoint, is called a **partition** of S. The previous proposition can be run the other direction as well:

Proposition: Let S be a set, and let X be a set of subsets of S, so that X is a partition of S. Define a *relation* $\sim$ on S by $x \sim y$ if and only if there is $X \in \mathcal{X}$ so that $x \in X$ and $y \in X$. That is, $x \sim y$ if and only if they both lie in the same element of X. Then $\sim$ is an *equivalence relation*, and its equivalence classes are the elements of X.

Proof: Since the union of the sets in X is the whole set S, each element $x \in S$ is contained in *some* $X \in \mathcal{X}$. Thus, we have the reflexivity property $x \sim x$. If $x \sim y$ then there is $X \in \mathcal{X}$ containing both x and y, and certainly $y \sim x$, so we have symmetry.

Finally, the mutual disjointness of the sets in X assures that each $y \in S$ lies in just one of the sets from X. For $y \in S$, let X be the *unique* set from X which contains y. If $x \sim y$ and $y \sim z$, then it must be that $x \in X$ and $z \in X$, since y lies in no other subset from X. Then x and z both lie in X, so $x \sim z$, and we have transitivity.

Verification that the equivalence classes are the elements of X is left as an exercise.   ///

6.7   The integers modulo m

Now it will be possible (among other things) to prove that we can reduce mod m (or not) whenever we wish in the course of an arithmetic computation involving only addition, subtraction, and multiplication, whose answer will be reduced modulo m at the end. This plausible-sounding (and true) fact is very clumsy to prove in 'raw' form. At the same time, before we become overly optimistic, it is important to note that *exponentiation* does not behave as simply. The complications in exponentiation modulo primes will be resolved by *Fermat's Little Theorem* a bit later.

If two integers x, y differ by a multiple of a non-zero integer m, we say that x is **congruent to** y **modulo** m, written

$$x \equiv y \bmod m$$

Any relation such as the latter is called a **congruence** modulo m, and m is the **modulus**. That is, $x \equiv y \bmod m$ if and only if $m|(x - y)$.

For example, $3 \equiv 18 \bmod 5$ because $5|(18 - 3)$. Yes, indeed, this is 'just' a different way of writing a divisibility assertion. But this notation (due to Gauss, almost 200 years ago) is meant to cause us to think of *congruence* as a variant of *equality*, with comparable features. That congruences do have properties similar to equality requires some proof, even though the proofs are not hard. In giving the statements of these properties the corresponding terminology is also introduced.

Proposition: For a fixed integer m, congruence modulo m is an *equivalence relation*. That is, as defined above
- *Reflexivity:* Always $x \equiv x \bmod m$ for any x.
- *Symmetry:* If $x \equiv y \bmod m$ then $y \equiv x \bmod m$.
- *Transitivity:* If $x \equiv y \bmod m$ and $y \equiv z \bmod m$ then $x \equiv z \bmod m$.

Proof: Since $x - x = 0$ and always $m|0$, we have reflexivity. If $m|(x - y)$ then $m|(y-x)$ since $y-x = -(x-y)$. Thus, we have symmetry. Suppose that $m|(x-y)$ and $m|(y-z)$. Then there are integers k, ℓ so that $mk = x - y$ and $m\ell = y - z$. Then
$$x - z = (x - y) + (y - z) = mk + m\ell = m \cdot (k + \ell)$$
This proves the transitivity.   ///

The **congruence class** (or **residue class** or **equivalence class**) of an integer x modulo m, denoted $\bar{x}$ (with only implicit reference to m!) is defined to be the set of all integers congruent to $x \bmod m$:
$$\bar{x} = \{y \in \mathbf{Z} : y = x \bmod m\}$$

The **integers mod** m, denoted $\mathbf{Z}/m$, is the collection of *congruence classes* of integers modulo m. For some $X \in \mathbf{Z}/m$, a choice of ordinary integer x so that $\bar{x} = X$ is called a **representative** for the congruence class X.

Thus, for example,
$$\mathbf{Z}/2 = \{\bar{0}, \bar{1}\}$$
$$\mathbf{Z}/3 = \{\bar{0}, \bar{1}, \bar{2}\}$$

But there is no imperative to use representatives which are reduced modulo the modulus. Thus, also,
$$\mathbf{Z}/2 = \{\bar{5}, \bar{8}\}$$
$$\mathbf{Z}/3 = \{\bar{6}, \bar{10}, \bar{101}\}$$

Remark: On many occasions, the bar is dropped, so that x-mod-m may be written simply as 'x' with only the *context* to make clear that this means x-mod-m and not the integer x. Also, of course, we can use symbols without bars for elements of the set $\mathbf{Z}/m$.

Thus, for example, modulo 12 we have
$$\bar{0} = \overline{12} = \overline{-12} = \overline{2400}$$
$$\bar{7} = \bar{7} = \overline{-5} = \overline{2407}$$
$$\bar{1} = \overline{13} = \overline{-11} = \overline{2401}$$

or, equivalently,

0-mod-12 = 12-mod-12 = −12-mod-12 = 2400-mod-12

7-mod-12 = 7-mod-12 = −5-mod-12 = 2407-mod-12

$$1\text{-mod-}12 = 13\text{-mod-}12 = -11\text{-mod-}12 = 2401\text{-mod-}12$$

Remark: There is one traditionally popular collection of representatives for the equivalence classes modulo m, namely

$$\{\bar{0}, \bar{1}, \bar{2}, \ldots \overline{m-2}, \overline{m-1}\}$$

In fact, some sources *define* integers-mod-m as being this set of things, but this is too naive an understanding of what kind of thing integers-mod-m really is. We should distinguish the set of integers *reduced* mod m (which really *is* $\{0, 1, 2, \ldots, m-1\}$!) from the set of integers *modulo* m, which is the set of equivalence classes of integers modulo m. The latter is a more abstract object. So while it is certainly true that (for example)

$$\mathbf{Z}/3 = \{\bar{0}, \bar{1}, \bar{2}\}$$

it is also true that

$$\mathbf{Z}/3 = \{\bar{9}, \overline{31}, \overline{-1}\}$$

and that there are many other ways of describing it as well.

Again: $\mathbf{Z}/m$ is *not* the set of integers $\{0, 1, 2, 3, \ldots, m-1\}$. Rather, $\mathbf{Z}/m$ is the set of *equivalence classes* modulo m. The set $\{0, 1, 2, 3, \ldots, m-1\}$ is the set of integers *reduced modulo* m (for which there is no special symbol). Still, it is true that

Proposition: Fix two integers x, x'. Let $x = qm + r$ and $x' = q'm + r'$ with integers q, q', r, r' and $0 \le r < |m|$ and $0 \le r' < |m'|$. Then $x \equiv x' \bmod m$ if and only if $r \equiv r' \bmod m$.

Proof: If $x \equiv x' \bmod m$ then there is an integer k so that $x' = x + km$. Then

$$r' = x' - q'm = (x + km) - q'm = x + m \cdot (k - q') = qm + r + m \cdot (k - q')$$

$$= r + m \cdot (q + k - q')$$

This proves that $r \equiv r' \bmod m$. The opposite direction of argument is similar. ///

And congruences behave very nicely with respect to the basic operations of addition, subtraction, and multiplication:

Proposition: Fix the modulus m. If $x \equiv x'$ then for all y

$$x + y \equiv x' + y \bmod m$$

$$xy \equiv x'y \bmod m$$

In fact, if $y \equiv y'$, then

$$x + y \equiv x' + y' \bmod m$$

$$x \cdot y \equiv x' \cdot y' \bmod m$$

Proof: It suffices to prove only the more general assertions. Since $x' \equiv x \bmod m$, $m|(x'-x)$, so there is an integer k so that $mk = x'-x$. That is, we have $x' = x+mk$. Similarly, we have $y' = y + \ell m$ for integer ℓ. Then

$$x' + y' = (x + mk) + (y + m\ell) = x + y + m \cdot (k + \ell)$$

Thus, $x' + y' \equiv x + y \bmod m$. And

$$x' \cdot y' = (x+mk) \cdot (y+m\ell) = x \cdot y + xm\ell + mky + mk \cdot m\ell = x \cdot y + m \cdot (k + \ell + mk\ell)$$

Thus, $x'y' \equiv xy \bmod m$.   ///

Remark: Don't become over-confident, though. For example, it is *not* true that

$$2^{10} = 2^{10\%5} \bmod 5$$

as we can check by noting that

$$2^{10}\%5 = 1024\%5 = 4$$

while

$$2^{10\%5}\%5 = 2^0\%5 = 1\%5 = 1$$

and $1 \neq 4$. That is, *exponents* can't be simply reduced modulo the modulus.

As a corollary of this last proposition, congruences immediately *inherit* some properties from ordinary arithmetic, simply because $x = y$ implies $x = y \bmod m$:

* *Distributivity:* $x(y + z) = xy + xz \bmod m$
* *Associativity of addition:* $(x + y) + z = x + (y + z) \bmod m$
* *Associativity of multiplication:* $(xy)z = x(yz) \bmod m$
* *Property of 1:* $1 \cdot x = x \cdot 1 = x \bmod m$
* *Property of 0:* $0 + x = x + 0 = x \bmod m$

Recall that we proved that a has a multiplicative inverse if and only if $\gcd(a, m) = 1$, in which case the Euclidean Algorithm is an effective means to actually *find* the inverse. There is a separate notation for the integers-mod-m which are relatively prime to m and hence have inverses:

$$(\mathbf{Z}/m)^\times = \{\bar{x} \in \mathbf{Z}/m : \gcd(x, m) = 1\}$$

The superscript is not an 'x' but is a 'times', making a reference to multiplication and multiplicative inverses mod m. Note also that $\gcd(x, m)$ is independent of the representative x of the equivalence class, so this is well-defined!

Proposition: The product xy of two integers x and y both prime to m is again prime to m.

Proof: One way to think about this would be in terms of *prime factorizations*, but let's do without that. Rather, let's use the fact that the *gcd* of two integers a, b can be expressed as

$$\gcd(a, b) = sa + tb$$

for some integers s, t. Thus, there are integers a, b, c, d so that

$$1 = ax + bm \qquad 1 = cy + dm$$

Then

$$1 = 1 \cdot 1 = (ax + bm)(cy + dm) = (ac)(xy) + (bcy + axd + bdm)m$$

Thus, 1 is expressible in the form $A(xy) + Bm$, so (by the sharp form of this principle!) necessarily xy and m are relatively prime.   ///

So in the batch of things denoted $(\mathbf{Z}/m)^\times$ we can multiply and take inverses (so, effectively, divide).

6.8 The finite field $\mathbf{Z}/p$ for p prime

The notion of 'field' is intended to abstract the properties of familiar collections of 'numbers', such as the rational numbers $\mathbf{Q}$, the real numbers $\mathbf{R}$, and the complex numbers $\mathbf{C}$. But more than 300 years ago it was noticed that other collections of number-like entities had analogous properties, and that what we know about more familiar numbers was still provably true about the less-familiar ones. After the example $\mathbf{F}_2 = \{0, 1\}$, the simplest examples of finite *fields* are the entities $\mathbf{Z}/p$ for p prime.

A **field** is a set F with two operations $+$ ('addition') and $\times$ ('multiplication'), with two special elements 1 ('one') and 0 ('zero'), with some obviously desirable properties

- Associativity of addition: $x + (y + z) = (x + y) + z$ for all $x, y, z \in F$.
- Associativity of multiplication: $x \times (y \times z) = (x \times y) \times z$ for all $x, y, z \in F$.
- Commutativity of addition: $x + y = y + x$ for all $x, y \in F$.
- Commutativity of multiplication: $x \times y = y \times x$ for all $x, y \in F$.
- Distributivity: $x \times (y + z) = x \times y + x \times z$ for all $x, y \in F$.
- Property of 1: $x \times 1 = 1 \times x = x$ for all $x \in F$.
- Property of 0: $x + 0 = 0 + x = x$ for all $x \in F$.
- Existence of additive inverses: for all x in F, there is $y \in F$ (usually denoted '$-x$') so that $y + x = 0$.
- Existence of multiplicative inverses: for $x \neq 0$ in F, there is $y \in F$ (usually denoted x^{-1}) so that $yx = 1$.
- $0 \neq 1$

(That last condition may seem completely unnecessary, but it would not follow from the other requirements, so we must impose it.)

Theorem: Let p be a prime. Then $\mathbf{Z}/p$ is a field.

Proof: We've already done most of the work to prove this. First, prior to proving any of these properties, there was the funny business verifying that addition and multiplication were 'well-defined' modulo p, meaning that the operations really made sense 'mod p'.

After the well-definedness is proven, the associativity and distributivity and commutativity are simply *inherited* by $\mathbf{Z}/p$ from the corresponding properties of the ordinary integers. The properties of $\bar{1} = 1\text{-mod-}p$ and $\bar{0} = 0\text{-mod-}p$ are likewise simply inherited.

The presence of an additive inverse is straightforward, unless we forget that $\mathbf{Z}/p$ is not simply $\{0, 1, 2, \ldots, p-1\}$. Indeed,

$$-\bar{x} = \overline{(-x)}$$

But, for example, if we try to find -2 among $\{0, 1, 2, 3, 4\}$ then we might mistakenly think that 2 has no additive inverse modulo 5. In reality, modulo 5,

$$-\bar{2} = \overline{(-2)} = \bar{3}$$

since $-2 = 3 \bmod 5$.

The only real issue is verifying that non-zero things x modulo p have multiplicative inverses. Note that 'non-zero modulo p' means that p does not divide x. Thus, $\gcd(x, p)$ is not p, but some *proper* divisor of p. But since p is prime there are few choices left: we must have $\gcd(x, p) = 1$. By the funny characterization of gcd's, there are integers a, b so that $ax + bp = 1$, and then (as we've discussed already on another occasion) a is a multiplicative inverse mod p. That is, $\bar{x}^{-1} = \bar{a}$.

                                                                                    ///

Corollary: For every prime integer p, there exists a finite field with p elements, denoted $\mathbf{F}_p$.

Proof: We can take $\mathbf{F}_p = \mathbf{Z}/p$.   ///

Remark: What is *not* clear is that there are no *other* finite fields with a prime number p of elements than $\mathbf{Z}/p$. In fact, it is true that a field F with a prime number p of elements is 'the same' as $\mathbf{Z}/p$, but this requires proof.

Collections of 'numbers' such as the ordinary integers $\mathbf{Z}$ don't quite have all the properties of a *field*, however. The particular missing property is that not every non-zero element of $\mathbf{Z}$ has a multiplicative inverse (*in* $\mathbf{Z}$). Such a collection which meets all the conditions above *except* possibly the requirement that every non-zero element has a multiplicative inverse is a **commutative ring**. If the commutativity of multiplication is also dropped, then we have a **ring**.

Remark: The entity $\mathbf{Z}/m$ is *not* a field for m not prime, although it is a commutative ring. Indeed, let $m = a \cdot b$ be a proper factorization of m. Then it's pretty easy to see that neither a nor b is actually 0 modulo m, but also that neither has a multiplicative inverse.

Remark: We will see later that for any prime *power* p^n there exists a finite field $\mathbf{F}_{p^n}$ with p^n elements. It is important to realize that for $n > 1$ it is *never* the case that $\mathbf{Z}/p^n$ gives a field, despite the fact that it has p^n elements. As in the previous remark, if $n > 1$ there are many non-zero elements in $\mathbf{Z}/p^n$ which have no multiplicative inverses, failing that important property of a field.

Remark: We could also spend time proving that in a field there is only *one* element that behaves like 0, only *one* element that behaves like 1, that additive or multiplicative inverses are *unique*, and such things, but since our viewpoint will be mostly computational, proof of these very unsurprising facts is not urgent.

6.9 Fermat's Little Theorem

When thinking about how ordinary operations of arithmetic behave modulo m, especially modulo primes p, it is important to be cautious. The result of this section may be counter-intuitive, but it is a basic fact about $\mathbf{Z}/p$.

More than 350 years ago Pierre de Fermat made many astute observations regarding prime numbers, factorization into primes, and related aspects of number theory (not to mention other parts of mathematics and science as well). About 300 years ago, Leonhard Euler systematically continued Fermat's work. Most of these things were prototypes for 'modern' mathematical ideas, and at the same time remain very much relevant to contemporary number theory and its applications.

Theorem: Let p be a prime number. Then for any integer x

$$x^p = x \bmod p$$

Corollary: Let p be a prime number. Then for any integer x prime to p,

$$x^{p-1} = 1 \bmod p$$

Remark: The corollary follows easily from the theorem by remembering that if $\gcd(x, p) = 1$ then x has a multiplicative inverse x^{-1} modulo p. Then multiply both sides of the equation $x^p = x \bmod p$ by x^{-1} to obtain the assertion of the corollary.

Proof: We will first prove that prime p divides the binomial coefficients

$$\binom{p}{i}$$

with $1 \le i \le p - 1$, keeping in mind that the extreme cases $i = 0$ and $i = p$ can't possibly also have this property, since

$$\binom{p}{0} = 1 \qquad \binom{p}{p} = 1$$

Indeed, from its definition,

$$\binom{p}{i} = \frac{p!}{i!\,(p-i)!}$$

Certainly p divides the numerator. Since $0 < i < p$, the prime p divides none of the factors in the factorials in the denominator. By unique factorization into primes, this means that p does not divide the denominator at all. Indeed,

$$\binom{p}{i} \cdot i! \cdot (p-i)! = p!$$

The prime p divides the right-hand side, so it divides the left-hand side. But p cannot divide $i!$ nor $(p-i)!$ (for $0 < i < p$) since these two numbers are products of integers smaller than p and hence not divisible by p. (And, even more important, we have seen that if a prime p does not divide a, b then p does not divide ab.)

The Binomial Theorem asserts that

$$(x + y)^p = \sum_{0 \leq i \leq p} \binom{p}{i} x^i y^{p-i}$$

In particular, since the coefficients of the left-hand side are integers the same must be true of the coefficients on the right-hand side. Thus, all the binomial coefficients are *integers*. We did not use the fact that p is prime to reach *this* conclusion.

Thus, the binomial coefficients with $0 < i < p$ are *integers* expressed as fractions whose numerators are divisible by p and whose denominators are *not* divisible by p. Thus, when all cancellation is done in the fraction, there must remain a factor of p in the numerator. This proves the desired fact about binomial coefficients. (One might notice that unique factorization is used here!)

Now we prove Fermat's Little Theorem for *positive* integers x by induction on x. First, certainly $1^p = 1 \mod p$. For the induction step, suppose that we already know for some particular x that

$$x^p = x \mod p$$

Then

$$(x + 1)^p = \sum_{0 \leq i \leq p} \binom{p}{i} x^i 1^{p-i} = x^p + \sum_{0 < i < p} \binom{p}{i} x^i + 1$$

All the coefficients in the sum in the middle of the last expression are divisible by p. Therefore,

$$(x + 1)^p = x^p + 0 + 1 = x + 1 \mod p$$

since our induction hypothesis is that $x^p = x \mod p$. This proves the theorem for positive x.   ///

6.10 Euler's theorem

Euler's theorem is an important extension of Fermat's Little Theorem. Here we give a proof of Euler's theorem which is in a different spirit than the proof above of Fermat's theorem. A little later we'll give an abstracted version of this in the context of Lagrange's theorem in group theory.

Again, for a positive integer n, the **Euler phi-function** $\varphi(n)$ is the number of integers b so that $1 \leq b \leq n$ and $\gcd(b, n) = 1$.

Theorem: *(Euler)* For x relatively prime to a positive integer n,

$$x^{\varphi(n)} = 1 \mod n$$

Remark: The special case that n is prime is just Fermat's Little Theorem, since for prime p we easily see that $\varphi(p) = p - 1$.

Proof: Let G be the collection of integers-mod-n which have multiplicative inverses (mod n, of course). We have already seen that these are exactly the integers modulo n which have multiplicative inverses modulo n. That is, $\varphi(n)$ counts the elements in G. In symbols,

$$|G| = \varphi(n)$$

We first note that the product

$$P = \prod_{g \in G} g = \text{product of all elements of } G$$

is again in G. Indeed, let $g_1, \ldots, g_t$ be a listing of all elements in G, so $P = g_1 \ldots g_t$. Then it should not be surprising that the inverse of $P = g_1 \ldots g_t$ is obtained by inverting the factors (and reversing the order!?):

$$(g_1 g_2 \ldots g_t) \cdot (g_t^{-1} \ldots g_2^{-1} g_1^{-1}) = 1 \bmod n$$

That is, P has a multiplicative inverse mod n, although we aren't trying to identify it.

Let x be an element of G. Then we claim that the map $f : G \to G$ defined by

$$f(g) = xg$$

is a bijection of G to itself. First, we should check that f really maps G to itself: indeed, for x and g both invertible mod n,

$$(xg)(g^{-1}x^{-1}) = 1 \bmod n$$

so $f(g) = xg$ is again in G. Next, check injectivity: if $f(g) = f(h)$, then by definition of f we have $xg = xh \bmod n$. Multiply this equality by $x^{-1} \bmod n$ to obtain $g = h \bmod n$, proving injectivity. Last, check surjectivity: given $g \in G$, let's find $h \in G$ so that $f(h) = g$. That is, find $h \in G$ so that $xh = g$. Well, taking $h = x^{-1}g$ works. This proves that f is a bijection as claimed.

Finally we get to the computational part of the argument. Again let P be the product of all elements of G. Then

$$P = \prod_{g \in G} g = \prod_{g \in G} f(g)$$

since the map f merely mixes around the elements of G. Then

$$P = \prod_{g \in G} f(g) = \prod_{g \in G} xg = x^{\varphi(n)} \prod_{g \in G} g = x^{\varphi(n)} \cdot P$$

where $\varphi(n)$ is the Euler phi-function of n. Since, as shown above, P is invertible mod n, we multiply through by $P^{-1} \bmod n$ to get

$$1 = x^{\varphi(n)} \bmod n$$

This proves Euler's Theorem.   ///

Remark: On one hand, this argument might hint that it is a mere shadow of some more systematic general approach. This is indeed the case. On the other hand, there are other equally important techniques toward which this little proof gives no hint.

6.11 Facts about primitive roots

In this section we simply *explain* what a **primitive root** is supposed to be, and state what is true. The proofs of *existence* (and non-existence) of primitive roots require more preparation, and are in fact a major part of the work we have to do.

Let n be a positive integer. An integer g relatively prime to n is a **primitive root modulo** n if for every x with $\gcd(x, n) = 1$ there is an integer ℓ so that $g^\ell = x \bmod n$. For fixed n, g, and x, the smallest non-negative integer ℓ with this property is the **discrete logarithm** or **index** of x base g modulo m.

Proposition: If g is a primitive root modulo n, then the smallest positive integer ℓ so that $g^\ell = 1 \bmod n$ is the value $\varphi(n)$ of Euler's phi-function at n.

Proof: Basically by the definition of $\varphi(n)$, the number of distinct residue classes $\bar{x}$ modulo n with x relatively prime to n is $\varphi(n)$. We claim that if ℓ is the smallest positive integer ℓ so that $g^\ell = 1 \bmod n$, then we can only get ℓ different values of $g^L \bmod n$ no matter what integer exponent L we use. Indeed, write $L = q\ell + r$ with $0 \le r < \ell$. Then

$$g^L = g^{q\ell+r} = (g^\ell)^q \cdot g^r = 1^q \cdot g^r = g^r \bmod n$$

That is, in fact, all possible values of $g^L \bmod n$ lie in the list

$$g^0, g^1, g^2, \ldots, g^{\ell-1}$$

This proves the proposition.   ///

For 'most' integers n there is *no* primitive root modulo n. The precise statement is

Theorem: The only integers n for which there is a primitive root modulo n are those of the forms
  * $n = p^e$ with an odd prime p, and $e \ge 1$
  * $n = 2p^e$ with an odd prime p, and $e \ge 1$
  * $n = 2, 4$

This will be proven later. In particular, the most important case is that there *do* exist primitive roots modulo *primes*. It is useful to make clear one important property of primitive roots:

Proposition: Let g be a primitive root modulo a prime p. Let ℓ be an integer so that

$$g^\ell = 1 \bmod p$$

Then $p - 1$ divides ℓ.

Proof: Using the division/reduction algorithm, we may write $\ell = q \cdot (p-1) + r$ with $0 \le r < p - 1$. Then

$$1 = g^\ell = g^{q \cdot (p-1)+r} = (g^{p-1})^q \cdot g^r = 1^q \cdot g^r = g^r \bmod p$$

Since g is a primitive root, $p - 1$ is the least positive exponent so that g raised to that power is 1 mod p. Thus, since $1 = g^r \bmod p$, it must be that $r = 0$. That is, $p - 1 | \ell$.   ///

6.12 Euler's criterion

One important type of corollary of the existence of primitive roots modulo primes is that we have a computational criterion (due to Euler) for whether integers are n^{th} powers modulo primes. Note that we've not yet proven that primitive roots exist modulo primes.

Fix a prime p. As usual, we say that an integer x is an nth power modulo p (or n^{th} *power residue*) if there is an integer y so that

$$y^n = x \bmod p$$

And then y is said to be an nth **root** of x modulo p. For example, since $2^7 = 11 \bmod 13$, 11 is a 7th power modulo 13 and 2 is a 7th root of 11 modulo 13.

Remark: It is safe to say that the intuition we have for powers and roots in real or complex numbers is not helpful in understanding roots and powers modulo p.

Example: Since $2^2 = 4 = -1 \bmod 5$, 2 is a square root of -1 modulo 5. Note that the fact that there is no *real* number which is a square root of -1 is no argument against the existence of a square root of -1 modulo 5.

Example: Since $4^2 = 16 = 5 \bmod 11$, 4 is a square root of 5 modulo 11.

Example: There is *no* $\sqrt{2}$ modulo 5: to be sure of this, we compute 5 cases:

$$0^2 = 0 \ne 2 \bmod 5$$
$$1^2 = 1 \ne 2 \bmod 5$$
$$2^2 = 4 \ne 2 \bmod 5$$
$$3^2 = 9 = 4 \ne 2 \bmod 5$$
$$4^2 = 16 = 1 \ne 2 \bmod 5$$

Since $\mathbf{Z}/5$ consists of just the 5 congruence classes $\bar{0}, \bar{1}, \bar{2}, \bar{3}, \bar{4}$, we don't need to check any further to know that there is no square root of 2 modulo 5.

From a naive viewpoint, it would appear that the only way to check whether an nth root of x modulo p exists is by *brute force*, taking the nth power of each element of $\mathbf{Z}/p$ in turn to see if by chance the value x appears among the squares. From this viewpoint, it would be especially laborious to be sure that something had *no* square root, since all of $\mathbf{Z}/p$ would have to be searched. The following criterion is better:

Theorem: Let p be a prime and n an integer so that $p = 1 \bmod n$. For an integer x so that $\gcd(x, p) = 1$, x is an nth power modulo p if and only if

$$x^{(p-1)/n} = 1 \bmod p$$

Proof: *(Easy half)* Suppose that $x = y^n \bmod p$. Then, invoking Fermat's Little Theorem,

$$x^{(p-1)/n} = (y^n)^{(p-1)/n} = y^{p-1} = 1 \bmod p$$

as claimed.

(*Hard half*) Now suppose that $x^{(p-1)/n} = 1 \bmod p$, and show that x is an nth power. Let g be a *primitive root* modulo p, and let ℓ be a positive integer so that $g^\ell = x$. We have

$$(g^\ell)^{(p-1)/n} = 1 \bmod p$$

From the discussion of primitive roots above, this implies that

$$(p-1) \,|\, \ell \cdot (p-1)/n$$

Let k be an integer such that

$$k \cdot (p-1) = \ell \cdot (p-1)/n$$

Then $kn = \ell$. Then

$$x = g^\ell = g^{kn} = (g^k)^n \bmod p$$

That is, x is the nth power of g^k.   ///

6.13 Fast modular exponentiation

Euler's criterion (and many other number-theoretic algorithms) would not be of much value if there were no underlying algorithm to exponentiate integers modulo m. In fact, this algorithm works in a great variety of contexts: integers modulo m, polynomials modulo P, and others. The idea of it is about 2500 years old.

The most naive version of exponentiation, in which to compute $x^n \% m$ one computes x^2, then $x^3 = x \cdot x^2$, then $x^4 = x \cdot x^3$, ..., $x^n = x \cdot x^{n-1}$ (all mod m), is very inefficient. Instead, to compute x^e we express e as a *binary* integer

$$e = e_o + e_1 \cdot 2^1 + e_2 \cdot 2^2 + ... + e_n \cdot e^n$$

with each e_i equal to 0 or 1, and compute power-of-two powers of x **by squaring**:

$$x^2 = x \cdot x$$
$$x^4 = (x^2)^2$$
$$x^8 = (x^4)^2$$
$$x^{2^4} = (x^8)^2$$
$$x^{2^5} = (x^{2^4})^2$$

$$\cdots$$

Then

$$x^e = x^{e_o} \, (x^2)^{e_1} \, (x^4)^{e_2} \, (x^8)^{e_3} (x^{2^4})^{e_4} \ldots (x^{2^n})^{e_n}$$

Again, the e_is are just 0 or 1, so in fact this notation is clumsy: we *omit* the factor x^{2^k} if $e_k = 0$ and *include* the factor x^{2^k} if $e_k = 1$.

A fairly good way of implementing this is the following, which we call the **Fast Modular Exponentiation** algorithm. To compute $x^e \% m$, we will keep track of a triple (X, E, Y) which initially is $(X, E, Y) = (x, e, 1)$. At each step of the algorithm:

- If E is odd then replace Y by $(X \times Y)\%m$ and replace E by $E - 1$
- If E is even then replace X by $(X \times X)\%m$ and replace E by $E/2$. When $E = 0$ the value of Y at that time is $x^e \% m$.

This algorithm takes at most $2 \log_2 E$ steps. Note that in the fast exponentiation modulo m, no number larger than m^2 will arise. Thus, for example, to compute something like

$$2^{1000} \% 1000001$$

would require no more than $2 \log_2 1000 \approx 2 \cdot 10 = 20$ multiplications of 6-digit numbers.

For example, let's directly evaluate $2^{1000} \bmod 89$. Setting this up as indicated just above, we have

X	E	Y	
2	1000	1	initial state
4	500	1	E was even: square X mod 89
16	250	1	E was even: square X mod 89
78	125	1	E was even: square X mod 89
78	124	78	E was odd: multiply Y by X mod 89
32	62	78	E was even: square X mod 89
45	31	78	E was even: square X mod 89
45	30	39	E was odd: multiply Y by X mod 89
67	15	39	E was even: square X mod 89
67	14	32	E was odd: multiply Y by X mod 89
39	7	32	E was even: square X mod 89
39	6	2	E was odd: multiply Y by X mod 89
8	3	2	E was even: square X mod 89
8	2	16	E was odd: multiply Y by X mod 89
64	1	16	E was even: square X mod 89
64	0	45	E was odd: multiply Y by X mod 89

We conclude that

$$2^{1000} \% 89 = 45$$

6.14 Sun-Ze's theorem

The result of this section is sometimes known as the **Chinese Remainder Theorem**, mainly because the earliest results (including and following Sun Ze's) were obtained in China. Sun Ze's result was obtained before 450, and the statement below was obtained by Chin Chiu Shao about 1250. Such results, with virtually the same proofs, apply to much more general 'numbers' than the integers **Z**.

First, an important special case.

Theorem: *(Sun-Ze)* Let m and n be relatively prime positive integers. Let r and s be integers such that

$$rm + sn = 1$$

Then the function

$$f : \mathbf{Z}/m \times \mathbf{Z}/n \to \mathbf{Z}/mn$$

defined by

$$f(x, y) = y \cdot rm + x \cdot sn$$

is a bijection. The inverse map

$$f^{-1} : \mathbf{Z}/mn \to \mathbf{Z}/m \times \mathbf{Z}/n$$

is simply

$$f^{-1}(z) = (x\text{-mod-}m, y\text{-mod-}n)$$

Proof: First, the peculiar characterization of the gcd(m, n) as the smallest positive integer expressible in the form $am + bn$ for integers a and b assures (since here gcd$(m, n) = 1$) that integers r and s exist such that $rm + sn = 1$. Second, we should check that the function f is well-defined, that is, that if $x' = x + am$ and $y' = y + bn$ for some integers a and b, then still

$$f(x', y') = f(x, y)$$

Indeed,

$$f(x', y') = y'rm + x'sn = (y + an)rm + (x + am)sn$$
$$= yrm + xsn + mn(ar + bs) = f(x, y) \bmod mn$$

This proves the well-definedness.

To prove surjectivity of f, for any integer z, let $x = z$ and $y = z$. Then

$$f(x, y) = zrm + zsn = z(rm + sn) = z \cdot 1 \bmod mn$$

To prove injectivity, we *could* use the fact that $\mathbf{Z}/m \times \mathbf{Z}/n$ and $\mathbf{Z}/mn$ are finite sets of the same size, so a surjective function is necessarily injective. But we can learn a little more by a more direct proof. Suppose that

$$f(x', y') = f(x, y)$$

Then modulo m the terms yrm and $y'rm$ are 0, so this asserts that

$$xsn = x'sn \bmod m$$

From $rm + sn = 1 \bmod mn$ we obtain $sn = 1 \bmod m$, so

$$x = x' \bmod m$$

Symmetrically,

$$y = y' \bmod n$$

This proves injectivity.

Finally, observe that (by the same reasoning)

$$f(x, y) = yrm + xsn = y \cdot 0 + x \cdot 1 \bmod m = x \bmod m$$

and similarly

$$f(x, y) = yrm + xsn = y \cdot 1 + x \cdot 0 \bmod n = y \bmod n$$

These facts, together with the identity $f(z, z) = z \bmod mn$ already proven, show that f^{-1} is as claimed. ///

The more general version is

Theorem: *(Sun-Ze)* For $m_1, \ldots, m_n$ mutually relatively prime, the map

$$g : \mathbf{Z}/(m_1 \ldots m_n) \to \mathbf{Z}/m_1 \times \mathbf{Z}/m_2 \times \ldots \times \mathbf{Z}/m_n$$

defined by

$$g(x) = (x \bmod m_1, x \bmod m_2, \ldots, x \bmod m_n)$$

is a *bijection*.

Proof: We'll do induction on the number n of moduli involved. The case $n = 2$ was just treated, and if $n = 1$ there is nothing to prove. So take $n > 2$. By induction on n, the map

$$g_o : \mathbf{Z}/m_2 \ldots m_n \to \mathbf{Z}/m_2 \times \mathbf{Z}/m_3 \times \ldots \times \mathbf{Z}/m_n$$

defined by

$$g_o(x\text{-mod-}m_2 \ldots m_n)$$

$$= (x\text{-mod-}m_2, x\text{-mod-}m_3, \ldots, x\text{-mod-}m_n)$$

is a bijection. Thus, the map

$$g_1 : \mathbf{Z}/m_1 \times \mathbf{Z}/m_2 \ldots m_n \to \mathbf{Z}/m_1 \times \mathbf{Z}/m_2 \times \mathbf{Z}/m_3 \times \ldots \times \mathbf{Z}/m_n$$

defined by

$$g_1(x\text{-mod-}m_1, x\text{-mod-}m_2 \ldots m_n)$$

$$= (x\text{-mod-}m_1, x\text{-mod-}m_2, x\text{-mod-}m_3, \ldots, x\text{-mod-}m_n)$$

is a bijection.

At the same time, invoking unique factorization (!), m_1 and the product $m_2 m_3 \ldots m_n$ are relatively prime, so the case $n = 2$ gives the bijectivity of the map

$$g_2 : \mathbf{Z}/m_1(m_2 \ldots m_n) \to \mathbf{Z}/m_1 \times \mathbf{Z}/m_2 \ldots m_n$$

defined by

$$g_2(x\text{-mod-}m_1(m_2 \ldots m_n)) = (x\text{-mod-}m_1, x\text{-mod-}m_2 \ldots m_n)$$

Therefore, the composite map

$$g = g_2 \circ g_1$$

is also a bijection.   ///

Now we paraphrase Sun-Ze's theorem in terms of solving several numerical congruences simultaneously. There are some similarities to the more elementary discussion of systems of linear equations, but there are critical differences as well.

To start with, let's take the smallest non-trivial systems, of the form

$$\begin{cases} x = a \bmod m \\ x = b \bmod n \end{cases}$$

where m, n are *relatively prime*, a, b are arbitrary integers, and we are to find all integers x which satisfy this system.

Notice that there are *two* congruences but just one *unknown*, which in the case of *equations* would probably lead to non-solvability immediately. But systems of congruences behave slightly differently. Our only concession is: **We'll only consider the case that the moduli m and n are** *relatively prime*, **that is, that** $\gcd(m, n) = 1$.

Using the Euclidean algorithm again, there are integers s, t so that

$$sm + tn = 1$$

since we supposed that $\gcd(m, n) = 1$. And this can be rearranged to

$$tn = 1 - sm$$

for example. **Here comes the trick:** the claim is that **the single congruence**

$$x_o = a(tn) + b(sm) \bmod mn$$

is equivalent to (has the same set of solutions) as the *system* of congruences above.

Let's check: modulo m, we have

$$x_o = (a(tn) + b(sm)) \bmod m = a(tn) + 0 \bmod m$$
$$= a(tn) \bmod m = a(1 - sm) \bmod m$$
$$= a(1) \bmod m = a \bmod m$$

The discussion of the congruence modulo n is nearly identical, with roles reversed. Let's do it:

$$x_o = (a(tn) + b(sm)) \bmod n = 0 + b(sm) \bmod m$$
$$= b(sm) \bmod n = b(1 - tn) \bmod n$$
$$= b(1) \bmod n = b \bmod n$$

Thus, anything congruent to this x_o modulo mn is a solution to the system.

On the other hand, suppose x is a solution to the system, and let's prove that it is congruent to x_o modulo mn. Since $x = a \bmod m$ and $x = b \bmod n$, we have

$$x - x_o = a - a = 0 \bmod m$$

and

$$x - x_o = b - b = 0 \bmod n$$

That is, both m and n divide $x - x_o$. Since m and n are *relatively prime*, we can conclude that mn divides $x - x_o$, as desired.

Note the process of sticking the solutions together via the formula above uses the Euclidean Algorithm in order to be computationally effective (rather than just theoretically *possible*).

For example, let's solve the system

$$\begin{cases} x = 2 \bmod 11 \\ x = 7 \bmod 13 \end{cases}$$

To glue these congruences together, we execute the Euclidean Algorithm on 11 and 13, to find

$$6 \cdot 11 - 5 \cdot 13 = 1$$

Thus, using the formula above, the single congruence

$$x = 2(-5 \cdot 13) + 7(6 \cdot 11) \bmod 11 \cdot 13$$

is equivalent to the given system. In particular, this gives the solution

$$x = -2 \cdot 5 \cdot 13 + 7 \cdot 6 \cdot 11 = 332 \bmod 11 \cdot 13$$

Quite generally, consider a system

$$\begin{cases} x = b_1 \bmod m_1 \\ x = b_2 \bmod m_2 \\ x = b_3 \bmod m_3 \\ \quad \cdots \\ x = b_n \bmod m_n \end{cases}$$

We'll only consider the scenario that m_i and m_j **are relatively prime** (for $i \neq j$). We solve it in steps: first, just look at the subsystem

$$\begin{cases} x = b_1 \bmod m_1 \\ x = b_2 \bmod m_2 \end{cases}$$

and use the method above to turn this into a single (equivalent!) congruence of the form

$$x = c_2 \bmod m_1 m_2$$

Then look at the system

$$\begin{cases} x = c_2 \bmod m_1 m_2 \\ x = b_2 \bmod m_3 \end{cases}$$

and use the method above to combine these two congruences into a single equivalent one, say

$$x = c_3 \bmod m_1 m_2 m_3$$

and so on.

6.15 Euler's phi-function

Euler's phi-function $\varphi(n)$ is defined to be the number of integers ℓ in the range $1 \leq \ell \leq n$ which are relatively prime to n. Thus, among other things, $\varphi(n)$ tells the number of integers x modulo n such that x has a multiplicative inverse modulo n. That is, $\varphi(n)$ is the cardinality of $(\mathbf{Z}/n)^\times$.

The definition of $\varphi(n)$ is very inefficient as a means to compute $\varphi(n)$. A significantly better approach is given by the formula of the following theorem, although this requires that n be factored into primes, which will become difficult or impossible for very large n.

Theorem: For m and n relatively prime

$$\varphi(mn) = \varphi(m) \cdot \varphi(n)$$

Let $n = p_1^{e_1} \ldots p_t^{e_t}$ be a factorization of n into primes, with the p_is distinct and with positive integers e_i. Then

$$\varphi(n) = (p_1 - 1)p_1^{e_1 - 1} \ldots (p_t - 1)p_t^{e_t - 1}$$

Corollary: *(of proof)* Sun-Ze's bijection

$$\mathbf{Z}/mn \to \mathbf{Z}/m \times \mathbf{Z}/n$$

gives a bijection

$$(\mathbf{Z}/mn)^\times \to (\mathbf{Z}/m)^\times \times (\mathbf{Z}/n)^\times$$

Proof: Note that we already proved several things relevant to this in our earlier discussion of Euler's theorem, such as the fact that $\varphi(n)$ is the cardinality of $(\mathbf{Z}/n)^\times$.

If we can prove the first formula, then by unique factorization it suffices to prove the second formula for prime powers $n = p^e$. Recall that Sun-Ze's theorem gives a bijection $\mathbf{Z}/m \times \mathbf{Z}/n \to \mathbf{Z}/mn$. In general, the cardinality of a cartesian product $A \times B$ of sets (meaning the set of ordered pairs (a, b) with $a \in A$ and $b \in B$) is the product of the cardinalities of A and B. By now we know that $(\mathbf{Z}/t)^\times$ exactly consists of x modulo t with $\gcd(x, t) = 1$. Combining these facts proves the first formula of the theorem.

Next, we prove the second formula for prime powers $n = p^e$ with e a positive integer. In this special case, $\gcd(\ell, p^e) > 1$ if and only if p divides ℓ. There are p^e/p multiples of p between (inclusive) 1 and p^e, so

$$\varphi(p^e) = p^e - p^{e-1} = (p-1)p^{e-1}$$

as claimed.   ///

Exercises

6.01 Factor the integers 1028 and 2057 into primes.

6.02 Find the reduction mod 99 of 1000. (*ans.*)

6.03 Find the reduction mod 88 of -1000. (*ans.*)

6.04 Prove that the reduction mod 10 of a positive integer N is simply the ones'-place digit of N in decimal expansion. (*ans.*)

6.05 Prove that the reduction mod 100 of a positive integer N is the two-digit number made up of the tens'-place and ones'-place digits of N.

6.06 Let m be any non-zero integer. Prove that the reduction mod $-m$ of N is the same as the reduction mod m of N.

6.07 Prove in general that if r is the reduction of N mod m, and if $r \neq 0$, then $m - r$ is the reduction of $-N$ mod m.

6.08 By brute force, find a multiplicative inverse to 13 mod 100. (*ans.*)

6.09 By brute force, check that among 1,2,...,25 the integers with multiplicative inverses modulo 26 are the *odd* integers in that range, excluding 13. Is there any shortcut here, by cleverness alone, without invoking any fancier mathematics?

6.10 (*) (This is a little hard to do without using anything further than what we have already!) Let m be a positive integer. Prove that for all integers x, y

$$((x\%m) + (y\%m))\%m = (x + y)\%m$$

and

$$((x\%m) \times (y\%m))\%m = (x \times y)\%m$$

6.11 Find all the divisors of 60. Why are you sure that you have them all? (*ans.*)

6.12 For all the numbers under 100, note either that they are prime, or factor them into primes.

6.13 Show directly from the definition of divisibility that if $d|m$ then $d|(-m)$. (*ans.*)

6.14 Prove directly, from the very definition of divisibility, that if $d|x$ and $d|y$ then $d|(x-y)$ and $d|(x+y)$.

6.15 Observe that 1331 and 14641 cannot be prime, without computation. (*ans.*)

6.16 Find the smallest divisor $d > 1$ of 10001. (*ans.*)

6.17 Find the smallest divisor $d > 1$ of 12344321. (*ans.*)

6.18 Find the least common multiple of $2, 4, 8, 16, 32, 64$, and 128. (*ans.*)

6.19 Show that for any integer n if $d|n$ and $d|(n+2)$ then $d|2$. (*ans.*)

6.20 Show that for any integer n the two integers n and $n+1$ are relatively prime.

6.21 Show that for any integer n exactly one of $n, n+2, n+4$ is divisible by 3. In particular, except for $3, 5, 7$, there are no triples of primes occurring in the pattern $n, n+2, n+4$. (*ans.*)

6.22 Show that for any integer n, the integers n and n^2+1 are relatively prime.

6.23 (*) Show that for any integer n the greatest common divisor of $16n^2+8n+1$ and $16n^2-8n+1$ is 1.

6.24 Prove that for any two integers m, n, the least common multiple $\operatorname{lcm}(m, n)$ exists, and is given by the formula $\operatorname{lcm}(m, n) = m \cdot n\gcd(m, n)$. (*Caution:* do not accidentally assume that the lcm exists to prove the formula.)

6.25 (**) How likely is it that two *randomly chosen positive integers* will be relatively prime? (*Hint:* Part of the issue is to make suitable sense of the question. First look in the range $1, \ldots, N$ with $N = p_1 \ldots p_t$ with distinct primes $p_1, \ldots, p_t$, and take a limit. Second, estimate the inaccuracy in this approach. There remains the question of evaluating

$$\prod_{p \text{ prime}} (1 - p^{-2}) = \sum_{n=1}^{\infty} \frac{1}{n^2}$$

6.26 Find a proper factor of $111, 111, 111, 111, 111$ without using a calculator. (*ans.*)

6.27 Find a proper factor of $101, 010, 101, 010, 101$ without using a calculator. (*ans.*)

6.28 Prove/observe that the ones'-place digit of a decimal number is not sufficient information (by itself) to determine whether the number is divisible by 3, or by 7.

6.29 Explain why $n^2 - 1$ cannot be prime for *any* $n > 2$. (*ans.*)

6.30 Explain why $3^n - 1$ cannot possibly be a prime number if $n > 1$.

6.31 Explain why $2^m + 1$ cannot possibly be a prime number unless m is a power of 2.

6.32 While we mostly know that $x^2 - y^2$ has a factorization, that $x^3 - y^3$ has a factorization, that $x^3 + y^3$ has, and so on, there is a factorization that seldom appears in high school algebra: $x^4 + 4y^4$ has a factorization into two quadratic pieces, each with 3 terms! Find this factorization. *Hint:*

$$x^4 + 4y^4 = (x^4 + 4x^2y^2 + 4y^4) - 4x^2y^2$$

6.33 Can $n^4 + 4$ be a prime if the integer n is bigger than 1?

6.34 Factor $x^6 - y^6$ in two different ways.

6.35 (*) *(Lagrange's identity)*: prove that

$$\left(\sum_i x_i y_i \right)^2 = \left(\sum_i x_i^2 \right) \left(\sum_i y_i^2 \right) - \sum_{i<j} (x_i y_j - x_j y_i)^2$$

6.36 (*) *(Euclid's proof that there are infinitely-many primes)* Suppose there were only finitely many primes $p_1, p_2, \ldots, p_n$. Consider the number $N = p_1 \ldots p_n + 1$. Show that none of the p_i can divide N. Conclude that there must be some other prime than those on this list, from which one would obtain a contradiction.

6.37 Find $\gcd(1112, 1544)$ and express it in the form $1112x + 1544y$ for some integers x and y by hand computation. *(ans.)*

6.38 Find $\gcd(10201, 32561)$, and express it in the form $10201x + 32561y$, by hand computation.

6.39 For an integer n, show that the greatest common divisor of the two integers $n^3 + n^2 + n + 1$ and $n^2 + n + 1$ is unavoidably just 1.

6.40 For an integer n, show that the greatest common divisor of the two integers $n^3 + n^2 + n + 1$ and $n^8 + n^7 + n^6 + n^5 + n^4 + n^3 + n^2 + n + 1$ is unavoidably just 1.

6.41 Show that the subset $\{(1,1), (2,2), (3,3), (1,2), (2,1)\}$ of $\{1,2,3\} \times \{1,2,3\}$ is an equivalence relation on the set $\{1,2,3\}$.

6.42 Show that the relation $x\,R\,y$ on real numbers, defined by $x\,R\,y$ if and only if $x \leq y$, is *not* an equivalence relation.

6.43 Let X be a set of non-empty subsets of a set S, whose union is all of S and which are mutually disjoint. (So X is a **partition**). Let $\sim$ be the equivalence relation defined by this partition. Prove that the equivalence classes are the elements of X.

6.44 How many equivalence relations are there on the set $\{1,2,3,4\}$? *(ans.)*

6.45 Take two positive integers n and N with n *not* dividing N. Find an integer x so that

$$(x \% N) \% n \neq x \% n$$

6.46 How many elements does the set $\mathbf{Z}/n$ have?   (*ans.*)

6.47 How many elements does the set $\mathbf{Z}/30^\times$ have?   (*ans.*)

6.48 Reduce $100,000,000,001$ modulo 10.

6.49 Compute and *reduce modulo* the indicated *modulus*: 110×124 modulo 3 and also $12 + 1234567890$ mod 10.

6.50 Compute $2^{1000} \% 11$. (*Hint:* In the first place, do manipulations in $\mathbf{Z}/11$, rather than thinking always of *reduction* mod 11. At the same time, to compute mod 11 there is never any reason to use numbers much larger than 11: for example, in computing powers of 2, we may as well *reduce modulo* 11 whenever it's *convenient*, although we are not *obliged* to reduce until the very end. Thus, compute

$$2, \ 2^2 = 4, \ 2^3 = 8, \ 2^4 = 16 = 5, \ 2^5 = 2 \cdot 2^4 = 2 \cdot 5 = 10$$

$$2^6 = 2 \cdot 2^5 = 2 \cdot 10 = 20 = 9, \ldots$$

Then use the 'law of exponents' $2^{ab} = (2^a)^b$.)

6.51 Compute the ones'-place digit in the decimal expansion of 3^{999}.   (*ans.*)

6.52 Find the multiplicative inverse of 3 modulo 100.   (*ans.*)

6.53 Find the multiplicative inverse of 1001 modulo 1234.   (*ans.*)

6.54 Find four distinct residue classes x modulo 15 so that $x^2 = 1$ mod 15.   (*ans.*)

6.55 Find three distinct residue classes x modulo 105 so that $x^2 = 1$ mod 105.   (*ans.*)

6.56 From the definition, find $\varphi(30)$, $\varphi(15)$, and $\varphi(24)$.   (*ans.*)

6.57 From the definition, find $\varphi(36)$, $\varphi(18)$, and $\varphi(28)$.

6.58 Factor $5^n - 1$ into primes for $1 \leq n \leq 11$.

6.59 Find a square root of 2 modulo 17.

6.60 Find a square root of 2 modulo 23. (*ans.*)

6.61 Find a square root of 3 modulo 1019. (*ans.*)

6.62 Find 11th roots of 2 and 3 modulo 127.   (*ans.*)

6.63 Find 11th roots of 2 and 3 modulo 101.

6.64 Find 11th roots of 141 and 162 modulo 199.

6.65 Find 11th roots of 141 and 162 modulo 199.

6.66 Show that 2 is *not* an 11th power mod 199.

6.67 By direct computation, check that 2 is *not* a primitive root modulo 17, but that 3 *is*.

6.68 Is 2 a square modulo 101?   (*ans.*)

6.69 Is 2 a square modulo 103?   (*ans.*)

6.70 Is 3 a square modulo 101?

6.71 Is 2 a cube modulo 103? (*ans.*)

6.72 Is 5 a cube modulo 103?

6.73 Is 2 a cube modulo 109?

6.74 Is 105 a 144th power modulo 1009?

6.75 Let p be a prime with $p = 3 \bmod 4$. Show that if b is a square modulo p then $b^{(p+1)/4}$ is a square root of b modulo p.   (*ans.*)

6.76 Let p be a prime with $p = 3 \bmod 4$. If b is a *not* a square modulo p then is $b^{(p+1)/4}$ a square root of b modulo p? What is it?

6.77 Let r be a prime, and let p be a prime with $r \nmid (p-1)$. Let s be a multiplicative inverse of r modulo $p - 1$. Show that b^s is an rth root of b modulo p.   (*ans.*)

6.78 Let r be a prime, and let p be a prime with $r \nmid (p - 1)$. Show that every element of $\mathbf{Z}/p$ has a unique r^{th} root.

6.79 Let r be a prime, and let p be a prime with $r|(p - 1)$ but $r^2 \nmid (p - 1)$. Let s be a multiplicative inverse of r modulo $(p - 1)/r$. Show that if b is an rth power modulo p then b^s is an rth root of b modulo p.   (*ans.*)

6.80 Show that $x^2 - y^2 = 102$ has no solution in integers. (*Hint:* Look at this equation modulo 4.)

6.81 Show that $x^3 + y^3 = 3$ has no solution in integers. (*Hint:* Look at this equation modulo 7.)

6.82 Show that $x^3 + y^3 + z^3 = 4$ has no solution in integers.

6.83 Show that $x^2 + 3y^2 + 6z^3 - 9w^5 = 2$ has no solution in integers.

7

Permutations and Interleavers

7.1 Permutations of sets

Intuitively, to apply a **permutation** to a bunch of things means just to move them around. More precisely, a **permutation** f **of a set** X is defined to be a *bijective* function f from X to itself.

The crudest question we can ask about permutations of X is *how many are there?* If X has n (distinct) elements $x_1, x_2, \ldots, x_n$ and $f : X \to X$ is a permutation of X, then there are n choices for what $f(x_1)$ can be, $n-1$ remaining choices for what $f(x_{n-1})$ can be (since it can't be whatever $f(x_n)$ was), and so on. Thus, there are $n!$ permutations of a set with n elements.

Another significant question is *how many times can a given permutation be applied before everything returns to its original position?* This is not only relevant in *card shuffling*, but also in thinking about random number generation and other things.

To study permutations themselves it doesn't matter much exactly what the elements of the set are so long as we can tell them apart, so let's just look at the set

$$\{1, 2, 3, \ldots, n-1, n\}$$

as a good prototype of a set with n (distinct) elements. The standard notation is to write S_n for the **set of permutations** of n things. This S_n is also called the **symmetric group** on n things.

A standard way to write permutations f of $\{1, 2, \ldots, n\}$ in order to describe in detail what f does is to effectively *graph* f but in the form of a list: write

$$f = \begin{pmatrix} 1 & 2 & 3 & \ldots & n \\ f(1) & f(2) & f(3) & \ldots & f(n) \end{pmatrix}$$

134

Thus, altering the notation just slightly, the permutation

$$g = \begin{pmatrix} 1 & 2 & 3 & \dots & n \\ i_1 & i_2 & i_3 & \dots & i_n \end{pmatrix}$$

is the one so that $g(\ell) = i_\ell$.

Always we have the **trivial permutation**

$$e = \begin{pmatrix} 1 & 2 & 3 & \dots & n \\ 1 & 2 & 3 & \dots & n \end{pmatrix}$$

which does not 'move' any element of the set. That is, for all i, $e(i) = i$.

Of course, one permutation may be applied after another. If g, h are two permutations, write

$$g \circ h$$

for the permutation that we get by first applying h and then applying g. This is the **composition** or **product** of the two permutations. It is important to appreciate that, *in general*

$$g \circ h \neq h \circ g$$

We'll see examples of this below. But in any case this notation is indeed compatible with the notation for (and the idea of) *composition of functions*. Thus, for $1 \leq i \leq n$, *by definition*

$$(g \circ h)(i) = g(h(i))$$

It is a consequence of the definition of permutations as (bijective) *functions* from a set to itself that *composition of permutations is associative:* for all permutations g, h, k of a set,

$$(g \circ h) \circ k = g \circ (h \circ k)$$

Indeed, for any element i of the set, the definition of composition of permutations gives

$$((g \circ h) \circ k)(x) = (g \circ h)(k(x)) \qquad \text{definition of } (g \circ h) \circ k, \text{ applied to } x$$

$$= g(h(k(x))) \qquad \text{definition of } g \circ h, \text{ applied to } k(x)$$

$$= g((h \circ k)(x)) \qquad \text{definition of } h \circ k, \text{ applied to } x$$

$$= (g \circ (h \circ k))(x) \qquad \text{definition of } g \circ (h \circ k), \text{ applied to } x$$

(This even works for infinite sets.)

And for any permutation g there is the **inverse** permutation g^{-1} which has the effect of reversing the permutation performed by g. That is,

$$g \circ g^{-1} = g^{-1} \circ g = e$$

Often the little circle indicating composition is suppressed, and we just write

$$g \circ h = gh$$

as if it were ordinary multiplication. The hazard is that we cannot presume that $gh = hg$, so a little care is required.

The graph-list notation for permutations is reasonably effective in computing the *product* of two permutations: to compute, for example,

$$\begin{pmatrix} 1 & 2 & 3 \\ 2 & 3 & 1 \end{pmatrix} \circ \begin{pmatrix} 1 & 2 & 3 \\ 3 & 2 & 1 \end{pmatrix}$$

we see what this composite does to each of $1, 2, 3$. The permutation on the right is applied first. It sends 1 to 3, which is sent to 1 by the second permutation (the one on the left). Similarly, 2 is sent to 2 (by the permutation on the right) which is sent to 3 (by the permutation on the left). Similarly, 3 is sent to 1 (by the permutation on the right) which is sent to 2 (by the permutation on the left). Graph-listing this information, we have

$$\begin{pmatrix} 1 & 2 & 3 \\ 2 & 3 & 1 \end{pmatrix} \circ \begin{pmatrix} 1 & 2 & 3 \\ 3 & 2 & 1 \end{pmatrix} = \begin{pmatrix} 1 & 2 & 3 \\ 1 & 3 & 2 \end{pmatrix}$$

If we multiply (compose) in the opposite order, we get something different:

$$\begin{pmatrix} 1 & 2 & 3 \\ 3 & 2 & 1 \end{pmatrix} \circ \begin{pmatrix} 1 & 2 & 3 \\ 2 & 3 & 1 \end{pmatrix} = \begin{pmatrix} 1 & 2 & 3 \\ 2 & 1 & 3 \end{pmatrix}$$

This is the simplest example of the **non-commutativity** of the 'multiplication' of permutations, that is, that $gh \neq hg$ in general.

It is certainly true that permutations, especially of big sets, can be very complicated things which are hard to visualize. Still, they can be broken up into simple pieces, as we'll see just below.

First, the simplest permutations are the **cycles** of various lengths. A **k-cycle** is a permutation f so that (for some numbers $i_1, \ldots, i_k$)

$$f(i_1) = i_2, \ \ f(i_2) = i_3, \ \ f(i_3) = i_4, \ldots, \ f(i_{k-1}) = i_k, \ \ f(i_k) = i_1$$

and so that $f(j) = j$ for any number j not in the list $i_1, \ldots, i_k$. Note that i_k is sent back to i_1. Thus, as the name suggests, f *cycles* the $i_1, \ldots, i_k$ among themselves. A more abbreviated notation is used for this: write

$$(i_1 \ \ i_2 \ \ \ldots \ \ i_{k-1} \ \ i_k)$$

for this k-cycle.

For example, comparing with the more general notation,

$$\begin{pmatrix} 1 & 2 & 3 \\ 2 & 1 & 3 \end{pmatrix} = (1 \ \ 2)$$

$$\begin{pmatrix} 1 & 2 & 3 \\ 3 & 2 & 1 \end{pmatrix} = (1 \ \ 3)$$

$$\begin{pmatrix} 1 & 2 & 3 \\ 2 & 3 & 1 \end{pmatrix} = (1\ 2\ 3)$$

These are, in order, two 2-cycles and a 3-cycle.

Unlike the more general notation, there is some *duplication* in the cycle notation: for example,

$$(1\ 2\ 3) = (2\ 3\ 1) = (3\ 1\ 2)$$

Generally, there are k different ways to write a k-cycle in this cycle notation. In a similar vein, it is pretty clear that
- If g is a k-cycle, then

$$g^k = e$$

meaning that applying g to the set k times has the net effect of *moving nothing*. How do cycles interact with each other? Well, generally not very well, but if $g = (i_1 \ldots i_k)$ and $h = (j_1 \ldots j_\ell)$ are a k-cycle and an ℓ-cycle with *disjoint* lists $\{i_1, \ldots, i_k\}$ and $\{j_1, \ldots, j_\ell\}$ interact nicely: *they commute with each other*, meaning that

$$gh = hg$$

in this special scenario. Such cycles are called (reasonably enough) **disjoint cycles**. Pursuing this idea, we have
- Any permutation can be written as a product of disjoint cycles, and in essentially just one way. The 'essentially' means that writing the same cycles in a different order is not to be considered different since after all they *commute*. This is called a **decomposition into disjoint cycles**.

Knowing the decomposition into disjoint cycles of a permutation g is the closest we can come to understanding the nature of g. Happily, this decomposition can be determined in a systematic way (effectively giving an explicit proof of this assertion). For example, consider

$$g = \begin{pmatrix} 1 & 2 & 3 & 4 & 5 & 6 & 7 \\ 4 & 3 & 2 & 5 & 7 & 6 & 1 \end{pmatrix}$$

We just trace the 'path' of elements under repeated applications of g. To start, let's see what happens to 1 under repeated application of g: first 1 goes to 4, which then goes to 5, which then goes to 7, which then goes to 1. Since we have returned to 1, we have *completed the cycle*: we see that one cycle occurring inside g is

$$(1\ 4\ 5\ 7)$$

Next, look at any number which didn't already occur in this cycle, for example 2. First 2 goes to 3, which then goes to 2, which already completes another cycle. Thus, there is also the 2-cycle

$$(2\ 3)$$

inside g. The only number which hasn't yet appeared in either of these cycles is 6, which is not moved by g. Thus, we have obtained the *decomposition into disjoint cycles*:

$$\begin{pmatrix} 1 & 2 & 3 & 4 & 5 & 6 & 7 \\ 4 & 3 & 2 & 5 & 7 & 6 & 1 \end{pmatrix} = (1\ 4\ 5\ 7)(2\ 3) = (2\ 3)(1\ 4\ 5\ 7)$$

The decomposition into disjoint cycles tells how many times a permutation must be repeated in order to have no net effect: *the least common multiple of the lengths of the disjoint cycles appearing in its decomposition.*

The **order** of a permutation is the number of times it must be applied in order to have *no net effect*. (Yes, there is possibility of confusion with other uses of the word 'order'). Thus,

- The order of a k-cycle is k. The order of a product of disjoint cycles is the least common multiple of the lengths.

We might imagine that permutations with larger orders *'mix better'* than permutations with smaller orders since more repetitions are necessary before the mixing effect is 'cancelled'. In this context, it may be amusing to realize that if a card shuffle is done perfectly, then after *some* number of repetitions the cards will be returned to their original order! But the number is pretty large with a 52-card deck, and it's not easy to do perfect shuffles anyway.

As an example, let's examine all the elements of S_7, determining their structure as products of disjoint cycles, counting the number of each kind, and noting their order.

First, let's count the 7-cycles $(i_1 \ldots i_7)$: there are 7 choices for i_1, 6 for i_2, and so on, but there are 7 different ways to *write* each 7-cycle, so there are $7!/7$ distinct 7-cycles altogether.

Next, 6-cycles $(i_1 \ldots i_6)$: there are 7 choices for i_1, 6 for i_2, and so on down to 2 choices for i_6, but there are 6 different ways to *write* each 6-cycle, so there are $7!/6$ distinct 6-cycles altogether.

Next, 5-cycles $(i_1 \ldots i_5)$: there are 7 choices for i_1, 6 for i_2, and so on down to 3 choices for i_5, but there are 5 different ways to *write* each 5-cycle, so there are $7!/(2!\,5)$ distinct 5-cycles altogether.

For variety, let's count the number of permutations writeable as a product of a disjoint 5-cycle and a 2-cycle. We just counted that there are $7!/(2!\,5)$ distinct 5-cycles. But each choice of 5-cycle leaves just one choice for 2-cycle disjoint from it, so there are again $7!/(2!\,5)$ distinct products of disjoint 5-cycle and 2-cycle. And we note that the *order* of a product of disjoint 5 and 2-cycle is $\mathrm{lcm}(2,5) = 10$.

There are $7!/(3!\,4)$ distinct 4-cycles, by reasoning similar to previous examples.

There are $7!/(3!\,4) \cdot 3!/2$ choices of disjoint 4-cycle and 2-cycle. The order of the product of such is $\mathrm{lcm}(2,4) = 4$.

There are $7!/(3!\,4) \cdot 3!/3$ choices of disjoint 4-cycle and 3-cycle. The order of the product of such is $\mathrm{lcm}(3,4) = 12$.

There are $7!/(4!\,3)$ distinct 3-cycles, by reasoning similar to previous examples.

There are $7!/(4!\,3) \cdot 4!/(2!\,2)$ choices of disjoint 3-cycle and 2-cycle. The order of the product of such is $\mathrm{lcm}(2,3) = 6$.

The number of disjoint 3-cycle, 2-cycle, and 2-cycle is slightly subtler, since *the two 2-cycles are indistinguishable.* Thus, there are

$$\frac{7!}{4!\,3} \frac{4!}{2!\,2} \frac{2!}{0!\,2} \cdot \frac{1}{2!}$$

where the last division by $2!$ is to take into account the $2!$ different orderings of the two 2-cycles, which make only a *notational* difference, *not* a difference in the permutation itself. The order of such a permutation is $\mathrm{lcm}(2,2,3) = 6$.

The number of disjoint pairs of 3-cycle and 3-cycle is similar: the two 3-cycles are not actually ordered although our 'choosing' of them gives the appearance that they are ordered. There are

$$\frac{7!}{4!\,3}\,\frac{4!}{1!\,3}\cdot\frac{1}{2!}$$

such pairs, where the last division by 2! is to take into account the 2! different orderings of the two 3-cycles, which make only a *notational* difference, *not* a difference in the permutation itself. The order of such a permutation is $\mathrm{lcm}(3,3,1)=3$.

There are $7!/(5!\,2)$ distinct 2-cycles, each of order 2.

There are $7!/(5!\,2)\cdot 5!/(3!\,2)\cdot 1/2!$ pairs of disjoint 2-cycles, where the last division by 2! is to take into account the possible orderings of the two 2-cycles, which affect the notation but not the permutation itself.

Finally, there are

$$\frac{7!}{5!\,2}\,\frac{5!}{3!\,2}\,\frac{3!}{1!\,2}\cdot\frac{1}{3!}$$

triples of disjoint 2-cycles, where the last division by 3! is to account for the possible orderings of the 3 2-cycles, which affects the notation but not the permutation itself. The order of such a permutation is just $\mathrm{lcm}(2,2,2)=2$.

As a by-product of this discussion, we see that the largest order of any permutation of 7 things is 12, which is obtained by taking the product of disjoint 3 and 4-cycles.

As a more extreme example of the counting issues involved, let's count the disjoint products of three 2-cycles and three 5-cycles in S_{24}. As above, this is

$$\frac{24!}{22!\,2}\,\frac{22!}{20!\,2}\,\frac{20!}{18!\,2}\,\frac{1}{3!}\cdot\frac{18!}{13!\,5}\,\frac{13!}{8!\,5}\,\frac{8!}{3!\,5}\,\frac{1}{3!}$$

where both of the divisions by 3! come from discounting the possible orderings of the 2-cycles, and the possible orderings of the 5-cycles. Note that since 2-cycles are distinguishable from 5-cycles, there is no further accounting necessary for the ordering of the 2-cycles *relative to the 5-cycles*, etc.

7.2 Shuffles

Overhand shuffles and riffle shuffles of decks of cards, viewed as permutations of the set of cards in the deck, are amenable to analysis. Some of the conclusions may be surprising. A mixing procedure identical to a riffle shuffle is used in interleaving *convolutional* codes.

The simplest type of **overhand shuffle** applied to a deck of n cards consists of choosing a random spot to break the deck in two, and then interchanging the two parts. For example, with a deck of just 6 cards labeled $0,1,2,3,4,5$, the deck might be broken into pieces $0,1$ and $2,3,4,5$. Then the two pieces are put back together as $2,3,4,5,0,1$. With a deck of n cards, the ith overhand shuffle f_i is defined as being the permutation that has the effect

$$0,1,2,3,\ldots,n-2,n-1 \;\to\; i,1+i,\ldots,n-2,n-1,0,1,2,3,\ldots,i-1$$

(respectively), meaning that the 0 is sent to the ith position, and so on. In the graph-listing notation above, starting the indexing with 0 rather than 1, this is

$$\begin{pmatrix} 0 & 1 & 2 & \ldots & n-1 \\ i & i+1 & i+2 & \ldots & (n-1+i)\%n \end{pmatrix}$$

That is, in terms of reduction of integers modulo n, as a function

$$f_i : \mathbf{Z}/n \to \mathbf{Z}/n$$

this shuffle is

$$f_i(x) = (x+i)\%n$$

where $y\%n$ denotes the reduction of y modulo n. That is, an overhand shuffle on a deck of n cards simply amounts to adding modulo n. In particular,

$$f_j(f_i(x)) = f_{i+j}(x)$$

That is, the effect of two overhand shuffles is identical to that of a single overhand shuffle. In particular, in that regard overhand shuffles are not very thorough mixers, since you can overhand shuffle a deck all day long and have no more effect than just doing a single overhand shuffle.

   It turns out that riffle shuffles are best described labeling the cards starting from 1, rather than starting from 0 as in the case of the simplest overhand shuffle. A good **riffle shuffle** of a deck of $2n$ cards consists of breaking the deck into two equal pieces

$$1, 2, 3, \ldots, n \quad n+1, n+2, \ldots, 2n-1, 2n$$

and then interleaving the cards from one half with the cards from the other as

$$n+1, 1, n+2, 2, n+3, 3, \ldots, 2n-1, n-1, 2n, n \text{ (good riffle)}$$

Note that the top and bottom cards do *not* stay in their original positions. There is a *bad* riffle shuffle, which may be useful in various card tricks, in which the top and bottom cards stay in the same position: the interleaving in the bad case is

$$1, n+1, 2, n+2, 3, n+3, 3, \ldots, n-1, 2n-1, n, 2n \text{ (bad riffle)}$$

This bad riffle shuffle is the same thing as a good riffle shuffle on the deck of cards obtained by removing the top and bottom cards from the deck. Also, note that there is really just one riffle shuffle, unlike the overhand shuffles where there is a parameter.

Proposition: The good riffle shuffle on a deck of $2n$ cards $1, 2, \ldots, 2n-1$ is the function

$$f(x) = (2 \cdot x)\%(2n+1)$$

That is, a good riffle shuffle is multiplication by 2 followed by reduction modulo $2n+1$.

Proof: On one hand, if $1 \le x \le n$, then by its definition the riffle shuffle sends x to the $2x^{\text{th}}$ spot in the deck, because of the interleaving. On the other hand, if $n < x \le 2n$, write $x = n + i$. Then by definition of the shuffle x is sent to the $(2i - 1)^{\text{th}}$ spot in the deck. We can re-express this as

$$f(n + i) = 2i - 1 = 2(n + i) - (2n + 1) = 2(n + i)\%(2n + 1)$$

since $2n + 1 < 2(n + i) < 2(2n + 1)$. This proves that the riffle shuffle is just multiplication by 2 modulo $2n + 1$, as claimed.   ///

Corollary: Let e be the order of 2 modulo $2n + 1$. That is, e is the smallest positive integer such that $2^e = 1 \bmod 2n + 1$. Then the good riffle shuffle on a deck of $2n$ cards returns all cards to their original position after e shuffles, and no earlier.

Proof: The xth card is put into position $2^t x \bmod 2n + 1$ by t applications of the riffle shuffle. The equations

$$2^t x = x \bmod 2n + 1$$

for $x = 1, 2, 3, \ldots, 2n$ include as a special case $x = 1$, which is

$$2^t = 1 \bmod 2n + 1$$

The smallest positive solution is $t = e$, and then indeed $2^e x = x \bmod 2n + 1$ for all x.   ///

7.3 Block interleavers

These permutations are used in concatenated error-correcting codes and in classical transposition ciphers. Rather like the riffle shuffles, there is an attractive analysis of these permutations.

Fix positive integers m, n. We will define a permutation, called the m-by-n **classic block interleaver**, on $N = m \cdot n$ things. (In fact, this is a *left-to-right, top-to-bottom* interleaver, for reasons that will become apparent.)

The physical description of the m-by-n block interleaver is quite straightforward: write the numbers $0, 1, 2, \ldots, N - 1$ *by row*, from left to right, top to bottom into an m-by-n rectangular array:

$$
\begin{array}{ccccc}
0 & 1 & 2 & \ldots & n - 1 \\
n & n + 1 & n + 2 & \ldots & 2n - 1 \\
& & \ldots & & \\
mn - n & mn - n + 1 & mn - n + 2 & \ldots & mn - 1
\end{array}
$$

Then read the numbers out by *by columns*, from left to right, top to bottom:

$$0, n, 2n, \ldots, mn - n, 1, n + 1, 2n + 1, \ldots, mn - n + 1, \ldots, mn - 1$$

This has the bad feature that 0 and $mn - 1$ are left in the same positions. This disadvantage is offset by some other positive features and simplicity. Variations on this idea can certainly avoid these fixed points.

From the physical description of the interleaver, we can get a formula for the effect of the m-by-n block interleaver: given x, let $x = qm + r$ with $0 \leq r < m$. Then the interleaver sends

$$qm + r = x \rightarrow q + rn$$

Indeed, notice that the row from which x is read out is the integer part of x/n and the column is $x\%n$. Writing into the array reverses the roles of column and row, and interchanges the roles of n and m.

For example, the 3-by-4 block interleaver is computed by creating the array

$$
\begin{array}{cccc}
0 & 1 & 2 & 3 \\
4 & 5 & 6 & 7 \\
8 & 9 & 10 & 11
\end{array}
$$

which is read out by columns to

$$0, 4, 8, 1, 5, 9, 2, 6, 10, 3, 7, 11$$

That is, we have the permutation

$$
\begin{pmatrix}
0 & 1 & 2 & 3 & 4 & 5 & 6 & 7 & 8 & 9 & 10 & 11 \\
0 & 4 & 8 & 1 & 5 & 9 & 2 & 6 & 10 & 3 & 7 & 11
\end{pmatrix}
$$

We can compute the cycle decomposition of this:

$$(1\ 4\ 5\ 9\ 3)\ (2\ 8\ 10\ 7\ 6)\ \ (0)\ (11)$$

By contrast, the 3-by-6 block interleaver is a 16-cycle (ignoring the fixed points 0 and 15, which give 1-cycles)

$$(1\ 6\ 2\ 12\ 4\ 7\ 8\ 14\ 16\ 11\ 15\ 5\ 13\ 10\ 9\ 3)$$

Proposition: Ignoring the obvious fixed point $mn - 1$, the m-by-n block interleaver acts on the set
$$\{0, 1, 2, 3, \ldots, mn - 2\}$$
by multiplication by n followed by reduction modulo $mn - 1$. That is

$$x \rightarrow (nx)\%(mn - 1)$$

Proof: Let $x = qm + r$, with $0 \leq r < m$. Then

$$n \cdot x = n(qm + r) = mn \cdot q + nr = (mn - 1)q + q + nr = q + nr \bmod (mn - 1)$$

This is the asserted formula.   ///

Exercises

7.01 Express the following permutation as a product of disjoint cycles and determine its order
$$\begin{pmatrix} 1 & 2 & 3 & 4 & 5 \\ 2 & 5 & 4 & 3 & 1 \end{pmatrix}$$

(*ans.*)

7.02 Express the following permutation as a product of disjoint cycles and determine its order
$$\begin{pmatrix} 1 & 2 & 3 & 4 & 5 & 6 & 7 \\ 2 & 5 & 4 & 7 & 1 & 3 & 6 \end{pmatrix}$$

7.03 Express the following permutation as a product of disjoint cycles and determine its order
$$\begin{pmatrix} 1 & 2 & 3 & 4 & 5 & 6 & 7 \\ 2 & 3 & 4 & 7 & 1 & 5 & 6 \end{pmatrix}$$

(*ans.*)

7.04 Express the following permutation as a product of disjoint cycles and determine its order
$$\begin{pmatrix} 1 & 2 & 3 & 4 & 5 & 6 & 7 & 8 & 9 \\ 2 & 3 & 4 & 8 & 9 & 7 & 1 & 5 & 6 \end{pmatrix}$$

7.05 Compute the product
$$\begin{pmatrix} 1 & 2 & 3 & 4 & 5 & 6 & 7 \\ 2 & 5 & 4 & 7 & 1 & 3 & 6 \end{pmatrix} \circ \begin{pmatrix} 1 & 2 & 3 & 4 & 5 & 6 & 7 \\ 2 & 3 & 4 & 7 & 1 & 5 & 6 \end{pmatrix}$$

(*ans.*)

7.06 Compute the product
$$\begin{pmatrix} 1 & 2 & 3 & 4 & 5 & 6 & 7 \\ 2 & 5 & 4 & 1 & 7 & 3 & 6 \end{pmatrix} \circ \begin{pmatrix} 1 & 2 & 3 & 4 & 5 & 6 & 7 \\ 2 & 4 & 3 & 7 & 5 & 1 & 6 \end{pmatrix}$$

7.07 How many distinct 3-cycles are there in the symmetric group S_5 of permutations of 5 things?   (*ans.*)

7.08 How many distinct 3-cycles are there in the symmetric group S_6 of permutations of 5 things?

7.09 Count the number of elements of S_4 of each possible order, by identifying them as products of disjoint cycles of various orders.

7.10 Count the number of elements of S_5 of all possible orders, by identifying them as products of disjoint cycles of various orders.

7.11 What is the largest *order* of any element of S_5? (*ans.*)

7.12   What is the largest *order* of any element of S_7? (*ans.*)

7.13   What is the largest *order* of any element of S_9? (*ans.*)

7.14   What is the largest *order* of any element of S_{14}?

7.15   A good **riffle shuffle** of a deck of $2n$ cards consists of breaking the deck into two equal pieces

$$1, 2, 3, \ldots, n \quad n+1, n+2, \ldots, 2n-1, 2n$$

and then interleaving the cards from one half with the cards from the other as

$$n+1, 1, n+2, 2, n+3, 3, \ldots, 2n-1, n-1, 2n, n$$

(The top and bottom cards do *not* stay in their original positions.) Show that if a good riffle shuffle on a deck of 50 cards is executed just 8 times in a row, then all cards return to their original positions. Show that if a perfect riffle shuffle on a deck of 52 cards is executed repeatedly, no card returns to its original position until the riffle shuffle has been executed 52 times.

7.16   Determine the disjoint cycle decomposition of a good riffle shuffle on a deck of 10 cards. (*ans.*)

7.17   Determine the disjoint cycle decomposition of a good riffle shuffle on a deck of 12 cards.

7.18   Determine the disjoint cycle decomposition of a good riffle shuffle on a deck of 14 cards. (*ans.*)

7.19   Determine the disjoint cycle decomposition of a good riffle shuffle on a deck of 48 cards.

7.20   Determine the disjoint cycle decomposition of a good riffle shuffle on a deck of 50 cards.

7.21   Determine the disjoint cycle decomposition of a good riffle shuffle on a deck of 52 cards.

7.22   On a deck of 12 cards, alternate a good riffle shuffle with an overhand shuffle that breaks the deck into two equal parts. How many times must this be repeated before the cards return to their original positions?

7.23   What is the disjoint cycle decomposition of the riffle shuffle followed by overhand shuffle in the previous exercise?

7.24   Find the cycle decomposition of the 2-by-6 (left-to-right, top-to-bottom) block interleaver.

7.25   Find the cycle decomposition of the 3-by-5 (left-to-right, top-to-bottom) block interleaver.

7.26   Find the cycle decomposition of the 3-by-7 (left-to-right, top-to-bottom) block interleaver.

7.27   Show that a 2-by-n left-to-right, **bottom-to-top** block interleaver has the same effect as a *good* riffle shuffle. Show that a 2-by-n left-to-right, **top-to-bottom** block interleaver has the same effect as a *bad* riffle shuffle.

8

Groups

Here we encounter the first instance of *abstract algebra* rather than the *tangible algebra* studied in high school. One way to think of the point of this is that it is an attempt to study the *structure* of things directly, without reference to irrelevant particular details.

This also achieves amazing efficiency (in the long run, anyway), since it turns out that the same underlying structures occur over and over again in mathematics. Thus, a careful study of these basic structures is amply repaid by allowing a much simpler and more unified mental picture of otherwise seemingly different phenomena.

8.1 Groups

The simplest (but maybe not most immediately intuitive) object in abstract algebra is a *group*. This idea is pervasive in modern mathematics. Many seemingly complicated or elusive issues seem to be merely secret manifestations of facts about groups. This is especially true in number theory, where it is *possible* to give 'elementary' proofs of many results, but only at the cost of having everything be complicated and so messy that it can't be remembered.

145

A **group** G is a set with an operation $g * h$, with a special element e called **the identity**, and with the properties:

- The property of the identity: for all $g \in G$, $e * g = g * e = g$.
- Existence of **inverses**: for all $g \in G$ there is $h \in G$ (the **inverse** of g) such that $h * g = g * h = e$.
- Associativity: for all $x, y, z \in G$, $x * (y * z) = (x * y) * z$.

If the operation $g * h$ is *commutative*, that is, if

$$g * h = h * g$$

then the group is said to be **abelian** (named after N.H. Abel, born on my birthday but 150 years earlier). In that case, often, but not always, the operation is written as *addition*. And if the operation is written as addition, then the identity is often written as 0 instead of e.

And in many cases the group operation is written as multiplication

$$g * h = g \cdot h = gh$$

This does not *preclude* the operation being abelian, but rather suggests only that there is no *presumption* that the operation is abelian. If the group operation is written as multiplication, then often the identity is written as 1 rather than e. Especially when the operation is written simply as *multiplication*, the **inverse** of an element g in the group is written as

$$\text{inverse of } g = g^{-1}$$

If the group operation is written as *addition*, then the inverse is written as

$$\text{inverse of } g = -g$$

In each of the following examples, it is easy to verify the properties necessary for the things to qualify as *groups*: we need an *identity* and we need *inverses*, as well as *associativity*.

- The integers **Z** with the operation being the usual addition $+$. The identity is 0 and the inverse of x is $-x$. This group is *abelian*.
- The *even* integers $2\mathbf{Z}$ with the usual addition $+$. The identity is 0 and the inverse of x is $-x$. This group is *abelian*.
- The set $7\mathbf{Z}$ of multiples of 7 among integers, with the usual addition $+$. The identity is 0 and the inverse of x is $-x$. This group is *abelian*.
- The set $\mathbf{Z}/m$ of integers-mod-m, with addition-mod-m as the operation. The identity is 0-mod-m and the inverse of x-mod-m is $(-x)$-mod-m. This group is *abelian*.
- The set $\mathbf{Z}/m^{\times}$ of integers mod m *relatively prime to* m, with multiplication-mod-m as the operation. The identity is 1-mod-m. In this example, a person unacquainted with arithmetic mod m would not realize that *there are multiplicative inverses*. We can compute them via the Euclidean algorithm. So this is the first 'non-trivial' example. This group is *abelian*.

- The collection of vectors in real n-space $\mathbf{R}^n$, with operation vector addition. The identity is just the 0 vector. Inverses are just negatives. (Note that we are literally *forgetting* the fact that there is a scalar multiplication).
- The set $GL(2, \mathbf{R})$ of invertible 2-by-2 real matrices, with group law matrix multiplication. Here the identity is the matrix

$$\begin{pmatrix} 1 & 0 \\ 0 & 1 \end{pmatrix}$$

The existence of inverses is just part of the definition. The fact that matrix multiplication is *associative* is not obvious from the definition, but this can either be checked by hand or inferred from 'higher principles', namely that the composition of functions is associative. The fact that the product of two invertible matrices is invertible is interesting: suppose that g, h both have inverses, g^{-1} and h^{-1}, respectively. Then you can check that $h^{-1}g^{-1}$ is an inverse of gh. This group is certainly not abelian.

Remark: Indeed, in general the best proof of associativity is by finding an interpretation as functions among sets, and invoking the associativity of functions.

- Permutations of a set, that is, bijective functions from the set to itself, form a group, with operation being *composition* (as functions) of permutations. The do-nothing permutation (the function which sends every element to itself) is the identity. The associativity follows because permutations are *functions*. If there are more than two things in the set, these permutations groups are certainly non-abelian.

8.2 Subgroups

Subgroups are subsets of groups which are groups 'in their own right'.

A subset H of a group G is said to be a **subgroup** if, with the same operation as that used in G, it is a group.

That is, if H contains the identity element $e \in G$, if H contains inverses of all elements in it, and if H contains products of any two elements in it, then H is a subgroup. (The associativity of the operation is assured since the operation was *assumed* associative for G itself to be a group.)

Another paraphrase: if $e \in H$, and if for all $h \in H$ the inverse h^{-1} is also in H, and if for all $h_1, h_2 \in H$ the product $h_1 h_2$ is again in H, then H is a subgroup of G.

Another cute paraphrase is: if $e \in H$, and if for all $h_1, h_2 \in H$ the product $h_1 h_2^{-1}$ is again in H, then H is a subgroup of G. (If we take $h_1 = e$, then the latter condition assures the existence of inverses! And so on.)

In any case, one usually says that H is **closed under inverses** and **closed under the group operation**. (These two conditions are independent of each other.)

For example, the collection of all *even* integers is a subgroup of the additive group of integers. More generally, for fixed integer m, the collection H of all multiples of m is a subgroup of the additive group of integers. To check this: first, the identity 0 is a multiple of m, so $0 \in H$. And for any two integers x, y divisible by m, write $x = ma$ and $y = mb$ for some integers a, b. Then using the 'cute' paraphrase, we see that

$$x - y = ma - mb = m(a - b) \in H$$

so H is *closed under inverses and under the group operation*. Thus, it is a subgroup of $\mathbf{Z}$.

8.3 Lagrange's Theorem

The theorem of this section is the simplest example of the use of group theory as *structured counting*. Although the discussion of this section is completely abstract, it gives the easiest route to (the very tangible) Euler's theorem proven as a corollary below.

A **finite group** is simply a group which is also finite. The **order** of a finite group is the number of elements in it. Sometimes the order of a group G is written as $|G|$. Throughout this section we will write the group operation simply as though it were ordinary multiplication.

Theorem: *(Lagrange)* Let G be a *finite* group. Let H be a subgroup of G. Then the order of H *divides* the order of G.

For the proof we need some other ideas which themselves will be reused later. For subgroup H of a group G, and for $g \in G$, the **left coset** of H by g or **left translate** of H by g is

$$gH = \{gh : h \in H\}$$

The notation gH is simply shorthand for the right-hand side. Likewise, the **right coset** of H by g or **right translate** of H by g is

$$Hg = \{hg : h \in H\}$$

Proof: First, we will prove that the collection of all left cosets of H is a *partition* of G, meaning that every element of G lies in *some* left coset of H, and if two left cosets xH and yH have non-empty intersection then actually $xH = yH$. (Note that this need not imply $x = y$.)

Certainly $x = x \cdot e \in xH$, so every element of G lies in a left coset of H.

Now suppose that $xH \cap yH \neq \phi$ for $x, y \in G$. Then for some $h_1, h_2 \in H$ we have $xh_1 = yh_2$. Multiply both sides of this equality on the right by h_2^{-1} to obtain

$$(xh_1)h_2^{-1} = (yh_2)h_2^{-1}$$

The right-hand side of this is

$$
\begin{aligned}
(yh_2)h_2^{-1} &= y(h_2 h_2^{-1}) \quad \text{(by associativity)} \\
&= y \cdot e \quad \text{(by property of inverse)} \\
&= y \quad \text{(by property of } e)
\end{aligned}
$$

Let $z = h_1 h_2^{-1}$ for brevity. By associativity in G,

$$y = (xh_1)h_2^{-1} = x(h_1 h_2^{-1}) = xz$$

Since H is a *subgroup*, $z \in H$.

Then

$$yH = \{yh : h \in H\} = \{(xz)h : h \in H\} = \{x(zh) : h \in H\}$$

On one hand, since H is closed under multiplication, for each $h \in H$ the product zh is in H. Therefore,

$$yH = \{x(zh) : h \in H\} \subset \{xh' : h' \in H\} = xH$$

Thus, $yH \subset xH$. But the relationship between x and y is completely symmetrical, so also $xH \subset yH$. Therefore $xH = yH$. (In other words, we have shown that the left cosets of H in G really do *partition* G.)

Next, we will show that the cardinalities of the left cosets of H are *all the same*. To do this, we show that there is a *bijection* from H to xH for any $x \in G$. In particular, define

$$f(g) = xg$$

(It is clear that this really does map H to yH.) Second, we prove *injectivity*: if $f(g) = f(g')$, then

$$xg = xg'$$

Left multiplying by x^{-1} gives

$$x^{-1}(xg) = x^{-1}(xg')$$

Using associativity gives

$$(x^{-1}x)g = (x^{-1}x)g'$$

Using the property $x^{-1}x = e$ of the inverse x^{-1} gives

$$eg = eg'$$

Since $eg = g$ and $eg' = g'$, by the defining property of the identity e, this is

$$g = g'$$

which is the desired injectivity. For *surjectivity*, we simply note that by its very definition the function f was arranged so that

$$f(h) = xh$$

Thus, any element in xH is of the form $f(h)$ for an element h of H. Thus, we have that f is bijective, and all left cosets of H have the same number of elements as does H itself.

150

So G is the union of all the different left cosets of H (no two of which overlap). Let i be the number of different cosets of H. We just showed that every left coset of H has $|H|$ elements. Then we can count the number of elements in G as

$$|G| = \text{sum of cardinalities of cosets} = i \times |H|$$

Both sides of this equation are integers, so $|H|$ divides $|G|$, as claimed.   ///

8.4 Index of a subgroup

Having introduced the idea of a *coset* in the proof of Lagrange's theorem, we can now define the *index* of a subgroup.

Let G be a group, and H a subgroup of G. The **index** of H in G, denoted

$$[G : H]$$

is the number of (left) cosets of H in G.

Corollary: *(of Lagrange's theorem)* For a finite group G and subgroup H,

$$|G| = [G : H] \cdot |H|$$

Proof: This is just a recapitulation of the counting done in proving Lagrange's theorem: we show that G is the disjoint union of the left cosets of H, and that each such coset has $|H|$ elements. Thus, the statement of this corollary is an assertion that counting the elements in G in two ways gives the same result.   ///

A closely related counting or divisibility principle is the following **multiplicative property** of indices of subgroups:

Corollary: Let G be a finite group, let H, I be subgroups of G, and suppose that $H \supset I$. Then

$$[G : I] = [G : H] \cdot [H : I]$$

Proof: We repeatedly use the previous corollary of Lagrange's theorem, and the fact that I is a subgroup of H as well as a subgroup of G. Thus, on one hand

$$|G| = [G : H] \cdot |H| = [G : H] \cdot ([H : I] \cdot |I|)$$

On the other hand

$$|G| = [G : I] \cdot |I|$$

Thus, equating these two expressions for $|G|$ gives

$$[G : I] \cdot |I| = [G : H] \cdot ([H : I] \cdot |I|)$$

Canceling the order of I gives the asserted result.   ///

8.5 Laws of exponents

It should be emphasized that the so-called *Laws of Exponents* are not 'laws' at all, but are *provable properties* of the exponential notation. And the exponential notation itself is basically nothing more than an abbreviation for repeated multiplication.

First, we prove something that one might have taken for granted all along, namely that there is just *one* inverse of a given element in a group. The following proposition actually proves slightly more.

Proposition: Let G be a group with identity e. Let $g \in G$. If x, y are elements of G such that

$$xg = e = gy$$

then $x = y$.

Proof: This is yet another direct if peculiar calculation.

$$x = xe = x(gy) = (xg)y = ey = y$$

as desired.   ///

Of course, we must be sure to be explicit about the *exponential notation* g^n for integer n, where g is an element of a group G. This is, after all, merely an abbreviation: first,

$$g^0 = e$$

and

$$g^n = \underbrace{g \cdot g \cdot \ldots \cdot g}_{n} \quad \text{(for } n \geq 0\text{)}$$

$$g^n = \underbrace{g^{-1} \cdot g^{-1} \cdot \ldots \cdot g^{-1}}_{|n|} \quad \text{(for } n \leq 0\text{)}$$

A more precise though perhaps less intuitive way of defining g^n is by **recursive definitions**:

$$g^n = \begin{cases} e & \text{for } n = 0 \\ g \cdot g^{n-1} & \text{for } n > 0 \\ g^{-1} \cdot g^{n+1} & \text{for } n < 0 \end{cases}$$

These are the definitions that lend themselves both to computation and to proving things.

While we're here, maybe we should check that the so-called *Laws of Exponents* really do hold:

Proposition: *(Laws of Exponents)* For g in a group G, for integers m, n
- $g^{m+n} = g^m \cdot g^n$
- $g^{mn} = (g^m)^n$

Proof: The least obvious thing to prove is that

$$\left(g^{-1}\right)^{-1} = g$$

Note that we absolutely cannot simply pretend to invoke 'laws of exponents' to prove this! Instead, to prove this, we must realize that the way that one checks that y is an inverse of x is to compute xy and yx and see that they are both just e. So to prove that x is the inverse of x^{-1}, we must compute both $x^{-1}x$ and xx^{-1}. By the property of x^{-1} these both are e, so by the definition of $(x^{-1})^{-1}$ we have $(x^{-1})^{-1} = x$.

The rest of the proof is an exercise in *induction* and is a bit tedious. And nothing really exciting happens.

Let's prove that

$$g^{m+n} = g^m \cdot g^n$$

for m and n non-negative integers. We prove this by induction on n. For $n = 0$ the assertion is true, since

$$g^{m+0} = g^m = g^m \cdot e = g^m \cdot g^0$$

Then for $n > 0$,

$$g^{m+n} = g^{(m+n-1)+1} = g^{m+n-1} \cdot g$$

by the recursive definition of g^{m+n}. By induction,

$$g^{m+n-1} = g^m \cdot g^{n-1}$$

Therefore,

$$g^{m+n-1} \cdot g = (g^m \cdot g^{n-1}) \cdot g = g^m \cdot ((g^{n-1}) \cdot g)$$

by associativity. Now from the recursive definition of g^n we obtain

$$g^m \cdot ((g^{n-1}) \cdot g) = g^m \cdot g^n$$

This proves the 'Law' for $m, n \geq 0$.   ///

Remark: If we are more tolerant of (potentially dangerously ambiguous) notation, we can give more intuitive near-proofs of these facts. For example,

$$g^m \cdot g^n = \underbrace{g \ldots g}_{m} \cdot \underbrace{g \ldots g}_{n} = \underbrace{g \ldots g}_{m+n} = g^{m+n}$$

and

$$(g^m)^n = \underbrace{g^m \ldots g^m}_{n} = \underbrace{\underbrace{g \ldots g}_{m} \ldots \underbrace{g \ldots g}_{m}}_{n} = \underbrace{g \ldots g}_{mn} = g^{mn}$$

apparently by simply regrouping. These symbolic manipulations certainly capture our intent and what we anticipate being true. The reason to have an objection to this admittedly appealing argument is that the use of the ellipses '...' in this fashion can lend itself to misuse by accidental misinterpretation or multiple interpretations of the ellipses. One way to legitimize the idea of this argument is by rewriting it as an induction, clunky though this may seem. Indeed, on occasion, insistence on a bit of extra care avoids pitfalls.

Remark: Note that in general it is *not* true that $(ab)^n = a^n b^n$, unless the group is *abelian*.

8.6 Cyclic subgroups, orders, exponents

For an element g of a group G, let

$$\langle g \rangle = \{g^n : n \in \mathbf{Z}\}$$

This is called the **cyclic subgroup of G generated by** g.
  The smallest positive integer n (if it exists!) so that

$$g^n = e$$

is the **order** or **exponent** of g. The order of a group element g is often denoted by $|g|$. Yes, we are reusing the terminology 'order', but it will turn out that these uses are compatible (just below).

Corollary: *(of Laws of Exponents)* For g in a group G, the sub*set* $\langle g \rangle$ of G really is a sub*group* of G.

Proof: The associativity is *inherited* from G. The *closure* under the group operation and the closure under taking inverses both follow immediately from the Laws of Exponents, as follows. First, the inverse of g^n is just g^{-n}, since

$$g^n \cdot g^{-n} = g^{n+(-n)} = g^0 = e$$

And closure under multiplication is

$$g^m \cdot g^n = g^{m+n}$$

$$/\!/\!/$$

Theorem: Let g be an element of a finite group G. Let n be the order of g. Then the order of g (as group *element*) is equal to the order of $\langle g \rangle$ (as subgroup). Specifically,

$$\langle g \rangle = \{g^0, g^1, g^2, \ldots, g^{n-1}\}$$

Generally, for arbitrary integers i, j,

$$g^i = g^j \quad \text{if and only if} \quad i \equiv j \bmod n$$

Proof: The last assertion easily implies the first two, so we'll just prove the last assertion. On one hand, if $i \equiv j \bmod n$, then write $i = j + \ell n$ and compute (using Laws of Exponents):

$$g^i = g^{j+\ell n} = g^j \cdot (g^n)^\ell = g^j \cdot e^\ell = g^j \cdot e = g^j$$

On the other hand, suppose that $g^i = g^j$. Without loss of generality, exchanging the roles of i and j if necessary, we may suppose that $i \leq j$. Then $g^i = g^j$ implies $e = g^{j-i}$. Using the Reduction/Division algorithm, write

$$j - i = q \cdot n + r$$

where $0 \leq r < n$. Then

$$e = g^{j-i} = g^{qn+r} = (g^n)^q \cdot g^r = e^q \cdot g^r = e \cdot g^r = g^r$$

Therefore, since n is the least positive integer so that $g^n = e$, it must be that $r = 0$. That is, $n | j - i$, which is to say that $i \equiv j \bmod n$ as claimed.   ///

Corollary: *(of Lagrange's theorem)* The order $|g|$ of an element g of a finite group G divides the order of G.

Proof: We just proved that $|g| = |\langle g \rangle|$. By Lagrange's theorem, $|\langle g \rangle|$ divides $|G|$, which yields this corollary.   ///

8.7 Euler's Theorem

Now we return to number theory, and give a clean and conceptual proof of Euler's identity, as a corollary of Lagrange's theorem and the discussion of Laws of Exponents and cyclic subgroups. Further, we can give a slightly refined form of it.

Let $\varphi(n)$ be Euler's phi-function, counting the number of integers ℓ in the range $0 < \ell \leq n$ that are relatively prime to n. The proof we give of this is simply the abstracted version of Euler's original argument.

Theorem: Let n be a positive integer. For $x \in \mathbf{Z}$ relatively prime to n,

$$x^{\varphi(n)} \equiv 1 \bmod n$$

Proof: The set $\mathbf{Z}/n^{\times}$ of integers-mod-n which are relatively prime to n has $\varphi(n)$ elements. By Lagrange's theorem and its corollaries just above, this implies that the order k of $g \in \mathbf{Z}/n^{\times}$ divides $\varphi(n)$. Therefore, $\varphi(n)/k$ is an integer, and

$$g^{\varphi(n)} = (g^k)^{\varphi(n)/k} = e^{\varphi(n)/k} = e$$

Applied to x-mod-n this is the desired result.   ///

Remark: This approach also gives another proof of Fermat's theorem, dealing with the case where n is prime, without mention of binomial coefficients.

Further, keeping track of what went into the proof of Euler's theorem in the first place, we have

Theorem: Let n be a positive integer. For $x \in \mathbf{Z}$ relatively prime to n, the smallest exponent ℓ so that

$$x^{\ell} \equiv 1 \bmod n$$

is a divisor of $\varphi(n)$. That is, the order of x in the multiplicative group $\mathbf{Z}/n^\times$ is a divisor of $\varphi(n)$.

Proof: The proof is really the same: the order x is equal to the order of the subgroup $\langle x \rangle$, which by Lagrange's theorem is a divisor of the order of the whole group $\mathbf{Z}/n^\times$.   ///

8.8   Exponents of groups

The idea of Euler's theorem can be made more precise and abstracted.

For a group G, the smallest positive integer ℓ so that for every $g \in G$

$$g^\ell = e$$

is the **exponent** of the group G. It is not clear from the definition that there really is such a positive integer ℓ. Indeed, for *infinite* groups G there may not be. But for *finite* groups the mere finiteness allows us to characterize the exponent:

Proposition: Let G be a finite group. Then the exponent of G exists, and in particular

$$\text{exponent of } G = \text{ least common multiple of } |g| \text{ for } g \in G$$

Proof: If $g^k = e$, then we know from discussion of cyclic subgroups above that $|g|$ divides k. And, on the other hand, if $k = m \cdot |g|$ then

$$g^k = g^{m \cdot |g|} = (g^{|g|})^m = e^m = e$$

Since G is finite, every element g of it is of finite order. Indeed, the list $g^1, g^2, \ldots,$ can contain at most $|G|$ distinct elements, so for some $i < j$ it must be that $g^i = g^j$. Then $g^{j-i} = e$, and we conclude that the order of g is at most $j - i$. And, since there are only finitely-many elements in G, the least common multiple M of their orders exists. From what we've just seen, surely $g^M = e$ for any g. Thus, G does have an exponent. And if $g^k = e$ for all $g \in G$ then k is divisible by the orders of all elements of G, so is divisible by their least common multiple. Thus, the exponent of G really is the least common multiple of the orders of its elements.   ///

Remark: The principle that a choice of N things from among n (with replacement) must result in duplication when $n < N$ is the *Pigeon-Hole Principle*.

And Lagrange's theorem gives a limitation on what we can expect the exponent to be:

Corollary: *(of Lagrange's theorem)* Let G be a finite group. Then the exponent of G divides the order $|G|$ of G.

Proof: From the proposition, the exponent is the least common multiple of the orders of the elements of G. From Lagrange's theorem, each such order is a divisor of $|G|$. The least common multiple of any collection of divisors of a fixed number is certainly a divisor of that number.   ///

8.9 Group homomorphisms

Group homomorphisms are the important maps between groups. They preserve the relevant structures of the group operations.

A *function* (or *map*)

$$f : G \to H$$

from one group G to another one H is a **group homomorphism** if

$$f(g_1 g_2) = f(g_1)\, f(g_2)$$

for all $g_1, g_2 \in G$. Let e_G be the identity in G and e_H the identity in H. The **kernel** of such a group homomorphism f is

$$\text{kernel of } f \ = \ker f = \{g \in G : f(g) = e_H\}$$

The **image** of f is just like the image of any function:

$$\text{image of } f \ = \operatorname{im} f = \{h \in H : \text{ there is } g \in G \text{ so that } f(g) = h\}$$

Let $f : G \to H$ be a group homomorphism. Let e_G be the identity in G and let e_H be the identity in H.

- Necessarily f carries the identity of G to the identity of H: $f(e_G) = e_H$.
- For $g \in G$, $f(g^{-1}) = f(g)^{-1}$.
- The *kernel* of f is a subgroup of G.
- The *image* of f is a subgroup of H.
- A group homomorphism $f : G \to H$ is *injective* if and only if the kernel is *trivial* (that is, is the trivial subgroup $\{e_G\}$).

Proof: The image $f(e_G)$ under f of the identity e_G in G has the property

$$f(e_G) = f(e_G \cdot e_G) = f(e_G) \cdot f(e_G)$$

using the property of the identity in G and the group homomorphism property. Left multiplying by $f(e_G)^{-1}$ (whatever this may be!), we get

$$f(e_G)^{-1} \cdot f(e_G) = f(e_G)^{-1} \cdot (f(e_G) \cdot f(e_G))$$

Simplifying and rearranging a bit, this is

$$e_H = (f(e_G)^{-1} \cdot f(e_G)) \cdot f(e_G) = e_H \cdot f(e_G) = f(e_G)$$

This proves that the identity in G is mapped to the identity in H.

To check that the image of an inverse is the image of an inverse, we simply compute

$$f(g^{-1}) \cdot f(g) = f(g^{-1} \cdot g)$$

by the homomorphism property, and this is

$$= f(e_G) = e_H$$

by the inverse property and by the fact just proven) that the identity in G is mapped to the identity in H by a group homomorphism. Likewise, we also compute that

$$f(g) \cdot f(g^{-1}) = e_H$$

so the image of an inverse is the inverse of the image, as claimed.

To prove that the kernel of a group homomorphism $f : G \to H$ is a subgroup of G, we must prove three things. First, we must check that the identity lies in the kernel: this follows immediately from the fact just proven that $f(e_G) = e_H$. Next, we must show that if g is in the kernel, then g^{-1} is also. Happily (by luck?) we just showed that $f(g^{-1}) = f(g)^{-1}$, so indeed if $f(g) = e_H$ then

$$f(g^{-1}) = f(g)^{-1} = e_H^{-1} = e_H$$

Finally, suppose both x, y are in the kernel of f. Then

$$f(xy) = f(x) \cdot f(y) = e_H \cdot e_H = e_H$$

so the 'product' is also in the kernel.

Now let X be a subgroup of G. Let

$$f(X) = \{f(x) : x \in X\}$$

To show that $f(X)$ is a subgroup of H, we must check the usual three things: presence of the identity, closure under taking inverses, and closure under products. Again, we just showed that $f(e_G) = e_H$, so the image of a subgroup contains the identity. Also, we showed that $f(g)^{-1}) = f(g^{-1})$, so the image of a subgroup is closed under inverses. And $f(xy) = f(x)f(y)$ by the defining property of a group homomorphism, so the image is closed under multiplication.

Finally, let's prove that a homomorphism $f : G \to H$ is injective if and only if its kernel is trivial. First, if f is injective, then at most one element can be mapped to $e_H \in H$. Since we know that at least e_G is mapped to e_H by such a homomorphism, it must be that *only* e_G is mapped to e_H. Thus, the kernel is trivial.

On the other hand, suppose that the kernel is trivial. We will suppose that $f(x) = f(y)$, and show that $x = y$. Left multiply the equality $f(x) = f(y)$ by $f(x)^{-1}$ to obtain

$$e_H = f(x)^{-1} \cdot f(x) = f(x)^{-1} \cdot f(y)$$

By the homomorphism property, this gives

$$e_H = f(x)^{-1} \cdot f(y) = f(x^{-1}y)$$

Thus, $x^{-1}y$ is in the kernel of f, so (by assumption) $x^{-1}y = e_G$. Left multiplying this equality by x and simplifying, we get $y = x$. This proves the injectivity.   ///

If a group homomorphism $f : G \to H$ is *surjective*, then H is said to be a **homomorphic image** of G. If a group homomorphism $f : G \to H$ is a *bijection*, then f is said to be an **isomorphism**, and G and H are said to be **isomorphic**.

Remark: At least from a theoretical viewpoint, two groups that are *isomorphic* are considered to be 'the same', in the sense that any *intrinsic* group-theoretic assertion about one is also true of the other. In practical terms, however, the *transfer of structure* via the isomorphism may be difficult to *compute*. That is, knowing that two groups are isomorphic is one thing, and knowing the isomorphism explicitly may be two quite different things.

8.10 Finite cyclic groups

A finite group G is **cyclic** if there is $g \in G$ so that $\langle g \rangle = G$. And such a g is a **generator** of G, and G is said to be **generated by** g. (The case of *infinite* cyclic groups will be considered in the next section.)

Finite cyclic groups are the simplest of all groups. First, note that a finite cyclic group is necessarily *abelian*, since by properties of exponents for any two integers a, b

$$g^a \cdot g^b = g^{a+b} = g^{b+a} = g^b \cdot g^a$$

Somewhat more refined features of finite cyclic groups can be readily understood as follows.

Let $N = |G|$. Since $G = \langle g \rangle$, also $N = |g|$. It is important to remember that (as proven a bit earlier)

- The elements $e = g^0, g^1, g^2, \ldots, g^{N-2}, g^{N-1}$ form a complete list of the *distinct* elements of $G = \langle g \rangle$.
- With arbitrary integers i, j, we have $g^i = g^j$ if and only if $i \equiv j \bmod N$.
- Given an integer j, let i be the *reduction of j* mod N. Then $g^j = g^i$.

Then the collections of all *subgroups* and of all *generators* can be completely understood in terms of elementary arithmetic:

- The *distinct* subgroups of G are exactly the subgroups $\langle g^d \rangle$ for all *divisors d* of N.
- For $d|N$ the order of the subgroup $\langle g^d \rangle$ is the order of g^d, which is just N/d.
- The order of g^k with arbitrary integer $k \neq 0$ is $N/\gcd(k, N)$.
- For any integer n we have

$$\langle g^n \rangle = \langle g^{\gcd(n,N)} \rangle$$

- The distinct generators of G are the elements g^r where $1 \leq r < N$ and $\gcd(r, N) = 1$. Thus, there are $\varphi(N)$ of them, where φ is Euler's phi function.
- The number of elements of order n in a finite cyclic group of order N is 0 unless $n|N$, in which case it is N/n.

Remark: Some aspects of this can be paraphrased nicely in words: for example, *Every subgroup of a finite cyclic group is again a finite cyclic group, with order dividing the order of the group. Conversely, for every divisor of the order of the group, there is a* **unique** *subgroup of that order.*

Proof: Let's prove that that the order of g^k is $N/\gcd(k, N)$. First, if $(g^k)^\ell = e = g^0$, then $k\ell \equiv 0 \bmod N$, from the simpler facts recalled above. That is, $N | k\ell$. That is, there is an integer m so that $k\ell = mN$. Then divide both sides of this equality by $\gcd(k, N)$, obtaining

$$\frac{k}{\gcd(k, N)} \cdot \ell = m \cdot \frac{N}{\gcd(k, N)}$$

Since now $N/\gcd(k, N)$ and $k/\gcd(k, N)$ are relatively prime, by unique factorization we conclude that

$$\frac{N}{\gcd(k, N)} \mid \ell$$

Therefore, the actual order of g^k is a multiple of $N/\gcd(k, N)$. On the other hand,

$$(g^k)^{N/\gcd(k,N)} = (g^N)^{k/\gcd(k,N)} = e^{k/\gcd(k,N)} = e$$

Note that we use the fact that $N/\gcd(k, N)$ and $k/\gcd(k, N)$ are both integers, so that all the expressions here have genuine content and sense. This finishes the proof that the order of g^k is $N/\gcd(k, N)$.

As a special case of the preceding, if $k|N$ then the order of g^k is $N/\gcd(k, N) = N/k$, as claimed above.

Since we know by now that $|\langle h \rangle| = |h|$ for any h, certainly

$$|\langle g^k \rangle| = |g^k| = N/\gcd(k, N)$$

Given integer k, let's show that

$$\langle g^k \rangle = \langle g^{\gcd(k,N)} \rangle$$

Let $d = \gcd(k, N)$, and let s, t be integers so that

$$d = sk + tN$$

Then
$$g^d = g^{sk+tN} = (g^k)^s \cdot (g^N)^t = (g^k)^s \cdot (e)^t = (g^k)^s \cdot e = (g^k)^s$$

so $g^d \in \langle g^k \rangle$. On the other hand,

$$g^k = (g^d)^{k/d}$$

since $d|k$. Thus, $g^k \in \langle g^d \rangle$. Therefore, since the subgroups $\langle g^k \rangle$ and $\langle g^d \rangle$ are closed under multiplication and under inverses, for any integer ℓ

$$(g^k)^\ell \in \langle g^d \rangle$$

and

$$(g^d)^\ell \in \langle g^k \rangle$$

But $\langle g^d \rangle$ *is* just the set of all integer powers of g^d (and similarly for g^k), so we have shown that

$$\langle g^d \rangle \subset \langle g^k \rangle$$

and *vice versa*, so we find at last that

$$\langle g^d \rangle = \langle g^k \rangle$$

Therefore, all the *cyclic* subgroups of $\langle g \rangle = G$ are of the form $\langle g^d \rangle$ for some positive d dividing $N = |G| = |g|$. And different divisors d give different subgroups. This proves the uniqueness.

Let H be an *arbitrary* subgroup of G. We must show that H is generated by some g^k (so is in fact cyclic). Let k be the smallest positive integer so that $g^k \in H$. We claim that $\langle g^k \rangle = H$. For any other $g^m \in H$, we can write

$$m = q \cdot k + r$$

with $0 \le r < k$. Then

$$g^r = g^{m - q \cdot k} = g^m \cdot (g^k)^q \in H$$

since H is a subgroup. Since k was the smallest positive integer so that $g^k \in H$, and $0 \le r < k$, it must be that $r = 0$. Therefore, m is a multiple of k, and g^k generates H.

As another particular case, notice that $\langle g^k \rangle = \langle g \rangle$ if and only if $\gcd(k, N) = 1$. And we may as well only consider $0 < k < N$, since otherwise we start repeating elements. That is, the distinct generators of $\langle g \rangle$ are the elements g^k with $0 < k < N$ and $\gcd(k, N) = 1$. So there certainly are $\varphi(N)$ of them.

Likewise, since

$$|g^k| = |\langle g^k \rangle| = |\langle g^{\gcd(k,N)} \rangle| = |g^{\gcd(k,N)}|$$

it is not hard to count the number of elements of a given order in $\langle g \rangle$.   ///

- *A homomorphic image of a finite cyclic group is finite cyclic.*

Proof: This follows by checking that the image of a generator is a generator for the image.   ////

- *A finite cyclic group of order N is isomorphic to $\mathbf{Z}/N$ with addition.* Specifically, for any choice of generator g of the cyclic group G, the map

$$f : n \to g^n$$

describes an isomorphism $f : \mathbf{Z}/N \to G$.

Proof: This is just a paraphrase of some of the other properties above.

A possibly disturbing issue here is that of proving that the map f as described above is **well-defined**. That is, we have some sort of formula which *appears* to describe a map, but there are hidden pitfalls. What we must show is that if $m = n \bmod N$ then $f(m) = f(n)$. (This has *nothing* to do with injectivity!) Well, it turns out that everything is ok, because we've already shown (in discussion of cyclic subgroups) that $g^m = g^n$ if and only if $m = n \bmod N$.

For emphasis, we'll write the group operation in the cyclic group G as $*$ rather than as multiplication or addition. The crucial property which must be demonstrated is the homomorphism property

$$f(m + n) = f(m) * f(n)$$

Indeed,

$$f(m + n) = f((m + n)\%N) = g^{m+n\%N} = g^{m+n}$$

since we proved (in the discussion of cyclic subgroups) that $g^i = g^j$ whenever $i = j \bmod N$. And then this is

$$= f(g^m) * f(g^n)$$

as desired.

To see that f is injective, suppose that $f(m) = f(n)$ for integers m, n. Then $g^m = g^n$. Again, this implies that $m = n \bmod N$, which says that $m(\bmod N) = n(\bmod N)$, as desired. So f is injective.

The surjectivity is easy: given $g^n \in \langle g \rangle$, $f(n) = g^n$.

Therefore, the map f is a bijective homomorphism, so by definition is an isomorphism.   ///

8.11   Roots, powers

In a cyclic group $G = \langle g \rangle$ of order n it is possible to reach very clear conclusions about the solvability of the equation $x^r = y$.

Let G be a cyclic group of order n with generator g. Fix an integer r, and define

$$f : G \to G$$

by

$$f(x) = x^r$$

Theorem: This map f is a group homomorphism of G to itself. If $\gcd(r, n) = 1$, then f is an *isomorphism*. That is, if $\gcd(r, n) = 1$, then every $y \in G$ has an rth root and has *exactly* one such root. Generally,

$$\text{order of kernel of } f = \gcd(r, n)$$

$$\text{order of image of } f = n/\gcd(r, n)$$

If an element y has an rth root, then it has exactly $\gcd(r, n)$ of them. There are exactly $n/\gcd(r, n)$ r^{th} powers in G.

Proof: Certainly

$$f(x \cdot y) = (xy)^r = x^r\, y^r \text{ (since } G \text{ is abelian)}$$

$$= f(x) \cdot f(y)$$

which shows that f is a homomorphism.

We may as well use the fact that G is isomorphic to $\mathbf{Z}/n$ with addition (proven just above.) This allows us to directly use things we know about $\mathbf{Z}/n$ and the relatively simple behavior of addition mod n to prove things about arbitrary finite cyclic groups. Thus, converting to the additive notation appropriate for $\mathbf{Z}/n$-with-addition, the map f is

$$f(x) = r \cdot x$$

We already know that if $\gcd(r, n) = 1$ then there is a multiplicative inverse r^{-1} to $r \bmod n$. Thus, the function

$$g(x) = r^{-1} \cdot x$$

gives an inverse function to f. This proves that f is both surjective and injective, so is a bijection, and thus an isomorphism.

For arbitrary r, let's look at the solvability of

$$r \cdot x = y \bmod n$$

for given y. Rewritten in more elementary terms, this is

$$n | (rx - y)$$

or, for some integer m,

$$mn = rx - y$$

Let $d = \gcd(r, n)$. Then certainly it is *necessary* that $d|y$ or this equation is impossible. On the other hand, suppose that $d|y$. Write $y = dy'$ with some integer y'. Then we want to solve

$$r \cdot x = dy' \bmod n$$

Dividing through by the common divisor d, this congruence is equivalent to

$$\frac{r}{d} \cdot x = y' \bmod \frac{n}{d}$$

The removal of the common divisor has made r/d relatively prime to n/d, so there is a multiplicative inverse $(r/d)^{-1}$ to $r/d \bmod n/d$, and

$$x = (r/d)^{-1} \cdot y' \bmod (n/d)$$

That is, any integer x meeting this condition is a solution to the original congruence. Letting x_0 be one such solution, the integers

$$x_0, \ x_0 + \frac{n}{d}, \ x_0 + 2 \cdot \frac{n}{d}, \ x_0 + 3 \cdot \frac{n}{d}, \ \ldots x_0 + (d-1) \cdot \frac{n}{d}$$

are also solutions, and are distinct mod n. That is, we have d distinct solutions mod n.

The necessary and sufficient condition $\gcd(r,n)|y$ for the equation $rx = y \bmod n$ to have a solution shows that there are exactly $n/\gcd(r,n)$ integers $y \bmod n$ which fulfill this condition. That is, there are exactly $n/\gcd(r,n)$ 'r^{th} powers'.

The kernel of f is the collection of x so that $rx = 0 \bmod n$. Taking out the common denominator $d = \gcd(r,n)$, this is $(r/d)x = 0 \bmod n/d$, which means $(n/d)|(r/d)x$. Since now r/d and n/d have no common factor, by unique factorization this implies that n/d divides x. Thus, mod n, there are d different solutions x. That is, the kernel of f has d elements. ///

Exercises

8.01 Prove that in any group G for any elements $h, x, y \in G$ we have $h(xy)h^{-1} = (hxh^{-1})(hyh^{-1})$. (*ans.*)

8.02 Prove (by induction) that in any group G for any elements $g, h \in G$ and for any integer n

$$hg^n h^{-1} = (hgh^{-1})^n$$

8.03 Make an addition table for $\mathbf{Z}/4$ and a multiplication table for $\mathbf{Z}/5^\times$.

8.04 Why isn't $\{1, 2, 3, 4, 5\}$ with operation *multiplication modulo* 6 a group? (*ans.*)

8.05 Prove by induction that in an *abelian* group G we have

$$(gh)^n = g^n h^n$$

for all $g, h \in G$, and for all positive integers n.

8.06 Show that

$$(gh)^2 = g^2 h^2$$

in a group if and only if $gh = hg$.

8.07 Prove that $(gh)^{-1} = h^{-1} g^{-1}$.

8.08 Prove that $(gh)^{-1} = g^{-1} h^{-1}$ if and only if $gh = hg$.

8.09 Prove that the intersection $H \cap K$ of two subgroups H, K of a group G is again a subgroup of G.

8.10 Show that in an *abelian* group G, for a fixed positive integer n the set X_n of elements g of G so that $g^n = e$ is a subgroup of G.

8.11 Find all 5 of the distinct subgroups of the group $\mathbf{Z}/16$ (with addition). (List each subgroup only once.) (*ans.*)

8.12 Find all 6 of the distinct subgroups of the group $\mathbf{Z}/12$ (with addition). (List each subgroup only once.)

8.13 There are 8 subgroups of the group $\mathbf{Z}/30^\times$. Find them all. (*ans.*)

8.14 Find all subgroups of the group $\mathbf{Z}/105^\times$. Find them all.

8.15 Check that the collection of matrices g in $GL(2, \mathbf{Q})$ of the form $g = \begin{pmatrix} a & 0 \\ 0 & d \end{pmatrix}$ (that is, with lower left and upper right entries 0) is a *subgroup* of $GL(2, \mathbf{Q})$.

8.16 Check that the collection of matrices g in $GL(2, \mathbf{Q})$ of the form $g = \begin{pmatrix} a & b \\ 0 & d \end{pmatrix}$ (that is, with lower left entry 0) is a *subgroup* of $GL(2, \mathbf{Q})$.

8.17 *(Casting out nines)* Show that

$$123456789123456789 + 234567891234567891$$

$$\neq 358025680358025680$$

(*Hint:* Look at things modulo 9: if two things are not equal mod 9 then they certainly aren't equal. And notice the funny general fact that, for example,

$$1345823416 \equiv 1 + 3 + 4 + 5 + 8 + 2 + 3 + 4 + 1 + 6 \bmod 9$$

since $10 \equiv 1 \bmod 9$, and $100 \equiv 1 \bmod 9$, and so on. The assertion is that a decimal number is congruent to the sum of its digits modulo 9! This is *casting out nines*, which allows detection of some errors in arithmetic).

8.18 By casting out nines, show that

$$123456789123456789 \times 234567891234567891$$

$$\neq 28958998683279996179682996625361999$$

Certainly in *this* case it's not easy to check *directly* by hand, and probably most calculators would overflow.

8.19 Prove that a group element and its inverse have the same order.

8.20 Without computing, show that in the group $\mathbf{Z}/100$ (with addition) the elements $1, 99$ have the same order, as do 11 and 89.   (*ans.*)

8.21 Find the orders of the following elements g, h of $GL(2, \mathbf{R})$:

$$g = \begin{pmatrix} 0 & -1 \\ 1 & 0 \end{pmatrix} \qquad h = \begin{pmatrix} 0 & 1 \\ -1 & -1 \end{pmatrix}$$

Compute the product gh, compute $(gh)^n$ for integers n, and then show that gh is necessarily of *infinite order* in the group.   (*ans.*)

8.22 Let G be a finite group. Let N be the *least common multiple* of the orders of the elements of G. Show that for all $g \in G$ we have $g^n = e$.

8.23 (*) Let G be an *abelian* group. Let m, n be relatively prime positive integers. Let g be an element of order m and let h be an element of order n. Show that $|gh| = mn$. More generally, show that without any relative primeness hypothesis on the orders of g, h show that $|gh|$ is the *least common multiple* of $|g|, |h|$.

8.24 Let x be an element of a group G and suppose that $x^{3 \cdot 5} = e$ and $x^3 \neq e$. Show that the order of x is either 5 or 15.

8.25 Show that any integer i so that $1 \leq i < 11$ is a generator for the additive group $\mathbf{Z}/11$ of integers modulo 11.

8.26 Check that $\mathbf{Z}/8^\times$ cannot be generated by a single element.   (*ans.*)

8.27 Prove that if an element g of a group G has order n and if d is a divisor of n then $g^{n/d}$ has order d. (Equivalently, g^d has order n/d.)

8.28 What is the kernel of the homomorphism

$$x \to x \bmod N$$

from $\mathbf{Z}$ (with addition) to $\mathbf{Z}/N$ (with addition modulo N)? (*Hint:* This may be easier than you think!)

8.29 Let M, N be positive integers, and suppose that $N|M$. What is the kernel of the map

$$x \bmod M \to x \bmod N$$

from $\mathbf{Z}/M$ (with addition modulo M) to $\mathbf{Z}/N$ (with addition modulo N)?

8.30 Let

$$\det : GL(2, \mathbf{Q}) \to \mathbf{Q}^\times$$

be the usual determinant map

$$\det \begin{pmatrix} a & b \\ c & d \end{pmatrix} = ad - bc$$

Show by direct computation that *det* is a group homomorphism.

8.31 Show that for any integer n and positive integer N the map

$$f : \mathbf{Z}/N \to \mathbf{Z}/N$$

defined by

$$f(x) = n \cdot x$$

is a group homomorphism (with addition mod N).

8.32 Show that for any integer n and positive integer N the map

$$f : \mathbf{Z}/N^\times \to \mathbf{Z}/N^\times$$

defined by

$$f(x) = x^n$$

is a group homomorphism.

8.33 Fix a positive integer N. Show that for any group homomorphism

$$f : \mathbf{Z}/N \to \mathbf{Z}/N$$

(with addition mod N) there is an integer n so that

$$f(x) = n \cdot x$$

Hint: Try $n = f(1)$, and use the fact that

$$f(x) = f(\underbrace{1 + \ldots + 1}_{x}) = \underbrace{f(1) + \ldots + f(1)}_{x}$$

8.34 Show that the map

$$t \to \begin{pmatrix} 1 & t \\ 0 & 1 \end{pmatrix}$$

is an isomorphism from $\mathbf{Q}$ (with addition) to a subgroup of $GL(2, \mathbf{Q})$.

8.35 Show that the map

$$\begin{pmatrix} a & b \\ 0 & d \end{pmatrix} \to a$$

is a *homomorphism* from the group of all matrices $\begin{pmatrix} a & b \\ 0 & d \end{pmatrix}$ in which a, d are *non-zero* rational numbers and b is *any* rational number, to the multiplicative group $\mathbf{Q}^{\times}$ of non-zero rational numbers. What is its kernel?

8.36 Show that

$$\begin{pmatrix} a & b \\ 0 & d \end{pmatrix} \to b$$

is *not* a homomorphism.

8.37 Define a map $E : \mathbf{Q} \to GL(2, \mathbf{Q})$ by

$$x \to \begin{pmatrix} 1 & x \\ 0 & 1 \end{pmatrix}$$

Show that E is a group homomorphism from $\mathbf{Q}$ with addition to a subgroup of $GL(2, \mathbf{Q})$.

8.38 Define a map $E : \mathbf{Q} \to GL(3, \mathbf{Q})$ by

$$x \to \begin{pmatrix} 1 & x & \frac{x^2}{2} \\ 0 & 1 & x \\ 0 & 0 & 1 \end{pmatrix}$$

Show that E is a group homomorphism from $\mathbf{Q}$ with addition to a subgroup of $GL(3, \mathbf{Q})$.

8.39 Define a map $r : \mathbf{R} \to GL(2, \mathbf{R})$ by

$$x \to \begin{pmatrix} \cos x & \sin x \\ -\sin x & \cos x \end{pmatrix}$$

Show that r is a group homomorphism from $\mathbf{R}$ with addition to a subgroup of $GL(2, \mathbf{R})$. What is its kernel?

8.40 Let n be an integer. Show that $f : \mathbf{Z} \to \mathbf{Z}$ defined by $f(x) = nx$ is a homomorphism.

8.41 Show that a homomorphism $f : G \to H$ always has the property that $f(g^{-1}) = f(g)^{-1}$ for $g \in G$.

9

Rings and Fields

9.1 Rings
9.2 Ring homomorphisms
9.3 Fields

This chapter introduces standard terminology necessary to talk more generally about *finite fields* a little later, and about *polynomials*. Much more can be said about rings and fields!

9.1 Rings

The idea of **ring** generalizes the idea of 'numbers', among other things, so maybe it is a little more intuitive than the idea of **group**. A **ring** R is a set with two operations, $+$ and $\cdot$, and with a special element 0 (**additive identity**) with most of the usual properties we expect or demand of 'addition' and 'multiplication'.

- The addition is **associative**: $a + (b + c) = (a + b) + c$ for all $a, b, c \in R$.
- The addition is **commutative**: $a + b = b + a$ for all $a, b \in R$.
- For every $a \in R$ there is an **additive inverse** denoted $-a$, with the property that $a + (-a) = 0$.
- The zero has the property that $0 + a = a + 0 = a$ for all $a \in R$.
- The multiplication is **associative**: $a(bc) = (ab)c$ for all $a, b, c \in R$.
- The multiplication and addition have left and right **distributive** properties: $a(b + c) = ab + ac$ and $(b + c)a = ba + ca$ for all $a, b, c \in R$.

When we write this multiplication, just as in high school algebra, very often we omit the dot and just write

$$ab = a \cdot b$$

Very often, a particular ring has some additional special features or properties:

- If there is an element 1 in a ring with the property that $1 \cdot a = a \cdot 1$ for all $a \in R$, then 1 is said to be **the (multiplicative) identity** or **unit** in the ring, and the ring is said to **have an identity** or **have a unit** or be a **ring with unit**. And 1 is **the unit** in the ring. We also demand that $1 \neq 0$ in a ring.

Remark: Sometimes the word 'unity' is used in place of 'unit' for the special element 1, but this cannot be relied upon.

- If $ab = ba$ for all a, b in a ring R, then the ring is said to be a **commutative ring**. That is, a ring is called *commutative* if and only if the *multiplication* is commutative.

Most often, but not always, our rings of interest will have units '1'. The condition of commutativity of multiplication is often met, but, for example, *matrix multiplication is not commutative*.

- In a ring R with 1, for a given element $a \in R$, if there is $a^{-1} \in R$ so that $a \cdot a^{-1} = 1$ and $a^{-1} \cdot a = 1$, then a^{-1} is said to be a **multiplicative inverse** for a. If $a \in R$ *has* a multiplicative inverse, then a is called **a unit** in R. The collection of all units in a ring R is denoted $R^\times$ and is called **the group of units in** R.
- A commutative ring in which every nonzero element is a *unit* is called a **field**.
- A not-necessarily commutative ring in which every nonzero element is a unit is called a **division ring**.
- In a ring R an element r so that $r \cdot s = 0$ or $s \cdot r = 0$ for some nonzero $s \in R$ is called a **zero divisor**. A commutative ring *without* nonzero zero-divisors is an **integral domain**.
- A commutative ring R has the **cancellation property** if, for any $r \neq 0$ in R, if $rx = ry$ for $x, y \in R$, then $x = y$. Most rings with which we're familiar have this property.

Remark: There is indeed an inconsistency in the use of the word *unit*. But that's the way the word is used. So *the* unit is 1, while *a* unit is merely something which has a multiplicative inverse. Of course, there are *no* multiplicative inverses unless there is a unit (meaning that there is a 1). *It is almost always possible to tell from context what is meant.*

It is very important to realize that the notations $-a$ for an additive inverse and a^{-1} for multiplicative inverse are meant to *suggest* 'minus a' and 'divide-by-a', but that at the moment we are *not justified* in believing any of the 'usual' high school algebra properties. *We have to prove that all the 'usual' things really do still work in this abstract situation.*

If we take a ring R with 0 and with its addition, then we get an abelian group, called **the additive group of** R.

The group of units $R^\times$ in a ring with unit certainly is a group. Its identity is the unit 1. This group is abelian if R is commutative.

In somewhat more practical terms: as our examples above show, very often a *group* really is just the *additive group* of a ring, or is the *group of units* in a ring. There are many examples where this is not really so, but many fundamental examples are of this nature.

The integers $\mathbf{Z}$ with usual addition and multiplication form a ring. This ring is certainly *commutative* and has a multiplicative identity '1'. The group of units $\mathbf{Z}^\times$ is just $\{\pm 1\}$. This ring is an integral domain.

The *even* integers $2\mathbf{Z}$ with the usual addition and multiplication form a commutative ring *without* unit. Just as this example suggests, very often the lack of a unit in a ring is somewhat artificial, because there is a 'larger' ring it sits inside which *does* have a unit. There are no units in this ring.

The integers mod m, denoted $\mathbf{Z}/m$, form a commutative ring with identity. *As the notation suggests,* the group of units really is $\mathbf{Z}/m^{\times}$: notice that we used the group-of-units notation in this case before we even introduced the terminology.

Take p to be a prime. The ring of integers mod p, denoted $\mathbf{Z}/p$, is a *field* if p is *prime*, since all positive integers less than p have a multiplicative inverse modulo p for p prime (computable by the Euclidean algorithm!). The group of units really is $\mathbf{Z}/p^{\times}$.

The collection of n-by-n real matrices (for fixed n) is a ring, with the usual matrix addition and multiplication. Except for the silly case $n = 1$, this ring is *non-commutative*. The group of units is the group $GL(n, \mathbf{R})$.

The rational numbers $\mathbf{Q}$, the real numbers $\mathbf{R}$, and the complex numbers $\mathbf{C}$ are all examples of *fields*, because all their nonzero elements have multiplicative inverses.

Just as in the beginning of our discussion of *groups*, there are some things which we might accidentally take for granted about how rings behave. In general these presumptions are reasonable, based on all our previous experience with numbers, etc. But it is certainly better to give the 'easy' little proofs of these things and to be conscious of what we believe, rather than to be unconscious.

Let R be a ring. We will prove the following fundamental properties:

- *Uniqueness of additive identity:* If there is an element $z \in R$ and another $r \in R$ so that $r + z = r$, then $z = 0$. (Note that we need this condition only for *one* other $r \in R$, not for *all* $r \in R$.)
- *Uniqueness of additive inverses:* Fix $r \in R$. If there is $r' \in R$ so that $r + r' = 0$, then actually $r' = -r$, the additive inverse of r.
- *Uniqueness of multiplicative identity:* Suppose that R has a unit 1. If there is $u \in R$ so that for all $r \in R$ we have $u \cdot r = r$, then $u = 1$. Or, if for all $r \in R$ we have $r \cdot u = r$, then $u = 1$. Actually, all we need is that *either* $1 \cdot u = 1$ *or* $u \cdot 1 = 1$ to assure that $u = 1$.
- *Uniqueness of multiplicative inverses:* If $r \in R$ has a multiplicative inverse r^{-1}, and if $r' \in R$ is such that $r \cdot r' = 1$, then $r' = r^{-1}$. Or, assuming instead that $r' \cdot r = 1$, we still conclude that $r' = r^{-1}$.
- For $r \in R$, we have $-(-r) = r$. That is, the additive inverse of the additive inverse of r is just r.

Proof: (*of uniqueness of additive identity*) If there is an element $z \in R$ and $r \in R$ so that $r + z = r$, add $-r$ to both sides of this equation to obtain

$$(r + z) - r = r - r = 0$$

by definition of additive inverse. Using the commutativity and associativity of addition, the left-hand side of this is

$$(r + z) - r = (z + r) - r = z + (r - r) = z + 0 = z$$

also using the property of the 0. That is, putting this together, $z = 0$, proving what we wanted.   ///

Proof: *(of uniqueness of additive inverses).* Fix $r \in R$. If there is $r' \in R$ so that $r + r' = 0$, then add $-r$ to both sides to obtain

$$(r + r') - r = 0 + (-r)$$

Using the commutativity and associativity of addition, the left-hand side of this is

$$(r + r') - r = (r' + r) - r = r' + (r - r) = r' + 0 = r'$$

Since the right-hand side is $0 + (-r) = -r$, we have $r' = -r$, as claimed.   ///

Proof: *(of uniqueness of multiplicative identity)* Suppose that *either* u is a left identity or u is a right identity. Let's just do one case, since the other is identical apart from writing things in the opposite order. Suppose that u is a left identity. Thus, in particular, $u \cdot 1 = 1$. Then, since $u \cdot 1 = u$ by the property of the multiplicative identity 1, we have $u = u \cdot 1 = 1$, the desired uniqueness.   ///

Proof: *(of uniqueness of multiplicative inverses)* Assume that $r \in R$ has a multiplicative inverse r^{-1}, and that $r' \in R$ is such that $r \cdot r' = 1$. Then multiply that latter equation by r^{-1} on the left to obtain

$$r^{-1} \cdot (r \cdot r') = r^{-1} \cdot 1 = r^{-1}$$

by the property of 1. Using the associativity of multiplication, the left-hand side is

$$r^{-1} \cdot (r \cdot r') = (r^{-1} \cdot r) \cdot r' = 1 \cdot r' = r'$$

by property of multiplicative inverses and of the identity. Putting this together, we have $r' = r^{-1}$ as desired.   ///

The proof that $-(-r) = r$ (that is, that the additive inverse of the additive inverse of r is just r) is identical to the argument given for *groups* that the inverse of the inverse is the original thing.

There are several 'slogans' that we all learned in high school or earlier, such as 'minus times minus is plus,' and 'zero times anything is zero'. It may be interesting to see that from the axioms for a ring we can *prove* those things. (We worried over the so-called 'laws of exponents' already a little earlier.)

These things are a little subtler than the 'obvious' things above, insofar as they involve the interaction of the multiplication and addition. These little proofs are good models for how to prove simple general results about rings.

Let R be a ring.

- For any $r \in R$, $0 \cdot r = r \cdot 0 = 0$.
- Suppose that there is a 1 in R. Let -1 be the additive inverse of 1. Then for any $r \in R$ we have $(-1) \cdot r = r \cdot (-1) = -r$, where as usual $-r$ denotes the additive inverse of r.
- Let $-x, -y$ be the additive inverses of $x, y \in R$. Then $(-x) \cdot (-y) = xy$.

Proof: Throughout this discussion, keep in mind that to prove that $b = -a$ means to prove just that $a + b = 0$.

Let's prove that 'zero times anything is zero': Let $r \in R$. Then

$$
\begin{aligned}
0 \cdot r &= (0+0) \cdot r \quad &&\text{(since } 0+0=0\text{)} \\
&= 0 \cdot r + 0 \cdot r \quad &&\text{(distributivity)}
\end{aligned}
$$

Then, adding $-(0 \cdot r)$ to both sides, we have

$$0 = 0 \cdot r - 0 \cdot r = 0 \cdot r + 0 \cdot r - 0 \cdot r = 0 \cdot r + 0 = 0 \cdot r$$

That is, $0 \cdot r$. The proof that $r \cdot 0 = 0$ is nearly identical.

Let's show that $(-1) \cdot r = -r$. That is, we are asserting that $(-1)r$ is the additive inverse of r, which by now we know is unique. So all we have to do is check that

$$r + (-1)r = 0$$

We have

$$r + (-1)r = 1 \cdot r + (-1) \cdot r = (1-1) \cdot r = 0 \cdot r = 0$$

by using the property of 1, using distributivity, and using the result we just proved, that $0 \cdot r = 0$. We're done.

Last, to show that $(-x)(-y) = xy$, we prove that $(-x)(-y) = -(-(xy))$, since we know generally that $-(-r) = r$. We can get halfway to the desired conclusion right now: we claim that $-(xy) = (-x)y$: this follows from the computation

$$(-x)y + xy = (-x+x)y = 0 \cdot y = 0$$

Combining these two things, what we want to show is that

$$(-x)(-y) + (-x)y = 0$$

Well,

$$(-x)(-y) + (-x)y = (-x)(-y+y) = (-x) \cdot 0 = 0$$

using distributivity and the property $r \cdot 0 = 0$ verified above. This proves that $(-x)(-y) = xy$.   ///

9.2 Ring homomorphisms

Quite analogous to *group homomorphisms*, ring homomorphisms are maps from one ring to another which preserve the ring structures. Precisely, a **ring homomorphism** $f : R \to S$ from one ring R to another ring S is a map such that for all r, r' in R we have

$$
\begin{aligned}
f(r+r') &= f(r) + f(r') \\
f(rr') &= f(r)\,f(r')
\end{aligned}
$$

That is, we would say that f *preserves* or *respects* both addition and multiplication. A ring homomorphism which is a bijection is an **isomorphism**. Two rings which are isomorphic are construed as 'the same' for all ring-theoretic purposes.

As in the case of groups and group homomorphisms, we do not make an attempt to use different notations for the addition and multiplication in the two different rings R and S in this definition. Thus, more properly put, f converts *addition in R* into *addition in S*, and likewise multiplication.

Very much like the case of groups, the **kernel** of a ring homomorphism $f : R \to S$ is

$$\ker f = \{r \in R : f(r) = 0\}$$

where (implicitly) the latter 0 is the additive identity in S.

Example: The most basic example of a ring homomorphism is

$$f : \mathbf{Z} \to \mathbf{Z}/n$$

given by

$$f(x) = x\text{-mod-}n$$

The assertion that this f is a ring homomorphism is the combination of the two assertions

$$(x\text{-mod-}n) + (y\text{-mod-}n) = (x + y)\text{-mod-}n$$

and

$$(x\text{-mod-}n) \cdot (y\text{-mod-}n) = (x \cdot y)\text{-mod-}n$$

Even though it is slightly misleading, this homomorphism is called the **reduction mod m homomorphism**.

Definition: A subset S of a commutative ring R is a **subring** if it contains 0, is closed under addition and additive inverses, and is closed under multiplication.

Remark: That is, as with groups and subgroups, a subset of a ring is called a subring if it is a ring in its own right, with the operations inherited from the ring inside which it sits. Thus, there is no need to reprove or reverify associativity or distributivity, since these are inherited.

Much as the kernels of group homormorphisms are not *arbitrary* subgroups but only *normal* subgroups, the kernels of ring homomorphisms are not arbitrary subrings.

Definition: A subring I of a commutative ring R is an **ideal** if

$$r \cdot i \in I$$

for all $r \in R$ and $i \in I$.

Now we prove

Proposition: the kernel of any ring homomorphism $f : R \to S$ is an ideal in R.

Proof: Let x be in the kernel, and $r \in R$. Then

$$f(rx) = f(r)f(x) = f(r) \cdot 0 = 0$$

since by now we've proven that in any ring the product of anything with 0 is 0. Thus, rx is in the kernel of f. And, for x, y both in the kernel,

$$f(x + y) = f(x) + f(y) = 0 + 0 = 0$$

That is, $x + y$ is again in the kernel. And $f(0) = 0$, so 0 is in the kernel. And for x in the kernel $f(-x) = -f(x) = -0 = 0$, so $-x$ is in the kernel.   ///

Example: Some homomorphisms which are very important in applications are **evaluation homomorphisms** or **substitution homomorphisms**, described as follows. Let R be a commutative ring, and $R[x]$ the polynomial ring in one variable with coefficients in R. Fix $r_0 \in R$. We want to talk about *evaluating* polynomials at r_0, or, equivalently, *substituting* r_0 for x in a polynomial. What is meant by this is that a polynomial

$$P(x) = a_n x^n + a_{n-1} x^{n-1} + \ldots + a_2 x^2 + a_1 x + a_0$$

should be mapped to

$$P(r_0) = a_n r_0^n + a_{n-1} r_0^{n-1} + \ldots + a_2 r_0^2 + a_1 r_0 + a_0$$

Let e_{r_0} denote this map, which is the **evaluation map**.
  - The evaluation map $e_{r_0} : R[x] \to R$ is a ring homomorphism from the polynomial ring $R[x]$ to the ring R.

Remark: Before proving this, note that our experience makes us anticipate the fact that such maps really are ring homomorphisms: indeed, we know that to evaluate the product or sum of two polynomials we can evaluate them individually and then multiply/add, or multiply/add first and then evaluate. This is exactly the assertion that evaluation is a ring homomorphism.

Proof: This is mostly just finding an effective notation. Let

$$
\begin{aligned}
P(x) &= \textstyle\sum_{0 \leq i \leq m} a_i x^i \\
Q(x) &= \textstyle\sum_{0 \leq i \leq n} b_i x^i
\end{aligned}
$$

be two polynomials with coefficients in a commutative ring R. First we show that evaluation e_{r_0} at $r_0 \in R$ respects the addition:

$$e_{r_0}(P + Q) = e_{r_0}\left(\sum_j (a_j + b_j)x^j\right) = \sum_j (a_j + b_j)r_0^j$$

$$= \sum_j a_j r_0^j + \sum_j b_j r_0^j = e_{r_0}(P) + e_{r_0}(Q)$$

where without harming anything we put $a_j = 0$ and $b_j = 0$ for any index outside the range for which the coefficients are defined. This proves that evaluation respects sums. For products:

$$e_{r_0}(P \cdot Q) = e_{r_0}\left(\sum_{i,j} (a_i \cdot b_j)x^{i+j}\right) = \sum_{i,j} (a_i \cdot b_j)r_0^{i+j} = e_{r_0}(P) \cdot e_{r_0}(Q)$$

This proves that multiplication is respected also by evaluation, so these evaluations really are ring homomorphisms. ///

Proposition: Let $f : R \to S$ be a ring homomorphism. Let $0_R, 0_S$ be the additive identities in R, S, respectively. Then $f(0_R) = 0_S$. That is, always the image of an additive identity under a ring homomorphism is the additive identity in the 'target' ring.

Proof: First,

$$f(0_R) + f(0_R) = f(0_R + 0_R)$$

by the defining property of 'group homomorphism'. Then

$$0_R + 0_R = 0_R$$

(by the property of the additive identity in R), so

$$f(0_R + 0_R) = f(0_R)$$

Thus, together, we have

$$f(0_R) + f(0_R) = f(0_R + 0_R) = f(0_R)$$

Add the additive inverse $-f(0_R)$ to both sides:

$$(f(0_R) + f(0_R)) - f(0_R) = f(0_R) - f(0_R) = 0_S$$

where the last equality uses the definition of additive inverse. Using associativity of addition,

$$(f(0_R) + f(0_R)) - f(0_R) = f(0_R) + (f(0_R) - f(0_R)) = f(0_R) + 0_S = f(0_R)$$

where we also use the defining property of 0_S. Putting these together (repeating a little):

$$f(0_R) = f(0_R) + f(0_R) - f(0_R) = f(0_R + 0_R) - f(0_R) = f(0_R) - f(0_R) = 0_S$$

as claimed. ///

• Let $f : R \to S$ be a *surjective* ring homomorphism. Suppose that R has a multiplicative identity 1_R. Then S has a multiplicative identity 1_S and

$$f(1_R) = 1_S$$

Remark: Notice that unlike the discussion about the additive identity here we need the further hypothesis of surjectivity. Otherwise the assertion is false: see the remark after the proof.

Proof: Given $s \in S$, let $r \in R$ be such that $f(r) = s$. Then

$$f(1_R) \cdot s = f(1_R) \cdot f(r) = f(1_R \cdot r) = f(r) = s$$

Thus, $f(1_R)$ behaves like the unit in S. By the already proven *uniqueness* of units, it must be that $f(1_R) = 1_S$.   ///

Remark: It is important to note that the image of the *multiplicative* identity 1_R under a ring homomorphism $f : R \to S$ is not necessarily the *multiplicative* identity 1_S of S. For example, define a ring homomorphism

$$f : \mathbf{Q} \to S$$

from the rational numbers $\mathbf{Q}$ to the ring S of 2-by-2 rational matrices by

$$f(x) = \begin{pmatrix} x & 0 \\ 0 & 0 \end{pmatrix}$$

Then the image of 1 is simply

$$\begin{pmatrix} 1 & 0 \\ 0 & 0 \end{pmatrix}$$

which is certainly not the same as the multiplicative identity

$$\begin{pmatrix} 1 & 0 \\ 0 & 1 \end{pmatrix}$$

in the ring S.

There are also examples in commutative rings where the unit is mapped to something other than the unit. For example, let $R = \mathbf{Z}/3$ and $S = \mathbf{Z}/6$, and define $f : R \to S$ by

$$f(r \bmod 3) = 4r \bmod 6$$

Check that this is well-defined: if $r = r' \bmod 3$, then $3|(4r - 4r')$ and $2|(4r - 4r')$ so surely $6|4(r - r')$, so indeed $4r = 4r' \bmod 6$. This proves well-definedness. Check that this is a homomorphism:

$$f(x + y) = 4(x + y) = 4x + 4y = f(x) + f(y)$$

This would have worked with *any* number, not just 4. To see that f preserves multiplication, the crucial feature of the situation is that

$$4 \cdot 4 = 4 \bmod 6$$

Then

$$f(x \cdot y) = 4(x \cdot y) = (4 \cdot 4)(x \cdot y) = (4x) \cdot (4y) = f(x) \cdot f(y)$$

Thus, f is a homomorphism. But $f(1) = 4 \neq 1 \bmod 6$.

9.3   Fields

An important subclass of commutative rings are called *fields*. Many of the familiar types of numbers such as complex numbers, real numbers, rational numbers, and $\mathbf{Z}$ modulo primes are all fields. But other familiar sets of numbers, such as the integers themselves, are not fields.

- A commutative ring R with unit 1 and such that any non-zero element of R has a multiplicative inverse (in R) is called a **field**.

The commutative ring of ordinary integers $\mathbf{Z}$ is *not* a field, because non-zero integers other than ± 1 do not have multiplicative inverses *in the integers* (though they have inverses in the larger ring $\mathbf{Q}$).

The commutative ring of rational numbers $\mathbf{Q}$ is a field, because every non-zero rational number a/b (with a and b non-zero integers) has the multiplicative inverse b/a.

The commutative ring of real numbers $\mathbf{R}$ is a field. The commutative ring of complex numbers $\mathbf{C}$ is a field.

The commutative ring $\mathbf{Z}/p$ with p prime is a field. To be sure of this let $x \neq 0 \bmod p$. Then p does not divide x. Always $\gcd(x, p)$ is a divisor of p (and of x), and since p is prime and does not divide x we have $\gcd(x, p) = 1$. Therefore, there are integers r and s such that $rx + sy = 1$. Then $rx = 1 \bmod p$, so r is a multiplicative inverse of x in $\mathbf{Z}/p$.

If n is a composite integer then $\mathbf{Z}/n$ is not a field. In particular, let d be a *proper* divisor of n. Then $d \neq 0 \bmod n$ but d has no multiplicative inverse modulo n.

Exercises

9.01 Check that the congruence class $\bar{1}$ of 1 modulo m really is the multiplicative identity '1' in the ring $\mathbf{Z}/m$.

9.02 Check that the subset $\{\bar{0}, \bar{3}\}$ of $\mathbf{Z}/6$ is a ring, and that $\bar{3}$ is the multiplicative identity '1'. (*ans.*)

9.03 Check that $\{\bar{0}, \bar{2}, \bar{4}, \bar{6}, \bar{8}\} \subset \mathbf{Z}/10$ is a ring, and that $\bar{6}$ is the multiplicative identity '1' in this ring.

9.04 Check that $\{\bar{0}, \bar{3}, \bar{6}, \bar{9}, \bar{12}\} \subset \mathbf{Z}/15$ is a ring, and that $\bar{6}$ is the multiplicative identity '1' in this ring.

9.05 Find the group of units in the rings $\mathbf{Z}/4$, $\mathbf{Z}/5$, $\mathbf{Z}/6$. (*ans.*)

9.06 Find the group of units in the ring $\mathbf{Z}/12$

9.07 Check that the collection $2\mathbf{Z}$ of all even integers is a ring, *without* unit.

9.08 Check that $\mathbf{Z}/n$ has nonzero zero divisors if n is composite.

9.09 Check that if p is prime then $\mathbf{Z}/p$ is an integral domain.

9.10 Show that a multiplicatively invertible element in a ring can never be a zero-divisor. (Recall that $1 \neq 0$.)

9.11 Let R be the collection of numbers of the form $a + bi$ where $a, b \in \mathbf{Q}$ and $i = \sqrt{-1}$. Just to keep in practice, check that R is 'closed' under multiplication and addition. Then, granting that R is a ring (meaning not to worry about associativity, etc.) show that R is a *field*. (*Hint:* Remember 'rationalizing denominators'?)

9.12 Let R be the collection of numbers of the form $a + b\sqrt{2}$ where $a, b \in \mathbf{Q}$. Check that R is 'closed' under multiplication and addition. Then, granting that R is a ring (meaning not to worry about associativity, etc.) show that R is a *field*. (*Hint:* 'Rationalizing denominators.')

9.13 Let R be the collection of numbers $a + bi$ with $a, b \in \mathbf{Z}$ and $i = \sqrt{-1}$. Check that R is 'closed' under multiplication and addition. Granting that it is a ring, then, find the *group of units*.

9.14 Let R be the collection of numbers $a + b\sqrt{-5}$ with $a, b \in \mathbf{Z}$. Check that R is 'closed' under multiplication and addition. Granting that it is a ring, then, find the *group of units*.

9.15 Show that in a ring the equation $r + r = r$ can hold only for $r = 0$.   (*ans.*)

9.16 Find several examples of *nonzero* elements x, y in the ring $\mathbf{Z}/15$ whose product is nevertheless 0.   (*ans.*)

9.17 Find several examples of *nonzero* elements x, y in the ring $\mathbf{Z}/21$ whose product is nevertheless 0.

9.18 Find several examples of *nonzero* elements x, y in the ring $\mathbf{Z}/16$ whose product is nevertheless 0.

9.19 Show that in the ring $\mathbf{Z}/n$ with n a *composite* (that is, not prime) number, the so-called *cancellation law* fails: that is, for such n, find (*non-zero*) elements $a, b, c \in \mathbf{Z}/n$ so that $ca = cb$ but $a \neq b$.

9.20 Fix an integer $N > 1$. Prove carefully that the map $f : \mathbf{Z} \to \mathbf{Z}/N\mathbf{Z}$ given by $f(x) = x + N\mathbf{Z}$ is a ring homomorphism. (We'd really known this all along.)

9.21 Let $f : R \to S$ be a *surjective* ring homomorphism (with R, S commutative, for simplicity). Let I be an ideal in R. Show that $J = \{f(i) : i \in I\}$ is an ideal in S.

9.22 Let $f : R \to S$ be a ring homomorphism (with R, S commutative, for simplicity). Let J be an ideal in I. Show that $I = \{i \in I : f(i) \in J\}$ is an ideal in S.

9.23 (*) Show that the only two two-sided ideals in the ring R of 2-by-2 rational matrices are $\{0\}$ and the whole ring R itself.

10

Polynomials

10.1 Polynomials

We need to understand polynomials algebraically, as being analogous in many regards to the ordinary integers. Thus, the intuition we have for the integers can be reused to a great extent in reasoning about polynomials with coefficients in a field.

Let k be a *field*, which we can think of as being a *finite* field $GF(q) = \mathbf{F}_q$ with q elements, especially $\mathbf{F}_p = \mathbf{Z}/p$ for prime p, or also possibly the rational numbers $\mathbf{Q}$, or real numbers $\mathbf{R}$, or complex numbers $\mathbf{C}$. For 'indeterminate' x, define the **polynomial ring over** k in one variable to be

$$k[x] = \{\text{polynomials with coefficients in } k\}$$

The ring $k[x]$ is a *commutative ring*, since it is a ring and polynomial multiplication is commutative.

We write a polynomial as a sum of 'constants' (from k) times non-negative integer powers of x:

$$f(x) = a_0 + a_1 x + a_2 x^2 + \ldots + a_m x^m$$

The a_is are the **coefficients** of the polynomial. The **constant coefficient** is a_0. If $a_n \neq 0$, then $a_n x^n$ is called **the highest-order term** and a_n is the **highest-order coefficient**. We refer to the summand $a_i x^i$ as the **degree i term**. Also sometimes i is called the **order** of the summand $a_i x^i$. The largest index i such that the coefficient a_i is non-zero is the **degree** of the polynomial. Equivalently, the degree of such a polynomial is the largest exponent i of x so that the ith coefficient

a_i is not 0. Note that just writing the term $a_n x^n$ does *not* imply that $a_n \neq 0$. A polynomial is said to be **monic** if its (*highest-order*) coefficient is 1.

Two polynomials in indeterminate x are **equal** if and only if the coefficients of respective powers of x are all equal.

Remark: At this point we must distinguish between polynomials and the functions given by them. In particular, we do *not* say that two polynomials are equal if they merely assume the same values for all inputs. While the latter principle is provably correct in the case that the possible inputs lie in an *infinite* field, it is definitely false when the inputs must be in a finite field. The simplest case is the polynomial

$$f(x) = x^p - x$$

with coefficients in $\mathbf{Z}/p$, with p a prime. Fermat's Little Theorem tells us that for all inputs x in $\mathbf{Z}/p$ this polynomial has *value* 0. Yet it is not the 0 polynomial.

We have the usual addition and multiplication of polynomials. Addition is easy to describe: the ith coefficient of the sum of two polynomials $f(x)$ and $g(x)$ is the sum of the ith coefficient of $f(x)$ and the ith coefficient of $g(x)$. (This is completely parallel to vector addition.) Multiplication is somewhat messier, but is reasonable: the coefficient of x^k in the product of

$$f(x) = a_0 + a_1 x + a_2 x^2 + \ldots + a_m x^m$$

and

$$g(x) = b_0 + b_1 x + b_2 x^2 + \ldots + b_n x^n$$

is the sum of the products $a_i b_j$ over all pairs of indices i, j that satisfy $i + j = k$. That is,

$$\text{coefficient of } x^k \text{ in } f \cdot g \; = \; \sum_{i+j=k} a_i \, b_j$$

Proposition: For polynomials P, Q with coefficients in a field k, the degree of the product is the sum of the degrees:

$$\deg(P \cdot Q) = \deg P + \deg Q$$

Remark: To make this true even when one of the two polynomials is the 0 polynomial, the 0 polynomial is by convention given degree $-\infty$.

Proof: The result is clear if either polynomial is the zero polynomial, so suppose that both are non-zero. Let

$$P(x) = a_m x^m + a_{m-1} x^{m-1} + \ldots + a_2 x^2 + a_1 x + a_0$$

$$Q(x) = b_n x^n + b_{n-1} x^{n-1} + \ldots + b_2 x^2 + b_1 x + b_0$$

where the *apparent* highest-degree coefficients a_m and b_n *really are* non-zero. Then in the product $P \cdot Q$ the highest-degree term is $a_m b_n x^{m+n}$, which occurs only in one way, as the product of the highest-degree terms from P and Q, so it has coefficient

$a_m \cdot b_n$. Since neither of these is 0, and since *the product of non-zero elements of a field is non-zero*, the coefficient of x^{m+n} is non-zero.   ///

Remark: From the latter proof we see that the crucial property is that $a \neq 0$ and $b \neq 0$ should imply $a \cdot b \neq 0$. We know that this is true in **Q**, **R**, and **C**, and we have verified earlier that this is true for $k = \mathbf{Z}/p$ for p prime. The latter fact comes from the key lemma that if a prime p divides a product ab, then either $p|a$ or $p|b$, which in turn is proven from the peculiar characterization of the gcd of a, p as the smallest positive integer of the form $sa + tp$.

Proposition: *(Cancellation property)* Let $A \cdot P = B \cdot P$ for some non-zero polynomial P, where all these polynomials have coefficients in a field k. Then $A = B$.

Proof: The equation $AP = BP$ gives $(A - B)P = 0$. Because the degree of the product is the sum of the degrees of the factors,

$$\deg(A - B) + \deg P = \deg 0 = -\infty$$

Since P is non-zero, $\deg P \geq 0$. The only possibility then is that $\deg(A-B) = -\infty$, so $A - B = 0$, and $A = B$, as desired.   ///

Remark: Sometimes polynomials are thought of as simply being a kind of *function*, but that is too naive. Polynomials *give rise to* functions, but they are more than just that. It *is* true that a polynomial

$$f(x) = c_n x^n + c_{n-1} x^{n-1} + \ldots + c_1 x + c_0$$

with coefficients in a field k *gives rise to* k-valued functions on the field k, writing as usual

$$f(a) = c_n a^n + c_{n-1} a^{n-1} + \ldots + c_1 a + c_0$$

for $a \in k$. That is, as usual, we imagine that the 'indeterminate' x is replaced by a everywhere (or 'a is substituted for x'). This procedure gives functions from k to k.

But polynomials themselves have features which may become invisible if we mistakenly think of them as just being functions. For example, suppose that we look at the polynomial $f(x) = x^3 + x^2 + x + \bar{1}$ in the polynomial ring $\mathbf{F}_2[x]$, that is, with coefficients in $GF(2) = \mathbf{F}_2 = \mathbf{Z}/2$. Then

$$f(0) = 0^3 + 0^2 + 1 + 1 = 0 \in \mathbf{F}_2$$

$$f(1) = 1^3 + 1^2 + 1 + 1 = 0 \in \mathbf{F}_2$$

That is, the *function* attached to the polynomial is the 0-function, but the polynomial is visibly not the zero polynomial.

As another example, consider $f(x) = x^3 - x$ as a polynomial with coefficients in $\mathbf{Z}/3$. Once again, $f(\bar{0})$, $f(\bar{1})$, $f(\bar{2})$ are all $\bar{0}$, but the polynomial is certainly not the zero polynomial.

Remark: We did not verify the associativity of addition, associativity of multiplication, distributivity, etc., to really prove that $k[x]$ is a commutative ring. It's not hard to do so just using the definitions above, but it's not very interesting.

10.2 Divisibility

In a polynomial ring $k[x]$ with k a *field*, there is a **division algorithm** and (therefore) there will be a **Euclidean algorithm** nearly identical *in form* to the analogous algorithms for the ordinary integers **Z**.

The division algorithm is just the usual *division of one polynomial by another*, with remainder, as we all learned in high school or earlier. It takes just a moment's reflection to see that the procedure we all learned does *not* depend upon the nature of the field that the coefficients are in, and that the degree of the remainder is indeed less than the degree of the divisor!

Proposition: Let k be a field and M a non-zero polynomial in $k[x]$. Let H be any other polynomial in $k[x]$. Then there are unique polynomials Q ('quotient') and R ('remainder') in $k[x]$ so that $\deg R < \deg M$ and

$$H = Q \cdot M + R$$

In this situation use the notation

$$R = H\%M = \text{ reduction of } H \text{ modulo } M$$

in parallel to the usage for integers.

Proof: Let X be the set of polynomials expressible in the form $H - S \cdot M$ for some polynomial S. Let $R = H - Q \cdot M$ be an element of X of minimal degree. We claim that $\deg R < \deg M$. If not, let a be the highest-degree coefficient of R, let b be the highest-degree coefficient of M, and define a polynomial

$$G = (ab^{-1}) \cdot x^{\deg R - \deg M}$$

Then the subtraction

$$R - G \cdot M$$

exactly removes the highest-order term of R, so

$$\deg(R - G \cdot M) < \deg R$$

But this modified version of R would still be in X, since

$$R - G \cdot M = (H - Q \cdot M) - G \cdot M = H - (Q + G) \cdot M$$

By choice of R this is impossible. Therefore, $\deg R < \deg M$. This proves existence. To prove uniqueness, suppose we had

$$H = Q \cdot M + R = Q' \cdot M + R'$$

Then subtract to obtain

$$R - R' = (Q' - Q) \cdot M$$

Since the degree of a product is the sum of the degrees, and since the degrees of R, R' are less than the degree of M, this is impossible unless $Q' - Q = 0$, in which case also $R - R' = 0$.   ///

A polynomial D **divides** another polynomial P if there is a polynomial Q so that $P = Q \cdot D$. Equivalently, P is a **multiple** of D. We may also say that D is a **divisor** of P. We use notation $D|P$ when D divides P. A divisor D of P is a **proper divisor** of P if

$$0 < \deg D < \deg P$$

A non-zero polynomial is **irreducible** ('prime') if it has no proper divisors.

Proposition: A polynomial M divides another polynomial H if and only if $H\%M = 0$.

Proof: Certainly if $H = Q \cdot M + R$ with $R = 0$, we have expressed H as a multiple of M. On the other hand, suppose $H = T \cdot M$ for some T. Then, by the uniqueness part of the reduction/division process, looking at this equality as $H = T \cdot M + 0$, it must be that T is the 'quotient' and 0 is the 'remainder'.   ///

For example: let's reduce $x^3 + 1$ modulo $x^2 + 1$, where we view the coefficients as being in $\mathbf{F}_2$, for example.

$$(x^3 + 1) - x \cdot (x^2 + 1) = x - 1$$

We're done with the reduction because the degree of $x - 1$ is (strictly) less than the degree of $x^2 + 1$.

Reduce $x^5 + 1$ modulo $x^2 + 1$, in stages:

$$(x^5 + 1) - x^3 \cdot (x^2 + 1) = -x^3 + 1$$
$$(-x^3 + 1) + x \cdot (x^2 + 1) = x + 1$$

which, summarized, gives the reduction

$$(x^5 + 1) - (x^3 - x) \cdot (x^2 + 1) = x + 1$$

Remark: Since the division algorithm works for polynomials with coefficients in a field, it is merely a *corollary* that we have a 'Euclidean algorithm'! If we think about it, the crucial thing in having the Euclidean algorithm work was that the division algorithm gave us progressively smaller numbers at each step. (And, indeed, each step of the Euclidean algorithm is just a division algorithm!)

The **greatest common divisor** of two polynomials A, B is the *monic* polynomial g of highest degree dividing both A and B.

Proposition: For polynomials f, g in $k[x]$, the monic polynomial of the form $sf + tg$ (for $s, t \in k[x]$) of smallest degree is the *gcd* of f, g. (In particular, greatest common divisors *exist*.)

Proof: Among the non-negative integer values $\deg(sf + tg)$ there is at least one which is minimal. (We reject any choice of s, t which gives $sf + tg = 0$, which has degree $-\infty$.) Let $h = sf + tg$ be such, and multiply through by the inverse of the highest-degree coefficient in order to make h monic. First, we must show that $h|f$ and $h|g$. Using the division/reduction algorithm, we have

$$f = q(sf + tg) + r$$

with $\deg r < \deg(sf + tg)$. Rearranging the equation, we obtain

$$r = (1 - qs)f + (-qt)g$$

So r itself is of the form $s'f + t'g$ with $s', t' \in k[x]$. Since $sf + tg$ had the smallest non-negative degree of any such expression, and $\deg r < \deg(sf + tg)$, it must be that $r = 0$. So $sf + tg$ divides f. Similarly, $sf + tg$ must divide g. This proves that $sf + tg$ is a divisor of both f and g. On the other hand if $d|f$ and $d|g$ then certainly $d|sf + tg$.   ///

Divide

$$x^7 + x^6 + x^5 + x^4 + x^3 + x^2 + 1$$

by

$$x^3 + x + 1$$

viewed as having coefficients in $GF(2) = \mathbf{F}_2 = \mathbf{Z}/2$. Written out in full:

$$
\begin{array}{r}
x^4 \ +x^3 \ +0 \ \ +x^1 \ +0 \ \ \text{R } x^1 + x^0 \\
\hline
x^3 \ \ +0 \ +x^1 +x^0 \, \big) \, x^7 \ +x^6 \ +x^5 \ +x^4 \ +x^3 \ +x^2 \ +0 \ \ +x^0 \\
x^7 \ \ +0 \ \ +x^5 \ +x^4 \ +0 \ \ +0 \ \ +0 \ \ +0 \\
\hline
x^6 \ \ +0 \ \ +0 \ \ +x^3 \ +x^2 \ +0 \ \ +x^0 \\
x^6 \ \ +0 \ \ +x^4 \ +x^3 \ +0 \ \ +0 \ \ +0 \\
\hline
x^4 \ \ +0 \ \ +x^2 \ +0 \ \ +x^0 \\
x^4 \ \ +0 \ \ +x^2 \ +x^1 \ +0 \\
\hline
x^1 \ \ +x^0
\end{array}
$$

So as a single step this would be

$$(x^7 + x^6 + x^5 + x^4 + x^3 + x^2 + 1) - (x^4 + x^3 + x)(x^3 + x + 1) = x + 1$$

If the field is not simply $\mathbf{Z}/2$, it can easily happen that a divisor D is not **monic**, that is, has highest-degree (non-zero) coefficient c_n not 1. In that case, the polynomial $c_n^{-1}D$ *is* monic, and we divide by $c_n^{-1}D$ instead. Then from an expression

$$F = Q \cdot (c_n^{-1}D) + R$$

for the reduction algorithm with divisor $c_n^{-1}D$ we immediately get

$$F = (Qc_n^{-1}) \cdot D + R$$

which is the reduction algorithm mod D, as desired.

The number of operations performed to divide by a non-monic polynomial is the same as the approach just indicated, but especially when executed by a human the approach of the previous paragraph seems to help avoid errors.

The naive way to compute the greatest commond divisor of two polynomials is to factor both of them (as in the following section) and determine all the common factors. However, this is suboptimal. It is better to use the *Euclidean algorithm*, discussed a little further below.

10.3 Factoring and irreducibility

Just as we factor ordinary (not too large) integers by trial division, we can factor polynomials (with coefficients in a field) into irreducible polynomials.

As in the naive primality/factoring approach for ordinary integers, for small-degree polynomials over a small finite field we can use a **naive** primality/factorization algorithm, **trial division**. Analogous to the fact that for ordinary integers

$$|xy| = |x| \cdot |y|$$

we need the fact (proven above) that

$$\deg(P \cdot Q) = \deg P + \deg Q$$

Again, a **proper divisor** D of a polynomial F is a polynomial divisor D of F so that

$$0 < \deg D < \deg F$$

(Note that the polynomials of degree 0 are the non-zero 'constants' k, viewed as polynomials with only an x^0 term.)

Proposition: If F has a proper divisor, then it has a proper divisor D with

$$0 < \deg D \leq \frac{1}{2} \deg F$$

Proof: If a proper divisor D of F has degree $\geq \frac{1}{2} \deg F$, then F/D has degree $\leq \frac{1}{2} \deg F$.   ///

Low-degree cases: Let k be a field.
- Every linear polynomial in $k[x]$ is irreducible, since there is no value of 'degree' between 1 and 0.
- If a quadratic polynomial factors properly, then it must be the product of two linear factors.
- If a cubic polynomial factors properly, then it must have at least one linear factor.
- If a quartic or higher-degree polynomial factors properly, it may nevertheless fail to have a linear factor.

Proposition: *(Testing for linear factors)* A polynomial $F(x)$ with coefficients in a field k has a linear factor $x - a$ (with $a \in k$) if and only if $F(a) = 0$.

Proof: If $x - a$ is a factor, then $F(x) = (x - a)G(x)$ for some polynomial G, and certainly

$$F(a) = (a - a)G(a) = 0 \cdot G(a)$$

On the other hand, suppose that $F(a) = 0$. Use the division algorithm to write

$$F(x) = Q(x) \cdot (x - a) + R$$

Since $\deg R < \deg(x - a) = 1$, R must be a constant. Evaluate both sides at a:

$$0 = F(a) = Q(a) \cdot (a - a) + R = Q(a) \cdot 0 + R = R$$

Therefore, $R = 0$ and so $x - a$ divides $F(x)$.   ///

This gives a slightly more economical way to test for linear factors.

There is only one degree 0 polynomial in $\mathbf{F}_2[x]$, namely the constant 1. The 0 polynomial has degree $-\infty$.

There are just two linear polynomials in $\mathbf{F}_2[x]$, namely x and $x + 1$. Since every linear polynomial is irreducible, they are irreducible.

For **quadratic** polynomials, there are 2 choices for the linear coefficient and 2 choices for the constant coefficient, so $2 \cdot 2 = 4$ quadratic polynomials in $\mathbf{F}_2[x]$. Testing for irreducibility, here the algebra is easy:

- Obviously $x^2 = x \cdot x$
- Obviously $x^2 + x = x \cdot (x + 1)$
- Less obviously $x^2 + 1 = (x + 1)^2$. Here use the fact that $2 = 0$, so $(x + 1)^2 = x^2 + 2x + 1 = x^2 + 0 + 1 = x^2 + 1$.
- $x^2 + x + 1$: Now it's a little easier to see whether or not this is 0 when values 0,1 are plugged in:

$$0^2 + 0 + 1 = 1 \neq 0$$

$$1^2 + 1 + 1 = 1 \neq 0$$

So $x^2 + x + 1$ is irreducible in $\mathbf{F}_2[x]$. It's the **only** irreducible quadratic polynomial in $\mathbf{F}_2[x]$.

For **cubic** polynomials with coefficients in $\mathbf{F}_2$, there are 2 choices for quadratic coefficient, 2 for linear coefficient, and 2 for constant, so 8 altogether. If we are looking only for irreducible ones, we should exclude those with constant coefficient 0, because they'll have value 0 for input 0 (equivalently, they'll have linear factor x). Also, those with an even number of non-zero coefficients will have value 0 for input 1, so will have a linear factor $x + 1$. Keep in mind that if a cubic is not irreducible then it has at least one linear factor.

We conclude that a cubic polynomial in $\mathbf{F}_2$ with constant coefficient 1 and with an odd total number of non-zero coefficients is necessarily irreducible. Thus, the only two irreducible cubics in $\mathbf{F}_2[x]$ are

$$x^3 + x^2 + 1$$

$$x^3 + x + 1$$

Irreducible quartic polynomials in $\mathbf{F}_2[x]$: there are $2^4 = 16$ choices for cubic, quadratic, linear, and constant coefficients. If the constant term is 0, or if the total number of non-zero coefficients is even, then there is a linear factor x or $x+1$. This leaves 4 possibilities for irreducible quartics:

$$x^4 + x^3 + x^2 + x + 1$$
$$x^4 + x^3 + 1$$
$$x^4 + x^2 + 1$$
$$x^4 + x + 1$$

None of these has a **linear** factor in $\mathbf{F}_2[x]$. But we must look for (irreducible!) **quadratic** factors. From above, the only irreducible quadratic in $\mathbf{F}_2[x]$ is x^2+x+1, so the only reducible quartic without linear factors **must** be

$$x^4 + x^2 + 1 = (x^2 + x + 1)^2$$

This leaves 3 irreducible quartics: $x^4 + x^3 + x^2 + x + 1$, $x^4 + x^3 + 1$, $x^4 + x + 1$.

Irreducible quintic polynomials in $\mathbf{F}_2[x]$: There are $2^5 = 32$ quintics in $\mathbf{F}_2[x]$. Excluding those with 0 constant coefficient (and therefore divisible by x) leaves $2^4 = 16$. Excluding those with an even total number of non-zero coefficients (divisible by $x + 1$) leaves

$$\binom{4}{3} + \binom{4}{1} = 4 + 4 = 8$$

This 8 is the number of quintics with no linear factors. The only way a quintic with no linear factors can be obtained as a product of lower-degree polynomials is

$$\text{irred quadratic} \cdot \text{irred cubic}$$

For example, if there were 2 irreducible quadratic factors, then that would leave room only for a linear factor, which we've assumed away. We've already found out that there is only one irreducible quadratic in $\mathbf{F}_2[x]$, and just 2 irreducible cubics, so there are exactly 2 reducible quintics without linear factors. They are

$$(x^2 + x + 1) \cdot (x^3 + x^2 + 1) = x^5 + x + 1$$
$$(x^2 + x + 1) \cdot (x^3 + x + 1) = x^5 + x^4 + 1$$

That leaves 6 irreducible quintics in $\mathbf{F}_2[x]$, which we obtain by listing anything not noted above to be reducible: they must have constant coefficient 1, an odd number of non-zero coefficients, and not be $x^5 + x + 1$ or $x^5 + x^4 + 1$. With exactly 5 non-zero coefficients, these are all irreducible

$$x^5 + 0 + x^3 + x^2 + x + 1$$
$$x^5 + x^4 + 0 + x^2 + x + 1$$
$$x^5 + x^4 + x^3 + 0 + x + 1$$
$$x^5 + x^4 + x^3 + x^2 + 0 + 1$$

With exactly 3 non-zero coefficients, avoiding the two reducible ones noted above, we have

$$x^5 + 0 + x^3 + 0 + 0 + 1$$
$$x^5 + 0 + 0 + x^2 + 0 + 1$$

10.4 Euclidean algorithm for polynomials

The form of the Euclidean algorithm for polynomials with coefficients in a field k is identical to that for the ordinary integers $\mathbf{Z}$. That is, each line is a division/reduction step: the divisor for the next step is the remainder from the previous step, and the dividend for the next step is the divisor from the previous. The algorithm terminates when the remainder is 0, and at that point the greatest common divisor is the remainder from the next-to-last step *divided by its highest-degree coefficient* to make it *monic*, since we require the gcd of two polynomials to be monic.

The Euclidean algorithm applied to two polynomials $f(x)$ and $g(x)$ runs as follows.

Initialize $(F(X), G(X), R(X)) = (f(x), g(x), f(x)\%g(x))$.

If $R(x) = 0$ we're done, and $\gcd(f(x), g(x)) = g(x)$.

   while $R(x) \neq 0$:

      Replace $(F(x), G(x), R(x))$ by $(G(x), R(x), G(x)\%R(x))$.

When $R(x) = 0$, the current value of $G(x)$ is the gcd.

The Euclidean algorithm is best explained by examples.

For example, to compute the *gcd* of $x^5 + x + 1$ and $x^3 + x + 1$ considered as polynomials in $\mathbf{F}_2[x]$:

$$
\begin{aligned}
(x^5 + x + 1) - (x^2 + 1)(x^3 + x + 1) &= x^2 \\
(x^3 + x + 1) - (x)(x^2) &= x + 1 \\
(x^2) - (x + 1)(x + 1) &= 1 \\
(x + 1) - (x + 1)(1) &= 0
\end{aligned}
$$

Since we have a 0 on the right-hand side, the algorithm terminates. The right-hand side of the next-to-last line is 1, so the greatest common divisor of these two polynomials is 1. That is, they are relatively prime.

To compute the *gcd* of $x^5 + x + 1$ and $x^3 + x + 1$ considered as polynomials in $\mathbf{F}_5[x]$:

$$
\begin{aligned}
(x^5 + x + 1) - (x^2 + 4)(x^3 + x + 1) &= 4x^2 + 2x + 2 \\
(x^3 + x + 1) - (4x + 3)(4x^2 + 2x + 2) &= 2x \\
(4x^2 + 2x + 2) - (2x + 1)(2x) &= 2 \\
(2x) - (x)(2) &= 0
\end{aligned}
$$

Since we have a 0 on the right-hand side, the algorithm terminates. The right-hand side of the next-to-last line is 2, a non-zero constant, so the greatest common divisor of these two polynomials is 1 because we take monic gcd's. That is, the two polynomials are relatively prime.

Remark: Yes, we need to know the context in order to determine what field the coefficients lie in. There is no way to simply look at the coefficients and know directly.

To compute the *gcd* of $x^7 + x^6 + x^4 + x^3 + x + 1$ and $x^5 + x^4 + x + 1$ considered as polynomials in $\mathbf{F}_2[x]$:

$$(x^7 + x^6 + x^4 + x^3 + x + 1) - (x^2)(x^5 + x^4 + x + 1) = x^4 + x^2 + x + 1$$
$$(x^5 + x^4 + x + 1) - (x + 1)(x^4 + x^2 + x + 1) = x^3 + x$$
$$(x^4 + x^2 + x + 1) - (x)(x^3 + x) = x + 1$$
$$(x^3 + x) - (x^2 + x)(x + 1) = 0$$

Since we have a 0 on the right-hand side, the algorithm terminates. The right-hand side of the next-to-last line is $x + 1$, a non-zero constant, so the greatest common divisor of these two polynomials is $x + 1$.

To compute the *gcd* of $x^7 + x^6 + x^4 + x^3 + x + 1$ and $x^6 + x^4 + x^2 + 1$ considered as polynomials in $\mathbf{F}_3[x]$:

$$(x^7 + x^6 + x^4 + x^3 + x + 1) - (x + 1)(x^6 + x^4 + x^2 + 1) = 2x^5 + 2x^2$$
$$(x^6 + x^4 + x^2 + 1) - (2x)(2x^5 + 2x^2) = x^4 + 2x^3 + x^2 + 1$$
$$(2x^5 + 2x^2) - (2x + 2)(x^4 + 2x^3 + x^2 + 1) = x + 1$$
$$(x^4 + 2x^3 + x^2 + 1) - (x^3 + x^2)(x + 1) = 1$$
$$(x + 1) - (x + 1)(1) = 0$$

Since we have a 0 on the right-hand side, the algorithm terminates. The right-hand side of the next-to-last line is 1, a non-zero constant, so the greatest common divisor of these two polynomials is 1.

Remark: Notice that in the last two examples the differing interpretation of 'where' the coefficients are has a big impact on what the greatest common divisor is!

Compute the greatest common divisor of the two polynomials $x^7 + x^5 + x^4 + x^3 + x + 1$ and $x^6 + x^3 + x^2 + x + 1$ (with coefficients in the finite field $GF(2) = \mathbf{F}_2 = \mathbf{Z}/2$ with just two elements) by the Euclidean algorithm.

$$
\begin{array}{rcl}
(x^7 + x^5 + x^4 + x^3 + x + 1) - (x) \cdot (x^6 + x^3 + x^2 + x + 1) &=& x^5 + x^2 + 1 \\
(x^6 + x^3 + x^2 + x + 1) - (x) \cdot (x^5 + x^2 + 1) &=& x^2 + 1 \\
(x^5 + x^2 + 1) - (x^3 + x + 1) \cdot (x^2 + 1) &=& x \\
(x^2 + 1) - (x) \cdot (x) &=& 1 \\
(x) - (x) \cdot (1) &=& 0
\end{array}
$$

Thus, since the last non-zero entry on the right-hand side is 1, the gcd of $x^7 + x^5 + x^4 + x^3 + x + 1$ and $x^6 + x^3 + x^2 + x + 1$ is 1.

With coefficients in $GF(2) = \mathbf{F}_2$, compute the *gcd* of $x^6 + x^5 + x^4 + x^3 + x^2 + 1$ and $x^5 + x^4 + x^3 + 1$.

$$
\begin{array}{rcl}
(x^6 + x^5 + x^4 + x^3 + x^2 + 1) - (x) \cdot (x^5 + x^4 + x^3 + 1) &=& x^3 + x^2 + x + 1 \\
(x^5 + x^4 + x^3 + 1) - (x^2) \cdot (x^3 + x^2 + x + 1) &=& x^2 + 1 \\
(x^3 + x^2 + x + 1) - (x + 1) \cdot (x^2 + 1) &=& 0
\end{array}
$$

Thus, the gcd of $x^6 + x^5 + x^4 + x^3 + x^2 + 1$ and $x^5 + x^4 + x^3 + 1$ is $x^2 + 1$, since the latter is the last non-zero right-hand side occurring.

10.5 Unique factorization of polynomials

In a manner entirely parallel to the proof of unique factorization in the ordinary integers $\mathbf{Z}$, we can prove that the polynomial ring $k[x]$ (coefficients in a *field* k) has unique factorization into irreducible ('prime') polynomials.

Theorem: Given a non-zero polynomial P in $k[x]$, with a field k, P can be expressed as a product

$$P = c \cdot P_1^{e_1} \ldots P_n^{e_n}$$

where c is a non-zero element of the field k, the P_i are irreducible monic polynomials, and the e_i are positive integers. This factorization is essentially unique, in the sense that any other factorization differs from this only in the ordering of the irreducible monic factors.

Proof: As in the case of $\mathbf{Z}$, we need a peculiar characterization of the greatest common divisor of two polynomials: we showed earlier that for polynomials f, g in $k[x]$, an element of the form $sf + tg$ (for $s, t \in k[x]$) with smallest degree is the *gcd* of f, g. And now the key lemma:

Lemma: Let P be an irreducible polynomial. For two other polynomials A, B, if $P|AB$ then $P|A$ or $P|B$. Generally, if an irreducible P divides a product $A_1 \ldots A_n$ of polynomials then P must divide one of the factors A_i.

Proof: It suffices to prove that if $P|AB$ and $P \nmid A$ then $P|B$. Since $P \nmid A$, and since P is irreducible, the *gcd* of P and A is just 1. Therefore, there are $s, t \in k[x]$ so that

$$1 = sA + tP$$

Then

$$B = B \cdot 1 = B \cdot (sA + tP) = s(AB) + (Bt)P$$

Since $P|AB$, surely P divides the right-hand side. Therefore, $P|B$, as claimed.

Generally, if P divides $A_1 \ldots A_n$, rewrite this as $(A_1)(A_2 \ldots A_n)$. By the first part, either $P|A_1$ or $P|A_2 \ldots A_n$. In the former case we're done. In the latter case, we continue: rewrite $A_2 \ldots A_n = (A_2)(A_3 \ldots A_n)$. So either $P|A_2$ or $P|A_3 \ldots A_n$. Continuing (induction!), we find that P divides at least one of the factors A_i.   ///

Now we prove the *existence* of factorizations into irreducibles. Suppose that some polynomial in $k[x]$ did not have a factorization. Then there is a $f \in k[x]$ without a factorization and with deg f *smallest* among all elements lacking a factorization. This f cannot be irreducible, or it has a factorization into irreducibles. If f is reducible, then of course it has a proper factorization $f = gh$. This means that $0 < \deg A < \deg f$ and $0 < \deg B < \deg f$. By the minimality of f among polynomials *not* having factorizations it must be that both A and B have prime factorizations. Then a prime factorization of f is obtained by multiplying together the prime factorizations for A and B.

Now we prove uniqueness of the factorization. Suppose that

$$h = c \cdot p_1^{e_1} \ldots p_m^{e_m}$$

and also

$$h = c' \cdot q_1^{f_1} \ldots q_n^{f_n}$$

with monic irreducibles p_i and q_i and constants c, c'.

First, since all the irreducibles are monic, the highest-degree coefficient of either of the products is simply the leading constant, c or c' in the two cases. But since both products are equal to h, c must equal c'.

By induction, we could assume that $\sum_{i=1}^{m} e_i$ is the *smallest* integer quantity for which there is a *different* factorization. Since p_1 divides $q_1^{f_1} \ldots q_n^{f_n}$ and p is prime, by the key lemma above p_1 must divide one of the q_i. By relabeling the q_is, we may suppose that $p_1 | q_1$. Since these are both monic irreducible, they are equal. Replacing q_1 by p_1, we get

$$p_1^{e_1} \ldots p_m^{e_m} = p_1^{f_1} q_2^{f_2} q_3^{f_3} \ldots q_n^{f_n}$$

Since $e_1 \geq 1$ and $f_1 \geq 1$, we can *cancel* at least one factor of p_1 from both sides.

But by induction, since we assumed that $\sum_{i=1}^{m} e_i$ was the smallest expression occurring in a factorization of some $h \in k[x]$ in two different ways, after removing the common factor of p_1 the remaining factorizations must be essentially the same.

///

Exercises

10.01 Factor $x^3 - x$ into linear factors in $\mathbf{F}_3[x]$.

10.02 Factor $x^5 - x$ into linear factors in $\mathbf{F}_5[x]$. (*ans.*)

10.03 Factor $x^5 + x + 1$ into irreducibles in $\mathbf{F}_2[x]$, by trial division. (*ans.*)

10.04 Factor $x^5 + x^4 + 1$ into irreducibles in $\mathbf{F}_2[x]$ by trial division.

10.05 Factor $x^6 + x^3 + x + 1$ into irreducibles in $\mathbf{F}_2[x]$ by trial division. (*ans.*)

10.06 Let $k[x]$ be the polynomial ring in one variable x over the field k. What is the **group of units** $k[x]^\times$ (meaning the collection of polynomials that have multiplicative inverses which are also polynomials)?

10.07 Find the greatest common divisor of $x^5 + x^4 + x^3 + x^2 + x + 1$ and $x^4 + x^2 + 1$ in the ring $\mathbf{Q}[x]$ of polynomials over $\mathbf{Q}$. (*ans.*)

10.08 Find the greatest common divisor of $x^6 + x^3 + 1$ and $x^2 + x + 1$ in the ring $k[x]$ of polynomials over the finite field $k = \mathbf{Z}/3$ with 3 elements.

10.09 Find the greatest common divisor of the two polynomials $x^6 + x^4 + x^2 + 1$ and $x^8 + x^6 + x^4 + x^2 + 1$ in the ring $k[x]$ of polynomials over the finite field $k = \mathbf{Z}/2$ with 2 elements.

10.10 Find the greatest common divisor of the two polynomials $x^5 + x + 1$ and $x^5 + x^4 + 1$ in the polynomial ring $\mathbf{F}_2[x]$. (*ans.*)

10.11 Find the greatest common divisor of the two polynomials $x^5+x^4+x^3+1$ and $x^5 + x^2 + x + 1$ in $\mathbf{F}_2[x]$.

10.12 Find the greatest common divisor of $x^7 + x^6 + x^5 + x^4 + 1$ and $x^6 + x^5 + x^4 + x^3 + x^2 + x + 1$ in $\mathbf{F}_2[x]$. (*ans.*)

10.13 Find the greatest common divisor of $x^5 + x^3 + x^2 + 1$ and $x^6 + x^5 + x + 1$ in $\mathbf{F}_2[x]$.

11

Finite Fields

Again, while we are certainly accustomed to (and entitled to) think of the *fields* rationals, reals, and complex numbers as 'natural' batches of numbers, it is important to realize that there are *many* other important and useful fields. Perhaps unexpectedly, there are many *finite* fields: For example, for a prime number p, the quotient $\mathbf{Z}/p$ is a *field* (with p elements).

On the other hand, for example, *there is no finite field with 6 or with 10 elements.* (Why?)

While it turns out that there *are* finite fields with, for example, 9 elements, 128 elements, or *any prime power* number of elements, it requires more preparation to 'find' them.

The simplest finite fields are the rings $\mathbf{Z}/p$ with p prime. For many different reasons, we want *more* finite fields than just these. One immediate reason is that for machine implementation (and for other computational simplifications) it is optimal to use fields *of characteristic 2*, that is, in which $1 + 1 = 2 = 0$. Among the fields $\mathbf{Z}/p$ only $\mathbf{Z}/2$ satisfies this condition. At the same time, for various reasons we might want the field to be *large*. If we restrict our attention to the fields $\mathbf{Z}/p$ we can't meet both these conditions simultaneously.

11.1 Making fields

Construction of finite fields, and computations in finite fields, are based upon polynomial computations.

For brevity, write $\mathbf{F}_q$ for the finite field with q elements (if it exists!) For a prime p at least we have one such finite field, namely $\mathbf{Z}/p = \mathbf{F}_p$. Again, another notation often seen is

$$GF(q) = \mathbf{F}_q$$

Here 'GF' stands for **Galois field**.

Remark: There is the issue of *uniqueness* of a finite field with a given number of elements. It is true that there is essentially at most one such, but this is not easy to prove. Also, in practice the various possible computational models of the same underlying abstract object have a great impact, so we will often be more concerned with the many different models themselves.

Remark: The present discussion continues to be entirely analogous to our discussion of $\mathbf{Z}/m$.

For a polynomial P (not necessarily irreducible), and for two other polynomials f, g, all with coefficients in $\mathbf{F}_p$, write

$$f = g \bmod P$$

if P **divides** $f - g$. This is completely analogous to congruences for ordinary integers. And, continuing with that analogy, define

$$\mathbf{F}_p[x]/P = \{\text{congruence classes mod } P\}$$

where the **congruence class** $\bar{f}$ mod P of a polynomial f is

$$\bar{f} = \{g \in \mathbf{F}_p[x] : g = f \bmod P\}$$

Usually one just writes 'f' rather than '$\bar{f}$'.

A polynomial f is **reduced mod** P if

$$\deg f < \deg P$$

Via the division/reduction algorithm in the polynomial ring $\mathbf{F}_p[x]$, every polynomial in $\mathbf{F}_p[x]$ is equal-mod-P to a reduced polynomial mod P: indeed, given f, by division-with-remainder we obtain polynomials Q and R with $\deg R < \deg P$ and so that

$$f = Q \cdot P + R$$

That is,

$$f - R = Q \cdot P$$

which is to say that $f = R \bmod P$.

Proposition: Two polynomials f, g which are reduced mod P are equal modulo P if and only if they are equal (in $\mathbf{F}_p[x]$).

Proof: Certainly if f and g are equal then they are equal modulo P, whether or not they are reduced. On the other hand, suppose that f and g are reduced modulo P and equal modulo P. Then

$$f - g = Q \cdot P$$

for some (quotient) polynomial Q. Looking at degrees,

$$\deg P > \max(\deg f, \deg g) \geq \deg(f - g) = \deg Q + \deg P$$

If all the degrees are integers, this is impossible. The only manner in which this can work out is that $Q = 0$, so (by convention) $\deg Q = -\infty$. Thus, actually $f - g = 0$.
///

Theorem: For irreducible polynomial P of degree n, the ring

$$\mathbf{F}_p[x]\text{-mod-}P = \mathbf{F}_p[x]/P$$

of polynomials mod P is a **field**, with p^n elements. The element x-mod-P is a root in $\mathbf{F}_p[x]/P$ of the equation
$$P(x) = 0 \bmod P$$

Proof: From the previous proposition, the set of polynomials $f(x)$ of degree strictly less than the degree of P is an irredundant set of representatives for $\mathbf{F}_p[x]/P$, whether or not $P(x)$ is irreducible. There are p choices (from $\mathbf{F}_p$) for each of the n coefficients of a polynomial of degree strictly less than n, so there are p^n choices altogether, and thus p^n elements in the quotient $\mathbf{F}_p[x]/P$.

Next, we prove existence of multiplicative inverses for non-zero elements f in $\mathbf{F}_p[x]/P$. Given $f \neq 0$ in $\mathbf{F}_p[x]/P$, we may suppose that $0 \leq \deg f < \deg P$. Since P does not divide f,
$$\deg \gcd(f, P) < \deg P$$

Since P is irreducible, $\gcd(f, P)$ cannot have *positive* degree, or it would be a *proper* factor of P. Thus,
$$\deg \gcd(f, P) = 0$$

That is, the gcd is a non-zero constant. Since we can adjust gcd's to be monic polynomials by multiplying through by non-zero constants, we have

$$\gcd(f, P) = 1$$

Therefore, from above, there are polynomials a, b such that

$$af + bP = 1$$

Then

$$a \cdot f = 1 \bmod P$$

giving a multiplicative inverse of f as desired. The other requirements of a field, namely the associativity, distributivity, and commutativity of addition and multiplication, and so on, follow from the analogous properties for polynomials themselves.

Last, we verify that $\alpha = x$-mod-P satisfies

$$P(\alpha) = 0 \bmod P$$

(This is easier than one might anticipate.) We will verify that for any polynomial M there is a polynomial N such that

$$P(x + M \cdot P) = N \cdot P$$

Actually, we will prove more, namely that for *any* polynomial h,

$$h(x + MP) = h(x) \bmod P$$

Indeed, by the Binomial Theorem for any exponent k

$$(x + MP)^k = x^k + \sum_{1 \le i \le k} \binom{k}{i} x^i (MP)^{k-i}$$

That is,

$$(x + MP)^k = x^k \bmod P$$

Adding together suitable constant multiples of powers gives

$$h(x + MP) = h(x) \bmod P$$

In particular,

$$P(x + MP) = P(x) = 0 \bmod P$$

That is, any polynomial differing from x by a multiple of P, when used as the input to P, gives 0 modulo P. That is, x-mod-P is a root of the equation $P(y) = 0$ in $\mathbf{F}_p[x]/P$, as claimed.   ///

Usually it is desirable in such a field $\mathbf{F}_p[x]/P$ to express anything in **reduced form**, since then it is easy to test two things for equality: just compare their coefficients.

Let k be a field. Another field K containing k is called an **extension field** of k, and k is a **subfield** of K. The **degree** of the extension K of k is the degree of the polynomial P used in the construction of K as $k[x]$ modulo P.

Remark: In this situation, thinking of

$$\alpha = x\text{-mod-}P$$

as 'existing in its own right' now, and being a root of the equation $P(x) = 0 \bmod P$, we say that we have **adjoined** a root of $P(x) = 0$ to k, and write

$$k[\alpha] = k[x] \bmod P$$

11.2 Examples of field extensions

Now we'll do some specific numerical examples of field extensions, using the set-up of the previous section.

Example: Let's see how to 'make' the complex numbers $\mathbf{C}$ as a **field extension** of the real number $\mathbf{R}$, *not* by presuming that there is a mysterious $\sqrt{-1}$ already existing 'out there somewhere'.

First, let's prove that $x^2 + 1 \in \mathbf{R}[x]$ is irreducible. Since the square of any real number is non-negative, the equation

$$x^2 + 1 = 0$$

has no roots in $\mathbf{R}$. Since the polynomial $x^2 + 1 \in \mathbf{R}[x]$ is quadratic, if it were to factor in $\mathbf{R}[x]$ it would have to factor into two linear factors (since the degree of the product is the sum of the degrees of the factors). But if $x^2 + 1$ had a linear factor then $x^2 + 1 = 0$ would have a root in $\mathbf{R}$, which it does not. Thus, in the polynomial ring $\mathbf{R}[x]$ the polynomial $x^2 + 1$ is irreducible, as claimed.

Then, from above we know that $\mathbf{R}[x]$ mod $x^2 + 1$ is a field, inside which we can view $\mathbf{R}$ as sitting, by viewing a real number r as being the constant polynomial r-mod-$x^2 + 1$. Also,

$$x^2 = -1 \bmod x^2 + 1$$

so x-mod-$(x^2 + 1)$ is a $\sqrt{-1}$.

We also showed (by showing that every element has a unique reduced representative) that any element β of the extension is expressible uniquely in the form $\beta = a + b\alpha$ for $a, b \in \mathbf{R}$. Of course we usually would write 'i' for the image of x in that extension field rather than 'α'.

Example: Let's adjoin a square root of 2 to the field $\mathbf{Z}/5$. First, note that there is no a in $\mathbf{Z}/5$ so that $a^2 = 5$. Thus, the quadratic polynomial $x^2 - 2$ does not factor in $\mathbf{Z}/5[x]$ (since if it did it would have a root in $\mathbf{Z}/5$, which it doesn't). Then $\mathbf{Z}/5[x]$ mod $x^2 - 2$ is a field, inside which we can view $\mathbf{Z}/5$ as sitting. And

$$x^2 = 2 \bmod x^2 - 2$$

so x-mod-$(x^2 - 2)$ is a square root of 2. Of course, we usually would write '$\sqrt{2}$' for x-mod-$(x^2 - 2)$, rather than 'α'.

Remark: Yes, these constructions might be viewed as anti-climactic, since the construction 'makes' roots of polynomials in a manner that seemingly is not as tangible as one would like. But in fact it's *good* that the construction is fairly straightforward, since that partly means that *it works well*, and computations can be efficiently done.

Example: Let's adjoining a cube root of 2 to $\mathbf{Z}/7$. First, note that there is no cube root of 2 in $\mathbf{Z}/7$. (Check by brute force. Or, by noting that $\mathbf{Z}/7^\times$ is cyclic of order 6, from earlier basic facts about cyclic groups $\mathbf{Z}/7^\times$ will have only two third powers, which we can directly observe are ± 1, so (by exclusion) 2 can't be a cube.)

Thus, the cubic polynomial $x^3 - 2$ is irreducible in $\mathbf{Z}/7[x]$, since if it were *reducible* then it would necessarily have a linear factor, and then $x^3 - 2 = 0$ would necessarily have a root in $\mathbf{Z}/7$, which it doesn't, as we check by brute force.

From this discussion, $\mathbf{Z}/7[x]$ mod $(x^3 - 2)$ is a field, and x-mod-$(x^3 - 2)$ is a cube root of 2. And every element β of this field extension of $\mathbf{Z}/7$ can be uniquely expressed in the form

$$\beta = a_0 + a_1\alpha + a_2\alpha^2$$

where we use α as an abbreviation for x-mod-$(x^3 - 2)$.

11.3 Addition mod P

Addition in $\mathbf{F}_p[x]/P$ is easy: just add the corresponding coefficients of polynomials. Since the degree of a sum of polynomials is less than or equal the max of their degrees, the sum of two *reduced* polynomials is still reduced.

For example, in $\mathbf{F}_2[x]/(x^4 + x + 1)$, adding $x^3 + x + 1$ and $x^2 + x + 1$ gives

$$(x^3 + x + 1) + (x^2 + x + 1) = x^3 + x^2 + 2x + 2 = x^3 + x^2 \bmod x^4 + x + 1$$

since $2 = 0$.

11.4 Multiplication mod P

Multiplication in $\mathbf{F}_p[x]/P$ is ordinary multiplication of polynomials followed by reduction modulo P.

For example, in $\mathbf{F}_2[x]/(x^4 + x + 1)$, multiplying $x^3 + x + 1$ and $x^2 + x + 1$ gives

$$(x^3 + x + 1) \cdot (x^2 + x + 1) = x^5 + x^4 + 2x^3 + 2x^2 + 2x + 1$$

$$= x^5 + x^4 + 1 = x^2 + 1 \bmod x^4 + x + 1$$

since $2 = 0$ and

$$(x^5 + x + 1) - (x)(x^4 + x + 1) = x^2 + 1$$

is the way that the reduction mod $x^4 + x + 1$ of $x^5 + x^4 + 1$ is computed.

Again: to multiply modulo P, multiply polynomials in the ordinary way and then reduce modulo P.

11.5 Multiplicative inverses mod P

This is the most complicated operation, requiring use of the Euclidean algorithm.

Now it is important that the modulus P be *irreducible*. To find the multiplicative inverse of f modulo P, that is, in $\mathbf{F}_p[x]/P$, with $f \neq 0 \bmod P$, use the extended Euclidean algorithm to find polynomials S, T so that

$$S \cdot f + T \cdot P = 1$$

Then

$$S \cdot f - 1 = T \cdot P$$

so by definition of equality-mod-P

$$S \cdot f = 1 \bmod P$$

That is,

$$f^{-1} = S \bmod P$$

Because f is not 0 mod P, and because P is irreducible, the gcd of the two is 1, so such S, T do exist.

For example, to find the multiplicative inverse of x in $\mathbf{F}_2[x]/(x^2 + x + 1)$, first do the Euclid Algorithm (which is very quick here)

$$(x^2 + x + 1) - (x + 1)(x) = 1$$

Thus, already we have the desired expression

$$(x + 1)(x) + (1)(x^2 + x + 1) = 1$$

from which

$$(x + 1)(x) = 1 \bmod x^2 + x + 1$$

In other words,

$$x^{-1} = x + 1 \bmod x^2 + x + 1$$

To find the multiplicative inverse of $x^2 + x + 1$ in $\mathbf{F}_2[x]/(x^4 + x + 1)$, first do the Euclidean Algorithm

$$(x^4 + x + 1) - (x^2 + x)(x^2 + x + 1) = 1$$

Thus, already we have the desired expression

$$(x^2 + x)(x^2 + x + 1) + (1)(x^4 + x + 1) = 1$$

from which

$$(x^2 + x)(x^2 + x + 1) = 1 \bmod x^4 + x + 1$$

In other words,

$$(x^2 + x + 1)^{-1} = x^2 + x \bmod x^2 + x + 1$$

Exercises

11.01 In the field $K = (\mathbf{Z}/2)[x]/(x^2 + x + 1)$ let α be the image of x, and compute in reduced form α^5. (*ans.*)

11.02 In the field $K = (\mathbf{Z}/2)[x]/(x^2 + x + 1)$ let α be the image of x, and compute in reduced form α^7.

11.03 In the field $K = (\mathbf{Z}/2)[x]/(x^3 + x + 1)$ let α be the image of x, and compute in reduced form α^5. (*ans.*)

11.04 In the field $K = (\mathbf{Z}/2)[x]/(x^3 + x^2 + 1)$ let α be the image of x, and compute in reduced form α^5.

11.05 In the field $K = (\mathbf{Z}/2)[x]/(x^2 + x + 1)$ let α be the image of x, and compute in reduced form α^{-1}. (*ans.*)

11.06 In the field $K = (\mathbf{Z}/2)[x]/(x^3 + x + 1)$ let α be the image of x and compute in reduced form $(1 + \alpha + \alpha^2)^{-1}$. (*ans.*)

11.07 In the field $K = (\mathbf{Z}/2)[x]/(x^5 + x^2 + 1)$ let α be the image of x and compute in reduced form $(1 + \alpha + \alpha^2 + \alpha^3)^{-1}$.

11.08 Show that there is no element $x \in \mathbf{F}_{13}$ so that $x^5 = 1$ except $x = 1$.

11.09 Factor $x^4 - x$ into irreducibles over $\mathbf{F}_2$. (*ans.*)

11.10 Factor $x^8 - x$ into irreducibles over $\mathbf{F}_2$. (*ans.*)

11.11 Factor $x^{16} - x$ into irreducibles over $\mathbf{F}_2$.

12

Linear Codes

It turns out to be hard to actually *make* good codes, meaning that they approach the bound indicated by Shannon's Noisy Coding Theorem. (They should also be relatively easy to encode and decode, in addition to their error-correcting facility.)

The class of codes easiest to study is that of **linear codes**, which does include some fairly good codes, and has enough structure so that encoding and decoding are not ridiculously complicated.

There are many standard introductory texts and references for coding theory, and we mention only a few: [MacWilliams Sloane 1977], [McEliece 1977], [Pless 1998], [Pretzel 1999], [Roman 1992], [Wells 1999], [Welsh 1988]. All the error-correcting coding material in the sequel is treated in most of these. There are many sorts of codes we have *not* treated, and these are treated in various of these sources.

12.1 An ugly example

Before systematically introducing linear codes, we first give a very explicit and awkward example to illustrate several points. One point is the senselessness of exact computation rather than robust approximations. Another is the computational awkwardness of non-linear codes.

Let the codewords be 0001, 0110, and 1100, emitted with equal probabilities. The **Hamming distance** between two binary words (of the same length) is defined to be the number of positions at which they differ. Here, the first word is Hamming distance 3 from the other two, which are Hamming distance 2 from each other.

Suppose that a binary symmetric channel has bit error probability $p = 1/10$. Using this code over that channel (or really its *fourth extension*, so that we send 4 bits at a time) **what is the probability of an uncorrectible error?** We are using minimum distance decoding, so the question means **what is the probability that a codeword will get mangled into a 4-bit word that is closer (in Hamming distance) to some** *other* **codeword than to the** *original* **codeword?**

We'll first compute this in the most obvious but labor-intensive approach. The naive aspect will be that we'll try to get an exact answer, but this exactness will not really be relevant to anything, so is a bit silly. And the more trouble it takes to preserve this needless exactness the sillier it becomes. So we'll do a second computation in which we only get an **estimate** rather than striving for an expensive and pointless precision.

Let's make a table of all possible 4-bit words and their Hamming distances from the 3 codewords. Each 4-bit word would be decoded/corrected as the closest codeword to it. The minimum distances are in boldface.

	0001	0110	1100	
0000	**1**	2	2	
0001	**0**	3	3	
0010	2	**1**	3	
0011	**1**	2	4	
0100	2	**1**	**1**	ambiguous decoding
0101	**1**	2	2	
0110	3	**0**	2	
0111	2	**1**	3	
1000	2	3	**1**	
1001	**1**	4	2	
1010	3	**2**	**2**	ambiguous decoding
1011	**2**	3	3	
1100	3	2	**0**	
1101	2	3	**1**	
1110	4	**1**	**1**	ambiguous decoding
1111	3	**2**	**2**	ambiguous decoding

There are exactly 4 cases where there would be **ambiguous** decoding, that is, where the minimum distance of the received word to a codeword is achieved for two different codewords. These received words cannot be corrected (with certainty) in any case.

A possibly multi-bit error in a 4-bit word is not correctible if *either* the received word is one of those whose smallest distance to a codeword occurs for two different codewords, *or* if the received word is closer (or equal) to another codeword than to the original codeword.

The probability that a codeword gets mangled into a given 4-bit word is completely computable just from knowledge of the number of bit errors that would turn the codeword into the received word, that is, from the Hamming distance between the codeword and the received word. With error probability p, the probability of a specific 0-bit error in a 4-bit word is $(1-p)^4$, the probability of a specific 1-bit error is $(1-p)^3 p$, the probability of a specific 2-bit error is $(1-p)^2 p^2$, of a specific 3-bit error is $(1-p)p^3$, and of a specific 4-bit error is p^4. With $p = 1/10$, these numbers are approximately

$$
\begin{aligned}
P(\text{no error}) &= 0.6561 \\
P(\text{specific 1-bit error}) &= 0.0729 \\
P(\text{specific 2-bit error}) &= 0.0081 \\
P(\text{specific 3-bit error}) &= 0.0009 \\
P(\text{specific 4-bit error}) &= 0.0001
\end{aligned}
$$

And note that there are no binomial coefficients appearing here since after all it's not just *any* error that turns a given codeword into a given received word. For example, to turn codeword 0001 into 0111, there must be bit errors at the two middle bit positions, and no other errors.

Now rewrite the table above, writing the probabilities that the 4-bit words will arise as mangled versions of codewords *other than* the codewords closest to them. We also include the cases that the received word is closest to two or more codewords. That is, we are tabulating the probabilities of various mistakes in decoding:

	0001	0110	1100	
0000	-	.0081	.0081	
0001	-	.0009	.0009	
0010	.0081	-	.0009	
0011	-	.0081	.0001	
0100	.0081	.0729	.0729	ambiguous decoding
0101	-	.0081	.0081	
0110	.0009	-	.0081	
0111	.0081	-	.0009	
1000	.0081	.0009	-	
1001	-	.0001	.0081	
1010	.0009	.0081	.0081	ambiguous decoding
1011	-	.0009	.0009	
1100	.0009	.0081	-	
1101	.0081	.0009	-	
1110	.0001	.0729	.0729	ambiguous decoding
1111	.0009	.0081	.0081	ambiguous decoding

Thus, under each codeword, the probabilities listed are that the codeword will get mangled into the 4-bit word on the left. The omitted cases are where the codeword gets slightly mangled, but only into a word that is still closer to the original codeword than to any other codeword.

Since the codewords are sent with equal probabilities, the probability of an uncorrectible (or falsely correctible) received word is

$$
\frac{1}{3}(\text{sum of first column}) + \frac{1}{3}(\text{sum of second column}) + \frac{1}{3}(\text{sum of third column})
$$

$$= \frac{1}{3}(5 \cdot 0.0081 + 4 \cdot 0.0009 + 1 \cdot 0.0001) + \frac{1}{3}(2 \cdot 0.0729 + 6 \cdot 0.0081 + 4 \cdot 0.0009 + 1 \cdot 0.0001)$$

$$+ \frac{1}{3}(2 \cdot 0.0729 + 6 \cdot 0.0081 + 4 \cdot 0.0009 + 1 \cdot 0.0001)$$

(We know that the last two subsums are the same, by symmetry.) This is

$$\frac{1}{3}(4 \cdot 0.0729 + 17 \cdot 0.0081 + 12 \cdot 0.0009 + 3 \cdot 0.0001) \approx 0.1468$$

That is, **the probability of an uncorrectible error is 0.8532**.

12.2 A better approach

Now let's recompute an approximate version of this in a style which avoids keeping track of so many details. The idea is that with a small bit error probability we should only pay attention to scenarios in which there are relatively few bit errors. This is certainly believable, considering that in our previous computation the 0.0009 and 0.0001 certainly didn't contribute much.

The idea that we don't need absolute precision can be clarified by thinking of the context. Note that the **rate** of this code is

$$\text{rate} = \frac{\log_2(\text{number codewords})}{\text{length codewords}} = \frac{\log_2(3)}{4} \approx 0.39624$$

The only reason to use a code with rate much below 1 would be to try to correct errors by adding redundancy. To judge the success of an attempt at error correction, we should make a comparison (for example) to the situation that we'd use *all* 4-bit words and see what the probability of uncorrectible error is in that case. In that case, *any* error is uncorrectible, so **using all 4-bit words as codewords**

$$P(\text{correctible error}) = P(\text{no error}) = (1 - \frac{1}{10})^4 \approx 0.6561$$

To make a *conservative* estimate (in a positive sense of the word) of correctible errors with our code, we can simply compute that sum of the probabilities that
- a codeword is not changed at all (0 bit errors)
- the codeword 0001 is changed by a 1-bit error
- codewords 0110 or 1100 are changed by a 1-bit error *other than* errors which give a received word the same distance from 0110 and 1100

These are simple-to-describe situations where the received word is correctible. It is important to remember the **triangle inequality**

$$d(x, y) \leq d(x, z) + d(z, y)$$

for the Hamming distance $d(,)$, which assures that *any* 4-bit word that differs by a single bit from 0001 must be at least distance 2 from 0110 and 1100 since

$$d(0001, 0110) = d(0001, 1100) = 3$$

And note that 0110 can be mangled to 0111 or 0010 by 1-bit errors, and that these are still closer to 0110 than to 1100. Likewise, 1100 can get mangled to 1101 or 1000 which are still closer to 1100 than to 0110. **For simplicity,** we just ignore any other possibilities of correctible errors. Thus, we'll know that the probability of a correctible error is **at least** the sum of these probabilities.

Computing:

$$P(\text{correctible error}) \geq P(\text{no error}) + P(0001 \text{ sent with any 1-bit error})$$

$$+ P(0110 \text{ sent, } 0111 \text{ or } 0010 \text{ received}) + P(1100 \text{ sent, } 1101 \text{ or } 1000 \text{ received})$$

$$= \left(\frac{9}{10}\right)^4 + \frac{1}{3}\binom{4}{1}\frac{1}{10}\left(\frac{9}{10}\right)^3 + \frac{1}{3}\cdot 2 \cdot \frac{1}{10}\left(\frac{9}{10}\right)^3 + \frac{1}{3}\cdot 2 \cdot \frac{1}{10}\left(\frac{9}{10}\right)^3$$

$$= \left(\frac{9}{10}\right)^4 + \frac{1}{3}\left(4 + 2 + 2\right)\frac{1}{10}\left(\frac{9}{10}\right)^3$$

$$\approx 0.6561 + 0.1944 = 0.8505$$

That is, **the probability that an error will be correctible is at least 0.8505**.

First, notice that 0.8505 is much higher than the 0.6561 probability of correctible error (no error) using all 4-bit words. So we've already proven that this code is significantly better in terms of error correction, even though we don't know *exactly* the probability of errors being correctible.

Second, we had earlier computed that the 'exact' probability that an error is correctible is 0.8532. The difference is less than 1% of the actual number. In this context, such an error of 1% in computing a probability is completely irrelevant!

So we conclude that we could have done the easier second computation and skipped all the work of constructing *complete* tables of Hamming distances, etc., and all the arithmetic.

12.3 An inequality from the other side

Let's continue with the idea that with relatively small probability of single-bit error we can get a very good approximation of probability of uncorrectible error without looking at the details of errors involving more than one bit.

That is, so far we have computed rather simply that

$$P(\text{uncorrectible error}) \leq 0.15$$

This is the right sort of inequality to have for **quality assurance**. That is, if we want to convince people that the code is good, we want to be able to guarantee a limit to the probability of errors.

On the other hand, at the same time, we don't want to undersell our code: if we really have probability of error less than 1% we don't want to only say that the probability of error is less than 10%. That assertion would be true, of course, but it would be *needlessly weak.*

So in the present example let's see whether we can give a simple computational approach to show that our approximation

$$P(\text{uncorrectible error}) \leq 0.15$$

is *not* needlessly weak. That is, we'll find a relatively simple approach to obtain an inequality of the form

$$P(\text{uncorrectible error}) \geq \text{number}$$

and hope that the number on the right-hand side is close to 0.15.

We'll only pay attention to uncorrectible single-bit errors. As a complement to the earlier discussion of *correctible* single-bit errors, we know 4 uncorrectible single-bit errors:

0110 sent   1110 received
0110 sent   0100 received
1100 sent   1110 received
1100 sent   0100 received

These are uncorrectible because they are Hamming distance 1 from both 0110 and 1100. These are disjoint events, so the probability that at least one of them occurs is the sum of the separate probabilities: this probability is

$$\frac{1}{3} \cdot \frac{1}{10} \left(\frac{9}{10}\right)^3 + \frac{1}{3} \cdot \frac{1}{10} \left(\frac{9}{10}\right)^3 + \frac{1}{3} \cdot \frac{1}{10} \left(\frac{9}{10}\right)^3 + \frac{1}{3} \cdot \frac{1}{10} \left(\frac{9}{10}\right)^3 \approx 0.0972$$

Then we can say

$$P(\text{uncorrectible error}) \geq P(\text{those 4 specific uncorrectible errors}) \approx 0.0972$$

Combining this inequality with the earlier one, we have

$$0.0972 \leq P(\text{uncorrectible error}) \leq 0.15$$

The right-hand inequality gives a quality assurance, while the left-hand inequality tells us that we are not wastefully underselling the quality of the code. And, again, we get this **estimate** on the probability of an uncorrectible error without looking at anything beyond single-bit errors.

12.4 The Hamming binary [7, 4] code

Shannon's theorem on noisy coding gives no indication of how to *make* good codes in any systematic manner. Further, there is the additional issue of efficient *decoding*, which is not directly addressed by Shannon's theorem: a code might be very good at correcting errors, but very expensive in terms of the trouble it takes to do the decoding. The first *constructions* of codes that were not only pretty good but also easily decodable occurred about 1952 and were due to Hamming. By the way, the notation [7, 4] refers to the fact that the codewords are length 7, while the *dimension* (defined precisely later) of the code is 4. The latter roughly means that each 7-bit codeword carries 4 bits of information.

Hamming's **binary** $[7, 4]$ **code** starts with an alphabet or vocabulary of the $16 = 2^4$ binary words of length 4: 0001, 0010, 0011, 0100, 0101, 0110, etc. To each such word $abcd$ (with each of a, b, c, d being 0 or 1) Hamming's $[7, 4]$ code adds some **redundancy bits** in a clever pattern:

$$abcd \text{ becomes } abcdefg$$

where

$$e = b + c + d$$

$$f = a + c + d$$

$$g = a + b + d$$

viewing a, b, c, d as being in the finite field $\mathbf{F}_2$. The notation $[7, 4]$ refers to the fact that the initial *source words* were all the binary words of length 4, and the *codewords* are of length 7.

For example, the Hamming $[7, 4]$ code would encode

$$
\begin{array}{ccc}
1000 & \rightarrow & 1000011 \\
0100 & \rightarrow & 0100101 \\
0010 & \rightarrow & 0010110 \\
0001 & \rightarrow & 0001111
\end{array}
$$

The **Hamming decoding** procedure is one of the good features of this code. First, we'll write all the codewords as **vectors**, like

$$1000011 = (1, 0, 0, 0, 0, 1, 1)$$

$$0100101 = (0, 1, 0, 0, 1, 0, 1)$$

(Keep in mind that the *components* of these vectors are in $\mathbf{F}_2$.) Define auxiliary vectors by

$$
\begin{array}{rcl}
r & = & (0, 0, 0, 1, 1, 1, 1) \\
s & = & (0, 1, 1, 0, 0, 1, 1) \\
t & = & (1, 0, 1, 0, 1, 0, 1)
\end{array}
$$

(No, it's not at all clear why these are the right things...) We'll use the **inner product** (also called **dot** or **scalar** product) on vectors, defined as usual by the expression

$$(x_1, \ldots, x_n) \cdot (y_1, \ldots, y_n) = x_1 y_1 + x_2 y_2 + \ldots + x_n y_n$$

although in the present context all the indicated arithmetic is done inside the finite field $\mathbf{F}_2$ rather than the real or complex numbers. Then for a source word such as 0100 the Hamming $[7, 4]$ code encodes it as $x = 0100101$, or, equivalently, as the vector $x = (0, 1, 0, 0, 1, 0, 1)$. Suppose that a binary symmetric channel transmits the word as $y = (1, 1, 0, 0, 1, 0, 1)$, that is, with a single bit error (in this example it's

in the first position). To do **Hamming decoding**, compute the 3 inner products
(in $\mathbf{F}_2$!)

$$
\begin{aligned}
y \cdot r &= (1,1,0,0,1,0,1) \cdot (0,0,0,1,1,1,1) = 0 \\
y \cdot s &= (1,1,0,0,1,0,1) \cdot (0,1,1,0,0,1,1) = 0 \\
y \cdot t &= (1,1,0,0,1,0,1) \cdot (1,0,1,0,1,0,1) = 1
\end{aligned}
$$

Then interpret the triple of inner products as a **binary integer**:

$$001 = 0 \cdot 2^2 + 0 \cdot 2^1 + 1 \cdot 2^0 = 1 \text{ (in decimal)}$$

The Hamming decoding procedure says that this should be interpreted as indicating
that *the received word had a bit error in the first position.*

Similarly, suppose that the same word $x = (0,1,0,0,1,0,1)$ was sent, but that
$y = (0,1,1,0,1,0,1)$ was received (that is, with a bit error in the third position).
Then the same computation gives

$$
\begin{aligned}
y \cdot r &= (0,1,1,0,1,0,1) \cdot (0,0,0,1,1,1,1) = 0 \\
y \cdot s &= (0,1,1,0,1,0,1) \cdot (0,1,1,0,0,1,1) = 1 \\
y \cdot t &= (0,1,1,0,1,0,1) \cdot (1,0,1,0,1,0,1) = 1
\end{aligned}
$$

As a binary integer, the 011 is

$$011 = 0 \cdot 2^2 + 1 \cdot 2^1 + 1 \cdot 2^0 = 3 \text{ (in decimal)}$$

which tells us that the *third* bit is wrong.

Further, even if *two* bits change, the Hamming [7, 4] code can *detect* this,
although a 2-bit error is beyond the power of this code to *correct.*

*Now let's compare the effectiveness of the Hamming [7, 4] code to the cases of
doing nothing, and also to merely adding a parity-check bit.*

On a binary symmetric channel with bit error probability 1/8, with source
words consisting of the 16 binary words of length 4, the word error probability is
simply

$$\text{word error} = 1 - \text{ probability that } no \text{ bit is flipped}$$

$$= 1 - (7/8)^4 \approx 1 - 0.5862 \approx 0.4138$$

That is, there is a quite high chance that a 4-bit word won't be transmitted intact,
and we'd have no way of knowing.

If we add a parity-check bit, then the probability of an *uncorrectable* error goes
up, since the parity-check bit itself may get flipped, too. But now we can *detect*
the presence of a single bit error, but won't know which bit was changed.

When the Hamming code is used, the probability of a correctable error is the
sum of the probabilities of the cases of *no* errors and the case of a single bit error:

$$\text{word error probability} = 1 - \left(\frac{7}{8}\right)^7 - \binom{7}{1}\left(\frac{7}{8}\right)^6\left(\frac{1}{8}\right)$$

$$\approx 1 - 0.3436 - 0.3436 \approx 0.2146$$

If the bit error probability goes down to 1/12, then the word error probability with the do-nothing encoding is

$$1 - (11/12)^4 \approx 0.2939$$

while for the Hamming $[7, 4]$ code it is

$$1 - \left(\left(\frac{11}{12} \right)^7 + \binom{7}{1} \left(\frac{11}{12} \right)^6 \frac{1}{12} \right) \approx 0.1101$$

With word error further reduced to 1/20, the word error for do-nothing encoding is

$$1 - (19/20)^4 \approx 0.18549$$

while for the Hamming $[7, 4]$ code it iss

$$1 - \left(\left(\frac{19}{20} \right)^7 + \binom{7}{1} \left(\frac{19}{20} \right)^6 \frac{1}{20} \right) \approx 0.0444$$

Remark: The Hamming $[7, 4]$ code can correct single bit errors, by converting 4-bit words into 7-bit words in a clever manner. This is much better than simply repeating messages, but what about 2-bit errors, etc?

12.5 Some linear algebra

We will need some basic terminology regarding vector and matrix operations. This will be applied mostly when the entries of the vectors and matrices in question are in a finite field $\mathbf{F}_q$ with q elements. There are subtler underlying issues of well-definedness which have been relegated to the appendix on linear algebra, in which linear algebra is treated more abstractly rather than just in terms of matrices and row and column vectors. But all we need for our immediate purposes is the matrix version, if one is willing to accept certain foundational results.

Let F denote the 'scalars'. Thus, F could be the real numbers $\mathbf{R}$, the complex numbers $\mathbf{C}$, the rational numbers $\mathbf{Q}$, the finite field $\mathbf{F}_2$, the finite field $\mathbf{Z}/p = \mathbf{F}_p$ for p prime, and other things as well.

Remark: In fact, all this works for a quite broad abstract class of 'scalars': F could be any **field**. Recall that, as defined earlier in general, a *field* is a commutative ring in which every non-zero element has a multiplicative inverse.

A **vector** of **dimension** n is an ordered n-tuple of scalars, separated by commas and with parentheses on the ends. For example, $(1, 2, 3, 4, 5, 6, 7)$ is a 7-dimensional vector, and $(0, 0, 1, 0)$ is a 4-dimensional vector. The set of n-dimensional vectors with entries in F is denoted

$$F^n = \{n\text{-dimensional vectors over } F\}$$

The context should provide adequate clues about what kind of scalars the entries in a vector are. The scalars in the vector are called the **entries** or **components**.

Sometimes the ith component of a vector v is denoted by means of a subscript, such as v_i, but this is absolutely not a reliable indicator. It is necessary to pay attention to the context.

The **zero vector** (of whatever dimension) is the ordered tuple consisting of all 0s. It is denoted 0. Yes, in real life we are not required to put an arrow on top of it. We will have to depend upon the context to tell whether '0' refers to a 0-vector or simply a scalar 0.

The **(vector) sum** of two vectors $x = (x_1, \ldots, x_n)$ and $y = (y_1, \ldots, y_n)$ is obtained by adding component-wise:

$$x + y = (x_1, \ldots, x_n) + (y_1, \ldots, y_n) = (x_1 + y_1, x_2 + y_2, \ldots, x_n + y_n)$$

The **scalar multiple** cx of a vector $x = (x_1, \ldots, x_n)$ by a scalar c is obtained by multiplying each component by the scalar:

$$cx = (cx_1, \ldots, cx_n)$$

A **linear combination** of a collection of vectors $v_1, \ldots, v_t$ (all of the same length) is any other vector w expressible as

$$w = c_1 v_1 + c_2 v_2 + \ldots + c_t v_t$$

with scalars $c_1, \ldots, c_t$. A collection $v_1, \ldots, v_t$ of vectors (all of the same length) is **linearly dependent** if there is some linear combination (not with all coefficients c_is being 0) which is the zero vector:

$$0 = c_1 v_1 + c_2 v_2 + \ldots + c_t v_t$$

Likewise, a collection $v_1, \ldots, v_t$ of vectors (all of the same length) is **linearly independent** if there is *no* linear combination (except that with all coefficients 0) which is the zero vector.

Example: In F^3 the 2 vectors $u = (1, 0, 0)$ and $v = (0, 1, 0)$ are linearly independent. We can verify this by solving for scalars x, y in the equation

$$(0, 0, 0) = xu + yv = x(1, 0, 0) + y(0, 1, 0)$$

That is, by carrying out the indicated operations, we must solve

$$(0, 0, 0) = (x, y, 0)$$

Since **two vectors are equal if and only if all their components are equal**, this equality can hold if and only if both $x = 0$ and $y = 0$. This proves that the two given vectors are linearly independent.

Remark: In general, it requires some work to check linear independence, or to express a given vector as a linear combination of some given ones, or even to ascertain whether there *exists* such an expression without necessarily finding it. The row reduction (Gaussian elimination) of the next section will provide one systematic approach.

The **dot product** or **scalar product** or **inner product** of two vectors $x = (x_1, \ldots, x_n)$ and $y = (y_1, \ldots, y_n)$ is

$$x \cdot y = x_1 y_1 + x_2 y_2 + \ldots + x_n y_n$$

Say that two vectors are **orthogonal** if their dot product is 0.

Remark: When the scalars are real numbers or complex numbers, the dot product has geometric significance, but when the scalars are $\mathbf{F}_2$ or other things, the geometric interpretation is less elementary. Likewise, while 2-dimensional or 3-dimensional vectors over the real numbers have popular and important physical interpretations as arrows or points in the plane or space, we have no such interpretation here. But the *mathematical* operations are the same.

For positive integers m and n, an m-by-n **matrix** with entries in F is simply a block of numbers with m rows and n columns, with big parentheses enclosing it. The ij^{th} **entry** or **component** is the entry in the ith row and j^{th} column. For matrix M, very often the ij^{th} component is denoted by M_{ij}. For example,

$$M = \begin{pmatrix} 11 & 12 & 13 \\ 21 & 22 & 23 \end{pmatrix}$$

is a 2-by-3 matrix. Here $M_{11} = 11$, $M_{12} = 12$, etc.

The **diagonal** of a matrix M is the upper-left to lower-right diagonal, consisting of the entries M_{11}, M_{22}, M_{33}, etc.

The **transpose** M^t of an m-by-n matrix M is an n-by-m matrix obtained by flipping M across the **diagonal**, whose ij^{th} entry is the ji^{th} entry of the original. For example,

$$\begin{pmatrix} 11 & 12 & 13 \\ 21 & 22 & 23 \end{pmatrix}^t = \begin{pmatrix} 11 & 21 \\ 12 & 22 \\ 13 & 23 \end{pmatrix}$$

The **size-n identity matrix** I_n is the n-by-n matrix with 1s on the diagonal and 0s off the diagonal. For example,

$$I_1 = \begin{pmatrix} 1 \end{pmatrix}$$
$$I_2 = \begin{pmatrix} 1 & 0 \\ 0 & 1 \end{pmatrix}$$
$$I_3 = \begin{pmatrix} 1 & 0 & 0 \\ 0 & 1 & 0 \\ 0 & 0 & 1 \end{pmatrix}$$
$$I_4 = \begin{pmatrix} 1 & 0 & 0 & 0 \\ 0 & 1 & 0 & 0 \\ 0 & 0 & 1 & 0 \\ 0 & 0 & 0 & 1 \end{pmatrix}$$

Notice that this makes sense regardless of what kind of scalars we are using. At the same time, looking at an identity matrix doesn't give any clue as to what the scalars are. The n-by-n **zero matrix** consists entirely of zeros.

A **row vector** of **dimension** n is a 1-by-n matrix. A **column vector** of **dimension** n is an n-by-1 matrix. Sometimes for typographical or other reasons the entries in a row vector are separated by commas: for example,

$$(1 \quad 2 \quad 3 \quad 4 \quad 5) = (1, 2, 3, 4, 5)$$

Remark: In any case, the idea of a vector as ordered n-tuple is slightly more abstract than the tangible notational manifestations as 'row' or 'column' vectors. For most purposes, there is little reason to try to worry about whether a vector is *'naturally'* a row vector versus column vector. We will consider these as just being different notational devices for the same underlying thing.

12.6 Row reduction: a review

Row reduction is one of the fundamental algorithms in linear algebra, arising in many contexts.

Elementary row operations are simple transformations of matrices which are best described by treating the rows of the matrix as vectors. The elementary row operations are:

- Adding a scalar multiple of one row to another row
- Multiplying a row by a non-zero scalar
- Interchanging two rows

Elementary column operations are analogous simple transformations of matrices which are best described by treating the *columns* of the matrix as vectors. The elementary column operations are:

- Adding a scalar multiple of one column to another column
- Multiplying a column by a non-zero scalar
- Interchanging two columns

It is sometimes very useful to realize that row operations on a matrix M correspond to *matrix multiplication* of M on the left by certain special matrices. For example, interchanging the second and third rows of the 3-by-2 matrix

$$M = \begin{pmatrix} a & b \\ c & d \\ e & f \end{pmatrix}$$

is the same as left-multiplying M by

$$\begin{pmatrix} 1 & 0 & 0 \\ 0 & 0 & 1 \\ 0 & 1 & 0 \end{pmatrix}$$

As another example, adding t times the third row of M to the first row of M is achieved by left-multiplying M by

$$\begin{pmatrix} 1 & 0 & t \\ 0 & 1 & 0 \\ 0 & 0 & 1 \end{pmatrix}$$

(To prove that this is so in general is an exercise in notation and the definition of matrix multiplication.)

The **row space** of an m-by-n matrix M is the subset of F^n consisting of all linear combinations of rows of M (viewed as n-dimensional vectors). Similarly, the **column space** of an m-by-n matrix M is the subset of F^m consisting of all linear combinations of columns of M (viewed as m-dimensional vectors).

An m-by-n matrix matrix M is **(strongly) row reduced** if the following slightly complicated but important condition is met. Look at the ith row of M, which has entries M_{i1}, M_{i2}, ..., M_{in}. If all these entries are 0, then there is no condition. If not all these entries are 0, let j_i be the smallest integer so that $M_{ij_i} \neq 0$. Call this the **leading entry** of the ith row, or **pivot** in the ith row. For M to be **(strongly) row reduced** we require that for every row index i

$$M_{i\,j_i} = 1$$

and

$$M_{i'\,j_i} = 0 \quad \text{for } i' \neq i$$

Further, we require that

$$j_i < j_{i'} \quad \text{for } i < i'$$

In words, the pivot in each row is 1, and the entries above and below each pivot are 0s. Further, as we go down the rows, the leading entries occur further and further to the right.

There is also a more relaxed definition of **row reduced** which needs less labor to obtain, and is sometimes good enough for applications. Using the terminology above, for M to be **(weakly) row reduced** we require that for every row index i

$$M_{i\,j_i} = 1$$

and

$$M_{i'\,j_i} = 0 \quad \text{for } i' > i$$

Further, we require that

$$j_i < j_{i'} \quad \text{for } i < i'$$

In words, the pivot in each row is 1, and the entries below each pivot are 0s. Further, as we go down the rows, the leading entries occur farther and farther to the right.

The only difference between the two notions of 'row reduced' is that in the latter, weaker sense the entries *above* a pivot are not required to be 0. For example, the matrix

$$\begin{pmatrix} 1 & 0 & 0 & 0 & 1 & 1 \\ 0 & 1 & 0 & 0 & 1 & 0 \\ 0 & 0 & 0 & 1 & 1 & 1 \end{pmatrix}$$

is row reduced (in the strong sense): the leading entry in the top row occurs in the first column, and all the other entries in the first column are 0. The leading entry in the second row occurs in the second column, and all the other entries in the second column are 0. The leading entry of the third row occurs in the fourth column, and all other entries in that column are 0. The fact that the third column is *all* 0s is irrelevant. Also, the contents of the fifth and sixth columns are irrelevant to the question of whether or not the matrix is row-reduced. And the leading entries occur farther and farther to the right as we go down the rows. On the other hand, the matrix

$$\begin{pmatrix} 1 & 0 & 0 & 0 & 1 & 1 \\ 0 & 1 & 0 & 0 & 1 & 0 \\ 1 & 0 & 0 & 1 & 1 & 1 \end{pmatrix}$$

is *not* row reduced (in either sense): in the first column there are two 1s. That is, the leading entry in both the first and third row occurs in the first column. Also, the matrix

$$\begin{pmatrix} 0 & 0 & 1 & 0 & 1 & 1 \\ 0 & 1 & 0 & 0 & 1 & 0 \\ 1 & 0 & 0 & 1 & 1 & 1 \end{pmatrix}$$

is *not* row reduced, since the leading entries do *not* occur farther to the right as we move down the rows. That is, the leading entry in the second row is in the second column, which is farther to the left than the leading entry of the first row, which is in the third column. Likewise, the leading entry of the third row occurs still farther to the left of the leading entry in the second column.

- **Elementary row operations can be used to put a matrix into row-reduced form** (in either the stronger or the weaker sense). Reasonably enough, the process of doing elementary row operations to put a matrix into row-reduced form is called **row reduction.**

(Strong) row reduction is easy to illustrate in an example. Let's start with the matrix

$$\begin{pmatrix} 0 & 1 & 1 & 0 & 1 & 1 \\ 1 & 1 & 1 & 0 & 1 & 0 \\ 1 & 0 & 0 & 1 & 1 & 1 \end{pmatrix}$$

with entries in the field with two elements $\mathbf{F}_2$. First look in the first column: there is a non-zero entry, but it's not in the first row, so we *interchange* the first and second rows, to get

$$\begin{pmatrix} 1 & 1 & 1 & 0 & 1 & 0 \\ 0 & 1 & 1 & 0 & 1 & 1 \\ 1 & 0 & 0 & 1 & 1 & 1 \end{pmatrix}$$

to make a non-zero entry occur in the first row. (We could also have interchanged the first and third rows.) Then, since there is still a non-zero entry in the third row, we *subtract* the first row from the third, obtaining

$$\begin{pmatrix} 1 & 1 & 1 & 0 & 1 & 0 \\ 0 & 1 & 1 & 0 & 1 & 1 \\ 0 & 1 & 1 & 1 & 0 & 1 \end{pmatrix}$$

So the first column looks the way it should.

Next, look in the second column, but only below the first row. There are two 1s, and in particular there is a 1 in the second row, so we don't need to interchange any rows. Thus, the leading term in the second row occurs in the second column. But there are two other non-zero entries in the second column (in both first and third rows), so we subtract the second row from both first and third rows, obtaining

$$\begin{pmatrix} 1 & 0 & 0 & 0 & 0 & 1 \\ 0 & 1 & 1 & 0 & 1 & 1 \\ 0 & 0 & 0 & 1 & 1 & 0 \end{pmatrix}$$

So the second column is arranged the way it should be. The third row has its leading entry not in the third column, but in the fourth. (So we just don't worry about what's going on in the third column.) And, in fact, the other entries of the fourth column are already 0s, so we don't have to do any further work. That is, the matrix is now in row-reduced form.

Remark: The weaker version of row reduction merely omits some work by not bothering to do the row operations to make the entires *above* a pivot 0. This approximately cuts in half the total number of operations necessary, and is sometimes a good-enough version of row reduction.

Remark: The term *row reduced* in the literature is ambiguous, and one must look at the context to discern whether it is *strongly* or *weakly* row reduced. For many purposes it does not matter much which sense is taken.

We can describe the row-reduction process for an m-by-n matrix M a little more abstractly. Start with two auxiliary indices s, t both set equal to 1. While $s \leq m$ and $t \leq n$ repeat the following:

- If the $s, s+1, s+2, \ldots, m$ entries in the tth column are all 0, replace t by $t+1$ and restart this block.
- Else if the $(s,t)^{\text{th}}$ entry is non-zero, divide the sth row by the $(s,t)^{\text{th}}$ entry and then go to the next block.
- Else if the $(s,t)^{\text{th}}$ entry is 0, but the $(s',t)^{\text{th}}$ entry is non-zero (with $s' > s$), then divide the s'^{th} row by the $(s',t)^{\text{th}}$ entry, interchange the sth and s'^{th} rows, and go to the next block of operations.
- For every $s' \neq s$, if the $(s',t)^{\text{th}}$ entry is not 0, then subtract $(s',t)^{\text{th}}$-entry times the sth row from the s'^{th} row. (This applies also to the indices $s' < s$.)
- After all these subtractions, replace s by $s+1$.
- Go back to the previous block (as long as $s \leq m$).

When finally $s = m+1$ or $t = n+1$, the matrix will be in row-reduced form.

Remark: In the special case that the field is $\mathbf{F}_2$, the above process is simpler, since any non-zero element is already 1, so no division is ever necessary.

Remark: Again, if the weaker version of row reduction will suffice in a given application, then simply don't bother to subtract a lower row from a higher row. That is, don't bother to do the row operations to make entries *above* a pivot 1.

Remark: Most often these algorithms are studied in contexts in which floating-point real numbers are used. In that setting, the issue of loss of precision is critical. But in the present scenario, as well as when computing with 'numbers' from arbitrary finite fields, we effectively have *infinite precision*, so we need not worry about round-off error, etc. This avoids many of the technical worries which require lengthy consideration in the floating-point case.

One problem we need to solve is the following: let

$$
\begin{aligned}
v_1 &= (v_{11}, v_{12}, \ldots, v_{1,n}) \\
v_2 &= (v_{21}, v_{22}, \ldots, v_{2,n}) \\
v_3 &= (v_{31}, v_{32}, \ldots, v_{3,n}) \\
&\cdots \\
v_m &= (v_{m1}, v_{m2}, \ldots, v_{m,n})
\end{aligned}
$$

be n-tuples of elements of a **field** k. The field k may be the rational numbers $\mathbf{Q}$, the real numbers $\mathbf{R}$, finite fields $\mathbf{F}_p = \mathbf{Z}/p$ (with p prime), or any other field. We will operate as though we know the numbers **exactly**, or as some would say **with infinite precision**. This hypothesis is usually not fulfilled if the numbers are real numbers which arise from measurements, but for our applications this hypothesis *will* hold.

The question is to find a **linear dependence relation** (if any exists) among the vectors v_i. That is, we want to find elements $c_1, \ldots, c_m$ in k, not all 0, so that

$$
c_1 v_1 + \ldots + c_m v_m = 0 \text{ (zero vector)}
$$

where the indicated multiplications are scalar multiplication

$$
c \cdot (x_1, x_2, \ldots, x_n) = (cx_1, cx_2, \ldots, cx_m)
$$

and the 0 on the right-hand side is the **zero vector**

$$
0 = \underbrace{(0, \ldots, 0)}_{n}
$$

of size n. The **dimension** of vectors represented as n-tuples is (as expected) n.

Remark: In a systematic development of basic linear algebra, one of the first results proven would be that *if the number of vectors is greater than the dimension, then there is a linear dependency relation.* We will not directly use this fact, except to assure ourselves that the algorithm we present does what it claims to do. This fact is proven in the appendix on linear algebra.

First, we form an m-by-n matrix from the components of the vectors: let

$$
M = \begin{pmatrix}
v_{11} & v_{12} & \cdots & v_{1,n} \\
v_{21} & v_{22} & \cdots & v_{2,n} \\
v_{31} & v_{32} & \cdots & v_{3,n} \\
& & \cdots & \\
v_{m1} & v_{m2} & \cdots & v_{m,n}
\end{pmatrix}
$$

Recall that an m-by-m **identity matrix** I_m is an m-by-m matrix with 1s on the (upper-left to lower-right) **diagonal** and 0s off this diagonal:

$$
I_m = \begin{pmatrix}
1 & 0 & 0 & \cdots & 0 \\
0 & 1 & 0 & \cdots & 0 \\
0 & 0 & 1 & \cdots & 0 \\
& & \cdots & & \\
0 & 0 & 0 & \cdots & 1
\end{pmatrix}
$$

Then form a larger matrix from M by sticking an m-by-m **identity matrix** onto its right end: from now on we look at the matrix

$$\widetilde{M} = \begin{pmatrix} v_{11} & v_{12} & \cdots & v_{1,n} & 1 & 0 & 0 & \cdots & 0 \\ v_{21} & v_{22} & \cdots & v_{2,n} & 0 & 1 & 0 & \cdots & 0 \\ v_{31} & v_{32} & \cdots & v_{3,n} & 0 & 0 & 1 & \cdots & 0 \\ & & \cdots & & & & & & \\ v_{m1} & v_{m2} & \cdots & v_{m,n} & 0 & 0 & 0 & \cdots & 1 \end{pmatrix}$$

That identity matrix (or, really, what it turns into subsequently) will keep track of the operations we perform. This type of larger matrix created from M is sometimes called an **augmented matrix**, but this terminology is nonspecific so you shouldn't rely upon it.

The goal is to do elementary row operations until the matrix M (as a part of the larger matrix $\widetilde{M}$) has one or more rows which are all 0s, *if possible*. (The identity matrix stuck onto M on the right can never have this property...) That is, the leftmost m entries of one or more rows of $\widetilde{M}$ should be 0, if possible.

Doing the weak version of row reduction will accomplish this. We go through it again: Starting in the leftmost column, if the top entry is 0, but if there is *some* entry in the first column that is non-zero, interchange rows to put the non-zero entry at the top. Divide through by the leftmost entry in the (new) first row so that the leftmost entry is now 1. Let a_{i1} be the leftmost entry in the ith row. Then for $i > 1$ subtract a_{i1} times the top row from all other rows. This has the effect of making all entries in the first column 0 except for the top entry. (If the leftmost or any other column is all 0s, just ignore it.)

Next look at the second column. If necessary, interchange the second row with another row below it in order to arrange that the second entry of the second row is not 0. (The first entries of all rows below the top one have already been made 0.) Divide through the second row by the second entry, so that the second row starts $0, 1$. Let a_{i2} be the ith entry from the top in the second column. Then subtract a_{i2} times the second row from all lower rows.

Continue this with the third, fourth, up to m^{th} columns, or until any remaining among the first m columns are all 0s. Suppose that the row-reduced version of $\widetilde{M}$ is

$$\widetilde{M}_{\text{red}} = (M_{\text{red}} \quad A)$$

where the M_{red} is the reduced version of M, and the m-by-m matrix A is what I_m turns into by this process.

Let w_i be the left n entries of the ith row of the new matrix M_{red}. (So these are length-n row vectors.) Then what we have is

$$A \begin{pmatrix} v_1 \\ v_2 \\ \cdots \\ v_m \end{pmatrix} = \begin{pmatrix} w_1 \\ w_2 \\ \cdots \\ w_m \end{pmatrix}$$

If $m > n$, then at least the last $m - n$ of the w_is will be the zero vector. For example w_m will certainly be the length-n zero vector. That is, we have

$$a_{m1}v_1 + a_{m2}v_2 + a_{m3}v_3 + \ldots + a_{mm}v_m = (0, \ldots, 0)$$

It is important that (due to the way we obtained the matrix A) for each index i at least one a_{ij} is nonzero.

In other words, we have found a linear combination of the vectors v_i which is zero. (And not all the coefficients in the linear combination are zero.)

Further, it may happen that there is more than one row of the reduced matrix M_{red} which is all 0s. So, quite generally, if the ith row of M_{red} is all 0s, then

$$a_{i1}v_1 + a_{i2}v_2 + a_{i3}v_3 + \ldots + a_{im}v_m = (0, \ldots, 0)$$

A numerical example: Find a (non-trivial) linear dependence relation among the five 4-dimensional binary vectors

$$1101, 1011, 1100, 1111, 0110$$

First, stack these up as the rows of a matrix

$$\begin{pmatrix} 1 & 1 & 0 & 1 \\ 1 & 0 & 1 & 1 \\ 1 & 1 & 0 & 0 \\ 1 & 1 & 1 & 1 \\ 0 & 1 & 1 & 0 \end{pmatrix}$$

and then form the augmented matrix by sticking a 5-by-5 identity matrix onto the right of the previous:

$$\begin{pmatrix} 1 & 1 & 0 & 1 & 1 & 0 & 0 & 0 & 0 \\ 1 & 0 & 1 & 1 & 0 & 1 & 0 & 0 & 0 \\ 1 & 1 & 0 & 0 & 0 & 0 & 1 & 0 & 0 \\ 1 & 1 & 1 & 1 & 0 & 0 & 0 & 1 & 0 \\ 0 & 1 & 1 & 0 & 0 & 0 & 0 & 0 & 1 \end{pmatrix}$$

Now do (weak) row reduction. We already have the proper pivot in the first row, so subtract the first row from the second, third, and fourth (but not fifth) to make the other entries in the first column 0:

$$\begin{pmatrix} 1 & 1 & 0 & 1 & 1 & 0 & 0 & 0 & 0 \\ 0 & 1 & 1 & 0 & 1 & 1 & 0 & 0 & 0 \\ 0 & 0 & 0 & 1 & 1 & 0 & 1 & 0 & 0 \\ 0 & 0 & 1 & 0 & 1 & 0 & 0 & 1 & 0 \\ 0 & 1 & 1 & 0 & 0 & 0 & 0 & 0 & 1 \end{pmatrix}$$

The pivot in the second row is already prepared as well. Then we want to make all the *lower* entries in the second column 0. (We don't care about the *higher* ones because we're doing the weaker form of row reduction.) Thus, just subtract the second from the last row:

$$\begin{pmatrix} 1 & 1 & 0 & 1 & 1 & 0 & 0 & 0 & 0 \\ 0 & 1 & 1 & 0 & 1 & 1 & 0 & 0 & 0 \\ 0 & 0 & 0 & 1 & 1 & 0 & 1 & 0 & 0 \\ 0 & 0 & 1 & 0 & 1 & 0 & 0 & 1 & 0 \\ 0 & 0 & 0 & 0 & 1 & 1 & 0 & 0 & 1 \end{pmatrix}$$

In the third column to get a pivot into the right spot we must interchange the third and fourth rows:

$$\begin{pmatrix} 1 & 1 & 0 & 1 & 1 & 0 & 0 & 0 & 0 \\ 0 & 1 & 1 & 0 & 1 & 1 & 0 & 0 & 0 \\ 0 & 0 & 1 & 0 & 1 & 0 & 0 & 1 & 0 \\ 0 & 0 & 0 & 1 & 1 & 0 & 1 & 0 & 0 \\ 0 & 0 & 0 & 0 & 1 & 1 & 0 & 0 & 1 \end{pmatrix}$$

In this case all the entries below that 1 in the $(3,3)$ position are already 0s, so no subtractions are necessary. In the fourth column the pivot is already in the right spot, and there is only a 0 below it, so no subtractions are necessary. Likewise, in the fifth column we already have a pivot, and no subtractions are necessary.

By this point, looking at the left 4 columns only of this big reduced matrix (since the original vectors were length/dimension 4):

$$\begin{pmatrix} 1 & 1 & 0 & 1 \\ 0 & 1 & 1 & 0 \\ 0 & 0 & 1 & 0 \\ 0 & 0 & 0 & 1 \\ 0 & 0 & 0 & 0 \end{pmatrix}$$

we see that we succeeded in getting a row of 0s along the bottom. Thus, taking the bottom row 11001 of the right part of the large reduced matrix as coefficients for a linear combination of the original vectors, we have (as predicted)

$$1 \times 1101 + 1 \times 1011 + 0 \times 1100 + 0 \times 1111 + 1 \times 0110 = 0000$$

This is the desired linear dependency relation.

12.7 Linear codes

Linear codes form the simplest class of codes, both because they are analyzable, and because they are reasonable to implement. The alphabet used is a fixed choice of a finite field $GF(q) = \mathbf{F}_q$ with q elements. The special case of $GF(2) = \mathbf{F}_2$ is the case of **binary codes**.

A **generating matrix** G for a **linear** $[n, k]$ code over $\mathbf{F}_q$ is a k-by-n matrix with entries in the finite field $\mathbf{F}_q$, whose rows are *linearly independent*. Two generating matrices G_1 and G_2 are **equivalent** if one can be transformed into the other by elementary row operations and by permuting columns. A k-by-n generating matrix is in **standard form** or **systematic form** or **(strong) row-reduced form** or **reduced echelon form** if it is of the form

$$G = (I_k A)$$

where I_k is the k-by-k identity matrix, and A is a k-by-$(n-k)$ matrix. The **code generated by** G is, by definition, the row space of G.

Example: The generating matrix for the Hamming binary $[7, 4]$ code has standard form

$$\begin{pmatrix} 1 & 0 & 0 & 0 & 0 & 1 & 1 \\ 0 & 1 & 0 & 0 & 1 & 0 & 1 \\ 0 & 0 & 1 & 0 & 1 & 1 & 0 \\ 0 & 0 & 0 & 1 & 1 & 1 & 1 \end{pmatrix}$$

Proposition: Any k-by-n generating matrix G can be put in standard form by elementary row operations and by permuting columns. The resulting standard form is called a **standard form of G**.

Proof: We will take for granted that row reduction can put any matrix into a (strongly) row-reduced form. (One could prove this by induction.) That is, each non-zero row begins with a 1, that 1 has only 0s above and below it, and, last, these leading 1s are farther and farther to the right as one goes down the rows. By permuting the columns we may move the columns in which these leading 1s occur as far left as possible, putting the matrix into a form like

$$\begin{pmatrix} 1 & 0 & 0 & \cdots & 0 & * & \cdots & * \\ 0 & 1 & 0 & \cdots & 0 & * & \cdots & * \\ 0 & 0 & 1 & \cdots & 0 & * & \cdots & * \\ \vdots & \vdots & \vdots & \ddots & \vdots & \vdots & & \vdots \\ 0 & 0 & 0 & 0 & 1 & * & \cdots & * \\ 0 & 0 & 0 & 0 & 0 & 0 & \cdots & 0 \\ \vdots & \vdots & \vdots & 0 & \vdots & \vdots & & \vdots \\ 0 & 0 & 0 & 0 & 0 & 0 & \cdots & 0 \end{pmatrix}$$

That is, the upper left corner is an identity matrix, to the right of this there is an unpredictable rectangular matrix, and below these everything is 0. If not for the possibility of rows of 0s at the bottom, this would be the desired form.

The hypothesis that the k rows of the original matrix are linearly independent will assure that there can be no rows of 0s. Elementary row operations do not change the row space, and permutations of columns do not change the *dimension* of the row space. Thus, the dimension of the row space of the matrix above must still be k, the number of its rows. Thus, since dimension of a vector (sub-) space is well-defined, it cannot be that a k-dimensional space is spanned by fewer than k non-zero vectors. That is, there can be *no* rows of 0s in the reduced form. Thus, with suitable permutations of columns, we have the standard form as claimed. ///

For a generating matrix G of size k-by-n, the associated **linear $[n, k]$-code** C consists of all linear combinations of rows of G other than the zero vector. That is, the **codewords** of the code C are exactly the vectors in k^n which are linear combinations of the rows of G. Such codes are **linear codes**. The set of all linear combinations of rows of a matrix is the **row space** of the matrix.

Remark: A not-necessarily linear code over alphabet $\mathbf{F}_q$ is *any* subset of $\mathbf{F}_q^n$, as opposed to being describable as a row space, as in the case of linear codes.

If G is in standard form, then the first k entries of a codeword are called the **information positions** or **information symbols**, and the remaining $n-k$ entries are called the **parity check positions** or **parity-check symbols**.

Associated to a k-by-n generating matrix G is an **encoding (map)**

$$f : \mathbf{F}_q^k \to \text{ row space of } G$$

defined by

$$f(v_1, v_2, \ldots, v_k) = (\begin{matrix} v_1 & v_2 & v_3 & \ldots & v_k \end{matrix})\, G$$

Thus, the **source words** are taken to be all k-length words over $\mathbf{F}_q$ (other than all 0s), and the encoding is by n-length words over $\mathbf{F}_q$.

Remark: In the special case that the code is *binary*, instead of saying 'k-length' and 'n-length', we can say 'k-bit' and 'n-bit'.

Remark: Note that if G is in standard form then the first k positions of the encoded word are the same as the word itself:

$$f(v_1, v_2, \ldots, v_k) = (v_1, v_2, \ldots, v_k, \ldots)$$

Therefore, for G in standard form, the information positions of a vector in the associated code completely determine the parity-check symbols. In particular, if

$$G = (\begin{matrix} I_k & A \end{matrix})$$

and $v = (v_1, \ldots, v_k)$ is a k-tuple of scalars, then (viewing v as a *row* vector)

$$f(v) = vG = v(\begin{matrix} I_k & A \end{matrix}) = (\begin{matrix} vI_k & vA \end{matrix}) = (\begin{matrix} v & vA \end{matrix})$$

That is, the parity-check positions are obtained from the information positions by matrix multiplication.

Remark: In general, for a k-by-n generating matrix G not necessarily in standard form, a bunch of k indices i in the range $1 \le i \le n$ is called a **set of information positions** if values of a codeword at these entries completely determines the other symbols in the codeword. A code is called **systematic on** a set of positions if that set of positions is a set of information positions for the code.

As defined earlier, the **(Hamming) distance** between two vectors $v = (v_1, \ldots, v_n)$ and $w = (w_1, \ldots, w_n)$ in $\mathbf{F}_q^n$ is the number of indices i so that

$$v_i \ne w_i$$

This is *not* the usual notion of distance, but it is appropriate for linear codes. And, again, the **Hamming weight** of a binary vector is the number of non-zero components (that is, the number of components which are 1). The **minimum distance** of a linear $[n, k]$ code C is the minimum of $d(v, w)$ for two vectors v, w in C. (Recall that a linear $[n, k]$ code is a particular kind of subset of $\mathbf{F}_q^n$, being the row space of a generating matrix.)

Proposition: The Hamming distance on $\mathbf{F}_q^n$ has the formal properties of a distance function: for $u, v, w \in \mathbf{F}_q^n$,

- *Positivity:* $d(v, w) \geq 0$.
- *Symmetry:* $d(v, w) = d(w, v)$.
- *Positivity:* $d(v, w) = 0$ if and only if $v = w$.
- *Triangle inequality:* $d(u, w) \leq d(u, v) + d(v, w)$ if and only if $v = w$.

Proof: The first three assertions are immediate. The reason the fourth is true is that if u and w differ at the ith position, then any vector v must differ from at least one of the two at the ith position.   ///

Minimum distance decoding of a code C is done by choosing the *closest* vector x in C to a received word y, using the Hamming distance, and declaring y as the decoding of x. (If there are two closest codewords, then either pick one arbitrarily, or 'refuse' to decode.)

Remark: There still remains the issue of how to do the decoding *efficiently*. We'll address this shortly in discussing so-called **syndrome decoding**.

As earlier, let floor(t) denote the **floor function** of t, which is the largest integer less-than-or-equal t, for real numbers t.

Theorem: Using minimum distance decoding, a linear code C with *minimum distance d* can **correct** floor($\frac{d-1}{2}$) errors, and **detect** floor($\frac{d}{2}$) errors.

Proof: Suppose a transmitted vector x is received as y, with e symbol errors, with $e \leq$ floor$\frac{d-1}{2}$. That is, since e is an integer, $e \leq \frac{d-1}{2}$, or $2e \leq d - 1$, so $2e < d$. The first claim is that there is no other codeword x' as close to y as y is to x. That is, we claim that

$$d(x, y) < d(x', y)$$

for every codeword x' other than x. Suppose, to the contrary, that $d(x', y) \leq e$ as well. We use the triangle inequality (proven just above) in a slightly clever (but completely standard!) way:

$$d(x, x') \leq d(x, y) + d(y, x') \leq e + e = 2e$$

But this contradicts

$$2e < d \leq d(x, x')$$

Thus, it could not have been that y was as close to x' as to x. Thus, with $2e < d$, e symbol errors can be corrected by minimum-distance decoding.

Similarly, if $e \leq$ floor($\frac{d}{2}$), then $2e \leq d$. To be sure to *detect* this error, it must be that y is still at least as close to x (in Hamming distance) as y is to any other codeword. That is, it must be that

$$d(x, y) \leq d(x', y)$$

for every *other* codeword x'. Suppose, to the contrary, that $d(x', y) < e$. Then we use the triangle equality as we did just above:

$$d(x, x') \leq d(x, y) + d(y, x') < e + e = 2e$$

But this contradicts

$$2e \le d \le d(x, x')$$

Thus, it could not have been that y was closer to x' than to x. Thus, with $2e < d$, e symbol errors can be corrected by minimum-distance decoding.   ///

Proposition: For linear codes C, the minimum distance of C is also equal to

$$\min_{v \in C} \text{Hamming weight}(v)$$

Proof: Let $x = (x_1, \ldots, x_n)$ and $y = (y_1, \ldots, y_n)$. The Hamming distance $d(x, y)$ is defined to be the number of indices i so that $x_i \ne y_i$. This is the same as the number of indices so that $x_i - y_i \ne 0$. Since the code is linear, $x - y$ is another codeword.   ///

Remark: It remains to see a practical approach to decoding. The **syndrome decoding** below is not so bad. The more serious issue is **finding good codes**.

12.8 Dual codes, syndrome decoding

For linear codes there is a not-so-bad decoding method, called **syndrome decoding**. (In colloquial English, a *syndrome* is a group of related or coincident things.) This is just the beginning of a study of vastly better and vastly subtler decoding algorithms.

The proofs of several of the results here are not trivial, being roughly equivalent to some standard results from linear algebra, proven in the appendix on linear algebra. Thus, the proofs here relate the problems at hand to more standard linear algebra issues rather than proving things from scratch.

Let G be a generating matrix for a linear $[n, k]$ code C over alphabet $\mathbf{F}_q$. The **dual code** $C^\perp$ is defined to be

$$C^\perp = \{w \in \mathbf{F}_q^n : v \cdot w = 0 \quad \text{for all} \quad v \in C\}$$

Proposition: The dual of a linear $[n, k]$ code over $\mathbf{F}_q$ is a linear $[n, n - k]$ code over $\mathbf{F}_q$.

Proof: In the terminology of the appendix on linear algebra, for fixed vector w of length n, the map $v \to v \cdot w$ is a *linear functional* on the vector space of length-n vectors. That is, we are identifying the *dual space* V^* of the space V of all length-n vectors with V itself via the dot product. Thus, with this identification, the dual code is the orthogonal complement of the original code, in the sense of that appendix. And, from that appendix, we have the relation

$$\dim C + \dim C^\perp = n$$

Thus, for $\dim C = k$, we have $\dim C^\perp = n - k$.   ///

Theorem: For a linear code C, the dual code of the dual code is again C itself. In symbols:

$$(C^\perp)^\perp = C$$

Proof: The fact that the second dual of a subspace W is W itself again is proven in the appendix on linear algebra.   ///

Proposition: If G is in standard form $G = (I_k \ \ A)$, then a generating matrix $G^\perp$ for the *dual code* $C^\perp$ to the code C associated to G is

$$G^\perp = (-A^t \ \ I_{n-k})$$

Proof: Multiplying matrices in blocks, we have

$$G\,(G^\perp)^t = (I_k \ \ A)(-A^t \ \ I_k)^t = (I_k \ \ A)\begin{pmatrix} -A \\ I_k \end{pmatrix} = -A + A = 0_k$$

Thus, the rowspace of $(-A^t \ \ I_k)$ is a subspace of the orthogonal complement to the rowspace of G. On the other hand, from the appendix on linear algebra, if the rowspace of $(-A^t \ \ I_k)$ is strictly smaller than the orthogonal complement to the rowspace of G, then (reversing order of inclusion)

$$(\text{rowspace } (-A^t \ \ I_k))^\perp \subset ((\text{rowspace } G)^\perp)^\perp$$

but

$$(\text{rowspace } (-A^t \ \ I_k))^\perp \neq ((\text{rowspace } G)^\perp)^\perp$$

Recall also from the appendix that

$$G^{\perp\perp} = G$$

Thus, if the rowspace of $(-A^t \ \ I_k)$ is strictly smaller than the orthogonal complement to the rowspace of G, then

$$(\text{rowspace } (-A^t \ \ I_k))^\perp \subset \text{rowspace } G$$

but

$$(\text{rowspace } (-A^t \ \ I_k))^\perp \neq \text{rowspace } G$$

But the same reason as in the beginning of this proof shows that

$$(\text{rowspace } (-A^t \ \ I_k))^\perp \supset \text{rowspace } G$$

Thus, in fact

$$(\text{rowspace } (-A^t \ \ I_k))^\perp = \text{rowspace } G$$

which proves the result.   ///

Let $y_1, \ldots, y_{n-k}$ be the rows of a generating matrix for the dual code $C^\perp$ of a linear $[n, k]$ code C over $\mathbf{F}_q$. Then the last result implies that a vector x in $\mathbf{F}_q^n$ is in the code C if and only if

$$v \cdot y_i = 0 \quad \text{for all} \quad y_i$$

Each such condition is a **parity-check condition** for v to lie in C. An entire generating matrix H for the dual code is called a **(parity) check matrix** for the original code. Note that a parity-check matrix for an $[n, k]$ code is $(n-k)$-by-n. And the simultaneous conditions imposed by all the separate parity-check equations is equivalent to the matrix equation

$$v \, H^t = 0$$

where the last 0 is a zero *vector*.

For a code C with parity-check matrix H, for $v \in \mathbf{F}_q^n$ the vector

$$v \, H^t \quad \text{(matrix multiplication)}$$

is the **syndrome** of v. By the theorem above that asserts that the dual of the dual is the original code, the syndrome xH^t of a *codeword* x is the zero-vector. Thus, if a vector y is received which is a codeword x with an error vector e added,

$$y = x + e$$

then the syndrome of y and e are the same, as is easily verified by a little algebra:

$$yH^t = (x + e)H^t = xH^t + eH^t = 0 + eH^t = eH^t$$

since $xH^t = 0$ (because x is a codeword).

A **coset** or **syndrome** of C in $\mathbf{F}_q^n$ is a subset of $\mathbf{F}_q^n$ of the form (with *fixed* $v_o \in \mathbf{F}_q^n$)

$$\{v_o + v : v \in C\}$$

The standard notation for this coset (equivalently, *syndrome*) is

$$v_o + C = \{v_o + v : v \in C\}$$

This is also called **the $v_o{}^{\text{th}}$ coset** or **syndrome** of C.

Proposition: Let C be a binary linear $[n, k]$ code. For vectors v, w in $\mathbf{F}_2^n$,
- A vector v is in C if and only if $v + C = C$.
- If $(v + C) \cap (w + C) \neq \phi$, then $v + C = w + C$.
- There are exactly 2^{n-k} distinct cosets (syndromes) of C.

Proposition: Fix an n-bit binary linear code C in $\mathbf{F}_q^n$. For a *sent* codeword x *received* as vector y with *error* $e = y - x$, we have an equality of cosets

$$e + C = y + C$$

To prepare in advance for **syndrome decoding**, in each **coset** $e + C$ choose a vector e_{min} of **smallest Hamming weight**. This vector is called a **coset leader** in $e + C$. It may happen that there is more than one coset leader (that is, vector of minimal weight). In that case choose from among the coset leaders (minimal weight vectors in that coset) at random.

Remark: The coset leaders for a given code C only need to be computed once for a given code, rather than being recomputed each time the code C is used.

Then the **syndrome decoding** procedure is as follows. Given a received vector $y \in \mathbf{F}_q^n$, let e_{min} be a coset leader in the coset $y + C$, and **decode** y as $y - e_{min}$.

Proposition: The coset $y + C$ is uniquely determined by the syndrome $yH^\top$, where H is a check matrix for the linear code C.

Proof: On one hand, if $y + C = z + C$ then $y + 0 = z + w$ for some $w \in C$, then $y - z = w$ is a codeword, and $(y - z)H^\top = 0$. That is, by matrix algebra, $yH^\top = zH^\top$. On the other hand, this argument is reversible. That is, if $yH^\top = zH^\top$, then $(y - z)H^\top = 0$. Since $wH^\top = 0$ if and only if w is a codeword, $y - z = w$ is a codeword. Thus, $y = z + w$ and

$$y + C = \{y + v : v \in C\} = \{z + w + v : v \in C\} = \{z + v : v \in C\} = z + C$$

since C is closed under addition.   ///

Thus, in our one-time initial computation, we compute $eH^\top$ for each of the coset leaders e, and when we receive a word y we compute $yH^\top$ and compare to the list of values $eH^\top$ for coset leaders e. By the previous proposition the value $yH^\top$ will match exactly *one* of the values $eH^\top$, and we decode y as $y - e$.

Remark: An obvious approach to implementing the decoding of any code is simply to make a **look-up table** which tells how to decode every possible received vector. But for an n-bit code this gives 2^n look-up entries. By contrast, syndrome decoding achieves a significant improvement, needing 'only' 2^{n-k} look-up entries associated to each of the possible values $yH^\top$.

Theorem: Syndrome decoding is equivalent to minimum-distance decoding (which is equivalent to maximum-likelihood decoding), assuming that the bit error probability is less than $1/2$.

Proof: Note that of course the hypothesis that the bit error probability is less than $1/2$ would hold in any interesting or realistic situation.

The first assertion is straightforward, as follows. Given a received word y, let e be a coset leader for the coset $y + C$. That is, $e \in y + C$ and e has minimum Hamming weight for all words in that coset $y + C$. Write e in the form $y + x$ for $x \in C$. Then syndrome decoding says to decode y as $y - e$, which is

$$y - e = y - (y + x) = -x \in C$$

The Hamming distance from y to $-x$ is the Hamming weight of

$$y - (-x) = y - (y - e) = e$$

Thus, minimizing the Hamming weight of e is equivalent to minimizing the Hamming distance from y to an element $x \in C$. This makes the equivalence of syndrome decoding and minimum distance decoding clear. (And we had earlier verified the equivalence of minimum distance decoding and maximum likelihood decoding.) ///

Remark: Of course a coset $y + C$ with more than one coset leader is **bad**, because the presence of more than one coset leader means that maximum likelihood decoding is *ambiguous*, so has a good chance of failure, in the sense that such an error is *detected* but cannot be *corrected*. But this is *inescapable* for the worst cosets in most codes.

Exercises

12.01 Encode the 4-bit word 1101 using the Hamming $[7, 4]$ code.

12.02 Decode the 7-bit word 1101111 using the Hamming $[7, 4]$ code.

12.03 What is the *rate* of the Hamming $[7, 4]$ code?   (*ans.*)

12.04 What is the *word error probability* using the Hamming $[7, 4]$ code and a binary symmetric channel with *bit error probability* 1/6?

12.05 Express $(1, 2)$ as a linear combination of $(3, 4)$ and $(5, 7)$ (with real scalars). (*ans.*)

12.06 Express $(2, 1)$ as a linear combination of $(3, 4)$ and $(5, 7)$ (with rational scalars).

12.07 Express $(1, 2, 3)$ as a linear combination of $(8, 3, 2)$, $(4, 2, 1)$, $(3, 1, 1)$ (with rational scalars).

12.08 Express $(1, 0, 1)$ as a linear combination of $(8, 3, 2)$, $(4, 2, 1)$, $(3, 1, 1)$ (with rational scalars). (*ans.*)

12.09 Express $(1, 1, 1)$ as a linear combination of $(1, 0, 1)$, $(0, 0, 1)$, $(0, 1, 1)$ (with scalars $\mathbf{F}_2$). (*ans.*)

12.10 Express $(1, 0, 1)$ as a linear combination of $(1, 1, 1)$, $(0, 1, 1)$, $(1, 1, 0)$ (with scalars $\mathbf{F}_2$).

12.11 Express $(1, 0, 1, 1)$ as a linear combination of $(1, 1, 1, 0)$, $(0, 1, 1, 1)$, $(1, 1, 0, 1)$, $(1, 1, 1, 1)$ (with scalars $\mathbf{F}_2$). (*ans.*)

12.12 Express $(1, 1, 0, 1)$ as a linear combination of $(1, 0, 0, 1)$, $(0, 1, 1, 1)$, $(1, 1, 0, 1)$, $(1, 1, 1, 1)$ (with scalars $\mathbf{F}_2$).

12.13 What is the rate of a binary linear $[n, k]$ code?

12.14 Let

$$G = \begin{pmatrix} 1 & 0 & 0 & 1 \\ 0 & 1 & 1 & 1 \end{pmatrix}$$

be a generator matrix for a binary linear code C. What is the minimum distance of the code C? How many errors can it *detect*? How many errors can it *correct*? (*ans.*)

12.15 Let

$$G = \begin{pmatrix} 1 & 0 & 0 & 0 & 1 & 1 \\ 0 & 1 & 1 & 1 & 0 & 1 \\ 0 & 0 & 1 & 1 & 1 & 0 \end{pmatrix}$$

be a generator matrix for a code C. What is the minimum distance of the associated binary linear code? How many errors can it detect? How many errors can it *correct*?

12.16 Let C be the binary linear code with parity-check matrix

$$H = \begin{pmatrix} 1 & 1 & 1 & 0 \\ 0 & 1 & 0 & 1 \end{pmatrix}$$

Compute the syndrome of the received vector $y = (1 \quad 1 \quad 0 \quad 1)$. (*ans.*)

12.17 Let C be the binary linear code with parity-check matrix

$$H = \begin{pmatrix} 1 & 1 & 1 & 0 \\ 0 & 1 & 0 & 1 \end{pmatrix}$$

Compute the syndrome of the received vector $y = (1 \quad 0 \quad 0 \quad 1)$.

12.18 Let C be the binary linear code with parity-check matrix

$$H = \begin{pmatrix} 1 & 0 & 1 & 1 \\ 0 & 1 & 0 & 1 \end{pmatrix}$$

Find a generator matrix G for the code C. (*ans.*)

12.19 Let C be the binary linear code with parity-check matrix

$$H = \begin{pmatrix} 1 & 0 & 1 & 1 & 0 \\ 0 & 1 & 0 & 1 & 1 \end{pmatrix}$$

Find a generator matrix G for the code C.

12.20 Let C be the binary linear code with parity-check matrix

$$H = \begin{pmatrix} 1 & 1 & 0 \\ 1 & 0 & 1 \end{pmatrix}$$

Find the coset leaders.

13

Bounds for Codes

There are some general facts that can be proven about codes without actual construction of any codes themselves, giving us guidance in advance about what may be possible and what is impossible.

13.1 Hamming (sphere-packing) bound

The inequality proven here applies to all codes, not just linear ones. Roughly, it gives a limit on how good a code can be. In fact, even this bound is rarely reachable, but it is much harder to give more accurate estimates of how good we might hope a code to be. In that context, the Hamming bound is nice because we can understand it in physical terms, despite its not being the most precise thing that could be said.

Let's use an alphabet $\mathbf{F}_q$ which is a finite field with q elements. Let $\mathbf{F}_q^n$ denote the set of all length-n vectors made from the alphabet. As usual, the **Hamming weight** $\mathrm{wt}(v)$ of such a vector

$$v = (v_1, \ldots, v_n)$$

is the number of entries v_i which are not 0. The **Hamming distance** $d(v, w)$ between two such vectors is the number of positions at which they're different. That is, the Hamming *distance* between v and w is the Hamming *weight* of the difference

$$d(v, w) = \mathrm{wt}(v - w)$$

So with $w = (w_1, \ldots, w_n)$ and $v = (v_1, \ldots, v_n)$

$$d(v, w) = \mathrm{wt}(v_1 - w_1, v_2 - w_2, \ldots, v_n - w_n)$$

The **ball of radius** r in $\mathbf{F}_q^n$ centered at a vector v is the collection of all vectors w so that $d(v, w) \leq r$. The **volume** of this ball is the number of vectors in it.

Lemma: The volume of a ball of radius r in $\mathbf{F}_q^n$ is

volume of ball of radius r centered at v

$$= 1 + (q-1)\binom{n}{1} + (q-1)^2\binom{n}{2} + \ldots + (q-1)^r\binom{n}{r}$$

where $\binom{n}{k}$ is the binomial coefficient

$$\binom{n}{k} = \frac{n!}{k!\,(n-k)!}$$

Proof: The '1' counts the vector v itself. Next we count vectors which differ at *one* position from v: there are $\binom{n}{1} = n$ positions at which they might be different and $q-1$ choices for the other character to appear at the chosen position. Next we count vectors which differ at *two* positions from v: there are $\binom{n}{2}$ positions at which they might be different, and $q-1$ choices for each of the other two characters at the chosen positions:

$$\text{number of vectors at distance 2 from } v = (q-1)^2\binom{n}{2}$$

Continue: finally we count vectors which differ at r positions from v: there are $\binom{n}{r}$ positions at which they might be different, and $q-1$ choices for each of the other r characters at the chosen positions:

$$\text{number of vectors at distance } r \text{ from } v = (q-1)^r\binom{n}{r}$$

Adding these all up gives the indicated formula.   ///

Lemma: Let x and y be two vectors in $\mathbf{F}_q^n$ with $d(x, y) > 2e$ for some integer e. Then for another vector z with $d(x, z) \leq e$, it must be that $d(y, z) > e$.

Proof: This is a standard use of the **triangle inequality**

$$d(x, y) \leq d(x, z) + d(z, y)$$

for all vectors x, y, z. In this case

$$d(x, y) \leq d(x, z) + d(z, y)$$

Using $d(z, x) \leq e$ and $d(x, y) > 2e$ gives

$$2e < e + d(z, y)$$

which gives $e < d(z, y)$.   ///

Corollary: Given vectors x, y with $d(x, y) > 2e$, the balls of radius e centered at x and at y are **disjoint**.

Proof: If x' is in the ball of radius e centered at x, then apply the previous lemma to see that its distance from y must be $> e$, so x' cannot lie in the ball of radius e centered at y.   ///

Theorem: *(Hamming (sphere-packing) bound)* Consider a code which is a subset of $\mathbf{F}_q^n$, has minimum distance $2e + 1$, and has ℓ codewords. Then

$$\ell \cdot \left(1 + (q-1)\binom{n}{1} + (q-1)^2\binom{n}{2} + \ldots + (q-1)^e\binom{n}{e}\right) \le q^n$$

Proof: Since the minimum distance is $2e + 1$, by the triangle inequality corollary above any two spheres of radius e centered at codewords will be *disjoint*. Thus, the sum of the volumes of these ℓ disjoint spheres will be less than or equal to the total 'volume' of the whole set, namely q^n.   ///

A code which achieves *equality* in this bound is called **perfect**. There are few perfect *linear* codes, although this isn't so easy to prove (see [Tietavainen 1973]). The Hamming single-error-correcting codes are perfect, as are the two Golay codes. [Vasilyev 1962] found some *non-linear* perfect codes. See [MacWilliams Sloane 1977] for discussion and many further references.

13.2 Gilbert-Varshamov bound

This bound goes in the opposite direction to the Hamming bound: it asserts *existence* of a linear code with certain parameters, assuming that an inequality is met which in effect says that we're not being too greedy. This bound applies only to *linear* codes.

Consider a linear code with alphabet $\mathbf{F}_q$, block size n, dimension k, and minimum distance d. That is, a **generating matrix** would be k-by-n: we are looking at $[n, k, d]$ codes.

Theorem: If

$$q^{n-k} - 1 > (q-1)\binom{n-1}{1} + \ldots + (q-1)^{d-3}\binom{n-1}{d-3} + (q-1)^{d-2}\binom{n-1}{d-2}$$

then an $[n, k, d]$ code over alphabet $\mathbf{F}_q$ exists. That is, the block size is n, the dimension is k, and the minimum distance is d.

Specializing to the case $q = 2$ gives a simpler-looking assertion:

Corollary: If

$$2^{n-k} - 1 > \binom{n-1}{1} + \binom{n-1}{2} + \ldots + \binom{n-1}{d-3} + \binom{n-1}{d-2}$$

then a *binary* $[n, k, d]$-code exists.   ///

Remark: Although this theorem is a concrete assurance that good codes exist, it does *not* give any efficient procedure to find them (nor to decode them).

Remark: There is *no* assertion that this is the *best* that a code can do, only that we can expect *at least* this level of performance.

Proof: The starting point for the proof is the fundamental fact, proven in the next chapter, that for a linear code the minimum distance is d if and only if any $d-1$ columns of a check matrix are linearly independent. Granting that, consider the process of choosing n columns in a check matrix so that any $d-1$ of them are linearly independent. The code is the row space of a k-by-n generating matrix. Its check matrix is an $(n-k)$-by-n matrix of full rank, that is, of rank $n-k$. (That means that if you do row reduction there will *not* be any row of all 0's when you're done.)

We just do the binary case for simplicity.

Let's suppose that in the construction of a check matrix we have successfully chosen ℓ columns so far, with $\ell \geq d-2$, so that no $d-1$ of them are linearly dependent. Now we want to choose an $(\ell+1)^{\text{th}}$ column. The choice must be made from among column vectors of size $n-k$. There are 2^{n-k} such elements. We must *exclude* the all-0-column, exclude any previous column, exclude the sum of any previous two columns, exclude the sum of any previous three columns, and so on up to excluding the sum of any previous $d-2$ columns. In the worst case, all these things that we must exclude are *different*. This is the case we consider. That is, at worst there might be only

$$2^{n-k} - \left(1 + \binom{\ell}{1} + \binom{\ell}{2} + \ldots + \binom{\ell}{d-2} \right)$$

available vectors. Thus, to be *sure* that a choice is available, this number must be *positive*.

For $i < d$, the inequality that must be satisfied in order to be able to choose the ith column is

$$2^{n-k} \geq 1 + \binom{i-1}{1} + \binom{i-1}{2} + \ldots + \binom{i-1}{i-1}$$

By the binomial theorem, the right-hand side is just 2^i. Since

$$i \leq d - 1 \leq n - k$$

(the columns have to have length at least $d-1$), this inequality certainly holds.

The binomial coefficients $\binom{\ell}{i}$ are *increasing* as ℓ increases. Thus, if

$$2^{n-k} > 1 + \binom{\ell}{1} + \binom{\ell}{2} + \ldots + \binom{\ell}{d-2}$$

for $\ell = n - 1$ (to try to choose the nth column) then the inequality is certainly satisfied for smaller ℓ. Thus, we obtain the condition of the theorem.   ///

Remark: That is, if the Gilbert-Varshamov inequality holds then in principle we could make a code with the given $[n, k, d]$. However, so far as seems to be known currently, the construction would be no better than an extremely labor-intensive brute force search. That is, there does *not* seem to be any algorithmic approach here.

Remark: The converse assertion is false. That is, there *may* exist linear codes *exceeding* what the theorem guarantees, although such codes would be very good indeed. In fact, certain of the *geometric Goppa codes* were proven by Tsfasman, Vladut, and Zink to exceed the Gilbert-Varshamov bound.

13.3 Singleton bound

The Singleton bound below applies to arbitrary codes, not only linear ones, but our interest is primarily in linear codes. This bound can only prove *non-existence*, not *existence* of a code with given parameters.

Theorem: Let C be a code with codewords of length n using alphabet $\mathbf{F}_q$ with minimum distance d and ℓ codewords. Then

$$q^{n-(d-1)} \geq \ell$$

Remark: If the code is linear, for example is an $[n, k]$ code, then the number of codewords is $\ell = q^k$, and by taking logarithms base q the Singleton bound becomes

$$n - (d - 1) \geq k$$

or, alternatively,

$$n + 1 \geq k + d$$

Thus, on the other hand, if $k + d \leq n$ then *no* such code can exist.

Proof: Since every pair of codewords differs in at least d positions, even if we ignore the last $d - 1$ positions no two codewords will be the same in the first $n - (d - 1)$ codewords. So if we just chop off the last $d-1$ positions all the ℓ codewords are still different. So we'll get a code with ℓ codewords and block length $n - (d - 1)$. Since there are $q^{n-(d-1)}$ words of length $n - (d - 1)$ altogether, certainly $\ell \leq q^{n-(d-1)}$. This is the desired inequality.   ///

If a code meets the Singleton bound, then it is called a **minimum distance separating** code, or **MDS** code.

Exercises

13.01 Is there a binary code with 17 codewords, with minimum distance 3, and with length 7?   (*ans.*)

13.02 Is there a binary code with 29 codewords, with minimum distance 3, and with length 8?

13.03 Is there a binary code with 7 codewords, with minimum distance 5, and with length 8? (*ans.*)

13.04 Is there a binary linear code of dimension 2, with minimum distance 3, and with block length 5? (*ans.*)

13.05 Is there a binary linear code of dimension 3, with minimum distance 3, and with block length 6?

13.06 Is there a binary linear code of dimension 3, with minimum distance 3, and with block length 5? (*ans.*)

13.07 Is there a binary linear code of dimension 3, with minimum distance 4, and with block length 8?

13.08 Is there a binary linear code of dimension 2, with minimum distance 4, and with block length 7? (*ans.*)

13.09 Is there a binary code with 9 codewords, with minimum distance 3, and with length 5?

13.10 Is there a binary code with 17 codewords, with minimum distance 5, and with length 8?

14

More on Linear Codes

14.1 Minimum distances in linear codes

We know that a code (linear or not) with minimum distance $2d+1$ can correct any d symbol errors. In the case of *linear* codes we can give a linear algebra criterion that makes determining minimum distance much easier.

Theorem: Let C be a *linear* code with generating matrix G and check matrix H. Let d be the largest integer such that any d of the **columns** of H are linearly independent. Then C has minimum distance $d+1$. (Conversely, if C has minimum distance $d+1$ then any d columns of H are linearly independent.)

Proof: Since the code is linear, the minimum distance between two codewords is also the minimum distance from the 0 codeword to any other codeword. Let the columns of the check matrix H be

$$H = (\,r_1 \quad r_2 \quad \ldots \quad r_n\,)$$

and let $v = (\,c_1, \ldots, c_n\,)$ be a codeword. Then

$$0 = v \cdot H^\top = \sum_i c_i r_i^\top$$

If *any* d of the r_is are linearly independent, then for *any* codeword v there must be at least $d+1$ non-zero c_is. On the other hand, if *some* d of the r_is are linearly dependent, then for *some* codeword v there must be at most d non-zero c_is.   ///

Remark: This theorem finally gives an idea of how to look for *linear* codes that can correct many errors. The issue is converted to looking for (check) matrices H so that any e columns are linearly independent. This is what motivates the construction of Hamming codes, BCH (Bose-Chaudhuri-Hocquenghem) codes, RS (Reed-Solomon) codes, and Goppa codes.

Corollary: If any $2e$ columns of the check matrix are linearly independent, then the code can correct any e errors, and *vice versa*.

Proof: By the theorem, the minimum distance is $2e + 1$ if any $2e$ columns of the check matrix are linearly independent. We already know that this implies that the code can correct e errors. The converse is equally clear.   ///

Corollary: For a binary linear code, if no 2 columns of a check matrix are the same, and if no column of the check matrix is 0, then the code can correct any single error.

Proof: The case of two binary vectors being linearly independent is especially simple: this means that neither is a multiple of the other. And because the scalars are just the field with two elements, if the columns are not all 0's then the only possible scalar multiple would be by the scalar 1, so to be scalar multiples and non-zero two columns would actually have to be the *same*.   ///

Corollary:
- A linear code can correct any 2 errors if and only if no 4 columns (or fewer) of a check matrix are linearly dependent.
- A linear code can correct any 3 errors if and only if no 6 columns (or fewer) of a check matrix are linearly dependent.

14.2   Cyclic codes

In fact, many of the linear codes whose check matrix we can analyze are of an especially simple and highly structured form.

Let $v = (v_1, \ldots, v_n)$ be a vector of length n over a finite field $\mathbf{F}_q$. Let G be a matrix whose rows are (in order)

$$(v_1, v_2, v_3, \ldots, v_n)$$
$$(v_n, v_1, v_2, \ldots, v_{n-1})$$
$$(v_{n-1}, v_n, v_1, \ldots, v_{n-2})$$
$$\ldots$$

That is, the rows are obtained from v by cycling to the right and wrapping around. That is, the row space of G consists of all linear combinations of these cycled versions of v.

Remark: In general, it can happen that some of those cycled rows are linearly *dependent*. Then how do we systematically determine the *dimension* of a cyclic code C manufactured in such manner? That is, what is the k so that C will be an $[n, k]$-code?

To answer this question about the dimension of a cyclic code, we identify vectors $(b_0, \ldots, b_{n-1})$ with polynomials with coefficients in $\mathbf{F}_q$, this time in *ascending* degree:

$$(b_0, \ldots, b_{n-1}) \rightarrow b_0 + b_1 x + b_2 x^2 + b_3 x^3 + \ldots + b_{n-1} x^{n-1}$$

(Notice how we altered the indexing of the vector to match the exponents in the polynomial.) With this convention, the vector v' obtained from a given vector v by cycling the symbols of v to the right (and wrapping around) is simply described as

$$v'(x) = (x \cdot v(x))\%(x^n - 1) \quad \text{(polynomial multiplication)}$$

where $A\%B$ denotes the reduction of A modulo B. Thus, the set of all such cycled-and-wrapped versions of v is the set of all polynomials

$$(x^i \cdot v(x))\%(x^n - 1)$$

And since the code is *linear*, we can add any number of these cycled vectors together. Thus, the code C is exactly the collection of all vectors expressible (in polynomial terms) in the form

$$(P(x) \cdot v)\%(x^n - 1)$$

where $P(x)$ is any polynomial. Further, if a linear combination

$$\sum_i c_i x^i v$$

of the rows of G is 0, this is the same as saying

$$\left(\left(\sum_i c_i x^i\right) v\right)\%(x^n - 1) = 0$$

- Therefore, the dimension k of the cyclic linear code C generated by a vector v is $n - \deg h$, where h is the lowest-degree polynomial such that

$$(h(x) \cdot v)\%(x^n - 1) = 0$$

- Further, let

$$h(x) = c_0 + c_1 x + c_2 x^2 + \ldots + c_\ell x^\ell$$

be such a polynomial (with $k + \ell = n$). We claim that a **checksum matrix** H for C is given by

$$H = \begin{pmatrix} c_\ell & c_{\ell-1} & c_{\ell-2} & c_{\ell-3} & \cdots & c_1 & c_0 & 0 & \cdots & 0 \\ 0 & c_\ell & c_{\ell-1} & c_{\ell-2} & \cdots & c_2 & c_1 & c_0 & \cdots & 0 \\ 0 & 0 & c_\ell & c_{\ell-1} & \cdots & & & & & \\ 0 & 0 & 0 & c_\ell & c_{\ell-1} & \cdots & & & & \\ & & & \cdots & & & & & & \\ 0 & 0 & \cdots & c_\ell & c_{\ell-1} & \cdots & c_2 & c_1 & c_0 & 0 \\ 0 & 0 & \cdots & 0 & c_\ell & c_{\ell-1} & \cdots & c_2 & c_1 & c_0 \end{pmatrix}$$

That is, the top row is made from the coefficients of h in *descending* order, and they are cycled to the right (with wrap-around).

Proof: Since we'll see just below that there is no loss of generality in taking $g(x) = b_k x^k + \ldots + b_1 x + b_0$ to be a divisor of $x^n - 1$, we assume so now. Then we have $g(x)h(x) = x^n - 1$. By the very definition of polynomial multiplication, the coefficient of x^m in the product $g(x)h(x) = x^n - 1$ is

$$\sum_{i+j=m} b_i c_j = \begin{cases} 1 & \text{(if } m = n) \\ -1 & \text{(if } m = 0) \\ 0 & (0 < m < n) \end{cases}$$

Note that the set of the $n - 1$ of these expressions with $0 < m < n$ is the same as the set of expressions for entries of $GH^\top$, that is, scalar products of rows of H and G, though the set of scalar products of the rows has many repeats of the same thing. Thus, $g(x)h(x) = x^n - 1$ implies that $GH^\top = 0$. However, this does not quite assure that H is a check matrix, since without any further information it is conceivable that there would be a vector v of length n *not* in the code (the rowspace of G) but with $vH^\top = 0$. We will show that this does not happen, invoking some standard linear algebra. In particular, for a vector subspace C of the length n vectors $\mathbf{F}_q^n$, define the *orthogonal complement*

$$C^\perp = \{w \in \mathbf{F}_q^n : w \cdot v = 0 \text{ for all } v \in C\}$$

From the appendix on linear algebra, we have

$$\dim C + \dim C^\perp = n$$

Since the rowspace of H is *contained in* the orthogonal complement $C^\perp$ of the rowspace C of G, and since visibly

$$\dim \text{ rowspace } G + \dim \text{ rowspace } H = n$$

we find that

$$\dim \text{ rowspace } H = \dim C^\perp$$

Again, $H \subset C^\perp$, so necessarily $H = C^\perp$. That is, $vH^\top = 0$ implies $v \in C$. That is, H is a check matrix for the code with generator matrix G. ///

To find the smallest-degree polynomial h so that $h \cdot v\%(x^n - 1) = 0$ we take

$$h(x) = (x^n - 1)/\gcd(v, x^n - 1)$$

where gcd is **greatest common divisor**. The greatest common divisor of two polynomials is easily found via the **Euclidean algorithm** for polynomials.

- In fact, continuing this line of thought, *every cyclic code of block length n is obtainable by taking $g(x)$ to be a divisor of $x^n - 1$*. With

$$k = n - \deg g$$

we obtain an $[n, k]$-code. The check polynomial $h(x)$ is

$$h(x) = \frac{x^n - 1}{g(x)}$$

Proof: Given arbitrary $g(x)$ as a generator polynomial, from above we see that a check polynomial is

$$h(x) = \frac{x^n - 1}{\gcd(g(x), x^n - 1)}$$

That is, the dual code is generated by the collection of all shifts (with wrap-around) of the coefficients of $h(x)$ (padded by 0s). (If the coefficients of $g(x)$ are arranged by *ascending* degree, then those of $h(x)$ are arranged by *descending* degree, and *vice versa*.) Similarly, the dual code to the dual has generator polynomial

$$f(x) = \frac{x^n - 1}{\gcd(h(x), x^n - 1)} = \frac{x^n - 1}{h(x)}$$

since $h(x)$ divides $x^n - 1$. We have shown earlier that the dual of the dual is the original code. Thus, the cyclic code with generator polynomial $f(x)$ is identical to the original code with generator $g(x)$. That is, we could as well have taken $f(x)$ in the first place. Since $f(x) = (x^n - 1)/h(x)$ we have $f(x) \cdot h(x) = x^n - 1$ and thus it is clear that the generator polynomial could have been chosen to be a divisor of $x^n - 1$.   ///

In this situation, the smaller the degree of $h(x)$, the bigger the code (so the higher the rate).

Exercises

14.01 Find the dimension of the row space of $\begin{pmatrix} 1 & 1 & 1 & 0 & 0 & 0 \\ 0 & 1 & 1 & 1 & 0 & 0 \\ 0 & 0 & 1 & 1 & 1 & 0 \\ 0 & 0 & 0 & 1 & 1 & 1 \\ 1 & 0 & 0 & 0 & 1 & 1 \\ 1 & 1 & 0 & 0 & 0 & 1 \end{pmatrix}$ (*ans.*)

14.02 Find the dimension of the row space of the matrix

$$\begin{pmatrix} 1 & 1 & 1 & 0 & 0 & 0 & 0 & 0 & 0 \\ 0 & 1 & 1 & 1 & 0 & 0 & 0 & 0 & 0 \\ 0 & 0 & 1 & 1 & 1 & 0 & 0 & 0 & 0 \\ 0 & 0 & 0 & 1 & 1 & 1 & 0 & 0 & 0 \\ 0 & 0 & 0 & 0 & 1 & 1 & 1 & 0 & 0 \\ 0 & 0 & 0 & 0 & 0 & 1 & 1 & 1 & 0 \\ 0 & 0 & 0 & 0 & 0 & 0 & 1 & 1 & 1 \\ 1 & 0 & 0 & 0 & 0 & 0 & 0 & 1 & 1 \\ 1 & 1 & 0 & 0 & 0 & 0 & 0 & 0 & 1 \end{pmatrix}$$

14.03 Let C be the binary cyclic code of length 9 with generator polynomial 100111011 (coefficients ordered by ascending degree). Find a check matrix for C. (*ans.*)

14.04 Let C be the binary cyclic code of length 9 with generator polynomial 010001011 (coefficients ordered by ascending degree). Find a check matrix for C.

14.05 Let C be the binary cyclic code of length 9 with generator polynomial 011010001 (coefficients ordered by ascending degree). Find a check matrix for C.

15

Primitive Roots

15.1 Primitive elements in finite fields

As preparation for construction of more sophisticated codes, we need to be aware of a bit of abstract algebra.

Suppose that P is an *irreducible* polynomial of degree n with coefficients in $\mathbf{F}_q$. An element A of $\mathbf{F}_q[x]/P$ is a **primitive element** if

$$A^{q^n - 1} = 1 \bmod P$$

but for every prime r dividing $q^n - 1$

$$A^{(q^n - 1)/r} \neq 1 \bmod P$$

Remark: Note that a primitive element mod P can be identified as an ordinary *polynomial* of degree strictly less than the degree of P, satisfying the equations just above. This description is not completely satisfactory for later purposes, but is a reasonable first approximation.

Theorem:
- For P irreducible of degree n with coefficients in $\mathbf{F}_q$, there exists a primitive element in $\mathbf{F}_q[x]/P$.
- For a primitive element g mod P, the powers

$$g^0, g^1, g^2, g^3, g^4, \ldots, g^{q^n - 1}$$

run through all the non-zero elements of $\mathbf{F}_q[x]/P$.

This theorem is not easy to prove. The subsequent discussion of primitive roots and cyclotomic polynomials gives the proof. The following lemma is an easy component of the argument we will give.

Lemma: For P *irreducible* of degree n with coefficients in $\mathbf{F}_q$, for any polynomial A not divisible by P,

$$A^{q^n - 1} = 1 \bmod P$$

Proof: The best proof is as a special case of a corollary to *Lagrange's theorem* from group theory! This invocation of Lagrange's theorem in a context that did not mention group theory is very typical of the ubiquitous if hidden applicability of the result. ///

How to find primitive elements? Well, it turns out that usually at least 1/4 or more of the elements in $\mathbf{F}_q[x]/P$ are primitive, so naive searching won't take very long. Note, however, that it is important to use the fast exponentiation algorithm or the search would take much longer. First just guess that x-mod-P is primitive, and check the conditions. The lemma just above says that the first condition defining a primitive element is always satisfied if we know that the polynomial modulus is *irreducible*.

15.2 Characteristics of fields

Let k be a field. The **characteristic** char k of k is the smallest positive integer n (if there *is* one) so that

$$\underbrace{1_k + 1_k + \ldots + 1_k}_{n} = 0_k$$

where 1_k is the unit in k and 0_k is the zero. As usual, we abbreviate

$$\ell \cdot 1_k = \underbrace{1_k + 1_k + \ldots + 1_k}_{\ell}$$

for positive integers ℓ.

If there is *no* such positive integer n, then the characteristic is said to be 0. Thus,

$$\text{char } \mathbf{Q} = 0$$

By contrast,

$$\text{char } \mathbf{Z}/p = p$$

Proposition: The characteristic of a field is a prime number, if it is non-zero. For a field of characteristic p with p prime, if for some positive integer n

$$\underbrace{1_k + 1_k + \ldots + 1_k}_{n} = 0_k$$

then p divides n.

Proof: Suppose that

$$\underbrace{1_k + 1_k + \ldots + 1_k}_{n} = 0_k$$

with n *minimal* to achieve this effect, and that n had a factorization

$$n = a \cdot b$$

with positive integers a and b. Then

$$\underbrace{(1_k + 1_k + \ldots + 1_k)}_{a} \cdot \underbrace{(1_k + 1_k + \ldots + 1_k)}_{b} = \underbrace{1_k + 1_k + \ldots + 1_k}_{n} = 0_k$$

Since a field has no proper zero-divisors, it must be that either $a \cdot 1_k = 0$ or $b \cdot 1_k = 0$. By the hypothesis that n was minimal, if $a \cdot 1_k = 0$ then $a = n$, and similarly for b. Thus, the factorizaton $n = a \cdot b$ was not *proper*. Since n has no proper factorization, it is prime.

Suppose that $n \cdot 1_k = 0_k$. By the division algorithm, we have $n = qp + r$ with $0 \leq r < p$. Then

$$0_k = n \cdot 1_k = q(p \cdot 1_k) + r \cdot 1_k = 0_k + r \cdot 1_k$$

From this, $r \cdot 1_k = 0_k$. Since $r < p$ and p was the least positive integer with $p \cdot 1_k = 0_k$, it follows that $r = 0$ and p divides n.   ///

Fields with positive characteristic p have a peculiarity which is at first counter-intuitive, but which plays an important role in both theory and applications:

Proposition: Let k be a field of positive characteristic p. Then for any polynomial

$$f(x) = a_n x^n + a_{n-1} x^{n-1} + \ldots + a_2 x^2 + a_1 x + a_0$$

in $k[x]$ we have

$$f(x)^p = a_n^p x^{pn} + a_{n-1}^p x^{p(n-1)} + \ldots + a_2^p x^{2p} + a_1^p x^p + a_0^p$$

Proof: Recall that p divides binomial coefficients $\binom{p}{i}$ with $0 < i < p$. Therefore, for $0 < i < p$,

$$\binom{p}{i} \cdot 1_k = 0_k$$

Thus, for $a_n \in k$ and any polynomial $g(x)$ with coefficients in k,

$$(a_n x^n + g(x))^p = (a_n x^n)^p + \sum_{0<i<p} \binom{p}{i} (a_n x^n)^{p-i} g(x)^i + g(x)^p$$

All the middle terms have a coefficient

$$\binom{p}{i} \cdot 1_k = 0_k$$

so they disappear. Thus,

$$(a_n x^n + g(x))^p = a_n^p x^{pn} + g(x)^p$$

The same assertion applies to $g(x)$ itself. Take

$$g(x) = a_{n-1} x^{n-1} + h(x)$$

Then

$$g(x)^p = a_{n-1}^p x^{p(n-1)} + h(x)^p$$

Continuing (that is, doing an induction), we obtain the result for f.   ///

For example, with coefficients in $k = \mathbf{Z}/p$ with p prime, we have

$$(x + 1)^p = x^p + \sum_{0<i<p} \binom{p}{i} x^i + 1 = x^p + 1$$

Also

$$(x^2 + 1)^p = x^{2p} + 1$$

$$(x^2 + x + 1)^p = x^{2p} + x^p + 1$$

and such things.

15.3 Multiple factors in polynomials

There is a very simple device to detect repeated occurrence of a factor in a polynomial (with coefficients in a field). This is very useful both theoretically and in computational situations.

Let k be a *field*. For a polynomial

$$f(x) = c_n x^n + \ldots + c_1 x + c_0$$

with coefficients c_i in k, we *define* the **algebraic derivative** $f'(x)$ of $f(x)$ by

$$f'(x) = n c_n x^{n-1} + (n-1) c_{n-1} x^{n-2} + \ldots + 3 c_3 x^2 + 2 c_2 x + c_1$$

Remark: Note that we simply *define* a 'derivative' this way, purely algebraically, without taking any limits. Of course (!) this formula is still supposed to yield a thing with familiar properties, such as the product rule. So we've simply used our calculus experience to make a 'good guess'.

Lemma: For two polynomials f, g in the collection $k[x]$ of polynomials in x with coefficients in k, and for $r \in k$,

- $(r \cdot f)' = r \cdot f'$
- $(f + g)' = f' + g'$
- $(fg)' = f'g + fg'$

Proof: The first assertion is easy: let $f(x) = a_m x^m + \ldots + a_0$, and compute

$$(r \cdot (a_m x^m + \ldots + a_0))' = (ra_m x^m + ra_{m-1}x^{m-1} + \ldots + ra_0)'$$

$$= m \cdot (ra_m)x^{m-1} + (m-1) \cdot (ra_{m-1})x^{m-2} + \ldots + ra_1 + 0$$

$$= r\left(m \cdot (a_m)x^{m-1} + (m-1) \cdot (a_{m-1})x^{m-2} + \ldots + a_1 + 0\right) = r \cdot f'(x)$$

The second assertion is also not hard: let $f(x) = a_m x^m + \ldots + a_0$ and $g(x) = b_n x^n + \ldots + b_0$. Padding the one of smaller degree with terms of the form $0 \cdot x^\ell$, we can suppose without loss of generality that $m = n$. (This simplifies notation considerably!) Then

$$(f(x) + g(x))' = ((a_n + b_n)x^n + \ldots + \ldots + (a_1 + b_1)x + (a_0 + b_0)x^0)'$$

$$= n(a_n + b_n)x^{n-1} + (n-1)(a_{n-1} + b_{n-1})x^{n-2} + \ldots + 1(a_1 + b_1)x^0 + 0 \cdot x^0$$

$$= \left(na_n x^{n-1} + (n-1)a_{n-1}x^{n-2} + \ldots + 1 \cdot a_1 x^0\right)$$

$$+ \left(nb_n x^{n-1} + \ldots + (n-1)b_{n-1}x^{n-2} + \ldots + 1 \cdot b_1 x^0\right)$$

$$= f'(x) + g'(x)$$

For the third property, let's first see what happens when f and g are *monomials*, that is, are simply $f(x) = ax^m$, $g(x) = bx^n$. On one hand, we have

$$(fg)' = (ax^m \cdot bx^n)' = (abx^{m+n})' = ab(m+n)x^{m+n-1}$$

On the other hand,

$$f'g + fg' = amx^{m-1} \cdot bx^n + ax^m \cdot bnx^{n-1} = ab(m+n)x^{m+n-1}$$

after simplifying. This proves the product rule for monomials.

To approach the general product rule, let

$$f(x) = a_m x^m + \ldots + a_0$$

$$g(x) = b_n x^n + \ldots + b_0$$

The coefficient of x^ℓ in the product $f(x)g(x)$ is

$$\sum_{i+j=\ell} a_i \cdot b_j$$

Then the coefficient of $x^{\ell-1}$ in the derivative of the product is

$$\ell \sum_{i+j=\ell} a_i \cdot b_j$$

On the other hand, the coefficient of $x^{\ell-1}$ in $f'g$ is

$$\sum_{i+j=\ell} (i a_i) \cdot b_j$$

and the coefficient of $x^{\ell-1}$ in fg' is

$$\sum_{i+j=\ell} a_i \cdot j b_j$$

Adding these two together, we find that the coefficient of $x^{\ell-1}$ in $f'g + fg'$ is

$$\sum_{i+j=\ell} a_i \cdot b_j \cdot (i+j) = \ell \sum_{i+j=\ell} a_i \cdot b_j$$

which matches the coefficient in $(fg)'$. This proves the product rule.   ///

A field k is called **perfect** if either the characteristic of k is 0, as is the case for $\mathbf{Q}$, $\mathbf{R}$, and $\mathbf{C}$, or if for characteristic $p > 0$ there is a pth root $a^{1/p}$ in k for every $a \in k$.

Remark: By Fermat's little theorem, the finite field $\mathbf{Z}/p$ (for p prime) is perfect. Similarly, any *finite* field is perfect.

Proposition: Let f be a polynomial with coefficients in a field k, and P an irreducible polynomial with coefficients in k. If P^2 divides f then P divides $\gcd(f, f')$. On the other hand, if k is *perfect*, then P^2 divides f if P divides $\gcd(f, f')$.

Proof: On one hand, suppose $f = P^2 \cdot g$. Then, using the product rule,

$$f' = 2PP' \cdot g + P^2 \cdot g' = P \cdot (2P'g + Pg')$$

which is certainly a multiple of P. This half of the argument did not use the irreducibility of P.

On the other hand, suppose that P divides both f and f' (and show that actually P^2 divides f). Dividing the polynomial f/P by P, we obtain

$$f/P = Q \cdot P + R$$

with the degree of R less than that of P. Then $f = QP^2 + RP$. Taking the derivative, we have

$$f' = Q'P^2 + 2QPP' + R'P + RP'$$

By hypothesis P divides f'. All the terms on the right-hand side except possibly RP' are divisible by P, so P divides RP'. Since P is irreducible and it divides the product RP', it must divide either R or P'. If it divides R, then we've shown that P^2 divides f, so we're done.

If P fails to divide R then P must divide P'. Since P' is of lower degree than P, if P divides it then P' must be the zero polynomial. Let's see that this is impossible for P irreducible. Let

$$P(x) = a_n x^n + a_{n-1} x^{n-1} + \ldots + a_2 x^2 + a_1 x + a_0$$

Then

$$P'(x) = n a_n x^{n-1} + (n-1) a_{n-1} x^{n-2} + \ldots + 2 a_2 x^1 + a_1 + 0$$

For this to be the zero polynomial it must be that for all indices ℓ

$$\ell \cdot a_\ell = 0$$

That is, for any index ℓ with $a_\ell \neq 0$, $\ell \cdot 1_k = 0_k$. Since at least one coefficient of P is non-zero, this implies that the *characteristic* of k is not 0, so the characteristic is a prime p. From above, $\ell \cdot 1_k = 0_k$ implies that p divides ℓ. That is, the characteristic p divides ℓ if the coefficient a_ℓ is non-zero. So we can write

$$P(x) = a_{pm} x^{pm} + a_{p(m-1)} x^{p(m-1)} + a_{p(m-2)} x^{p(m-2)} + \ldots + a_{2p} x^{2p} + a_p x^p + a_0$$

Using the general property that (because the characteristic is p)

$$(A + B)^p = A^p + B^p$$

we recognize the expression for $P(x)$ as being the pth power of

$$b_{pm} x^n + b_{p(m-1)} x^{(m-1)} + b_{p(m-2)} x^{(m-2)} + \ldots + b_{2p} x^2 + b_p x + b_0$$

where b_i is a pth root of a_i. But if P is a pth power it is certainly not irreducible. Therefore, for P irreducible it cannot be that P' is the zero polynomial. Therefore, $R = 0$, which is to say that P^2 divides f, as claimed.   ///

15.4 Cyclotomic polynomials

For b in a field k, the **exponent** of b is the smallest positive integer n (if it exists at all) so that $b^n = 1$. That is, $b^n = 1$ but $b^d \neq 1$ for $0 < d < n$. In other words, b is a root of the polynomial $x^n - 1$ but not of $x^d - 1$ for any smaller d. Our goal here is to show that there is a polynomial $\varphi_n(x)$ such that b is of exponent n if and only if

$$\varphi_n(b) = 0$$

This polynomial will be the nth **cyclotomic polynomial**.

Fix a field k.

Lemma: For m, n two integers (divisible by the characteristic or not)

$$\gcd(x^m - 1, x^n - 1) = x^{\gcd(m,n)} - 1$$

Proof: We do induction on the maximum of m and n. First, if by chance $m = n$, then $x^m - 1 = x^n - 1$ and we are certainly done. Second, if either $m = 1$ or $n = 1$ then the one polynomial divides the other and again we're done.

Now we come to the more substantial part of the argument. For $m > n$, doing a fragment of a division we have

$$x^m - 1 - x^{m-n} \cdot (x^n - 1) = x^{m-n} - 1$$

So if D is a polynomial dividing both $x^m - 1$ and $x^n - 1$, then D divides $x^{m-n} - 1$ as well. By induction,

$$\gcd(x^{m-n} - 1, x^n - 1) = x^{\gcd(m-n,n)} - 1$$

But

$$\gcd(m, n) = \gcd(m - n, n)$$

and

$$x^m - 1 = x^{m-n} \cdot (x^n - 1) + x^{m-n} - 1$$

so

$$\gcd(x^m - 1, x^n - 1) = \gcd(x^{m-n} - 1, x^n - 1)$$

If $m < n$ we reverse the roles of m and n: let's repeat the argument. Doing a fragment of a division:

$$x^n - 1 - x^{n-m} \cdot (x^m - 1) = x^{n-m} - 1$$

So if D is a polynomial dividing both $x^m - 1$ and $x^n - 1$ then D divides $x^{n-m} - 1$ as well. By induction,

$$\gcd(x^{n-m} - 1, x^n - 1) = x^{\gcd(n-m,n)} - 1$$

But

$$\gcd(m, n) = \gcd(n - m, n)$$

and

$$x^n - 1 = x^{n-m} \cdot (x^m - 1) + x^{n-m} - 1$$

so

$$\gcd(x^m - 1, x^n - 1) = \gcd(x^{n-m} - 1, x^m - 1)$$

This completes the induction step.   ///

Remark: Note that the analogous formula for least common multiples would be false in general. For example,

$$\text{lcm}(x^4 - 1, x^6 - 1) = \frac{(x^4 - 1)(x^6 - 1)}{\gcd(x^4 - 1, x^6 - 1)}$$

because of the general fact that

$$\operatorname{lcm}(A, B) = \frac{A \cdot B}{\gcd(A, B)}$$

By the result just above,

$$\operatorname{lcm}(x^4 - 1, x^6 - 1) = \frac{(x^4 - 1)(x^6 - 1)}{\gcd(x^4 - 1, x^6 - 1)} = \frac{(x^4 - 1)(x^6 - 1)}{x^2 - 1}$$

$$= (x^2 + 1)(x^6 - 1) = x^{12} + x^6 - x^2 - 1 \neq x^{12} - 1 = x^{\operatorname{lcm}(4,6)} - 1$$

Lemma: Let n be a positive integer not divisible by the characteristic of the field k. (This is *no* condition if the characteristic is 0.) Then the polynomial $x^n - 1$ has no repeated factors.

Proof: From above, it suffices to check that the *gcd* of $x^n - 1$ and its derivative nx^{n-1} is 1. Since the characteristic of the field does not divide n, $n \cdot 1_k$ has a multiplicative inverse t in k. Then, doing a division with remainder,

$$(x^n - 1) - (tx) \cdot (nx^{n-1}) = -1$$

Thus, the *gcd* is 1.   ///

Now suppose that n is not divisible by the characteristic of the field k, and define the nth **cyclotomic polynomial** $\varphi_n(x)$ (with coefficients in k) by

$$\varphi_1(x) = x - 1$$

and for $n > 1$, inductively,

$$\varphi_n(x) = \frac{x^n - 1}{\text{lcm of all } x^d - 1 \text{ with } 0 < d < n, \, d \text{ dividing } n}$$

where the least common multiple is taken to be *monic*.

Theorem:
- φ_n is monic (and truly is a polynomial).
- For α in a field, $\varphi_n(\alpha) = 0$ if and only if $\alpha^n = 1$ and $\alpha^t \neq 1$ for all $0 < t < n$.
- $\gcd(\varphi_m, \varphi_n) = 1$ for $m < n$ with neither m nor n divisible by the characteristic of the field k.
- The degree of φ_n is $\varphi(n)$ (Euler's phi-function)
- There is a more efficient description of $\varphi_n(x)$:

$$\varphi_n(x) = \frac{x^n - 1}{\prod_{1 \leq d < n, d \mid n} \varphi_d(x)}$$

- The polynomial $x^n - 1$ factors as

$$x^n - 1 = \prod_{1 \leq d \leq n, d \mid n} \varphi_d(x)$$

Proof: First, we really should check that the least common multiple of the $x^d - 1$ with $d < n$ and $d|n$ divides $x^n - 1$, so that φ_n is a polynomial. We know that $d|n$ (and $d > 0$) implies that $x^d - 1$ divides $x^n - 1$ (either by high school algebra or from the lemma above). Therefore, using the *unique factorization* of polynomials with coefficients in a field, it follows that the least common multiple of a collection of things each dividing $x^n - 1$ will also divide $x^n - 1$.

Next, the assertion that φ_n is *monic* follows from its definition, since it is the quotient of the monic polynomial $x^n - 1$ by the monic *lcm* of polynomials.

For α in a field, $x - \alpha$ divides $\varphi_n(x)$ if and only if α is a root of the equation $\varphi_n(x) = 0$, from unique factorization of polynomials in one variable with coefficients in a field. Similarly, $\alpha^t = 1$ if and only if $x - \alpha$ divides $x^t - 1$. Thus, having shown that $\varphi_n(x)$ truly is a polynomial, the definition

$$\varphi_n(x) = \frac{x^n - 1}{lcm \text{ of all } x^d - 1 \text{ with } 0 < d < n, \ d \text{ dividing } n}$$

shows that $\varphi_n(\alpha) = 0$ implies that $\alpha^n = 1$ and $\alpha^t \neq 1$ for all $0 < t < n$, as claimed in the theorem.

To determine the *gcd* of φ_m and φ_n, let $d = \gcd(m, n)$. Observe that φ_m divides $x^m - 1$ and φ_n divides $x^n - 1$, so

$$\gcd(\varphi_m, \varphi_n) \text{ divides } \gcd(x^m - 1, x^n - 1)$$

In the lemma above we computed that

$$\gcd(x^m - 1, x^n - 1) = x^{\gcd(m,n)} - 1 = x^d - 1$$

Since

$$d \leq m < n$$

d is a *proper* divisor of n. Thus, from

$$\varphi_n(x) = \frac{x^n - 1}{lcm \text{ of all } x^d - 1 \text{ with } 0 < d < n, \ d \text{ dividing } n}$$

we see that $\varphi_n(x)$ divides $(x^n - 1)/(x^d - 1)$. Since $x^n - 1$ has no repeated irreducible factors, $\varphi_n(x)$ has no factors in common with $x^d - 1$. Thus, in summary, the *gcd* of $\varphi_m(x)$ and $\varphi_n(x)$ divides $x^d - 1$, but $\varphi_n(x)$ has no factor in common with $x^d - 1$, so $\gcd(\varphi_m, \varphi_n) = 1$.

Next, we use induction to prove that

$$x^n - 1 = \prod_{1 \leq d \leq n, \ d|n} \varphi_d(x)$$

For $n = 1$ the assertion is true. From the definition of φ_n, we have

$$x^n - 1 = \varphi_n(x) \cdot lcm\{x^d - 1 : d|n, 0 < d < n\}$$

By induction, for $d < n$

$$x^d - 1 = \prod_{0 < e \le d, e|d} \varphi_e(x)$$

Since we have already shown that for $m < n$ the gcd of φ_m and φ_n is 1, we have

$$\text{lcm}\{x^d - 1 : d|n, 0 < d < n\} = \prod_{d|n, d<n} \varphi_d(x)$$

Thus,

$$x^n - 1 = \varphi_n(x) \cdot \prod_{d|n, d<n} \varphi_d(x)$$

as claimed.

The assertion about the degree of φ_n follows from the identity proven below for Euler's phi-function:

$$\sum_{d|n, d>0} \varphi(d) = n$$

This completes the proof of the theorem.   ///

Proposition: Let $\varphi(x)$ be Euler's phi-function

$$\varphi(x) = \sum_{1 \le \ell \le x; \gcd(\ell, x)=1} 1$$

Then for m and n relatively prime

$$\varphi(mn) = \varphi(m) \cdot \varphi(n) \quad \text{(weak multiplicativity)}$$

For p prime and ℓ a positive integer

$$\varphi(p^\ell) = (p - 1) \cdot p^{\ell-1}$$

And

$$\sum_{d|n, d>0} \varphi(d) = n$$

Proof: For the first statement, note that by unique factorization

$$\gcd(t, mn) = \gcd(t, m) \cdot \gcd(t, n)$$

In particular, t is relatively prime to mn if and only if t is relatively prime to both m and n. Recall that the gcd of m and n is the smallest positive integer expressible as $rm + sn$. By Sun-Ze's theorem, the map

$$f : \{0, 1, \ldots, m - 1\} \times \{0, 1, \ldots, n - 1\} \to \mathbf{Z}/mn$$

by

$$f : (x, y) \to rmy + snx$$

is a *bijection*. From $rm + yn = 1$, $rm = 1 \bmod n$ so rm is relatively prime to n, and $sn = 1 \bmod m$ so sn is relatively prime to m. Thus, $rmy + snx$ has a common factor with m if and only if x does, and $rmy + snx$ has a common factor with n if and only if y does. Thus, f also gives a bijection

$$\{x : 1 \le x < m, \gcd(x, m) = 1)\} \times \{y : 1 \le y < n, \gcd(y, n) = 1)\}$$

$$\to \{z : 1 \le z < mn, \gcd(z, mn) = 1)\}$$

is a bijection. This proves that for $\gcd(m, n) = 1$

$$\varphi(mn) = \varphi(m) \cdot \varphi(n)$$

Using unique factorization, this reduces the calculation of $\varphi()$ to its evaluation on prime powers p^e (p prime). This is easy, as an integer x in the range $1 \le x < p^e$ is relatively prime to p^e if and only if it is not divisible by p, so there are

$$\varphi(p^e) = p^e - p^{e-1} = (p - 1)p^{e-1}$$

such x, as claimed.

To obtain the formula

$$\sum_{d|n, d>0} \varphi(d) = n$$

start with the case that n is a prime power p^e, in which case

$$\sum_{d|p^e} \varphi(d) = \sum_{0 \le k \le e} \varphi(p^k) = 1 + \sum_{1 \le k \le e} (p-1)p^{k-1} = 1 + (p-1)(p^e - 1)/(p-1) = p^e$$

Then use the weak multiplicativity and unique factorization of divisors into their prime power factors. Let $n = p_1^{e_1} \ldots p_t^{e_t}$ be the prime factorization of n into powers of distinct primes p_i. We have

$$\sum_{d|n} \varphi(d) = \prod_{i=1,\ldots,t} \left(\sum_{d|p_i^{e_i}} \varphi(d) \right) = \prod_{i=1,\ldots,t} \varphi(p_i^{e_i}) = \varphi(\prod_i p_i^{e_i}) = \varphi(n)$$

This proves the desired identity for φ.   ///

15.5 Primitive elements in finite fields: proofs

Now we can prove that the multiplicative group $k^\times$ of a finite field k is a *cyclic group*. A generator of $k^\times$ is sometimes called a *primitive root* for k. This property of $k^\times$ is essential. (Note that the superscript is a cross $\times$, not an x.)

Theorem: Let k be a finite field. Then $k^\times$ is a cyclic group.

Proof: Let q be the number of elements in k. The group of units $k^\times$ is a group. Since k is a field, any $b \neq 0$ has a multiplicative inverse in k. So the order of $k^\times$ is $q - 1$. Thus, by corollaries to Lagrange's theorem, for $b \neq 0$,

$$b^{q-1} = 1$$

That is, any non-zero element of k is a root of the polynomial $f(x) = x^{q-1} - 1$. On the other hand, by a fundamental theorem from algebra, a polynomial with coefficients in a field k has at most as many roots (in k) as its degree, so this polynomial has at most $q - 1$ roots in k. Therefore, it has *exactly $q - 1$* (distinct) roots in k.

Let p be the characteristic of k. Certainly p cannot divide $q - 1$, since if it did then the derivative of $f(x) = x^{q-1} - 1$ would be zero, so $\gcd(f, f') = f$ and f would have multiple roots. We have just noted that f has $q - 1$ distinct roots, so this doesn't happen.

Since the characteristic of k does not divide $q - 1$, we can apply the results from just above concerning cyclotomic polynomials. Thus,

$$x^{q-1} - 1 = \prod_{d|q-1} \varphi_d(x)$$

Since $x^{q-1} - 1$ has $q - 1$ roots in k, and since the φ_d's here are relatively prime to each other, each φ_d with $d|q-1$ must have a number of roots (in k) equal to its degree. Thus, φ_d for $d|q-1$ has $\varphi(d) > 0$ roots in k (Euler's phi-function).

Finally, the roots of $\varphi_{q-1}(x)$ are those field elements b so that $b^{q-1} = 1$ and no smaller positive power than $q - 1$ has this property. The primitive roots are exactly the roots of $\varphi_{q-1}(x)$. The cyclotomic polynomial φ_{q-1} has $\varphi(q - 1)$ roots. Therefore, there are $\varphi(q - 1) > 0$ primitive roots. Thus, the group $k^\times$ has a generator. That is, the group $k^\times$ is cyclic.   ///

15.6 Primitive roots in $\mathbf{Z}/p$

We emphasize that the multiplicative group $\mathbf{Z}/p^\times$ of the finite field $\mathbf{Z}/p$ with p elements is a *cyclic group*. Any generator of it is called a *primitive root* for $\mathbf{Z}/p$. This property of $\mathbf{Z}/p$ (and other finite fields) is essential in primality tests and factorization algorithms.

Theorem: Let k be the finite field $\mathbf{Z}/p$ with p prime. Then $\mathbf{Z}/p^\times$ is a cyclic group.

Proof: As a corollary of our study of cyclotomic polynomials, we've already proven that the multiplicative group $k^\times$ of any finite field k is cyclic. Therefore, all we need do is check that $\mathbf{Z}/p$ is a field. That is, we must check that any non-zero element $b \in \mathbf{Z}/p$ has a multiplicative inverse.

Let's repeat the important explanation of why there is a multiplicative inverse, even though we've given it before in other contexts. Indeed, since p is prime, if $b \neq 0 \bmod p$, then $\gcd(p, b) = 1$. Thus, there are integers s, t so that $sp + tb = 1$.

Then, looking at the latter equation modulo p, we see that t is a multiplicative inverse to b modulo p. ///

15.7 Primitive roots in $\mathbf{Z}/p^e$

To prove that there is a primitive root in $\mathbf{Z}/p^e$ for p an odd prime is not difficult once we know that there is a primitive root for $\mathbf{Z}/p$. A minor adaption of this applies as well to $\mathbf{Z}/2p^e$.

Theorem: For an odd prime p, $\mathbf{Z}/p^e$ and $\mathbf{Z}/2p^e$ have primitive roots. That is, the multiplicative groups $\mathbf{Z}/p^{e\times}$ and $\mathbf{Z}/2p^{e\times}$ are *cyclic*.

The following proposition is of interest in its own right, and is necessary to prove the theorem on primitive roots. Its point is that understanding the order of *certain* types of elements in $\mathbf{Z}/p^{e\times}$ is much more elementary than the trouble we went through to show that $\mathbf{Z}/p$ has a primitive root. We'll prove this proposition before proving the theorem.

Proposition: Let p be an odd prime. For integers $1 \le k \le e$ and for an integer x with $p \nmid x$, the order of an element $1 + p^k x$ in $\mathbf{Z}/p^{e\times}$ is p^{e-k}. Moreover, for $p \nmid x$ and $k \ge 1$,

$$(1 + p^k x)^{p^\ell} = 1 + p^{k+\ell} y$$

with $y = x \bmod p$.

Proof: *(of proposition)* The main trick here is that a prime p divides the binomial coefficients

$$\binom{p}{1}, \binom{p}{2}, \ldots, \binom{p}{p-2}, \binom{p}{p-1}$$

Also, the hypothesis that $p > 2$ is essential.

Let's first compute

$$(1 + p^k x)^p = 1 + \binom{p}{1}p^k x + \binom{p}{2}p^{2k}x^2 + \ldots + \binom{p}{p-1}p^{(p-1)k}x^{p-1} + p^{pk}x^p$$

$$= 1 + p^{k+1} \cdot \underbrace{\left(x + \binom{p}{2}p^{2k-(k+1)}x^2 + \ldots + p^{pk-(k+1)}x^p\right)}_{y}$$

Since p divides those binomial coefficients, the expression y differs from x by a multiple of p. Looking at the very last term, $p^{pk-(k+1)}x^p$, we see that it is necessary that $pk - (k+1) \ge 1$ for this to work. This inequality fails if $k = 1$ and $p = 2$. This explains why the argument fails for the prime 2. So we have proven that

$$(1 + p^k x)^p = 1 + p^{k+1} y$$

with $y = x \bmod p$. Repeating this argument (that is, doing an induction), we get

$$(1 + p^k x)^{p^\ell} = 1 + p^{k+\ell} y$$

with $y = x \bmod p$. This is the formula in the proposition.

Now let's see that this formula gives the assertion about orders. First we must see what the order in $\mathbf{Z}/p^{e\times}$ of elements of the form $1 + px$ can be. To do this we will invoke Lagrange's theorem. So we have to count the number of elements of $\mathbf{Z}/p^{e\times}$ expressible as $1 + px$. In the first place, for any integer x the integer $1 + px$ is relatively prime to p, so gives an element of $\mathbf{Z}/p^{e\times}$. On the other hand, if

$$1 + px = 1 + px' \bmod p^e$$

then $p^e|(1 + px - 1 - px')$. That is, $p^{e-1}|x - x'$. So the integers $1 + px$ and $1 + px'$ give the *same* element of $\mathbf{Z}/p^{e\times}$ only if $x = x' \bmod p^{e-1}$. Thus, the p^{e-1} integers $x = 0, 1, 2, \dots p^{e-1} - 1$ give all the elements of $\mathbf{Z}/p^{e\times}$ expressible as $1 + px$.

By Lagrange's theorem, the order of any element $1 + px$ in $\mathbf{Z}/p^{e\times}$ must divide p^{e-1}.

This limitation allows our computation of $(1+p^k x)^{p^{\ell}}$ to give a definitive answer to the question of order: for $p \nmid x$,

$$(1 + p^k x)^{p^{\ell}} = 1 + p^{k+\ell} y$$

with $y = x \bmod p$, so this is not $1 \bmod p^e$ unless $k + \ell \geq e$. (And if $k + \ell \geq e$ it *is* $1 \bmod p^e$.) Thus,

$$\text{(multiplicative) order of } 1 + p^k x \bmod p^e \text{ is } p^{e-k}$$

This proves the proposition.   ///

Proof: (of theorem) The assertion of the corollary is stronger than the theorem, so it certainly suffices to prove the more specific assertion of the corollary in order to prove the theorem.

Before the most serious part of the proof, let's see why an integer g which is a primitive root for $\mathbf{Z}/p^e$ will also be a primitive root for $\mathbf{Z}/2p^{e\times}$. The main point is that for an odd prime p

$$\varphi(2p^e) = (2 - 1)(p - 1)p^{e-1} = (p - 1)p^{e-1} = \varphi(p^e)$$

Let g be a primitive root modulo p^e. Then $\ell = \varphi(p^e)$ is the smallest exponent so that $g^{\ell} = 1 \bmod p^e$. Thus, surely there is no *smaller* exponent ℓ so that $g^{\ell} = 1 \bmod 2p^e$, since $p^e|2p^e$. Therefore, a primitive root mod p^e also serves as a primitive root modulo $2p^e$.

Now the central case, that of primitive roots for $\mathbf{Z}/p^e$. That is, we want to show that the multiplicative group $\mathbf{Z}/p^{e\times}$ is of the form $\langle g \rangle$ for some g. Let g_1 be a primitive root mod p, which we already know exists for *other* reasons. The plan is to *adjust* g_1 suitably to obtain a primitive root mod p^e. It turns out that at most a single adjustment is necessary altogether.

If (by good luck?)

$$g_1^{p-1} = 1 + px$$

with $p \nmid x$, then let's show that g_1 is already a primitive root mod p^e for any $e \geq 1$. By Lagrange's theorem, the order of g_1 in $\mathbf{Z}/p^{e\times}$ is a divisor of $\varphi(p^e) = (p-1)p^{e-1}$. Since $p - 1$ is the smallest positive exponent ℓ so that $g_1^\ell = 1 \mod p$, $p - 1$ divides the order of g_1 in $\mathbf{Z}/p^{e\times}$ (from our discussion of cyclic subgroups). Thus, the order of g_1 is in the list

$$p - 1, \ (p-1)p, \ (p-1)p^2, \ \ldots, \ (p-1)p^{e-1}$$

Thus, the question is to find the smallest positive ℓ so that

$$g_1^{(p-1)p^\ell} = 1 \mod p^e$$

We are assuming that

$$g_1^{p-1} = 1 + px$$

with $p \nmid x$, so the question is to find the smallest positive ℓ so that

$$(1 + px)^{p^\ell} = 1 \mod p^e$$

From the proposition, the smallest positive ℓ with this property is $\ell = e - 1$. That is, we have proven that g_1 is a primitive root mod p^e for *every* $e \geq 1$.

Now suppose that

$$g_1^{p-1} = 1 + px$$

with $p | x$. Then consider

$$g = (1 + p)g_1$$

Certainly g is still a primitive root mod p, because $g = g_1 \mod p$. And we compute

$$(1+p)^{p-1} = 1 + \binom{p-1}{1}p + \binom{p-1}{2}p^2 + \ldots + \binom{p-1}{p-2}p^{p-2} + p^{p-1}$$

$$1 + p \cdot \underbrace{\left(\binom{p-1}{1} + \binom{p-1}{2}p + \binom{p-1}{3}p^2 + \ldots \right)}_{y} = 1 + py$$

Since

$$\binom{p-1}{1} = p - 1$$

we see that

$$y = p - 1 \mod p$$

so $p \nmid y$. Thus,

$$g^{p-1} = ((1+p)g_1)^{p-1} = (1 + py)(1 + px) = 1 + p(y + x + pxy)$$

Since $p | x$, we have

$$y + x + pxy = y \mod p$$

In particular, $p \nmid y + x + pxy$. Thus, by adjusting the primitive root a bit, we have returned to the first case above, that g^{p-1} is of the form $g^{p-1} = 1 + pz$ with $p \nmid z$. In that case we already saw that such g is a primitive root mod p^e for any $e \geq 1$.

This finishes the proof of existence of primitive roots in $\mathbf{Z}/p^e$ for p an odd prime.   ///

Corollary: *(of proof)* In fact, for an integer g which is a primitive root mod p, either g is a primitive root mod p^e and mod $2p^e$ for all $e \geq 1$, or else $(1+p)g$ is. In particular, if $g^{p-1} \neq 1 \bmod p^2$, then g is a primitive root mod p^e and mod $2p^e$ for all $e \geq 1$. Otherwise, $(1+p)g$ is.

15.8 Counting primitive roots

After proving *existence* of primitive roots, it is at least equally interesting to have an idea *how many* there are.

Theorem: If $\mathbf{Z}/n$ has a primitive root, then there are exactly

$$\varphi(\varphi(n))$$

primitive roots mod n. (Yes, that is Euler's *phi* of Euler's *phi* of n.) For example, there are

$$\varphi(\varphi(p)) = \varphi(p-1)$$

primitive roots modulo a prime p, and there are

$$\varphi(\varphi(p^e)) = \varphi(p-1) \cdot (p-1)p^{e-2}$$

primitive roots mod p^e for an odd prime p and $e \geq 2$.

Proof: The hypothesis that $\mathbf{Z}/n$ has a primitive root is that the multiplicative group $\mathbf{Z}/n^\times$ is *cyclic*. That is, for some element g (the 'primitive root')

$$\mathbf{Z}/n^\times = \langle g \rangle$$

Of course, the order $|g|$ of g must be the order $\varphi(n)$ of $\mathbf{Z}/n^\times$. From general discussion of cyclic subgroups, we know that

$$g^0, g^1, g^2, g^3, \ldots, g^{\varphi(n)-1}$$

is a complete list of all the different elements of $\langle g \rangle$. And from general properties of *cyclic groups*

$$\text{order of } g^k = \frac{\text{order of } g}{\gcd(k, |g|)}$$

So the generators for $\langle g \rangle$ are exactly the elements

$$g^k \text{ with } 1 \leq k < |g| \text{ and } k \text{ relatively prime to } |g|$$

By definition of Euler's φ-function, there are $\varphi(|g|)$ of these. Thus, since $|g| = \varphi(n)$, there are $\varphi(\varphi(n))$ primitive roots.   ///

Corollary: For an odd prime p, the fraction $\varphi(p-1)/p$ of the elements of $\mathbf{Z}/p^{e\times}$ consists of primitive roots.

Proof: From the theorem just proven the ratio of primitive roots to all elements is

$$\frac{\varphi(\varphi(p^e))}{\varphi(p^e)} = \frac{\varphi(p-1)\cdot(p-1)p^{e-2}}{(p-1)p^{e-1}} = \frac{\varphi(p-1)}{p}$$

as claimed.   ///

Remark: Thus, there are relatively *many* primitive roots modulo p^e.

15.9 Non-existence of primitive roots

For *generic* integers n, there is *no* primitive root in $\mathbf{Z}/n$.

Theorem: If n is *not* 2, 4, nor of the forms p^e, $2p^e$ for p an odd prime (and e a positive integer), then there is *no* primitive root modulo n.

Proof: First, let's look at $\mathbf{Z}/2^e$ with $e \geq 3$. Any $b \in \mathbf{Z}/2^{e\times}$ can be written as $b = 1 + 2x$ for integer x. Then

$$(1+2x)^2 = 1 + 4x + 4x^2 = 1 + 4x(x+1)$$

The peculiar feature here is that for any integer x, the expression $x(x+1)$ is divisible by 2. Indeed, if x is even surely $x(x+1)$ is even, and if x is odd then $x+1$ is even and $x(x+1)$ is again even. Thus,

$$(1+2x)^2 = 1 \bmod 8$$

(rather than merely modulo 4). And from the pattern

$$(1+2^k x)^2 = 1 + 2^{k+1}x + 2^{2k}x^2$$

we can prove by induction that

$$(1+8x)^{2^{e-3}} = 1 \bmod 2^e$$

Putting this together, we see that

$$(1+2x)^{2^{e-2}} = 1 \bmod 2^e$$

But $2^{e-2} < 2^{e-1} = \varphi(2^e)$. That is, there cannot be a primitive root modulo 2^e with $e > 2$.

Now consider n not a power of 2. Then write $n = p^e m$ with p an odd prime not dividing m. By Euler's theorem, we know that

$$b^{\varphi(p^e)} = 1 \bmod p^e$$

$$b^{\varphi(m)} = 1 \bmod m$$

Let $M = \mathrm{lcm}(\varphi(p^e), \varphi(m))$. Then (as usual)

$$b^M = (b^{\varphi(p^e)})^{M/\varphi(p^e)} = 1^{M/\varphi(p^e)} = 1 \bmod p^e$$

and

$$b^M = (b^{\varphi(m)})^{M/\varphi(m)} = 1^{M/\varphi(m)} = 1 \bmod m$$

Thus, certainly

$$b^M = 1 \bmod p^e\, m$$

But a primitive root g would have the property that no smaller exponent ℓ than $\varphi(p^e m)$ has the property that $g^\ell = 1 \bmod p^e m$. Therefore, unless $\gcd(\varphi(p^e), \varphi(m)) = 1$ we'll have

$$\mathrm{lcm}(\varphi(p^e), \varphi(m)) < \varphi(p^e)\, \varphi(m) = \varphi(p^e\, m)$$

which would deny the possibility that there is a primitive root.

Thus, we need $\varphi(m)$ relatively prime to $\varphi(p^e) = (p-1)p^{e-1}$. Since $p-1$ is even, this means that $\varphi(m)$ must be odd. If an odd prime q divides m, then $q-1$ divides $\varphi(m)$, which would make $\varphi(m)$ even, which is impossible. Thus, no odd prime can divide m. Further, if any power of 2 greater than just 2 itself divides m, again $\varphi(m)$ would be even, and no primitive root could exist.

Thus, except for the cases where we've already proven that a primitive root *does* exist, there is no primitive root mod n.　　　　　///

15.10　An algorithm to find primitive roots

If we know the factorization of $p-1$ for a prime p, then there is a reasonable algorithm to *find* a primitive root modulo p.

First we give an efficient criterion to *check* whether or not a candidate b is a primitive root modulo p or not. This uses knowledge of the factorization of $p-1$.

Lemma: Let p be a prime. An integer b is a primitive root modulo p if and only if $b^{(p-1)/q} \neq 1 \bmod p$ for all primes q dividing $p-1$.

Proof: If b is a primitive root, certainly the conditions of the lemma are met. On the other hand, suppose that the conditions of the lemma are fulfilled for a particular b. Let q^e be the exact power of q dividing $p-1$, and let t be the order of q in $\mathbf{Z}/p^\times$. Then $t | p-1$ by Fermat's Little Theorem. If q^e did not divide t, then still t would divide $(p-1)/q$. But by hypothesis t does not divide $(p-1)/q$. Therefore, $q^e | t$. Since this is true for every prime q dividing $p-1$, the least common multiple m of all these prime powers *also* divides t, by unique factorization of integers. Of course, the least common multiple of all prime powers dividing any number $p-1$ is that number itself. Thus, $m = p-1$, and $p-1$ divides t. Since t divides $p-1$, this gives $t = p-1$. That is, b is a primitive root modulo p.　　　　　///

Remark: Note that the number of primes dividing $p-1$ is well below $\log_2 p$.

Remark: And recall that the number of primitive roots modulo p (for p prime) is $\varphi(p-1)$, which is typically greater than $(p-1)/4$. Thus, choosing primitive root candidates at random has roughly a 1/4 chance of success. Thus, by a typical expected value computation, as a heuristic, we should usually expect to find a primitive root after about 4 tries.

The algorithm to find a primitive root b modulo a prime p, using knowledge of the factorization of $p - 1$, and to *verify* that b really is a primitive root, is as follows:

- Pick a random b.
- For each prime q dividing $p - 1$, compute $b^{(p-1)/q} \bmod p$.
- If *any* of these values is 1 mod p, reject b and try a different random candidate.
- Else if *none* of these values is 1 mod p, then b is a primitive root modulo p.

Remark: Again, roughly a quarter or more of the elements of $\mathbf{Z}/p^\times$ are primitive roots, so random guessing will succeed in finding a primitive root very quickly. And the lemma above justifies the fairly efficient procedure to verify whether or not a given candidate is a primitive root. And of course we take for granted that we use an efficient exponentiation algorithm.

Remark: Very often 2 or 3 is a primitive root. For example, among the 168 primes under 1000, only 60 have the property that neither 2 nor 3 is a primitive root. Among the 168 primes under 1000, only the 7 moduli 191, 311, 409, 439, 457, 479, and 911 have the property that none of 2,3,5,6,7,10,11 is a primitive root.

Exercises

15.01 Find a prime $p > 2$ such that 2 is *not* a primitive root modulo p.

15.02 Find all the primitive roots in $\mathbf{Z}/17$. (*ans.*)

15.03 Find all the primitive roots in $\mathbf{Z}/19$.

15.04 Find any repeated factors of $x^4 + x^2 + 1$ in $\mathbf{F}_2[x]$. (*ans.*)

15.05 Find any repeated factors of $x^6 + x^4 + x^2 + 1$ in $\mathbf{F}_2[x]$.

15.06 Determine the cyclotomic polynomials φ_2, φ_3, φ_4, φ_5, φ_6. (*ans.*)

15.07 Determine the cyclotomic polynomials φ_8, φ_9, φ_{12}.

15.08 Use a bit of cleverness to avoid working too much, and determine the cyclotomic polynomials φ_{14}, φ_{16}, φ_{18}. (*ans.*)

15.09 Use a bit of cleverness to avoid working too much, and determine the cyclotomic polynomials φ_{20}, φ_{24}, φ_{25}.

15.10 Use some cleverness as well as perseverance to determine the cyclotomic polynomials φ_{15}, φ_{21}.

15.11 Find a primitive root in $\mathbf{F}_2[x]$ modulo $x^2 + x + 1$. (*ans.*)

15.12 Find a primitive root in $\mathbf{F}_2[x]$ modulo $x^3 + x + 1$. (*ans.*)

15.13 Find a primitive root in $\mathbf{F}_2[x]$ modulo $x^3 + x^2 + 1$.

15.14 Find a primitive root in $\mathbf{F}_2[x]$ modulo $x^4 + x + 1$.

15.15 (*) Find a cyclotomic polynomial that has coefficients other than $0, +1, -1$. (*ans.*)

16

Primitive Polynomials

The notion of **primitivity** of a polynomial with coefficients in $\mathbf{F}_2$ or some other finite field $\mathbf{F}_q$ is very important in many different applications. Unfortunately, it is not particularly intuitive.

We give two applications here: length of period of linear feedback shift registers, and two-bit error detections by cyclic redundancy checks.

16.1 Definition of primitive polynomials

Primitive polynomials and primitive roots in finite fields have a complementary relationship to each other.

A polynomial P of degree N in $\mathbf{F}_q[x]$ is **primitive** if P is irreducible and

$$x^{q^N-1} = 1 \bmod P$$

and

$$x^\ell \neq 1 \bmod P$$

for $0 < \ell < q^N - 1$.

Proposition: An irreducible polynomial P of degree N in $\mathbf{F}_q[x]$ is **primitive** if and only if x-mod-P is a primitive *element* in the finite field $\mathbf{F}_q[x]/P$.

Proof: The only thing to worry about is that $\mathbf{F}_q[x]/P$ should be a field. This requires exactly that P be irreducible. ///

Theorem: An irreducible polynomial P of degree N in $\mathbf{F}_q[x]$ is primitive if and only if P divides the $(q^N - 1)^{\text{th}}$ cyclotomic polynomial in $\mathbf{F}_q[x]$.

Proof: On one hand, suppose that P is primitive. By definition, this means that

$$x^{q^N-1} = 1 \bmod P$$

but that no smaller positive exponent will do. That is, P divides $x^{q^N-1} - 1$ but not $x^M - 1$ for any positive M smaller than $q^N - 1$. We have seen that

$$\varphi_\ell(x) = \frac{x^\ell - 1}{\text{lcm of all } x^t - 1 \text{ with } t | \ell}$$

By unique factorization of polynomials (in one variable, with coefficients in a field), we conclude that P divides the $(q^N - 1)^{\text{th}}$ cyclotomic polynomial.

On the other hand, suppose that P is irreducible of degree N and divides the $(q^N - 1)^{\text{th}}$ cyclotomic polynomial. The multiplicative group of non-zero elements of the field $\mathbf{F}_q[x]/P$ has $q^N - 1$ elements, so by Lagrange's theorem and its corollaries

$$x^{(q^N-1)} = 1 \bmod P$$

That is, P divides $x^{(q^N-1)} - 1$. We must prove that P does not divide $x^t - 1$ for any divisor t of $q^N - 1$ smaller than $q^N - 1$ itself. Note that the characteristic of the field (the prime dividing the prime power q) certainly does not divide $q^N - 1$. Thus, $x^{(q^N-1)} - 1$ has no repeated roots. Thus, again using the definition of the cyclotomic polynomial quoted just above, and again using unique factorization, $P(x)$ has no common factors with $x^t - 1$ for divisors t of $a^N - 1$ with $t < q^N - 1$. In particular, P does not divide $x^t - 1$ for any divisor t of $q^N - 1$ with $0 < t < q^N - 1$. Thus, x is of order exactly $q^N - 1$ modulo P, rather than of order any proper divisor of $q^N - 1$. That is, P is primitive.   ///

Remark: In fact, a little further preparation would allow proof that for $N = 2, 3, 4, 5, 6, \ldots$ the irreducible factors of the $(q^N - 1)^{\text{th}}$ cyclotomic polynomial in $\mathbf{F}_q[x]$ are all of degree exactly N.

The **order** of a polynomial Q modulo P is the smallest positive integer M so that

$$Q^M = 1 \bmod P$$

Thus, paraphrasing the previous proposition, an irreducible polynomial P of degree N in $\mathbf{F}_q[x]$ is primitive if and only if the order of x mod P is $q^N - 1$. In any case, by Lagrange's theorem, the order of Q mod P is always a divisor of $q^N - 1$.

16.2 Examples mod 2

For applications, some of the most important polynomials are those with coefficients in $\mathbf{F}_2$. Here we'll look at low-degree **primitive polynomials** modulo 2.

A **linear** polynomial in $\mathbf{F}_2[x]$ is primitive, by definition, if it is irreducible and divides the $(2^1 - 1)^{\text{th}}$ cyclotomic polynomial, which is

$$\varphi_1 = x - 1 = x + 1$$

This directly shows that the linear polynomial $x + 1$ *is* primitive, while x is *not*.

A **quadratic** polynomial in $\mathbf{F}_2[x]$ is primitive, by definition, if it is irreducible and divides the $(2^2 - 1)^{\text{th}}$ cyclotomic polynomial, which is

$$\varphi_{2^2-1} = \varphi_3 = \frac{x^3 - 1}{x - 1} = x^2 + x + 1$$

which is by coincidence quadratic itself. It's easy to check (by trial division) that $x^2 + x + 1$ is irreducible, so $x^2 + x + 1$ is the only primitive quadratic polynomial mod 2.

A **cubic** polynomial in $\mathbf{F}_2[x]$ is primitive, by definition, if it is irreducible and divides the $(2^3 - 1)^{\text{th}}$ cyclotomic polynomial, which is

$$\varphi_{2^3-1} = \varphi_7 = \frac{x^7 - 1}{x - 1} = x^6 + x^5 + x^4 + x^3 + x^2 + x + 1$$

From earlier (trial division), we know that the irreducible cubics mod 2 are exactly

$$x^3 + x^2 + 1 \quad x^3 + x + 1$$

Just checking, multiply out

$$(x^3 + x^2 + 1) \cdot (x^3 + x + 1) = x^6 + x^5 + x^4 + x^3 + x^2 + x + 1$$

We conclude that both the irreducible cubics are primitive.

A **quartic** polynomial in $\mathbf{F}_2[x]$ is primitive, by definition, if it is irreducible and divides the $(2^4 - 1)^{\text{th}}$ cyclotomic polynomial, which is

$$\varphi_{2^4-1} = \varphi_{15} = \frac{x^{15} - 1}{\varphi_1(x)\,\varphi_3(x)\,\varphi_5(x)} = \frac{x^{15} - 1}{\varphi_3(x)\,(x^5 - 1)} = \frac{x^{15} - 1}{(x^2 + x + 1)(x^5 - 1)}$$

$$= x^8 + x^7 + x^5 + x^4 + x^3 + x + 1$$

From earlier (trial division), we know that the irreducible quartics mod 2 are exactly the 3
$$x^4 + x^3 + x^2 + x + 1 \quad x^4 + x^3 + 1 \quad x^4 + x + 1$$

If we make a lucky (?!) guess that the second two are the primitive ones (since they are somewhat related to each other) then we check:

$$(x^4 + x^3 + 1) \cdot (x^4 + x + 1) = x^8 + x^7 + x^5 + x^4 + x^3 + x + 1$$

Yes, these two are the primitive quartics mod 2. So 2 out of 3 irreducible quartics are primitive.

Note that we might have recognized that $x^4 + x^3 + x^2 + x + 1$ is not primitive by the fact that it is in fact exactly φ_5. That implies that every root λ of it has order 5 rather than 15.

A **quintic** polynomial in $\mathbf{F}_2[x]$ is primitive, by definition, if it is irreducible and divides the $(2^5 - 1)^{\text{th}}$ cyclotomic polynomial, which is

$$\varphi_{2^5-1} = \varphi_{31} = \frac{x^{31} - 1}{x - 1}$$

This is of degree 30, so if we imagine that it's exactly the product of the primitive quintics, then there should be 6 of them.

But in fact we already saw (by trial division) that there are exactly 6 irreducible quintics,

$$x^5 + 0 + x^3 + x^2 + x + 1$$
$$x^5 + x^4 + 0 + x^2 + x + 1$$
$$x^5 + x^4 + x^3 + 0 + x + 1$$
$$x^5 + x^4 + x^3 + x^2 + 0 + 1$$
$$x^5 + x^3 + 1$$
$$x^5 + x^2 + 1$$

A person who cared enough could really check that the product of these is φ_{31}.

A **sextic** polynomial in $\mathbf{F}_2[x]$ is primitive, by definition, if it is irreducible and divides the

$$(2^6 - 1)^{\text{th}} = 63^{\text{th}} = (3 \cdot 3 \cdot 7)^{\text{th}}$$

cyclotomic polynomial, which is of degree

$$\varphi(2^6 - 1) = \varphi(3 \cdot 3 \cdot 7) = (3 - 1)3(7 - 1) = 42$$

So if we imagine that it's exactly the product of the primitive sextics, then there should be $42/6 = 7$ of them.

How many irreducible sextics are there mod 2? It turns out (as we will see later in our discussion of the Frobenius automorphism and other further structure of finite fields) that there are

$$\frac{2^6 - 2^3 - 2^2 + 2^1}{6} = \frac{54}{6} = 9$$

So *two* irreducible sextics are *not* primitive. Which two?

A **septic** polynomial in $\mathbf{F}_2[x]$ is primitive, by definition, if it is irreducible and divides the

$$(2^7 - 1)^{\text{th}} = 127^{\text{th}}$$

cyclotomic polynomial, which is of degree

$$\varphi(2^7 - 1) = 127 - 1 = 2 \cdot 3 \cdot 3 \cdot 7$$

(since 127 is prime). So if we imagine that it's exactly the product of the primitive septics, then there should be $2 \cdot 3 \cdot 3 = 18$ of them.

How many irreducible septics are there mod 2? It turns out that there are

$$\frac{2^7 - 2^1}{7} = \frac{126}{7} = 18$$

So all irreducible septics mod 2 are primitive.

An **octic** polynomial in $\mathbf{F}_2[x]$ is primitive, by definition, if it is irreducible and divides the

$$(2^8 - 1)^{\text{th}} = 255^{\text{th}} = (3 \cdot 5 \cdot 17)^{\text{th}}$$

cyclotomic polynomial, which is of degree

$$\varphi(2^8 - 1) = (3 - 1)(5 - 1)(7 - 1) = 2\dot{4} \cdot 6 = 48$$

So if we imagine that it's exactly the product of the primitive octics, then there should be $48/8 = 6$ of them.

How many irreducible octics are there mod 2? It turns out that there are

$$\frac{2^8 - 2^4}{8} = 2^5 - 2 = 30$$

So only 6 of the 30 irreducible octics are primitive.

16.3 Testing for primitivity

For large degree d, it is not good to test for primitivity of polynomials in $\mathbf{F}_q[x]$ by actually computing the $(p^d - 1)^{\text{th}}$ cyclotomic polynomial, since the degree of this grows exponentially in d, and too much memory would be needed to do this! There is a better approach expressible as an algorithm, which uses hardly any memory.

Theorem: Let P be an irreducible polynomial of degree n in $\mathbf{F}_q[x]$. Let $N = p^n - 1$. Then P is primitive if and only if

$$x^{N/r} \neq 1 \bmod P$$

for every prime number r dividing N.

Remark: As usual, the way we test whether a polynomial f is 1 **mod P** is to divide-with-remainder f by P, and see whether or not the remainder is 1.

Remark: Of course, we should use the fast exponentiation algorithm here.

Remark: The fast exponentiation algorithm in $\mathbf{F}_2[x]$ runs especially fast, since all that is necessary to square such a polynomial is to double the exponents (of terms which actually occur). For example, in $\mathbf{F}_2[x]$,

$$(x^5 + x^4 + x + 1)^2 = x^{10} + x^8 + x^2 + 1$$

Example: Let's verify that the nonic (degree nine polynomial) $1 + x^4 + x^9$ is primitive, while the nonic $1 + x + x^9$ is irreducible but not primitive. In both cases, we'll take the irreducibility for granted. Also, for brevity, let's express polynomials in $\mathbf{F}_2[x]$ as arrays of non-negative integers, where an integer i occurs if and only if x^i occurs in the polynomial. (Of course this trick is special to the case that the coefficients are in $\mathbf{F}_2$.) For example, $x^3 + x + 1$ would be denoted by $[0, 1, 3]$.

First, note that

$$2^9 - 1 = 7 \cdot 73$$

so (by Lagrange's theorem, etc.) it might be that

$$x^7 = 1 \bmod \text{ irred nonic}$$

or

$$x^{73} = 1 \bmod \text{ irred nonic}$$

if the nonic is not primitive. In the first case, x^7 is already reduced modulo any nonic polynomial, so it cannot be that $x^7 = 1$ modulo any nonic. Next, compute $x^{73} \bmod 1 + x^4 + x^9$ via the Fast Modular Exponentiation Algorithm: initiate $(X, E, Y) = (x, 73, 1)$ and at each step in the algorithm we list the triple of values (X, E, Y) at that point. When $E = 0$ the algorithm terminates and the value of Y is the desired x^{73} modulo the polynomial.

[1]	73	[0]
[1]	72	[1]
[2]	36	[1]
[4]	18	[1]
[8]	9	[1]
[8]	8	[0, 4]
[2, 6, 7]	4	[0, 4]
[0, 3, 5, 7]	2	[0, 4]
[1, 4, 6]	1	[0, 4]
[1, 4, 6]	0	[4, 6, 8]

Thus,

$$x^{73} = x^4 + x^6 + x^8 \bmod 1 + x^4 + x^9$$

which is not $1 \bmod 1 + x^4 + x^9$.

Just to check, let's verify that $x^{511} = 1 \bmod 1 + x^4 + x^9$. Of course, taking advantage of the power-of-2 situation, it would be smarter to verify that $x^{512} = x \bmod 1 + x^4 + x^9$. We again use the Fast Modular Exponentiation Algorithm, displaying the values of (X, EY) at successive steps in the execution:

[1]	512	[0]
[2]	256	[0]
[4]	128	[0]
[8]	64	[0]
[2, 6, 7]	32	[0]
[0, 3, 5, 7]	16	[0]
[1, 4, 6]	8	[0]
[2, 3, 7, 8]	4	[0]
[0, 2, 5, 7]	2	[0]
[1]	1	[0]
[1]	0	[1]

So that $x^{512} = x \bmod 1 + x^4 + x^9$ as it should.

Remark: If for some nonic P it happened that

$$x^{2^9} \neq x \bmod P$$

then we would know that the nonic P was **reducible**. (Why?) For example, with

$$P(x) = 1 + x^9 = (1 + x^3)(1 + x^3 + x^6)$$

$$= (1 + x)(1 + x + x^2)(1 + x^3 + x^6)$$

we compute $x^{512} \bmod P$ (here there is an unusual shortcut):

$$x^{512} = x^{9 \cdot 56 + 8} = (x^9)^{56} \cdot x^8$$

$$= 1 \cdot x^8 = x^8 \bmod x^9 + 1$$

which is not $x \bmod x^9 + 1$, so we have proven indirectly that $x^9 + 1$ is not irreducible.

On the other hand, let's look at the second nonic mentioned above, $1 + x + x^9$. Compute $x^{73} \bmod 1 + x + x^9$ by fast exponentiation, with the abbreviation used above:

$[1]$	73	$[0]$
$[1]$	72	$[1]$
$[2]$	36	$[1]$
$[4]$	18	$[1]$
$[8]$	9	$[1]$
$[8]$	8	$[0, 1]$
$[7, 8]$	4	$[0, 1]$
$[5, 6, 7, 8]$	2	$[0, 1]$
$[1, 2, 3, 4, 5, 6, 7, 8]$	1	$[0, 1]$
$[1, 2, 3, 4, 5, 6, 7, 8]$	0	$[0]$

That is,

$$x^{73} = 1 \bmod 1 + x + x^9$$

which proves that $1 + x + x^9$ is *not* primitive.

Just to check, let's compute $x^{512} \bmod 1 + x + x^9$:

$[1]$	512	$[0]$
$[2]$	256	$[0]$
$[4]$	128	$[0]$
$[8]$	64	$[0]$
$[7, 8]$	32	$[0]$
$[5, 6, 7, 8]$	16	$[0]$
$[1, 2, 3, 4, 5, 6, 7, 8]$	8	$[0]$
$[1, 3, 5, 7]$	4	$[0]$
$[1, 5]$	2	$[0]$
$[1]$	1	$[0]$
$[1]$	0	$[1]$

Thus, $x^{512} = x$ modulo $1 + x + x^9$, as it should because $1 + x + x^9$ is irreducible. (Why?)

16.4 Periods of LFSRs

Linear feedback shift registers, LFSR's, are among the simplest mechanisms by which to generate a stream of **pseudo-random numbers**. The very first requirement would be that the generator **not repeat itself** for a long time. This requirement can be completely addressed by looking at the **generating polynomial** for the shift register, and asking how close it is to being **primitive**.

Fix a size N, a modulus m (often $m = 2$), and choose **coefficients** $c = (c_0, \ldots, c_{N-1})$. Also choose a **seed** or **initial state** $s = (s_0, s_1, s_2, s_3, \ldots, s_{N-1})$. This will be the beginning of the keystream, as well. Then we recursively define, for $n + 1 \geq N$,

$$s_{n+1} = c_0\, s_n + c_1\, s_{n-1} + c_2\, s_{n-2} + \ldots + c_{N-1}\, s_{n-(N-1)} \ \% \ m$$

For example, with size $N = 2$, modulus 2, coefficients $c = (1,1)$, and seed $s = (s_0, s_1) = (0, 1)$ we have the Fibonacci sequence modulo 2, namely

$$
\begin{aligned}
s_0 &= 0 \\
s_1 &= 1 \\
s_2 &= s_1 + s_0 = 1 + 0 = 1 \\
s_3 &= s_2 + s_1 = 1 + 1 = 0 \\
s_4 &= s_3 + s_2 = 0 + 1 = 1 \\
s_5 &= s_4 + s_3 = 1 + 0 = 1 \\
s_6 &= s_5 + s_4 = 1 + 1 = 0 \\
&\cdots
\end{aligned}
$$

In this example it is apparent (and can be proven by induction) that the pattern repeats in blocks of 3 bits, with each block being 0, 1, 1.

As another example, with size $N = 3$, modulus 2, coefficients $c = (1, 1, 1)$, and seed $s = (s_0, s_1, s_2) = (0, 0, 1)$ we have

$$
\begin{aligned}
s_0 &= 0 \\
s_1 &= 0 \\
s_2 &= 1 \\
s_3 &= s_2 + s_1 + s_0 = 1 + 0 + 0 = 1 \\
s_4 &= s_3 + s_2 + s_1 = 1 + 1 + 0 = 0 \\
s_5 &= s_4 + s_3 + s_2 = 0 + 1 + 1 = 0 \\
s_6 &= s_5 + s_4 + s_3 = 0 + 0 + 1 = 1 \\
s_7 &= s_6 + s_5 + s_4 = 1 + 0 + 0 = 1 \\
&\cdots
\end{aligned}
$$

and the pattern repeats in blocks of 0011. With the seed 101 and the same coefficients we have

$$
\begin{aligned}
s_0 &= 1 \\
s_1 &= 0 \\
s_2 &= 1 \\
s_3 &= s_2 + s_1 + s_0 = 1 + 0 + 1 = 0 \\
s_4 &= s_3 + s_2 + s_1 = 0 + 1 + 0 = 1 \\
s_5 &= s_4 + s_3 + s_2 = 1 + 0 + 1 = 0 \\
s_6 &= s_5 + s_4 + s_3 = 0 + 1 + 0 = 1 \\
s_7 &= s_6 + s_5 + s_4 = 1 + 0 + 1 = 0 \\
&\cdots
\end{aligned}
$$

so there is a shorter time-to-repeat with this seed, in blocks of 01.

By contrast, with size $N = 3$, modulus 2, coefficients $c = (1, 0, 1)$, and seed $s = (s_0, s_1) = (0, 0, 1)$ we have

$$
\begin{aligned}
s_0 &= 0 \\
s_1 &= 0 \\
s_2 &= 1 \\
s_3 &= s_2 + s_0 = 1 + 0 = 1 \\
s_4 &= s_3 + s_1 = 1 + 0 = 1 \\
s_5 &= s_4 + s_2 = 1 + 1 = 0 \\
s_6 &= s_5 + s_3 = 0 + 1 = 1 \\
s_7 &= s_6 + s_4 = 1 + 1 = 0 \\
s_8 &= s_7 + s_5 = 0 + 0 = 0 \\
s_9 &= s_8 + s_6 = 0 + 1 = 1
\end{aligned}
$$

and thereafter the pattern repeats. Note that with size $N = 3$ this example repeats in blocks of 7, by contrast to the previous example.

The kind of recursive definition used to define the keystream here can be written in terms of matrices. For simplicity, let's just suppose that $N = 4$. From coefficients $c = (c_0, c_1, c_2, c_3)$, we make a matrix

$$
C = \begin{pmatrix}
c_0 & c_1 & c_2 & c_3 \\
1 & 0 & 0 & 0 \\
0 & 1 & 0 & 0 \\
0 & 0 & 1 & 0
\end{pmatrix}
$$

and the recursion relation can be written as

$$
\begin{pmatrix}
s_{n+1} \\
s_n \\
s_{n-1} \\
s_{n-2}
\end{pmatrix}
= C \cdot
\begin{pmatrix}
s_n \\
s_{n-1} \\
s_{n-2} \\
s_{n-3}
\end{pmatrix}
\qquad \text{(all modulo } m)
$$

For example suppose the modulus is $m = 2$ and the coefficients are

$$
c_0 = 1, c_1 = 0, c_2 = 0, c_3 = 1
$$

so that the output stream is produced by

$$s_{i+1} = c_0 \cdot s_i + c_1 \cdot s_{i-1} + c_2 \cdot s_{i-2} + c_3 \cdot s_{i-3}$$

$$= 1 \cdot s_i + 0 \cdot s_{i-1} + 0 \cdot s_{i-2} + 1 \cdot s_{i-3} = s_i + s_{i-3}$$

With seed

$$(s_0, s_1, s_2, s_3) = (1, 1, 0, 0)$$

the whole stream produced (including the initial $(1, 1, 0, 0)$) is

$$1, 1, 0, 0, 1, 0, 0, 0, 1, 1, 1, 1, 0, 1, 0, 1, 1, 0, 0, 1, 0, 0, 0, \ldots$$

In this case, if an earlier occurring pattern of 4 consecutive bits recurs, then the stream will repeat itself, since the four previous values completely determine the next one. Here the initial $(1, 1, 0, 0)$ recurred after 15 steps.

The possibility of expressing the computation of the output stream in terms of matrices is both convenient for computations and as an exploitable vulnerability for cryptanalytic attacks.

It is possible that for *some* choices of seed the keystream has a large period, but for other choices of seed the keystream has a short period, both with the same coefficients c. For this reason, in some scenarios the coefficients $c_0, c_1, c_2, \ldots$ should be chosen carefully, and only the seed $(s_0, s_1, s_2, \ldots)$ chosen 'at random'.

Theorem: If the **generating polynomial**

$$x^N - c_0 x^{N-1} - c_1 x^{N-2} - c_2 x^{N-3} - \ldots - c_{N-1}$$

in $\mathbf{F}_q[x]$ is primitive, then the linear feedback shift register with coefficients $c_0, \ldots, c_{N-1}$ has period $q^N - 1$ for *any* initial state $s_0, s_1, \ldots, s_{N-1}$ (other than all 0's).

Remark: If that polynomial is *not* primitive, then the period will be less, *and* there will be several 'bad' initial states which will cause the LFSR to have a *much* smaller period.

Proof: Define the **transition matrix** L by

$$L = \begin{pmatrix} c_0 & c_1 & c_2 & \ldots & c_{N-2} & c_{N-1} \\ 1 & 0 & 0 & \ldots & 0 & 0 \\ 0 & 1 & 0 & \ldots & 0 & 0 \\ 0 & 0 & 1 & \ldots & 0 & 0 \\ & & \ldots & & & \\ 0 & 0 & \ldots & 0 & 1 & 0 \end{pmatrix}$$

That is, the top row consists of the coefficients (note the ordering of them!) and everything else is 0 except for the 1's on the subdiagonal. Then

$$L \cdot \begin{pmatrix} s_n \\ s_{n-1} \\ \ldots \\ s_{n-(N-2)} \\ s_{n-(N-1)} \end{pmatrix} = \begin{pmatrix} s_{n+1} \\ s_n \\ \ldots \\ s_{n-(N-3)} \\ s_{n-(N-2)} \end{pmatrix}$$

As is standard in linear algebra, the *idea* is to express the initial state

$$\begin{pmatrix} s_{N-1} \\ s_{N-2} \\ \ldots \\ s_1 \\ s_0 \end{pmatrix}$$

as a **linear combination**

$$\begin{pmatrix} s_{N-1} \\ s_{N-2} \\ \ldots \\ s_1 \\ s_0 \end{pmatrix} = a_1 \cdot v_1 + \ldots + a_n \cdot v_n$$

of **eigenvectors** v_i of L with corresponding eigenvalue λ_i, thereby being easily able to evaluate L^k:

$$L^k \begin{pmatrix} s_{N-1} \\ s_{N-2} \\ \ldots \\ s_1 \\ s_0 \end{pmatrix} = \lambda_1^k a_1 \cdot v_1 + \ldots + \lambda_n^k a_n \cdot v_n$$

If you understand how determinants work, then you can see that the **characteristic polynomial** of a matrix of the special form that L has is just

$$P_L(x) = x^N - c_0 x^{N-1} - c_1 x^{N-2} - c_2 x^{N-3} - \ldots - c_{N-1}$$

But we cannot expect to 'solve' high-degree polynomial equations explicitly.

Instead of being so explicit, we could demand that all the eigenvalues λ_i have the largest possible order(s). That is, the smallest positive integer ℓ so that $\lambda_i^\ell = 1$ is as large as possible.

Remark: A possible problem here is that if we've only discussed the finite fields $\mathbf{F}_p$ and no others then we don't know where to look to find these eigenvalues, since we probably *cannot* solve the characteristic equation in $\mathbf{F}_p$! We need to understand finite fields more generally to understand what's going on with LFSR's, even though we don't mention finite fields in the definition of LFSR! But let's not worry too much.

Assuming (as we did) that P_L is irreducible, these eigenvalues lie in the finite field $\mathbf{F}_{p^N}$ (since P_L is of degree N). In the discussion of primitive roots, we actually showed that the multiplicative group of *any* finite field is cyclic, so $F_{p^N}^\times$ is cyclic, of order $p^N - 1$. That is, every non-zero element of $\mathbf{F}_{p^N}$ satisfies

$$x^{p^N - 1} - 1 = 0$$

But we want to exclude elements with smaller orders (so by Lagrange's theorem having order *proper* divisors of P_L). That is, we want to look at the polynomial that's left after removing from $x^{p^N-1} - 1 = 0$ all its common factors with polynomials $x^d - 1$ where d is a proper divisor of $p^N - 1$. From the discussion of cyclotomic polynomials, what remains after such common factors are removed is exactly the $(p^N - 1)^{\text{th}}$ **cyclotomic polynomial**.

Therefore the hypothesis that P_L is irreducible and divides the $(p^N - 1)^{\text{th}}$ cyclotomic polynomial assures that the order of each eigenvalue is $p^N - 1$.

Then look at the periodicity condition

$$\lambda_1^{i+\ell} a_1 \cdot v_1 + \ldots + \lambda_n^{i+\ell} a_n \cdot v_n = \lambda_1^i a_1 \cdot v_1 + \ldots + \lambda_n^i a_n \cdot v_n$$

This simplifies to

$$(\lambda_1^{i+\ell} - \lambda_1^i)v_1 + \ldots + (\lambda_N^{i+\ell} - \lambda_N^i)v_N = 0$$

or

$$(\lambda_1^\ell - 1)\lambda_1^i v_1 + \ldots + (\lambda_N^\ell - 1)\lambda_N^i v_N = 0$$

Certainly if $p^N - 1$ divides ℓ then the quantities in parentheses are all 0, so the sum is 0.

To prove the other half, that this vector sum being zero implies that every $\lambda_i^\ell - 1 = 0$, we need a bit more information about eigenvectors. First, in this situation we know that P_L has **distinct roots**, since P_L is a divisor of the $(p^N - 1)^{\text{th}}$ cyclotomic polynomial, which we know to have distinct roots. Now we claim that for an N-by-N matrix M with *distinct* eigenvalues $\lambda_1, \ldots, \lambda_N$, any relation

$$a_1 v_1 + \ldots + a_N v_N = 0$$

among corresponding eigenvectors v_i must have all coefficients a_i equal to 0. To prove this, make the clever hypothesis that we have such a relation, and that among all such relations it has the fewest non-zero a_i's. Apply M to both sides of that relation, obtaining

$$\lambda_1 a_1 v_1 + \ldots + \lambda_N a_N v_N = 0$$

Multiplying the first relation by λ_j and subtracting from the second gives a vector relation

$$(\lambda_1 - \lambda_j)a_1 v_1 + \ldots + (\lambda_N - \lambda_j)a_N v_N = 0$$

This has the effect of getting rid of the jth term. Note that since the eigenvalues are all distinct none of the quantities $\lambda_i - \lambda_j$ is 0 except for $i = j$. Thus, we can obtain a relation with fewer non-zero coefficients by using this trick to kill off some non-zero coefficient. Contradiction.

Thus, in the case at hand,

$$(\lambda_1^\ell - 1)\lambda_1^i v_1 + \ldots + (\lambda_N^\ell - 1)\lambda_N^i v_N = 0$$

if and only if *all* coefficients $(\lambda_i^\ell - 1)\lambda_i$ are 0. Since $\lambda_i^{p^N-1} = 1$, λ_i is non-zero itself, so the condition is that

$$\lambda_i^\ell - 1 = 0 \text{ (for all } i)$$

Since every λ_i has order $p^N - 1$, this holds if and only if ℓ divides $p^N - 1$. That is, we've proven that the order of such a LFSR is $p^N - 1$.   ///

Remark: We did *not* prove above that every vector can be expressed as a linear combination

$$v = a_1 v_1 + \ldots + a_N v_N$$

of eigenvectors v_i. Since the eigenvalues are all different from each other, this *is* true. We proved above that eigenvectors attached to different eigenvalues are linearly independent. On the other hand, N linearly independent vectors in an N-dimensional space implies that these vectors are a basis. (See the appendix on linear algebra.)

16.5 Two-bit errors in CRCs

The question of which two-bit errors are detected by a **cyclic redundancy check** (CRC) can be completely answered in terms of **primitivity** (or not) of the **generator polynomial**.

First let's recall how a CRC works. Given data expressed as a stream of bits such as 11100010100, create a **data polynomial** with coefficients in the finite field $\mathbf{F}_2$ from it by using the 0's and 1's as coefficients: from this string of bits, make polynomial

$$11100010100 \to x^{10} + x^9 + x^8 + x^4 + x^2$$

A CRC-computing algorithm is specified by its **generating polynomial**, which is also a polynomial with coefficients in the finite field $\mathbf{F}_2$. For example, we might take generating polynomial

$$x^3 + x + 1$$

Then the CRC of the data is computed by **finding the remainder when the data polynomial is divided by the generating polynomial**: With data polynomial and generating polynomial as above, we'd get

$$
\begin{array}{r}
x^7 + x^6 + 0 + 0 + x^3 + 0 + 0 + 1 \quad R \; x^2 + x^1 + x^0 \\
\hline
x^3 + 0 + x^1 + x^0 \big) \; x^{10} + x^9 + x^8 + 0 + 0 + 0 + x^4 + 0 + x^2 + 0 + 0 \\
x^{10} + 0 + x^8 + x^7 + 0 + 0 + 0 + 0 + 0 + 0 + 0 \\
\hline
x^9 + 0 + x^7 + 0 + 0 + x^4 + 0 + x^2 + 0 + 0 \\
x^9 + 0 + x^7 + x^6 + 0 + 0 + 0 + 0 + 0 + 0 \\
\hline
x^6 + 0 + x^4 + 0 + x^2 + 0 + 0 \\
x^6 + 0 + x^4 + x^3 + 0 + 0 + 0 \\
\hline
x^3 + x^2 + 0 + 0 \\
x^3 + 0 + x^1 + x^0 \\
\hline
x^2 + x^1 + x^0
\end{array}
$$

Thus, the remainder is $x^2 + x + 1$, which we translate back to bits as 111. That is

CRC with generating polynomial $x^3 + x + 1$ computed for $11100010100 = 111$

As discussed earlier, when a piece of data is expressed as a stream of 0's and 1's, a change of any 0 to a 1 or *vice versa* is a **bit error**. In general, the number of 0-to-1 or 1-to-0 changes in a chunk of data (viewed as a stream of 0's and 1's) is the **number of bit errors**.

Theorem: Let $g(x)$ be a CRC generating polynomial with coefficients in $\mathbf{F}_2$ and non-zero constant coefficient. Suppose that $g(x)$ has a factor $h(x)$ which is **primitive**, of degree N. Then for this CRC to fail to detect some two-bit error it must be that the two altered bits are a distance apart which is a multiple of 2^N.

Proof: Let $e(x) = x^m - x^n = x^n(x^{m-n} - 1)$ be the error viewed as a polynomial, with $m > n$. To fail to be detected by the CRC with generator $g(x)$ it must be that $g(x)$ divides $e(x)$. Since $g(x)$ has non-zero constant coefficient, it has no factor of x, so to divide $x^n(x^{m-n} - 1)$ it must be that $g(x)$ divides $x^d - 1$, where $d = m - n$ is the distance apart of the two single-bit errors. By the definition of primitivity, $s = 2^N - 1$ is the smallest exponent such that $h(x)$ divides $x^s - 1$. Since $g(x)$ divides $x^d - 1$, the primitive polynomial $h(x)$ of degree N must also divide $x^d - 1$. Invoking the division algorithm, write $d = qs + r$ with $0 \le r < |s|$. Then

$$x^d = x^{qs+r} = (x^s)^q \cdot x^r = 1^q \cdot x^r = x^r \bmod h(x)$$

because $x^s = 1 \bmod h(x)$. But also $x^d = 1 \bmod h(x)$, so $x^r = 1 \bmod h(x)$. Since s was the smallest positive exponent with this property, it must be that $r = 0$, and thus $s = 2^N - 1$ divides d, the distance apart.   ///

Remark: Thus, it is desirable to have a CRC generating polynomial be divisible by a pretty-high-degree primitive polynomial.

Exercises

16.01 Find the (multiplicative) order of x mod $x^3 + x + 1$ with coefficients in $\mathbf{Z}/2$. (*ans.*)

16.02 Find the (multiplicative) order of $x + 1$ mod $x^3 + x + 1$ with coefficients in $\mathbf{Z}/2$.

16.03 Find the (multiplicative) order of $x^2 + x + 1$ mod $x^3 + x + 1$ with coefficients in $\mathbf{Z}/2$.

16.04 Find the (multiplicative) order of x mod $x^4 + x^3 + x^2 + x + 1$ with coefficients in $\mathbf{Z}/2$. (*ans.*)

16.05 Find the (multiplicative) order of x mod $x^4 + x + 1$ with coefficients in $\mathbf{Z}/2$.

16.06 Find the (multiplicative) order of $x^2 + x + 1$ mod $x^4 + x + 1$ with coefficients in $\mathbf{Z}/2$.

16.07 Find an element of order 63 in $\mathbf{F}_{64}$, where $\mathbf{F}_{64}$ is modeled as $\mathbf{F}_2[x]$ modulo 1010111 where those are the coefficients in order of decreasing degree. (*ans.*)

16.08 Find an element of order 63 in $\mathbf{F}_{64}$, where $\mathbf{F}_{64}$ is modeled as $\mathbf{F}_2[x]$ modulo 1110101 where those are the coefficients in order of decreasing degree.

16.09 Define a linear feedback shift register by

$$s_{n+1} = s_n + s_{n-1} + s_{n-2} + s_{n-3}$$

where for an index n the state is a list of 4 bits (or elements of $\mathbf{F}_2$) $(s_n, s_{n-1}, s_{n-2}, s_{n-3})$. With initial state $(s_3, s_2, s_1, s_0) = (1, 1, 1, 1)$, after how many steps will the state return to this? (*ans.*)

16.10 Define a linear feedback shift register by

$$s_{n+1} = s_n + s_{n-3}$$

where for an index n the state is a list of 4 bits (or elements of $\mathbf{F}_2$) $(s_n, s_{n-1}, s_{n-2}, s_{n-3})$. With initial state $(s_3, s_2, s_1, s_0) = (1, 1, 1, 1)$, after how many steps will the state return to this? (*ans.*)

16.11 Define a linear feedback shift register by

$$s_{n+1} = s_{n-2} + s_{n-4}$$

where for an index n the state is a list of 5 bits $(s_n, s_{n-1}, s_{n-2}, s_{n-3}, s_{n-4})$. With initial state $(s_4, s_3, s_2, s_1, s_0) = (1, 1, 1, 1, 1)$, after how many steps will the state return to this? (*ans.*)

16.12 Define a linear feedback shift register by

$$s_{n+1} = s_{n-1} + s_{n-4}$$

where for an index n the state is a list of 5 bits $(s_n, s_{n-1}, s_{n-2}, s_{n-3}, s_{n-4})$. With initial state $(s_4, s_3, s_2, s_1, s_0) = (1, 0, 0, 0, 0)$, after how many steps will the state return to this?

16.13 Define a linear feedback shift register by

$$s_{n+1} = s_{n-3} + s_{n-4}$$

where for an index n the state is a list of 5 bits $(s_n, s_{n-1}, s_{n-2}, s_{n-3}, s_{n-4})$. With initial state $(s_4, s_3, s_2, s_1, s_0) = (1, 0, 0, 0, 0)$, after how many steps will the state return to this? (*ans.*)

16.14 Define a linear feedback shift register by

$$s_{n+1} = s_{n-3} + s_{n-3} + s_{n-4} + s_{n-5}$$

where for index n the state is a list of 6 bits $(s_n, s_{n-1}, s_{n-2}, s_{n-3}, s_{n-4}, s_{n-5})$. With initial state $(s_5, s_4, s_3, s_2, s_1, s_0) = (1, 0, 0, 0, 0)$, after how many steps will the state return to this?

16.15 Define a linear feedback shift register by

$$s_{n+1} = s_{n-4} + s_{n-5}$$

where for index n the state is a list of 6 bits $(s_n, s_{n-1}, s_{n-2}, s_{n-3}, s_{n-4}, s_{n-5})$. With initial state $(s_5, s_4, s_3, s_2, s_1, s_0) = (1, 0, 0, 0, 0)$, after how many steps will the state return to this?

16.16 Let $\mathbf{F}_{16}$ be modeled as $\mathbf{F}_2[x]$ modulo 10011, the latter indicating coefficients in order of decreasing degree. Find two roots of the equation $y^2 + y + 1 = 0$ in this field. (*ans.*)

16.17 Let $\mathbf{F}_{16}$ be modeled as $\mathbf{F}_2[x]$ modulo 10111, the latter indicating coefficients in order of decreasing degree. Find two roots of the equation $y^2 + y + 1 = 0$ in this field.

17

RS and BCH Codes

So far in our story we have *not* been very succesful in making error-correcting codes. Yet Shannon's Noisy Coding Theorem assures us of the *existence* of codes which correct as close to 100% of errors as we want (with chosen *rate*, also). It is simply hard to *find* these codes.

We know that a *linear* code can correct e errors if and only if any $2e$ columns of its check matrix are linearly independent. This transformation of the question is much more helpful than the more primitive (though entirely correct) idea that to correct e errors the **minimum distance** must be $2e + 1$. (Equivalently, for linear codes, the minimum weight of non-zero vectors in the code must be $2e + 1$.) The linear algebra condition about linear independence is more accessible. For example we can use this criterion to easily construct the **Hamming** $[7, 4]$ **code** which can correct any single error. The next immediate question is how to achieve this linear independence property for correction of multiple errors.

The examples we give here are not merely linear, but *cyclic*. The simplest ones after the Hamming codes are **Reed-Solomon codes** or **RS codes**, and *do* achieve correction of arbitrarily large numbers of errors. Generalizing these somewhat are the **BCH codes**. They were created by Bose, Chaudhuri, and independently by Hocquengham, about 1959–60, and were considered big progress at the time. All of these can be viewed as a certain kind of generalization of Hamming codes. In the end, these codes are *not* so good, but, still, they are the simplest examples of multiple-error-correcting codes. (Actually, we'll only consider *primitive, narrow-sense* BCH codes.)

To construct these codes we need *larger and larger* finite fields, at least for auxiliary purposes. Our little friend $\mathbf{F}_2 = \{0, 1\}$ is unfortunately not adequate. One approach is simply to use $\mathbf{Z}$-mod-$p = \mathbf{Z}/p$ for large prime numbers p. From a theoretical viewpoint this is fine, but from some practical viewpoints we would much prefer to be able to rearrange everything as a *binary* code in the end. This will require us to use finite fields $\mathbf{F}_{2^n} = GF(2^n)$ with 2^n elements.

Remark: It is very important to realize that we *cannot* realize finite fields $\mathbf{F}_{2^n}$ by using simply **Z**-mod-something:

$$\mathbf{Z}/2^n \neq \mathbf{F}_{2^n} \quad (\text{unless } n = 1)$$

Instead, we need an **irreducible polynomial** $P(x)$ of degree n with coefficients in $\mathbf{F}_2$, and then

$$\mathbf{F}_{2^n} = \mathbf{F}_2[x]/P = \mathbf{F}_2[x] \text{ modulo } P(x)$$

- It is important to realize that the issue is not so much the *number* of errors corrected, but rather the *ratio*

$$\textbf{relative error correction } = \frac{\text{number of errors correctible}}{\text{block length}}$$

  and maintaining a high *rate*. After all, correcting 2 errors but needing a block size of 1000000 is not very good, since it is quite likely that more than 2 errors will occur in a block that size! Thus, a code can be a failure even if its rate is high, and even if it corrects many errors, if its block length is just too long by comparison.

  Despite having been used for decades in engineering applications, from an abstract viewpoint the Hamming, RS, and BCH codes are very limited successes. Specifically, as we try to use these ideas to correct more and more errors, the block size goes up too fast, and the *relative* error correction goes to 0.

17.1 Vandermonde determinants

So: a linear code can correct e errors if and only if any $2e$ columns of its check matrix are linearly independent. How to achieve this effect? From basic linear algebra we may know that ℓ vectors of length ℓ are linearly independent if and only if the determinant of the matrix made by sticking them together is *not* 0. But determinants are not easy or cheap to evaluate in general. What is needed is some easy and systematic trick to know that a whole class of determinants is non-zero, to be exploited in making suitable **check matrices** for cyclic codes later. We will introduce the two standard types of Vandermonde matrix and note that under very simple hypotheses their determinants are **not 0**.

A move in the right direction to use this is to 'recall' that n vectors

$$(v_{11}, v_{12}, v_{13}, v_{14}, \ldots, v_{1n})$$
$$(v_{21}, v_{22}, v_{23}, v_{24}, \ldots, v_{2n})$$
$$(v_{31}, v_{32}, v_{33}, v_{34}, \ldots, v_{3n})$$
$$\ldots$$
$$(v_{n1}, v_{n2}, v_{n3}, v_{n4}, \ldots, v_{nn})$$

are linearly independent if and only if the **determinant** of the n-by-n matrix made by sticking the vectors in (either as rows or columns) is *non-zero*:

$$\det \begin{pmatrix} v_{11} & v_{12} & v_{13} & v_{14} & \cdots & v_{1n} \\ v_{21} & v_{22} & v_{23} & v_{24} & \cdots & v_{2n} \\ v_{31} & v_{32} & v_{33} & v_{34} & \cdots & v_{3n} \\ & & \cdots & & & \\ v_{n1} & v_{n2} & v_{n3} & v_{n4} & \cdots & v_{nn} \end{pmatrix} \neq 0$$

But whether you remember how to evaluate such a determinant or not, it is a fact that it is a pain to evaluate big determinants, and you should try to avoid evaluating big determinants.

And, in the present case, we don't really need its value, but only the assurance that it's not 0. Since the entries of our matrices will be elements of a finite field, we effectively know the entries with infinite precision, so round-off errors are not the issue here.

Not surprisingly, over the centuries various *special* matrices arose in practice which luckily could be evaluated easily. One such type is a **Vandermonde matrix**. One version of Vandermonde matrix is any matrix of the form

$$M = \begin{pmatrix} 1 & 1 & 1 & 1 & \cdots & 1 \\ x_1 & x_2 & x_3 & x_4 & \cdots & x_n \\ x_1^2 & x_2^2 & x_3^2 & x_4^2 & \cdots & x_n^2 \\ x_1^3 & x_2^3 & x_3^3 & x_4^3 & \cdots & x_n^3 \\ x_1^4 & x_2^4 & x_3^4 & x_4^4 & \cdots & x_n^4 \\ & & & \cdots & & \\ x_1^{n-1} & x_2^{n-1} & x_3^{n-1} & x_4^{n-1} & \cdots & x_n^{n-1} \end{pmatrix}$$

where the $x_1, x_2, \ldots, x_n$ are 'numbers' or 'indeterminates', or nearly anything. That is, the ith column is formed by taking successively increasing powers of the ith entity x_i. The determinant of a Vandermonde matrix is called a **Vandermonde determinant**.

The amazing fact is that there is a simple general formula for the determinant of such a matrix:

$$\det M = (-1)^{n(n-1)/2} \prod_{i<j} (x_i - x_j)$$

More to the point, for example if the x_i's lie in a **field**, then

- If for all $i < j$ we have $x_i \neq x_j$ then the corresponding Vandermonde determinant is not 0.

Remark: Keep in mind that in greatest generality the product of a bunch of non-zero things can nevertheless be 0. But this counter-intuitive phenomenon certainly does not occur in *fields*, for example. More generally, recall that a commutative ring in which $ab = 0$ only when either a or b is 0 is an *integral domain*. Every field is an integral domain. The ordinary integers $\mathbf{Z}$ are an example of an integral domain which is not a field.

For example, for α in a field k, assuming that all the quantities 1, α, α^2, α^3, ..., α^ℓ are different from each other, by taking $x_i = \alpha^{i-1}$, we get a non-zero determinant

$$\det \begin{pmatrix} 1 & 1 & 1 & 1 & \ldots & 1 \\ 1 & \alpha & \alpha^2 & \alpha^3 & \ldots & \alpha^{n-1} \\ 1 & \alpha^2 & (\alpha^2)^2 & (\alpha^3)^2 & \ldots & (\alpha^{n-1})^2 \\ 1 & \alpha^3 & (\alpha^2)^3 & (\alpha^3)^3 & \ldots & (\alpha^{n-1})^3 \\ 1 & \alpha^4 & (\alpha^2)^4 & (\alpha^3)^4 & \ldots & (\alpha^{n-1})^4 \\ & & & \ldots & & \\ 1 & \alpha^{n-1} & (\alpha^2)^{n-1} & (\alpha^3)^{n-1} & \ldots & (\alpha^{n-1})^{n-1} \end{pmatrix} \neq 0$$

More generally, there is no reason that the different powers of α have to be consecutive: the only requirement is that they're not equal to each other. That is, for a non-zero element α of a field and for integers $\ell_1, \ldots, \ell_n$ so that

$$\alpha^{\ell_1}, \ \alpha^{\ell_2}, \ \alpha^{\ell_3}, \ \ldots, \ \alpha^{\ell_n}$$

are distinct, we have a non-zero determinant

$$\det \begin{pmatrix} 1 & 1 & 1 & 1 & \ldots & 1 \\ 1 & \alpha^{\ell_1} & \alpha^{\ell_2} & \alpha^{\ell_3} & \ldots & \alpha^{\ell_{n-1}} \\ 1 & (\alpha^{\ell_1})^2 & (\alpha^{\ell_2})^2 & (\alpha^{\ell_3})^2 & \ldots & (\alpha^{\ell_{n-1}})^2 \\ 1 & (\alpha^{\ell_1})^3 & (\alpha^{\ell_2})^3 & (\alpha^{\ell_3})^3 & \ldots & (\alpha^{\ell_{n-1}})^3 \\ 1 & (\alpha^{\ell_1})^4 & (\alpha^{\ell_2})^4 & (\alpha^{\ell_e})^4 & \ldots & (\alpha^{\ell_{n-1}})^4 \\ & & & \ldots & & \\ 1 & (\alpha^{\ell_1})^{n-1} & (\alpha^{\ell_2})^{n-1} & (\alpha^{\ell_3})n-1 & \ldots & (\alpha^{\ell_{n-1}})^{n-1} \end{pmatrix} \neq 0$$

- A fundamental property of determinants is that if a row or column of a matrix is multiplied by β, then the whole determinant is multiplied by β.

This property allows us to certify that a still larger class of determinants is non-zero. From the fact that

$$M = \begin{pmatrix} 1 & 1 & 1 & 1 & \ldots & 1 \\ x_1 & x_2 & x_3 & x_4 & \ldots & x_n \\ x_1^2 & x_2^2 & x_3^2 & x_4^2 & \ldots & x_n^2 \\ x_1^3 & x_2^3 & x_3^3 & x_4^3 & \ldots & x_n^3 \\ x_1^4 & x_2^4 & x_3^4 & x_4^4 & \ldots & x_n^4 \\ & & & \ldots & & \\ x_1^{n-1} & x_2^{n-1} & x_3^{n-1} & x_4^{n-1} & \ldots & x_n^{n-1} \end{pmatrix} \neq 0$$

for distinct $x_1, \ldots, x_n$ we can multiply through the ith column by x_i to obtain

$$M = \begin{pmatrix} x_1 & x_2 & x_3 & x_4 & \ldots & x_n \\ x_1^2 & x_2^2 & x_3^2 & x_4^2 & \ldots & x_n^2 \\ x_1^3 & x_2^3 & x_3^3 & x_4^3 & \ldots & x_n^3 \\ x_1^4 & x_2^4 & x_3^4 & x_4^4 & \ldots & x_n^4 \\ x_1^5 & x_2^5 & x_3^5 & x_4^5 & \ldots & x_n^5 \\ & & & \ldots & & \\ x_1^n & x_2^n & x_3^n & x_4^n & \ldots & x_n^n \end{pmatrix} \neq 0$$

for the $x_1, \ldots, x_n$ all different from each other, and non-zero. This type of matrix is also called a **Vandermonde matrix**.

17.2 Variant check matrices for cyclic codes

We already saw that for cyclic codes of block length n we can easily write down one kind of check matrix. This works over arbitrary finite fields $\mathbf{F}_q$ with q elements, as follows.

Every cyclic code of block length n can be given by a generator polynomial $g(x)$ for some polynomial $g(x)$ dividing $x^n - 1$. The collection of all codewords specified by $g(x)$ is the collection of all polynomials of degree $< n$ which are polynomial multiples of $g(x)$. This gives an $[n, k]$ code with

$$k = n - \deg g$$

Let

$$g(x) = c_o + c_1 x + \ldots + c_s x^s$$

Then the code has generator matrix

$$G = \begin{pmatrix} c_o & c_1 & \ldots & c_s & 0 & 0 & \ldots & 0 \\ 0 & c_o & \ldots & c_{s-1} & c_s & 0 & \ldots & 0 \\ 0 & 0 & \ldots & c_{s-2} & c_{s-1} & c_s & \ldots & 0 \\ & & & \ldots & & & & \end{pmatrix}$$

Let

$$h(x) = \frac{x^n - 1}{g(x)} = b_o + b_1 x + \ldots + b_t x^t$$

(with $s + t = n$). We can easily make *one* kind of check matrix, as we saw earlier works for any *cyclic* code, by

$$H = \begin{pmatrix} b_t & b_{t-1} & b_{t-2} & b_{t-3} & \ldots & b_1 & b_o & 0 & \ldots & 0 \\ 0 & b_t & b_{t-1} & b_{t-2} & \ldots & b_2 & b_1 & b_o & \ldots & 0 \\ 0 & 0 & b_t & b_{t-1} & \ldots & b_3 & b_2 & b_1 & \ldots & 0 \\ & & & \ldots & & & & & & \end{pmatrix}$$

Now we'll make a different kind of check matrix for such a cyclic code, which illustrates better the error-correction possibilities via the linear independence of columns condition. Suppose that the above discussion took place with all coefficients b_i and c_j in a finite field $\mathbf{F}_q$. Let $\mathbf{F}_{q^m}$ be a larger finite field containing the finite field $\mathbf{F}_q$ and large enough so that the polynomial $g(x)$ factors into linear factors when we allow coefficients in $\mathbf{F}_{q^m}$. To be sure that this happens, we need the following proposition.

Proposition: Given a non-constant polynomial $g(x)$ with coefficients in $\mathbf{F}_q$, there is a larger finite field $\mathbf{F}_{q^m}$ in which $g(x)$ factors into linear factors.

Proof: Let $f(x)$ be an irreducible factor of $g(x)$, of degree $d > 1$. Then from our discussion of finite fields and polynomial rings the quotient rign $\mathbf{F}_q[x]/f(x)$ is a field, with q^d elements. (In fact, $f(x)$ factors into linear polynomials in this field, but seeing this requires more effort than we can exert at the moment, so we must continue as though we did not know this.) Let α be the image of x in this quotient. Then as seen earlier $f(\alpha) = 0$. Thus, by unique factorization of polynomials, $x - \alpha$ is a factor of $f(x)$, hence of $g(x)$. Thus, we can divide, obtaining a polynomial of lower degree

$$h(x) = g(x)/(x - \alpha)$$

What we have shown so far is that if a polynomial does not already factor into linear factors then we can enlarge the finite field so as to find a further linear factor. We repeat this process (by induction on degree) to enlarge the field sufficiently to factor $g(x)$ into linear factors entirely.   ///

Factor $g(x)$ into irreducible polynomials

$$g(x) = f_1(x)f_2(x)\ldots f_\ell(x)$$

where each f_i has coefficients in $\mathbf{F}_q$. For the subsequent discussion **we need to assume that no factor f_i occurs more than once.** An easy way to be sure that this is so is to **require that** $\gcd(n, q) = 1$, for example.

Let β_i be a root of the ith irreducible factor f_i in $\mathbf{F}_{q^m}$. We claim that

$$H = \begin{pmatrix} 1 & \beta_1 & \beta_1^2 & \beta_1^3 & \cdots & \beta_1^{n-1} \\ 1 & \beta_2 & \beta_2^2 & \beta_2^3 & \cdots & \beta_2^{n-1} \\ 1 & \beta_3 & \beta_3^2 & \beta_3^3 & \cdots & \beta_3^{n-1} \\ & & \cdots & & & \\ 1 & \beta_\ell & \beta_\ell^2 & \beta_\ell^3 & \cdots & \beta_\ell^{n-1} \end{pmatrix}$$

is a check matrix for G.

Proof: The ith row of the cyclic generator matrix G, interpreted as the coefficients of polynomials ordered by ascending degree, is $x^{i-1}g(x)$. Thus, $G \cdot H^\top = 0$ if and only if

$$\beta_j^{i-1} g(\beta_j) = 0$$

for all indices j and i. Since none of the β_js is 0, this is equivalent to the set of equations

$$g(\beta_j) = 0$$

for all indices j. Since the β_js are roots of this equation, certainly $G \cdot H^\top = 0$.

Now we prove that $v \cdot H^\top = 0$ implies that v is in the code. Since β_j is a root of $f_j(x) = 0$ with $f_j(x)$ irreducible, as in our earlier discussion of field extensions we can take

$$\beta_j = x \bmod f_j(x)$$

Again interpreting v as a polynomial, the condition $v \cdot H^\top = 0$ is equivalent to

$$v(\beta_j) = 0$$

(for all j) which by the previous remark is equivalent to

$$v(x) = 0 \bmod f_j(x)$$

for all j. Thus $f_j(x)$ divides $v(x)$ for all indices j. Since the $f)j(x)$s have no common factor, their least common multiple is simply their product, and we conclude that $g(x)$ divides $v(x)$. That is, $v(x)$ is a linear combination of $x^i g(x)$s. That is, v is in the rowspace of G, so by definition is in the code.   ///

17.3 Reed-Solomon codes

We can use the linear algebra from the Vandermonde determinant story to make progress in constructing linear codes to correct several errors. The first examples are **Reed-Solomon codes**. These are **cyclic (linear) codes**.

Let $\mathbf{F}_q$ be a finite field. For example, if q is simply a prime number (rather than a *power* of a prime number), then we can take

$$\mathbf{F}_q = \mathbf{Z}/q = \mathbf{Z}\text{-mod-}q$$

We will make codes over $\mathbf{F}_q$ of block length $n = q - 1$.

Let β be a **primitive root** (equivalently, **primitive element**) in $\mathbf{F}_q$. As usual, this means that $\beta^{q-1} = 1$ but no smaller positive power of β is 1. And

$$1, \beta, \beta^2, \beta^3, \beta^4, \ldots, \beta^{q-3}, \beta^{q-2}$$

are all distinct. Further, since every non-zero element of $\mathbf{F}_q$ is a power of β,

$$x^{q-1} - 1 = (x - 1)(x - \beta)(x - \beta^2)(x - \beta^3)\ldots(x - \beta^{q-3})(x - \beta^{q-2})$$

For chosen t in the range $2 \le t \le q - 1$, define a degree $t - 1$ polynomial by

$$g(x) = (x - \beta)(x - \beta^2)(x - \beta^3)\ldots(x - \beta^{t-2})(x - \beta^{t-1})$$

The cyclic code specified by this will be a $[n, n - t + 1]$-code using the alphabet $\mathbf{F}_q$ rather than just $\{0, 1\}$. This is a **Reed-Solomon code** over $\mathbf{F}_q$. The t is called the **designed distance**.

- The Reed-Solomon code C over $\mathbf{F}_q$ with generating polynomial

$$g(x) = (x - \beta)(x - \beta^2)(x - \beta^3)\ldots(x - \beta^{t-2})(x - \beta^{t-1})$$

(where β is a primitive root in $\mathbf{F}_q$) has minimum distance at least t.

Remark: Thus, calling t the *designed distance* is reasonable at least in the sense that we are sure that the minimum distance is at least t.

Corollary: With $t = 2e + 1$, the minimum distance $2e + 1$ assures that the Reed-Solomon $[q - 1, q - 1 - 2e]$ code with alphabet $\mathbf{F}_q$ can correct any e errors.   ///

Proof: We will make a variant-type check matrix for C in which any t columns are linearly independent. This linear independence will be proven by observing that the t-by-t matrix consisting of any t columns is a Vandermonde determinant.

Let

$$H = \begin{pmatrix} 1 & \beta & \beta^2 & \beta^3 & \cdots & \beta^n \\ 1 & \beta^2 & (\beta^2)^2 & (\beta^3)^2 & \cdots & (\beta^n)^2 \\ 1 & \beta^3 & (\beta^2)^3 & (\beta^3)^3 & \cdots & (\beta^n)^3 \\ 1 & \beta^4 & (\beta^2)^4 & (\beta^3)^4 & \cdots & (\beta^n)^4 \\ & & \cdots & & & \\ 1 & \beta^{t-1} & (\beta^2)^{t-1} & (\beta^3)^{t-1} & \cdots & (\beta^n)^{t-1} \end{pmatrix}$$

The jth column consists of powers of β^{j-1}. Since β is a primitive root, the entries of the top row are distinct. Thus, any $t-1$ columns together form a Vandermonde matrix with non-zero determinant! This proves linear independence, and by earlier discussions proves the minimum distance assertion.   ///

Example: Let's make a code that will correct 2 errors. For this, we'll need *designed distance* $t = 5$. Since we need $t \le q - 1$, we need $5 \le q - 1$. For simplicity we'll have q be a prime number, so to satisfy $5 \le q - 1$ take $q = 7$. Let β be a primitive root mod 7, for example $\beta = 3$. Then take a generating polynomial

$$g(x) = (x - 3)(x - 3^2)(x - 3^3)(x - 3^4)$$

$$= (x - 3)(x - 2)(x - 6)(x - 4) = x^4 + 6x^3 + 3x^2 + 2x + 4$$

Thus, this will make a $[6, 2]$-code, since $\deg g = t - 1 = 4$ and $2 = 6 - 4$. A generating matrix is

$$G = \begin{pmatrix} 4 & 2 & 3 & 6 & 4 & 0 \\ 0 & 4 & 2 & 3 & 6 & 4 \end{pmatrix}$$

To obtain a check matrix in the usual form for cyclic codes, take

$$h(x) = \frac{x^6 - 1}{g(x)} = (x - 1)(x - 5) = x^2 + x + 5$$

Then the check matrix is (note, as usual, the reversal of order of coefficients)

$$H = \begin{pmatrix} 1 & 1 & 5 & 0 & 0 & 0 \\ 0 & 1 & 1 & 5 & 0 & 0 \\ 0 & 0 & 1 & 1 & 5 & 0 \\ 0 & 0 & 0 & 1 & 1 & 5 \end{pmatrix}$$

Evidently any 4 columns are linearly independent. To verify this directly we'd have to check $\binom{6}{4} = 15$ different possibilities, which would be too tedious. But our variant check matrix proves this for us *indirectly!* This gives us a $[6, 2]$-code with alphabet $\mathbf{Z}/7$ which can correct any 2 errors. The rate is $2/6$.

Example: Let's make a Reed-Solomon code that can correct any 3 errors, with alphabet $\mathbf{F}_q$. For this, we need *designed distance* $t = 2 \cdot 3 + 1 = 7$. Since we must have $t \le q - 1$, we take $q = 11$, so $\mathbf{F}_q = \mathbf{Z}/11$. This will make a code of block length $q - 1 = 11 - 1 = 10$ with alphabet $\mathbf{Z}/11$. Let β be a *primitive root* mod 11. For example, take $\beta = 2$. Then use generating polynomial of degree $t - 1 = 6$ given by

$$g(x) = (x-2)(x-2^2)(x-2^3)(x-2^4)(x-2^5)(x-2^6) = x^6+9x^5+9x^4+7x^3+x^2+4x+8$$

The other polynomial is

$$h(x) = (x - 2^7)(x - 2^8)(x - 2^9)(x - 1) = x^4 + 5x^3 + 9x^2 + 2x + 5$$

Together,

$$g(x)h(x) = x^{10} - 1$$

A generating matrix is

$$G = \begin{pmatrix} 8 & 4 & 1 & 7 & 9 & 9 & 1 & 0 & 0 & 0 \\ 0 & 8 & 4 & 1 & 7 & 9 & 9 & 1 & 0 & 0 \\ 0 & 0 & 8 & 4 & 1 & 7 & 9 & 9 & 1 & 0 \\ 0 & 0 & 0 & 8 & 4 & 1 & 7 & 9 & 9 & 1 \end{pmatrix}$$

A check matrix is (note, as usual, the reversal of order of coefficients)

$$H = \begin{pmatrix} 1 & 5 & 9 & 2 & 5 & 0 & 0 & 0 & 0 & 0 \\ 0 & 1 & 5 & 9 & 2 & 5 & 0 & 0 & 0 & 0 \\ 0 & 0 & 1 & 5 & 9 & 2 & 5 & 0 & 0 & 0 \\ 0 & 0 & 0 & 1 & 5 & 9 & 2 & 5 & 0 & 0 \\ 0 & 0 & 0 & 0 & 1 & 5 & 9 & 2 & 5 & 0 \\ 0 & 0 & 0 & 0 & 0 & 1 & 5 & 9 & 2 & 5 \end{pmatrix}$$

It's not obvious, but evidently any 6 columns of H are linearly independent. Thus, this [10, 4]-code over alphabet $\mathbf{Z}/11$ can correct any 3 errors. It has rate 4/10.

Remark: The **rate** of the Reed-Solomon code with parameters q, $n = q - 1$, and designed distance $t \leq q - 1$ is computable in the standard manner by which the rate of any cyclic code is determined:

$$\text{rate} = \frac{n - \deg g}{n} = \frac{q - t}{q - 1} = 1 - \frac{t - 1}{q - 1}$$

Taking $t = 2e + 1$ to correct e errors, this is

$$\text{rate} = 1 - \frac{2e}{q - 1}$$

At the same time, the **relative error correction** is

$$\text{relative error correction} = \frac{2e}{\text{block length}} = \frac{2e}{q - 1}$$

Thus, we can either correct lots of errors per block length, or maintain a high rate, but not both.

Remark: The Reed-Solomon codes are **maximum-distance separating** codes, meaning that they meet the **Singleton bound**.

Remark: And, although now we finally have examples where arbitrary numbers of errors can be corrected, these are not *binary* codes. For practical applications we might be compelled to have a *binary* code, which is one of the possibilities of the **BCH codes** treated below.

17.4 Hamming codes

Let's see how we can make **binary** codes which correct single errors, from the viewpoint of the new sort of check matrix above. These are **binary Hamming codes**. The discussion can easily be extended to non-binary codes, but our point here is to avoid endlessly changing alphabets (as the Reed-Solomon codes require) and manage instead to obtain *binary* codes.

Fix the block length $n = 2^k - 1$. Let g be a *primitive* polynomial of degree k. Let β be a root of $g(x) = 0$, so β is a primitive element in $\mathbf{F}_{2^k}$. Let C be the cyclic code generated by $g(x)$. From our discussion of cyclic codes, this is an $[n, n-k]$-code. Specifically, it is a $[2^k - 1, 2^k - 1 - k]$-code.

Motivated by the idea of the variant check matrices above, we could take an extreme simple form of check matrix

$$H = \begin{pmatrix} 1 & \beta & \beta^2 & \cdots & \beta^{n-1} \end{pmatrix}$$

Since any two columns of this check matrix are linearly independent, simply by not being multiples of each other, the minimum distance of the code arising from this is at least 3 (and it can correct any single error: $(3-1)/2 = 1$).

Proof: We want to prove directly in this example that the minimum distance is at least 3. Since the code is linear, this is equivalent to the assertion that the minimum *weight* is at least 3. Suppose not. Then there is at least one vector v in the code with weight 2, that is, with only two non-zero entries say at the ith and j^{th} places (indexing from 0 to $n-1$). Then

$$0 = v \cdot H^t = \beta^i + \beta^j$$

Without loss of generality, $i < j$. Then

$$\beta^{j-i} + 1 = 0$$

That is, seemingly β satisfies an equation of degree $j - i$ with coefficients in $\mathbf{F}_2$. But by hypothesis $g(x) = 0$ is the lowest-degree equation satisfied by β, and g has degree $n > j \geq j - i$, so this is impossible. Thus, the minimum distance is at least 3.   ///

Example: For example, with $k = 3$, $n = 2^3 - 1 = 7$, we can easily find a *primitive* cubic polynomial: $g(x) = x^3 + x + 1$ will do. (The other primitive cubic is $x^3 + x^2 + 1$.)

The cyclic code generated by this should give a binary $[7,4]$-code correcting any single error. A generating matrix is made from the coefficients 1101 (in ascending order) of $g(x)$:

$$G = \begin{pmatrix} 1 & 1 & 0 & 1 & 0 & 0 & 0 \\ 0 & 1 & 1 & 0 & 1 & 0 & 0 \\ 0 & 0 & 1 & 1 & 0 & 1 & 0 \\ 0 & 0 & 0 & 1 & 1 & 0 & 1 \end{pmatrix}$$

This is *not* in the 'standard form', but since the code is cyclic, we have an easy way to make the check matrix. We will not make the 'variant' check matrix as just above, but rather the general type applicable to *any* cyclic code. Take

$$h(x) = \frac{x^7 - 1}{g(x)} = \frac{x^7 - 1}{x^3 + x + 1} = x^4 + x^2 + x + 1 = (x+1)(x^3 + x^2 + 1)$$

Then a check matrix is given by (note the reversal of the coefficient order)

$$H = \begin{pmatrix} 1 & 0 & 1 & 1 & 1 & 0 & 0 \\ 0 & 1 & 0 & 1 & 1 & 1 & 0 \\ 0 & 0 & 1 & 0 & 1 & 1 & 1 \end{pmatrix}$$

From examination of the variant-type check matrix we know that the code has minimum distance at least 3, so we know *without directly checking* that any two columns of this H are linearly independent. This can also be verified directly, but it would be silly to do so.

The **rate** of this code is dimension/length $= 4/7$.

Example: With $k = 4$, $n = 2^4 - 1 = 15$, we need a primitive quartic. We can use $g(x) = x^4 + x + 1$ (or $x^4 + x^3 + 1$) as the generating polynomial. This will make a binary cyclic $[15, 11]$-code, since $15 = 2^4 - 1$ and $11 = 2^4 - 1 - 4$. Using the coefficient of $g(x)$ in ascending order, a generating matrix is

$$G = \begin{pmatrix} 1 & 1 & 0 & 0 & 1 & 0 & 0 & 0 & 0 & 0 & 0 & 0 & 0 & 0 & 0 \\ 0 & 1 & 1 & 0 & 0 & 1 & 0 & 0 & 0 & 0 & 0 & 0 & 0 & 0 & 0 \\ 0 & 0 & 1 & 1 & 0 & 0 & 1 & 0 & 0 & 0 & 0 & 0 & 0 & 0 & 0 \\ 0 & 0 & 0 & 1 & 1 & 0 & 0 & 1 & 0 & 0 & 0 & 0 & 0 & 0 & 0 \\ 0 & 0 & 0 & 0 & 1 & 1 & 0 & 0 & 1 & 0 & 0 & 0 & 0 & 0 & 0 \\ 0 & 0 & 0 & 0 & 0 & 1 & 1 & 0 & 0 & 1 & 0 & 0 & 0 & 0 & 0 \\ 0 & 0 & 0 & 0 & 0 & 0 & 1 & 1 & 0 & 0 & 1 & 0 & 0 & 0 & 0 \\ 0 & 0 & 0 & 0 & 0 & 0 & 0 & 1 & 1 & 0 & 0 & 1 & 0 & 0 & 0 \\ 0 & 0 & 0 & 0 & 0 & 0 & 0 & 0 & 1 & 1 & 0 & 0 & 1 & 0 & 0 \\ 0 & 0 & 0 & 0 & 0 & 0 & 0 & 0 & 0 & 1 & 1 & 0 & 0 & 1 & 0 \\ 0 & 0 & 0 & 0 & 0 & 0 & 0 & 0 & 0 & 0 & 1 & 1 & 0 & 0 & 1 \end{pmatrix}$$

The rate of this code is 11/15. Note that as the size of these Hamming codes grows the rate approaches 1. But on the other hand the **relative error correction**

$$\frac{\text{number of errors correctible}}{\text{block size}}$$

goes to 0 as the block size grows. This is bad. Thus, the useful codes among the Hamming codes are the relatively small ones.

17.5   BCH codes

The Reed-Solomon codes require an alphabet consisting of larger and larger finite fields in order to correct more errors. If we want *binary* codes, or even just codes over a *fixed alphabet*, this is unacceptable. Among other accomplishments, the **BCH codes** overcome this objection. They continue to make use of Vandermonde determinants. These **Bose-Chaudhuri-Hocquengham** codes can correct multiple errors. BCH codes are **cyclic (linear) codes** generalizing the construction of Reed-Solomon codes. Unfortunately, they suffer from the same shortcoming as do the Hamming and Reed-Solomon codes: as the block size increases, they become worse and worse in the sense that the relative error correction rate goes to 0, as just above.

Start with a finite field $\mathbf{F}_q$ with q elements. Very often we will be thinking of the case $q = 2$, but the development of the idea does not depend upon this. Choose a block size n. For simplicity, we'll suppose that n and q are relatively prime. In the case $q = 2$, that means we will always look at *odd* block sizes.

In particular, trying to correct any two errors by having any 4 columns be linear independent, imagine that we could have a (variant-type) check matrix like

$$H = \begin{pmatrix} 1 & \alpha & \alpha^2 & \alpha^3 & \cdots & \alpha^{n-1} \\ 1 & \alpha^2 & (\alpha^2)^2 & (\alpha^3)^2 & \cdots & (\alpha^{n-1})^2 \\ 1 & \alpha^3 & (\alpha^2)^2 & (\alpha^3)^3 & \cdots & (\alpha^{n-1})^3 \\ 1 & \alpha^4 & (\alpha^2)^4 & (\alpha^3)^4 & \cdots & (\alpha^{n-1})^4 \end{pmatrix}$$

with α possibly lying in some larger field $\mathbf{F}_{q^m}$. We suppose that $1, \alpha, \alpha^2, \alpha^3,$ $\ldots, \alpha^{n-1}$ are all distinct and non-zero, and that $n - 1 \geq 4$, so $n \geq 5$. The discussion of Vandermonde determinants above implies that the determinant of any 4-by-4 matrix made from 4 different columns of this matrix is non-zero. Thus, the corresponding linear code will correct 2 errors, since the minimum distance is $4 + 1 = 5$ and a code with minimum distance d will correct any number of errors $< d/2$.

Further, we can just as well make check matrices with any 6 columns linear independent (so any 3 errors correctible), any 8 columns linearly independent (so any 4 errors correctible), and so on. This much was already done by Reed-Solomon codes, as long as the alphabet $\mathbf{F}_q$ was sufficiently large.

The new ingredient is that we want to allow the element α to be in a larger field $\mathbf{F}_{q^m}$ than just the field $\mathbf{F}_q$ which is used as the actual alphabet for the code. This would be in contrast to the Reed-Solomon codes where we never went outside the finite field $\mathbf{F}_q$ used as the code alphabet. Staying inside $\mathbf{F}_q$ was what required that Reed-Solomon codes use larger and larger $\mathbf{F}_q$ as the block size goes up. Instead, if we can make check matrices over *larger* fields but keep the code alphabet itself *fixed*, we can make multiple-error-correcting codes using small alphabets. Such possibilities were already hinted at in the discussion of variant check matrices, and illustrated in a rather trivial case in the reconstruction of Hamming codes above.

Certainly allowing α to be in a larger field than $\mathbf{F}_q$ is *necessary* to construct *binary* codes correcting many errors, since if the only choices for α are 0,1 it will be impossible to arrange that $1, \alpha, \alpha^2, \alpha^3, \ldots, \alpha^{n-1}$ are all different, unless we just take $n = 2$, which would not be enough.

Let α lie in the finite field $\mathbf{F}_{q^m}$ with q^m elements. Take α to be a **primitive element** in $\mathbf{F}_{q^m}$, so $\alpha^{q^m-1} = 1$ but no smaller exponent will do, and all smaller positive powers of α are distinct. For simplicity, take

$$\text{block length } = n = q^m - 1$$

Then for any integer t with $t < n = q^m - 1$ the matrix

$$H = \begin{pmatrix} 1 & \alpha & \alpha^2 & \alpha^3 & \cdots & \alpha^{n-1} \\ 1 & \alpha^2 & (\alpha^2)^2 & (\alpha^3)^2 & \cdots & (\alpha^{n-1})^2 \\ 1 & \alpha^3 & (\alpha^2)^3 & (\alpha^3)^3 & \cdots & (\alpha^{n-1})^3 \\ & & & \cdots & & \\ 1 & \alpha^{t-2} & (\alpha^2)^{t-2} & (\alpha^3)^{t-2} & \cdots & (\alpha^{n-1})^{t-2} \\ 1 & \alpha^{t-1} & (\alpha^2)^{t-1} & (\alpha^3)^{t-1} & \cdots & (\alpha^{n-1})^{t-1} \end{pmatrix}$$

has the property that the $(t-1)$-by-$(t-1)$ matrix formed from any $t-1$ columns has non-zero determinant. This follows from properties of Vandermonde matrices.

• In this notation, the quantity t is the **designed distance**, because if we make a code with this check matrix then it will have minimum distance *at least t*. This generalizes the use of the terminology in the Reed-Solomon case.

We would need to connect such a variant check matrix with generating polynomials for a cyclic code. For $1 \le i \le t-1$, let f_i be the irreducible polynomial with coefficients in $\mathbf{F}_q$ so that

$$f_i(\alpha^i) = 0$$

Since α lies in $\mathbf{F}_{q^m}$ (and is primitive besides), by Lagrange's theorem (or even more elementary reasoning) each irreducible $f_i(x)$ must be a factor of $x^{q^m-1} - 1$. Then let

$$g(x) = \text{ least common multiple of } (f_1, \ldots, f_{t-1})$$

This will be a polynomial (with coefficients in $\mathbf{F}_q$) dividing $x^n - 1$.

• Since by assumption $n = q^m - 1$ and q are relatively prime, $x^{q^m-1} - 1$ has no repeated factors, so unless two or more of the f_i are simply *the same*, their least common multiple is their *product*. The lack of repeated factors follows from the fact that any repeated factor of a polynomial $f(x)$ must also be a factor of the derivative $f'(x)$ of $f(x)$, as observed earlier: if $f = P^2 Q$ with polynomials P, Q, then

$$f' = 2PP'Q + P^2Q' = P \cdot (2P'Q + PQ)$$

Using the Euclidean algorithm, we can compute without great difficulty that the gcd of $x^n - 1$ and nx^{n-1} is 1 when $n \ne 0$ in the field $\mathbf{F}_q$.

So the generating polynomial $g(x)$ for the code C with the check matrix H above is the product of the different irreducible polynomials f_i which have roots

α^i $(1 \le i < t)$, **not** repeating a given polynomial f_i if two different α^i and α^j are roots of the same f_i. Then the question is: given q, m, block length $n = q^m - 1$, primitive element α, and designed distance t,

* How can we nicely determine $g(x)$ as a function of t?

The answer to this question cannot be described well by a simple formula, but *can* be answered systematically.

* For a in the finite field $\mathbf{F}_{q^m}$, the **Frobenius map** $\mathbf{F}_{q^m} \to \mathbf{F}_{q^m}$ is defined to be

$$a \to a^q$$

(There is no completely standard symbol for this map!)

Theorem: For a, b in the finite field $\mathbf{F}_{q^m}$, the **Frobenius map** $a \to a^q$ has the properties

* $(xy)^q = x^q \, y^q$
* $(x + y)^q = x^q + y^q$
* For a polynomial f with coefficients in $\mathbf{F}_q$, suppose the equation $f(x) = 0$ has root $a \in \mathbf{F}_{q^m}$. Then also $f(a^q) = 0$.

(Let's not worry about the proof of all this right now. It's not very hard in any case.)

In particular, this means that not only is $\alpha = \alpha^1$ a root of f_1, but also α^q, α^{q^2}, etc. are all roots of f_1. Of course this is not really an infinite list, because $\alpha^{q^m} = \alpha$ so the list cycles on itself. And α^2, $(\alpha^2)^q$, $(\alpha^2)^{q^2}$, etc. are roots of f_2. Further, α^3, $(\alpha^3)^q$, $(\alpha^3)^{q^2}$, etc. are roots of f_3. And so on.

The key question is: among $\alpha, \alpha^2, \ldots, \alpha^{t-1}$, how many *different* polynomials f_i do we need? The more we need, the *larger* the degree of g, and thus the *smaller* the quantity

$$n - \deg g$$

which occurs in the expression for the *rate* of the code

$$\text{rate} \;=\; 1 - \frac{\deg g}{n}$$

In the worst-case scenario, even with designed distance t much less than the block length n, it can be that by accident $g(x)$ must be

$$g(x) = \frac{x^n - 1}{x - 1} = \frac{x^{q^m - 1} - 1}{x - 1}$$

which would leave us a code with rate $\frac{1}{n}$. This would be bad.

Another key point is that

* The degree of each irreducible factor f_i of $x^n - 1 = x^{q^m - 1} - 1$ is $\le m$.

So, conceivably, with designed distance t

$$t \approx 1 + \frac{q^m - 1}{m}$$

if no two of the $\alpha, \alpha^2, \ldots, \alpha^{t-1}$ are roots of the same irreducible factor f_i, then the degree of the generating polynomial g for the code is

$$\deg g = (t-1) \cdot m \approx q^m - 1 = \deg x^n - 1 \ (= \deg x^{q^m-1} - 1)$$

so the code is low-dimensional and has a very low rate.

Let's illustrate this by a simple example. We'll be interested in **binary** codes, that is, with code alphabet $\mathbf{F}_2$.

Suppose we want block size $n = 2^3 - 1 = 7$. (So $m = 3$ in the notation above). What designed distance t will give something worthwhile by this constuction? Certainly we must have $t < n = 7$. Let's make a binary code that corrects any 2 errors, so we have to take designed distance $t = 5$. To specify a primitive element α in $\mathbf{F}_{2^3}$ we describe $\mathbf{F}_{2^3}$ as

$$\mathbf{F}_{2^3} = \mathbf{F}_2[x]/P$$

for some primitive cubic polynomial P (coefficients in $\mathbf{F}_2$), and let

$$\alpha = x\text{-mod-}P(x)$$

For example, we can use the primitive polynomial

$$P(x) = x^3 + x + 1$$

Thus, our generalized check matrix is

$$H = \begin{pmatrix} 1 & \alpha & \alpha^2 & \cdots & \alpha^6 \\ 1 & \alpha^2 & (\alpha^2)^2 & \cdots & (\alpha^2)^6 \\ 1 & \alpha^3 & (\alpha^3)^2 & \cdots & (\alpha^3)^6 \\ 1 & \alpha^4 & (\alpha^4)^2 & \cdots & (\alpha^4)^6 \end{pmatrix}$$

Here the polynomial $x^n - 1 = x^7 - 1$ factors as

$$x^7 - 1 = (x - 1)(x^3 + x + 1)(x^3 + x^2 + 1)$$

(by trial-and-error!). By testing, all three irreducible factors are primitive. (We used one of them to define the field $\mathbf{F}_{2^3}$.) The α, α^2, and $\alpha^4 = (\alpha^2)^2$ are obtained by applying the Frobenius automorphism to α, so these must all be roots of $x^3 + x + 1 = 0$. The α^3 cannot be obtained in this manner, yet is not simply 1 (since α is primitive!), so by default must be a zero of the other factor $x^3 + x^2 + 1$ of $x^7 - 1$. (After all, since $\alpha^7 = 1$, surely $(\alpha^3)^7 = 1$ as well.) Thus, the generating polynomial for this code must be the product of these two cubics:

$$g(x) = (x^3 + x + 1)(x^3 + x^2 + 1) = x^6 + x^5 + x^4 + x^3 + x^2 + x + 1$$

A generating matrix must be

$$G = (1 \ \ 1 \ \ 1 \ \ 1 \ \ 1 \ \ 1 \ \ 1)$$

Too bad: this is disappointing. It has collapsed back to a majority-logic repetition code: send each bit 7 times, and evidently look at the 7 bits received and decode by taking the most common received bit. This is nothing new. (Also, the *rate* is low, only 1/7.)

Try again in another example: enlarge the block size to $n = 2^4 - 1 = 15$. (So $m = 4$.) What designed distance t will give something worthwhile by this construction? Certainly we must have $t < n = 15$. Let's try again to make a *binary* code that corrects any 2 errors, so we have to take designed distance $t = 5$. To specify a primitive element α in $\mathbf{F}_{2^4}$ we describe $\mathbf{F}_{2^4}$ as

$$\mathbf{F}_{2^4} = \mathbf{F}_2[x]/P$$

for some primitive quartic polynomial P (coefficients in $\mathbf{F}_2$), and let

$$\alpha = x\text{-mod-}P(x)$$

For example, we can use the primitive polynomial

$$P(x) = x^4 + x + 1$$

Thus, our generalized check matrix is H =

$$\begin{pmatrix} 1 & \alpha & \alpha^2 & \cdots & \alpha^{14} \\ 1 & \alpha^2 & (\alpha^2)^2 & \cdots & (\alpha^2)^{14} \\ 1 & \alpha^3 & (\alpha^3)^2 & \cdots & (\alpha^3)^{14} \\ 1 & \alpha^4 & (\alpha^4)^2 & \cdots & (\alpha^4)^{14} \end{pmatrix}$$

Here the polynomial $x^n - 1 = x^{15} - 1$ factors as

$$x^{15} - 1 = (x - 1)(x^2 + x + 1)(x^4 + x^3 + x^2 + x + 1)(x^4 + x + 1)(x^4 + x^3 + 1)$$

(by trial and error!). By testing, only the last two polynomials are primitive. (We used one of them to define the field $\mathbf{F}_{2^4}$.)

So we need to identify which among the factors

$$(x - 1), \ (x^2 + x + 1), \ (x^4 + x^3 + x^2 + x + 1), \ (x^4 + x + 1), \ (x^4 + x^3 + 1)$$

get used to make equations of which the $\alpha, \alpha^2, \alpha^3, \alpha^4$ are roots. Since here $q = 2$, the image α^2 of α under the Frobenius map is just the next power of α in the sequence, and also $\alpha^4 = (\alpha^2)^2$. That's good. But to have α^3 be a root we need another polynomial.

For the moment let's shirk the general problem of determining such polynomials, and try to be a little lucky: we know that $\alpha^{15} = 1$, so surely

$$(\alpha^3)^5 = 1$$

The polynomial $x^5 - 1$ factors a little (over any field, though we use $-1 = +1$ here):

$$x^5 - 1 = (x^4 + x^3 + x^2 + x + 1)(x + 1)$$

Since $\alpha^3 \neq 1$ (since α is primitive) it must be that

$$\alpha^4 + \alpha^3 + \alpha^2 + \alpha + 1 = 0$$

Thus, the generating polynomial is

$$g(x) = (x^4 + x + 1)(x^4 + x^3 + x^2 + x + 1) = x^8 + x^4 + x^2 + x + 1$$

Arranging this in descending order, and cycling suitably, this gives generating matrix

$$\begin{pmatrix}
1 & 1 & 1 & 0 & 1 & 0 & 0 & 0 & 1 & 0 & 0 & 0 & 0 & 0 & 0 \\
0 & 1 & 1 & 1 & 0 & 1 & 0 & 0 & 0 & 1 & 0 & 0 & 0 & 0 & 0 \\
0 & 0 & 1 & 1 & 1 & 0 & 1 & 0 & 0 & 0 & 1 & 0 & 0 & 0 & 0 \\
0 & 0 & 0 & 1 & 1 & 1 & 0 & 1 & 0 & 0 & 0 & 1 & 0 & 0 & 0 \\
0 & 0 & 0 & 0 & 1 & 1 & 1 & 0 & 1 & 0 & 0 & 0 & 1 & 0 & 0 \\
0 & 0 & 0 & 0 & 0 & 1 & 1 & 1 & 0 & 1 & 0 & 0 & 0 & 1 & 0 \\
0 & 0 & 0 & 0 & 0 & 0 & 1 & 1 & 1 & 0 & 1 & 0 & 0 & 0 & 1
\end{pmatrix}$$

This is a *binary* $[15, 7]$-code and has minimum distance at least 5, by construction, so can correct any 2 errors.

Remark: Notice that it was not so easy to predict from the specification that the resulting binary code would be $[15, 7]$. Indeed, since the generalized check matrix had only 4 rows and had block size 15, a person might have mistakenly thought that the code would have dimension $15 - 4 = 11$ rather than just 7. The difference is accounted for in a subtle way by the fact that we get a *binary* code, not a code with alphabet $\mathbf{F}_{16}$, but the check matrix uses $\mathbf{F}_{16}$.

One more example: let's make a code with **designed distance** $t = 7$, to make a binary code to correct any 3 errors. We can use the block size $n = 15 = 2^4 - 1$ again, and check matrix

$$H = \begin{pmatrix}
1 & \alpha & \alpha^2 & \cdots & \alpha^{14} \\
1 & \alpha^2 & (\alpha^2)^2 & \cdots & (\alpha^2)^{14} \\
1 & \alpha^3 & (\alpha^3)^2 & \cdots & (\alpha^3)^{14} \\
1 & \alpha^4 & (\alpha^4)^2 & \cdots & (\alpha^4)^{14} \\
1 & \alpha^5 & (\alpha^5)^2 & \cdots & (\alpha^5)^{14} \\
1 & \alpha^6 & (\alpha^6)^2 & \cdots & (\alpha^6)^{14}
\end{pmatrix}$$

The generating polynomial $g(x)$ will be the 'minimal' polynomial so that

$$g(\alpha) = 0, \; g(\alpha^2) = 0, \; g(\alpha^3) = 0, \; g(\alpha^4) = 0, \; g(\alpha^5) = 0, \; g(\alpha^6) = 0$$

By applying the Frobenius map and the little theorem above, we see that $\alpha, \alpha^2, \alpha^4$ will all be roots of a single irreducible factor of $x^{16} - 1$, namely $x^4 + x + 1 = 0$ since α was effectively defined as a root of this. Likewise, α^3 and $\alpha^6 = (\alpha^3)^2$ will both be roots of the irreducible polynomial $x^4 + x^3 + x^2 + x + 1$ which has α^3 as a root (determined by luck above). All that is left is α^5. We'll again try to be lucky rather than systematic. Since $\alpha^{15} = 1$, we have $(\alpha^5)^3 = 1$, or

$$((\alpha^5)^2 + (\alpha^5) + 1)(\alpha^5 + 1) = 0$$

Since $\alpha^5 \neq 1$, because α was primitive, necessarily

$$(\alpha^5)^2 + (\alpha^5) + 1 = 0$$

Thus,

$$g(x) = (x^4 + x + 1)(x^4 + x^3 + x^2 + x + 1)(x^2 + x + 1) = x^{10} + x^9 + x^8 + x^6 + x^5 + x^2 + 1$$

Thus, we managed to add 2 to the designed distance (by adding 2 rows) while only increasing the degree of g by 2.

This gives the generating matrix

$$G = \begin{pmatrix}
1 & 0 & 1 & 0 & 0 & 1 & 1 & 0 & 1 & 1 & 1 & 0 & 0 & 0 & 0 \\
0 & 1 & 0 & 1 & 0 & 0 & 1 & 1 & 0 & 1 & 1 & 1 & 0 & 0 & 0 \\
0 & 0 & 1 & 0 & 1 & 0 & 0 & 1 & 1 & 0 & 1 & 1 & 1 & 0 & 0 \\
0 & 0 & 0 & 1 & 0 & 1 & 0 & 0 & 1 & 1 & 0 & 1 & 1 & 1 & 0 \\
0 & 0 & 0 & 0 & 1 & 0 & 1 & 0 & 0 & 1 & 1 & 0 & 1 & 1 & 1
\end{pmatrix}$$

This is a binary $[15, 5]$-code that can correct any 3 errors. The fact that the rate is only $5/15 = 1/3$ might be disappointing. Also, the **relative** error correction rate is only $3/15 = 1/5$.

One more example: using block size $n = 2^5 - 1 = 31$, let's try again to correct 3 errors, so we need designed distance $t = 7$. Thus, the check matrix is

$$H = \begin{pmatrix}
1 & \alpha & \alpha^2 & \cdots & \alpha^{30} \\
1 & \alpha^2 & (\alpha^2)^2 & \cdots & (\alpha^2)^{30} \\
1 & \alpha^3 & (\alpha^3)^2 & \cdots & (\alpha^3)^{30} \\
1 & \alpha^4 & (\alpha^4)^2 & \cdots & (\alpha^4)^{30} \\
1 & \alpha^5 & (\alpha^5)^2 & \cdots & (\alpha^5)^{30} \\
1 & \alpha^6 & (\alpha^6)^2 & \cdots & (\alpha^6)^{30}
\end{pmatrix}$$

where α is a primitive element in $\mathbf{F}_{32}$. For example, let's model $\mathbf{F}_{32} = \mathbf{F}_2[x]/P(x)$ where $P(x)$ is the primitive quintic

$$P(x) = x^5 + x^2 = 1$$

Then $\alpha, \alpha^2, \alpha^4$ are all roots of $P(x) = 0$, α^3, α^6 go together, and α^5 is by itself. Since $31 = 2^5 - 1$ is prime, all these elements are again *primitive*, so we need 2 more distinct irreducible quintics as factors to be able to have $\alpha, \alpha^2, \alpha^3, \alpha^4, \alpha^5, \alpha^6$ as roots: without worrying about determining these quintics, we do know

$$\deg g = 3 \cdot 5 = 15$$

Therefore, we get a binary $[31, 16]$-code, since $16 = 31 - 15$. This gives a rate above $1/2$ again. But now the **relative** error correction is only $3/31 < 1/10$.

Remark: Although our success here was very limited, we *did* manage to make a relatively straightforward class of multiple-error-correcting codes. Since they are *linear*, the decoding (for example, by *syndrome decoding*) is reasonably efficient. Unfortunately, as with the Reed-Solomon codes which are generalized by these BCH codes, as block size becomes larger we *cannot* keep both a good rate *and* good relative error correction: one or the other must go to 0.

Finally, we give an algorithm to determine the dimensiona and to estimate the minimum distance of BCH codes. It is reasonably efficient to proceed as follows.

First, the Frobenius automorphism $x \rightarrow x^p$ (over the finite field $GF(p)$) is applied repeatedly to the rows of the initial check matrix H for the BCH code, making a larger check matrix, called the *Frobenius-stable* check matrix (after all the different possibilities are included, but without repetition). The row rank of this Frobenius-stable check matrix is the 'true' row rank, in the sense that

dimension of BCH code = length − row rank of Frob-stable check matrix

Further, a better estimate of the minimum distance can be obtained from the Frobenius stable check matrix: let t' be the largest integer so that contiguous exponents $1, 2, 3, \ldots, t'-2, t'-1$ appear as exponents (of the primitive root) in the second column of the Frobenius-stable check matrix. Then the minimum distance is *at least* t'. (We cannot easily reach a stronger conclusion about minimum distance since we have only the Vandermonde determinant criterion for linear independence of columns.)

More efficiently, given the set of exponents (of the primitive root) in the second column of the usual check matrix for a length n BCH code using $GF(p^m)$ over $GF(p)$, to determine the set of such exponents in the Frobenius-stable version we repeatedly multiply these exponents by p (reducing modulo $p^m - 1$). Let r be the number of exponents in the Frobenius-stabilized set: then the actual dimension k of the code is $k = n - r$. That is, there is no need to write the whole rows of any check matrix, but only the exponents occurring in the second column, since that exponent determines the whole row.

For example, to determine the dimension and estimate the minimum distance of the BCH code of length 26 constructed with designed distance 9 using the field extension $GF(3^3)$ of the finite field $GF(3)$, proceed as indicated above. Here, the initial set of exponents in the second column of the check matrix is $1, 2, 3, \ldots, 8$ (going up to design distance t less 1). Repeatedly multiplying by 3 (effectively applying the Frobenius) gives the Frobenius-stable set

$$1, 2, 3, 4, 5, 6, 7, 8, 9, 10, 11, 12, 15, 18, 19, 20, 21, 24$$

which has 18 elements. Thus, the row rank of the Frobenius-stable check matrix is 18, and the dimension of the BCH code is (with length 26)

$$26 - 18 = 8$$

The largest t' so that contiguous exponents $1, 2, \ldots, t'-1$ is visibly 13. Thus, we can conclude that the actual minimum distance is *at least* 13.

As another example, determine the dimension and minimum distance of the BCH code of length 24 constructed with designed distance 11 using the field extension $GF(5^2)$ of the finite field $GF(5)$. The initial set of exponents in the second column of the check matrix is $1, 2, 3, \ldots, 10$ (going up to design distance t less 1). Repeatedly multiplying by 5 (applying the Frobenius) gives the Frobenius-stable set

$$1, 2, 3, 4, 5, 6, 7, 8, 9, 10, 11, 15, 16, 20, 21$$

which has 15 elements. Thus, the row rank of the Frobenius-stable check matrix is 15, and the dimension of the BCH code is (with length 24)

$$24 - 15 = 9$$

The largest t' so that contiguous exponents $1, 2, \ldots, t' - 1$ is visibly 12. Thus, we can conclude that the actual minimum distance is *at least* 12.

Exercises

17.01 Compute the determinant of $\begin{pmatrix} 1 & 2 \\ 7 & 8 \end{pmatrix}$ (*ans.*)

17.02 Compute the determinant of $\begin{pmatrix} 3 & 5 \\ 7 & 8 \end{pmatrix}$

17.03 Compute the determinant of $\begin{pmatrix} 1 & 2 & 3 \\ 4 & 5 & 6 \\ 7 & 8 & 9 \end{pmatrix}$ (*ans.*)

17.04 Compute the determinant of $\begin{pmatrix} 1 & 2 & 3 \\ 4 & 3 & 2 \\ 7 & 0 & 8 \end{pmatrix}$

17.05 Compute the determinant of $\begin{pmatrix} 1 & 1 & 1 & 1 \\ 1 & 2 & 3 & 4 \\ 1 & 4 & 9 & 16 \\ 1 & 8 & 27 & 64 \end{pmatrix}$ (*ans.*)

17.06 Compute the determinant of $\begin{pmatrix} 1 & 1 & 1 & 1 \\ 5 & 6 & 7 & 8 \\ 25 & 36 & 49 & 64 \\ 125 & 216 & 343 & 512 \end{pmatrix}$

17.07 Using the alphabet $GF(13)$ find a generator matrix for a Reed-Solomon code correcting any 5 bit errors. Use primitive root 2 mod 13. (*ans.*)

17.08 Using the alphabet $GF(17)$ find a generator matrix for a Reed-Solomon code correcting any 7 bit errors. (Use primitive root 3 mod 17.)

17.09 Using the alphabet $GF(11)$ find a generator matrix for a Reed-Solomon code correcting any 4 bit errors. (Use primitive root 2 mod 11.)

17.10 Using the alphabet $GF(19)$ find a generator matrix for a Reed-Solomon code correcting any 8 bit errors. (Use primitive root 2 mod 19.)

17.11 Determine the dimension and minimum distance of the BCH code of length 48 constructed with designed distance 9 using the field extension $GF(7^2)$ of the finite field $GF(7)$. (*ans.*)

17.12 Determine the dimension and minimum distance of the BCH code of length 31 constructed with designed distance 7 using the field extension $GF(2^5)$ of the finite field $GF(2)$.

17.13 Determine the dimension and minimum distance of the BCH code of length 124 constructed with designed distance 9 using the field extension $GF(5^3)$ of the finite field $GF(5)$.

17.14 For a polynomial f with coefficients in $\mathbf{F}_q$, suppose the equation $f(x) = 0$ has root $a \in F_{q^m}$. Prove that also $f(a^q) = 0$.

18

Concatenated Codes

In this chapter we first give a *non-constructive* proof that there exist infinite families of linear codes with information rate 1/2 and minimum distance at least 1/10 of the length, all lying in a very restricted class of linear codes. That is, both the information rate and the error correction rate (ratio of minimum length to length) are bounded away from 0. We say that such an infinite family of codes is **asymptotically good**. RS and BCH codes do *not* have this property. But the non-constructive nature of this proof means basically that we cannot *find* these codes or *describe* them in any useful manner.

But there is a clever adaptation of the idea of that proof to make tangible examples of asymptotically good codes, due to Justesen. This was achieved relatively recently, in the late 1970s. The codes Justesen made were examples of **concatenated codes**, meaning that they are made by combining simpler building-block codes in a way that has a synergistic effect on the error-correction properties, etc.

Concatenated codes were apparently introduced by G.D. Forney in about 1966 (in the context of *convolutional* codes rather than block codes). The general idea is simple enough: repeatedly encode a message. Of course working out the details in a way to make it advantageous is the whole trick of it.

For now, this is the only known way to make a *constructive* infinite family of longer and longer codes so that *neither* the information rate nor the relative error correction go to 0 as the length goes to ∞.

18.1 Mirage codes

We call these codes 'mirage' codes because they are out of reach: we have no way (at present) to find them explicitly, much as in Shannon's theorem. That is, we can prove that they exist, but no one knows how to construct them. A funny situation.

This is a simple and well-known example. We'll make an infinite family of binary codes, all with information rate 1/2, whose minimum distance is at least 1/10 of the length.

Fix an integer n. Choose an irreducible polynomial $P(x)$ of degree n in $\mathbf{F}_2[x]$. Then we know that $\mathbf{F}_2[x]/P(x)$ is a **finite field** $\mathbf{F}_{2^n} = GF(2^n)$ with 2^n elements. Further, in the same way that we often choose representatives $0, 1, 2, \ldots, p-1$ for $\mathbf{Z}/p$, we can choose representatives for $\mathbf{F}_2[x]/P(x)$ consisting of polynomials of degrees $< n$. Then we can express elements

$$\alpha = a_0 + a_1 x + \ldots + a_{n-1} x^{n-1} \in GF(2^n)$$

in reduced form (mod $P(x)$) as being the binary length n vector of the coefficients:

$$\alpha \longleftrightarrow (a_0, a_1, \ldots, a_{n-1})$$

For fixed n and $\alpha \in GF(2^n)$, define a length $2n$ code

$$C_{2n}(\alpha) = \{(v, \alpha v) : v \in \mathbf{F}_2^n\}$$

depending on α, where the expression αv means to view v as being in $\mathbf{F}_{2^n}$ (as above) and multiply it by α (and then turn it back into a binary vector).

Theorem: For any integer $n \geq 4$ there is a choice of $\alpha \in \mathbf{F}_{2^n}$ so that the length $2n$ code $C_n(\alpha)$ has *information* rate $\frac{1}{2}$ and minimum distance at least $n/10$.

Proof: The idea of the proof is to *count* the number of α's which give relatively low minimum Hamming weight, and see that there are many α's left over. These leftovers must necessarily give relatively good codes.

Notice that any single non-zero binary word $(v, \alpha v)$ in the code $C_{2n}(\alpha)$ determines α, by the relation

$$\alpha = (v\alpha) \cdot v^{-1}$$

where inverse and multiplication are as elements of $\mathbf{F}_{2^n}$. Fix a real number c in the range $0 < c < 1/2$. If the code has minimum weight $< c \cdot 2n$, then there is a non-zero word $(v, \alpha v)$ in $C_{2n}(\alpha)$ with Hamming weight $< c \cdot 2n$, so α is expressible as $\alpha = (\alpha v) \cdot v^{-1}$ for some v so that $(v, \alpha v)$ is in $C_{2n}(\alpha)$ and has Hamming weight $< c \cdot 2n$.

The number of $(v, \alpha v)$'s in $C_{2n}(\alpha)$ with Hamming weight $< c \cdot 2n$ is certainly at most the number of binary vectors of length $2n$ with Hamming weight $< c \cdot 2n$ (that is, without assuming they're in $C_{2n}(\alpha)$). Thus,

$$(\text{number of } (v, \alpha v)\text{'s with Hamming weight} < c \cdot 2n) \leq \sum_{i \leq c \cdot 2n} \binom{2n}{i}$$

since there are $\binom{2n}{i}$ locations to put i 1s in a length $2n$ vector. From the lemma below, we have a slightly subtle estimate of this sum of binomial coefficients

$$\sum_{i < c \cdot 2n} \binom{2n}{i} \leq 2^{2n \cdot H(c)}$$

where as usual
$$H(c) = -c \log_2 c - (1 - c) \log_2 (1 - c)$$

We wish to choose c such that the number of these *bad* α's is $\leq 2^n - 2$, so, since there are $2^n - 1$ αs available altogether, not all the αs would be bad. That is, there would be at least one α so that $C_{2n}(\alpha)$ has minimum weight $\geq c \cdot 2n$.

That is, we want
$$2^{H(c) \cdot 2n} \leq 2^n - 2$$

so must choose c such that $H(c)$ is somewhat less than $1/2$. Some numerical experimentation yields

$$H(0.1) \approx 0.46899559358928122 < \frac{1}{2}$$

Therefore, certainly asymptotically as n becomes large we have the desired inequality. In fact, already for $n \geq 4$ we have the inquality, by numerical computation:

$$2^{H(0.1) \cdot 2 \cdot 4} \approx 13.472678057860175 \leq 2^4 - 2$$

The derivative

$$\frac{d}{dt} \left[2^t - 2 - 2^{H(0.1) \cdot 2 \cdot t} \right] = t \ln 2 \left(1 - 2 \cdot H(c) \right) \cdot \left[2^t - 2 - 2^{H(0.1) \cdot 2 \cdot t} \right]$$

is likewise positive for $t \geq 4$ since for this value of c

$$1 - 2 \cdot H(c) > 0$$

Thus, the desired inequality holds for all $n \geq 4$. That is, for $n \geq 4$ there is α such that the length $2n$ code C_{2n} has minimum distance at least $c \cdot 2n = 2n/10$.   ///

Now we prove the lemma giving the necessary estimate on sums of binomial coefficients used in the proof above.

Lemma: Fix $0 \leq c \leq 1/2$. As usual let

$$H(c) = -c \log_2 c - (1 - c) \log_2 (1 - c)$$

For positive integers ℓ,

$$\sum_{i < c\ell} \binom{\ell}{i} \leq 2^{\ell \cdot H(c)}$$

Proof: By the binomial theorem,

$$1 = 1^\ell = (c + (1 - c))^\ell = \sum_{0 \leq i \leq \ell} \binom{\ell}{i} c^i (1 - c)^{\ell - i}$$

$$\geq \sum_{0 \leq i \leq c\ell} \binom{\ell}{i} c^i (1 - c)^{\ell - i}$$

Now note that

$$c^i (1-c)^{\ell-i} = \left(\frac{c}{1-c}\right)^i (1-c)^\ell \geq \left(\frac{c}{1-c}\right)^{c\ell} (1-c)^\ell$$

since $i \leq c\ell$ and since $c/(1-c) \leq 1$ (because $0 \leq c \leq 1/2$). Therefore,

$$1 \geq \sum_{0\leq i\leq c\ell} \binom{\ell}{i} \left(\frac{c}{1-c}\right)^{c\ell} (1-c)^\ell = \left(\frac{c}{1-c}\right)^{c\ell} (1-c)^\ell \sum_{0\leq i\leq c\ell} \binom{\ell}{i}$$

Take logarithm base 2 of the factor in front:

$$\log_2 \left(\left(\frac{c}{1-c}\right)^{c\ell} (1-c)^\ell\right) = c\ell \log_2 c - c\ell \log_2 (1-c) + \ell \log_2 (1-c)$$

$$= \ell[c\log_2 c + (1-c)\log_2 (1-c)] = -\ell \cdot H(c)$$

Thus,

$$1 \geq 2^{-\ell \cdot H(c)} \cdot \sum_{0\leq i\leq c\ell} \binom{\ell}{i}$$

Moving the power of 2 to the other side gives the inequality.   ///

Example: Let's make a length 8 binary code with information rate 1/2 and determine its minimum distance by brute force. Model $\mathbf{F}_8$ as $\mathbf{F}_2[x]/(x^3 + x + 1)$. Let β be the image of x in that field. First try $\alpha = \beta$ and make the corresponding binary code. The encoding of $\mathbf{F}_8$ in binary is by encoding $v = a + b\beta + c\beta^2$ as (a, b, c). Then, starting to compute the encodings of the 7 non-zero length-3 words, we have

100	$\rightarrow$	1	$\rightarrow$	$(1, \beta)$	$\rightarrow$	100010
010	$\rightarrow$	β	$\rightarrow$	(β, β^2)	$\rightarrow$	010001
001	$\rightarrow$	β^2	$\rightarrow$	$(\beta^2, 1+\beta)$	$\rightarrow$	001110
110	$\rightarrow$	$1+\beta$	$\rightarrow$	$(1+\beta, \beta+\beta^2)$	$\rightarrow$	110011
101	$\rightarrow$	$1+\beta^2$	$\rightarrow$	$(1+\beta^2, 1)$	$\rightarrow$	101100
011	$\rightarrow$	$\beta+\beta^2$	$\rightarrow$	$(\beta+\beta^2, 1+\beta+\beta^2)$	$\rightarrow$	011111

It is clear that using $\alpha = \beta$ has the disadvantage that some weight-1 length-3 codewords v will give $(v, \alpha v)$ of weight only 2, not enough to correct even a single error. Thus, we try this again with $\alpha = \beta + 1$:

100	$\rightarrow$	1	$\rightarrow$	$(1, 1+\beta)$	$\rightarrow$	100110
010	$\rightarrow$	β	$\rightarrow$	$(\beta, \beta+\beta^2)$	$\rightarrow$	010011
001	$\rightarrow$	β^2	$\rightarrow$	$(\beta^2, 1+\beta+\beta^2)$	$\rightarrow$	001111
110	$\rightarrow$	$1+\beta$	$\rightarrow$	$(1+\beta, 1+\beta^2)$	$\rightarrow$	110101
101	$\rightarrow$	$1+\beta^2$	$\rightarrow$	$(1+\beta^2, \beta^2)$	$\rightarrow$	101001
011	$\rightarrow$	$\beta+\beta^2$	$\rightarrow$	$(\beta+\beta^2, 1)$	$\rightarrow$	011100

This is a relative success, in the sense that we have achieved a minimum distance 3, so one bit error can be corrected. This is *not* as good as the Hamming $[7, 4]$ code, however, since the information rate of the present code is $1/2$ while that of the Hamming code is $4/7 > 1/2$.

Example: Now make a length 8 code of information rate $1/2$, hoping to have a minimum distance greater than 3. Model $\mathbf{F}_{16}$ as $\mathbf{F}_2[x]/(x^4 + x + 1)$. Let β be the image of x in the field. Encode

$$a + b\beta + c\beta^2 + d\beta^3 \rightarrow (a, b, c, d)$$

To avoid having the weight-1 length-4 binary words encode as weight 3 or less, we try

$$\alpha = 1 + \beta + \beta^2$$

The weight-1 words encode as

$$
\begin{array}{ccccccc}
1000 & \rightarrow & 1 & \rightarrow & (1, 1 + \beta + \beta^2) & \rightarrow & 10001110 \\
0100 & \rightarrow & \beta & \rightarrow & (\beta, \beta + \beta^2 + \beta^3) & \rightarrow & 01000111 \\
0010 & \rightarrow & \beta^2 & \rightarrow & (\beta^2, 1 + \beta + \beta^2 + \beta^3) & \rightarrow & 00101111 \\
0001 & \rightarrow & \beta^3 & \rightarrow & (\beta^3, 1 + \beta^2 + \beta^3) & \rightarrow & 00011011
\end{array}
$$

We get no word with Hamming weight less than 4. Continuing with our brute-force computations, encoding weight-2 length-4 words we have

$$
\begin{array}{ccc}
0011 & \rightarrow & 00110100 \\
0101 & \rightarrow & 01011100 \\
1001 & \rightarrow & 10010101 \\
0110 & \rightarrow & 01101000 \\
1010 & \rightarrow & 10100001 \\
1100 & \rightarrow & 11001001
\end{array}
$$

Unfortunately, the fourth one encodes as a weight-3 codeword. Indeed, the Hamming bound says that this attempt is too optimistic, because a length 8 binary code with $2^4 = 16$ codewords and minimum distance would have to satisfy

$$2^8 \geq 2^4 \cdot \left(1 + \binom{8}{1} + \binom{8}{2} \right)$$

which is false. Thus, we would need to consider longer mirage codes to achieve minimum distance 5 and correction of two bit errors. The computations are not illuminating, and we might concede once again that we do not understand how to explicitly construct good codes.

18.2 Concatenated codes

Now we introduce the idea of putting together simpler codes to make bigger *concatenated* ones. This was first introduced in the somewhat different context of **convolutional codes** by [Forney 1966].

The basic idea of a **concatenated code**, in our context, is that the symbols in the *alphabet* of the **outer code** C_{out} are interpreted as being the *words* of the **inner code** C_{in}, and after the outer encoding is applied the inner encoding is applied to each alphabet symbol. Sometimes such a process is also called **superencoding**, and the concatenated code is sometimes called a **supercode**.

We'll take both codes to be *linear*. More specifically, let C_{out} be a linear code with alphabet $\mathbf{F}_{2^k}$, and let C_{in} be a *binary* linear code of length n. (To identify elements of $\mathbf{F}_{2^k}$ with binary vectors of length k, as usual choose an irreducible polynomial $P(x)$ in $\mathbf{F}_2[x]$ of degree k so that we have a model for $\mathbf{F}_{2^k}$ as $\mathbf{F}_2[x]/P(x)$). If the outer code C_{out} is an (N, K, D) code (with alphabet $\mathbf{F}_{2^k}$) and the inner code C_{in} is a binary (n, k, d) code, then a word

$$a = (a_0, a_1, \ldots, a_{K-1}) \in \mathbf{F}_{2^k}^K$$

is encoded by the outer code as some N-tuple

$$b = (b_0, b_1, \ldots, b_{N-1}) \in \mathbf{F}_{2^k}^N$$

Then each $b_i \in \mathbf{F}_{2^k}$ is rewritten as some binary vector

$$b_i = (b_{i,0}, b_{i,1}, b_{1,2}, \ldots, b_{i,k-1}) \in \mathbf{F}_2^k$$

(for a choice of irreducible degree k polynomial $P(x) \in \mathbf{F}_2[x]$), and encoded by the inner code to

$$c_i = (c_{i,0}, c_{i,1}, c_{1,2}, \ldots, c_{i,n-1}) \in \mathbf{F}_2^n$$

Proposition: The concatenated code made from an outer (N, K, D) code with alphabet $\mathbf{F}_{2^k}$ and an inner binary (n, k, d) code is essentially a *binary* (nN, kK)-code. That is, the information rate of such a concatenated code is equal to the product of the rates of the inner and outer codes.

Proof: This is almost clear from the very definition of the concatenated code.

$$\text{information rate} = \frac{\log_2(\text{number of codewords})}{\log_2(\text{all words})} = \frac{kK}{nN}$$

$$= \frac{\log_{2^k}((2^k)^K)}{\log_{2^k}((2^k)^N)} \cdot \frac{\log_2(2^k)}{\log_2(2^n)} = (\text{outer info rate}) \cdot (\text{inner info rate})$$

$$/\!/\!/$$

Also we have an easy-to-prove fact about minimum distances:

Proposition: The minimum distance of a concatenated code is *at least* the product of the minimum distances of the outer and inner codes.

Proof: Let D be the minimum distance of the outer code and d the minimum distance of the inner code. Let $w = (\alpha_0, \ldots, \alpha_{N-1})$ be a codeword in $\mathbf{F}_{2^k}^N$. Then there are at least D nonzero entries among the α_i. Now viewing each α_i as a binary vector, if α_i is non-zero then it has at least d non-zero entries. Thus, the length

Nn binary version of w has at least Dd non-zero entries, which is to say that the minimum distance is at least Dd, as claimed.   ///

Remark: As it stands, there is no visible reason to use concatenated codes, but Justesen found a further trick.

18.3 Justesen codes

The Justesen codes are a practical version of the non-constructive codes discussed above, made by a sort of *variable* concatenation of codes. It turns out that a clever compromise in the mirage code description makes it possible to constructively describe the Justesen codes, and at the same time retain the virtues of the mirage codes.

To make an example following Justesen, using the description of a concatenated code above, we will take the outer code C_{out} to be a Reed-Solomon code, and the inner code C_{in} to be *variable* depending on the position of the symbol in a word of the outer code. Indeed, there is no compulsion to encode the symbols in different positions the same way.

Fix a degree k irreducible polynomial $P(x)$ in $\mathbf{F}_2[x]$, and view $\mathbf{F}_{2^k}$ as

$$\mathbf{F}_{2^k} = \mathbf{F}_2[x]/P(x)$$

Let $N = 2^m - 1$ for some integer m, and take the outer code C_{out} to be an (N, K, D) Reed-Solomon code over $\mathbf{F}_{2^k}$. That is, a codeword in C_{out} is an N-tuple of elements of $\mathbf{F}_{2^k}$. A message word

$$a = (a_0, \ldots, a_{K-1}) \in \mathbf{F}_{2^k}^K$$

gets encoded by the outer Reed-Solomon code as some codeword

$$b = (b_0, \ldots, b_{N-1}) \in \mathbf{F}_{2^k}^N$$

Let g be a primitive element in the finite field $\mathbf{F}_{2^k}$. Then for each position $0 \le i \le N - 1$ we have a code $C_{\text{in}}(i)$ which encodes

$$b_i \rightarrow (b_i, g^i \cdot b_i) \in \mathbf{F}_{2^k}^2$$

So the outer-code codeword b gets encoded by this aggregate inner code as

$$(b_0, g^0 b_0, b_1, g^1 b_1, b_2, g^2 b_2, b_3, g^3 b_3, \ldots, b_{N-1}, g^{N-1} b_{N-1})$$

The code obtained by this *variable* concatenation is a **Justesen code**.

Remark: These varying inner codes are the codes discussed earlier, among which the really good ones are *mirages* since we cannot readily locate them. But the idea is that even the *average* is good enough so that the supercode is still pretty good. But of course we need to verify some details.

Theorem: There is an infinite family of Justesen codes with information rates at least 1/4 and with minimum distance asymptotically at least 1/40 of the block length.

Remark: The particular number 1/5 and 1/90 are not so interesting in themselves, and not so terrific in terms of performance, either. The point is that we can demonstrate in a *computationally effective* manner a family of longer and longer codes whose performance does not deteriorate.

Proof: A Reed-Solomon (N, K, D) code always has minimum distance at least $D = N - K + 1$, regardless of what finite field we use as its alphabet. So out of the N symbols of each codeword of the outer code, at least D are not 0. But we have no idea *which* of the N codeword symbols are the non-zero ones, so we must prove that among *any* D of the inner codes enough of them are good enough so that the minimum distance of the binary supercode is a definite positive fraction of its length $Nn = N \cdot 2k$.

In discussing the mirage codes we noted that a two-tuple $(v, \alpha v)$ with $v \in \mathbf{F}_{2^k}$ non-zero determines α. And we can get an upper bound for the number of bad α's for which $(v, \alpha v)$ has Hamming weight $\leq c \cdot 2k$, by counting the number of ways of distributing $\leq c \cdot 2k$ 1's among the $2k$ positions in the binary vector $(v, \alpha v)$. Using binomial coefficients to count this, we get

$$(\text{number of } \alpha\text{'s with some } (v, \alpha v) \text{ of weight less than } c \cdot 2k) \leq \sum_{i < c \cdot 2k} \binom{2k}{i}$$

In the discussion of the mirage codes we proved a lemma asserting the inequality

$$\sum_{i < c \cdot 2k} \binom{2k}{i} \leq 2^{H(c) \cdot 2k}$$

We know that at least D/N of the codeword symbols from the outer code are not 0, and we want to use this inequality to estimate how good or bad the *better* half of the *worst* D/N fraction of the inner codes can be. That is, we are interested in guessing a fraction $0 < c < 1/2$ so that at most the fraction $\frac{1}{2} \cdot D/N$ of the inner codes have minimum distance $< c \cdot 2k$. That is, using the lemma, we want to find c so that

$$2^{H(c) \cdot 2k} \leq \frac{1}{2} \cdot \frac{D}{N} \cdot N$$

This simplifies to

$$2^{H(c) \cdot 2k} \leq \frac{1}{2} \cdot D$$

Since at least $\frac{1}{2} \cdot D/N$ of the inner codes have minimum distance $\geq c \cdot 2k$, then we'll get a lower bound for the minimum distance of the supercode:

$$\text{min distance for supercode} \geq (c \cdot 2k) \cdot (\frac{1}{2} \cdot D)$$

and the lower bound for ratio of minimum distance to length is

$$\frac{\text{min distance}}{\text{length}} \geq \frac{(c \cdot 2k) \cdot (\frac{1}{2} \cdot D)}{2k \cdot N} = \frac{c \cdot D}{2N} = \frac{c \cdot D}{2(2^k - 1)} \geq \frac{c \cdot D}{2^{k+1}}$$

(A Reed-Solomon code over the field $\mathbf{F}_{2^k}$ has length $N = 2^k - 1$.)

If we try taking

$$D = \frac{1}{2} \cdot 2^k \approx \frac{1}{2} \cdot N$$

then we require

$$2^{H(c) \cdot 2k} \leq \frac{1}{2} \cdot D \leq \frac{1}{2} \cdot \frac{1}{2} \cdot 2^k = \frac{1}{4} \cdot 2^k$$

If we take c so that $H(c) < 1/2$, then for *sufficiently large* k this inequality will hold. Specifically, for

$$k \geq \frac{2}{1 - 2 \cdot H(c)}$$

the inequality holds. For example, as with the mirage codes earlier, taking $c = 1/10$ gives

$$H(c) = H(0.1) \leq 0.469 < \frac{1}{2}$$

Then with this choice of D and c we want k large enough such that

$$\frac{1}{2} \cdot D - 2^{H(c) \cdot 2k} \geq \frac{1}{4} \cdot 2^k - 2^{0.469 \, 2k}$$

For $k \geq 33$ this holds. In any case, to get $H(c) < 1/2$ we must take $c < 0.11$, since

$$H(0.11) \approx 0.4999 \approx \frac{1}{2}$$

Thus, for $k \geq 33$ and $c \leq 1/10$ for example, with $D = 2^k/2$, the minimum distance is at least

$$(c \cdot 2k) \cdot (\frac{1}{2} \cdot D) \geq \frac{1}{10} \cdot 2k \cdot \frac{1}{2} \cdot \frac{1}{2} \cdot 2^k = k \cdot 2^k/20$$

The length of the binary supercode is $2k \cdot (2^k - 1) \leq 2k \cdot 2^k$, so we have

$$\frac{\text{min distance}}{\text{length}} \geq \frac{k \cdot 2^k/20}{2k \cdot 2^k} = \frac{1}{40}$$

From the relation $D = N - K + 1$ for a Reed-Solomon code, we see that the information rate for the outer code is $K/N \approx 1/2$. The inner code information rates are all $1/2$, so the information rate of the concatenated code is about $1/4$. (The information rate goes to $1/4$ as k goes to infinity.)

That is, for $k = 33, 34, 35, \ldots$ we can make concatenated binary codes of lengths $2k \cdot (2^k - 1)$, with information rate going to $1/4$ in the limit, and with minimum distance asymptotically at least $1/40$ of the length. ///

18.4 Some explicit irreducible polynomials

As an afterthought we might want to see if we can really create an infinite family of irreducible polynomials in $\mathbf{F}_2[x]$, in order to make the creation of the Justesen codes really computationally constructive. It turns out that this is not so hard, given what we know about primitive roots in finite fields.

Remark: We will use the fact that if α is a root of $f(x) = 0$ for irreducible $f(x) \in \mathbf{F}_2[x]$ then α^2 is also, and in fact the complete list of roots is

$$\alpha, \alpha^2, \alpha^{2^2}, \alpha^{2^3}, \alpha^{2^4}, \alpha^{2^5}, \ldots, \alpha^{2^{t-1}}$$

where the degree of the polynomial is t.

Proposition: Let ℓ be a positive integer. Let $m = 3^\ell$ for any positive integer ℓ. Then the polynomial

$$x^{2m} + x^m + 1$$

in $\mathbf{F}_2[x]$ is irreducible.

Proof: First, we check that the order t of 2 modulo $3^{\ell+1}$ is exactly $2 \cdot 3^\ell = \varphi(3^{\ell+1})$. By Euler's theorem and Lagrange's theorem, t is a *divisor* of $2 \cdot 3^\ell$. So what we want to show is that 2 is a primitive root in $\mathbf{Z}/3^{\ell+1}$. From our discussion of primitive roots, we know that it suffices to show that 2 is a primitive root mod 3^2. And, indeed, $2^3 = -1 \neq 1 \bmod 3^2$, $2^2 = 4 \neq 1 \bmod 3^2$, so 2 is a primitive root as desired.

Next, let P be *any* irreducible polynomial of degree $2m = 2 \cdot 3^\ell$ over $\mathbf{F}_2$, so that we have a concrete model

$$\mathbf{F}_{2^{2m}} \approx \mathbf{F}[x]/P(x)$$

(Note that we do *not* have to give a constructive proof that P exists! Why?) Since 3^ℓ divides $2^{2m} - 1$ (that is, since the order of 2 mod $3^{\ell+1}$ is $2 \cdot 3^\ell = 2m$) and since there is a primitive root g in $\mathbf{F}_{2^{2m}}$, the element

$$\xi = g^{(2^{2m}-1)/3^\ell}$$

is of order 3^ℓ. Since the field $\mathbf{F}_2$ is of characteristic 2, if α is a root of a polynomial then α^2, α^{2^2}, α^{2^3}, ... are roots as well. Since the order of 2 mod 3^ℓ is exactly $2 \cdot 3^\ell$, we obtain roots

$$\xi, \xi^2, \xi^{2^2}, \xi^{2^3}, \ldots, \xi^{2^{2m-1}}$$

of the irreducible polynomial of which ξ is a root. In particular, that irreducible polynomial is of degree at least $2m$, since it has at least these $2m$ distinct roots. Since 2 is relatively prime to 3^ℓ, all these elements ξ^{2^i} are also of order $m = 3^\ell$. Now the polynomial

$$x^{3^\ell} - 1$$

has roots in $\mathbf{F}_{2^m}$ consisting of all elements whose orders are powers of 3 less than or equal 3^ℓ. The element of order 1 (namely 1 itself) is a root of $x - 1$, the elements of order 3 are roots of

$$(x^3 - 1)/(x - 1) = x^2 + x + 1$$

and generally the elements of order 3^i are roots of $x^{3^i} - 1$ but not $x^{3^{i-1}} - 1$, so by unique factorization are roots of

$$\frac{x^{3^i} - 1}{x^{3^{i-1}} - 1} = x^{2 \cdot 3^{i-1}} + x^{3^{i-1}} + 1$$

Thus, we find factors of $x^{3^\ell} - 1$

$$(x - 1)(x^2 + x + 1)(x^6 + x^3 + 1)(x^{18} + x^9 + 1) \ldots (x^{2m} + x^m + 1)$$

By good luck here, the sum of the degrees is

$$1 + 2 + 2 \cdot 3 + 2 \cdot 3^2 + 2 \cdot 3^3 + \ldots + 2 \cdot 3^\ell = 1 + \frac{2 \cdot (3^\ell - 1)}{3 - 1} = 3^\ell$$

That is, we've found a factorization of $x^{3^\ell} - 1$. Since every factor but the last has degree strictly less than $2m$, and since the irreducible polynomial of which ξ is a root is a divisor of $x^{3^\ell} - 1$, the last factor must be the irreducible polynomial of which ξ is a root. This proves the proposition.   ///

Remark: A similar argument works for other primes p in place of 3, such as 5 (but not 7) for which 2 is a primitive root modulo p^2. That is, for such p, let

$$m = p^\ell$$

Then

$$x^{(p-1)m} + x^{(p-2)m} + \ldots + x^{3m} + x^{2m} + x^m + 1 \in \mathbf{F}_2[x]$$

is irreducible.

Exercises

18.01 Let α be the image of x in $\mathbf{F}_4 = \mathbf{F}_2[x]/(x^2 + x + 1)$. Write out the 3 non-zero codewords of the corresponding mirage code and observe the minimum distance. (*ans.*)

18.02 Let α be the image of $x + 1$ in $\mathbf{F}_4 = \mathbf{F}_2[x]/(x^2 + x + 1)$. Write out the 3 non-zero codewords and observe the minimum distance.

18.03 Let $\mathbf{F}_8 = \mathbf{F}_2[x]/(x^3 + x^2 + 1)$, let α be the image of $1 + x$, and write out the encoding of the corresponding mirage code of length 6 and information rate $1/2$. Note the minimum distance.

18.04 Can you find $\alpha \in \mathbf{F}_{32}$ to give a mirage code of length 10 with minimum distance at least 4?

18.05 Find a constant c such that

$$\sum_{i < c \cdot 3n} \binom{3n}{i} < 2^{2n}$$

(*ans.*)

18.06 In a variant on mirage codes, encode binary n-bit strings v by $v \rightarrow (v, \alpha v, \beta v)$ viewing v as lying in $\mathbf{F}_{2^n}$ and with α, β chosen in $\mathbf{F}_{2^n}$ to make a binary code of length $3n$ with information rate 1/3. As with the mirage codes, prove a lower bound on the error-correction rate for such a code, with optimal (but inexplicit) α and β. (*ans.*)

18.07 Prove that the minimum distance of a concatenated code is at least the product of the minimum distances of the inner and outer code.

19

More on Rings and Fields

Here we develop in greater detail some aspects of ring theory touched upon very briefly earlier.

19.1 Ideals in commutative rings

The concept of **ideal** in a commutative ring is a sort of generalization of the concept of *number*. In fact, originally there was a closely related notion of *ideal number* which extended the usual notion of number. This phrase has since been shortened simply to 'ideal'.

Let R be a commutative ring with unit 1. An **ideal** in R is a subset I of R so that

- For all $r \in R$ and $i \in I$ we have $r \cdot i \in I$. (Closure under multiplication by ring elements)
- For all $x, y \in I$ we have $x + y \in I$. (Closure under addition)
- For all $x \in I$ we have $-x \in I$. (Closure under inverse)

The second and third conditions can be capsulized as requiring that I-with-addition must be a subgroup of the additive group R-with-addition.

The first condition may seem a little peculiar. For one thing, it is a stronger requirement than that I be a *subring* of R, since we require that I be closed under multiplication by elements of R, not merely by elements of I itself.

Example: The basic example is the following. In the ring $\mathbf{Z}$, for any fixed n, the set $n \cdot \mathbf{Z}$ consisting of all multiples of n is an ideal. Indeed, if $x = mn$ is a multiple of n, and if $r \in \mathbf{Z}$, then $r \cdot x = r(mn) = (rm)n$ is still a multiple of n. Likewise, 0 is contained in $n\mathbf{Z}$, $n\mathbf{Z}$ is closed under sums, and $n\mathbf{Z}$ is closed under taking additive inverses.

Example: Let $R = k[x]$ be the ring of polynomials in one variable x with coefficients in a field k. Fix a polynomial $P(x)$, and let $I \subset R$ be the set of all polynomial multiples $M(x) \cdot P(x)$ of $P(x)$. Verification that I is an ideal is identical in form to the previous example.

Example: Abstracting the previous two examples: let R be any commutative ring with unit 1, and fix $n \in R$. Then the set $I = n \cdot R = \{rn : r \in R\}$ consisting of all multiples of m is an ideal, called the **principal ideal generated by** n. The same argument proves that it is an ideal. Such an ideal is called a **principal ideal**.

Example: In any ring, the **trivial ideal** is just the set $I = \{0\}$. Consistent with typical usage in mathematics, an ideal I is **proper** if it is neither the trivial ideal $\{0\}$ nor the whole ring R (which is also an ideal).

The following proposition is an important basic principle.

Proposition: Let I be an ideal in a commutative ring R with unit 1. If I contains any element $u \in R^\times$, then $I = R$.

Proof: Suppose I contains $u \in R^\times$. The fact that u is a unit means that there is a multiplicative inverse u^{-1} to u. Then, for any $r \in R$,

$$r = r \cdot 1 = r \cdot (u^{-1} \cdot u) = (r \cdot u^{-1}) \cdot u$$

That is, r is a multiple of u. Since I is an ideal, it must contain every multiple of u, so I contains r. Since this is true of every element $r \in R$, it must be that $R = I$.   ///

Corollary: Let I be an ideal in a polynomial ring $k[x]$ where k is a field. If I contains any non-zero 'constant' polynomial, then $I = k[x]$.

Proof: This will follow from the previous proposition if we check that non-zero constant polynomials are units (that is, have multiplicative inverses). Indeed, for $a \in k$ with $a \neq 0$, since k is a field there is $a^{-1} \in k \subset k[x]$. Thus, certainly a is invertible in the polynomial ring $k[x]$.   ///

We can recycle the notation we used for cosets to write about ideals in a more economical fashion. For two subsets X, Y of a *ring* R, write

$$X + Y = \{x + y : x \in X, \, y \in Y\}$$

$$X \cdot Y = X\,Y$$

$$= \{\text{finite sums } \sum_i x_i\, y_i : x_i \in X, \, y_i \in Y\}$$

Note that in the context of *ring* theory the notation $X \cdot Y$ has a different meaning than it does in *group* theory. Then we can say that *an ideal I in a commutative ring R is an additive subgroup so that $R\,I \subset I$.*

Proposition: Every ideal I in $\mathbf{Z}$ is principal, that is, of the form $I = n \cdot \mathbf{Z}$. In particular, the integer n so that this is true is the least positive element of I unless $I = \{0\}$, in which case $n = 0$.

Proof: If $I = \{0\}$, then certainly $I = \mathbf{Z} \cdot 0$, and we're done. So suppose I is non-zero. Since I is closed under taking additive inverses, if I contains $x < 0$ then it also contains $-x > 0$. So a non-trivial ideal I does indeed contain *some* positive element. Let n be the least element of I. Let $x \in I$, and use the Division Algorithm to get $q, r \in \mathbf{Z}$ with $0 \le r < n$ and

$$x = q \cdot n + r$$

Certainly qn is still in I, and then $-qn \in I$ also. Since $r = x - qn$, we conclude that $r \in I$. Since n was the smallest positive element of I, it must be that $r = 0$. Thus, $x = qn \in n \cdot \mathbf{Z}$, as desired.   ///

Proposition: Let k be a field. Let $R = k[x]$ be the ring of polynomials in one variable x with coefficients in k. Then every ideal I in R is principal, that is, is of the form $I = k[x] \cdot P(x)$ for some polynomial P. In particular, $P(x)$ is the monic polynomial of smallest degree in I, unless $I = \{0\}$, in which case $P(x) = 0$.

Proof: If $I = \{0\}$, then certainly $I = k[x] \cdot 0$, and we're done. So suppose I is non-zero. Suppose that $Q(x) = a_n x^n + \ldots + a_0$ lies in I with $a_n \ne 0$. Since k is a field, there is an inverse a_n^{-1}. Then, since I is an ideal, the polynomial

$$P(x) = a_n^{-1} \cdot Q(x) = x^n + a_n^{-1} a_{n-1} x^{n-1} + \ldots + a_n^{-1} a_0$$

also lies in I. That is, there is indeed a *monic* polynomial of lowest degree of any element of the ideal. Let $x \in I$, and use the Division Algorithm to get $Q, R \in k[x]$ with $\deg R < \deg P$ and

$$x = Q \cdot P + R$$

Certainly $Q \cdot P$ is still in I, and then $-Q \cdot P \in I$ also. Since $R = x - Q \cdot P$, we conclude that $R \in I$. Since P was the monic polynomial in I of smallest degree, it must be that $R = 0$. Thus, $x = Q \cdot P \in n \cdot k[x]$, as desired.   ///

Remark: The proofs of these two propositions can be abstracted to prove that every ideal in a *Euclidean ring* is *principal.*

Example: Let R be a commutative ring with unit 1, and fix two elements $x, y \in R$. Then

$$I = R \cdot x + R \cdot y = \{rx + sy : r, s \in R\}$$

is an ideal in R. This is checked as follows. First,

$$0 = 0 \cdot x + 0 \cdot y$$

so 0 lies in I. Second,

$$-(rx + sy) = (-r)x + (-s)y$$

so I is closed under inverses. Third, for two elements $rx + sy$ and $r'x + s'y$ in I (with $r, r', s, s' \in R$) we have

$$(rx + sy) + (r'x + s'y) = (r + r')x + (s + s')y$$

so I is closed under addition. Finally, for $rx + sy \in I$ with $r, s \in R$, and for $r' \in R$,

$$r' \cdot (rx + sy) = (r'r)x + (r's)y$$

so $R \cdot I \subset I$ as required. Thus, this type of I is indeed an ideal. The two elements x, y are the **generators** of I.

Example: Similarly, for fixed elements $x_1, \ldots, x_n$ of a commutative ring R, we can form an ideal

$$I = R \cdot x_1 + \ldots + R \cdot x_n$$

Example: To construct new, larger ideals from old, smaller ideals we can proceed as follows. Let I be an ideal in a commutative ring R. Let x be an element of R. Then let

$$J = R \cdot x + I = \{rx + i : r \in R, \ i \in I\}$$

Let's check that J is an ideal. First

$$0 = 0 \cdot x + 0$$

so 0 lies in J. Second,

$$-(rx + i) = (-r)x + (-i)$$

so J is closed under inverses. Third, for two elements $rx + i$ and $r'x + i'$ in J (with $r, r' \in R$ and $i, i' \in I$) we have

$$(rx + i) + (r'x + i') = (r + r')x + (i + i')$$

so J is closed under addition. Finally, for $rx + i \in J$ with $r \in R$, $i \in I$, and for $r' \in R$,

$$r' \cdot (rx + i) = (r'r)x + (r'i)$$

so $R \cdot J \subset J$ as required. Thus, this type of set J is indeed an ideal.

Remark: In the case of rings such as $\mathbf{Z}$, where we know that every ideal is principal, the previous construction does not yield any more general type of ideal.

Remark: In some rings R, it is definitely the case that *not* every ideal is principal. That is, there are some ideals that cannot be expressed as $R \cdot x$. The simplest example is the following. Let

$$R = \{a + b\sqrt{-5} : a, b \in \mathbf{Z}\}$$

It is not hard to check that this is a ring. Let

$$I = \{x \cdot 2 + y \cdot (1 + \sqrt{-5}) : x, y \in R\}$$

With just a little bit of cleverness, one can show that this ideal is not principal. This phenomenon is closely related to the *failure of unique factorization* into primes in this ring. For example, we have two apparently different factorizations

$$2 \cdot 3 = 6 = (1 + \sqrt{-5}) \cdot (1 - \sqrt{-5})$$

(All the numbers 2, 3, $1 + \sqrt{-5}$, $1 - \sqrt{-5}$ are 'prime' in the naive sense that they can't be further factored in the ring R.) These phenomena are not of immediate relevance, but did provide considerable motivation in the historical development of algebraic number theory.

Remark: In rings R that are not necessarily commutative, there are *three different kinds* of ideals. A **left ideal** I is an additive subgroup so that $R I \subset I$, a **right ideal** I is an additive subgroup so that $I R \subset I$, and a **two-sided ideal** I is an additive subgroup so that $R I R \subset I$. Mostly we'll only care about ideals in *commutative* rings, so we can safely ignore this complication most of the time.

19.2 Ring homomorphisms

Quite analogous to *group homomorphisms*, ring homomorphisms are maps from one ring to another which preserve the ring structures.

A ring homomorphism $f : R \to S$ from one ring R to another ring S is a map such that for all r, r' in R we have

$$f(r + r') = f(r) + f(r')$$

$$f(rr') = f(r)\, f(r')$$

That is, we would say that f *preserves* or *respects* both addition and multiplication.

A ring homomorphism which is a bijection is an **isomorphism**. Two rings which are isomorphic are construed as 'the same' for all ring-theoretic purposes.

As in the case of groups and group homomorphisms, we do not make an attempt to use different notations for the addition and multiplication in the two different rings R and S in this definition. Thus, more properly put, f converts *addition in R* into *addition in S*, and likewise multiplication.

Very much like the case of groups, the **kernel** of a ring homomorphism $f : R \to S$ is

$$\ker f = \{r \in R : f(r) = 0\}$$

where (implicitly) the latter 0 is the additive identity in S.

Example: The most basic example of a ring homomorphism is

$$f : \mathbf{Z} \to \mathbf{Z}/n$$

given by

$$f(x) = x\text{-mod-}n$$

The assertion that this f is a ring homomorphism is the combination of the two assertions

$$(x\text{-mod-}n) + (y\text{-mod-}n) = (x + y)\text{-mod-}n$$

and
$$(x\text{-mod-}n) \cdot (y\text{-mod-}n) = (x \cdot y)\text{-mod-}n$$
Even though it is slightly misleading, this homomorphism is called the **reduction mod n homomorphism.**

Now we prove that

- The kernel of any ring homomorphism $f : R \to S$ is an ideal in R.

Let x be in the kernel, and $r \in R$. Then
$$f(rx) = f(r)f(x) = f(r) \cdot 0 = 0$$
since by now we've proven that in any ring the product of anything with 0 is 0. Thus, rx is in the kernel of f. And, for x, y both in the kernel,
$$f(x + y) = f(x) + f(y) = 0 + 0 = 0$$
That is, $x + y$ is again in the kernel. And $f(0) = 0$, so 0 is in the kernel. And for x in the kernel $f(-x) = -f(x) = -0 = 0$, so $-x$ is in the kernel.   ///

Example: Some homomorphisms which are very important in applications are **evaluation homomorphisms** or **substitution homomorphisms**, described as follows. Let R be a commutative ring and $R[x]$ the polynomial ring in one variable with coefficients in R. Fix $r_o \in R$. We want to talk about *evaluating* polynomials at r_o, or, equivalently, *substituting* r_o for x in a polynomial. What is meant by this is that a polynomial
$$P(x) = a_n x^n + a_{n-1} x^{n-1} + \ldots + a_2 x^2 + a_1 x + a_0$$
should be mapped to
$$P(r_o) = a_n r_o^n + a_{n-1} r_o^{n-1} + \ldots + a_2 r_o^2 + a_1 r_o + a_0$$
Let e_{r_o} denote this map, which is the **evaluation map.**

- The evaluation map $e_{r_o} : R[x] \to R$ is a ring homomorphism from the polynomial ring $R[x]$ to the ring R.

Before proving this, note that our experience makes us anticipate the fact that such maps really are ring homomorphisms: indeed, we know that to evaluate the product or sum of two polynomials we can evaluate them individually and then multiply/add, or multiply/add first and then evaluate. This is exactly the assertion that evaluation is a ring homomorphism.

Proof: Let $g(x) = \sum_i a_i x^i$ and $h(x) = \sum_i b_i x^i$ be two polynomials. That addition is preserved is easy:
$$e_{r_o}(g + h) = \sum_i (a_i + b_i) r_o^i = \sum_i a_i r_o^i + \sum_i b_i r_o^i = e_{r_o}(g) + e_{r_o}(h)$$
Multiplication is potentially more complicated notationally, but is also not difficult:
$$e_{r_o}(g \cdot h) = \sum_k \left(\sum_{i+j=k} (a_i \cdot b_i) \right) r_o^k = \left(\sum_i a_i r_o^i \right) \cdot \left(\sum_j b_j r_o^j \right) = e_{r_o}(g) \cdot e_{r_o}(h)$$

$///$

- Let $f : R \to S$ be a ring homomorphism. Let $0_R, 0_S$ be the additive identitites in R, S, respectively. Then $f(0_R) = 0_S$. That is, always the image of an additive identity under a ring homomorphism is the additive identity in the 'target' ring.

Proof: (that $f(0_R) = 0_S$.) First,

$$f(0_R) + f(0_R) = f(0_R + 0_R)$$

by the defining property of 'group homomorphism'. Then

$$0_R + 0_R = 0_R$$

(by the property of the additive identity in R), so

$$f(0_R + 0_R) = f(0_R)$$

Thus, together, we have

$$f(0_R) + f(0_R) = f(0_R + 0_R) = f(0_R)$$

Add the additive inverse $-f(0_R)$ to both sides:

$$(f(0_R) + f(0_R)) - f(0_R) = f(0_R + 0_R) - f(0_R)$$

$$= f(0_R) - f(0_R) = 0_S$$

where the last equality uses the definition of additive inverse. Using associativity of addition,

$$(f(0_R) + f(0_R)) - f(0_R) = f(0_R) + (f(0_R)) - f(0_R)) = f(0_R) + 0_S = f(0_R)$$

where we also use the defining property of 0_S. Putting these together (repeating a little):

$$f(0_R) = f(0_R) + f(0_R) - f(0_R) = f(0_R + 0_R) - f(0_R) = f(0_R) - f(0_R) = 0_S$$

as claimed. $///$

- Let $f : R \to S$ be a *surjective* ring homomorphism. Suppose that R has a multiplicative identity 1_R. Then S has a multiplicative identity 1_S and

$$f(1_R) = 1_S$$

Remark: Notice that, unlike the discussion about the additive identity, here we need the further hypothesis of surjectivity. Otherwise the assertion is false: see the remark after the proof.

Proof: Given $s \in S$, let $r \in R$ be such that $f(r) = s$. Then

$$f(1_R) \cdot s = f(1_R) \cdot f(r) = f(1_R \cdot r) = f(r) = s$$

Thus, $f(1_R)$ behaves like the unit in S. By the already proven *uniqueness* of units, it must be that $f(1_R) = 1_S$.   ///

Remark: It is important to note that it is not necessarily true that the image of the *multiplicative* identity 1_R under a ring homomorphism $f : R \to S$ has to be the *multiplicative* identity 1_S of S. For example, define a ring homomorphism

$$f : \mathbf{Q} \to S$$

from the rational numbers $\mathbf{Q}$ to the ring S of 2-by-2 rational matrices by

$$f(x) = \begin{pmatrix} x & 0 \\ 0 & 0 \end{pmatrix}$$

Then the image of 1 is simply

$$\begin{pmatrix} 1 & 0 \\ 0 & 0 \end{pmatrix}$$

which is certainly not the same as the multiplicative identity

$$\begin{pmatrix} 1 & 0 \\ 0 & 1 \end{pmatrix}$$

in the ring S.

There are also examples in commutative rings where the unit is mapped to something other than the unit. For example, let $R = \mathbf{Z}/3$ and $S = \mathbf{Z}/6$, and define $f : R \to S$ by

$$f(r \bmod 3) = 4r \bmod 6$$

Check that this is well-defined: if $r = r' \bmod 3$, then $3|(r - r')$. Then surely $6|4(r-r')$, so indeed $4r = 4r' \bmod 6$. This proves well-definedness. Check that this is a homomorphism:

$$f(x + y) = 4(x + y) = 4x + 4y = f(x) + f(y)$$

This would have worked with *any* number, not just 4. To see that f preserves multiplication, the crucial feature of the situation is that

$$4 \cdot 4 = 4 \bmod 6$$

Then

$$f(x \cdot y) = 4(x \cdot y) = (4 \cdot 4)(x \cdot y) = (4x) \cdot (4y) = f(x) \cdot f(y)$$

Thus, f is a homomorphism. But $f(1) \neq 1$.

19.3   Quotient rings

Now we give a construction of new rings from old in a manner that includes as a special case the construction of $\mathbf{Z}/n$ from $\mathbf{Z}$.

Let R be a commutative ring with unit 1. Let I be an ideal in R. The **quotient ring** R/I ('R mod I') is defined to be the set of cosets

$$r + I = \{r + i : i \in I\}$$

We define operations of addition and multiplication on R/I by

$$(r + I) + (s + I) = (r + s) + I$$

$$(r + I) \cdot (s + I) = (r \cdot s) + I$$

The zero in this quotient will be $0_{R/I} = 0 + I$, and the unit will be $1_{R/I} = 1 + I$.

Example: The basic example is that $\mathbf{Z}/n$ is the quotient ring $\mathbf{Z}/I$ where $I = n \cdot \mathbf{Z}$.

But, just as we had to check that the operations of addition and multiplication in $\mathbf{Z}/n$ were *well-defined*, we must do so here as well. The point is that the set $r + I$ typically can be named in several different ways, and we want the alleged addition and multiplication operations not to depend on the way the coset is *named*, but only on *what it is*. This is what well-definedness is about.

So suppose $r + I = r' + I$ and $s + I = s' + I$. That is, we have two cosets, each named in two possibly different ways. To prove well-definedness of addition we need to check that

$$(r + s) + I = (r' + s') + I$$

and to prove well-definedness of multiplication we must check that

$$(r \cdot s) + I = (r' \cdot s') + I$$

Since $r' + I = r + I$, in particular $r' = r' + 0 \in r + I$, so r' can be written as $r' = r + i$ for some $i \in I$. Likewise, $s' = s + j$ for some $j \in I$. Then

$$(r' + s') + I = (r + i + s + j) + I = (r + s) + (i + j + I)$$

The sum $k = i + j$ is an element of I. We claim that for any $k \in I$ we have $k + I = I$. Certainly since I is closed under addition, $k + I \subset I$. On the other hand, for any $x \in I$ we can write

$$x = k + (x - k)$$

with $x - k \in I$, so also $k + I \supset I$. Thus, indeed, $k + I = I$. Thus,

$$(r' + s') + I = (r + s) + I$$

which proves the well-definedness of addition in the quotient ring. Likewise, looking at multiplication:

$$(r' \cdot s') + I = (r + i) \cdot (s + j) + I = (r \cdot s) + (rj + si + I)$$

Since I is an ideal, rj and si are again in I, and then $rj + si \in I$. Therefore, as just observed in the discussion of addition, $rj + si + I = I$. Thus,

$$(r' \cdot s') + I = (r \cdot s) + I$$

and multiplication is well-defined.

The proofs that $0 + I$ is the zero and $1 + I$ is the unit are similar.

And in this situation the **quotient homomorphism**

$$q : R \to R/I$$

is the natural map

$$q(r) = r + I$$

In fact, the discussion just above proves

Proposition: For a commutative ring R and ideal I, the quotient map $R \to R/I$ is a ring homomorphism.   ///

19.4 Maximal ideals and fields

Now we see how to make fields by taking suitable quotients by maximal ideals. This is a fundamental construction.

Let R be a commutative ring with unit 1. An ideal M in R is **maximal** if $M \neq R$ and if for any other ideal I with $I \supset M$ it must be that $I = R$. That is, M is a maximal ideal if there is no ideal strictly larger than M (containing M) except R itself.

Proposition: For a commutative ring R with unit, and for an ideal I, the quotient ring R/I is a *field* if and only if I is a *maximal* ideal.

Proof: Let $x + I$ be a non-zero element of R/I. Then $x + I \neq I$, so $x \notin I$. Note that the ideal $Rx + I$ is therefore strictly larger than I. Since I was already maximal, it must be that $Rx + I = R$. Therefore, there are $r \in R$ and $i \in I$ so that $rx + i = 1$. Looking at this last equation modulo I, we have $rx \equiv 1 \bmod I$. That is, $r + I$ is the multiplicative inverse to $x + I$. Thus, R/I is a field.

On the other hand, suppose that R/I is a field. Let $x \in R$ but $x \notin I$. Then $x + I \neq 0 + I$ in R/I. Therefore, $x + I$ has a multiplicative inverse $r + I$ in R/I. That is,

$$(r + I) \cdot (x + I) = 1 + I$$

From the definition of the multiplication in the quotient, this is $rx + I = 1 + I$, or $1 \in rx + I$, which implies that the ideal $Rx + I$ is R. But $Rx + I$ is the smallest ideal containing I and x. Thus, there cannot be any proper ideal strictly larger than I, so I is maximal.   ///

19.5 Field extensions

Now we'll make the construction above more concrete, making 'bigger' fields by taking quotients of polynomial rings with coefficients in 'smaller' fields. This is a very basic procedure.

Let k be a field. Another field K containing k is called an **extension field** of k, and k is a **subfield** of K.

Theorem: Let k be a field and $P(x)$ an irreducible polynomial in $k[x]$ (other than the zero polynomial). Then the principal ideal $I = k[x] \cdot P(x)$ is *maximal*. Thus, the quotient ring $k[x]/I$ is a *field*. Further, the composite map

$$k \to k[x] \to k[x]/I$$

is *injective*, so we may consider the field k as a subset of the field $k[x]/I$. Now let $\alpha = x + I$ be the image in $k[x]/I$ of the indeterminate x. Then (in the quotient $k[x]/I$)

$$P(\alpha) = 0$$

Last, any element $\beta \in k[x]/I$ can be *uniquely* expressed in the form

$$\beta = R(\alpha)$$

where R is a polynomial with coefficients in k and of degree strictly less than the degree of P.

Remark: The **degree** of the extension K of k is the degree of the polynomial P used in the construction.

Remark: In this situation, thinking of α as 'existing' now and being a root of the equation $P(x) = 0$, we say that we have **adjoined** a root of $P(x) = 0$ to k, and write

$$k[\alpha] = k[x]/I$$

Remark: As a notational convenience, often a quotient

$$k[x]/k[x] \cdot P(x)$$

is written as

$$k[x]/P(x)$$

where it is meant to be understood that the quotient is by the *ideal* generated by $P(x)$. This is entirely consistent with the notation $\mathbf{Z}/n$ for $\mathbf{Z}/\mathbf{Z} \cdot n$.

Remark: An element β of $k[x]/I$ expressed as a polynomial $R(\alpha)$ with R of degree less than the degree of P is **reduced**. Of course, since $k[x]/I$ is a ring, *any* polynomial $R(\alpha)$ in α gives something in $k[x]/I$. But everything can be expressed by a polynomial of degree less than that of P, and *uniquely* so. This is exactly analogous to the fact that every equivalence class in the quotient ring $\mathbf{Z}/n$ has a unique representative among the integers reduced modulo n, namely $\{0, 1, 2, \ldots, n-1\}$.

Proof: Let J be a polynomial not in the ideal $I = k[x] \cdot P$. We want to show that the ideal $k[x] \cdot J + I$ is $k[x]$, thereby proving the maximality of I. Since P is irreducible, the gcd of J and P is just 1. Therefore, by the Euclidean Algorithm in $k[x]$, there are polynomials A, B in $k[x]$ so that

$$A \cdot P + B \cdot J = 1$$

That is, $k[x] \cdot J + I$ contains 1. Then for *any* polynomial M we have

$$M = M \cdot 1 = M \cdot (A \cdot P + B \cdot J) = (M \cdot A) \cdot P + (M \cdot B) \cdot J$$

which lies in $k[x] \cdot J + k[x] \cdot P$. That is, M is in the ideal $k[x] \cdot J + k[x] \cdot P$, so the latter ideal is the whole ring $k[x]$. This proves the maximality of $k[x] \cdot J + k[x] \cdot P$.

Next, we show that the composite map

$$k \to k[x] \to k[x]/k[x] \cdot P$$

is an injection. Let $I = k[x] \cdot P$. The first map $k \to k[x]$ is the obvious one, which takes $a \in k$ to the 'constant' polynomial a. Suppose $a, b \in k$ so that $a + I = b + I$. Then, by subtracting, $(a - b) + I = 0 + I$, which gives

$$a - b = (a - b) + 0 \in (a - b) + I = I$$

so $a - b \in I$. That is, $a - b$ is a multiple of P. Thus, either $a - b = 0$ or $\deg(a - b) \geq \deg P$, because the degree of a product of polynomials is the sum of the degrees, and degrees are non-negative integers except in the case of the 0 polynomial. Thus, since $\deg P > 0$ and $\deg(a - b) \leq 0$, it must be that $a - b = 0$.

Next, we prove that $P(\alpha) = 0$. Let $q : k[x] \to k[x]/I$ be the quotient homomorphism. Write out P as

$$P(x) = a_n x^n + a_{n-1} x^{n-1} + \ldots + a_2 x^2 + a_1 x + a_0$$

To show that $P(\alpha) = 0$ in the quotient, we compute

$$P(\alpha) = a_n \alpha^n + a_{n-1} \alpha^{n-1} + \ldots + a_2 \alpha^2 + a_1 \alpha + a_0$$

$$= a_n q(x)^n + a_{n-1} q(x)^{n-1} + \ldots + a_2 q(x)^2 + a_1 \alpha + a_0$$

$$= q(a_n x^n + a_{n-1} x^{n-1} + \ldots + a_2 x^2 + a_1 x + a_0) = q(P(x))$$

since q is a ring homomorphism and since the 'constants' in k are essentially unchanged in mapping to the quotient. Since $P(x) \in I$, the image $q(P(x))$ of it under q is 0. That is, we have proven that $P(\alpha) = 0$.

Finally, we prove that any element of the quotient $k[x]/I$ is uniquely expressible as a polynomial in $\alpha = x + I$, of degree less than the degree of P. Indeed, given $\beta \in k[x]/I$ there is some polynomial J so that $q(J(x)) = \beta$. Using the Division Algorithm for polynomials in one variable over a field, we have

$$J(x) = Q(x) \cdot P(x) + R(x)$$

where $\deg R < \deg P$. Then, under the homomorphism q we have

$$\beta = q(J(x)) = q(Q(x)) \cdot q(P(x)) + q(R(x)) = q(Q(x)) \cdot 0 + R(q(x)) = R(\alpha)$$

since $q(P(x)) = P(\alpha) = 0$, and of course using the ring homomorphism properties. Thus, every element in the quotient is representable as claimed. For uniqueness, suppose that $q(R(x)) = q(S(x))$ for two polynomials R, S of degrees less than the degree of P. Then $R(x) = S(x) \bmod P(x)$, which is to say that $P(x)$ divides $R(x) - S(x)$. Since the degree of $R(x) - S(x)$ is strictly less than that of $P(x)$, this can happen only for $R(x) = S(x)$. This is the desired result.   ///

Corollary: When the field k is finite with q elements, for an irreducible polynomial P of degree n, the field extension $K = k[x]/P(x)$ has q^n elements.

Proof: Let α be the image of x in K. We use the fact that every element of K has a unique expression as $R(\alpha)$ for a polynomial R of degree less than n. There are q choices for each of the n coefficients (for powers of α ranging from 0 to $n-1$), so there are q^n elements altogether.   ///

Remark: A field extension $k[x]/P(x)$ with irreducible polynomial P is called **quadratic** if P is quadratic, **cubic** if P is cubic, **quartic** if P is quartic, **quintic** if P is quintic, etc.

19.6 The Frobenius automorphism

One essential higher-level structural feature of finite fields is the presence of **Frobenius maps**, which play a central technical role. Several basic theorems about finite fields which don't mention the Frobenius maps directly nevertheless make use of the Frobenius maps in their proofs. In this section we will think about finite fields more abstractly and rely less upon specific models of them depending upon choices of irreducible polynomials. In fact this more abstract study will be used to give proofs of the counting assertions about irreducible and primitive polynomials.

In this section we also briefly develop just a few aspects of the idea of *automorphism group* of a larger field over a smaller field, in the context of finite fields. This is a forerunner of *Galois theory*, which is the systematic study of such automorphism groups.

Let $k = \mathbf{F}_q = GF(q)$ be a finite field with q elements, where $q = p^n$ is a power of a prime number p. Fix an integer $N > 1$ and suppose we have a larger finite field $K = \mathbf{F}_{q^N} = GF(q^N)$ containing k. The **Frobenius map** of K **over** k is simply

$$\Phi(\alpha) = \alpha^q$$

This is also sometimes called the **Frobenius automorphism** of K **over** k, for reasons that will be clarified somewhat in what follows. Since K is closed under multiplication, it is clear that Φ maps K to itself.

Remark: Yes, Φ is just the map that takes the qth power of things inside K, where q is the cardinality of the littler field k inside K. And, yes, the way we're writing it the notation does not forcefully tell us what the corresponding K and k are. This implicit reference to K and k is harmless, though, because we won't be doing anything devious with Φ.

Proposition: The Frobenius map Φ of $K = \mathbf{F}_{q^N}$ over $k = \mathbf{F}_q$ is a bijection of K to K. In particular,

$$\Phi^N = \underbrace{\Phi \circ \Phi \circ \ldots \circ \Phi}_{N}$$

is the identity map on K (which maps every element of K to itself).

Proof: Again, since the Frobenius map Φ is just taking q^{th} powers and K is closed under multiplication, Φ maps K to itself. What needs more attention is the injectivity and surjectivity. One way to prove injectivity is to note that the kernel of Φ^N (or of any power of Φ) is $\{0\}$, so Φ^N is injective, by the trivial kernel criterion for injectivity of a ring homomorphism. And for functions from a finite set to itself, injectivity implies surjectivity. Also, some thought should make clear that proving Φ^N is the identity map on K certainly is sufficient to prove that Φ is both injective and surjective.

The multiplicative group $\mathbf{K}^\times$ is of order $q^N - 1$, so by Lagrange's theorem and its corollaries the order of any $\beta \in K^\times$ is a divisor of $q^N - 1$, and

$$\beta^{q^N - 1} = 1$$

Therefore, for nonzero β in K,

$$\Phi(\beta) = \beta^{q^N} = \beta \cdot \beta^{q^N - 1} = \beta \cdot 1 = \beta$$

This proves the proposition.   ///

Proposition: The Frobenius map Φ restricted to k is the identity map. That is, for every α in $k = \mathbf{F}_q$, $\Phi(\alpha) = \alpha$. If $\alpha \in K$ has the property that $\Phi(\alpha) = \alpha$, then in fact $\alpha \in k$.

Proof: Half of the proposition is really just a corollary of Lagrange's theorem. The first point is that the multiplicative group $k^\times$ of nonzero elements in k has $q - 1$ elements. So, by Lagrange's theorem and its corollaries, the *order* of any element α in k is a divisor d of $q - 1$, and, further, $\alpha^{q-1} = 1$ for that reason. Then for nonzero $\alpha \in k$ we have

$$\Phi(\alpha) = \alpha^q = (\alpha)^{q-1} \cdot \alpha = 1 \cdot \alpha = \alpha$$

And certainly $0^q = 0$, so this proves half of the proposition.

Now suppose that $\alpha \in K$ and $\Phi(\alpha) = \alpha$. By the definition of Φ this means that α is a solution of the equation $x^q - x = 0$ lying inside the field K. By unique factorization of polynomials (with coefficients in a field), we know that a polynomial equation of degree q has at most q roots in a field. We already found q roots of this equation, namely the elements of the smaller field k sitting inside K. So there simply can't be any other roots of that equation other than the elements of k. This shows that $\Phi(\alpha) = \alpha$ implies $\alpha \in k$, which is the second half of the proposition. ///

Lemma: Let 1_K be the multiplicative identity in K. Then

$$\underbrace{1_K + \ldots + 1_K}_{p} = 0$$

As a consequence, for any α in K,

$$\underbrace{\alpha + \ldots + \alpha}_{p} = 0$$

Remark: A more systematic development of general *field theory* would make the result of the last lemma much clearer, but would have taken more time altogether than the funny proof given below.

Proof: By Lagrange's theorem and its corollaries, in the group obtained by taking K with its addition (ignoring for the moment its multiplication), the order of any element α is a divisor of the order q^N of the group, and

$$q^N \cdot \alpha = \underbrace{\alpha + \ldots + \alpha}_{q^N} = 0$$

Since $q = p^n$, this is

$$p^{nN} \cdot \alpha = \underbrace{\alpha + \ldots + \alpha}_{p^{nN}} = 0$$

For the moment, use the abbreviation

$$t = \underbrace{1_K + \ldots + 1_K}_{p}$$

Taking $\alpha = 1_K$ in the formula above,

$$0 = \underbrace{1_K + \ldots + 1_K}_{q^N} = t^{nN}$$

Since K is a field, whenever the product of several elements is 0, one of the factors is itself 0. Thus, t is 0, as asserted in the lemma. And then

$$\underbrace{\alpha + \ldots + \alpha}_{p} = \underbrace{1_K \cdot \alpha + \ldots + 1_K \cdot \alpha}_{p} = \underbrace{(1_K + \ldots + 1_K)}_{p} \cdot \alpha = 0 \cdot \alpha = 0$$

This proves the lemma.   ///

Proposition: The Frobenius map Φ of K over k has the property that for any α, β in K

$$\Phi(\alpha + \beta) = \Phi(\alpha) + \Phi(\beta)$$
$$\Phi(\alpha \cdot \beta) = \Phi(\alpha) \cdot \Phi(\beta)$$

That is, Φ preserves addition and multiplication. Since we already saw that Φ is bijective, Φ is said to be a **ring isomorphism**.

Proof: The second assertion, about preserving multiplication, is simply the assertion that the qth power of a product is the product of the qth powers. This is true in great generality as long as the multiplication is commutative, which it is here. This doesn't depend at all on what the particular exponent is.

   The proof that Φ preserves addition makes quite sharp use of the fact that the exponent is q, which is a power of a prime number p. This wouldn't work for other exponents. To start with, we claim that for α, β in K

$$(\alpha + \beta)^p = \alpha^p + \beta^p$$

Expanding by the binomial theorem, the left-hand side is

$$\alpha^p + \binom{p}{1}\alpha^{p-1}b + \binom{p}{2}\alpha^{p-2}b^2 + \ldots + \binom{p}{p-1}\alpha^1 b^{p-1} + \beta^p$$

Here the multiplication of elements of K by positive integers means repeated addition. As observed in the proof of Fermat's Little Theorem, all those binomial coefficients in the middle of the expansion are integers divisible by p, so by the previous lemma all the middle terms of the expansion are 0 in K. Thus, we have proven that

$$(\alpha + \beta)^p = \alpha^p + \beta^p$$

Then, repeatedly invoking this result,

$$(\alpha + \beta)^{p^2} = (\alpha^p + \beta^p)^p = a^{p^2} + b^{p^2}$$

$$(\alpha + \beta)^{p^3} = (\alpha^p + \beta^p)^{p^2} = (a^{p^2} + b^{p^2})^p = \alpha^{p^3} + \beta^{p^3}$$

and so on, so by induction we could prove that

$$(\alpha + \beta)^{p^{nN}} = \alpha^{p^{nN}} + \beta^{p^{nN}}$$

as asserted. That is, the Frobenius map preserves addition.   ///

Proposition: Let $P(x)$ be a polynomial with coefficients in $k = \mathbf{F}_q$. Let $\alpha \in K$ be a root of the equation $P(x) = 0$. Then $\Phi(\alpha) = \alpha^q$, $\Phi^2(\alpha) = \Phi(\Phi(\alpha)) = \alpha^{q^2}$, ... are also roots of the equation.

Proof: Let P have coefficients

$$P(x) = c_n x^n + c_{n-1}x^{n-1} + \ldots + c_2 x^2 + c_1 x + c_0$$

with all the c_i's in k. Apply the Frobenius map to both sides of the equation

$$0 = c_n \alpha^n + c_{n-1}\alpha^{n-1} + \ldots + c_2 \alpha^2 + c_1 \alpha + c_0$$

to obtain

$$\Phi(0) = \Phi(c_n)\Phi(\alpha)^n + \Phi(c_{n-1})\Phi(\alpha)^{n-1} + \ldots + \Phi(c_2)\Phi(\alpha)^2 + \Phi(c_1)\Phi(\alpha) + \Phi(c_0)$$

since Φ preserves addition and multiplication in K, in the sense of the previous proposition. The coefficients c_i are in k, as is the 0 on the left-hand side, so Φ doesn't change them. Thus, in fact we have

$$0 = c_n \Phi(\alpha)^n + c_{n-1}\Phi(\alpha)^{n-1} + \ldots + c_2 \Phi(\alpha)^2 + c_1 \Phi(\alpha) + c_0$$

That is, we have

$$0 = P(\Phi(\alpha))$$

That proves that $\Phi(\alpha)$ is a root of $P(x) = 0$ if α is. By repeating this, we obtain the assertion of the proposition.   ///

Proposition: Let

$$A = \{\alpha_1, \ldots, \alpha_t\}$$

be a set of (t distinct) elements of K, with the property that for any α in A, $\Phi(\alpha)$ is again in A. Then the polynomial

$$(x - \alpha_1)(x - \alpha_2) \ldots (x - \alpha_t)$$

(when multiplied out) has coefficients in k.

Proof: For a polynomial

$$P(x) = c_n x^n + c_{n-1} x^{n-1} + \ldots + c_2 x^2 + c_1 x + c_0$$

with coefficients in the larger field K, define a new polynomial $\Phi(P)$ by letting Φ just act on the coefficients:

$$\Phi(P)(x) = \Phi(c_n)x^n + \Phi(c_{n-1})x^{n-1} + \ldots + \Phi(c_2)x^2 + \Phi(c_1)x + \Phi(c_0)$$

Since Φ preserves addition and multiplication in K, it is not hard to check that it also preserves addition and multiplication of polynomials with coefficients in K, in the sense that for two such polynomials P and Q

$$\begin{aligned} \Phi(P + Q) &= \Phi(P) + \Phi(Q) \\ \Phi(P \cdot Q) &= \Phi(P) \cdot \Phi(Q) \end{aligned}$$

Then applying Φ to the product

$$(x - \alpha_1)(x - \alpha_2) \ldots (x - \alpha_t)$$

will merely mix around the factors, by the hypothesis that Φ just permutes the elements of the set A. The order in which the factors are multiplied certainly doesn't matter here, so we have

$$\Phi((x - \alpha_1)(x - \alpha_2) \ldots (x - \alpha_t)) = (x - \alpha_1)(x - \alpha_2) \ldots (x - \alpha_t)$$

That means that the multiplied-out version

$$(x - \alpha_1)(x - \alpha_2) \ldots (x - \alpha_t) = c_n x^n + c_{n-1} x^{n-1} + \ldots + c_2 x^2 + c_1 x + c_0$$

has the property that

$$c_n x^n + c_{n-1} x^{n-1} + \ldots + c_2 x^2 + c_1 x + c_0$$

$$= \Phi(c_n)x^n + \Phi(c_{n-1})x^{n-1} + \ldots + \Phi(c_2)x^2 + \Phi(c_1)x + \Phi(c_0)$$

The meaning of 'equality' for polynomials is that the corresponding coefficients are equal, so the previous inequality implies that $\Phi(c_i) = c_i$ for all indices i. By now we know that this implies that $c_i \in k$, for all indices i.   ///

Proposition: Let α be an element of $K = k[x]/Q$. There is exactly one monic irreducible polynomial P in $k[x]$ so that α is a root of $P(x) = 0$, namely

$$P(x) = (x - \alpha)(x - \Phi(\alpha))(x - \Phi^2(\alpha)) \ldots (x - \Phi^{d-1}(\alpha))$$

where d is the smallest positive integer so that $\Phi^d(\alpha) = \alpha$.

Proof: Consider the successive images $\Phi^i(\alpha)$ of α under the Frobenius map. Since the field is finite, at some point $\Phi^i(\alpha) = \Phi^j(\alpha)$ for some $0 \le i < j$. Since Φ is a bijection of K to K, it has an inverse map Φ^{-1}. Applying this inverse i times to the equation $\Phi^i(\alpha) = \Phi^j(\alpha)$, we find

$$\alpha = \Phi^0(\alpha) = \Phi^{j-i}(\alpha)$$

That is, in fact $i = 0$. That means that for the smallest j so that $\Phi^j(\alpha)$ is already $\Phi^j(\alpha) = \Phi^i(\alpha)$ for $1 \le i < j$, in fact this duplication occurs as

$$\Phi^j(\alpha) = \alpha$$

rather than duplicating some *other* element farther along on the list. Let

$$\alpha, \ \Phi(\alpha), \ \ldots, \ \Phi^{d-1}(\alpha)$$

be the distinct images of α under the Frobenius map. We just saw that $\Phi^d(\alpha) = \alpha$. Let
$$P(x) = (x - \alpha)(x - \Phi(\alpha))(x - \Phi^2(\alpha)) \ldots (x - \Phi^{d-1}(\alpha))$$

As just above, application of Φ to P only permutes the factors on the right-hand side, by shifting indices forward by one, and wrapping around at the end since $\Phi^d(\alpha) = \alpha$. Thus, when multiplied out, the polynomial P is unchanged by application of Φ, so has coefficients in the smaller field k. We saw this phenomenon already in the discussion of the Frobenius map. And visibly α is a root of the equation $\mathbf{P}(x) = 0$.

From just above, if β is a root in K of a polynomial equation with coefficients in the smaller field k, then $\Phi(\beta)$ is also a root. So *any* polynomial with coefficients in k of which α is a zero must have factors $x - \Phi^i(\alpha)$ as well, for $1 \le i < d$. By unique factorization of polynomials with coefficients in a field, this shows that this is the *unique* such polynomial.

In particular, P must be irreducible in $k[x]$, because if it properly factored in $k[x]$ as $P = P_1 P_2$ then (by unique factorization) α would be a root of either $P_1(x) = 0$ or $P_2(x) = 0$, and then all the d distinct elements $\Phi^i(\alpha)$ would be roots of the same equation as well. Since the number of roots is at most the degree, there cannot be any proper factorization, so P is irreducible in $k[x]$.   ///

Corollary: Let β be the image of x in $K = \mathbf{F}_q[x]/Q$, and let n be the degree of Q. Then

$$Q(x) = (x - \beta)(x - \Phi(\beta))(x - \Phi^2(\beta))\ldots(x - \Phi^{n-1}(\beta))$$

We have $\Phi^n(\beta) = \beta$, and n is the smallest positive integer so that this is so.

Proof: This is a special case of the proposition.   ///

We need to develop one further abstraction. Let e denote the identity map of $K = \mathbf{F}_q[x]/Q$ to itself, and let

$$G = \{e, \Phi, \Phi^2, \ldots, \Phi^{n-1}\}$$

where Q is of degree n. This is a set of maps of K to itself. As noted above, each one of these maps when restricted to $\mathbf{F}_q$ is the identity map on $\mathbf{F}_q$. Since each Φ^i is the identity on $\mathbf{F}_q$ and maps K bijectively to itself, we say that G is a set of **automorphisms** of K over $\mathbf{F}_q$.

Proposition: This set G of automorphisms of K over $\mathbf{F}_q$ is a *group*, with identity e.

Proof: Let β be the image of x in K. We first check that $\Phi^n(\alpha) = \alpha$ for any α in K. We know that we can express α as a polynomial in β with coefficients in $\mathbf{F}_q$, say $\alpha = R(\beta)$. Then because Φ preserves addition and multiplication, and because $\Phi^n(\beta) = \beta$ by the previous corollary,

$$\Phi^n(\alpha) = \Phi^n(R(\beta)) = R(\Phi^n(\beta)) = R(\beta) = \alpha$$

Since $\Phi^n = e$, for any integer ℓ

$$\Phi^\ell = \Phi^{\ell \% n}$$

as a function from K to itself, where as usual $\% n$ means reduction modulo n. Therefore, the set G is closed under multiplication (meaning composition of functions):

$$\Phi^i \circ \Phi^j = \Phi^{(i+j)\% n}$$

Further, this shows that G is closed under inverses:

$$(\Phi^i)^{-1} = \Phi^{n-i}$$

The associativity follows as a consequence of the associativity of composition of functions from a set to itself. That the identity element of the group is the identity *map e* is clear.   ///

Keeping in mind that G acts on K, for α in K, the **stabilizer subgroup** G_α of α in G is defined to be

$$G_\alpha = \{g \in G : g(\alpha) = \alpha\}$$

Of course, we should verify that this really is a subgroup of G:

Proposition: For α in K the stabilizer subgroup G_α of α is a subgroup of G.

Proof: Certainly G_α contains the identity map e. Suppose that $g \in G$ so that $g(\alpha) = \alpha$. Applying the function g^{-1} to this equality gives

$$\alpha = g^{-1}(g(\alpha)) = g^{-1}(\alpha)$$

so G_α is closed under inverses. If g and h are both in G_α, then

$$g(h(\alpha)) = g(\alpha) = \alpha$$

which proves closure under multiplication. Thus, G_α really is a group.   ///

Proposition: Given α in $K = \mathbf{F}_q[x]/Q$, the number of distinct images $\Phi^i(\alpha)$ of α under repeated applications of the Frobenius map is a divisor of the degree n of Q.

Proof: What we should really claim here is that the collection of distinct images $\Phi^i(\alpha)$ is naturally in bijection with the collection of cosets G/G_α where G_α is the stabilizer subgroup of α in the automorphism G. Indeed, if $g \in G$ and $h \in G_\alpha$, then

$$(gh)(\alpha) = g(h(\alpha)) = g(\alpha)$$

This proves that $gG_\alpha \to g(\alpha)$ is well-defined. And if $g(\alpha) = g'(\alpha)$, then $\alpha = g^{-1}g'(\alpha)$, so $g^{-1}g'$ is in the stabilizer subgroup G_α. This proves that no two distinct cosets gG_α and $g'G_\alpha$ of G_α send α to the same thing.   ///

Corollary: For α in the field $K = k[x]/Q$, the degree of the unique monic irreducible polynomial P with coefficients in k so that $P(\alpha) = 0$ is a divisor of the degree n of Q.

Proof: From above,

$$P(x) = (x - \alpha)(x - \Phi(\alpha))(x - \Phi^2(\alpha))\ldots(x - \Phi^{d-1}(\alpha))$$

where α, $\Phi(\alpha)$, $\Phi^2(\alpha)$, ..., $\Phi^{d-1}(\alpha)$ are the distinct images of α and d is then the degree of P. As was shown in the course of the proof of Lagrange's theorem and its corollaries, all cosets of G_α have the same cardinality. By this and by the previous proposition,

$$\operatorname{card}(G) = d \cdot \operatorname{card}(G_\alpha)$$

Likewise, in the special case of the image β of x in K, the stabilizer subgroup is just $\{e\}$, so

$$\operatorname{card}(G) = n \cdot 1$$

so $\operatorname{card}(G) = n$. This proves that d is a divisor of n.   ///

Remark: In the discussion of this section we did *not* make any assumptions about the uniqueness of 'the' finite fields $\mathbf{F}_q$ and $\mathbf{F}_{q^N}$. Rather, we just used this notation as an occasional reminder of the number of elements in the finite fields k and K.

19.7 Counting irreducibles

Knowing that finite fields have primitive roots enables us to *count* the number of irreducible polynomials of a given degree. We make essential use of facts we've developed about Frobenius maps. Along the way, it is inevitable that we develop more structural properties of finite fields, and these are of interest in their own right.

An integer is usually said to be **square-free** if it is not divisible by the square of any prime number. Recall that the Möbius function μ is defined on positive integers by

$$\mu(n) = \begin{cases} (-1)^t & \text{if } n \text{ is square-free, divisible by exactly } t \text{ primes} \\ 1 & \text{if } n = 1 \\ 0 & \text{if } n \text{ is divisible by the square of some prime} \end{cases}$$

Theorem: The number of irreducible monic polynomials in $\mathbf{F}_q[x]$ of degree n is

$$\frac{1}{n} \sum_{1 \le d \le n,\ d|n} \mu(d)\, q^{n/d}$$

That is, this number is

$$\frac{1}{n} \cdot \left(q^n - \sum_{p_1|n} q^{n/p_1} + \sum_{p_1,p_2|n} q^{n/p_1 p_2} - \sum_{p_1,p_2,p_3|n} q^{n/p_1 p_2 p_3} + \cdots \right)$$

where the sums are over collections of *distinct* prime divisors of n.

We can specialize this formula to some interesting and more memorable special cases:

Corollary: If $n = p_1$ is prime, then there are

$$\frac{q^n - q}{n}$$

irreducible monic polynomials of degree n in $\mathbf{F}_q[x]$.   ///

Corollary: If $n = p_1 p_2$ is a product of two distinct primes p_1 and p_2, then there are

$$\frac{q^{p_1 p_2} - q^{p_1} - q^{p_2}}{p_1 p_2}$$

irreducible monic polynomials of degree $n = p_1 p_2$ in $\mathbf{F}_q[x]$.   ///

Corollary: If $n = p_1^e$ is a power of a prime p_1, then there are

$$\frac{q^{p_1^e} - q^{p_1^{e-1}}}{n}$$

irreducible monic polynomials of degree $n = p_1^e$ in $\mathbf{F}_q[x]$.   ///

Let Q be a fixed irreducible monic polynomial of degree n in $\mathbf{F}_q[x]$. We know that $K = \mathbf{F}_q[x]/Q$ is a field with q^n elements. Let

$$\Phi(\gamma) = \gamma^q$$

be the Frobenius automorphism of K over $k = \mathbf{F}_q$. From the discussion of the Frobenius automorphism above, we know that for any α in K there is a unique monic irreducible polynomial P with coefficients in $k = \mathbf{F}_q$ so that $P(\alpha) = 0$, and in fact

$$P(x) = (x - \alpha)(x - \Phi(\alpha))(x - \Phi^2(\alpha))\ldots(x - \Phi^{d-1}(\alpha))$$

where d is the number of distinct images of α under repeated applications of the Frobenius automorphism Φ of K over $k = \mathbf{F}_q$. We have a converse:

Proposition: Let P be an irreducible monic polynomial of degree d with d dividing the degree n of irreducible Q. Then $P(x) = 0$ has d distinct roots in $K = k[x]/Q$, so $P(x)$ factors into distinct linear factors in K.

Proof: The quotient ring $L = k[x]/P$ is a field. Let α be the image of x there. We know that $P(\alpha) = 0$, and from discussion of the Frobenius map we know that

$$P(x) = (x - \alpha)(x - \Phi(\alpha))(x - \Phi^2(\alpha))\ldots(x - \Phi^{d-1}(\alpha))$$

By Lagrange's theorem and its corollaries, we know that $\alpha^{q^d-1} = 1$, since the order of $L^\times$ is $q^d - 1$. By unique factorization of polynomials with coefficients in a field, this implies that $P(x)$ divides $x^{q^d-1} - 1$ as polynomials with coefficients in $k = \mathbf{F}_q$.

On the other hand, the existence of a primitive root g in K means exactly that $g^{q^n-1} = 1$ but no smaller positive exponent makes this true. And, thus, the elements $g^1, g^2, g^3, \ldots, g^{q^n-1}$ are all distinct (and nonzero). For any integer t

$$(g^t)^{q^n-1} = (g^{q^n-1})^t = 1^t = 1$$

so these $q^n - 1$ elements are all roots of $x^{q^n-1} - 1 = 0$. On the other hand, this equation is of degree $q^n - 1$, so has at most $q^n - 1$ roots. We conclude that

$$x^{q^n-1} - 1 = (x - g^1)(x - g^2)(x - g^3)\ldots(x - g^{q^n-1})$$

in $K[x]$, that is, allowing coefficients in the larger field K.

For d dividing n, we have a basic algebra identity

$$q^n - 1 = (q^d - 1)(q^{(n-d)} + q^{(n-2d)} + q^{(n-3d)} + \ldots + q^d + 1)$$

Thus, $q^d - 1$ divides $q^n - 1$, and by the same basic identity $x^{q^d-1} - 1$ divides $x^{q^n-1} - 1$. As $P(x)$ divides $x^{q^d-1} - 1$, $P(x)$ divides $x^{q^n-1} - 1$. Thus, $P(x) = 0$ has d roots in K, since $x^{q^n-1} - 1$ factors into *linear* factors in $K[x]$.   ///

Proof: (of theorem) At last we can count the elements of K by grouping them in d-tuples of roots of elements of irreducible monic polynomials with coefficients in

$k = \mathbf{F}_q$, where d runs over positive divisors of n including 1 and n. Let N_d be the number of irreducible monic polynomials of degree d with coefficients in $k = \mathbf{F}_q$. Then this grouping and counting argument gives

$$q^n = \sum_{d|n} d \cdot N_d$$

By *Möbius inversion* we obtain the formula

$$n \cdot N_n = \sum_{d|n} \mu(d)\, q^{n/d}$$

which gives the assertion of the theorem.   ///

19.8 Counting primitives

Our more refined discussion of finite fields just above also allows us to prove the counting formula for primitive polynomials, as a corollary of the characterization of primitive polynomials as irreducible factors of cyclotomic polynomials.

Fix a power q of a prime number, and let $k = \mathbf{F}_q$ be a finite field with q elements. Recall that a polynomial Q with coefficients in k of degree n is *primitive* if

$$x^{q^n - 1} = 1 \bmod Q(x)$$

and no smaller positive integer will do in place of this n. For brevity, let

$$N = q^n - 1$$

Theorem: A primitive polynomial Q of degree n in $\mathbf{F}_q[x]$ is an irreducible factor of the $(q^n - 1)^{\text{th}}$ cyclotomic polynomial. Conversely, every irreducible factor of the $(q^n - 1)^{\text{th}}$ cyclotomic polynomial is of degree n, and is primitive.

Let φ be Euler's phi-function. Recall that the degree of the Nth cyclotomic polynomial φ_N is $\varphi(N)$. Again, the counting corollary of the latter theorem is

Corollary: There are $\varphi(q^n - 1)/n$ primitive polynomials of degree n in the polynomial ring $\mathbf{F}_q[x]$.

Proof: By the theorem, every such primitive polynomial is an irreducible factor of the cyclotomic polynomial φ_N, where $N = q^n - 1$. And every irreducible factor of φ_N is primitive of degree n. Because $q^n - 1$ is relatively prime to the *characteristic* p of the fields in question, φ_N has no repeated factors, so no irreducible factor appears more than once. Since the degree of a product is the sum of the degrees, we have

$$\text{degree } \varphi_N = (\text{number of primitives of degree } n) \cdot n$$

from which we obtain the formula of the corollary.   ///

Proof: Without loss of generality, we only consider the case $n > 1$, since the linear case can be treated separately and easily. In particular, this excludes the case that an irreducible polynomial is divisible by x.

On one hand, suppose that Q divides the $(q^n - 1)^{\text{th}}$ cyclotomic polynomial φ_N and the degree of Q is n. Since φ_N divides $x^{q^n-1} - 1$, certainly

$$x^{q^n-1} = 1 \bmod Q(x)$$

If any smaller positive integer t were to have the property that

$$x^t = 1 \bmod Q(x)$$

then $Q(x)$ would divide $x^t - 1$. But from the discussion of cyclotomic polynomials, since p and $q^n - 1$ are relatively prime, φ_N and $x^t - 1$ have no common factor for $t < q^n - 1$. Thus, we see that the smallest power of x which is 1 modulo $Q(x)$ is $q^n - 1$, so Q is primitive of degree n.

On the other hand, suppose that Q is primitive of degree n. The condition

$$x^{q^n-1} = 1 \bmod Q(x)$$

is by definition equivalent to asserting that $Q(x)$ is a divisor of $x^{q^n-1} - 1$. Likewise, the condition that no smaller power of x is 1 modulo Q asserts that $Q(x)$ does *not* divide $x^N - 1$ for any smaller N. From the discussion of cyclotomic polynomials, using unique factorization, if we remove from $x^{q^n-1} - 1$ any factors that it has in common with $x^N - 1$ for $N < q^n - 1$, then what remains is the cyclotomic polynomial φ_N. Thus, primitive Q of degree n divides the $(q^n - 1)^{\text{th}}$ cyclotomic polynomial φ_N.

Now we will prove that all the irreducible factors of φ_N have degree n. Let Q be any irreducible factor of φ_N. Then $L = \mathbf{F}_q[x]/Q$ is a field, and the image α of x is of order $N = q^n - 1$ in the multiplicative group $L^\times$, by construction of the cyclotomic polynomial φ_N. Therefore, if d is the degree of Q, by Lagrange's theorem and its corollaries,

$$q^n - 1 \ \text{ divides } \ q^d - 1$$

In particular, $d \geq n$. That is, on one hand, any irreducible factor of φ_N has degree at least n. On the other hand, let Φ be the Frobenius map

$$\Phi(\beta) = \beta^q$$

of L over $\mathbf{F}_q$. The statement

$$x^{q^n-1} = 1 \bmod Q$$

is

$$\alpha^{q^n-1} = 1$$

which is equivalent to

$$\alpha^{q^n} = \alpha$$

which is
$$\Phi^n(\alpha) = \alpha$$

From the discussion of the Frobenius automorphism, this implies that the unique monic irreducible polynomial $f(x)$ in $\mathbf{F}_q[x]$ so that $f(\alpha) = 0$ is of degree at most n. At the same time, in the construction of finite fields we saw that $Q(\alpha) = 0$ as well. As a corollary of the discussion of the Frobenius automorphism, there is exactly *one* monic irreducible polynomial f so that $f(\alpha) = 0$, so $Q = f$. Since f has degree at most n, the degree of Q is at most n. Thus, all the irreducible factors of φ_N are of degree n, where $N = q^n - 1$.

Finally, we observe that primitive polynomials are necessarily irreducible. Indeed, a primitive polynomial Q of degree n in $\mathbf{F}_q[x]$ divides the cyclotomic polynomial φ_N with $N = q^n - 1$. Just above we proved that all the irreducible factors of φ_N are of degree n, so by unique factorization Q has no alternative but to be irreducible.   ///

Exercises

19.01 Let N be an integer. Prove carefully that $N \cdot \mathbf{Z}$ is an *ideal* in $\mathbf{Z}$.

19.02 Fix an integer $N > 1$. Prove carefully that the map $f : \mathbf{Z} \to \mathbf{Z}/N\mathbf{Z}$ given by $f(x) = x + N\mathbf{Z}$ is a ring homomorphism.

19.03 Show that $x^2 - y^2 = 102$ has no solution in integers. (*ans.*)

19.04 Show that $x^3 + y^3 = 3$ has no solution in integers.   (*ans.*)

19.05 Show that $x^3 + y^3 + z^3 = 4$ has no solution in integers. (*ans.*)

19.06 Show that $x^2 + 3y^2 + 6z^3 - 9w^5 = 2$ has no solution in integers.

19.07 Let I, J be two ideals in a ring R. Show that $I \cap J$ is also an ideal in R.

19.08 Let I, J be two ideals in a ring R. Let
$$I + J = \{i + j : i \in I \quad \text{and} \quad j \in J\}$$
Show that $I + J$ is an ideal.

19.09 Let $f : R \to S$ be a *surjective* ring homomorphism (with R, S commutative, for simplicity). Let I be an ideal in R. Show that $J = \{f(i) : i \in I\}$ is an ideal in S.

19.10 Let $f : R \to S$ be a ring homomorphism (with R, S commutative, for simplicity). Let J be an ideal in I. Show that $I = \{i \in I : f(i) \in J\}$ is an ideal in S.

19.11 Show that there is no element $x \in \mathbf{F}_{13}$ so that $x^4 + x^3 + x^2 + x + 1 = 0$. (*ans.*)

19.12 Show that there is no solution to $x^2 + 1$ in $\mathbf{F}_{11}$.

19.13 Consider the polynomial ring $\mathbf{Z}[x]$ in one variable over the ring of integers. Show that the ideal
$$I = \mathbf{Z}[x] \cdot 2 + \mathbf{Z}[x] \cdot x$$

generated by 2 and x is not *principal*, that is, that there is no single polynomial $f(x)$ such that I consists of all polynomial multiples of $f(x)$.   (*ans.*)

19.14 Let k be a field. Show that in the polynomial ring $k[x,y]$ in two variables
the ideal $I = k[x,y] \cdot x + k[x,y] \cdot y$ is not principal.

19.15 (*) Show that the maximal ideals in $R = \mathbf{Z}[x]$ are all of the form $I = R \cdot p + R \cdot f(x)$ where p is a prime and $f(x)$ is a monic polynomial which is
irreducible modulo p.

20

Curves and Codes

The material of this chapter is significantly more difficult than earlier ones, and we are very far from giving a complete treatment. Indeed, the theory of algebraic curves over fields of positive characteristic was only developed within the last 60 years or so, and is not elementary. An introductory treatment of the applications to coding theory, at a similar level, is to be found in [Walker 2000].

The discovery described in [Tsfasman Vladut Zink 1982] of codes exceeding the Gilbert-Varshamov bound was sensational not only because these codes were so good, but also because their construction used such esoteric mathematics.

We cannot pretend to do justice to the theory of algebraic curves or to the additional mathematics necessary to fully explain these codes, but can only give an approximate idea of the more accessible aspects of these ideas.

20.1 Plane curves

We have the idea from analytic geometry that the graph of a single equation describes a 'curve' in the plane. This idea can be pushed a little bit to have the benefit of 'geometric intuition' in the analysis of solutions of polynomial equations over *finite fields* rather than solutions in **R** or **C**.

Let k be a field (such as **R**, **C**, $\mathbf{F}_q$) and let $k[x, y]$ denote the polynomial ring in two variables with coefficients in k. For a polynomial $f(x, y)$ other than the 0 polynomial, the (**algebraic**) **curve** X_f attached to f **defined over** k is

$$X_f = \{(x, y) \in \mathbf{F}_q : f(x, y) = 0\}$$

We may add the modifier 'algebraic' to the word 'curve' to emphasize that we use only algebra to define this set of points, rather than transcendental functions such as e^x, which might not work right over finite fields anyway. The field k is sometimes called the **field of definition** of the curve.

Remark: Often we say 'the curve $f(x,y) = 0$' rather than the more proper 'the curve *defined by* $f(x,y) = 0$'. But do not be deceived: an equation is not a curve.

Actually, what we have defined here is the set of k-**rational points** on a curve. For example, taking k to be the real numbers **R** the curve $x^2 + y^2 = -1$ has no (real-valued) points on it at all, since the square of a real number is non-negative. Yet taking k to be the *complex* numbers **C** it has infinitely many.

Remark: Unlike the family of examples $y = f(x)$, in general it is a highly non-trivial problem to figure out what rational points lie on a curve, or even whether there are any at all.

Example: Consider the curve X defined over the rational numbers **Q** by $x^2 + y^2 = 1$. This is the set of points on the usual unit circle in the plane $\mathbf{R}^2$ which happen to have rational coordinates (here 'rational' means in **Q**). We can systematically find *all* the rational points on this curve, as follows. First, there is at least one 'easy' point to notice on the curve: $(1,0)$ is such. Second, and this is considerably more subtle, it turns out that if we consider any (straight) line $y = -t \cdot (x - 1)$ passing through the point $(1,0)$ with *rational* slope $-t$, then the *other* point in which this line intersects the circle is *also* rational. (The converse is easier: for any other *rational* point on the curve, the straight line connecting it to $(1,0)$ will have rational slope.) Let's verify the claim that the second point of intersection is rational: we want to solve the system of equations

$$\begin{cases} x^2 + y^2 &= 1 \\ y &= -t(x-1) \end{cases}$$

where t is viewed as a fixed parameter. The situation suggests that we replace y by $t(x-1)$ in the first equation, to obtain

$$x^2 + t^2(x-1)^2 = 1$$

This might look unpromising, but we know in advance that this quadratic equation in x has *one* root $x = 1$. Recall that the *discriminant* Δ of a quadratic equation $ax^2 + bx + c = 0$ is defined to be

$$\Delta = \sqrt{b^2 - 4ac}$$

and the quadratic formula (obtained really by simply *completing the square*) gives a formula for the roots of the quadratic equation $ax^2 + bx + c = 0$: the roots are

$$\text{roots} = \frac{-b \pm \sqrt{b^2 - 4ac}}{2a}$$

Since the parameter t is rational, the *discriminant* of the quadratic equation is rational. Thus, the *other* root must also be rational, however unclear this is from the equation itself. This should give us sufficient courage to go ahead with the computation. Rearrange the equation to the standard form

$$(1+t^2)x^2 - 2t^2 x + (t^2 - 1) = 0$$

Then, invoking the quadratic formula,

$$\{\text{roots of } x^2 + t^2(x-1)^2 = 1 \} = \frac{2t^2 \pm \sqrt{(2t^2)^2 - 4(1+t^2)(t^2-1)}}{2(1+t^2)}$$

$$= \frac{t^2 \pm \sqrt{t^4 + (1+t^2)(1-t^2)}}{1+t^2}$$

$$= \frac{t^2 \pm \sqrt{t^4 + 1 - t^4}}{1+t^2} = \frac{t^2 \pm 1}{t^2 + 1} = \left\{ \frac{t^2+1}{t^2+1}, \frac{t^2-1}{t^2+1} \right\} = \left\{ 1, \frac{t^2-1}{t^2+1} \right\}$$

That is, the *other* solution is

$$x = \frac{t^2 - 1}{t^2 + 1}$$

Then the corresponding y value is

$$y = t(x-1) = t \left(\frac{t^2-1}{t^2+1} - 1 \right) = \frac{2t}{t^2+1}$$

Thus, every rational point on the curve is of the form

$$(x, y) = \left(\frac{t^2-1}{t^2+1}, \frac{2t}{t^2+1} \right)$$

This formula has been known for about 2500 years.

Remark: Another way to think about the previous example is that the sum of the roots of a *monic* quadratic equation $x^2 + ax + b = 0$ is $-a$. Thus, rearranging the equation $x^2 + t^2(x-1)^2 = 1$ to a monic version

$$x^2 + \frac{-2t^2}{t^2+1} + \frac{t^2-1}{t^2+1} = 0$$

shows that the sum of the two roots is $2t^2/(t^2+1)$. We know that one of the two roots is 1, so the other root is

$$\frac{2t^2}{t^2+1} - 1 = \frac{t^2-1}{t^2+1}$$

Remark: In the last example we used the fact that a quadratic equation has (at most) two roots, and that if the coefficients of the equation are rational, and if one root is rational, then so is the other root. More generally, as a consequence of *unique factorization* of polynomials with coefficients in a field, we have:

Proposition: Let $f(x)$ be a polynomial of degree n with coefficients in a field k. If the equation $f(x) = 0$ has $n - 1$ distinct roots $\alpha_1, \ldots, \alpha_{n-1}$ in k, then it has a further root α_n in k.

Proof: We have earlier observed that α is a root of the equation $f(x) = 0$ if and only if the linear polynomial $x - \alpha$ *divides* the polynomial $f(x)$. From this, and from unique factorization, we conclude that each $x - \alpha_1$, $x - \alpha_2$, $\ldots$, $x - \alpha_{n-1}$ divides $f(x)$, and so does the product

$$(x - \alpha_1)(x - \alpha_2) \ldots (x - \alpha_{n-1})$$

We also know by now that the degree of $f(x)$ divided by this product will be the difference of their degrees, hence just 1. That is, this division will leave a *linear* factor $c(x - \alpha_n)$ (with $c \neq 0$). Since the computation takes place inside $k[x]$, the coefficients c and $c\alpha$ are in k. Thus, α is necessarily in k, since c is non-zero. This α_n is the last root of the equation.   ///

Example: Consider the equation $y^2 = 1 - x^3$ defined over **Q**. By design, this has two rational points that are easy to observe by trial and error: $(1, 0)$ and $(0, 1)$. The straight line passing through two points (x_1, y_1) and (x_2, y_2) is easily parametrized as

$$(x, y) = (tx_1 + (1 - t)x_2,\ ty_1 + (1 - t)y_2)$$

In the present simple case the line through $(1, 0)$ and $(0, 1)$ is just

$$(x, y) = (t, 1 - t)$$

We already know that this line meets the cubic curve in the two given (rational!) points. Let's find a third point: replacing x by t and y by $1 - t$, from the parametrization, will give a cubic equation in t, with coefficients in **Q**, for which we already know 2 roots in **Q**. By the proposition, we anticipate that there will be a third rational root. Doing the computation, we have

$$(1 - t)^2 = 1 - t^3$$

Both sides have a factor of $t - 1$, corresponding to the point $(1, 0)$. Removing this factor and simplifying gives

$$t(t + 2) = 0$$

The solution $t = 0$ corresponds to the other previously known point $(0, 1)$. The *new* point is at $t = -2$, which gives $(-2, 3)$.

Already in the case of **Q** plane curves $f(x, y) = 0$ have many points that are not rational. For example, $y^2 = 3x^2 + 1$ does have some points with coordinates in **Q**, such as $(0, 1)$, $(0, -1)$, and in general

$$(x, y) = \left(\frac{-2t}{t^2 - 3}, \frac{-t^2 - 3}{t^2 - 3} \right)$$

by the method above. But it also has many more points in $\mathbf{R}^2$ that are *not* rational, such as $(2, \sqrt{13})$. Indeed, for *any* real value of x since $3x^2 + 1$ is positive there will be two real square roots y of that expression, although only occasionally will these square roots be *rational*.

This phenomenon is even more pronounced over finite fields $\mathbf{F}_q$. For example, over $\mathbf{F}_5 = \mathbf{Z}/5$ the equation

$$y^2 = x^5 - x + 2$$

has no rational points at all: by Fermat's little theorem $x^5 - x = 0$ for every x in $\mathbf{F}_5$, so for x, y in $\mathbf{F}_5$ the equation is equivalent to $y^2 = 2$. But 2 is not a square in $\mathbf{Z}/5$, so there is no such y in $\mathbf{F}_5$. Thus, the set of *rational points* of this 'curve' is the *empty set*. This might correctly seem to be missing some information, and it is indeed so. We should consider the *family* of all finite fields $\mathbf{F}_{5^n}$ containing the little field $\mathbf{F}_5$ in this case, and ask about points (x, y) with x, y in $\mathbf{F}_{5^n}$ satisfying $y^2 = x^5 - x + 2$ as n gets larger and larger.

We can give a preliminary imprecise definition: an **algebraic closure** of $\mathbf{F}_q$ is 'the union' of all the extension fields $\mathbf{F}_{q^n}$ of it.

Thus, without worrying about how to organize that definition properly and make it precise, we should anticipate that we might care about points on a curve (defined over $\mathbf{F}_q$) *with coordinates in the algebraic closure* of $\mathbf{F}_q$.

Remark: We should also be sure that up to inessential differences there is only *one* finite field $\mathbf{F}_{p^n}$ with p^n elements for p prime. There is more to be said here!

20.2   Singularities of curves

The notion of whether a curve has sharp corners or self-intersections makes sense intuitively when we do analytic geometry in $\mathbf{R}^2$, but has less obvious meaning if the 'curves' in question are defined over a finite field $\mathbf{F}_q$ so that pictures don't really apply literally.

Example: The equation $y^2 = x^2$ defines two crossing lines in the plane. Away from the point $(0, 0)$, if we look at a piece of this 'curve', since we only see one of the two lines what we see really does look like a smooth curve. However, if we look at $(0, 0)$ and nearby it, we see the crossed lines, and might consider the crossing point 'bad'.

Example: The curve $y^2 = x^3 + x^2$ is much more complicated than the previous example of two crossed lines but, nevertheless, near $(0, 0)$ it looks roughly like two crossed lines. A *heuristic* to understand this is that for very small real values of x the x^3 is much smaller than the x^2 term, so is 'negligible', and we're back in the previous case $y^2 = x^2$. But we'd want a computationally effective procedure that doesn't require visualizing things.

For a polynomial $f(x, y)$ in two variables with coefficients in a field k, let

$$f_x(x, y) = f_1(x, y) = \frac{\partial f}{\partial x}(x, y)$$

$$f_y(x, y) = f_2(x, y) = \frac{\partial f}{\partial y}(x, y)$$

be the partial derivatives with respect to the first and second inputs, respectively.

Remark: Most often the first input will be x, and likewise most often the second input will be y, but it is slightly dangerous to rely upon this, and even to use the notation f_x which presumes this. The notation f_i for the partial derivative with respect to the ith input is more reliable.

While derivative-taking as a *limit* is familiar in case the underlying field k is $\mathbf{R}$ or $\mathbf{C}$, we *cannot possibly* define derivatives in such manner when the underlying field is a finite field $\mathbf{F}_q$. Rather, as done in the one-variable case earlier to look at the issue of multiple factors, the *formulas* that we *prove* in the familiar case will be taken as the *definition* in the abstract case. That is, *bring the exponent down into the coefficient and subtract one from the exponent:*

$$\frac{\partial}{\partial x}\left(\sum_{i,j} c_{ij}\, x^i\, y^j\right) = \sum_{i,j} i \cdot c_{ij}\, x^{i-1}\, y^j$$

$$\frac{\partial}{\partial y}\left(\sum_{i,j} c_{ij}\, x^i\, y^j\right) = \sum_{i,j} j \cdot c_{ij}\, x^i\, y^{j-1}$$

Unfortunately, it requires proof to know that this direct algebraic definition really does have the other properties to which we're accustomed. *It does!*

A plane curve defined by a single equation $f(x, y) = 0$ is **non-singular** at a point (x_0, y_0) on the curve if and only if (in addition to the condition $f(x_0, y_0) = 0$) we have

$$f_x(x_0, y_0) \neq 0 \quad \text{or} \quad f_y(x_0, y_0) \neq 0$$

If *both* of these partial derivatives vanish, then the point (x_0, y_0) is a **singular point** of the curve. That is, the point (x_0, y_0) is a non-singular point of the curve if and only if the **gradient**

$$\nabla f(x_o, y_o) = \left(\frac{\partial f(x_o, y_o)}{\partial x}, \frac{\partial f(x_o, y_o)}{\partial y}, \right)$$

evaluated at (x_o, y_o) is *not* the zero vector.

Remark: These conditions on partial derivatives should remind an astute observer of the implicit function theorem.

Over the rational numbers $\mathbf{Q}$, the real numbers $\mathbf{R}$, and even more so in the case of finite fields $\mathbf{F}_q$, there may be singular points which are not rational over the field of definition. An example is

$$y^2 = (x^2 - 3)^2$$

which has a singular point at $(\sqrt{3}, 0)$.

A plane curve defined over $\mathbf{F}_q$ is **non-singular** if it has no singular points over *any* extension field $\mathbf{F}_{q^n}$. That is, it is non-singular if it has no singular points over an *algebraic closure* of $\mathbf{F}_q$.

Example: Consider $f(x, y) = x^2 + y^2 - 1$. Since over the real numbers the equation $f(x, y) = 0$ defines a circle, which is plausibly non-singular, we hope that this curve is non-singular. We can practice the partial derivative criterion to verify this computationally, as follows. To find singular points (x, y), solve the system

$$\begin{cases} f(x, y) &= 0 \\ f_x(x, y) &= 0 \\ f_y(x, y) &= 0 \end{cases}$$

In the present case this is

$$\begin{cases} x^2 + y^2 &= 1 \\ 2x &= 0 \\ 2y &= 0 \end{cases}$$

From the last two equations, if $2 \neq 0$ in the field, the only possible singular point is $(0, 0)$, but it doesn't lie on the curve. Therefore, there are no singular points if $2 \neq 0$ in the field. (If $2 = 0$ in the field, this curve degenerates.)

Example: Consider $f(x, y) = x^2 - y^2 - 1$. Since over the real numbers the equation $f(x, y) = 0$ defines a hyperbola, which is plausibly non-singular, we expect that this curve is non-singular. Again, we use the partial derivative criterion to verify this computationally. To find singular points (x, y), solve the system

$$\begin{cases} x^2 - y^2 &= 1 \\ 2x &= 0 \\ -2y &= 0 \end{cases}$$

Again, from the last two equations, if $2 \neq 0$ in the field, then the only possible singular point is $(0, 0)$, but it doesn't lie on the curve. Therefore, there are no singular points. (If $2 = 0$ in the field, this curve degenerates.)

Example: Consider $f(x, y) = x^3 - y^2$. Use the partial derivative criterion to find singular points, if any. To find singular points (x, y), solve the system

$$\begin{cases} x^3 - y^2 &= 0 \\ 3x^2 &= 0 \\ -2y &= 0 \end{cases}$$

From the last two equations, if neither $2 = 0$ nor $3 = 0$ in the field, then the only possible singular point is $(0, 0)$, which does lie on the curve. Therefore, if neither $2 = 0$ nor $3 = 0$ in the field, then the only singular point is $(0, 0)$.

Example: A general family of curves whose non-singularity can be verified systematically is those of the form

$$y^2 = f(x)$$

where f is a polynomial in $k[x]$ *without repeated factors* (even over extension fields). These are called **hyperelliptic**. (The cases that the degree of f is 1, 2, 3, or 4 are special: the degree 2 curves are called **rational** curves, and the degree 3 and 4 curves are called **elliptic curves**.) The system of equations to be solved to find singularities is

$$\begin{cases} y^2 &= f(x) \\ 0 &= f_x(x) \\ 2y &= 0 \end{cases}$$

The last equation shows that the only possible singularities occur at points with y-coordinate 0 if $2 \neq 0$ in k. Substituting that into the first equation and carrying along the second equation gives a system

$$\begin{cases} 0 &= f(x) \\ 0 &= f_x(x) \end{cases}$$

We have already observed that if this system has a solution x_0 then at least the square $(x - x_0)^2$ of the linear factor $x - x_0$ must divide $f(x)$. That is, $f(x)$ would have a repeated factor, contrary to assumption. Thus, the curve has no singularities in the plane (at least if $2 \neq 0$ in the field).

Remark: On the other hand, in the previous example, if the underlying field does have $2 = 0$, as happens in the case that $k = \mathbf{F}_2$, then the curve degenerates. It turns out that a more proper analogue of hyperelliptic curve in characteristic 2 (that is, when $2 = 0$) is a modifed equation of the form

$$y^2 + ay + bxy = f(x)$$

with at least one of a, b non-zero.

20.3 Projective plane curves

To make counting arguments about intersections of lines and curves come out more symmetrically, we might find motivation to introduce some idealized **points at infinity**. However, to avoid merely fooling ourselves, we should do this in a manner that can be legitimized, as follows.

As the simplest example of what we'd like to 'fix up', recall the fact that *either* two (distinct) lines in the plane meet in a single point *or* they are parallel. The special parallel case might be irksome, and we might attempt to 'fix' it by saying (optimistically?!) that two parallel lines *do* have a common point, *at infinity*. Then we would have a prettier assertion, that two lines always meet in a point. But there is the obvious danger that maybe this 'point at infinity' is complete nonsense. Thus, we must take some care to formalize this without presuming the conclusion we want to reach.

Let k be any field, including $\mathbf{C}$ and $\mathbf{R}$ and also finite fields $\mathbf{F}_q$. Let

$$k^\times = \{\text{non-zero elements in } k\}$$

Let

$$\Omega = \{(x, y, z) \in k^3 : \text{not all } x, y, z \text{ are } 0\}$$

That is, Ω is k^3 with the origin removed. Define an **equivalence relation** $\sim$ on Ω by

$$(x, y, z) \sim (x', y', z') \ \text{ if, for some } \lambda \in k^\times, \ \ (x, y, z) = (\lambda x', \lambda y', \lambda z')$$

The **projective plane** $\mathbf{P}^2$ (over k) is defined to be the set of $\sim$-equivalence classes in Ω:

$$\mathbf{P}^2 = \Omega / \sim$$

The coordinates (x, y, z) are called **homogeneous coordinates** for points in $\mathbf{P}^2$. Emphatically, if two points (x_1, y_1, z_1) and (x_2, y_2, z_2) are in the relation

$$(x_1, y_1, z_1) \sim (x_2, y_2, z_2)$$

then we consider them to be *the same*.

For example, with $k = \mathbf{Q}$, using homogeneous coordinates on $\mathbf{P}^2$,

$$(1, 2, 3) \sim (4, 8, 12) \sim (-1, -2, -3)$$

$$(0, 2, 0) \sim (0, 1, 0) \sim (0, -1, 0)$$

Remark: There is simply more than one way to give coordinates to a point in projective space, in the same way that there is more than one way to specify a fraction

$$\frac{1}{2} = \frac{3}{6} = \frac{7}{14}$$

and in the same way that there is more than one way to specify a residue class mod m:

$$3 = 3 + m \bmod m = 3 + 2m \bmod m = 3 - 7m \bmod m = \ldots$$

Remark: The projective plane $\mathbf{P}^2$ can also be thought of as the collection of **lines in three-space**, by identifying a point (a, b, c) in homogeneous coordinates with the line through the origin defined by the equation $ax + by + cz = 0$. Note that changing the representative (a, b, c) by multiplying through by a non-zero scalar does not change the line.

The **affine plane** k^2 **embeds** into $\mathbf{P}^2$ nicely by

$$(x, y) \to (x, y, 1)$$

Note that $(x, y, 1) \sim (x', y', 1)$ if and only if $(x, y) = (x', y')$.

Thus, for example, the point $(3, 4)$ in the (affine) plane is identified with $(3, 4, 1)$ in homogeneous coordinates on the projective plane $\mathbf{P}^2$.

A point given in projective coordinates (x, y, z) with $z = 0$ is called the **point at infinity**, and the **line at infinity** is the set of points (x, y, z) in $\mathbf{P}^2$ with $z = 0$. That is,

all points at infinity = line at infinity $= \{(x, y, 0) :$ not both x, y are 0 $\}$

One justification for this terminology is that no such point lies in the embedded copy of the (affine) plane k^2, so whatever they are these points at infinity really do lie outside the usual plane.

The **total degree** of a term $c_{ijk} x^i y^j z^k$ (with $c_{ijk} \neq 0$) is simply the sum $i+j+k$ of the exponents. The total degree $\deg(f)$ of a polynomial f is the *maximum* of the total degrees of all the summands in it. A polynomial in 3 variables x, y, z is **homogeneous of degree** N if there is a non-negative integer N so that every term $c_{ijk} x^i y^j z^k$ (with $c_{ijk} \neq 0$) has the same total degree N, that is,

$$i + j + k = N$$

Given an affine curve $f(x, y) = 0$, we create the corresponding **projective curve** as follows. First we must create the corresponding **homogeneous equation** $F(x, y, z) = 0$ to replace $f(x, y) = 0$. To **homogenize** each term $c_{ij}x^i y^j$ we replace it by

$$c_{ij}x^i y^j z^{\deg(f)-i-j}$$

That is, we insert powers of z termwise so that the *total degree* of each term is equal to the maximum. Thus, an 'inhomogeneous' polynomial

$$f(x, y) = \sum_{i,j} c_{ij}x^i y^j$$

is replaced by the corresponding 'homogeneous' polynomial

$$F(x, y, z) = \sum_{i,j} c_{ij}x^i y^j z^{\deg(f)-i-j}$$

The original curve is $F(x, y, 1) = 0$.

Example: Starting with the affine curve $y^2 = x^3 - 1$, we see that the total degree is 3. Thus, filling in z's in every summand to make the degree equal to the maximum, we have the homogeneous equation

$$y^2 z = x^3 - z^3$$

Proposition: Let $F(x, y, z)$ be the homogeneous polynomial attached to a polynomial $f(x, y)$ in two variables, and let x, y, z in k satisfy $F(x, y, z) = 0$. Then for any $t \in k^\times$

$$F(tx, ty, tz) = 0$$

That is, the equation $F(x, y, z) = 0$ (not including the point $(0, 0, 0)$) specifies a *well-defined* subset of $\mathbf{P}^2$. And the intersection of this set with the imbedded *affine* plane F^2 is the original affine curve $f(x, y) = 0$.

Proof: One basic feature of the 'homogenization' process is that for any x, y, z

$$F(tx, ty, tz) = t^{deg(f)} \cdot F(x, y, z)$$

The other basic feature is that

$$F(x, y, 1) = f(x, y)$$

The first property makes clear the first assertion of the proposition, and then the second makes clear the second assertion of the proposition.   ///

Now we give the beginning of better justification of the terminology and construction by returning to the simple example of two lines in the plane. From the equation of a straight line L

$$ax + by + c = 0$$

in the usual coordinates on k^2 (with not both a, b zero), we create the **associated homogenized equation**

$$ax + by + cz = 0$$

If (x, y, z) satisfies this equality, then so does $(\lambda x, \lambda y, \lambda z)$ for any $\lambda \in k^\times$. That is, the homogenized equation defines a **curve** $\tilde{L}$ in the *projective plane* $\mathbf{P}^2$. And it has the desirable property that under the embedding of k^2 into $\mathbf{P}^2$ the original line L is mapped to a subset of $\tilde{L}$.

What **points at infinity** are there on the extended version $\tilde{L}$ of L? This amounts to looking for solutions to $ax + by + cz = 0$ with $z = 0$: That means $ax + by = 0$. Since not both a, b are zero, without loss of generality we may suppose that $b \neq 0$ and get $y = (-a/b)x$. Thus, we get points

$$(x, -ax/b, 0) \sim (1, -a/b, 0)$$

on $\tilde{L}$. That is, these are just different homogenous coordinates for the same point: there is a single point at infinity lying on a given line.

We really do have the smoothed-out symmetrical assertion:

Theorem: Any two (distinct) lines in the projective plane $\mathbf{P}^2$ intersect in exactly one point.

Proof: Let the two lines in $\mathbf{P}^2$ be, in homogeneous coordinates,

$$\begin{aligned} ax + by + cz &= 0 \\ a'x + b'y + c'z &= 0 \end{aligned}$$

The assumption on the lines is that (a, b, c) is not a scalar multiple of (a', b', c') (and equivalently (a', b', c') is not a scalar multiple of (a, b, c)). We must solve this system of equations for (x, y, z).

Suggested by basic linear algebra, we might view this as hunting for a vector (x, y, z) so that

$$\begin{aligned} (x, y, z) \cdot (a, b, c) &= 0 \\ (x, y, z) \cdot (a', b', c') &= 0 \end{aligned}$$

with the usual **dot product**. Suggested by basic linear algebra over the real numbers, we might anticipate that the **cross product** of $(a, b, c,)$ and (a', b', c') is a solution: try

$$(x, y, z) = (bc' - b'c, -ac' + a'c, ab' - a'b)$$

Indeed,

$$\begin{aligned} a(bc' - b'c) + b(-ac' + a'c) + c(ab' - a'b) &= 0 \\ a'(bc' - b'c) + b'(-ac' + a'c) + c'(ab' - a'b) &= 0 \end{aligned}$$

Note that it is the fact that (a, b, c) and (a', b', c') are not scalar multiples of each other that makes $(x, y, z) \neq (0, 0, 0)$.

A little more work, as in the preceding proposition, would show that the collection of all solutions is exactly the collection of scalar multiples of a given solution. Thus, in $\mathbf{P}^2$ there is a unique solution.   ///

Example: Consider the affine quadratic curve $x^2 - 3xy + 2y^2 + 3x + 5y + 7 = 0$. The homogenization of this equation is $x^2 - 3xy + 2y^2 + 3xz + 5yz + 7z^2 = 0$. The *points at infinity* lying on this curve are the points (x, y, z) with $z = 0$ (and not both x, y zero). Setting $z = 0$ gives the equation

$$x^2 - 3xy + 2y^2 = 0$$

for points $(x, y, 0)$ on the curve. If $y = 0$ then from the equation also $x = 0$, which is impossible since we are talking about homogeneous coordinates on projective space. If $y \neq 1$, then we may as well take $y = 1$ without loss of generality, since

$$(x, y, 0) \sim (x/y, 1, 0)$$

Then the equation becomes
$$x^2 - 3x + 2 = 0$$

This gives two solutions, 3 and 2, which give points at infinity $(3, 1, 0)$ and $(2, 1, 0)$. That is, there are two points at infinity on the projectivized version of this curve.

Example: A cubic curve with equation $y^2 = x^3 + ax + b$ has **homogeneous form**

$$y^2 z = x^3 + axz^2 + bz^3$$

The point is that we insert factors of z into each term, so that each term is of degree 3. This has the effect that if (x, y, z) satisfies the homogenized equation, then so does $(\lambda x, \lambda y, \lambda z)$ for any $\lambda \in k^\times$. Let's see what **points at infinity** lie on the extended cubic curve: set $z = 0$ and solve.

$$0 \cdot y^2 = x^3 + 0^2 \cdot ax + 0^3 \cdot c$$

or

$$0 = x^3$$

Therefore, the only point at infinity is given by the homogeneous coordinates $(0, 1, 0)$.

Finally, we might wonder about determination of the **singularity** or not of a projective curve defined by a projective equation $F(x, y, z) = 0$, especially near points at infinity. Fortunately, this can be reduced to the more intuitive affine case we've already treated, as follows. Given an equivalence class representative (x_1, y_1, z_1) for a point on the curve attached to the homogeneous equation $F(x, y, z) = 0$, at least one of x_1, y_1, z_1 is not 0, by the definition of the projective plane. To say that the point (x_1, y_1, z_1) is *at infinity* is exactly to say that $z_1 = 0$. Then one or the other of x_1 and y_1 is necessarily non-zero. Without loss of generality, we can suppose that $y_1 \neq 0$, so then take representative $(x_1/y_1, 1, z_1/y_1)$ instead, and consider the dehomogenized equation

$$f(x, z) = F(x, 1, z) = 0$$

to study the part of the curve near (x_1, y_1, z_1) with $y_1 \neq 0$. Thus, reasonably declaring a projective curve to be **non-singular** if all these affine parts of it are non-singular in the usual affine sense, we see that

Proposition: A projective curve given by a single homogeneous equation $F(x, y, z) = 0$ is non-singular if and only if at every point (x_0, y_0, z_0) on the curve the gradient

$$\nabla F = \left(\frac{\partial F}{\partial x}, \frac{\partial F}{\partial y}, \frac{\partial F}{\partial z} \right)$$

does not vanish.   ///

The following theorem is a very nice justification of the introduction of the projective plane and points at infinity, and is the beautiful generalization of the assertion that two (distinct) lines always intersect in a single point.

Theorem: (*Bezout's Theorem*) Let $F(x, y, z) = 0$ and $G(x, y, z) = 0$ be two homogeneous equations, of total degrees $\deg(F)$ and $\deg(G)$, respectively. (Assume that F and G have no common factor.) Then the number of points of intersection of the two corresponding projective curves is

$$\text{number of points in intersection } = \deg(F) \cdot \deg(G)$$

(where points are counted including *multiplicities*).

Proof: Omitted.

Remark: The notion of *multiplicity* is familiar in the case of polynomials in a single variable, where the left-hand side of a polynomial equation $f(x) = 0$ may have repeated linear factors, as in the case

$$(x - 1)^2 \cdot (x - 2) = x^3 - 4x^2 + 5x - 2 = 0$$

which has a *double root* at $x = 1$. In the case at hand, the spirit of the idea of multiplicity is similar, but is more complicated to define precisely and so as to make Bezout's theorem exactly true. Perhaps one may view the notion of multiplicity as a technical refinement to deal with somewhat special or extreme cases, since generically there will be *no* multiple points, in the same way that it is unusual for a polynomial in a single variable to have a multiple root.

Corollary: Let $f(x, y) = 0$ and $g(x, y) = 0$ be two equations, of total degrees $\deg(f)$ and $\deg(g)$, respectively. (Assume that f and g have no common factor.) Then the number of points of intersection of the two corresponding affine curves is

$$\text{number of points in intersection } \leq \deg(f) \cdot \deg(g)$$

Proof: (*of corollary*) Affine plane curves will have the same points of intersection as the corresponding projective plane curves, except that they'll be missing any points of intersection that are points at infinity. Thus, instead of the equality that we get in Bezout's theorem for projective curves, we merely get an inequality, since we may have 'lost' some points (*and* we may have failed to properly count multiplicities).   ///

20.4 Curves in higher dimensions

Certainly it is intuitively clear that 'curves' exist in 3-space and in higher dimenensions, but one immediate complication is that in such generality curves cannot be defined by single equations. Thus, the algebra becomes more complicated. Here we briefly comment on some of the difficulties.

Not every 'projective algebraic curve' can be imbedded into 2-space (projective or not) without introducing *singularities*. This is not so easy to see. It is even less easy to see that curves whose natural definition imbeds them in high-dimensional spaces (rather than the plane) include those with relatively large numbers of *rational points*. The latter fact makes consideration of this more complicated scenario inescapable in the long run. There are of course technical complications.

Following the general intuition that the 'dimension' of something might be the 'number of variables' minus the 'number of conditions', we would first guess that a curve in n-space would need $n-1$ equations to define it. This is nearly true, but not quite: in some cases a greater number of defining equations is necessary. Further, the technical question of ascertaining whether a set of (non-linear!) *polynomial* equations in several variables is 'independent' is much more complicated than in the simple case of *linear* equations.

If we turn to alternatives, in analogy with multi-variable calculus we might hope to be able to *parametrize* curves in n-space. Unfortunately, already in the case of *plane* curves, the only ones which are parametrizable are *quadratic* ones.

It *is* possible to consider algebraic curves imbedded in higher-dimensional spaces, but the technical demands exceed our resources at this point.

20.5 Genus, divisors, linear systems

Here we do a blisteringly fast sketch of some essential ideas from the basic theory of algebraic curves, just enough to explain the idea of the geometric Goppa codes subsequently.

The **field of rational functions $\mathbf{F}_q(x,y)$ in two variables** over $\mathbf{F}_q$ is the collection of ratios

$$\frac{h(x,y)}{g(x,y)}$$

where h and g are polynomials in $\mathbf{F}_q[x,y]$, and g is not the zero polynomial.

Remark: Notice that the only notational device that distinguishes this field of rational functions from the ring of polynomials is the use of ('round') parentheses rather than ('square') brackets.

Let X be an affine plane curve defined by an equation $f(x,y) = 0$ over $\mathbf{F}_q$. We suppose that $f(x,y)$ has no repeated factors. (It is in fact a little tricky to understand what this means, since we're talking about polynomials in *two* variables, not *one*.) For two other polynomials $r(x, y)$ and $s(x, y)$, we write

$$r(x, y) = s(x, y) \bmod f(x, y)$$

if $r(x, y) - s(x, y)$ is a polynomial *multiple of* $f(x, y)$. Note that there is *no* division/reduction algorithm for polynomials in *two* variables, so that we cannot be so glib about 'dividing' one polynomial by another in this context as we were in the one-variable context. Further, for two rational functions $r_1(x, y)/s_1(x, y)$ and $r_2(x, y)/s_2(x, y)$, we write

$$\frac{r_1(x, y)}{s_1(x, y)} = \frac{r_2(x, y)}{s_2(x, y)} \bmod f(x, y)$$

if

$$r_1(x, y) \cdot s_2(x, y) = r_2(x, y) \cdot s_1(x, y) \bmod f(x, y)$$

That is, two 'fractions' are equal modulo f if and only if we have equality when we 'multiply out' the fractions to have simply polynomials.

Recall that non-zero elements r, s in a commutative ring R are *zero divisors* if $r \cdot s = 0$. The **field of fractions** of a commutative ring R without zero divisors is the field consisting of all 'fractions' r/s with $r \in R$, $0 \neq s \in R$, where

$$\frac{r}{s} = \frac{r'}{s'} \quad \text{if } rs' = sr'$$

(The latter is the expected condition for equality of fractions.) Addition, multiplication, and inversion of fractions are by the usual formulas

$$\frac{a}{b} + \frac{c}{d} = \frac{ad + bc}{bd}$$

$$\frac{a}{b} \cdot \frac{c}{d} = \frac{ac}{bd}$$

$$1 / \left(\frac{a}{b} \right) = \frac{b}{a} \quad \text{(for } a \neq 0\text{)}$$

One should verify that the axioms for a field are met. As perhaps expected, assuming that R has a unit 1, there is an injective ring homomorphism of the original ring R into this field of fractions by $r \to r/1$.

The **field of rational functions** on the plane curve X defined by $f(x, y) = 0$ is defined to be the **field of fractions of**

$$\mathbf{F}_q[x, y] \bmod f(x, y)$$

That is, it consists of all ratios of polynomials-modulo-$f(x, y)$. This field is denoted $\mathbf{F}_q(X)$.

Remark: So every 'rational function' on a plane curve X is *expressible* as a ratio of polynomials, but *in more than one way*, since two such ratios are 'equal on X' if they are equal modulo $f(x, y)$.

Thinking about it in a 'projective' context, we would define the **field of functions** on the *projective plane* $\mathbf{P}^2$ to be the collection of ratios of homogeneous polynomials in 3 variables where the degree of the numerator is equal to the degree of the denominator. On the face of it, this is a different thing than the field of rational functions in two variables defined above. But they are in fact essentially the same thing: every ratio of not necessarily homogeneous polynomials in *two* variables may be converted to a ratio of homogeneous polynomials (with degree of numerator equal to degree of denominator) simply by homogenizing both numerator and denominator (and adding extra factors of z to either numerator or denominator in order to make the degrees equal). The process can likewise be reversed.

The idea of field-of-functions on a plane curve has a *projective* version as well. Everything here is predictable, in principle, from thinking about the proper way to 'projectivize' the affine case discussed just above. But we'll repeat it in the projectivized setting just for emphasis. Let X be a projective curve defined by a homogeneous equation $F(x, y, z) = 0$ over $\mathbf{F}_q$. We suppose that $F(x, y, z)$ has no repeated factors (!?). For two other homogeneous polynomials $R(x, y, z)$ and $S(x, y, z)$, say

$$R(x, y, z) = S(x, y, z) \bmod F(x, y, z)$$

if $R(x, y, z) - S(x, y, z)$ is a polynomial *multiple* of $F(x, y, z)$. For two ratios $r_1(x, y, z)/s_1(x, y, z)$ and $r_2(x, y, z)/s_2(x, y, z)$ of homogeneous polynomials, we write

$$\frac{r_1(x, y, z)}{s_1(x, y, z)} = \frac{r_2(x, y, z)}{s_2(x, y, z)} \bmod F(x, y, z)$$

if

$$r_1(x, y, z) \cdot s_2(x, y, z) = r_2(x, y, z) \cdot s_1(x, y, z) \bmod F(x, y, z)$$

That is, two 'fractions' are equal modulo F if and only if we have equality when we 'multiply out' the fractions to have simply polynomials.

The **field of rational functions** on the projective curve X defined by $F(x, y, z) = 0$ is defined to be

$$\mathbf{F}_q(x, y, z) \bmod F(x, y, z)$$

That is, it consists of all ratios of homogeneous polynomials *and* two such ratios are 'the same' if they are equal modulo $F(x, y, z)$. This field is denoted $\mathbf{F}_q(X)$.

Remark: So every 'rational function' on a projective plane curve X is *expressible* as a ratio of homogeneous polynomials in the three 'projective' coordinates, but *in more than one way*, since two such ratios are 'equal on X' if they are equal modulo $F(x, y, z)$.

Example: Consider the projective plane curve C given by $x^2 + y^2 + z^2 = 0$. The gradient ∇F of $F(x, y, z) = x^2 + y^2 + z^2$ is simply $(2x, 2y, 2z)$. Thus, if $2 \neq 0$ in the field, the gradient never vanishes and the curve is non-singular. The rational function $f(x, y, z) = xy/z^2$ is the same rational function on C as $g(x, y, z) = -xy/(x^2 + y^2)$ since

$$x^2 + y^2 = -z^2$$

is the defining relation of the curve. In general, things need not be quite so simple.

Let $P_1, P_2, \ldots, P_n$ be a set of distinct points on a projective curve X defined over $\mathbf{F}_q$. A **divisor** on X is an expression

$$D = \ell_1 \cdot P_1 + \ldots + \ell_n \cdot P_n$$

with integers ℓ_i. Such a thing once would have been called a 'formal finite sum of points'. However, rather than misguidedly wasting our time trying to legitimize this by imagining what 'adding points' might mean, or what 'multiplying points by integers' might mean, we make sense of this as follows. A divisor on X is an integer-valued function ℓ on X, which takes the value 0 at all but finitely many points. That is certainly legal. Then the expression above is really the sum

$$\sum_{P \in X} \ell(P) \cdot P$$

and the notation is that $\ell(P_i) = \ell_i$.

Example: Let C be the projective plane curve defined by the homogeneous equation $x^3 + y^3 + z^3 = 0$. The points $P_1 = (1, -1, 0)$, $P_2 = (1, 0, -1)$, $P_3 = (0, 1, -1)$ are distinct points on the projective plane, and all lie on the curve C. Thus, the expression

$$5 \cdot P_1 - 17 \cdot P_2 + 11 \cdot P_3$$

is a divisor on the curve.

Remark: The previous expression does *not* indicate scalar multiplication or vector addition, but rather operations inside a more abstract object (which is a group).

The **degree** of a divisor is just the sum of the coefficients:

$$\deg\left(\ell_1 \cdot P_1 + \ldots + \ell_n \cdot P_n \right) = \ell_1 + \ldots + \ell_n$$

Assuming that the points P_i are distinct, the coefficient ℓ_i corresponding to the point P_i is the **multiplicity** of the divisor **at** P_i. The **support** of a divisor is the set of points at which the divisor has non-zero multiplicity. A non-zero divisor is **positive** if all its multiplicities are non-negative.

Example: Let C again be the projective plane curve defined by the homogeneous equation $x^3 + y^3 + z^3 = 0$, with points $P_1 = (1, -1, 0)$, $P_2 = (1, 0, -1)$, $P_3 = (0, 1, -1)$ on it. The degree of the divisor

$$D = 5 \cdot P_1 - 17 \cdot P_2 + 11 \cdot P_3$$

is

$$\deg D = 5 - 17 + 11 = -1$$

Let C_1 and C_2 be two projective plane curves (defined by single equations *without a common factor*). Then by Bezout's theorem the intersection is a finite set of points $P_1, \ldots, P_n$, whose number is equal to the product of the degrees (being sure to count multiplicities). The **intersection divisor** is the divisor which is the 'sum' of all the points in this intersection, counting multiplicities:

$$\mathrm{div}(C_1 \cap C_2) = \sum_i P_i$$

Let $\varphi = g/h$ be a rational function on a projective plane curve X, with homogeneous polynomials g and h of the same degree. Let Z_g be the projective curve defined by $g(x, y, z) = 0$, and let Z_h be the curve defined by $h(x, y, z) = 0$. We have

$$\textit{zeros of } \varphi \textit{ on } X = \mathrm{div}(Z_g \cap X)$$

$$\textit{poles of } \varphi \textit{ on } X = \mathrm{div}(Z_h \cap X)$$

One should think of the *poles* as being where the function *blows up*. The **divisor** $\mathrm{div}(f)$ φ is

$$\mathrm{div}(f) = \mathrm{div}(Z_g \cap X) - \mathrm{div}(Z_h \cap X)$$

That is, roughly, the divisor of a function is simply the 'formal sum' of zeros *minus* poles.

The **linear system** $L(D)$ attached to a divisor D on a projective plane curve X is

$$L(D) = \{f \in \mathbf{F}_q(X) : \mathrm{div}(f) + D \text{ is a positive divisor}\}$$

By convention, we also include the zero function in any such linear system. This linear system is a *vector space* over $\mathbf{F}_q$, in the sense that any two elements of it can be added, there are additive inverses, and there is a scalar multiplication. Thus, there is a corresponding notion of *dimension* of $L(D)$.

Remark: The integer g, the 'genus', occurring in the following theorem, has a more intuitive origin that is described afterward, but in reality its importance lies in such things as the more technical content of this theorem.

Theorem: (*Riemann-Roch*) Let X be a non-singular projective plane curve. There is a non-negative integer g such that for any divisor D,

$$\text{dimension of vector space } L(D) \geq \deg(D) + 1 - g$$

and in fact if $\deg(D) > 2g - 2$, we have the equality

$$\text{dimension of vector space } L(D) = \deg(D) + 1 - g$$

Example: Suppose that X is the usual line with the added point at infinity. (That is, X is the *projective line*.) The point at infinity we will suggestively denote by ∞. Then for a positive integer ℓ the linear system $L(\ell \cdot \infty)$ consists of the polynomial functions of degree less than or equal ℓ. In particular, the functions in that linear system are not allowed to have poles anywhere but at ∞, and the order of pole at ∞ is bounded by ℓ.

It is not possible to give a complete-yet-accurate description of where 'genus' came from, but a heuristic description is possible, along with a family of examples.

First, a curve defined over $\mathbf{C}$, with points at infinity properly inserted, is provably geometrically 'equivalent' to a sphere with a number of 'handles' attached. For example, attaching a single handle gives a geometric thing 'equivalent' to the surface of a doughnut (called a **torus**). Attaching *no* handles leaves us simply with a sphere. Any number of handles may be attached, and in fact in slightly different ways, but for the moment all we care about is the **number** of handles attached, in effect. If a curve X over $\mathbf{C}$ is described as a sphere with g handles attached, then the curve X is said to have **genus** g. In some cases there is a computationally effective way to determine genus: for *hyperelliptic* curves

$$y^2 = f(x) \quad \text{(with } f(x) \text{ having no repeated factors)}$$

(after desingularizing this curve at infinity when the degree of f is odd) the genus is

$$\text{genus of } \{y^2 = f(x)\} = \begin{cases} \frac{\deg f - 2}{2} & (\deg f \text{ even}) \\ \frac{\deg f - 1}{2} & (\deg f \text{ odd}) \end{cases}$$

This *geometric* discussion doesn't quite make sense if the defining field is $\mathbf{F}_q$, and in that case the abstracted version of genus is a trickier thing. Nevertheless, for hyperelliptic curves, for example, the formula for genus is the same as for complex curves.

20.6 Geometric Goppa codes

First, we reconsider the Reed-Solomon codes from a viewpoint that suggests how to try some interesting generalizations. Then we describe geometric Goppa codes in terms of linear systems on curves.

Let $L(k-1)$ be the collection of all polynomials in $\mathbf{F}_q[x]$ of degree less than or equal $k-1$. (This set can be viewed as a vector space of dimension k over $\mathbf{F}_q$.) Let $\alpha_1, \ldots, \alpha_{q-1}$ be the $q-1$ non-zero elements in $\mathbf{F}_q$. Then a way of describing the simplest Reed-Solomon ('RS') code attached to q, k slightly different from our earlier matrix-oriented approach is as

$$C = \{(f(\alpha_1), \ldots, f(\alpha_{q-1})) : f \in L(k)\}$$

That is, the code consists of all ordered sets of values of these polynomials f at the non-zero elements of $\mathbf{F}_q$. We want to view the collection of non-zero elements of $\mathbf{F}_q$ as being points other than 0 and ∞ on *a line*, which then we'll view as a very special case of an algebraic curve. This is the germ of Goppa's idea (although it's certainly not clear from this whether or not such things would give rise to *good* codes).

Here is Goppa's generalization. Let X be a non-singular projective plane curve over $\mathbf{F}_q$, and D a divisor on X. Let $P_1, \ldots, P_n$ be a set of n distinct $\mathbf{F}_q$-rational points on X. Assume that no one of the P_i is in the support of D. Then the **algebraic geometry code** $C(X, D, \{P_i\})$ attached to this data is

$$C(X, D, \{P_i\}) = \{(f(P_1), \ldots, f(P_n)) : f \in L(D)\}$$

Theorem: (*Goppa*) Let X be a non-singular projective plane curve of genus g defined over $\mathbf{F}_q$. Let $\{P_1,\ldots,P_n\}$ be a set of n distinct $\mathbf{F}_q$-rational points on X. Let D be a divisor on X satisfying

$$2g - 2 < \deg(D) < n$$

Then the algebraic-geometry code $C(X, D, \{P_i\})$ defined just above is of length n, dimension

$$k = \deg(D) + 1 - g$$

and minimum distance

$$\text{minimum distance } d \ \geq n - \deg(D)$$

Thus, such a code $C = C(X, D, \{P_i\})$ has

$$\text{information rate } = \frac{\deg(D) + 1 - g}{n}$$

$$\text{relative min distance } \geq \frac{n - \deg(D)}{n}$$

We would want both of these to be large. Or, as a sort of compromise, we'd want the *sum* to be large. Here

$$\text{information rate } + \text{ relative min distance } \geq \frac{N + 1 - g}{n} = 1 + 1/n - g/n$$

Planning to take longer and longer codes, we have

$$\lim_{n \to \infty} \text{ information rate } + \text{ relative min distance } \geq 1 - g/n$$

We want g/n to become small, or, equivalently, n/g to become large. In particular, this means that we want the curves to have a 'large' number of $\mathbf{F}_q$-rational points available to use as the P_i's.

20.7 The Tsfasman-Vladut-Zink-Ihara bound

In 1982, Tsfasman, Vladut, and Zink found a sequence of curves designed so that the associated geometric Goppa codes surpass the Gilbert-Varshamov bound. This was big news! Ihara generalized that result considerably soon after.

First, there is an inequality that tells an upper bound for the number of rational points there may be on an algebraic curve. The critical invariant attached to a curve is not really the *degree*, which would be harder to define for curves imbedded in higher-dimensional spaces anyway, but rather the **genus**. And the following very serious result exactly uses 'genus':

Theorem: (*Hasse-Weil Inequality*) Let X be a projective non-singular curve defined over $\mathbf{F}_q$ of genus g, with N rational points over $\mathbf{F}_q$. Then

$$|N - (q + 1)| \leq 2g\sqrt{q}$$

A curve that achieves the maximum allowed by this inequality is the **hermitian curve**

$$y^q z + y z^q = x^{q+1}$$

over the field $\mathbf{F}_{q^2}$ with q^2 elements.

Theorem: (*Tsfasman, Vladut, Zink, Ihara*) Let q be an even power of a prime. There is a *constructible* infinite sequence of curves X_i defined over $\mathbf{F}_q$ so that

$$\lim_{i \to \infty} \frac{\text{number of } \mathbf{F}_q\text{-rational points on } X_i}{\text{genus of } X_i} = \sqrt{q} - 1$$

Remark: Thus, if we trace back the implications of this for the geometric Goppa codes, and compare *asymptotically* with the Gilbert-Varshamov bound, we would see that we've done better!

Remark: The curves constructed to exceed the Gilbert-Varshamov bound are **modular curves,** meaning that they are very special among algebraic curves, in particular admitting a very sharp analysis of their rational points!

Exercises

20.01 Find all solutions (x, y) to $x^2 - 2y^2 = 1$ with x, y in $\mathbf{Q}$. (*ans.*)

20.02 Find all solutions (x, y) to $x^2 - 3y^2 = 1$ with x, y in $\mathbf{Q}$.

20.03 Find all solutions (x, y) to $x^2 + xy + y^2 = 1$ with x, y in $\mathbf{Q}$.

20.04 Determine all the points at infinity of the projectivization of the curve $x^2 - 2y^2 = 1$. (*ans.*)

20.05 Determine singular points of the affine curve $x^2 - 2y^2 = 1$. (*ans.*)

20.06 Are the points at infinity of the projectivization of $x^2 - 2y^2 = 1$ singular? (*ans.*)

20.07 Determine all the points at infinity of the projectivization of the curve $x^2 + xy + y^2 = 1$. Which are singular points?

20.08 Over a field of characteristic 2, show that $y^2 + y = x^3 + x + 1$ is non-singular. Find all the points at infinity and show that they are non-singular. Determine the genus.

20.09 Prove **Euler's identity:** for a homogeneous polynomial $f(x_1, \ldots, x_n)$ of total degree d, prove that

$$\sum_{i=1}^{n} \frac{\partial}{\partial x_i} f = d \cdot f$$

20.10 Show that the hermitian curve $y^q z + y z^q = x^{q+1}$ over the field $\mathbf{F}_{q^2}$ with q^2 elements is non-singular and has a unique point at infinity.

20.11 Determine the *genus* of the hermitian curve $y^q z + y z^q = x^{q+1}$.

Appendix: Stirling's Formula

The properties of the **factorial** function

$$n! = 1 \cdot 2 \cdot 3 \cdot 4 \cdot 5 \cdot \ldots \cdot (n-2) \cdot (n-1) \cdot n$$

are important to understand, considering that many counting problems have answers involving factorials, or in terms of binomial coefficients (which are made from factorials).

The most obvious feature of the factorial function $n!$ is that it grows very rapidly as a function of n. Therefore, in many situations the question is not to compute factorials *exactly*, but rather only to express them in terms of simpler functions whose size (large though it may be) we can discuss more easily. The approximation we obtain here is nearly the simplest case of **Stirling's Approximation**, but suffices for our purposes. The proof itself is fairly memorable.

(This estimate also plays a role in elementary approaches to the Prime Number Theorem.)

Proposition: The limit

$$\lim_{n \to \infty} \frac{n!}{n^{n+\frac{1}{2}} e^{-n}}$$

exists. Its value is $\sqrt{2\pi}$. Further, in fact, for $n \geq 2$

$$\sqrt{2\pi}\, n^{n+\frac{1}{2}} e^{-n} \cdot e^{\frac{1}{12(n+1)}} < n! < \sqrt{2\pi}\, n^{n+\frac{1}{2}} e^{-n} \cdot e^{\frac{1}{12n}}$$

Proof: The proof starts by comparing

$$\ln(n!) = \ln 1 + \ln 1 + \ln 3 + \ldots + \ln n$$

to the integrals

$$\int_1^{n+1} \ln x \, dx = [x \ln x - x]_1^{n+1} = (n+1)\ln(n+1) - (n+1)$$

and

$$\int_0^n \ln x \, dx = [x \ln x - x]_0^n = n \ln n - n$$

(The latter integral is 'improper' at 0, but converges.) First, for each $n = 2, 3, 4, \ldots$, since $\ln$ is an increasing function,

$$\int_{t-1}^t \ln x \, dx \leq \ln t \leq \int_t^{t+1} \ln x \, dx$$

From this we get

$$n \ln n - n \leq \ln n! \leq (n+1) \ln(n+1) - (n+1)$$

Already this is interesting: if we exponentiate we get

$$n^n e^{-n} \leq n! \leq (n+1)^{n+1} e^{-(n+1)}$$

The key quantity to consider is $(n + \frac{1}{2}) \ln n - n$, which is a moderately clever choice of an average between the lower and upper bounds we just obtained. Then let

$$E_n = \ln n! - \left[\left(n + \frac{1}{2} \right) \ln n - n \right]$$

be the error in estimating $\ln n!$ by this average. We have

$$E_n - E_{n+1}$$

$$= \ln n! - \left[\left(n + \frac{1}{2} \right) \ln n - n \right] - \left[\ln (n+1)! - \left[\left(n + 1 + \frac{1}{2} \right) \ln(n+1) - (n+1) \right] \right]$$

$$= \left(n + \frac{1}{2} \right) \ln \left(1 + \frac{1}{n} \right) - 1$$

after simplifying and rearranging. Next use the Taylor expansion

$$\ln(1+x) = x - \frac{x^2}{2} + \frac{x^3}{3} - \frac{x^4}{4} + \dots$$

to obtain

$$E_n - E_{n+1}$$

$$= \left(n + \frac{1}{2} \right) \left(\frac{1}{n} - \frac{1}{2n^2} + \frac{1}{3n^3} - \dots \right) - 1$$

$$= \left(\frac{1}{1} - \frac{1}{2n} + \frac{1}{3n^2} - \dots \right) + \frac{1}{2} \left(\frac{1}{n} - \frac{1}{2n^2} + \frac{1}{3n^3} - \dots \right) - 1$$

$$= \left(\frac{1}{3} - \frac{1}{4} \right) \frac{1}{n^2} + \left(-\frac{1}{4} + \frac{1}{6} \right) \frac{1}{n^3} + \left(\frac{1}{5} - \frac{1}{8} \right) \frac{1}{n^4} + \left(-\frac{1}{6} + \frac{1}{10} \right) \frac{1}{n^5} + \dots$$

by cancelling the '1' and the $\frac{1}{2n}$. For any $n \geq 1$ this is an alternating decreasing sequence.

Recall that for an alternating decreasing sequence

$$a_1 - a_2 + a_3 - a_4 + \dots$$

(that is, with each $a_i > 0$ and $a_i > a_{i+1}$ for all i), we have identities such as

$$a_1 - a_2 < a_1 - a_2 + a_3 - a_4 + \dots < a_1 - a_2 + a_3$$

Therefore,

$$\frac{1}{12}\left(\frac{1}{n^2} - \frac{1}{n^3}\right) < E_n - E_{n+1} < \frac{1}{12n^2} - \frac{1}{12n^3} + \frac{1}{40n^4}$$

In particular, since the left-hand side is always positive, each of the values $E_n - E_{n+1}$ is *positive*, so the sequence E_n itself is *decreasing*.

Subtracting $\frac{1}{12n}$ and adding $\frac{1}{12(n+1)}$ to the right-hand inequality here, we get

$$\left(E_n - \frac{1}{12n}\right) - \left(E_{n+1} - \frac{1}{12(n+1)}\right) < \frac{1}{12n^2} - \frac{1}{12n^3} + \frac{1}{40n^4} - \frac{1}{12n} + \frac{1}{12(n+1)}$$

The right-hand side (miraculously) simplifies to

$$\frac{12 - 28n}{12 \cdot 40 \cdot n^3(n+1)}$$

which is *negative* for all $n \geq 1$. Therefore, the sequence $E_n - \frac{1}{12n}$ is *increasing*.

Since E_n is decreasing and $E_n - \frac{1}{12n}$ is increasing, and since $\frac{1}{12n}$ goes to 0, we conclude that E_n is a *bounded* decreasing sequence, so has a limit C. This limit is actually $\sqrt{2\pi}$, but we'll not prove that just now.

Similarly, subtracting $\frac{1}{12(n+1)}$ and adding $\frac{1}{12((n+1)+1)}$ to the left-hand inequality, we have

$$\frac{1}{12}\left(\frac{1}{n^2} - \frac{1}{n^3}\right) - \frac{1}{12(n+1)} + \frac{1}{12((n+1)+1)}$$

$$< \left(E_n - \frac{1}{12(n+1)}\right) - \left(E_{n+1} - \frac{1}{12((n+1)+1)}\right)$$

The left-hand side simplifies (not as miraculously as the previous episode) to

$$\frac{2n^2 - n - 2}{n^3 \cdot 12(n+1) \cdot 12((n+1)+1)}$$

The numerator satisfies

$$2n^2 - n - 2 = 2 \cdot \left[\left(n - \frac{1}{4}\right)^2 - \frac{1}{16} - 1\right] \geq 2 \cdot \left[\left(2 - \frac{1}{4}\right)^2 - \frac{17}{16}\right] = 4 > 0$$

for $n \geq 2$. Therefore, at least starting with $n \geq 2$, the sequence

$$E_n - \frac{1}{12(n+1)}$$

is *decreasing*.

In summary,

$$\lim_n E_n = C$$

and since the sequences $\frac{1}{12n}$ and $\frac{1}{12(n+1)}$ go to 0,

$$E_n - \frac{1}{12n} \quad \text{increases to} \quad C$$

$$E_n - \frac{1}{12(n+1)} \quad \text{decreases to} \quad C$$

Therefore, for $n \geq 2$,

$$C + \frac{1}{12(n+1)} < E_n < C + \frac{1}{12n}$$

That is,

$$C + \frac{1}{12(n+1)} + \left(n + \frac{1}{2}\right) \ln n - n < \ln n! < C + \frac{1}{12n} + \left(n + \frac{1}{2}\right) \ln n - n$$

This is the statement of the proposition.   ///

Appendix: Linear Algebra

This appendix consists entirely of proofs of some basic linear algebra results. Even though our immediate interests are in tangible linear algebra involving row vectors, row spaces, and other concrete versions of vectors and operations upon them, it turns out to be economical to give relatively abstract proofs of some important basic properties of them.

A.1 Basics

This section gives definitions for 'abstract' vector spaces over arbitrary fields that subsume concrete definitions in terms of matrices, row-vectors, and column-vectors.

Let k be a field, whose elements we may also call **scalars**. A **vector space** *over* k is a set V with a special element 0 (the **zero vector**) and with a **vector addition** denoted '+' with the expected properties

$$
\begin{array}{lll}
0 + v = v + 0 & \text{for all } v \in V & \text{(property of 0)} \\
v + w = w + v & \text{for all } v, w \in V & \text{(commutativity)} \\
(u + v) + w = u + (v + w) & \text{for all } u, v, w \in V & \text{(associativity)}
\end{array}
$$

and for every $v \in V$ there is $-v \in V$ such that

$$
v + (-v) = 0 \quad \text{(additive inverse)}
$$

There is a **scalar multiplication** of vectors by scalars, written αv of $\alpha \cdot v$ for $\alpha \in k$ and $v \in V$, with properties

$$
\begin{array}{lll}
\alpha(v + w) = \alpha v + \alpha w & \text{for all } v, w \in V,\ \alpha \in k & \text{(distributivity)} \\
(\alpha + \beta)v = \alpha v + \beta v & \text{for all } v \in V,\ \alpha\beta \in k & \text{(distributivity)} \\
\alpha(\beta v) = (\alpha\beta)v & \text{for all } v \in V,\ \alpha\beta \in k & \text{(associativity)} \\
1 \cdot v = v & \text{for all } v \in V & \text{(property of 1)}
\end{array}
$$

Remark: The last axiom may seem unnecessary, but in abstract situations it is not automatically satisfied, and must be explicitly required.

A familiar vector space over a field k is the space of ordered n-tuples of elements from k

$$k^n = \{(x_1, \ldots, x_n) : x_1, \ldots, x_n \in k\}$$

with component-wise addition and scalar multiplication. The 0-vector is

$$0 = (0, \ldots, 0)$$

Remark: Note the use of the word 'over' in the above definition to tell what the field of scalars is. This is a peculiar but standard mathematical usage.

Remark: Ignoring the scalar multiplication, a vector space V is an *abelian group*. Thus, some basic properties of groups could be recycled here to immediately deduce some properties of vector spaces.

- There is exactly one vector in V with the property of the zero vector 0.

Proof: Let $z \in V$ also have the property that $z + v = v$ for even a single $v \in V$. Then, using associativity and the definition of $-v$,

$$z = z + 0 = z + (v + (-v)) = (z + v) + (-v) = v + (-v) = 0$$

as claimed.   ///

- The additive inverse of a vector $v \in V$ is unique.

Proof: Let $x, y \in V$ be such that $x + v = 0$ and $y + v = 0$. Then, using associativity,

$$y = y + 0 = y + (v + x) = (y + v) + x = 0 + x = x$$

as claimed.   ///

- The 0 scalar multiple $0 \cdot v$ of any vector is the zero vector 0:

$$0 \cdot v = 0$$

Proof: From the distributivity property,

$$0 \cdot v = (0 + 0) \cdot v = 0 \cdot v + 0 \cdot v$$

Then add $-(0 \cdot v)$ to both sides (without assuming anything about what this may be!) to obtain, via associativity and the property of the additive inverse,

$$0 = 0 \cdot v - (0 \cdot v) = (0 \cdot v + 0 \cdot v) - (0 \cdot v)$$

$$= 0 \cdot v + (0 \cdot v) - (0 \cdot v)) = 0 \cdot v + 0 = 0 \cdot v$$

as claimed.   ///

- For any scalar α, $\alpha \cdot 0 = 0$.

Proof: Using distributivity

$$\alpha \cdot 0 = \alpha \cdot (0 + 0) = \alpha \cdot 0 + \alpha \cdot 0$$

Then add $-(\alpha \cdot 0)$ (whatever the latter is!) to both sides to obtain, via associativity and the property of the additive inverse,

$$0 = \alpha \cdot 0 - (\alpha \cdot 0) = (\alpha \cdot 0 + \alpha \cdot 0) - (alf \cdot 0)$$

$$= \alpha \cdot 0 + (\alpha \cdot 0) - (\alpha \cdot 0)) = \alpha \cdot 0 + 0 = \alpha \cdot 0$$

as claimed.   ///

- The additive inverse $-v$ of a vector v is $(-1) \cdot v$:

$$-v = (-1) \cdot v$$

Proof: From the previous result, $0 \cdot v = 0$, so by distributivity

$$0 = 0 \cdot v = (1 - 1) \cdot v = 1 \cdot v + (-1) \cdot v = v + (-1) \cdot v$$

invoking the property of scalar multiplication by 1. By uniqueness of inverses, proven above, $(-1) \cdot v = v$.   ///

A **(vector) subspace** W of a vector space V is a subset of V with the following **closure** properties.
- For $w \in W$ the inverse $-w$ is in W.
- For $v, w \in W$ the sum $v + w$ is in W.
- For $v \in W$ and $\alpha \in k$ the scalar multiple $\alpha \cdot v$ is in W. Note that since $0 = w + (-w)$ it follows that $0 \in W$. The whole vector space V itself is surely a subspace, as is the subset consisting solely of the zero vector, $\{0\}$. The latter is the **trivial subspace** of V. A subspace is *proper* if it is not the whole space.
- The intersection of a (non-empty) set of subspaces of a vector space V is a subspace.

Proof: This is surprisingly easy. Let $\{W_i : i \in I\}$ be a set of subspaces of V, where I is any index set. For w lying in every W_i, since W_i is a subspace the additive inverse $-w$ lies in W_i. Thus, $-w$ lies in the intersection. The same sort of argument proves the other two properties of subspaces.   ///

A **linear combination** of vectors $v_1, \ldots, v_n$ in a vector space V with **coefficients** $c_1, \ldots, c_n$ in the scalars k is the vector

$$c_1 \cdot v_1 + \ldots + c_n \cdot v_n$$

The vectors $v_1, \ldots, v_n$ are **linearly dependent** if there is a set of coefficients $c_1, \ldots, c_n$ *not all zero* such that the corresponding linear combination is the zero vector:

$$c_1 \cdot v_1 + \ldots + c_n \cdot v_n = 0$$

Conversely, vectors $v_1, \ldots, v_n$ are **linearly independent** if

$$c_1 \cdot v_1 + \ldots + c_n \cdot v_n = 0$$

implies that all the coefficients c_i are 0.

The **subspace spanned** by a set X of vectors in a vector space V is the intersection of all subspaces containing all the vectors in X. Since the whole space V contains X, this intersection is non-empty. By the last bulleted point above this intersection is indeed a subspace.

- The subspace spanned by a set X of vectors in a vector space V is the collection of all linear combinations of vectors from X.

Proof: Since a vector subspace is closed under scalar multiplication and vector addition, certainly every linear combination of vectors taken from X must lie in any vector subspace containing X. On the other hand, we must show that any vector in the intersection of all subspaces containing X is expressible as a linear combination of vectors in X. But it is not hard to check that the collection of these linear combinations *is* a vector subspace of V, and certainly contains X. Therefore, the intersection is no larger than this set of linear combinations.   ///

A *linearly independent* set of vectors *spanning* a subspace W of V is a **basis** for W.

Proposition: Given a basis $e_1, \ldots, e_n$ for a vector space V, there is *exactly one* expression for an arbitrary vector $v \in V$ as a linear combination of $e_1, \ldots, e_n$.

Proof: That there is *at least one* such expression follows from the spanning property. If

$$\sum_i a_i e_i = v = \sum_i b_i e_i$$

are two expressions for v, then subtract to obtain

$$\sum_i (a_i - b_i) e_i = 0$$

Since the e_i are linearly independent, this implies that $a_i = b_i$ for all indices i. ///

A.2   Dimension

The first main results involve the notion of *dimension*. The conclusions of this section are not surprising, but must be considered carefully for subsequent discussions to be well-founded.

The argument in the proof of the following fundamental theorem is sometimes called the *Lagrange replacement principle*. This is the first and main non-trivial result in linear algebra.

Theorem: Let $v_1, \ldots, v_m$ be a linearly independent set of vectors in a vector space V, and let $w_1, \ldots, w_n$ be a basis for V. Then $m \leq n$, and (renumbering the vectors w_i if necessary!) the vectors

$$v_1, \ldots, v_m, w_{m+1}, w_{m+2}, \ldots, w_n$$

are a basis for V.

Proof: Since the w_i's are a basis, we may express v_1 as a linear combination

$$v_1 = c_1 w_1 + \ldots + c_n w_n$$

of them. Not all the coefficients can be 0, since v_1 is not 0. Renumbering the w_i's if necessary, we can suppose that $c_1 \neq 0$. It is at this point that we use the fact that the scalars k are a *field*, namely that every non-zero element has a multiplicative inverse. Thus, we can rearrange, expressing w_1 in terms of v_1 and $w_2, \ldots, w_n$, as

$$w_1 = c_1^{-1} v_1 + (-c_1^{-1} c_2) w_2 + \ldots + (-c_1^{-1} c_2) w_n$$

This proves that (replacing w_1 by v_1) the vectors $v_1, w_2, w_3, \ldots, w_n$ span V. They are still linearly independent, since if v_1 were a linear combination of $w_2, \ldots, w_n$ then the expression for w_1 in terms of $v_1, w_2, \ldots, w_n$ would show that w_1 was a linear combination of $w_2, \ldots, w_n$. This would contradict the linear independence of $w_1, \ldots, w_n$.

Continuing, suppose inductively that $v_1, \ldots, v_i, w_{i+1}, \ldots, w_n$ form a basis for V, with $i < n$. Express v_{i+1} as a linear combination

$$v_{i+1} = a_1 v_1 + \ldots + a_i v_i + b_{i+1} w_{i+1} + \ldots + b_n w_n$$

Some b_j must be non-zero, or else v_i is a linear combination of $v_1, \ldots, v_i$, contradicting the linear independence of the v_j's. By renumbering the w_j's (again!) if necessary, we may assume that $b_{i+1} \neq 0$. Then rewrite this to express w_{i+1} as a linear combination of $v_1, \ldots, v_i, w_{i+1}, \ldots, w_n$:

$$w_{i+1} = (-b_{i+1}^{-1} a_1) v_1 + \ldots + (-b_{i+1}^{-1} a_i) v_i + (b_{i+1}^{-1}) v_{i+1}$$

$$+ (-b_{i+1}^{-1} b_{i+2}) w_{i+2} + \ldots + (-b_{i+1}^{-1} b_n) w_n$$

Thus, $v_1, \ldots, v_{i+1}, w_{i+2}, \ldots, w_n$ span V. We claim that these vectors are linearly independent. Indeed, if for some coefficients a_j and b_j

$$a_1 v_1 + \ldots + a_{i+1} v_{i+1} + b_{i+2} w_{i+2} + \ldots + b_n w_n = 0$$

then some a_{i+1} must be non-zero, because of the (inductively assumed) linear independence of $v_1, \ldots, v_i, w_{i+1}, \ldots, w_n$, thus surely of the subcollection $v_1, \ldots, v_i, w_{i+2}, \ldots, w_n$. Thus, we can rearrange to express v_{i+1} as a linear combination of $v_1, \ldots, v_i, w_{i+2}, \ldots, w_n$. Then the expression for w_{i+1} in terms of $v_1, \ldots, v_i, v_{i+1}, w_{i+2}, \ldots, w_n$ becomes an expression for w_{i+1} as a linear combination of $v_1, \ldots, v_i, w_{i+2}, \ldots, w_n$. But this would contradict the (inductively assumed) linear independence of $v_1, \ldots, v_i, w_{i+1}, w_{i+2}, \ldots, w_n$.

Consider the possibility that $m > n$. Then, by the above argument, $v_1, \ldots, v_n$ is a basis for V. Thus, v_{n+1} is a linear combination of $v_1, \ldots, v_n$, contradicting their linear independence. Therefore, $m \leq n$, and $v_1, \ldots, v_m, w_{m+1}, \ldots, w_n$ is a basis for V, as claimed.   ///

The previous theorem allows us to define the **dimension** of a vector space to be the number of elements in a basis for it, since the theorem says that this number is the same for any basis. Write

$$\dim V = \text{ dimension of } V$$

A vector space is **finite-dimensional** if it has a finite basis. What we actually proved is only the finite-dimensional case of this well-definedness, but we will not need the infinite-dimensional case.

Corollary: A linearly independent set of vectors in a finite-dimensional vector space can be augmented to be a basis.

Proof: Let $v_1, \ldots, v_m$ be the linearly independent set of vectors, let $w_1, \ldots, w_n$ be a basis, and apply the theorem.   ///

Corollary: The dimension of a *proper* subspace of a finite-dimensional vector space is strictly less than the dimension of the whole space.

Proof: Let $w_1, \ldots, w_m$ be a basis for the subspace. By the theorem, it can be extended to a basis $w_1, \ldots, w_m, v_{m+1}, \ldots, v_n$ of the whole space. It must be that $n > m$, or else the subspace is the whole space.   ///

Corollary: The dimension of k^n is n.

Proof: The vectors

$$\begin{aligned}
e_1 &= (1, 0, 0, \ldots, 0, 0) \\
e_2 &= (0, 1, 0, \ldots, 0, 0) \\
e_3 &= (0, 0, 1, \ldots, 0, 0) \\
&\cdots \\
e_n &= (0, 0, 0, \ldots, 0, 1)
\end{aligned}$$

spans k^n, since

$$(c_1, \ldots, c_n) = c_1 e_1 + \ldots + c_n e_n$$

On the other hand, a linear dependence relation

$$0 = c_1 e_1 + \ldots + c_n e_n$$

gives

$$(c_1, \ldots, c_n) = (0, \ldots, 0)$$

from which each c_i is 0. Thus, these vectors are a basis for k^n.   ///

Remark: The vectors in the latter proof are the **standard basis** for k^n.

A.3 Homomorphisms and duals

Now we can introduce vector space homomorphisms, their kernels, their images, and prove a fundamental result about how dimensions behave in this situation. The *dual* of a vector space is an important special case of this discussion.

A vector space **homomorphism** $f : V \to W$ from a vector space V over a field k to a vector space W over the same field k is a function f such that

$$
\begin{aligned}
f(v_1 + v_2) &= f(v_1) + f(v_2) & \text{(for all } v_1, v_2 \in V) \\
f(\alpha \cdot v) &= \alpha \cdot f(v) & \text{(for all } \alpha \in k, \, v \in V)
\end{aligned}
$$

The **kernel** of f is

$$
\ker f = \{v \in V : f(v) = 0\}
$$

and the **image** of f is

$$
\operatorname{Im} f = \{f(v) : v \in V\}
$$

Vector space homomorphisms are also called **linear**. A homomorphism is an **isomorphism** if it is *one-to-one* (injective) and *onto* (surjective).

- A vector space homomorphism $f : V \to W$ sends 0 (in V) to 0 (in W).

Proof: First,

$$
f(0) = f(0 + 0) = f(0) + f(0)
$$

Then add $-f(0)$ (whatever it may be) to both sides, obtaining

$$
0 = -f(0) + f(0) = -f(0) + (f(0) + f(0)) = (-f(0) + f(0)) + f(0) = 0 + f(0) = f(0)
$$

proving what was claimed.   ///

- For a vector space homomorphism $f : V \to W$, for $v \in V$,

$$
f(-v) = -f(v)
$$

Proof: Above we saw that $-v = (-1) \cdot v$. Thus,

$$
f(-v) = f((-1) \cdot v) = (-1) \cdot f(v) = -f(v)
$$

using the linearity of f.   ///

Proposition: The kernel and image of a vector space homomorphism $f : V \to W$ are vector subspaces of V and W, respectively.

Proof: Regarding the kernel, the previous proposition shows that it contains 0. The last bulleted point observed that additive inverses of elements in the kernel are again in the kernel. And for $x, y \in \ker f$

$$
f(x + y) = f(x) + f(y) = 0 + 0 = 0
$$

so the kernel is closed under addition. Finally, for $\alpha \in k$ and $v \in V$

$$
f(\alpha \cdot v) = \alpha \cdot f(v) = \alpha \cdot 0 = 0
$$

so the kernel is closed under scalar multiplication. Thus, the kernel is a vector subspace.

Similarly, $f(0) = 0$ shows that 0 is in the image of f. For $w = f(v)$ in the image of f and $\alpha \in k$

$$\alpha \cdot w = \alpha \cdot f(v) = f(\alpha v) \in \operatorname{Im} f$$

For $x = f(u)$ and $y = f(v)$ both in the image of f,

$$x + y = f(u) + f(v) = f(u + v) \in \operatorname{Im} f$$

And from above

$$f(-v) = -f(v)$$

Thus, the image is a vector subspace.   ///

Corollary: A linear map $f : V \to W$ is *one-to-one* (injective) if and only if its kernel is the trivial subspace $\{0\}$.

Proof: If $f(x) = f(y)$ for $x, y \in V$, then

$$f(x - y) = f(x) - f(y) = 0$$

Thus, if f is not injective, for some $x \neq y$ we have $f(x) = f(y)$, so $x - y \neq 0$ is in the kernel of f. On the other hand, if f is injective, then $f(x) = 0$ implies that $f(x) = f(0)$, so $x = 0$ (by injectivity), and the kernel is $\{0\}$.   ///

Corollary: Let $f : V \to W$ be a vector space homomorphism, with V finite-dimensional. Then

$$\dim \ker f + \dim \operatorname{Im} f = \dim V$$

Proof: Let $v_1, \ldots, v_m$ be a basis for $\ker f$, and, invoking the theorem, let $w_{m+1}, \ldots, w_n$ be vectors in V such that $v_1, \ldots, v_m, w_{m+1}, \ldots, w_n$ form a basis for V. We claim that the images $f(w_{m+1}), \ldots, f(w_n)$ form a basis for $\operatorname{Im} f$. First, show that these vectors *span* the image. Indeed, for $f(v) = w$, express v as a linear combination

$$v = a_1 v_1 + \ldots + a_m v_m + b_{m+1} w_{m+1} + \ldots + b_n w_n$$

and apply f, using its linearity

$$w = a_1 f(v_1) + \ldots + a_m f(v_m) + b_{m+1} f(w_{m+1}) + \ldots + b_n f(w_n)$$

$$= a_1 \cdot 0 + \ldots + a_m \cdot 0(v_m) + b_{m+1} f(w_{m+1}) + \ldots + b_n f(w_n)$$

$$= b_{m+1} f(w_{m+1}) + \ldots + b_n f(w_n)$$

since the v_i's are in the kernel. This shows that the $f(w_j)$'s *span* the image. For linear independence, suppose that

$$0 = b_{m+1} f(w_{m+1}) + \ldots + b_n f(w_n)$$

Then

$$0 = f(b_{m+1}w_{m+1} + \ldots + b_n w_n)$$

Then, $b_{m+1}w_{m+1}+\ldots+b_n w_n$ would be in the kernel of f, so would be a linear combination of the v_i's, which would contradict the fact that $v_1,\ldots,v_m,w_{m+1},\ldots,w_n$ is a basis, unless all the b_j's were 0. Thus, the images $f(w_j)$ are linearly independent, so form a basis for $\operatorname{Im} f$. ///

Proposition: An isomorphism $f : V \to W$ sends a basis for V to a basis for W.

Proof: Let $e_1,\ldots,e_n$ be a basis for V. Given $w \in W$, let $v \in V$ be such that (by the surjectivity) $f(v) = w$. Write $v = \sum_i c_i e_i$. Then

$$w = f(v) = f\left(\sum_i c_i e_i\right) = \sum_i f(c_i e_i) = \sum_i c_i f(e_i)$$

by the linearity of f, showing that w is a linear combination of the images $f(e_i)$. On the other hand, suppose that

$$\sum_i c_i f(e_i) = 0$$

Then

$$0 = \sum_i c_i f(e_i) = \sum_i f(c_i e_i) = f\left(\sum_i c_i e_i\right)$$

Since f is injective $\sum_i c_i e_i = 0$. Since the e_i form a basis for V, it must be that all c_i's are 0. This proves that the $f(e_i)$'s are linearly independent. ///

A **(linear) functional** $\lambda : V \to k$ on a vector space V over k is a linear map from V to the field k itself, viewed as a one-dimensional vector space over k. The collection V^* of all such linear functionals is the **dual space** of V.

Proposition: The collection V^* of linear functionals on a vector space V over k is itself a vector space over k, with the addition

$$(\lambda + \mu)(v) = \lambda(v) + \mu(v)$$

and scalar multiplication

$$(\alpha \cdot \lambda)(v) = \alpha \cdot \lambda(v)$$

Proof: The 0-vector in V^* is the linear functional which sends every vector to 0. The additive inverse $-\lambda$ is defined by

$$(-\lambda)(v) = -\lambda(v)$$

The distributivity properties are readily verified:

$$(\alpha(\lambda+\mu))(v) = \alpha(\lambda+\mu)(v) = \alpha(\lambda(v)+\mu(v)) = \alpha\lambda(v)+\alpha\mu(v) = (\alpha\lambda)(v)+(\alpha\mu)(v)$$

and

$$((\alpha + \beta) \cdot \lambda)(v) = (\alpha + \beta)\lambda(v) = \alpha\lambda(v) + \beta\lambda(v) = (\alpha\lambda)(v) + (\beta\lambda)(v)$$

as desired.   ///

Let V be a finite-dimensional vector space, with a basis $e_1, \ldots, e_n$ for V. A **dual basis** $\lambda_1, \ldots, \lambda_n$ for V^* (and $\{e_i\}$) is a basis for V^* with the property that

$$\lambda_j(e_i) = \begin{cases} 1 & \text{(for } i = j) \\ 0 & \text{(for } i \ne j) \end{cases}$$

From the definition alone it is not at all clear that a dual basis exists, but the following proposition proves that it does.

Proposition: The dual space V^* to an n-dimensional vector space V (with n a positive integer) is also n-dimensional. Given a basis $e_1, \ldots, e_n$ for V, there exists a unique corresponding **dual basis** $\lambda_1, \ldots, \lambda_n$ for V^*, namely a basis for V^* with the property that

$$\lambda_j(e_i) = \begin{cases} 1 & \text{(for } i = j) \\ 0 & \text{(for } i \ne j) \end{cases}$$

Proof: Proving the existence of a dual basis corresponding to the given basis will certainly prove the dimension assertion. Using the *uniqueness* of expression of a vector in V as a linear combination of the basis vectors, we can unambiguously define a linear functional λ_j by

$$\lambda_j \left(\sum_i c_i e_i \right) = c_j$$

These functionals certainly have the desired relation to the basis vectors e_i. We must prove that the λ_j are a basis for V^*. If

$$\sum_j b_j \lambda_j = 0$$

then apply this functional to e_i to obtain

$$b_i = \left(\sum_j b_j \lambda_j \right)(e_i) = 0(e_i) = 0$$

This holds for every index i, so all coefficients are 0, proving the linear independence of the λ_j. To prove the spanning property, let λ be an arbitrary linear functional on V. We claim that

$$\lambda = \sum_j \lambda(e_j) \cdot \lambda_j$$

Indeed, evaluating the left-hand side on $\sum_i a_i e_i$ gives $\sum_i a_i \lambda(e_i)$, and evaluating the right-hand side on $\sum_i a_i e_i$ gives

$$\sum_j \sum_i a_i\, \lambda(e_j)\, \lambda_j(e_i) = \sum_i a_i \lambda(e_i)$$

since $\lambda_j(e_i) = 0$ for $i \neq j$. This proves that any linear functional is a linear combination of the λ_j.   ///

Let W be a subspace of a vector space V over k. The **orthogonal complement** $W^\perp$ of W in V^* is

$$W^\perp = \{\lambda \in V^* : \lambda(w) = 0, \text{ for all } w \in W\}$$

- The orthogonal complement $W^\perp$ of a subspace W of a vector space V is a vector subspace of V^*.

Proof: Certainly $W^\perp$ contains 0. If $\lambda(w) = 0$ and $\mu(w) = 0$ for all $w \in W$, then certainly $(\lambda + \mu)(w) = 0$. Likewise, $(-\lambda)(w) = \lambda(-w)$, so $W^\perp$ is a subspace.   ///

Corollary: Let W be a subspace of a finite-dimensional vector space V over k.

$$\dim W + \dim W^\perp = \dim V$$

Proof: Let $e_1, \ldots, e_m$ be a basis of W, and extend it to a basis $e_1, \ldots, e_m,$ $f_{m+1}, \ldots, f_n$ of V, invoking the results above. Let $\lambda_1, \ldots, \lambda_m, \mu_{m+1}, \ldots, \mu_n$ be the corresponding dual basis of V^*. To prove the corollary it would suffice to prove that $\mu_{m+1}, \ldots, \mu_n$ form a basis for $W^\perp$. First, these functionals do lie in $W^\perp$, since they are all 0 on the basis vectors for W. To see that they span $W^\perp$, let

$$\lambda = \sum_{1 \leq i \leq m} a_i \lambda_i + \sum_{m+1 \leq j \leq n} b_j \mu_j$$

be a functional in $W^\perp$. Evaluating both sides on $e_\ell \in W$ gives

$$0 = \lambda(e_\ell) = \sum_{1 \leq i \leq m} a_i \lambda_i(e_\ell) + \sum_{m+1 \leq j \leq n} b_j \mu_j(e_\ell) = a_\ell$$

by the defining property of the dual basis. That is, every functional in $W^\perp$ is a linear combination of the μ_j, and thus the latter form a basis for $W^\perp$. Then

$$\dim W + \dim W^\perp = m + (n - m) = n = \dim V$$

as claimed.   ///

The **second dual** V^{**} of a vector space V is the dual of its dual. There is a natural vector space homomorphism $\varphi : V \to V^{**}$ of a vector space V to its second V^{**} by

$$\varphi(v)(\lambda) = \lambda(v)$$

for $v \in V$, $\lambda \in V^*$.

Corollary: Let V be a finite-dimensional vector space. Then the natural map of V to V^{**} is an isomorphism.

Proof: If v is in the kernel of the linear map $v \to \varphi(v)$, then $\varphi(v)(\lambda) = 0$ for all λ, so $\lambda(v) = 0$ for all λ. But if v is non-zero then v can be part of a basis for V, which has a dual basis, among which is a functional λ such that $\lambda(v) = 1$. Thus, for $\varphi(v)(\lambda)$ to be 0 for all λ it must be that $v = 0$. Thus, the kernel of φ is $\{0\}$, so (from above) φ is an injection. From the formula

$$\dim \ker \varphi + \dim \operatorname{Im} \varphi = \dim V$$

it follows that $\dim \operatorname{Im} \varphi = \dim V$. We showed above that the dimension of V^* is the same as that of V, since V is finite-dimensional. Likewise, the dimension of $V^{**} = (V^*)^*$ is the same as that of V^*, hence the same as that of V. Since the dimension of the image of φ in V^{**} is equal to the dimension of V, which is the same as the dimension of V^{**}, the image must be all of V^{**}. Thus, $\varphi : V \to V^{**}$ is an isomorphism.   ///

Corollary: Let W be a subspace of a finite-dimensional vector space V over k. Let $\varphi : V \to V^{**}$ be the isomorphism of the previous corollary. Then

$$(W^\perp)^\perp = \varphi(W)$$

Proof: First, show that

$$\varphi(W) \subset (W^\perp)^\perp$$

Indeed, for $\lambda \in W^\perp$,

$$\varphi(w)(\lambda) = \lambda(w) = 0$$

On the other hand,

$$\dim W + \dim W^\perp = \dim V$$

and likewise

$$\dim W^\perp + \dim(W^\perp)^\perp = \dim V^* = \dim V$$

Thus, $\varphi(W) \subset (W^\perp)^\perp$ and

$$\dim(W^\perp)^\perp = \dim \varphi(W)$$

since φ is an isomorphism. Therefore, $\varphi(W) = (W^\perp)^\perp$.   ///

As an illustration of the efficacy of the present viewpoint, we can prove a useful result about matrices.

Corollary: Let M be an m-by-n matrix with entries in a field k. Let R be the subspace of k^n spanned by the rows of M. Let C be the subspace of k^m spanned by the columns of M. Let

$$\begin{aligned} \text{column rank of } M &= \dim C \\ \text{row rank of } M &= \dim R \end{aligned}$$

Then

$$\text{column rank of } M = \text{row rank of } M$$

Proof: The matrix M gives a linear transformation $T : k^n \to k^m$ by $T(v) = Mv$ where v is a column vector of length n. It is easy to see that the column space of M is the image of T. It is a little subtler that the row space is $(\ker T)^\perp$. From above,

$$\dim \ker T + \dim \operatorname{Im} T = \dim V$$

and also

$$\dim \ker T + \dim (\ker T)^\perp = \dim V$$

Thus,

$$\text{column rank } M = \dim \operatorname{Im} T = \dim (\ker T)^\perp = \text{ row rank } M$$

as claimed.   ///

A.4 Scalar products

It turns out that the familiar properties of inner products can be treated in abstraction. This is very useful in applications.

An **inner product** or **scalar product** or **dot product** on a vector space V over k is a k-valued function of two V-variables, written $v \cdot w$ or $\langle v, w \rangle$, with the following properties for $u, v, w \in V$ and $\alpha \in k$

- (Symmetry) $\langle u, v \rangle = \langle v, u \rangle$
- (Linearity in first argument) $\langle u+v, w \rangle = \langle u, w \rangle + \langle v, w \rangle$ and $\langle \alpha u, v \rangle = \alpha \langle u, v \rangle$
- (Non-degeneracy in first argument) For all $v \neq 0$ in V there is $w \in V$ such that $\langle v, w \rangle \neq 0$

Remark: From the symmetry it follows that there are corresponding linearity and non-degeneracy properties for the *second* argument, as well:

$$\langle u, v + w \rangle = \langle u, w \rangle + \langle u, v \rangle \qquad \text{and} \qquad \langle u, \alpha v \rangle = \alpha \langle u, v \rangle$$

and for all $w \neq 0$ in V there is $v \in V$ such that $\langle v, w \rangle \neq 0$.

Remark: When the scalars are the complex numbers $\mathbf{C}$, often a variant of the symmetry condition is useful, namely a *hermitian* condition that $\langle u, v \rangle = \overline{\langle v, u \rangle}$ where the bar denotes complex conjugation.

Remark: When the scalars are real, sometimes the non-degeneracy condition is usefully replaced by a *positive-definiteness* condition, namely that $\langle v, v \rangle \geq 0$ and is 0 only for $v = 0$. An analogous condition is likewise often appropriate in the complex-scalar case.

When a vector space V has a scalar product $\langle , \rangle$, there is a natural linear map $v \to \lambda_v$ from V to its dual V^* given by

$$\lambda_v(w) = \langle v, w \rangle$$

That λ_v is a linear functional on V is an immediate consequence of the linearity of $\langle,\rangle$ in its second argument, and the linearity of the map $v \to \lambda_v$ itself is an immediate consequence of the linearity of $\langle,\rangle$ in its first argument.

Corollary: Let V be a finite-dimensional vector space. The linear map $v \to \lambda_v$ above is an isomorphism $V \to V^*$.

Proof: The non-degeneracy in the first argument means that for $v \neq 0$ the linear functional λ_v is not 0, since there is $w \in V$ such that $\lambda_v(w) \neq 0$. Thus, the linear map $v \to \lambda_v$ has kernel $\{0\}$, so $v \to \lambda_v$ is *injective*. Since V is finite-dimensional, from above we know that it and its dual have the same dimension. Let $L(v) = \lambda_v$. Since (from above)

$$\dim \operatorname{Im} L + \dim \ker L = \dim V$$

the image of V under $v \to \lambda_v$ in V is that of V. Since (from above) proper subspaces have strictly smaller dimension it must be that $L(V) = V^*$.   ///

Corollary: Let V be a finite-dimensional vector space. Under the isomorphism $v \to \lambda_v$ of V to its dual V^*

$$L\left(\{v \in V : \langle v, w \rangle = 0 \text{ for all } w \in W\}\right) = W^\perp$$

Proof: Suppose that $L(v) \in W^\perp$. Thus, $\lambda_v(w) = 0$ for all $w \in W$. That is, $\langle v, w \rangle = 0$ for all $w \in W$. On the other hand, suppose that $\langle v, w \rangle = 0$ for all $w \in W$. Then $\lambda_v(w) = 0$ for all $w \in W$, so $\lambda_v \in W^\perp$.   ///

Corollary: Redefine

$$W^\perp = \{v \in V : \langle v, w \rangle = 0 \text{ for all } w \in W\}$$

Then

$$\dim W + \dim W^\perp = \dim V$$

and

$$W^{\perp\perp} = W$$

Proof: With our original definition of $W^\perp_{\text{orig}}$ as

$$W^\perp_{\text{orig}} = \{\lambda \in V^* : \lambda(w) = 0 \text{ for all } w \in W\}$$

we had proven

$$\dim W + \dim W^\perp_{\text{orig}} = \dim V$$

We just showed that $L(W^\perp) = W^\perp_{\text{orig}}$, and since the map $L : V \to V^*$ by $v \to \lambda_v$ is an isomorphism

$$\dim W^\perp = \dim W^\perp_{\text{orig}}$$

Thus,

$$\dim W + \dim W^\perp = \dim V$$

as claimed. Next, we claim that $W \subset W^{\perp\perp}$. Indeed, for $w \in W$ it is certainly true that for $v \in W^\perp$

$$\langle w, v \rangle = \langle v, w \rangle = 0$$

That is, we see easily that $W \subset W^{\perp\perp}$. On the other hand, from

$$\dim W + \dim W^\perp = \dim V$$

and

$$\dim W^\perp + \dim W^{\perp\perp} = \dim V$$

we see that $\dim W^{\perp\perp} = \dim W$. Since W is a subspace of $W^{\perp\perp}$ with the same dimension, the two must be equal (from our earlier discussion).   ///

A.5 Vandermonde determinants

Granting facts about polynomials in several variables, we can compute Vandermonde determinants. We had already stated that

$$\det \begin{pmatrix} 1 & 1 & \cdots & 1 \\ x_1 & x_2 & \cdots & x_n \\ x_1^2 & x_2^2 & \cdots & x_n^2 \\ x_1^3 & x_2^3 & \cdots & x_n^3 \\ \vdots & \vdots & & \vdots \\ x_1^{n-1} & x_2^{n-1} & \cdots & x_n^{n-1} \end{pmatrix} = (-1)^{n(n-1)/2} \cdot \prod_{i<j} (x_i - x_j)$$

where the $\prod$ means product over the indicated indices, just as $\sum$ means sum. A matrix of that form is a **Vandermonde** matrix, and its determinant is a **Vandermonde determinant**. Granting some standard facts about determinants, the *idea* of the proof of this formula is straightforward. However, to make the idea fully legitimate, it is necessary to do some further work, namely verify that polynomial rings in several variables are *unique factorization domains*. We do that in the following appendix.

    The idea of the proof of the identity is as follows. First, we note that whatever the determinant is it is a polynomial in $x_1, \ldots, x_n$. It is a standard fact that if two columns of a matrix are the same, then the determinant is 0. From this we conclude (!) that for $i \neq j$ the determinant is divisible by $x_i - x_j$. Since $x_i - x_j$ and $x_j - x_i$ only differ by ± 1 and we do not want inadvertently to include the same factor twice, we conclude (!) that the determinant is divisible by the product

$$\prod_{i<j} (x_i - x_j)$$

We want to argue that the determinant can have no further polynomial factors, so up to a constant (which we'll determine) is equal to the latter product. The notion of **total degree** is useful. The total degree of a monomial $x_1^{m_1} \ldots x_n^{m_n}$ is $m_1 + \ldots + m_n$. The total degree of a polynomial is the maximum of the total degrees of the monomials occurring in it. We grant for the moment the result of the proposition below, that the total degree of a product is the sum of the total degrees of the factors. The total degree of our product is

$$\sum_{1\le i<j\le n} 1 = \sum_{1\le i<n} n - i = \frac{1}{2}n(n-1)$$

To determine the total degree of the determinant, we invoke a standard formula for the determinant of a matrix M with entries M_{ij}, namely that

$$\det M = \sum_p \sigma(p)\, M_{1p(1)} M_{2p(2)} \ldots M_{np(n)}$$

where p runs over permutations of n things and $\sigma(p)$ is the *sign* or *parity* of p, that is, $\sigma(p)$ is $+1$ if p is a product of an *even* number of 2-cycles and is -1 if p is the product of an *odd* number of 2-cycles. Qualitatively, up to ± 1, this expresses the determinant as a sum of products of elements from the first, second, third, $\ldots$, n^{th} columns, no two in the same row. In particular, since the matrix is square, there must be *exactly* one factor from each row. In a Vandermonde matrix all the top row entries have total degree 0, all the second row entries have total degree 1, and so on. Thus, in this sort of sum for a Vandermonde determinant, each summand has total degree

$$0 + 1 + 2 + \ldots + (n-1) = \frac{1}{2}n(n-1)$$

That is, the total degree of the determinant is equal to the total degree of the product

$$\sum_{1\le i<j\le n} 1 = \sum_{1\le i<n} n - i = \frac{1}{2}n(n-1)$$

Thus, we conclude (!) that

$$\det \begin{pmatrix} 1 & 1 & \cdots & 1 \\ x_1 & x_2 & \cdots & x_n \\ x_1^2 & x_2^2 & \cdots & x_n^2 \\ x_1^3 & x_2^3 & \cdots & x_n^3 \\ \vdots & \vdots & & \vdots \\ x_1^{n-1} & x_2^{n-1} & \cdots & x_n^{n-1} \end{pmatrix} = \text{constant} \cdot \prod_{i<j} (x_i - x_j)$$

Granting this, to determine the constant it suffices to compare a single monomial in both the determinant and the product expression. Among many other reasonable choices, we will compare the coefficients of

$$x_1^{n-1} x_2^{n-2} x_3^{n-3} \ldots x_{n-1}^1 x_n^0$$

In the product expression, the only way we can get x_1^{n-1} is by taking all the x_1s in the linear factors $x_1 - x_j$ with $1 < j$. After this, the only way to get x_2^{n-2} is by taking all the x_2s in the linear factors $x_2 - x_j$ with $2 < j$. Continuing in this manner, we get a coefficient of $+1$ in the product.

In the determinant, the only way to obtain this monomial is as the product of entries from lower left to upper right. The indices of these entries are $(n, 1)$, $(n-1, 2), \ldots, (2, n-1), (1, n)$. Thus, the coefficient of this monomial is $(-1)^t$ where t is the number of 2-cycles necessary to obtain the permutation p with the property

$$p(i) = n + 1 - i$$

There are at least two ways to count this. We might observe that this permutation is expressible as a product of two-cycles

$$p = \begin{cases} (1\,n)(2\,n-1)\,(3\,n-3)\ldots(\frac{n}{2}\,\frac{n}{2}+1) & \text{(for n even)} \\ (1\,n)(2\,n-1)\,(3\,n-3)\ldots(\frac{n-1}{2}\,\frac{n+1}{2}) & \text{(for n odd)} \end{cases}$$

Thus, for n even there are $n/2$ two-cycles, and for n odd there are $(n-1)/2$ two-cycles. We might insist on arranging a closed form for this. Since these numbers will be the exponent on -1, we only care about their values modulo 2. Thus, because of the division by 2, we only care about n modulo 4, and we have values

$$\begin{cases} n/2 & = & 0 \bmod 2 & \text{(for $n = 0 \bmod 4$)} \\ (n-1)/2 & = & 0 \bmod 2 & \text{(for $n = 1 \bmod 4$)} \\ n/2 & = & 1 \bmod 2 & \text{(for $n = 3 \bmod 4$)} \\ (n-1)/2 & = & 1 \bmod 2 & \text{(for $n = 1 \bmod 4$)} \end{cases}$$

After some experimentation, we find a closed expression for this, namely

$$n(n-1)/2 \bmod 2$$

Thus, finally, have determined the leading constant

$$(-1)^{n(n-1)/2}$$

in the expression for the Vandermonde determinant.　　　　　　　　　///

Now we verify the property of total degree used above.

Proposition: Let $f(x_1, \ldots, x_n)$ and $g(x_1, \ldots, x_n)$ be polynomials in $k[x_1, \ldots, x_n]$ where k is a field. Then the total degree of the product is the sum of the total degrees:

total degree $f \cdot g = $ (total degree f) + (total degree g)

Proof: The fact that the total degree of the product is less than or equal the sum of the total degrees is clear. However, it is less clear that there cannot be any cancellation which might cause the total degree of the product to be strictly less than the sum of the total degrees. It is true that such cancellation does not occur, but the proof is a little less clear than in the single-variable case. One way to demonstrate the non-cancellation is as follows.

Let $x_1^{e_1} \ldots x_n^{e_n}$ and $x_1^{f_1} \ldots x_n^{f_n}$ be two monomials of highest total degree t occurring with non-zero coefficients in f and g, respectively. We can assume without loss of generality that the exponents e_1 and f_1 of x_1 in the two expressions are the largest among all monomials of total degree t in f and g, respectively. Similarly, we can assume without loss of generality that the exponents e_2 and f_2 of x_2 in the two expressions are the largest among all monomials of total degree t in f and g, respectively, and so on. We claim that the coefficient of the monomial

$$M = x^{e_1+f_1} \ldots x_n^{e_n+f_n}$$

is simply the product of the coefficients of $x_1^{e_1} \ldots x_n^{e_n}$ and $x_1^{f_1} \ldots x_n^{f_n}$, so non-zero. Let $x_1^{u_1} \ldots x_n^{u_n}$ and $x_1^{v_1} \ldots x_n^{v_n}$ be two other monomials occurring in f and g such that for all indices i we have $u_i + v_i = e_i + f_i$. By the maximality assumption on e_1 and f_1, we have $e_1 \geq u_1$ and $f_1 \geq v_1$, so the only way that the necessary power of x_1 can be achieved is that $e_1 = u_1$ and $f_1 = v_1$. Among exponents with these maximal exponents of x_1, e_2 and f_2 are maximal, so $e_2 \geq u_2$ and $f_2 \geq v_2$, and again it must be that $e_2 = u_2$ and $f_2 = v_2$ in order to obtain the exponent of x_2. Continuing inductively, we find that $u_i = e_i$ and $v_i = f_i$ for all indices. That is, the only terms in f and g which contribute to the coefficient of the monomial M in the product $f \cdot g$ are the two monomials $x_1^{e_1} \ldots x_n^{e_n}$ and $x_1^{f_1} \ldots x_n^{f_n}$. Thus, the coefficient of the monomial M is non-zero, and the total degree is indeed as large as claimed.   ///

Appendix: Polynomials

The goal here is to prove that rings of polynomials in several variables with coefficients in a field are *unique factorization domains*, meaning that such polynomials can be factored essentially uniquely into irreducible polynomials. We will make this precise. Among other uses, this fact is necessary in discussion of Vandermonde determinants, and is useful in the proof that the *parity* (or *sign*) of a permutation is well-defined.

For precision, we need some definitions. Let R be a commutative ring R with 1. For r, s in R, r *divides* s, written $r|s$, if there is $t \in R$ such that $s = tr$. Such R is said to be a *domain* or *integral domain* if for $r, s \in R$ the equation $r \cdot s = 0$ implies that either r or s is 0. The *units* $R^{\times}$ in R are the elements in R with multiplicative inverses. An *irreducible* element p in R is a non-unit with the property that if $p = xy$ for $x, y \in R$ then either x or y is a unit.

Remark: Sometimes irreducible elements are called *prime* elements, although equally often the terminology is used to make an important distinction. Namely, to prove *uniqueness* of factorization (not to prove *existence*) into irreducible elements in a ring R it is critical that we be able to prove that if an irreducible element p divides a product ab in R, then $p|a$ or $p|b$. This does *not* hold in all rings, but we will be able to prove it in the case at hand. Sometimes only elements p with the property that $p|ab$ implies either $p|a$ or $p|b$ are called *prime*.

Remark: Quite generally, in a domain R elements p with the property that $p|ab$ implies either $p|a$ or $p|b$ are *irreducible*. Indeed, suppose p has this property and p factors as $p = xy$. Then certainly $p|xy$, so either $p|x$ or $p|y$ by the definition of primality. Suppose without loss of generality that $p|x$, so $x = ap$ for some $a \in R$. Then

$$p = xy = (ap)y$$

As observed earlier, since R is a domain, the cancellation property holds, namely, that $ax = bx$ and $x \neq 0$ implies $a = b$. Indeed, $ax = bx$ implies that $(a - b)x = 0$, and since R is a domain and $x \neq 0$ it must be that $a - b = 0$. Thus, $1 = ay$, and y is a unit. By contrast, already in the examples given earlier to illustrate the failure of unique factorization in more exotic rings, elements *do* have factorizations into irreducibles, but these irreducibles may fail to be prime, thus allowing a failure of unique factorization in such rings.

Definition: Two irreducible elements p and q in a domain R are *equivalent* if they differ by a unit, that is, if $p = uq$ for some $u \in R^{\times}$. This is easily seen to be an equivalence relation.

Definition: A *factorization* of an element r into irreducibles in an integral domain

R is an expression for r of the form

$$r = u \cdot p_1^{e_1} \ldots p_m^{e_m}$$

where u is a unit, p_1 through p_m are *inequivalent* irreducible elements, and the e_is are positive integers.

Definition: Two factorizations

$$r = u \cdot p_1^{e_1} \ldots p_m^{e_m}$$

$$r = v \cdot q_1^{f_1} \ldots q_n^{f_n}$$

into irreducibles p_i and q_j with units u, v are *equivalent* if $m = n$ and (after possibly renumbering the irreducibles) q_i is equivalent to p_i for all indices i. Here we assume that

Definition: A domain R is a *unique factorization domain* if any two factorizations are equivalent.

Theorem: (*Gauss*) Let R be a commutative ring with 1 that is a unique factorization domain. Then the polynomial ring in one variable $R[x]$ is a unique factorization domain.

Remark: The idea of the proof is to factor a given polynomial $f(x)$ in $R[x]$ in the larger ring $k[x]$ where k is the field of fractions of R (reviewed below), and rearrange constants to get all coefficients to be in R rather than k. Uniqueness of the factorization should follow from the uniqueness of factorization in R together with the uniqueness of factorization in $k[x]$. Moving back and forth between $R[x]$ and $k[x]$ requires some finesse, for which we must prepare.

Corollary: A polynomial ring $k[x_1, \ldots, x_n]$ in a finite number of variables x_1, $\ldots$, x_n over a field k is a unique factorization domain. (*Proof by induction via the theorem.*) ///

Before proving the theorem itself, we must explicitly observe that unique factorization does allow us to recover some of our usual ideas about divisibility.

Definition: Given $r, s \in R$ not both 0, an element $g \in R$ dividing both r and s, such that any divisor d of both r and s also divides g, is a *greatest common divisor* of r and s, denoted $g = \gcd(r, s)$.

Remark: It is of course not at all clear that such greatest common divisors exist in general rings. Indeed, in general they do not.

Proposition: Let R be a unique factorization domain. For r, s in R not both 0 there exists $\gcd(r, s)$ and it is unique up to an element of $R^{\times}$. We have a formula for the greatest common divisor, as follows. Factor both r and s into irreducibles

$$r = u \cdot p_1^{e_1} \ldots p_m^{e_m}$$

$$s = v \cdot p_1^{f_1} \ldots p_m^{f_n}$$

where u and v are units and where the p_i are mutually inequivalent irreducibles, but we allow the exponents to be 0, so that we can use a common set of irreducibles to express both r and s. Then the greatest common divisor has exponents which are the minima of those of r and s

$$\gcd(r, s) = p_1^{\min(e_1, f_1)} \dots p_m^{\min(e_m, f_m)}$$

Proof: Let

$$g = p_1^{\min(e_1, f_1)} \dots p_m^{\min(e_m, f_m)}$$

First, it is easy to see that g does divide both r and s. On the other hand, let d be any common divisor of both r and s. Enlarge the collection of inequivalent irreducibles p_i if necessary such that d can be expressed as

$$d = w \cdot p_1^{h_1} \dots p_m^{h_m}$$

with a unit w and non-negative integer exponents. To say that $d|r$ is to say that there is $D \in R$ such that $dD = r$. Let

$$D = W \cdot p_1^{H_1} \dots p_m^{H_m}$$

Then we find

$$wW \cdot p_1^{h_1 + H_1} \dots p_m^{h_m + H_m} = d \cdot D = r = u \cdot p_1^{e_1} \dots p_m^{e_m}$$

Then unique factorization (and the non-equivalence of the p_is) implies that the exponents are the same: for all indices i we have

$$h_i + H_i = e_i$$

Thus, $h_i \le e_i$. The same argument applies with r replaced by s, so $h_i \le f_i$, and $h_i \le \min(e_i, f_i)$. Thus, $d|g$. For uniqueness, observe that any other greatest common divisor h would have $g|h$, but also $h|r$ and $h|s$. Using the (unique up to units) factorizations, it is immediate that the exponents of the irreducibles in g and h must be the same, so g and h must differ only by a unit.   ///

Proposition: Let R be a unique factorization domain. For r, s in R, let $g = \gcd(r, s)$. Then

$$\gcd(r/g, \, s/g) = 1$$

Proof: The characterization of the greatest common divisor given in the previous proposition shows that for each irreducible p in factorizations of r and s at least one of the exponents of p in r/g and s/g is 0.   ///

Definition: The **field of fractions** k of R is the collection of fractions a/b with $a, b \in R$ and $b \ne 0$ and with the usual rules for addition and multiplication. More precisely, we might say that k is the set of ordered pairs (a, b) with $a, b \in R$ and $b \ne 0$, modulo the equivalence relation that

$$(a, b) \sim (c, d)$$

if and only if $ad - bc = 0$. (This corresponds to the ordinary rule for equality of two fractions.) Multiplication and addition would be simply the encoded version of the usual rules, namely

$$(a, b) \cdot (c, d) = (ac, bd)$$

$$(a, b) + (c, d) = (ad + bc, bd)$$

And we identify $r \in R$ with $(r, 1)$ (thinking of the fraction $r/1$). One should note that the assumption that R is a *domain* (meaning has no non-zero 0-divisors) is needed to make this work as stated. From now on we write a/b rather than (a, b) modulo $\sim$. Further, since R is a unique factorization ring, whenever we want we can suppose without loss of generality that fractions a/b are *in lowest terms*, meaning that $\gcd(a, b) = 1$, by dividing both a and b by their greatest common divisor. We saw in the last proposition just above that this effectively removes any common factors from a and b.

We extend the notions of divisibility and of greatest common divisor so as to apply to elements of the fraction field k of R. First, say that $x|y$ for two elements x and y in k if there is $r \in R$ such that $s = rx$. That is, x divides y if y is an R-multiple of x. And, continuing this parallel for $r_1, \ldots, r_n$ in k, not all 0, a greatest common divisor $\gcd(r_1, \ldots, r_n)$ is an element $g \in k$ such g divides each r_i and such that if $d \in k$ divides each r_i then $d|g$.

Remark: Note that for non-zero r in the domain R, $rx|ry$ if and only if $x|y$. Indeed, if $ry = m \cdot rx$ then by cancellation (using the domain property), $y = m \cdot x$. And of course $y = m \cdot x$ implies $ry = m \cdot rx$ directly.

Proposition: In the field of fractions k of a unique factorization domain R greatest common divisors exist.

Proof: We reduce this to the case when everything is inside the ring R. Given a list of elements $x_i = a_i/b_i$ in k with a_i and b_i all in R, take $0 \neq r \in R$ such that $rx_i \in R$ for all indices i. For example, taking r to be the product of the denominators b_i would do. Let G the the greatest common divisor of the rx_i, and then put $g = G/r$. We claim that this g is the greatest common divisor of the original x_is. This is straightforward. On one hand, from $G|rx_i$ it follows immediately that $g|x_i$. On the other hand, if $d|x_i$ then $rd|rx_i$, so rd divides $G = rg$ and then $d|g$. ///

Definition: The **content** $\text{cont}(f)$ of a polynomial f in $k[x]$ is the greatest common divisor of the coefficients of f.

The following lemma is the crucial point in proving the theorem.

Lemma: *(Gauss)* Let f and g be two polynomials in $k[x]$. Then

$$\text{cont}(fg) = \text{cont}(f) \cdot \text{cont}(g)$$

Remark: The values of the content function are only well-defined up to units $R^\times$. Thus, the content of Gauss' lemma more properly concerns the equivalence classes of irreducibles dividing the respective coefficients.

Proof: From the remark just above we see that for any $c \in k^\times$

$$\text{cont}(c \cdot f) = c \cdot \text{cont}(f)$$

Thus, from the proposition above which notes that

$$\gcd\left(\frac{a}{\gcd(a,b)}, \frac{b}{\gcd(a,b)}\right) = 1$$

we can assume without loss of generality that $\text{cont}(f) = 1$ and $\text{cont}(g) = 1$ and must prove that $\text{cont}(fg) = 1$. Suppose not. Then there is a a non-unit irreducible element p of R dividing all the coefficients of fg. Put

$$f(x) = a_0 + a_1 x + a_2 x^2 + \ldots$$

$$g(x) = b_0 + b_1 x + b_2 x^2 + \ldots$$

But p does not divide all the coefficients of f, nor all those of g. Let i be the smallest integer such that p does not divide a_i. Let j be the largest integer such that p does not divide b_j. Now consider the coefficient of x^{i+j} in fg. It is

$$a_0 b_{i+j} + a_1 b_{i+j-1} + \ldots + a_{i-1} b_{j-1} + a_i b_j + a_{i+1} b_{j-1} + \ldots + a_{i+j-1} b_1 + a_{i+j} b_0$$

In all the summands to the left of $a_i b_j$ the factor a_k with $k < i$ is divisible by p, and in all the summand to the right of $a_i b_j$ the factor b_k with $k < j$ is divisible by p. This leaves only the summand $a_i b_j$ to consider. Since the whole sum is divisible by p, it follows that $p | a_i b_j$. Since R is a unique factorization domain, either $p | a_i$ or $p | b_j$, contradiction. Thus, it could not have been that p divided all the coefficients of fg.   ///

Corollary: Let f be a polynomial in $R[x]$. If f factors properly in $k[x]$ then f factors properly in $R[x]$. More precisely, if f factors as $f = g \cdot h$ with g and h polynomials in $k[x]$ both of positive degree, then there is $c \in k\times$ such that $cg \in R[x]$ and $h/c \in R[x]$, and then

$$f = (cg) \cdot (h/c)$$

is a factorization of f in $R[x]$.

Proof: Since f has coefficients in R, $\text{cont}(f)$ is in R. By replacing f by f/c we may suppose that $\text{cont}(f) = 1$. Then, by Gauss' lemma above,

$$\text{cont}(g) \cdot \text{cont}(h) = \text{cont}(f) = 1$$

Let $\text{cont}(g) = c$. Then $\text{cont}(h) = 1/c$, and $\text{cont}(g/c) = 1$ and $\text{cont}(c \cdot h) = 1$, so both g/c and ch are in $R[x]$, and $(g/c) \cdot (ch) = f$. Thus f is reducible in $R[x]$.   ///

Corollary: The irreducibles in $R[x]$ are of two sorts, namely irreducibles in R and polynomials f in $R[x]$ with $\text{cont}(f) = 1$ which are irreducible in $k[x]$.

Proof: If an irreducible p in R were to factor in $R[x]$ as $p = gh$, then the degrees of both g and h would be 0 (since degrees add under polynomial multiplication), so g and h would lie in R. The irreducibility of p in R would imply that one or the other of g or h would be a unit. Thus, irreducibles in R remain irreducible in $R[x]$.

Now suppose p were an irreducible in $R[x]$ of positive degree. If $\text{cont}(p)$ were a non-unit g, then $p = (p/g) \cdot g$ would be a proper factorization of p, contradiction. Thus, $\text{cont}(p) = 1$. The previous corollary to Gauss' lemma shows that p is irreducible in p.

Last suppose that f is irreducible in $k[x]$, and has $\text{cont}(f) = 1$. The irreducibility in $k[x]$ implies that if $f = gh$ in $R[x]$ then the degree one of g or h must be 0. Without loss of generality suppose the degree of g is 0, so $\text{cont}(g) = g$. Since

$$1 = \text{cont}(f) = \text{cont}(g)\text{cont}(h)$$

We see that g is a unit in R, so this is not a proper factorization after all, and f is irreducible in $R[x]$. ///

Proof: (*of theorem*) We can now combine the corollaries of Gauss' lemma to prove the theorem. Given a polynomial f in $R[x]$, let $c = \text{cont}(f)$, so from above $\text{cont}(f/c) = 1$. The hypothesis that R is a unique factorization domain allows us to factor u into irreducibles in R, and we showed just above that these irreducibles remain irreudicble in $R[x]$.

Replace f by $f/\text{cont}(f)$ to assume now that $\text{cont}(f) = 1$. Factor f into irreducibles in $k[x]$ as

$$f = u \cdot p_1^{e_1} \cdots p_m^{e_m}$$

where u is in $k^\times$, the p_is are irreducibles in $k[x]$, and the e_is are positive integers. We can replace each p_i by $p_i/\text{cont}(p_i)$ and replace u by

$$u \cdot \text{cont}(p_1)^{e_1} \cdots \text{cont}(p_m)^{e_m}$$

so then the new p_is are in $R[x]$ and have content 1. Since content is multiplicative, from $\text{cont}(f) = 1$ we find that $\text{cont}(u) = 1$, so u is a unit in R. The previous corollaries demonstrate the irreducibility of the (new) p_is in $R[x]$, so this gives a factorization of f into irreducibles in $R[x]$. That is, we have an explicit *existence* of a factorization into irreducibles.

Now suppose that we have two factorizations

$$f = u \cdot p_1^{e_1} \cdots p_m^{e_m} = v \cdot q_1^{f_1} \cdots q_n^{f_n}$$

where u, v are in R (and have unique factorizations there) and the p_i and q_j are irreducibles in $R[x]$ of positive degree. From above, all the contents of these irreducibles must be 1. Looking at this factorization in $k[x]$, it must be that $m = n$ and up to renumbering p_i differs from q_i by a constant in $k^\times$, and $e_i = f_i$. Since all these polynomials have content 1, in fact p_i differs from q_i by a unit in R. By equating the contents of both sides, we see that u and v differ by a unit in $R^\times$. Thus, by the unique factorization in R their factorizations into irreducibles in R (and, from above, in $R[x]$) must be essentially the same. Thus, we obtain uniqueness of factorization in $R[x]$. ///

Bibliography

The fundamental paper from which nearly all these things originate is [Shannon 1948]. There are several other introductory texts on coding, meeting various tastes, mostly emphasizing the error-correction aspects and omitting discussion of compression. [Roman 1992] includes both. Some devoted mostly to error correction are [Berlekamp 1968], [Lidl Niederreiter 1986], [van Lint 1998], [McEliece 1977], [Pless 1998], [Pretzel 1999], [Wells 1999], [Welsh 1988]. Discussion of compression appears in its own right in other sources such as [Salomon 1998] and [Sayood 1996]. An encyclopedic reference for error-correction is [MacWilliams Sloane 1977]. The collection [Verdu McLaughlin 2000] contains many tutorial and historical articles. [Conway Sloane 1988] discusses lattices and sphere packing and applications to coding, among many other uses.

[Berlekamp 1968] E. R. Berlekamp, *Algebraic Coding Theory*, McGraw-Hill, New York, 1968.

[Conway Sloane 1988] J. H. Conway, N.J.A. Sloane, *Sphere Packings, Lattices, and Groups*, Springer-Verlag, New York, 1988.

[Forney 1966] G. D. Forney, *Concatenated Codes*, M.I.T Press, Cambridge, MA, 1966.

[Justesen 1972] J. Justesen, *A class of constructive asymptotically good algebraic codes*, IEEE Trans. Info. Theory **18** (1972), pp. 652–656.

[Lidl Niederreiter 1986] R. Lidl, H. Niederreiter, *Introduction to finite fields and their applications*, University Press, Cambridge, 1986.

[van Lint 1998] J. H. van Lint, *Introduction to Coding Theory*, third edition, Springer-Verlag, New York, 1998.

[MacWilliams Sloane 1977] F. J. MacWilliams, N. A. J. Sloane, *The Theory of Error-Correcting Codes*, North-Holland, Amsterdam, 1977.

[McEliece 1977] R. J. McEliece, *The Theory of Information and Coding*, Encyclopedia of Math. and its Applications, Vol. 3, Addison-Wesley, Reading, MA, 1977.

[Pless 1998] V. Pless, *Introduction to the Theory of Error-Correcting Codes*, third edition, John Wiley & Sons, New York, 1998.

[Pretzel 1999] O. Pretzel, *Error-Correcting Codes and Finite Fields*, student edition, Clarendon Press, Oxford, 1999.

[Roman 1992] S. Roman, *Coding and Information Theory*, Springer-Verlag, New York, 1992.

[Salomon 1998] D. Salomon, *Data Compression, the Complete Reference*, Springer-Verlag, New York, 1998.

[Sayood 1996] K. Sayood, *Introduction to Data Compression*, Morgan Kaufmann, San Francisco, 1996.

[Shannon 1948] C. E. Shannon, *A mathematical theory of communication*, Bell Syst. Tech. J. **27** (1948), pp. 379–423, 623–656.

[Tietavainen 1973] A. Tietavainen, *On the nonexistence of perfect codes over finite fields*, SIAM J. Appl. Math. **24** (1973), pp. 88–96.

[Tsfasman Vladut Zink 1982] M. A. Tsfasman, S. G. Vladut, T. Zink, *Modular curves, Shimura curves, and Goppa codes, better than Vashamov-Gilbert bound* Math. Nachr. **109** (1982), pp. 21–28.

[van der Geer van Lint 1988] G. van der Geer, J. H. van Lint, *Introduction to Coding Theory and Algebraic Geometry*, Birkhäuser, Basel, 1988.

[Vasilyev 1962] J. L. Vasilyev, *On nongroup close-packed codes* (Russian), Probl. Kibernet. **8** (1962), pp. 337–339, translated in Probleme der Kybernetik **8** (1965), pp. 375–378.

[Verdu McLaughlin 2000] S. Verdu, S. McLaughlin, *Information Theory, Fifty Years of Discovery*, IEEE Press, Piscataway, NJ, 2000.

[Walker 2000] J. Walker, *Codes and Curves*, Amer. Math. Soc., Providence, RI, 2000.

[Wells 1999] R. B. Wells, *Applied Coding and Information Theory for Engineers*, Prentice Hall, Upper Saddle River, NJ, 1999.

[Welsh 1988] D. Welsh, *Codes and Cryptography*, Clarendon Press, Oxford, 1988.

Selected Answers

1.01 5, 7, 6 elements, respectively.

1.02 $\{1, 2, 3, 4, 5, 6, 7\}$, $\{3, 4, 5\}$, $\{1, 2\}$, respectively.

1.03 $\{\}$, $\{1\}$, $\{2\}$, $\{3\}$, $\{1, 2\}$, $\{1, 3\}$, $\{2, 3\}$, $\{1, 2, 3\}$.

1.04 $(1, 2)$, $(1, 3)$, $(2, 2)$, $(2, 3)$, $(3, 2)$, $(3, 3)$

1.05 4 choices for the first element, for each such choice $4 - 1$ choices for the second, for each such choices $4 - 2$ for the third, and finally $4 - 3$ for the last. This is $4! = 24$.

1.06 10 choices for the first, for each such choice $10 - 1$ for the second, for each choice $10 - 2$ for the third, and then divide by $3!$ since ordering does not matter. Thus, $\binom{10}{3} = 120$.

1.07 $\binom{7}{4} = 35$

1.08 $\binom{10}{2}$, $10 \cdot 9$, respectively.

1.09 For each of the 3 possible inputs there are 4 possible outputs, so $4^3 = 64$.

1.10 4 choices for the image of 1, for each such choice, $4 - 1$ choices for the image of 2 (since it must be different from the image of 1), for each such choices, $4 - 1$ choices for the image of 3 (since it must be different from the images of 1 and 2). Thus, $4 \cdot 3 \cdot 2$.

1.12 Since the target set has just one fewer element than the source set, there are exactly two elements among the source set which must be sent to the same element of the target. There are $\binom{4}{2}$ choices for a two-element subset of the source. For each such choice, there are $3!$ choices for how to allocate the source elements to different target set elements. Thus, $\binom{4}{2} \cdot 3! = 36$.

1.20 Hint: consider the expansion of $(1 + 1)^n$ via the Binomial Theorem.

1.22 Go down the list of all elements in the set: for each one you have 2 choices, to *include* it or to *exclude* it. Altogether 2^n choices.

1.23 $\binom{8}{3} \cdot \binom{8-3}{3} = \frac{8!}{3!\,3!\,2!}$

1.24 Send $2n$ to n.

1.25 Send 0 to 0, send $n > 0$ to $2n$, and $n < 0$ to $2|n| - 1$.

1.28 $\binom{10}{3} 2^{-10}$

1.29 $\frac{1}{2}\left(1 - 2^{-10}\binom{10}{5}\right)$, $\frac{1}{2}\left(1 - 2^{-20}\binom{20}{10}\right)$,

1.30 $\left(\frac{3}{3+7}\right)^2$

1.39 The correct answer as well as intuitively appealing answer is $\frac{3}{7} \cdot 20$, but justification is needed. Invoke the theorem which says that the expected value of a sum of random variables is the sum of the expected values, applied to a sum of much simpler random variables whose sum computes the desired total.

1.40 $\sum_{i=0}^{\infty} i \cdot 2^{-(i+1)} = 1$ (This equality is not obvious.)

1.53 Use Chebysheff's inequality.

1.54 Use Chebysheff's inequality.

1.55 Use Chebysheff's inequality.

1.56 Use Chebysheff's inequality.

2.01 $\frac{15}{8}$

3.01 Start from the Kraft-MacMillan inequality. With lengths ℓ at most 5, the smallest possible value of the summands $2^{-\ell}$ in Kraft-MacMillan is 2^{-5}. Thus, we can have at most $2^5 = 32$ of these.

3.03 By the Noiseless Coding Theorem, the average word length for *any* encoding is at least the entropy $H(p_1, \ldots, p_n)$ where the p_i are the probabilities of the codewords. Granting that for fixed n the maximum value of this occurs for all the p_i equal, we have $p_i = 1/n$, and the entropy is $\log_2 n$. Then $\log_2 n \geq 4$ implies that the number of codewords is $n \geq 16$.

3.04 One Huffman coding is to encode the probability $\frac{1}{2}$ source word as '1', $\frac{1}{4}$ as '01', $\frac{1}{8}$ as '001', $\frac{1}{16}$ as '0001', and the second $\frac{1}{16}$ as '0000'.

3.07 There will be a length 1 codeword if and only if there is a source word of probability at least $1/2$. There will be 2 of length 2 if and only if there are two source words the sum of whose probabilities is at least $1/2$. There will be 4 of length 3 if and only if there are four source words the sum of whose probabilities is at least $1/2$.

4.01 $1 - (1/4)^2$

4.02 $1 - (1/6)^4$

4.03 Hint: one should really use the theorem that the expected value of a

sum of random variables is the sum of the expected values. The intuitively reasonable answer Np is indeed correct, but does not actually follow easily from the definition of expected value.

4.08 $\frac{\log_2 2^4}{5} = \frac{4}{5}$

4.09 $1/2$

4.10 Hint: This is the probability that a non-trivial error occurs in the first 4 bits and exactly the same as the error occurs in the second 4 bits. There are $\binom{4}{i}$ different patterns of i bit errors in the first 4 bits, and the probability of each one is $p^i(1-p)^{4-i}$. The probability that the same pattern of errors occurs in the second 4 bits is $p^i(1-p)^{4-i}$. Thus, the sum over $i = 1, 2, 3, 4$ of $\binom{4}{i}p^{2i}(1-p)^{8-2i}$ is the probability of undetected error.

5.05 0000

5.07 Divide the given polynomial into $x^4 - 1$ and see that the remainder is 0. One might even recall the algebra identity that $(x-1)(x^3 + x^2 + x + 1)$ equals $x^4 - 1$.

6.02 10

6.03 56

6.04 For $N = a_0 + 10a_1 + 100a_2 + \ldots$ with each a_i an integer in the range $0 \leq a_i < 10$, the ones'-place digit is a_0. Dividing by 10 shows that the remainder is a_0.

6.08 77

6.11 1, 2, 3, 4, 5, 6, 10, 12, 15, 20, 30, 60 and their negatives. To be sure that these are all we can give a slightly higher-level argument to *count* the number of factors, as follows. Since $60 = 2^2 \cdot 3 \cdot 5$ is the prime factorization of 60, to make a positive divisor of 60 we use the same prime factors raised to (non-negative integer) powers less than or equal to those occurring in this prime factorization. Thus, we have 3 choices (0, 1, or 2) of how many factors of 2 to include, 2 choices (0 or 1) of how many factors of 3 to include, and similarly 2 choices of how many factors of 5 to include. $3 \cdot 2 \cdot 2 = 12$ positive factors.

6.13 To say that $d|m$ is to say that there is an integer k such that $k \cdot d = m$. Then $-k \cdot d = -m$, which shows that d divides $-m$.

6.15 One really should recognize the binomial coefficients: $1331 = (1+10)^3$ and $14641 = (1+10)^4$.

6.16 73

6.17 11

6.18 128

6.19 Since $d|n$ there is an integer a such that $ad = n$. Likewise, there is an integer b such that $bd = n + 2$. Subtracting, $(b - a)d = (n + 2) - n = 2$. Thus $d|2$.

6.21 We must treat three cases. If n is divisible by 3, we are done. Otherwise, either $n = 3N + 1$ or $n = 3N + 2$ for some N. In the case $n = 3N + 1$, $n + 2 = 3N + 1 + 2$ is divisible by 3. Similarly, in the case $n = 3N + 2$, $n + 4 = 3N + 2 + 4$ is divisible by 3.

6.26 This is the product of 111 and $1,001,001,001,001$.

6.27 This is the product of 101 and $1,000,100,010,001$.

6.29 $n^2 - 1 = (n-1)(n+1)$ and both the right-hand-side factors are integers larger than 1 if $n > 2$.

6.37 Via the extended Euclidean Algorithm, $8 = 15 \cdot 1112 - 18 \cdot 1544$.

6.44 It may be more conceptual to count the number of partitions of this four-element set, and to group these by the sizes of the mutually disjoint subsets which appear. There is 1 partition with one subset, there are $\binom{4}{3}$ partitions with a 3-element and 1-element subsets, $\binom{4}{2}/2!$ with two 2-element subsets, $\binom{4}{2}$ with a 2-element and two 1-element subsets, and 1 with four 1-element subsets. Adding these up, there are 15 partitions, hence 15 equivalence relations.

6.46 n

6.47 8

6.51 Since $3^2 = -1 \bmod 10$, we have $3^4 = (-1)^2 = 1 \bmod 10$. Since $999 = 4 \cdot 249 + 3$, $3^{999} \bmod 10$ is $3^{4 \cdot 249 + 3} = (3^4)^{249} \cdot 3^3$ modulo 10, which simplifies to $1^{249} \cdot 3^3$ modulo 10, since $3^4 = 1 \bmod 10$.

6.52 67 Brute force is plausible here. Or the Extended Euclidean Algorithm.

6.53 This is less palatable by brute force, but the Extended Euclidean Algorithm works well and gives -143, equivalently, 1091.

6.54 Obvious solutions 1 and 14, and less obvious are 4 and 11.

6.55 In addition to the obvious 1 and 104, there are also the less obvious 29, 34, 41, 64, 71, and 76.

6.56 8, 8, and 8

6.60 18

6.61 375

6.62 4 and 83

6.68 No, by Euler's criterion, since $2^{(101-1)/2} = -1 \bmod 101$.

6.69 Yes, by Euler's criterion, since $2^{(103-1)/2} = 1 \bmod 103$.

6.71 No, by Euler's criterion, since $2^{(103-1)/3} = 46 \bmod 103$.

6.75 Let a be such that $a^2 = b \bmod p$. Then, modulo p,

$$(b^{(p+1)/4})^2 = a^{p+1} = a \cdot a = b$$

since $a^p = a \bmod p$ by Fermat's Little Theorem, so $b^{(p+1)/4}$ really is a square root of b.

6.77 Fermat's Little Theorem. Let $rs = 1 + k(p-1)$ for some integer k.

$$(b^s)^r = b^{1+k(p-1)} = b \cdot 1$$

since $b^{p-1} = 1$ modulo p by Fermat's Little Theorem.

6.79 Let $rs = 1 + k(p-1)/r$ for some integer k, and $a^r = b \bmod p$. Then

$$(b^s)^r = (a^r)^{1+k(p-1)/r} = b \cdot (a^{p-1})^k = b$$

since $a^{p-1} = 1$ modulo p by Fermat's Little Theorem.

7.01 $(1\,2\,5) \cdot (3\,4)$ of order $\mathrm{lcm}(2,3) = 6$

7.03 $(1\,2\,3\,4\,7\,6\,5)$ of order 7

7.05

$$\begin{pmatrix} 1 & 2 & 3 & 4 & 5 & 6 & 7 \\ 5 & 4 & 7 & 6 & 2 & 1 & 3 \end{pmatrix}$$

7.07 $\frac{5 \cdot 4 \cdot 3}{3} = 20$

7.11 $6 = \mathrm{lcm}(2,3)$

7.12 $12 = \mathrm{lcm}(3,4)$

7.13 $20 = \mathrm{lcm}(4,5)$

7.16 Labeling by position modulo $11 = 10+1$, a 10-cycle $(1\,2\,4\,8\,5\,10\,9\,7\,3\,6\,1)$ since 2 is a primitive root modulo $11 = 10 + 1$.

7.18 Note that 15 has no primitive root. $(1\,2\,4\,8) \circ (3\,6\,12\,9) \circ (5\,10) \circ (7\,14\,13\,11)$

8.01 Roughly, $h(xy)h^{-1} = (hx)e(yh^{-1})$ $= (hx)(h^{-1}h)(yh^{-1}) = (hxh^{-1})(hyh^{-1})$

8.04 The elements 2, 3, 4 have no multiplicative inverses.

8.11 $\{0\}$, $\{0,8\}$, $\{0,4,8,12\}$, $\{0,2,4,6,8,10,12,14\}$, and the whole $\{0,1,2,\ldots,15\}$.

8.13 $\{1\}$, $\{1,11\}$, $\{1,7,19,13\}$, $\{1,19\}$, $\{1,29\}$, $\{1,17,19,23\}$, $\{1,19,29,11\}$, $\{1,7,11,13,17,19,23,29\}$

8.20 An element and its inverse have the same order.

8.21 4, 3

8.26 All elements are of order 1 or 2.

9.02 Closedness under addition and multiplication is easy. What may be surprising is that 3 functions as a multiplicative identity, namely $3 \cdot 3 = 3 \bmod 6$, and $3 \cdot 0 = 0 \bmod 6$.

9.05 $\{1,3\}$, $\{1,2,3,4\}$, $\{1,5\}$, respectively.

9.15 Add $-r$ to both sides to obtain (using associativity) $0 + r = 0$, from which $r = 0$.

9.16 3 and 5, 6 and 5, 3 and 10, etc.

10.02 $x(x-1)(x-2)(x-3)(x-4)$ (Fermat's Little Theorem may suggest this.)

10.03 $(x^3 + x^2 + 1)(x^2 + x + 1)$

10.05 $(x+1)^3(x^3 + x^2 + 1)$

10.07 $x^4 + x^2 + 1$

10.10 $x^2 + x + 1$

10.12 $x^3 + x^2 + 1$

11.01 $\alpha + 1$

11.03 $\alpha^2 + \alpha + 1$

11.05 $\alpha + 1$

11.06 α^2

11.09 $x(x+1)(x^2+x+1)$

11.10 $x(x+1)(x^3+x+1)(x^3+x^2+1)$

12.03 $4/7$

12.05 $(1,2) = -3(3,4) + 2(5,7)$

12.08 $(1,0,1) = -(8,3,2) + 3(3,1,1)$

12.09 $(1,0,1) + (0,0,1) + (0,1,1)$

12.11 $(1,1,1,0)+(0,1,1,1)+(1,1,0,1)+$
$(1,1,1,1)$

12.14 C is the rowspace of G, just 4 vectors, $(0,0,0,0)$, $(1,0,0,1)$, $(0,1,1,1)$, and $(0,1,1,0)$. By direct observation, the minimum distance to $(0,0,0,0)$ of the others is 2. So single-bit errors are detected but not corrected.

12.16 $yH^\top = (0\ 0)$ (y is a codeword)

12.18

$$G = \begin{pmatrix} 1 & 0 & 1 & 0 \\ 1 & 1 & 0 & 1 \end{pmatrix}$$

13.01 No. Hamming bound violated: $2^7 - 17 \cdot (1+7) < 0$.

13.03 No. Hamming bound violated: $2^8 - [7 \cdot (1+8+8 \cdot 7/2)] < 0$.

13.04 Yes, by Gilbert-Varshamov: $2^{(5-2)} - 1 - (5-1) > 0$.

13.06 No, the Hamming bound is violated. There are 2^3 codewords, and $2^5 - 2^3 \cdot (1+5) < 0$.

13.08 Yes, by Gilbert-Varshamov: $2^{(7-2)} - 1 - (7-1) - (7-1)(7-2)/2 > 0$.

14.01 4

14.03

$$\begin{pmatrix} 1 & 0 & 0 & 1 & 0 & 0 & 1 & 0 & 0 \\ 0 & 1 & 0 & 0 & 1 & 0 & 0 & 1 & 0 \\ 0 & 0 & 1 & 0 & 0 & 1 & 0 & 0 & 1 \end{pmatrix}$$

15.02 3 is one such, and then odd powers of 3, since $\varphi(17) = 16$: 3, 10, 5, 11, 14, 7, 12, 6. This computation is easier than testing all elements modulo 17.

15.04 $x^2 + x + 1$

15.06 $\varphi_2(x) = x+1$, $\varphi_3(x) = x^2+x+1$, $\varphi_4(x) = x^2+1$, $\varphi_5(x) = x^4+x^3+x^2+x+1$, $\varphi_6(x) = x^2 - x + 1$

15.08 $x^6 - x^5 + x^4 - x^3 + x^2 - x + 1$, $x^8 + 1$, $x^6 - x^3 + 1$

15.11 x modulo $x^2 + x + 1$

15.12 x modulo $x^3 + x + 1$

15.15 $\varphi_{105}(x)$ has some coefficients ± 2.

16.01 7

16.04 5

16.07 Not x, as $x^{21} = 1$ modulo the polynomial. Rather, $x + 1$ works.

16.09 By brute force, with initial state 1111, the subsequent states are 0111, 1011, 1101, 1110, 1111, so the initial state reappears on the 5th step.

16.10 Brute force would be tedious here. Instead, observe that the associated polynomial $x^4 + x^3 + 1$ is *primitive* of degree 4, so for *any* non-zero initial state it will take $2^4 - 1 = 15$ steps to return to the initial state.

16.11 The associated polynomial $x^5 + x^2 + 1$ is primitive, so for any non-zero initial state it will take $2^5 - 1 = 31$ steps to return to the initial state.

16.13 The associated polynomial $x^5 + x + 1$ is the product of two primitive polynomials $x^2 + x + 1$ and $x^3 + x^2 + 1$, so for any non-zero initial state it will take

$\text{lcm}((2^2-1),(2^3-1))=21$ steps to return to the initial state.

16.16 $x^2 + x$ modulo 10011 and $x^2 + x + 1$ modulo 10011. These are x^5 and x^{10} reduced modulo 10011, and note that $y^2 + y + 1 = (y^3 - 1)/(y - 1)$.

17.01 $1 \cdot 8 - 2 \cdot 7 = -6$

17.03 $1 \cdot 5 \cdot 9 + 2 \cdot 6 \cdot 7 + 3 \cdot 4 \cdot 8 - 7 \cdot 5 \cdot 3 - 8 \cdot 6 \cdot 1 - 9 \cdot 4 \cdot 2 = 0$

17.05 A Vandermonde determinant: $(1 - 2)(1 - 3)(1 - 4)(2 - 3)(2 - 4)(3 - 4) = 12$

17.07 To correct e errors the minimum distance must be $\geq 2 \cdot e + 1$, so to correct 5 bit errors, take designed distance $2 \cdot 5 + 1 = 11$. For an RS code take generating polynomial $g(x) = (x - 2)(x - 2^2)(x - 2^3)(x - 2^4) \ldots (x - 2^{11-2})(x - 2^{11-1})$. The length of an RS code using alphabet $GF(13)$ is $13 - 1 = 12$. By Fermat's little theorem $x^{12} - 1$ is the product of all the linear polynomials $x - 2^k$ with $1 \leq k \leq 13 - 1$, namely $x^{12} - 1 = (x - 2)(x - 2^2)(x - 2^3)(x - 2^4) \ldots (x - 2^{13-2})(x - 2^{13-1})$. To get the check polynomial $h(x)$ we divide $x^{12} - 1$ by $g(x)$ $h(x) = (x - 2^{11})(x - 2^{13-1}) = x^2 + 5x + 7$. The generator polynomial is $g(x) = (x^{12} - 1)/h(x)$, or $g(x) = x^{10} + 8x^9 + 5x^8 + 10x^7 + 6x^6 + 4x^5 + 3x^4 + 9x^3 + 12x^2 + 7x + 11$ Insert the coefficients in descending order into a 2-by-12 matrix, padding at the right with 0s in the first line and cycling to the right until the constant coefficient bumps against the right edge to obtain generating matrix

$$\begin{pmatrix} 11 & \ldots & 8 & 1 & 0 \\ 0 & 11 & \ldots & 8 & 1 \end{pmatrix}$$

17.11 The exponents in the second column of the check matrix are 1, 2, 3, ..., 8. Repeatedly multiplying by 7 gives Frobenius-stable set 1, 2, 3, 4, 5, 6, 7, 8, 14, 21, 28, 35, 42 with 13 elements so the rank of the Frobenius-stable check matrix is 13 and the dimension of the code is $48 - 13 = 35$. Adjacent exponents $1, 2, \ldots, t' - 1$ appear for $t' = 9$, so the minimum distance is ≥ 9.

18.01 Use binary coordinates (a, b) for $a + b\alpha$ in $\mathbf{F}_4$. The 3 non-zero words v are $(1, 0)$, $(0, 1)$, and $(1, 1)$. Keep in mind that $\alpha^2 = 1 + \alpha$. The 3 codewords $(v, \alpha v)$ are $(1, \alpha)$ which has binary encoding $(1, 0, 0, 1)$, $(\alpha, 1 + \alpha)$ which has binary encoding $(0, 1, 1, 1)$, and $(1 + \alpha, 1)$ which has binary encoding $(1, 1, 1, 0)$. Thus, the minimum distance is 2.

18.05 Use the lemma which asserts that

$$\sum_{i < c \cdot N} \binom{N}{i} \leq 2^{N \cdot H(c)}$$

where

$$H(c) = -c \log_2 c - (1 - c) \log_2 (1 - c)$$

Thus, we want $H(c) < 2/3$. Numerical experimentation yields $H(.1667) \approx 0.65$.

18.06 Imitate the proof for the mirage codes. There are $(2^n - 1) \cdot (2^n - 1)$ choices for (α, β), and we want the number of *bad* pairs to be less than the total:

$$\sum_{i < c \cdot 3n} \binom{3n}{i} \leq (2^n - 1)^2 - 1$$

By the lemma, we want

$$2^{3n \cdot H(c)} \leq (2^n - 1)^2 - 1$$

Use $(2^n - 1)^2 - 1 > 2^{2n-1}$. From $3n \cdot H(c) \leq 2n - 1$ we see that we want $H(c) < 2/3$. As computed above $H(.1667)$ works. With this value of c, for $n \geq 4$

$$2^{3n \cdot H(c)} \leq (2^n - 1)^2 - 1$$

That is, for $n \geq 4$ there is a choice of α, β such that the code has minimum distance at least $c \cdot 3n \approx \frac{1}{6} \cdot 3n = n/2$. The error-correction rate is at least $1/6$, and the information rate is $1/3$.

19.03 Look at this equation modulo 4, and realize (check!) that the only squares mod 4 are $0, 1$.

19.04 Look at this modulo 7. The cubes modulo 7 are 0 and ± 1.

19.05 Look at this modulo 9.

19.11 Hint: the polynomial $x^4 + x^3 + x^2 + x + 1$ is the 5th cyclotomic polynomial, and $\mathbf{F}_{13}^{\times}$ is a cyclic group of order 12 while 5 is relatively prime to 12.

19.13 First, show that 1 is not in I: if $1 = g(x) \cdot 2 + h(x) \cdot x$, then modulo x we have $1 = g(0) \cdot 2$, but this would say that 1 is an even integer, which it is not. Next, observe that the quotient ring $\mathbf{Z}[x]/I$ is $\mathbf{Z}/2$, since in the homomorphism to the quotient polynomials lose their higher-degree terms since x goes to 0. Likewise, 2 goes to 0. (But 1 does not go to 0.)

20.01 The point $(1, 0)$ is an obvious point on the curve. Consider the line of slope t through $(1, 0)$, $y = t(x - 1)$. We find its intersection with the curve $x^2 - 2y^2 = 1$ by substituting for y, obtaining $x^2 - 2t(x - 1)^2 = 1$. This quadratic equation has the root $x = 1$ and another root $x =$

$(2t^2 + 1)/(2t^2 - 1)$. The corresponding $y = t(x - 1)$ is $2t/(2t^2 - 1)$. Thus, every rational t gives a solution. Conversely, any solution other than $(1, 0)$ gives a line of rational slope, hence is of this form for some t.

20.04 The projectivization is given by the homogenized equation $x^2 - 2y^2 = z^2$. The points at infinity are those where $z = 0$, namely given by the equation $x^2 - 2y^2 = 0$. If there is a square root α of 2 in whatever the field is, then the points $(\pm\alpha, 1, 0)$ (in projective coordinates) are the points at infinity. If there is no square root in the underlying field then there are no points at infinity.

20.05 The gradient of the function $f(x, y) = x^2 - 2y^2$ is $(2x, -4y)$. If the characteristic of the underlying field is not 2, this vector is the zero vector only for x, y both 0, which is a point not on the curve. That is, there are no singular points in the affine plane.

20.06 From an earlier exercise, just above, if there is no square root of 2 in the underlying field, then there are no points at infinity. If there is a square root α of 2, then there are points $(\pm\alpha, 1, 0)$. If the characteristic of the field is not 2, then the gradient $(2x, -4x, -2z)$ of $f(x, y, z) = x^2 - 2y^2 - z^2$ does not vanish there, so these points are non-singular.

Index